5th Edition

Clinical Psychology

Concepts, Methods, and Profession

Related Titles

Abnormal Psychology

Abnormal Psychology: An Integrative Approach
    by Barlow/Durand
Abnormal Psychology: An Introduction
    by Durand/Barlow
Exploring Psychological Disorders, a CD-ROM for Mac and Windows
    by Chute/Bliss
Seeing Both Sides: Classic Controversies in Abnormal Psychology
    by Lilienfeld

Psychopathology

Exploring Psychological Disorders, a CD-ROM for Mac and Windows
    by Chute/Bliss
Seeing Both Sides: Classic Controversies in Abnormal Psychology
    by Lilienfeld
Culture and Mental Illness
    by Castillo
Meanings of Madness: A Reader
    by Castillo

Forthcoming Titles

Abnormal Child Psychology
    by Wolfe/Mash

5th Edition

Clinical Psychology

Concepts, Methods, and Profession

E. Jerry Phares

Kansas State University

Timothy J. Trull

University of Missouri-Columbia

 Brooks/Cole Publishing Company

I(T)P® An International Thomson Publishing Company

Pacific Grove • Albany • Bonn • Boston • Cincinnati • Detroit • London • Madrid • Melbourne • Mexico City
New York • Paris • San Francisco • Singapore • Tokyo • Toronto • Washington

Sponsoring Editor: *Marianne Taflinger*
Editorial Assistant: *Laura Donahue/Scott Brearton*
Production Editor: *Tessa A. McGlasson*
Marketing Team: *Deborah Petit/Lauren Harp*
Manuscript Editor: *Jennifer McClain*
Permissions Editor: *Lillian Campobasso*

Interior and Cover Design: *Katherine Minerva*
Art Editor: *Lisa Torri*
Photo Editor: *Robert Western*
Indexer: *Matthew Spence*
Typesetting: *ColorType, San Diego*
Cover Printing: *Lehigh Press*
Printing and Binding: *Quebecor/Fairfield*

For more information, contact:

BROOKS/COLE PUBLISHING COMPANY
511 Forest Lodge Road
Pacific Grove, CA 93950
USA

International Thomson Editores
Seneca 53, Col. Polanco
México, D. F., México
C. P. 11560

International Thomson Publishing Europe
Berkshire House 168-173
High Holborn
London WC1V 7AA
England

International Thomson Publishing GmbH
Königswinterer Strasse 418
53227 Bonn
Germany

Thomas Nelson Australia
102 Dodds Street
South Melbourne, 3205
Victoria, Australia

International Thomson Publishing Asia
221 Henderson Road
#05-10 Henderson Building
Singapore 0315

Nelson Canada
1120 Birchmount Road
Scarborough, Ontario
Canada M1K 5G4

International Thomson Publishing Japan
Hirakawacho Kyowa Building, 3F
2-2-1 Hirakawacho
Chiyoda-ku, Tokyo 102
Japan

Printed in the United States of America

10   9   8   7   6   5   4   3   2   1

Library of Congress Cataloging-in-Publication Data

Phares, E. Jerry.
    Clinical psychology : concepts, methods, profession / E. Jerry
Phares, Timothy J. Trull. — 5th ed.
        p.   cm.
    Includes bibliographical references and indexes.
    ISBN 0-534-26298-8
    1. Clinical psychology.   2. Psychotherapy.   I. Trull, Timothy J.,
1960–   . II. Title.
RC467.P48   1996
616.89—dc20
                                                          96-33547
                                                          CIP

About the Authors

E. Jerry Phares received his B.A. in Psychology, with honors, from the University of Cincinnati and his M.S. and then Ph.D. in clinical psychology from The Ohio State University. He is a Fellow of the American Psychological Association (Divisions 8 and 12) and is a member of the Department of Psychology at Kansas State University in Manhattan, Kansas. He is also the author of *Introduction to Personality*.

Timothy J. Trull is Associate Professor of Psychology and Director of Clinical Training at the University of Missouri—Columbia. He received his B.A. from Baylor University and his M.A. and Ph.D in clinical psychology from the University of Kentucky. Dr. Trull is co-author (along with Tom Widiger) of a structured interview, the Structured Interview for the Five Factor Model of Personality (SIFFM), that assesses both adaptive and maladaptive personality features. Dr. Trull teaches a variety of courses in clinical psychology, including abnormal psychology, adult psychopathology, and psychometrics. In addition to his academic pursuits, he is a practicing clinical psychologist. Finally, he does his best to keep up with two active daughters under the age of seven, as well as to improve his three-point shot.

Brief Contents

Contents

4 Research Methods in Clinical Psychology 80

5 Abnormal Behavior and Psychopathology 110

II Clinical Assessment   139

6 The Assessment Interview   141

7   The Assessment of Intelligence   173

8   Personality Assessment   201

9 Behavioral Assessment   239

10 Clinical Judgment   263

13 Psychotherapy: Phenomenological and Humanistic-Existential Perspectives   350

14 Psychotherapy: Behavioral and Cognitive-Behavioral Perspectives   376

17 Health Psychology and Behavioral Medicine   452

Preface

These are interesting times for the field of clinical psychology. First, the scope of the field is expanding, leading, in some cases, to a blurring of boundaries between clinical psychology and other disciplines. Although it is fairly easy to identify some of the major activities of clinical psychologists (for example, psychological assessment, diagnosis of mental disorders, intervention), professionals from other fields perform many of these same duties as well. This raises several issues. How is clinical psychology different from other disciplines that focus on behavioral and mental health? Should clinical psychologists expand the domain of their interest and practice to that of health in general? Should clinical psychologists pursue prescription priveledges, or is this role more appropriate for physicians?

Second, a variety of training models for clinical psychologists is available, ranging from those that focus almost exclusively on the development of clinical skills to those that primarily emphasize the development of research skills. Which training models should be preferred? How important is it for clinical psychologists in training to learn to conduct and evaluate research?

Finally, the managed care industry is shaping the way that clinical psychology is practiced. Clinicians are increasingly faced with limitations on the number of treatment sessions that are reimbursable as well as with the need to document the efficacy of their interventions.

This is just a sample of the issues confronting clinical psychologists today. This edition of *Clinical Psychology* has been thoroughly updated to present both contemporary trends in the field as well as to incorporate recent empirical evidence relevant to major assessment and intervention approaches used by clinical psychologists. Its audience includes advanced undergraduates seeking a comprehensive overview of the field, as well as beginning clinical psychology graduate students. Because we are concerned about the apparent rift between practitioners and researchers, we have attempted to highlight how research and practice actually complement each other.

In addition to thoroughly updating the discussion of the various aspects of clinical psychology, this new edition takes an in-depth look at the utility and effectiveness of major forms of clinical assessment and clinical intervention. Empirically validated assessment methods and interventions are emphasized, as are briefer forms of psychotherapy. Descriptions of the new diagnostic manual, DSM-IV, have been incorporated. New examples and case studies have been provided. Finally, contemporary issues like the impact of managed health care are discussed throughout the book.

Specifically, the major changes made in this edition include:

- Updated information regarding demographic trends in clinical psychology, career options, and applying to graduate school
- Discussion of various training models (for example, scientist-practitioner, Psy.D., clinical scientist models) for clinical psychologists
- Discussion of the impact of managed care on the field of clinical psychology
- Discussion of the advantages and disadvantages of psychologists seeking prescription priveleges
- Updated ethical principles
- New sections on what constitutes "abnormal behavior," the advantages and disadvantages of various definitions of abnormal behavior, the relationship between abnormal behavior and mental illness, the importance of diagnosis, the DSM–IV classification system, and the issue of sex bias in diagnosis

As for the format of the book, a new chapter, "Current Issues in Clinical Psychology" (Chapter 3) has been added, whereas the fourth edition's Chapter 3 ("The Role of Personality Theory") and Chapter 16 ("Psychotherapy and Behavior Change: The Research Perspective") no longer appear. The material from these two chapters has been integrated throughout the book. At the end of each chapter Focus Questions and Key Terms appear as study aids.

Also, several ancillary materials for instructors are published with this edition. A Test Bank is available. In addition, a home page on the World Wide Web is in the planning stages. This will be accessible to both instructors and students and will include figures, text, and links to other web pages relevant to the topics in the textbook.

Our hope is that students and instructors using this textbook will find the field of clinical psychology both exciting and challenging.

Acknowledgments

I am grateful to E. Jerry Phares for asking me to serve as co-author of this leading clinical psychology textbook, and I look forward to our collaborations in the future. I would also like to express my appreciation to Meg, Molly, and Janey for allowing me to participate in this project and for tolerating my frequent absences from home. I feel fortunate to have such a loving, supportive, and entertaining family. Several clinical psychology colleagues have directly or indirectly influenced what is in this book, especially Tom Widiger, Ken Sher, Lizette Peterson-Homer, David Dubois, Meg Klein-Trull, and Brick Johnstone. I also thank the Department of Psychology at the University of Missouri-Columbia for its support, especially Tom DiLorenzo and Mark Thelen. In addition, I want to thank my current clinical graduate students for their understanding given all the time crunches they witnessed and, unfortunately, experienced to some extent. A number of other individuals were helpful in various aspects of putting this edition together, especially Jay Farrar, Terri Kennedy, David Knipp, David Lowery, and Krista Shouse.

I want to express my appreciation to the Brooks/Cole staff involved in this project: Marianne Taflinger, senior editor; Tessa McGlasson, production editor; Jennifer McClain, copyeditor; Roy Neuhaus, design editor; Deborah Petit, advertising; Lisa Torri, art editor; Bob Western, photo editor; and Lillian Campobasso, permissions editor. It has been a pleasure to work with this group of enthusiastic and competent professionals.

Finally, I want to thank the reviewers of various chapters of this edition: Debora Bell-Dolan, University of Missouri-Columbia; Martha E. Bernal, Arizona State University; David Dubois, University of Missouri-Columbia; Jess Feist, McNeese State University; R. Edward Geiselman, University of California at Los Angeles; Martin Heinstein, San Francisco State University; William P. Henry, University of Utah; Chris Kearney, University of Nevada, Las Vegas; Jack M. McGuire, University of Central Florida; Scott M. Monroe, University of Oregon; Beverly B. Palmer, California State University, Dominguez Hills; Catherine A. Perz, University of Houston at Victoria; Gretchen Reevy, California State University at Hayward; Phillip Rice, Moorhead State University; Rick Snyder, University of Kansas; Mary Spiers, Drexel University; Peter Zachar, Auburn University at Montgomery; and R. Fred Zuker, University of Dallas.

Timothy J. Trull

5th Edition

Clinical Psychology

Concepts, Methods, and Profession

I

FOUNDATIONS OF CLINICAL PSYCHOLOGY

1

Clinical Psychology: An Introduction

One of the tried-and-true methods of uncovering a person's feelings is said to be the old word-association technique. Most of us are quite familiar with it: "I am going to say a word and I want you to respond with the first word that comes to mind." Maybe such an approach can tell us what people think about clinical psychologists. In this spirit, some 30 undergraduates in psychology classes were once asked to give their associations to the stimulus *clinical psychologist.* Here is a sample of their responses:

potato head	strange	help
crazy	psychoanalysis	shaman
a person who helps others	therapist	mind
shrink	doctor	couch
APA member	medical man	

This list is probably a fairly representative mixture of the stereotypes, distortions, humor, and truths that characterize the public's perceptions of clinical psychologists (Peterson, 1995). After all these years, people still confuse them with medical doctors. Some continue to believe that clinical psychology and psychoanalysis are synonymous. Others see a bit of the witch doctor in clinical psychologists while still others view them as somewhat peculiar. Fortunately, there are many who regard them as researchers, therapists, or even members of professional societies. Perhaps all of these perceptions, diverse as they are, do tap into some of the essence of clinical psychology.

In a recent attempt to define and describe clinical psychology, Resnick (1991) proposed the following definition and description:

> The field of clinical psychology involves research, teaching, and services relevant to the applications of principles, methods, and procedures for understanding, predicting, and alleviating intellectual, emotional, biological, psychological, social and behavioral maladjustment, disability and discomfort, applied to a wide range of client populations. (p.7)

According to Resnick, the skill areas that are considered to be essential for the field of clinical psychology include: assessment and diagnosis, intervention or treatment, consultation, research, and application of ethical and professional principles. Resnick further asserts that clinical psychologists are unique in their expertise in the areas of personality and psychopathology and in their integration of science, theory, and practice.

While this description tells what clinical psychologists do and what skills they possess, we must not forget how others may see the profession, and try to correct any false images. For example, very few clinical psychologists are psychoanalysts or medical doctors. The field yields neither shamans nor miracle workers. And one fervently hopes that even fewer clinical psychologists are crazy, strange, or even potato heads!

In any case, the main purpose of this first chapter is to clarify the nature of clinical psychology by describing what clinical psychologists do and where they do it, how they got to be clinicians, and how they differ from other professionals who also tend to the mental health needs of people. In the process, this should give us a better understanding of the field of clinical psychology.

■ Other Mental Health Professions

Before we examine the nature of clinical psychology, let us briefly review some of the other major professions in the mental health field. Following this review we can better present the characteristics that give clinical psychology its unique identity.

The psychiatrist

The *psychiatrist* is a physician. Psychiatry is rooted in the medical tradition and exists within the framework of organized medicine. Thus, psychiatrists are often accorded the power and status of the medical profession, even though their intellectual heritage comes from the nonmedical contributions of Freud, Jung, Adler, and others. Although the latter were physicians, they stepped out of the medical tradition to develop a psychoanalytic system of thought that had very little to do with medicine. The psychiatric profession has vocally and effectively pushed for a superior role in the mental health professional hierarchy, and much of the profession's argument has been based upon its medical background.

Because of their medical training, psychiatrists may function as physicians. They may prescribe medication, treat physical ailments, and give physical examinations. In fact, however, because of some psychiatrists' concentration on psychotherapy and psychiatric diagnosis, their medical skills may atrophy quickly. Psychiatrists do make extensive use of a variety of medications in treating the psychological difficulties of their patients. Furthermore, their medical training makes them potentially better able to recognize medical problems that may be contributing to the patient's psychological distress. But, as Box 1-1 suggests, even these traditional lines that have served to distinguish psychiatrists from clinical psychologists may become more blurred in the future.

Following the completion of the medical degree and the general medical internship required of all physicians, the typical psychiatrist-to-be receives psychiatric training during a three-year residency. This involves supervised work with

Box 1-1
But Is It The Right Prescription For Clinical Psychology?

Recently, a number of clinical psychologists have expressed the hope that they may eventually be accorded the same privilege of writing prescriptions that psychiatrists have long enjoyed. In particular, they want to prescribe the so-called psychotropic medications that affect mental activity, mood, or emotions. As Handler (1988) put it, they seem to want to "do what psychiatrists do, but do it better: a one-stop shopping approach in the best supermarket tradition . . . and thereby be more competitive in the marketplace (saving) our profession from becoming obsolete" (p. 44). Handler adds that the response of some to all this is to grumble, "If I wanted to be a psychiatrist I would have gone to medical school." For others it is, "Do you think we really could?" Overall, the responses of many seem highly supportive.

But others would urge caution here. They suggest that the best reason clinical psychology has flourished is for the very reason that it is different from psychiatry. Clinical psychologists have developed unique skills in psychological assessment. They have built a profession on a solid scientific basis. To mimic psychiatry by an ill-advised attempt to write prescriptions would help destroy clinical psychology's very uniqueness, they say.

Frequently, clinical psychologists stress to troubled clients their autonomy and the necessity that they, as clients, collaborate with the therapist in the change process. In contrast, psychiatrists may too often come from an authoritarian tradition. The doctor is an expert who tells the client/patient what is wrong and then prescribes medication to make things right. Traditionally, clinical psychologists have been committed to the power of words (the "talking cure") and to the process of thought and social learning. They do not subscribe to the credo of "better living through chemistry" when applied to psychological problems. While few clinical psychologists would argue that medication is *never* necessary, many would argue that ultimately, most clients must learn to come to grips psychologically with their problems in living. The bottom line seems to be that, at present, the field has not made up its mind about the value of prescription privileges. As yet, there is no consensus (Massoth, McGrath, Bianchi, & Singer, 1990), but clinical psychology's next frontier may well turn out to be prescription privileges (DeLeon, Fox, & Graham, 1991). If prescription privileges are pursued, there will be important implications for research, training, and practice. For example, major changes in graduate training will be required in order to prepare clinical psychologists for this new role.

What is the view of clinical training directors on this issue? Riley, Elliott, and Thomas (1992) conducted a survey of randomly selected psychology graduate and internship training directors regarding prescription privileges.

To the question, "Should psychology pursue prescription privileges?", the majority of training directors (66.4%) answered "definitely not," "probably not," or "unsure." Further, 66.3% of training directors indicated that their faculty would be unwilling to make changes to their respective programs if prescription privileges were granted. A majority (75%) of training directors also indicated that their programs would have to be lengthened by at least one year should prescription privileges be granted to psychologists, and 21.3% reported that their programs would have to be completely revamped. As this survey indicates, there appears to be a great amount of resistance from training directors to the idea of prescription privileges for psychologists. We will have more to say about this debate in Chapter 3.

patients in an outpatient or hospital setting and an apprenticeship that is sometimes accompanied by seminars, reading, discussion, and so on. The amount of formal psychiatric course work varies, but there can be little doubt that the core training experience is the treatment of patients with the supervision of a more experienced psychiatrist.

A 1977 editorial that appeared in the *American Psychologist* summarized the comparative training of psychiatrists and clinical psychologists:

> Psychiatrists receive standard medical training, little formal training in the study of human behavior, and practically no experience in research. Clinical psychologists, on the other hand, receive very little training in medicine (although many have strong backgrounds in neuroscience), rather standardized and extensive sets of experiences in research, and are engaged for 5 or more years in a broad study of human behavior. (Kiesler, 1977, p. 107)

Psychiatry no longer enjoys the prestige it once did. The proportion of medical school graduates who choose to become psychiatrists has dropped noticeably since 1968. Some say psychiatry is in a slump these days. The reasons are complex, but most reduce to economic issues. Health care systems have significantly lowered payments for mental health services and give priority to short-term therapy. This reduces professional income. Consequently, salaries for psychiatrists are relatively low compared to other medical specialties. Older psychoanalytic methods have been eclipsed by medication treatment, briefer therapies, and cognitive therapy. All of this has fostered a "remedicalization" of psychiatry, in which psychopharmacology and a renewed belief in the role of biological factors in mental illness have shown a resurgence (Dana & May, 1986). In fact, this biological perspective appears to be the dominant force in American psychiatry today.

The psychiatric social worker

The professional activities of *psychiatric social workers* often seem similar to those of psychiatrists and clinical psychologists. Many psychiatric social workers conduct psychotherapy on an individual or group basis and contribute to the diagnostic process as well.

In years past, social workers tended to deal with the social forces and the external agents that were contributing to the patient's difficulties. The social worker took the case history, interviewed employers and relatives, made arrangements for vocational placement, or counseled parents; the psychiatrist conducted psychotherapy with the patients; and the clinical psychologist tested them. However, these professional roles have blurred over the years.

Perhaps it was the close association with psychiatrists and psychologists that led many social workers to focus less on social or environmental factors and to become, like their colleagues, preoccupied with internal, psychological factors. Now, though, it appears that many social workers are moving away from psychoanalytic influences and returning to their earlier focus on the familial and social determinants of psychopathology.

The social work profession has been a leader in the utilization of supervised fieldwork as a learning device for students. Fieldwork placement is part of the program for the master's degree (usually the terminal degree for social workers), which typically requires two years. Compared to the training of clinical psychologists and psychiatrists, social work training is rather brief. This tends to ensure that the responsibilities of the social worker will not be as great as those of the psychiatrist or clinical psychologist. Characteristic of social workers is their intense involvement with the everyday lives and stresses of their patients. They are more likely to visit the home, the factory, or the street—the places where their patients spend the bulk of their lives. Their role tends to be active, and as a result, they are less concerned with the abstract, theoretical generalizations that can be drawn from a particular case than they are with the practical matters of living.

Many psychiatric social workers are employed by public agencies of one sort or another. Some find their way into private practice, where their work in individual or family therapy is often indistinguishable from that of psychiatrists or clinical psychologists. Other social workers function as part of the mental health team (psychiatrist, clinical psychologist, and psychiatric social worker) in hospitals, social service agencies, or mental health clinics.

The counseling psychologist

The activities of *counseling psychologists* overlap with those of clinical psychologists. Traditionally, counseling psychologists work with normal or moderately maladjusted individuals. Their work may involve group counseling or counseling with individuals. Their principal method of assessment is usually the interview, but counseling psychologists also do testing (for example, assessment of abilities, personality, interests, and vocational aptitude). Historically, they have done a great deal of educational and occupational counseling. More recently, many counseling psychologists have begun to employ cognitive-behavioral techniques and biofeedback. The most frequent employment arenas for counseling psychologists have been educational settings, especially colleges and universities; less frequently they work in hospitals, rehabilitation centers, mental health clinics, and industry. A good example of the kind of work they do is suggested in the heading that appeared above an article in a campus newspaper several years ago: "Counseling Center Responds to Married Students' Needs." The article described group counseling sessions designed to help students who are parents deal with the special problems that marriage and children create for them in pursuing their academic goals.

In general, counseling psychologists see themselves in the following activities: (a) preventive treatment, (b) consultation, (c) development of outreach programs, (d) vocational counseling, and (e) short-term counseling or therapy of from one to fifteen sessions (Tipton, 1983). However, younger counselors seem more and more to view themselves as engaged in activities such as psychotherapy that are in the traditional clinical province. Today they are frequently less interested in vocational or career counseling (Fitzgerald & Osipow, 1988) and more interested in private practice (Zook & Walton, 1989).

The December 1994 issue of the *American Psychologist* listed 64 doctoral training programs in counseling psychology that were accredited by the American Psychological Association (APA). It is estimated that over 500 doctoral degrees in counseling psychology are granted annually (Mayne, Norcross, & Sayette, 1994a).

The school psychologist

School psychologists work with educators and others to promote the intellectual, social, and emotional growth of school-age children. To do this, they may help to plan the learning environment. For example, they may generate programs to assist the development of children with special intellectual, emotional, or social needs. Often, they evaluate such children and recommend special programs, treatment, or placement if necessary. They also consult with teachers and school officials on issues of school policy or classroom management. Their work settings range from schools, nurseries, and day care centers to hospitals, clinics, and even penal institutions. A few are in private practice. In 1994, there were a total of 43 APA-accredited programs in school psychology, and it is estimated that less than 100 doctoral degrees in school psychology are awarded each year (Mayne et al., 1994).

The rehabilitation psychologist

In both research and practice, the focus of *rehabilitation psychologists* is on people who are physically or cognitively disabled. The disability may result from a birth defect or later illness or injury. Rehabilitation psychologists help individuals adjust to their disabilities and the physical, psychological, social, and environmental barriers that often accompany them. Their most frequent places of employment are in rehabilitation institutes and hospitals.

The health psychologist

In recent years, the field of health psychology has emerged and is growing rapidly (Brannon & Feist, 1997; Gatchel, Baum, & Krantz, 1989). *Health psychologists* are those who, through their research or practice, contribute to the promotion and maintenance of good health. They are also involved in the prevention and treatment of illness. They may design, execute, and study programs to help people stop smoking, manage stress, lose weight, or stay fit. Since this is an emerging field, those in it come from a variety of backgrounds: clinical psychology, counseling psychology, personality-social psychology, and others. Many health psychologists are employed in medical centers, but increasingly they are serving as consultants to business and industry—in any organization that recognizes the importance of keeping its employees or members well. As we will discuss in Chapter 3, this specialty is likely to profit most from the sweeping changes in health care.

Other mental health personnel

In recent years, the roles of other mental health personnel have been expanding. We have long been aware of the role of psychiatric nurses. Since they spend many hours in close contact with patients, they are not only in a position to provide information about their hospital adjustment patterns but they can also play a crucial and sensitive role in fostering an appropriate therapeutic environment. Working in close collaboration with the psychiatrist or the clinical psychologist, they—along with those they supervise (attendants, nurse's aides, volunteers, and so on)—can implement therapeutic recommendations through their behavior and that of their staff.

Most well-staffed hospitals employ a variety of other therapeutic personnel. There are occupational therapists, recreational therapists, horticultural therapists, and so on. By virtue of their training and experience, these people can play a vital adjunctive role in enhancing the adjustment patterns of patients. They can teach skills that will help patients in a variety of nonhospital settings. They can help make hospitalization a more tolerable experience, and they can provide outlets that increase the therapeutic value of institutions. Whether their role is to help put patients in touch with their feelings via art, music, gardening, or dancing or to enhance the personal and social skills of patients, the contributions of such therapeutic personnel are significant.

People who are trained to assist professional mental health workers are called *paraprofessionals,* and their role has expanded greatly in recent years. Volunteers are often provided short training sessions and then become the most visible personnel in crisis centers (both walk-in and telephone). Certain paraprofessional activities have become accepted practice. Research indicates strongly that the efforts of paraprofessionals can effectively supplement the work of professionals (Hattie, Sharpley, & Rogers, 1984). We will discuss this issue extensively in Chapter 16.

Now that we have briefly examined some of the other helping professions, let us turn to the work of the clinical psychologist.

■ The Clinical Psychologist

Trying to define clinical psychology in terms of the problems with which clinicians deal is hopeless. The number and kinds of problems are so extensive as to boggle the mind: depression, anxiety, psychosis, personality disorders, mental retardation, addictions, learning disabilities, juvenile delinquency, vocational problems, and sexual difficulties, to name but a few. This list does not cover the many so-called "normal" individuals who are treated in some way or another. Another approach to definition lies in the activities engaged in by clinical psychologists.

Clinical activities

Much of our information about clinical activities comes from a series of studies conducted between 1973 and 1995. Each study involved a random sample of members of Division 12—the Division of Clinical Psychology—of the American Psychological Association (APA). Garfield and Kurtz (1976) examined over 800 questionnaires collected in 1973; Norcross and Prochaska (1982) studied nearly 500 returns gathered in 1981; Norcross, Prochaska, and Gallagher (1989b) were able to analyze 579 questionnaires from 1986; and, finally, Norcross, Karg-Bray, and Prochaska (1995) surveyed 546 clinical psychologists in 1994 and 1995. The results of these four surveys are presented in Table 1-1.

From Table 1-1 it is apparent that *psychotherapy* of one sort or another is the activity engaged in most frequently and occupying the most time, as it has in all the cited surveys from 1973 to 1995. *Diagnosis and assessment* continue as major activities. *Research* activity has grown over the years (to around 10% of the 1995 respondents' time), and this is a bit surprising given that 40% of the 1995 sample was employed full-time in private practice. Still, it is important to note that some clinical psychologists never publish a research paper and that only 10 to 15% of all clinicians produce 40 to 50% of all the work published by clinical psychologists (Norcross et al., 1989b). *Teaching* is another relatively common activity among clinical psychologists. Unfortunately, time devoted to *administration* remains significant, perhaps reflecting the bureaucracy that is so prevalent in modern society. Let us now take a closer look at the six activities represented in Table 1-1.

Psychotherapy. It is clear from Table 1-1 that therapy is the activity that most frequently engages the typical clinician's efforts and to which the most time is devoted. The layperson often has an image of the therapy situation as one in which the client lies on a couch while the therapist, bearded and mysterious, sits

Table 1-1
Clinicians' activities.

Activity	Percentage Involved In	Mean Percentage of Time			
	1995	1995	1986	1981	1973
Psychotherapy	84	37	35	35	31
Diagnosis/Assessment	74	15	16	13	10
Teaching	50	9	14	12	14
Clinical Supervision	62	7	11	8	8
Research/Writing	47	10	15	8	7
Consultation	54	7	11	7	5*
Administration	52	11	16	13	13

*Garfield and Kurtz percentage is for "community consultation."

SOURCE: Based on data from "Clinical Psychologists in the 1990's," by J. C. Norcross, R. S. Karg-Bray, and J. O. Prochaska, 1995, unpublished manuscript.

behind with notepad and furrowed brow. Actually, therapy comes in many different sizes and shapes. Some therapists do use a couch, but more often the client sits in a chair adjacent to the therapist's desk. Most often therapy involves a one-to-one relationship, but today couple's therapy, family therapy, and group therapy are also very common. For example, a group of six or eight clients, all having trouble handling alcohol, may meet together with a therapist to work on their problems. Finally, a sizable proportion of therapists are women, not men.

In some instances, therapy involves mainly a search for insight into the origins of one's problems or the purposes served by one's undesirable behavior. In other cases, therapy consists primarily of a relationship between client and therapist designed to produce an atmosphere of trust that will help dissolve the client's debilitating defenses. Other forms of therapy are largely behavioral in the sense that the client learns new and more satisfying modes of adjustment. Sometimes the goals of therapy are sweeping: major changes in behavior are undertaken. On the other hand, some patients desire help only with a troublesome fear that prevents them from achieving certain goals. Therapy does, then, vary along many different dimensions.

Diagnosis/assessment.   All practicing clinicians engage in assessment of one form or another. Take, for example, the following cases:

- A child who is failing the fourth grade is administered an intelligence test. Is there an intellectual deficit?
- Personality tests are given to a client who is depressed and has lost all zest for life. Can the test results shed light on the underlying personality factors?
- It has been decided that a client will profit from therapy. But what form of therapy will be most suitable?
- A father has been charged with child abuse. He is interviewed and tested to determine whether he should receive a diagnosis of schizophrenia or some other disorder.

Common to all these examples is the effort to better understand the individual so that a more informed decision can be made or the most desirable course of action selected. Assessment, whether it be observation, testing, or interviewing, is a way of gathering information so that a problem can be solved. Of course, these problems are virtually infinite in variety, as the foregoing examples suggest. Assessment has long been a critical part of the clinical psychologist's role. Indeed, for many years assessment, especially testing, was the chief element in the clinician's professional identity.

Teaching.   Clinical psychologists who have full- or part-time academic appointments obviously devote a considerable amount of time to teaching. Those whose responsibilities are primarily in the area of graduate education teach courses in advanced psycho-pathology, psychological testing, interviewing, intervention, personality theory, experimental psychopathology, and so on. Some of them may also teach undergraduate courses such as introductory psychology, personality, abnormal psychology, introduction to clinical psychology, and psychology of aging, as well as others. Even clinicians whose primary appointments are in clinics or hospitals or who operate a private practice sometimes teach evening courses at a nearby college or university or may even have part-time appointments in graduate programs.

Much of the foregoing teaching is of the familiar classroom-lecture type. But a considerable amount of teaching is also done on a one-to-one supervisory basis. Clinical psychologists in clinical settings may also teach informal classes or do orientation work with other mental health personnel, such as nurses, aides, social workers, occupational therapists, and so on. In some cases, the clinician may go out into the community and lead workshops on various topics for police officers, volunteers, ministers, probation officers, and others.

Clinical supervision.   This activity is really another form of teaching. However, it typically involves more one-to-one teaching, small group approaches, and other less formal, non-classroom varieties of instruction. Whether in university, internship, or general clinical settings, clinical psychologists often spend significant portions of their time supervising students, interns, and others. Becoming skilled in the intricacies of therapy and assessment techniques requires more than just reading textbooks. It also involves seeing clients and then discussing their cases with a more experienced supervisor. In short, one learns by doing but under the controlled and secure conditions of a trainee-supervisor relationship. This kind of practicum teaching and supervision can occur both in university and internship settings and in postdoctoral programs as well.

Research.   Clinical psychology has grown out of an academic research tradition. As a result, when clinical training programs were first established after World War II, the scientist-practitioner model was adopted. This meant that, in contrast to other mental health workers such as psychiatrists or social workers, clinicians were to be trained both as scientists and as practitioners. While this research emphasis may not be so prominent in training programs as it once was, the fact remains that clinical psychologists are in a unique position both to evaluate research conducted by others as well as to conduct their own research. By virtue of their training in research, their extensive experience with people in distress, and their knowledge of both therapy and assessment, clinical psychologists have the ability to consume and to produce new knowledge.

The range of research projects carried out by clinicians is enormous. The studies deal with searching for the causes of mental disorders, development and validation of assessment devices, evaluation of therapy techniques, and so on. To provide something of the flavor of these efforts, Figure 1-1 shows the table of contents of a fairly recent issue of the *Journal of Consulting and Clinical Psychology,* a major publisher of research by clinical psychologists.

Consultation.   In both consultation and teaching, the goal is to increase the effectiveness of those to whom one's efforts are directed by imparting to them some degree of expertise. There are innumerable forms of consultation and settings in which it occurs. For example, one might consult with a colleague who is having difficulty with a therapy case. Such consultation might be a one-shot affair with someone who simply needs help with one specific case. In other instances,

April 1995   Volume 63, Number 2

Journal of
Consulting and Clinical Psychology

Copyright © 1995 by the American Psychological Association, Inc.

Figure 1-1

Sample table of contents from the *Journal of Consulting and Clinical Psychology.*
Copyright © 1995 by the American Psychological Association. Reprinted by
permission.

however, a clinician might be retained on a relatively permanent basis to provide the staff of an agency with help. Perhaps, for example, our consulting clinician is an expert on the problems of drug addicts. By working with the staff, the consultant can increase the effectiveness of the entire agency. Consultation could come in the form of case-by-case advice, or the consultant might be asked to discuss general problems associated with drug addiction. Further, more police departments have begun using clinical psychologists as consultants in hostage negotiations (Fuselier, 1989). Finally, a growing number of clinical psychologists serve as consultants to physicians who deliver primary care services (Pace, Chaney, Mullins, & Olson, 1995).

Consultation can run the gamut from clinical cases to matters of business, personnel, and profit. It can deal with individuals or entire organizations. Sometimes it is remedial; other times it is oriented toward prevention. Regardless of the setting in which it occurs or the particular purpose it has, consulting is becoming a significant activity of many clinical psychologists today.

Administration. It has been said half jokingly that no one in clinical psychology enjoys administrative work except masochists or those with obsessive-compulsive personalities. Nevertheless, nearly every clinician spends time on administrative tasks. Client records must be maintained, those infernal effort reports must be filled out each month, and research projects must be cleared by committees set up to guard the rights of human subjects. Clinical psychologists who work for agencies or institutions will likely serve on several committees: personnel, research, patient rights, or even the committee to select films for the patients' Friday night movies.

Some really hardy souls become full-time administrators. They do so for many reasons. Sometimes they are drafted by their colleagues who regard them as skillful in human relations. Others may grow a bit weary with therapy or assessment and want a change. Or maybe they have the fantasy that administration is the route to power and wealth. In any event, good administrators are the ones who keep their organization running smoothly and efficiently. Being sensitive to the needs and problems of people in the organization and having the patience to sometimes suffer in silence are useful attributes of the good administrator. The ability to communicate well with those under supervision is also important, as is a knack for selecting the right people for the right jobs.

It would be difficult to list all the sorts of administrative posts held by clinicians; however, here are a few examples: head of a university psychology department, director of a Veterans Administration clinic, vice president of a consulting firm, director of the psychological clinic in a university psychology department, chief psychologist in a state hospital, and director of a regional crisis center.

■ Employment Sites

Where are clinical psychologists employed? Data from the surveys noted previously will again help us answer this question. The data pertaining to work settings from the 1973 survey (Garfield & Kurtz, 1976) and the 1981, 1986, and 1995 surveys (Norcross & Prochaska, 1982; Norcross et al., 1989a; and Norcross et al., 1995, respectively) are shown in Table 1-2. It is evident that private

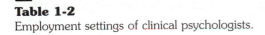

Table 1-2
Employment settings of clinical psychologists.

| | Percentage Employed | | | |
Employment Site	1995	1986	1981	1973
Psychiatric Hospital	5	9	8	8
General Hospital	4	5	8	6
Outpatient Clinic	4	4	5	5
Community Mental Health Center	4	5	6	8
Medical School	9	7	7	8
Private Practice	40	35	31	23
University, Psychology	15	17	17	22
University, Other	4	4	5	7
VA Medical Center	3	–	–	–
None	1	4	1	1
Other*	11	10	12	1

*This category includes professional schools, correctional facilities, managed care organizations, nursing homes, child and family services, rehabilitation centers, school systems, psychoanalytic institutes, and health maintenance organizations, and so on.

SOURCE: Based on data from "Clinical Psychologists in the 1990's," by J. C. Norcross, R. S. Karg-Bray, and J. O. Prochaska, 1995, unpublished manuscript.

practice has grown steadily over the years and is now the most frequent employment setting for clinical psychologists. University settings are the second most common employment sites. Although not shown in Table 1-2, the data from Norcross et al. (1995) indicate that, of those clinicians whose primary job was that of a full-time university professor, 66% are engaged in some part-time form of private practice or supervision.

From the information provided in Tables 1-1 and 1-2, the diversity of both the activities and the work settings of clinical psychologists is obvious. It is also evident in the increase over recent years in the numbers in the "Other" category in Table 1-2. This diversity can be illustrated in the background and activities of a hypothetical clinician presented in the next section.

■ A Week in the Life of Dr. Karen C.

Karen C. began her undergraduate career in journalism. However, following a course in general psychology she decided to switch to psychology. After fulfilling the requirements for the usual psychology major (courses in psychobiology, statistics, cognitive psychology, history and systems, personality, social psychology, and so on), she applied to seven graduate schools. With a strong grade point average and an equally strong set of scores on the Graduate Record Examination, she was accepted by four schools. She chose a large midwestern state university and later did her internship at a local state hospital.

Five years after enrolling, she was awarded the Ph.D. and began her career as a staff psychologist in a tri-county outpatient clinic. Four years later, we have a typical week in the life of Karen C.

MONDAY, WEDNESDAY, FRIDAY

8:00-9:00 A.M.: Staff meeting. This period is devoted to a variety of activities, including discussion of cases, agency policy and problems, insurance questions, and other administrative business.

9:00-10:00 A.M.: Psychotherapy. The current case is that of a moderately depressed 48-year-old woman who was recently divorced. Mrs. G. is showing gradual improvement, and the prospect of hospitalization seems to have passed. Dr. C. is using what might be termed an eclectic form of psychotherapy that is generally psychodynamic in flavor.

10:00-10:30 A.M.: Psychotherapy. This patient, Sam F., is 19 years old. He has a record of arrests for shoplifting, truancy, and public intoxication. His intellectual potential is limited, and his learning history is quite deprived. The therapy employed might be described as behavioral in character. The focus is on enhancing Sam F.'s repertoire of social skills and decreasing the frequency of his maladaptive behaviors.

10:30-12:00 P.M.: This period is reserved for psychological testing, both for Dr. C.'s patients and for the patients of other therapists. Typically, intelligence tests, projective tests, and self-report tests are employed. Occasionally, neuropsychological assessment is also done.

1:00-2:00 P.M.: Clinical supervision. The local university places several interns with Dr. C.'s agency. This period is devoted to supervising their psychotherapy and their diagnostic efforts. The supervision of two M.A.-level psychologists employed by the agency is also included here.

2:00-3:00 P.M.: Psychotherapy. Bob S. is a university student. His major difficulty might be termed alienation. Dr. C. has tried a variety of therapeutic techniques, but nothing has seemed to work. Although the patient has been able to continue with his classes thus far, the prospects of hospitalization seem to be increasing.

3:00-4:30 P.M.: Group psychotherapy. This period is devoted to the treatment of a group of six male alcoholics with heterogeneous backgrounds. The treatment approach is largely supportive.

4:30-5:00 P.M.: This time is typically devoted to report writing, administrative details, and so on.

TUESDAY, THURSDAY

8:00-10:00 A.M.: Dr. C. is engaged in a research project to determine whether certain psychological test responses (for example, from the Minnesota Multiphasic Personality Inventory) can be used to predict responsiveness to various forms of therapy. Dr. C. is using cases from her own agency along with cases from four other local clinics and institutions.

10:00-12:00 P.M.: Psychological testing.

1:00-3:00 P.M.: Dr. C. serves as a consultant to the local school system. She serves four schools and meets with teachers to discuss their handling of specific problem children. She provides consultation for the school psychologist as well.

3:00-5:00 P.M.: Dr. C. is advising a local institution for the mentally retarded on the establishment of a token economy. The goal is to upgrade the self-care habits of a group of moderately retarded children and young adults in the institution. It is hoped that the project can serve as a prototype demonstration for use throughout the institution.

7:00-8:30 P.M.: Two evenings a week, Dr. C. teaches a course in abnormal psychology at the local university. It is a fully accredited course and enrolls both full- and part-time students.

SATURDAY

9:00-1:00 P.M.: During this period, Dr. C. sees a series of patients in private practice. They are typically patients with a variety of so-called neurotic complaints (e.g., depression, anxiety). These patients are usually referred by local physicians and other professionals in the community who are aware of Dr. C.'s excellent work and reputation. Dr. C. also does some diagnostic testing on a referral basis during this time.

In contrast to Dr. C., a clinical psychologist who teaches at a major university might have a quite different schedule. Table 1-3 offers a glimpse of one such day for a new assistant professor.

Table 1-3
Wednesday at the university with Professor L.

8:30–9:00 A.M.
    Proofread test for class in introduction to clinical psychology

9:00–10:00 A.M.
    Research meeting with two graduate students

10:00–11:30 A.M.
    Teaching: Clinical practicum supervision

11:30–12:30 P.M.
    Jog at the track

12:30–1:00 P.M.
    Brown-bag lunch in the office (read journal articles)

1:00–2:00 P.M.
    Office hour for undergraduate students

2:00–2:30 P.M.
    Check the mail

2:30–4:00 P.M.
    Attend meeting of the campus committee on computer use

4:00–5:00 P.M.
    Work on a revision of a manuscript submitted earlier to a journal

7:00–9:00 P.M.
    Teaching: Seminar on therapy methods

9:30–11:00 P.M.
    Rest and rehabilitation

■ Some Demographic Notes

Several demographic characteristics have been noted by Norcross et al. (1995). First, in this survey of 546 randomly selected clinical psychologists from the APA Division 12 (clinical psychology) roster, roughly 28% were women. Further, only 7% of clinicians were members of racial minorities. Although these numbers seem low, they are roughly comparable to those published in 1993 by the APA Office of Demographic, Employment, and Educational Research (ODEER), suggesting the Norcross et al.'s sample was representative of Division 12 members. The mean age of the clinicians was 50 years old. The top ten universities that produced the greatest number of clinical psychology doctorates in this sample were: New York University, Pennsylvania State, Connecticut, Illinois, Iowa, Minnesota, Tennessee, Purdue, Ohio State, and Florida State.

As for primary *theoretical orientation,* 27% of the sample described themselves as eclectic/integrative, 24% as cognitive, 18% as psychodynamic, and 13% as behavioral. Table 1-4 presents the theoretical orientations of clinical psychologists in the Norcross et al. (1995) survey, as well as those identified in four other surveys dating back to 1960. As can be seen, the percentage of clinicians adhering to a psychodynamic orientation has declined over the years, whereas the corresponding percentage for a cognitive orientation has increased dramatically. The popularity of the eclectic orientation, while still strong, has decreased somewhat in recent years.

Finally, although hardly a demographic feature, it is reassuring to note that of all the clinical psychologists sampled, only 9% of them expressed any dissatisfaction with their choice of clinical psychology as a career (Norcross et al., 1995).

Table 1-4
Theoretical orientations of clinical psychologists.

Orientation	Percentage				
	1995	1986	1981	1973	1960
Behavioral	13	16	14	10	8
Cognitive	24	13	6	2	–
Eclectic/Integrative	27	29	31	55	36
Humanistic*	3	6	4	6	2
Interpersonal	4	–	–	–	–
Psychodynamic**	18	21	30	16	35
Rogerian	1	6	3	1	4
Sullivanian	1	2	2	3	10
Systems	4	4	4	–	–
Other	5	3	6	7	4

*Humanistic includes existential and gestalt.
**Psychodynamic includes psychoanalytic and psychodynamic. The corresponding 1960 and 1973 figures are for psychoanalysis and neo-Freudian.

SOURCE: Based on data from "Clinical Psychologists in the 1990's," by J. C. Norcross, R. S. Karg-Bray, and J. O. Prochaska, 1995, unpublished manuscript.

■ Research and the Scientific Tradition

Although clinical psychology is dedicated to the improvement of human welfare, it springs from a research tradition that emphasizes the quest for knowledge. This research tradition does not imply that every clinician ought to be *heavily* engaged in research or other scholarly pursuits. What it does suggest is that training in clinical psychology that incorporates courses and experience in research and statistical methods gives clinicians unique skills that help establish their professional identity. Such methodological training helps develop a capacity for evaluation and an attitude of caution and skepticism that permits clinical psychologists to become better, more perceptive diagnosticians and therapists, as well as researchers.

■ Art or Science?

Because clinical psychology deals with the problems of individuals, the focus of clinical psychology is often on individual differences rather than the commonalities among persons. Consider an example. Suppose that one of the authors is conducting an experiment on the effects of an attitude of personal control on problem solving. His goal is to develop certain principles that will indicate how a feeling of being in control of outcomes affects the ability to solve problems. Suppose, further, that he induces a feeling of control through verbal instructions. He instructs some subjects that they have much control and others that they have little. Several subjects may respond very differently from others in the same group. This, of course, increases the variance of the group and, statistically speaking, reduces the likelihood that significant differences between experimental groups will be found. As a result, the researcher will study ways to eliminate such variance.

In searching for general principles of behavior (the *nomothetic approach*), the research psychologist generally is less concerned with individual differences. The focus is on group differences that occur as a function of some experimental treatment or manipulation. The goal is the abstraction of general principles of behavior from the observation of many people.

The clinical, or *idiographic,* approach seeks the understanding of individual differences. Why is *this* patient so anxiety-ridden? Why is *this* patient unresponsive to certain reinforcements? This focus is perhaps responsible for the continuing debate over whether clinical psychology is an art or a science. For the more empirically oriented clinician it more often seems to be the former. Stated another way, there are clinicians who feel that when they make diagnostic judgments or therapeutic decisions, they do so largely on the basis of their own skill, experience, and subjective or intuitive awareness. Just as a person cannot be taught to paint a masterpiece, they believe, neither can one be taught to make highly sensitive and penetrating interpretations of a projective test or of a patient's report about a dream. Of course, the rudimentary elements of scoring a test or the basic mechanisms of therapy can be transmitted from one person to another. But these other high-level skills cannot be taught as such.

Yet other clinicians possess a more objective orientation. They argue that the answers lie in more research and in the objective application of the principles of human behavior to each case. Where subjectively oriented clinicians might seek the answer to a diagnostic problem in their own intuition, more empirically oriented clinicians may put their faith in the best possible statistical formula.

It is expected that through research and the development of general principles a greater level of understanding of specific patients will be attained. At the same time, just as there are individual differences among patients, so there are individual differences among clinicians. Some are smarter, more experienced, or harder working than others. The application of general principles to individual cases is not easy. The discovery of the sameness within diversity is difficult; but so too is locating the unique within the homogeneous. Furthermore, seeing the relevance of laboratory or field research to a person in distress is an important and difficult task that requires its own brand of sensitivity and intelligence.

In the final analysis, we must find ways to allow our "art" to complement our "science." The roles need not be antithetical. We will have more to say about this issue in Chapter 10.

■ Training: Toward a Clinical Identity

The preceding pages have provided a sketch of some of the activities, affiliations, and orientations of clinicians, touched upon the scientific tradition, and raised the issue of art versus science in clinical psychology. Now, let us turn to a discussion of the unique background and skills that set clinical psychologists apart from the other mental health professionals. None of this is set in stone, of course. The field is changing and, as always, there are disagreements among clinicians as to how to train students and in what direction the field should move. However, it is useful to remember that clinical psychology is but a specialized application of the more basic core of psychology (Matarazzo, 1987).

An overview

The typical clinical psychologist completes a bachelor's degree and then five years of graduate work. The latter typically includes training in assessment, research, diagnosis, and therapeutic skills along with an internship. Most often, this effort culminates in a Ph.D. (Doctor of Philosophy) degree from a university psychology department. In some instances, the degree awarded is the Psy.D. (Doctor of Psychology) from either a university department of psychology or from a training institution not affiliated with a university. There are also two-year programs that award the master's degree. Because of contemporary licensing laws which dictate who may practice independently as a psychologist, fewer individuals graduating from master's programs can achieve much in the way of professional independence; many of them hope to transfer to Ph.D. or Psy.D. programs later and, indeed, some are quite successful in doing so (Quereshi & Kuchan, 1988). Evidence suggests that subdoctoral clinicians are in less demand than doctoral-level clinicians, are paid less, and are perceived as less competent (Havens, Colliver, Dimond, & Wesley, 1982). In 1987, master's-level clinicians could be fully licensed to practice independently in psychology in only three states, while limited licensing was possible in fourteen (Dale, 1988). However, the number of master's programs as well as the number of master's degrees conferred appear to be growing. For example, in 1994, three times as many master's degrees were awarded in psychology as doctoral degrees (Murray, 1995).

Master's-level training in clinical psychology has always been somewhat controversial. Master's-level psychologists claim that research indicates that master's-level clinicians are as effective as doctoral-level clinicians. The American Psychological Association, however, accepts the doctoral degree alone as the key to work as an independent professional. The presidents of the American Psychological Association continue to assert that a *doctoral degree* is a prerequisite for the title "psychologist" and that it should be required for those who wish to practice psychology independently (Murray, 1995). Nevertheless, master's-level clinicians continue to work in a variety of service-delivery settings (Perlman, 1985). Further, the increasing influence of managed care in the mental health care marketplace may lead to a resurgence of the popularity of master's programs in clinical psychology (Sleek, 1995a). In general, master's-level practitioners charge lower fees, making them an attractive alternative (in the eyes of managed care insurers) to doctoral-level clinicians. It will be interesting to see how this controversial issue unfolds as lobbying efforts to give master's-level clinicians "psychologist" status increase and as increasing economic pressures come into play.

With this thumbnail sketch of training in clinical psychology we can now examine the content of doctoral training more closely.

Clinical training programs

The predominant training philosophy in clinical psychology today is still the *scientist-practitioner* model (Raimy, 1950). We shall have a good deal more to say about this model in the next chapter, and in Chapter 3 we will discuss alternative training models for clinical psychologists as well. For the moment, however, a brief overview of the scientist-practitioner training model will be useful.

Training programs that emerged after World War II were based on the principle that the scientist and practitioner roles could be combined in one person. The goal was the creation of a unique profession. More recently, this training model has come under attack as unrealistic and unresponsive to the needs of students who aspire only to clinical practice. Nevertheless, a majority of clinical programs still subscribe to it in varying degrees. And, it is certainly a model that differentiates clinical psychologists from the rest of the mental health pack.

A sample program. How does this translate into an actual program that trains clinicians? Table 1-5 presents a typical program of study.

Several things should be said about the program in Table 1-5. First, it is just a sample. Some programs place less emphasis on research and more on clinical techniques. Some are structured so that one can complete all work in four years, especially if summers can be devoted to course work. In some programs the internship comes in the fourth year, often before the dissertation has been completed. A few schools still require competency in a foreign language, although many now allow the student to substitute courses in statistics or computer technology. It is also true that each school tends to have its own personality. That is, some programs have a distinct cognitive-behavioral orientation that tends to emphasize such

■

Table 1-5
Sample Ph.D. program of study (scientist-practitioner model).

Year 1	Fall
	Statistics (Analysis of Variance)
	Systems of Psychotherapy
	Departmental Core Course: Social Psychology
	Introduction to Data Analysis
	M.A. Thesis Research
Year 1	Winter
	Statistics (Regression)
	Psychometrics (Test Construction)
	Assessment (Adult or Child)
	Introduction to Data Analysis
	M.A. Thesis Research
	Clinical Practicum
Year 2	Fall
	Ethical and Professional Issues
	Psychopathology
	M.A. Thesis Research
	Clinical Practicum
Year 2	Winter
	Departmental Core Course: Functional Neuroscience
	Elective: Family and Group Process
	M.A. Thesis Research
	Clinical Practicum
Year 3	Fall
	Departmental Core Course: Cognitive
	Elective: Experimental Psychopathology
	Dissertation Research
	Clinical Practicum
Year 3	Winter*
	Statistics (Latent Variables and Structural Equation Modeling)
	Departmental Core Course: Developmental
	Dissertation Research
	Clinical Practicum
Year 4	Fall
	Outside Course: Psychological Anthropology
	Dissertation Research
	History and Systems of Psychology
Year 4	Winter
	Outside Course: Violence in the Family
	Dissertation Research
Year 5	Fall and Winter
	Clinical Internship

*During the third year (usually in winter semester), students are expected to complete qualifying examinations.

techniques as cognitive therapy for depression. Others have a psychodynamic flavor and emphasize projective testing. Faculty interests in some programs center on children, while in others the focus is on adults. Although there is diversity among clinical programs, there is a great deal of commonality as well (O'Donohue, Plaud, Mowatt, & Fearon, 1989). A student applying for graduate work should investigate such emphases so as to make informed choices.

Course work. Clinical students normally must take a series of basic courses such as statistics and research design, biological foundations of behavior, social psychology, developmental psychology, and cognitive psychology. The exact number and content of these courses will vary somewhat from program to program. The intent is to give the student an understanding of the basics that underlie human behavior or that will permit us to investigate that same behavior. These courses provide a strong scientific foundation for the student's clinical training and give life to the scientist-practitioner model in clinical psychology. Depending upon the student's interests, several elective advanced courses and seminars in these same topics are often taken as well.

Clinical students also enroll in several courses that teach the fundamentals of clinical practice or deal with clinical topics at an advanced level. For example, there are often courses in psychopathology, theory and research in therapy, principles of cognitive-behavioral interventions, or seminars in such topics as schizophrenia, methods of family and group therapy, community psychology, or neuropsychological assessment.

Practicum work. Books and course work are fine, but ultimately one must learn by doing. As a result, all programs seek to build the student's clinical skills through exposure to *clinical practica.* The dictionary defines a practicum as "work done by an advanced student that involves the practical application of previously studied theory." In many instances, the practicum will combine academic content with practical experience. Typically, there are practica or clinics in assessment (intelligence, neuropsychology, personality, and so on), therapy (from psychodynamic treatment to cognitive-behavioral interventions), interviewing, and even methods of consulting with school officials, community agencies, or industry. Whatever the specific form or content of the practicum experience, it is a major vehicle for the acquisition of specific clinical skills. The student's practicum work is supervised by clinical faculty members or by clinicians in the community who have special skills. Most psychology departments that have clinical training programs also operate a *psychological clinic.* This clinic often provides assessment, therapy, and consulting services to university students, staff, and faculty, as well as to families of university personnel and to people in the surrounding community. Cases are accepted selectively in terms of their teaching value. Such a clinic may be staffed by a full-time secretary, a social worker, and clinical faculty.

Research. The implementation of the scientist-practitioner model requires that the student develop research competency. This is accomplished through courses in statistics, computer methods, and research methodology and by active participation in research projects. There are differences among schools as to the extent of their commitment to the scientist-practitioner approach to training. Therefore, differences also exist among departments in the emphasis they place upon research training and in the rewards they dispense to students for devotion to research. Most departments do, however, require the completion of a master's thesis (usually by the end of the second year). A dissertation reporting the results of an original research project is also required (by the end of either the fourth or fifth year, depending on the specific program). The dissertation is a more extensive project than the master's thesis, and it is designed to contribute significant new information to the field. Most programs continue to stress traditional experimental or correlational research for the dissertation (Shemberg, Keeley, & Blum, 1989).

Programs that emphasize the research commitment usually see to it that research experience is not confined to the thesis and dissertation. For example, in one department each clinical student joins the research "team" of a faculty member. The team consists of from four to eight graduate students who are at varying year levels in the program. The team meets one evening per week for two or three hours. Research topics are discussed, and research projects are designed. Thesis and dissertation proposals may be discussed and defended. The more advanced students can provide guidance and serve as role models for the younger students. In any case, the vigorous give-and-take of such meetings can go a long way toward building the research commitment.

The internship.   The internship is a vital part of any training program and could be described as a time of "professional adolescence." It is the capstone of the student's previous experiences in clinical courses and practica and provides the experience that begins to consolidate the scientist-practitioner role (Lipovsky, 1988). An internship of one sort or another is required of all students in clinical programs accredited by the APA. In the years immediately following World War II, the internship was most commonly taken during the third year of training. Now, however, so many programs are essentially five years in length that the internship most often seems to come at the end of graduate training (Davies, 1987). In a few instances, students may take half-time internships over a two-year period. Usually, an intern works at an independent facility off campus. However, some intern in such university facilities as counseling centers and medical schools. In 1994 there were 429 predoctoral internship sites fully approved by the American Psychological Association; these "approved" internship programs are listed each year in the December issue of the *American Psychologist*.

The values of the internship are many. For example, it allows the student to work full-time in a professional setting. New skills can be acquired; older ones can be sharpened. Experience in a professional setting gives the student a real taste of the demands of professional life. Students are also exposed to clinical psychologists who may have ideas and orientations different from those of their university faculty. Thus, the experience can help break down any provincialism that may have crept into the student's university training. Exposure to different kinds of clients can likewise enhance the student's competency. Ideally, the internship provides the opportunity to expand one's professional horizons and to integrate what one has learned at the university with the demands of the professional world. It becomes the final element in the three-dimensional world of academics, research, and experience.

The qualifying examination.   Most clinical programs require students to pass a *qualifying examination,* which is sometimes called the preliminary examination or the comprehensive examination. Whatever its title, many students regard it as the most anxiety-provoking experience in their training. It is a written examination that takes different forms at different universities. For example, in some cases three written examinations, each lasting four hours, are spaced over a week; others have a five-day examination. Some schools require an oral examination as well. In certain programs the tests cover all areas of psychology, whereas in others they are confined to the field of clinical psychology. Most often these examinations are taken during the third year. Qualifying examinations serve a very useful function in ensuring the student's overall academic competency. A few programs, however, employ innovative alternatives. For example, students might prepare a research grant application or perhaps complete several integrative literature reviews of important topics in clinical psychology (for example, the etiology of schizophrenia).

Given the foregoing descriptions of clinical training, it is reassuring to note that, in general, students express satisfaction with their training (Tibbits-Kleber & Howell, 1987).

■ Admission to Graduate Programs

The previous section described training in clinical psychology. But how does one get into graduate school in the first place? There are, of course, no guarantees, but the following pages should help answer some of the more frequently asked questions about admission to graduate training programs in clinical psychology.

Step 1. Know your program

To some degree, the purpose of graduate training is to challenge your intellect, open new vistas, and help you focus your aspirations. You should have a mental set receptive to new ideas. At the same time, you should be familiar with programs before you apply. Some have a psychodynamic orientation; others are cognitive-behavioral or perhaps eclectic; some emphasize research; some are more practice-oriented. Sayette and Mayne's 1990 survey of training programs provides some good information about clinical and research emphases. Also, it is interesting to note that among the many reasons applicants select particular graduate programs, three stand out: the amount of clinical supervision available; the emotional atmosphere of the program, and the reputation of the program (Walfish, Stenmark, Shealy, & Shealy, 1989).

No single authoritative source will tell you everything you need to know about graduate programs in clinical psychology. However, the more sources you check, the more likely it is that you will be able to make informed decisions. Here are some possibilities:

1. Talk to your psychology faculty, especially those who are clinical psychologists. They will have both formal information as well as informal impressions through which you can sift to arrive at your own ideas.
2. The APA annually publishes a list of graduate programs. Called *Graduate Study in Psychology,* it contains a wealth of information on each school including programs and degrees, addresses, application procedures, data on financial assistance, tuition charges, size of faculty, admission requirements, average test scores and GPAs of students admitted the previous year, and so on. Many psychology departments have a copy you can borrow, or you may purchase a copy from the APA.
3. Very often university libraries or psychology departments have copies of many catalogs from universities across the country. These are especially useful in discovering just what courses are offered and the names of the faculty as well.
4. Once you know who is on the faculty at a given school you can check the *APA Membership Directory* for additional information on faculty interests and background. Normally your psychology department office will have a copy of this directory.
5. A more laborious but sometimes more interesting strategy is to examine copies of journals that publish the research of clinical psychologists. This can give you an idea of who is active in research, the kind of research they do, and the programs with which they are affiliated.

Once you have completed your preliminary examination of programs, you will probably want to write to several schools for more detailed information and application forms. A good time to do this would be in September of the year preceding your planned enrollment. With this information in hand, you can further narrow your list of prospective schools.

Financing your education.   Because of economic pressure and shifting priorities, both the federal government and state governments are providing less money to help students finance their graduate education. Historically, money has been available from four major sources. *Loan programs* underwritten by the federal government allow students to borrow money at favorable interest rates and repay after leaving school. However, these loans have become increasingly difficult for graduate students to obtain as the federal government has begun to withdraw from the support of higher education. *Fellowships and scholarships* are available in a number of programs. These are outright grants given to strong students to help them finance their training. Again, with the country's changing priorities, these grants are harder to get than before. *Research and teaching assistantships* are also frequently available. Research assistantships are often financed through research grants obtained by faculty members and require the student to work on a particular research project. Teaching assistantships may involve a variety of duties, from grading papers or leading discussion sessions to actual classroom teaching. Both kinds of assistantships normally require up to twenty hours of work per week. Finally, *traineeships* in clinical psychology are sometimes available, although, again, there have been cutbacks in recent years. These are usually financed by the federal government, often in the form of grants to promising students.

It is clear that financing one's education is becoming more difficult. A number of schools do charge graduate assistants lower tuition rates, and students with fellowships or traineeships often pay no tuition at all. On the other hand, competition for all these forms of financial assistance is becoming increasingly keen. Information about financial matters will obviously be helpful in deciding where to apply for graduate study.

APA accreditation.   The APA maintains a Committee on Accreditation, which approves those programs that meet acceptable professional training standards. The list of approved schools is published each year in the December issue of the *American Psychologist*. The 1994 list contained 177 schools or sites with APA-approved programs in clinical psychology.

When to apply.   Schools vary in their deadlines, although most range from January 1 through February 15. However, students are advised to check carefully to make sure there is not, for example, a December deadline for a given school. While master's-level programs sometimes have deadlines as late as August, it is best not to gamble, since many schools enforce their deadlines rigidly.

Number of applications to submit.   There is no magic figure for the number of programs to which one should apply. A few students may apply to only one program and be accepted. Others may apply to twenty and be rejected by all of them. Obviously, the competition is fierce. Indeed, it has reached the point where the ratio of accepted applications to submitted ones is lower for clinical psychology programs offering a Ph.D. than for medical schools. It is not unusual for a school to receive 500 applications and accept fewer than 10.

The best strategy usually is to apply to as many schools as one can afford or can find the time and energy to prepare applications. Some schools have application fees as high as $40, although most are no higher than $25 and a few charge nothing at all. Furthermore, transcripts usually cost about a dollar and represent an added expense in the application process.

In view of all this, it is best to rank-order the schools you are willing to attend. From this list select several at or near the top, several from the middle, and a few others from the bottom tier. Thus, you will not have put all your eggs in one very small basket. To a certain extent, too, being accepted is an unpredictable event. It is not unusual for a student to be rejected by a program that has a modest national reputation and accepted by one that is highly recognized. Each school's selection committee has a somewhat different set of biases and guidelines. Therefore, do not give up hope when that first letter of rejection arrives.

Step 2. Application materials

Several elements compose one's completed application package. The elements summarized below are typical.

Test scores.   Virtually every school requires applicants to submit test scores. The test most frequently required is the *Graduate Record Examination* (GRE). In some cases the *Miller Analogies Test* (MAT) is required. Information about these tests is usually available from campus counseling centers or student personnel services as well as from your own psychology department. Additional information may be obtained by writing:

GRE: Graduate Record Examinations, Educational Testing Service, P.O. Box 6000, Princeton, NJ 08541-6000.
MAT: Psychological Corp., 304 East 4th St., New York, NY 10017.

The GRE consists of questions that tap quantitative, verbal, and analytical abilities. In addition, there is a Subject Test in psychology. Some schools require the psychology Subject Test, while others do not. The GRE is given in October, December, April, and June (General sections only). Since it takes up to six weeks for the results to be reported, most students choose the October date, which allows them to meet most schools' application deadlines. For the 1994-95 academic year, basic fees in the United States for the GRE were as follows: GRE General and Subject Tests—$112; General Test only—$56; Subject Test only—$56.

Transcripts.   Most schools require transcripts detailing your work at each institution you have attended. The application form may have a space for you to indicate your grade point average. Transcripts will be mailed by the institution's office of student records to those schools you request. Usually, a small fee is charged for the service.

Another point to consider is that some programs may require or strongly prefer course work in certain areas. For example, a recent survey (Mayne, Norcross, & Sayette, 1994b) indicated that the following courses were either required or recommended by at least one-third of the 108 APA-accredited clinical psychology doctoral programs sampled: statistics (94%); experimental methods/research design (68%); abnormal psychology (51%); physiological psychology/biopsychology (33%). Therefore, you will want to make sure that your transcript reflects that you have met any course requirements for a particular clinical program.

Letters of recommendation.   Three or four letters of recommendation are also required. The best persons to ask to write letters for you are professors who are familiar with your academic work and research experience. Letters from friends or relatives attesting to your high moral character are not very useful. The best letters are those from psychology professors with whom you have worked—not just in class but on special topics or research projects. A letter from a professor who taught you in a class of 249 others and who can only remember (by consulting the grade book) that you received an A is not nearly as useful as one from a professor with whom you worked on an independent project. A letter from a professional for whom you worked in a mental health-related job may also be quite helpful.

Unless you have specifically waived your right to see your letters of recommendation, the assumption by the readers of those letters will be that they are not confidential. Such readers will also be likely to assume that, if the letters are not confidential, you have seen them. It is often felt that such letters may be less frank and open than confidential statements in their assessment of your ability and potential. If you have doubts about how strong the letter of recommendation will be, you can always ask your potential reference for a candid assessment of your possibilities beforehand.

Personal statement.   Most application forms contain a section for a personal statement. This gives the selection committee a view of how you regard yourself in relation to clinical psychology. What are your motives? Why are you interested in clinical psychology and how did this interest develop? How have you prepared yourself and what are your career goals? Why are you interested in this particular clinical psychology program? These are just a few of the points often covered in such statements. They help to flesh out your application and also provide a glimpse of your verbal and writing abilities.

Experience.   Although not absolutely essential, evidence of research experience will usually be a definite plus and may give you a competitive edge. Such experience can be very helpful in your doctoral studies. Beyond that, however, research experience also suggests that you had the interest and motivation to seek out something beyond routine courses or ordinary classroom experience. It indicates that you are involved, and is usually taken as a positive sign of your potential for professional growth.

Likewise, practical experiences in mental health work can be helpful. Many students have been employed as aides in hospitals or as paraprofessionals in clinics, schools, community centers, crisis hotlines, and similar situations. Some have had practicum work associated with certain courses. Such experience suggests a greater level of sophistication—a sense that you already have some insight into what a career in the mental health field will be like. It also signifies something about your motivation.

■ Essential Qualifications

Students often ask about the minimum grade point average (GPA) required for admission or about the cutoff points for the GRE. These are difficult questions to answer, since programs vary considerably. The Mayne et al. survey, however, did indicate that 90% of all doctoral programs in clinical psychology use GRE scores to screen applicants (1994b). Therefore, for better or for worse, it appears that admissions committees do place a great deal of emphasis on GRE scores. In general, those schools that receive very large numbers of applications tend to require high GPA levels and GRE scores. Research-oriented Ph.D. programs tend to prefer higher GRE scores and GPAs than do practice-oriented Ph.D. programs or Psy.D. programs (Mayne et al., 1994b). As might be expected from these survey results, Mayne et al. report that it is much harder to gain admission into a research-oriented Ph.D. program in clinical psychology (acceptance rate = 6% of applicants) than into a Psy.D. program in clinical psychology (acceptance rate = 23%).

Some selection committees are concerned more with the student's GPA over the last two years rather than with that of the entire four years. A GPA of less than 3.5 on a 4.0 scale is, however, likely to make admission difficult. In the case of schools with a strong reputation, a GPA of 3.7 may be the minimum. High GRE scores are important. However, a number of schools will tolerate more modest scores if there are other compensating factors such as a high GPA or particularly strong letters of recommendation.

The foregoing comments do not apply to master's programs in clinical psychology. There is not as much competition for admission to these programs and, as a result, the GPA and GRE scores need not be as high. At the same time, it should be noted that completing such a program does not inevitably enhance one's chances of being admitted to a Ph.D. program later. In summarizing these matters, one clinical director at a major university had this to say about admission qualifications:

> First, and most important, is a psychology undergraduate degree with a high grade point average. Incidentally, we prefer a science/math-based array of courses rather than a soft set of courses. Approximately a fourth of our students enter with M.A. degrees, but this does not help them. We generally find that most everyone gets A's in M.A.-level programs, and thus we end up going back to the undergraduate record. Second, letters of recommendation are exceedingly important. Such letters are most informative when they are authored by people who truly know the applicant. Third, additional research or therapy experience is a plus. Fourth, good GRE scores are desirable but not absolutely necessary. In this latter vein, we are much more prone to weigh the undergraduate performance and letters of recommendation. (Personal communication)

■ A Profession in Movement

Clinical psychology is a profession in flux and ferment. Although clinical psychology retains its basic mission of applying psychological principles to the problems of individuals, the methods and the professional framework by which it seeks to accomplish this are undergoing change. Whether such change is good or reflects a major identity crisis that bodes ill for the profession is unclear. But one thing is certain. This is an exciting time to be a clinical psychologist and to participate in the ongoing shaping of a profession.

A recent demographic trend is important to note. Earlier in this chapter, we indicated that only approximately 25% of APA Division 12 (clinical psychology) members are women according to the most recent statistics available (ODEER, 1993). However, this percentage is likely to increase dramatically in the future. Increasingly, more women than men are receiving their doctorates in psychology, and this is especially true for clinical psychology (ODEER, 1993). Some have referred to this as the feminization of clinical psychology. What effect this change will have on the field is unclear. For example, it has been argued that the trend toward lower salaries for clinical psychologists in private practice may be directly related to the increased representation of women in clinical psychology (Philipson, 1993). On the other hand, it is clear that this change will serve to greatly advance the field because it will bring a broader range of perspectives to problems encountered in both clinical practice and clinical research.

There are training issues as well. Although the scientist-practitioner training model is still dominant, it is under fire. New models are beginning to emerge. Professional schools with no university affiliation have sprung up. New degree programs have been established within the structure of universities. For example, the *Doctor of Psychology* (Psy.D.) degree has become a more common alternative to traditional research-oriented Ph.D. degrees, and over 500 Psy.D. degrees in clinical psychology are awarded each year. The 1994 list of APA-accredited clinical programs that award the Psy.D. degree included 25 programs.

Others have called for a new model of training housed in university *professional schools* (Sechrest, 1985). Professional schools now award at least one-half of all doctorates in clinical psychology (personal communication, APA ODEER). Levy (1984) has even outlined a charter for a new human services psychology. This would be a generic training program composed of all the specialties concerned with promoting human welfare through psychological principles. Included would be clinical psychology, counseling psychology, school psychology, community psychology, health psychology, and other specialties. We discuss some of these alternative models in more detail in Chapter 3.

Increasingly, clinical psychologists are going into private practice. Issues of licensing and certification, participation in governmental health care programs, and other guild concerns seem to be preoccupying the clinical psychologist more and more. Paraprofessionals and subdoctoral mental health professionals are being employed with greater frequency in a variety of mental health settings. They are performing routine testing functions, assisting in group therapy, carrying out various administrative jobs in agencies, and so on. This trend has been reinforced by the fact that modern clinical psychologists are less and less willing to invest their time in diagnostic testing. Where once we had traditional individual psychotherapy and a bit of group psychotherapy, we now have brief therapy, cognitive-behavioral therapy, couple's therapy, gestalt therapy, family therapy, exposure therapy, rational-emotive therapy, and so on. It almost seems as if we could start a therapy-of-the-month club.

Some may find signs of the demise of clinical psychology in all of the foregoing; others may be excited by the sheer conflict of it all. But for the prospective student of clinical psychology the current situation offers an unparalleled opportunity to participate in shaping the future of a profession.

■ A Tolerance for Ambiguity

The orderly thing to do would be to conclude this chapter with a final, crisp definition of clinical psychology—one that would summarize and integrate our previous discussion and could readily be committed to memory. However, this does not seem possible or even useful. The problem resides in the range, diversity, and patterning of the interests and activities of clinical psychologists. To encompass such diversity a definition would have to be so lengthy or so general as to be essentially meaningless. For example, some feel that Resnick's (1991) definition that was presented at the beginning of this chapter is too broad and not specific to clinical psychology. Forty-five years ago, Shaffer and Lazarus (1952), in their textbook of clinical psychology, commented: "Nowhere is there real agreement over the exact role which should be played by the clinical psychologist"

(p. 25). Little has occurred in the meantime to persuade us to reject their evaluation. It might be well, then, to mention an important characteristic of the clinical psychologist—*the capacity to tolerate ambiguity.*

Assailed by some as charlatans, adored by others as saviors, depressed at times by their lack of knowledge about human behavior, exhilarated at other times by the remarkable improvement in their patients, bombarded by the conflicting claims of success made by cognitive behaviorists on the one hand and by humanistic psychologists on the other, criticized by academicians as being too applied and by other mental health colleagues as being too abstract or scientific—is it any wonder that a tolerance for ambiguity can be a helpful quality for clinicians? For those students who want all the answers about human behavior, clinical psychology can be a very disturbing enterprise. But for those who wish to participate in a search for increasingly effective means to improve the human condition, it can be rewarding indeed.

■ Focus Questions

1. What distinguishes a clinical psychologist from other mental health professionals?
2. How does a clinical psychologist integrate research and practice (i.e., clinical work)?
3. What current trends will likely affect the future roles of clinical psychologists?
4. What are the major components of a doctoral program in clinical psychology?
5. What are the general qualifications for graduate study in clinical psychology?

■ Key Terms

clinical praticum
clinical psychologist
counseling psychologist
doctoral degree
Graduate Record Examination
health psychologist
idiographic approach
internship
nomothetic approach
paraprofessional
professional schools

psychiatric social worker
psychiatrist
psychological clinic
Psy.D. degree
qualifying examination
rehabilitation psychologist
school psychologist
scientist-practitioner model of
    training
theoretical orientation

2

Historical Background: Chronology and Analysis

A particularly human characteristic is the need to know. Perhaps it is this need that has made the quest for insight through psychotherapy so enduring through the years. Achieving insight means understanding the origins of one's behavior. Only through an analysis of the past can the full import of the present come into focus. From the past we gain a sense of both the meaning and the reliability of the present and perhaps even some inklings of the future.

Likewise, a reflection on the roots of clinical psychology can promote a better understanding of the field. In this chapter, the reader will be offered a view of both the historical sweep of clinical psychology and some of the current issues that confront the field.

■ The Chronology

We will begin our survey of the background of clinical psychology with the chronology of diagnosis and assessment. First, we look at the historical roots of the field.

Historical roots

Establishing a certain time period as the beginning of clinical psychology or designating a particular person as its founder can be arbitrary if not downright misleading. One can certainly go back to Greek philosophers such as Thales, Hippocrates, or Aristotle who, long before the birth of Christ, were speculating about human beings and the nature of thought, sensation, and pathology (Shaffer & Lazarus, 1952). Since these philosophers are cited as antecedents of nearly every profession, movement, or system of thought in Western society, their citation here does little, perhaps, except to affirm our honorable beginnings.

For the years prior to 1890, there is really very little in the history of clinical psychology to separate it from the history of abnormal psychology or, as Zilboorg and Henry (1941) termed it, "medical psychology." Reisman (1976) finds it more useful to search for the roots of modern clinical psychology in the reform movements of the nineteenth century that ultimately resulted in improved care for the mentally ill. Such improvements, and the humanitarian impulses of those who encouraged them, fostered the faint beginnings of the mental health professions as we know them today (Hothersall, 1984). One of the major figures in this movement was Philippe Pinel, a French physician. Shocked by the senseless brutality that was the custom in the mental hospitals of his day, he managed to get himself appointed head of the asylum at Bicêtre, and later, Salpêtrière. He managed through kindness and humanity to accomplish much in a very difficult field. Whether Pinel's accomplishments should be regarded as personal achievements or as logical developments growing out of the philosophy of Rousseau and the idealism of the French Revolution is unclear. In any event, his work was a milestone in the development of psychiatry, the mental health approach, and, ultimately, of clinical psychology.

At about the same time, an Englishman, William Tuke, was devoting himself to the establishment of what might be called a model hospital for the humane treatment of the sick and troubled. In America, Eli Todd was laboring long and successfully to develop a retreat in Hartford for the mentally ill. Like his European counterparts, Todd emphasized the role of civilized care, respect, and morality. Through his efforts, it became less fashionable to regard mental patients as incurable. The search for psychological antecedents and an emphasis on treatment had begun to replace the routine harshness of custody.

Another American who had a profound effect on the mental health movement was Dorothea Dix. She campaigned for better facilities for the mentally ill. With determination and single-mindedness, Dix pushed, prodded, and cajoled until she got responses from government officials. Using the force of logic, facts, public sentiment, and good old-fashioned lobbying, she wrought her will. And in 1848, New Jersey responded by building a hospital for the insane—the first in a procession of over 30 states to do so.

Out of the efforts of such people, the groundwork was laid for a field of clinical psychology. But it would be a mistake to evaluate these contributions apart from the social forces and ideas of the time. In the nineteenth century, philosophers and writers were proclaiming the dignity and equality of all. Governments were beginning to respond. Even science, which was just coming into its own, contributed to the movement. An atmosphere of "knowledge through experimentation" began to prevail. A feeling that people can predict, understand, and perhaps even control the human condition began to replace older wisdom. This ferment in science, literature, politics, government, and reform combined to produce the first clear and unmistakable signs of new professions in what would come to be referred to as mental health.

These short sketches represent some of the roots of clinical psychology. In the following pages we will trace its development in the specific areas of diagnosis and assessment, intervention, research, and professional matters.

Diagnosis and assessment

The beginnings (1850–1899).   For many, the essence of clinical psychology has always been its emphasis on the differences among people. Much

Figure 2-1
Dorothea Dix traveled from state to state for 40 years campaigning for more humane
   treatment and better facilities for the insane and the retarded. During the Civil War
   she was chief of hospital nurses for the Union forces. *The Bettmann Archive*

of that emphasis can be traced to Francis Galton, an Englishman. Statistical analysis fascinated him, and he devoted a great deal of effort to the application of quantitative methods to understanding differences among people. Pursuing his interests
in sensory acuity, motor skills, and reaction time, he established an anthropomet-
ric laboratory in 1882.

   This tradition was further enhanced by the work of James McKeen Cattell,
an American. Despite the disapproval of Wilhelm Wundt, in whose laboratory he
assisted, Cattell turned his attention to reaction-time differences among people.
He believed, as did Galton, that this was a way of approaching the study of intelligence. In fact, he coined the term *mental tests* to describe his measures.
Through the use of a battery of ten tests Cattell hoped to discover the constancy
of mental processes, even predicting that such tests could be used in the selection
and training of people as well as in the detection of disease. From such early work
we can see the first halting steps of the testing movement.

   A related trend of the same general period is illustrated by the diagnostic
work of Emil Kraepelin in 1913. Few psychiatrists of the time could equal his professional stature. When Kraepelin divided mental illness into those types determined by exogenous factors (curable) and those caused by endogenous factors (incurable) he initiated a romance with classification schemes that persists even today.
His descriptions and classifications of patients were heuristic and have served to
stimulate an enormous amount of discussion about psychopathology.

The advent of the modern era (1900–1919). One of the major developments in this era was the rise of mental measurement or diagnostic psychological testing. The beginning may lie with Galton or Cattell, but the decisive impetus came from the work of Alfred Binet.

Binet was convinced that the key to the study of individual differences involved the notion of norms and deviations from those norms. His conviction was fortunate because, in 1904, a commission approached Binet and his collaborator Théodore Simon about developing a means of ensuring that defective children were properly educated. In order to objectively distinguish among various degrees of subnormality, the two men developed the 1908 Binet-Simon Scale. It is hard to overestimate the profound influence that this scale has exerted on the measurement of intelligence. Henry Goddard introduced the Binet tests to America, and Lewis Terman produced an American revision in 1916.

Some progress was also being made in the area of *personality testing.* Carl Jung began using word-association methods around 1905 to uncover unconscious complexes. In 1910, the Kent-Rosanoff Free Association Test was published. Even though Galton had been experimenting with such techniques as early as 1879, these free-association tests marked a significant advance in diagnostic testing.

In 1904 Charles Spearman offered the concept of a general intelligence that he termed g. Edward Thorndike countered with a conceptualization that emphasized the importance of separate abilities. Whatever the truth, the great debate regarding the nature of intelligence was on—a debate that still rages today.

When the United States entered World War I in 1917, the need arose to screen and classify the hordes of military recruits who were being pressed into service. A committee of five members from the American Psychological Association (APA) was appointed by the Medical Department of the Army. Its chairman was Robert Yerkes. The committee was charged with the task of creating a system for classifying men according to their ability levels. It designed the Army Alpha test in 1917. This verbal scale was quickly followed by a nonverbal version, the Army Beta test. In a similar vein, Robert Woodworth developed his Psychoneurotic Inventory in 1917. This was perhaps the first questionnaire designed to reveal abnormal behavior. With the advent of such rough screening instruments as Woodworth's Personal Data Sheet and the Army Alpha and Beta, the group testing movement was on its way.

Between the wars (1920–1939). Between the two world wars, there was substantial progress in diagnostic psychological testing. Pintner and Paterson introduced their nonverbal intelligence scale. In 1930, the Arthur Point Scale appeared, and in 1934 it was followed by the Cornell-Coxe test. In 1926, the Goodenough Draw-a-Man technique for measuring intelligence was published. The psychologist now had individual and group tests as well as verbal and nonverbal tests, and people were talking in the vernacular of intelligence quotients.

Aptitude testing, epitomized by the Seashore tests of musical ability, was now with us. Interest tests had also made their appearance by this time. In 1927, the Strong Vocational Interest Blank came upon the scene and was followed later by the Kuder Preference Record.

The continuing debate on theoretical issues in intelligence was further sparked in 1927 by Louis Thurstone's contribution based upon factor analysis.

Spearman, Thorndike, and Thurstone had all entered the intelligence arena with important concepts. In 1928, Gesell's developmental scales were published, and in 1936 Doll's Vineland Social Maturity Scale appeared. The latter was a scale that approached behavior not strictly in terms of intelligence but in terms of an individual's social maturity or competence.

A major development in the intelligence testing movement occurred in 1939. It was then that David Wechsler published the Wechsler-Bellevue test. Until then there had been no satisfactory individual measure of adult intelligence. Subsequent revisions of the Wechsler-Bellevue have kept it, to this day, the premier individual test for adult intelligence.

But tests of intelligence, interests, and abilities were not the only testing developments in these years. The field of personality testing was also making great strides. Woodworth's Personal Data Sheet was followed in 1921 by the Pressey X-0 Test for emotions and in 1923 by the Downey Will-Temperament Test. The Allport-Vernon Study of Values came along in 1931.

But the big news was projective testing. Some beginning progress had already been made through the word-association research of Galton, Jung, and Kent and Rosanoff. However, the major impetus for projectives occurred in 1921, when Hermann Rorschach, a Swiss psychiatrist, published *Psychodiagnostik*, which described his use of inkblots to diagnose psychiatric patients. Rorschach's work suggested that when people respond to an ambiguous test stimulus they will reveal something of their responses to real-life experiences. However, it was not until 1937, when S. J. Beck and Bruno Klopfer published their separate manuals and scoring procedures, that the Rorschach method really caught on. Then in 1939 L. K. Frank coined the term *projective techniques*. From that point on, a veritable flood of research publications, books, courses, and variations of techniques poured forth. Although the flood may have receded, the river still runs deep.

Another aspect of the projective movement is represented by the 1935 publication by Christiana Morgan and Henry Murray of the Thematic Apperception Test (TAT). This test requires the person to look at ambiguous pictures and then make up a story to describe the activities, thoughts, and feelings of the people in those pictures. The TAT has proved to be a widely used projective device, and it is probably second only to the Rorschach in popularity among projective tests. Then, in 1938, Lauretta Bender published her Bender-Gestalt Test. This test has been widely used both as a projective measure of personality and as a measure of brain dysfunction.

World War II and beyond (1940–present).

Clinical psychology's success with intelligence tests was largely responsible for its subsequent movement into personality assessment. As clinicians moved beyond the confines of public schools and institutions for the feebleminded and into penal institutions, mental hospitals, and clinics, referring physicians and psychiatrists gradually began to ask more complex questions. Questions such as, What is this patient's ability level? began to evolve into questions that dealt with differential diagnosis. Is this patient's level of functioning a product of constitutional intellectual limitations, or is a disease process such as schizophrenia eroding intellectual performance? Since answering such questions involved more than the sheer identification of an IQ level, new methods of examining the patient's performance on intelligence tests were developed. In many instances, the psychologist began to look at patterns of performance rather than just an overall score.

In 1943, the Minnesota Multiphasic Personality Inventory (MMPI) appeared (Hathaway, 1943). The MMPI was an objective self-report test whose major function initially seemed to be one of attaching psychiatric labels to patients. Other tests such as the Rorschach were often being put to similar uses.

The decades of the 1940s and 1950s witnessed a growing sophistication in our testing technology. Triggered by the development of the MMPI, debates over the relative effectiveness of clinical and statistical prediction began to occur (Meehl, 1954; Sarbin, 1943). Which was superior—the clinician's subjective impressions or hard, objective approaches based on crisp data such as test scores that were readily quantifiable? There were also sophisticated discussions of methods of validating tests and guarding against misleading test-taking attitudes on the part of subjects (Cronbach, 1946; Cronbach & Meehl, 1955). Assessment had come a long way since the crude instruments of the World War I era. Indeed, during this period we knew enough about constructing tests that the APA could promulgate standards for their proper development (American Psychological Association, 1954).

In the aftermath of World War II, the importance of intelligence testing continued. In 1949 Wechsler published another individual test. This one, the Wechsler Intelligence Scale for Children, was to become a serious alternative to the Stanford-Binet. Later, in 1955, the Wechsler Adult Intelligence Scale (a revision of the Wechsler-Bellevue scale) appeared. These tests marked the beginning of a whole series of revisions to the child and adult forms of the Wechsler scales.

From the 1940s through the 1950s there was an explosive growth of personality tests. This was especially true in the case of projective tests. The Rorschach and the TAT continued in a preeminent position. But many other devices were also published during these years (Anderson & Anderson, 1951). Clinical psychologists were seen as experts in psychodiagnosis, the use and interpretation of psychological test scores as a basis for diagnostic formulation as well as treatment planning. However, a rift was growing within the profession as to whether objective or projective assessment measures were better suited to accurately describe personality and psychopathology. Objective measures like the MMPI and the MMPI-2 (Butcher et al., 1989) are based on a nomothetic approach to assessment in which test scores are interpreted using empirically based rules involving the contrast between an obtained score and the average score obtained from a large representative sample. Responses from projective measures, in contrast, are often interpreted using an idiographic approach. The focus may be more on the individual, and often interpretations are guided as much by psychodynamic theory as they are by empirically supported rules. This rift between those who favor either objective or projective techniques continues to this day.

Surprisingly, however, the major challenger to personality testing came from outside these ranks. Beginning in the late 1950s, a movement termed radical behaviorism began to assert its influence. Those that adhered to this orientation held that only overt behavior can be measured and that it is not useful or desirable to infer the level or existence of personality traits from psychological test results; personality traits, according to the radical behaviorists, cannot be measured directly.

Personality assessment came under attack, and clinical psychology programs in the 1960s took on much more of a behavioral bent. In 1968, Walter Mischel made a strong case that traits existed more in the minds of observers than in the behavior of the observed. Situations, and not some nebulous set of traits, were said to be responsible for the ways we behaved. In tune with this view, the 1970s would witness the rise of *behavioral assessment.* Behaviors were understood within the context of the stimuli or situations that either preceded or followed them.

Did this in turn mark the death of personality assessment? Actually, it did not. The resurgence of interest that we saw in the 1980s and 1990s can be attributed to the presentation and coverage of a variety of *personality disorders* in the American diagnostic system for mental disorders; the introduction of a number of more contemporary and psychometrically sound personality inventories (e.g., the Millon Clinical Multiaxial Inventory; the NEO-Personality Inventory); and several empirical demonstrations that personality traits do appear to be fairly stable across time and across situations (e.g., Costa & McCrae, 1988; Epstein & O'Brien, 1985).

As we mentioned, the official American diagnostic classification system has influenced the clinical assessment field. The first edition of the American Psychiatric Association's *Diagnostic and Statistical Manual of Mental Disorders* (DSM-I) appeared in 1952. Revisions of this manual have appeared periodically, the last one in 1994. In addition to this diagnostic system's influence on the content of self-report inventories (i.e., new inventories were designed to measure the DSM mental disorders), it spurred the growth of another line of assessment tools—the structured diagnostic interviews. These interviews consist of a standard list of questions that are keyed to the diagnostic criteria for various disorders from the DSM. Clinicians (or researchers) that need to formulate a DSM diagnosis for a patient (or research participant) can use these interviews; it is no longer necessary to administer a psychological test and then infer a patient's diagnostic status from the test scores.

Finally, it is noteworthy that interest in *neuropsychological assessment* has grown tremendously as well. Neuropsychological assessment is used to evaluate relative strengths and deficits of patients based on empirically established brain-behavior (i.e., test responses) relationships. Several devices were introduced that were widely used to detect impaired brain functioning, including the Bender-Gestalt Test. In 1947, Halstead introduced an entire test battery to aid in the diagnosis of neuropsychological problems. Contemporary neuropsychological assessment typically involves one of two approaches. Some use a uniform group, or battery, of tests for all patients. Others use a small subset of tests initially and then, based on the results of these initial tests, employ additional tests to resolve and answer the referral questions. Some of the more popular neuropsychological test batteries include the Halstead-Reitan (Reitan, 1969) and the Luria-Nebraska Neuropsychological Battery (Golden, Purisch, & Hammeke, 1985). The field of neuropsychology is becoming increasingly sophisticated. Many neuropsychological tests are now computer-administered, more focus is being directed at the identification of neuropsychological correlates of mental disorder, and test results are integral components of rehabilitation planning (Golden, Zillmer, & Spiers, 1992; Jones & Butters, 1991).

Table 2-1

Highlights in the chronology of assessment.

1882	Galton establishes an anthropometric laboratory	1939	L. K. Frank coins the term *projective techniques*
1890	Cattell coins the term *mental test*	1939	The Wechsler-Bellevue Intelligence Scale is published
1904	Binet begins work on his intelligence scale	1943	The MMPI is published
		1947	Halstead introduces a neuropsychological test battery
1905	Jung begins using the word-association method		
1913	Kraepelin publishes his work on psychiatric diagnosis	1952	American Psychiatric Association publishes psychiatric diagnostic system (DSM-I)
1916	Terman produces an American version of the Binet scale		
		1970s	The rise of behavioral assessment
1917	The Yerkes committee develops the Army Alpha test	1980	DSM-III is published
		1980s	Resurgence of interest in personality assessment
1921	Rorschach publishes his work on the inkblot method		
		1980s	Proliferation of computer-based test interpretations (CBTIs)
1935	Morgan and Murray publish the TAT		
1938	Bender publishes her Bender-Gestalt Scale Test	1994	DSM-IV is published

A number of these assessment highlights are summarized in Table 2-1.

Interventions

The beginnings (1850–1899).   Kraepelin's focus was on the classification of psychoses, but others were investigating new treatments for neurotic patients such as suggestion and hypnosis. Specifically, Jean Charcot gained a widespread reputation for his investigations of hysterical patients. He was a master of the dramatic clinical demonstration with hypnotized patients. As a matter of fact, he believed that only hysterics could be hypnotized. However, he was probably investigating hypnosis rather than hysteria. Others, such as Hippolyte Bernheim and Pierre Janet, were critical of Charcot's work. Bernheim felt that the symptomatology of hysteria was nothing more than suggestibility. Janet, on the other hand, came to regard hysteria as a manifestation of a "split personality" and also as a kind of hereditary degeneration.

At about the same time, the momentous collaboration of Josef Breuer and Sigmund Freud began. In the early 1880s, Breuer was treating a young hysterical patient named "Anna O." Anna O.'s treatment presented many challenges but also led to theoretical breakthroughs that would influence psychotherapy practice

Figure 2-2
Jean Charcot demonstrates hypnosis with a patient called "Wit." Although trained as a
 neurologist, he employed a psychosocial approach in explaining hysteria. *The
 Bettmann Archive*

for years to come. Breuer discussed the case extensively with Freud, who became
so interested that he went to Paris to learn all that Charcot could teach him about
hysteria. To considerably shorten a long story, in 1895 Breuer and Freud published *Studies on Hysteria*. For a variety of reasons, the relationship between the
two men subsequently became quite strained. But their collaboration served as the
launching pad for *psychoanalysis*, the single most influential theoretical and treatment development in the history of psychiatry and clinical psychology.

    The advent of the modern era (1900–1919). Reformers such
as Clifford Beers have been important in the history of clinical psychology. Beers,
who was hospitalized in the wake of severe depression, passed into a manic phase
and began recording his experiences in the hospital. When he was free of his
manic-depressive symptoms he was released. But this release did not weaken his
resolve to write a book exposing the abuses in the hospital care of the mentally ill.
He very much wanted to generate a public movement to rectify those abuses. In
1908, *A Mind That Found Itself* was published, and the mental hygiene movement in America was launched.
    In 1900, shortly before Beers entered the hospital, Freud published *The In-
terpretation of Dreams*. With this event, the psychoanalytic movement was in full
swing. Concepts such as the unconscious, the Oedipus complex, and the ego began their ascendance, and sexuality became the coin of the psychological realm.

Figure 2-3
Clifford Beers wrote *A Mind That Found Itself,* which was a chronicle of his
  experiences while hospitalized as a mental patient. His efforts were instrumental
  in launching the mental hygiene movement. *The Bettman Archive*

Freud's ideas were by no means an overnight success. Recognition was slow in
coming, but converts did begin to beat a path to his door. Alfred Adler, Carl Jung,
and others began to take notice. Other books were published by Freud, and the
list of converts grew still longer—A. A. Brill, Paul Federn, Otto Rank, Ernest
Jones, Wilhelm Stekel, Sandor Ferenczi, and others.

Later in this chapter we will note Witmer's establishment of the first psychological clinic. But also important was William Healy's establishment of a child guidance clinic in Chicago in 1909. This clinic used a team approach involving psychiatrists, social workers, and psychologists. They directed their efforts toward what
would now be labeled juvenile delinquents rather than toward the learning problems
of children that had earlier attracted Witmer's attention. Furthermore, Healy's approach was much influenced by Freudian concepts and methods. Such an approach ultimately had the effect of shifting clinical psychology's work with children
in the dynamic direction of Freud rather than into an educational framework.

In 1905 Joseph Pratt, an internist, and Elwood Worcester, a psychologist,
began to use a method of supportive discussion among hospitalized mental patients. This was the forerunner of a variety of group therapy methods that gained
prominence in the 1920s and 1930s.

Between the wars (1920–1939).   The psychoanalysis of the early
twentieth century was largely devoted to the treatment of adults and was practiced

almost exclusively by analysts whose basic training was in medicine. Freud, however, argued that psychoanalysts did not need medical training. Despite Freud's protestations (Freud, 1959), the medical profession "captured" psychoanalytic therapy and in so doing made the subsequent entry of psychologists into the therapy enterprise quite difficult.

The eventual entry of psychologists into therapeutic activities was a natural outgrowth of their early work with children in various guidance clinics. At first, that work was largely confined to the evaluation of children's intellectual abilities, and this, of course, involved consultations with parents and teachers. But it is hard to separate intellectual functioning and school success from the larger psychological aspects of behavior. As a result, it was only natural that psychologists should begin to offer advice and make recommendations beyond the narrow analysis of abilities.

As psychologists looked for psychological principles to aid them in their efforts, the work of both Freud and Alfred Adler came to their attention. In particular the work of Adler impressed them; it had a more commonsense ring than that of Freud. Moreover, Freud's emphasis seemed to lie with adults and with the sexual antecedents of their problems, whereas Adler's de-emphasis of the role of sexuality in a person's psychological economy and his concomitant emphasis on the structure of family relationships seemed much more congenial to American mental health professionals in the field. By the early 1930s, Adler's (1930) ideas were firmly ensconced in those American clinics that dealt with children's problems.

A second trend that influenced early work with children—play therapy—was more directly derived from traditional Freudian principles. Play therapy is essentially a technique that relies on the curative powers of the release of anxiety or hostility through expressive play. In 1928, Anna Freud, the distinguished daughter of Sigmund Freud, described a method of play therapy derived from psychoanalytic principles.

Group therapy also began to attract attention. By the early 1930s the work of both J. L. Moreno and S. R. Slavson was having an impact. Another precursor of things to come was the technique of passive therapy described by Frederick Allen (1934). In this approach one could see some of the first stirrings of what became client-centered therapy. But there were other straws in the wind too. In 1920, John Watson described the famous case of Albert and the white rat, in which a young boy was conditioned to develop a neurotic-like fear of white, furry objects (Watson & Rayner, 1920). A few years later, Mary Cover Jones (1924) showed how such fears could be removed through conditioning. Still later, J. Levy (1938) described relationship therapy. These latter three events marked the beginnings of behavior therapy, a very popular and influential group of therapeutic methods used today.

World War II and beyond (1940–present).   World War II not only absorbed enormous numbers of men; it also contributed to the emotional difficulties that developed in many of them. The military physicians and psychiatrists were too few in number to cope with their problems. As a result, psychologists began to fill the mental health breach. At first, their role was ancillary and mainly involved group psychotherapy. But increasingly, they began to engage in individual psychotherapy, for they performed well in both the short-term goal of returning men to combat and in the longer-term goal of rehabilitation. Their successful performance of these activities, along with the research and testing skills they had already demonstrated, gradually produced an increasing acceptance of psychologists as mental health professionals.

This wartime experience whetted the appetites of psychologists for greater responsibility in the mental health field. It is uncertain whether this increasing focus on psychotherapy stemmed from a desire to gain greater professional responsibility, an awareness that they possessed the skills to perform mental health tasks, an embryonic disenchantment with the ultimate utility of diagnostic work, or some combination of the three. But the stage had been set.

An additional contributing factor to this chain of events was an outgrowth of the turmoil in Europe in the 1930s. The pressures of Nazi tyranny forced many European psychiatrists and psychologists to leave their homelands, and many of them ultimately settled in the United States. Through professional meetings, lectures, and other gatherings, the ideas of the Freudian movement generated excitement and gained increasing credence in psychology. Partly as the result of all this, clinical psychologists began to reduce their emphasis on the assessment of intelligence, ability testing, and the measurement of brain dysfunction. They became increasingly interested in personality development and its description. As intelligence testing receded in importance, psychotherapy and personality theory began to move into the foreground. A large part of the activity in these areas was psychoanalytic in character. But in 1950, John Dollard and Neal Miller published their book *Personality and Psychotherapy,* which was a seminal attempt to translate the psychoanalysis of Freud into the language of learning theory. Indeed, psychoanalysis was such a dominant force of the time that when Carl Rogers published *Client-Centered Therapy* in 1942, his was the first major alternative to psychoanalytic therapy up to that time. Rogers's book was an enormously significant development that had extensive repercussions in the world of psychotherapy and research.

A few years later Alexander and French (1946) published an influential book on briefer psychoanalytic interventions. Newer forms of therapy were beginning to proliferate. For example, Perls introduced Gestalt therapy (Perls, Hefferline, & Goodman, 1951) and Frankl (1953) talked about logotherapy and its relationship to existential theory. In 1958 Ackerman described family therapy, and in 1962 Ellis explained his rational-emotive therapy. At about the same time, along came Berne's (1961) transactional analysis, or TA. Therapy had surely become a growth industry. No better indication of the importance of psychotherapy in the professional lives of clinicians was there than the effect of Eysenck's (1952) critique of therapy. His scathing report on the ineffectiveness of psychotherapy alarmed many and inspired others to conduct research designed to prove him wrong.

But psychotherapy was not the whole story. The behaviorists were beginning to develop what they regarded as a more hardheaded brand of therapy. Andrew Salter (1949) wrote the book *Conditioned Reflex Therapy.* It was a pioneering work in what later evolved into desensitization methods. In 1953, B. F. Skinner

furthered the behavioral therapy cause when he outlined the application of operant principles to therapeutic and social interventions. Then in 1958 Joseph Wolpe
introduced systematic desensitization, a technique based on conditioning principles. The behavior therapy movement was now more firmly entrenched than ever.
Albert Bandura (1969) set the stage for the cognitive-behavioral movement by
demonstrating how behavior could be modified through the observation of others,
known as *modeling.*

Whereas psychoanalysis and psychodynamic psychotherapy were previously
the dominant forces, behavior therapy was now gaining in popularity among clinical psychologists. Its appeal stemmed from its focus on observable (and measurable) behavior, the shorter length or treatment required, and the emphasis on the
empirical evaluation of treatment outcome. Regarding the latter, behavior therapy
helped to stimulate the growth of the field of psychotherapy research. Previously,
only a select number of academics conducted studies of treatment efficacy. We
now see many researchers and practitioners who use empirical methods to investigate the effectiveness of various treatment techniques.

Several other trends in intervention are noteworthy. First, the number of
treatments employed by clinical psychologists has grown tremendously over the
years. These range from cognitive-behavioral approaches that have empirical support to trendier approaches like inner-child therapy that have no empirical support. Some have estimated that number of therapies available to be well over 400.
Fortunately, not all of these are "therapies-of-the-month," and many have empirical support. Perhaps because of this startling array of therapeutic orientations and
treatment choices, many clinical psychologists refer to themselves as *eclectics.*
These clinicians employ the techniques of more than one theoretical orientation;
selection is based on the particular problems presented by the individual client or
patient. Relatedly, many clinical psychologists are interested in integrating various
approaches into one therapeutic modality as well as identifying common factors
that underlie different approaches to treatment (Frank, 1971).

Second, *brief or time-effective therapy* (Budman & Gurman, 1988) is becoming a preferred mode of psychotherapeutic intervention for several reasons.
Many individuals cannot afford years of psychotherapy. Briefer forms of therapy
have been shown to be equally as effective, if not more effective, than traditional
psychotherapy. Further, managed care companies who control reimbursement for
mental health treatment are often unwilling to reimburse clinicians for more than
a handful of sessions. Along with the development of brief forms of therapy, manualized forms of treatment have been introduced into clinical work (Beck, Rush,
Shaw, & Emery, 1979; Strupp & Binder, 1984). These manuals are useful for
clinicians because they outline treatment goals for each session as well as techniques to be used, and, typically, the treatment "package" can be implemented
and completed in 10 to 15 sessions or less. Currently, treatment manuals are
available for a wide range of psychological problems including depression, anxiety
disorders, and personality disorders.

Finally, another line of intervention is important to highlight as well. By the
1950s, some clinicians had begun to be disenchanted with therapy methods that
dealt with one patient at a time (or even therapies involving ten patients at a time,

as in group therapy). They sought a more "preventive" approach. Their search culminated in the rise of community psychology in the 1960s and *health psychology* in the 1980s. A growing number of clinical psychologists provide services related to the prevention of health problems, mental health problems, and injury. The area of prevention is often associated with health psychology and will increasingly be in the spotlight in years to come as psychology is called upon by primary care physicians and managed care companies.

A summary of the major historical events relevant to interventions is presented in Table 2-2.

Research

The beginnings (1850–1899).   The academic research tradition in psychology owes much to the work of two men. Wilhelm Wundt, a German, is usually credited with establishing the first formal psychological laboratory in Leipzig in 1879. In that same decade, an American, William James, also established a laboratory, and in 1890 he published his classic text, *Principles of Psychology*. The work of both these men exemplifies the scholarly tradition. But their influence is also clearly discernible in the scientist-practitioner model that has served the field of clinical psychology for so many years.

The advent of the modern era (1900–1919).   During this period, Ivan Pavlov was lecturing on the conditioned reflex. His work on conditioning left an important legacy for clinical psychology. The notion of classical conditioning has become a central part of theory and research while also playing a significant role in a variety of therapeutic methods. Another important development was research on intelligence testing. In 1905 Binet and Simon offered some evidence for the validity of their new test, and in 1916 Terman's research on the Binet-Simon test appeared. This was also the era of the development of the Army Alpha and Beta tests, as noted previously.

Between the wars (1920–1939).   Clinical research was still in its infancy. Much of the noteworthy work comprised the development of tests. For example, as noted earlier, there was the 1939 publication of the Wechsler-Bellevue test along with all the personality testing work of the 1930s. On the academic research scene, both behaviorism and Gestalt psychology were prominent. Behaviorism taught clinicians the power of conditioning in the development and treatment of behavior disorders. Gestalt psychology emphasized the importance of understanding patients' unique perceptions as contributory to their problems.

World War II and beyond (1940–present).   By the mid-1960s, diagnosis and assessment had become less important for many clinicians. But in the 1950s you would hardly have predicted it. The journals were full of research studies dealing with both intelligence testing and personality assessment. Study after study dealt with various aspects of the Stanford-Binet and the Wechsler scales. Research on their validity and reliability, their use with various pathological groups, short forms, and implications for personality appeared in waves. The story was

■

Table 2-2
Highlights in the chronology of interventions.

1793	Pinel introduces humane care in French asylums	1950	Dollard and Miller publish *Personality and Psychotherapy*
1848	Efforts of Dix culminate in the construction of a hospital for the insane	1951	Rogers publishes *Client-Centered Therapy*
1895	Breuer and Freud publish *Studies on Hysteria*	1952	Eysenck publishes his critique of psychotherapy
1900	Freud publishes *The Interpretation of Dreams*	1953	Skinner outlines the application of operant principles
1908	Beers inaugurates the mental hygiene movement	1958	Wolpe describes the method of systematic desensitization
1909	Healy founds a child guidance clinic in Chicago	1965	A conference in Swampscott, Mass. gives birth to the community psychology movement
1920	Watson and Rayner describe the conditioning of fears		
1932	Moreno introduces the notion of group therapy	1980s	The rise of health psychology, an increasing focus on brief psychotherapy, and an increase in psychotherapy research

similar for projective tests. Literally hundreds of studies dealing with the Rorschach and TAT were published. Many of these studies also focused on issues of reliability and validity. Some observers attribute part of the subsequent decline in projective testing to the many negative validity studies that appeared in this time frame. Then, in 1940, data on the new MMPI test appeared.

Another very important research development during these years was the emergence of studies on the process and effectiveness of psychotherapy. As noted previously, Eysenck's critique sent clinicians scrambling to shore up psychotherapy's image through solid research evidence. One of the real pioneers in therapy research was Carl Rogers (1951). His use of recordings to study the process of therapy opened windows to an activity that had long been shrouded in mystery. Rogers and Dymond (1954) reported controlled research findings on the counseling process.

Another research landmark of this era was the publication of Julian Rotter's *Social Learning and Clinical Psychology* in 1954. It presented not only a social learning theory but also a series of controlled studies that provided an empirical foundation for the theory. Research on the theory's implications for assessment and therapy was also included. The work provided a solid foundation upon which subsequent social learning theorists could build.

The 1950s also witnessed the explicit beginnings of the more behaviorally oriented forms of intervention. Joseph Wolpe's research in South Africa on animal and human learning convinced him that his work was relevant to human emotional problems. This led him to develop the method of *systematic desensitization* (Wolpe, 1958). This is a behavioral method that seems to rely neither upon insight thought to be so necessary by the psychoanalysts nor on growth potential that is thought equally necessary by the client-centered school of therapy. Arnold Lazarus and Stanley Rachman were two others who helped facilitate this movement. Hans Eysenck was another influential figure in this behavioral research movement. He coined the term *behavior therapy* and wrote an important book on the topic in 1960.

As noted earlier, beginning in the 1950s, the effectiveness of psychotherapy had been questioned. But in 1977 Mary Smith and Gene Glass published a survey that supported the efficacy of therapy. This work laid the basis for a series of studies that has helped us better understand the way therapeutic methods affect patients. As we noted previously, the field of *psychotherapy research* continues to grow to this day.

Other areas of research that have grown tremendously are the fields of diagnosis and classification, as well as psychological testing and measurement. The introduction of DSM-III (APA, 1980) spurred an explosion of research aimed at evaluating the reliability, validity, and utility of specific criteria listed for the mental disorders included in this manual. In both psychiatry and psychology journals, multiple studies appeared whose focus was on the DSM-III criteria for syndromes like schizophrenia, major depression, and antisocial personality disorder. In addition, more clinical psychologists began conducting research aimed at identifying the *etiological* (i.e., causal) factors associated with the development of various mental disorders. The factors investigated ranged from genetic predispositions to traumatic childhood events like physical or sexual abuse.

Published research on psychological inventories, interviews, and rating scales has also increased. With the proliferation of psychological instruments available to both researchers and clinicians, there was a need to empirically evaluate the reliability and validity of these measures. An example of the growth of this research area is the splitting of a major clinical psychology journal, the *Journal of Consulting and Clinical Psychology* (JCCP), in two. Now we have the journal *Psychological Assessment* as well as JCCP, with the former being the primary outlet for research on psychological tests and measures that are used by clinical psychologists.

Because research is an important part of all of clinical psychology, we will be discussing research methods, research on particular topics, and the historical context of research in these areas throughout this book. Many of the research highlights mentioned in this section are summarized in Table 2-3.

The profession

The beginnings (1850–1899).   Two events of great significance in the development of clinical psychology as a profession occurred just as the nineteenth century was winding down. The first event was the founding of the American Psychological Association (APA) in 1892, with G. Stanley Hall as its first president. Although the membership of the association was still fewer than 100 by the close of the nineteenth century, the profession had truly begun.

■

Table 2-3

Highlights in the chronology of research.

1879	Wundt establishes the first psychological laboratory in Leipzig	1952	The Eysenck critique of psychotherapy appears
1890	James publishes his *Principles of Psychology*	1954	Rotter publishes his social learning theory
1905	Binet and Simon offer validity data for their test	1954	Rogers and Dymond report their research on the counseling process
1916	Terman research on the Binet scale appears	1977	Smith and Glass present their survey of therapy studies
1939	Wechsler publishes his research on the Wechsler-Bellevue scale	1980s	Psychopathology research shows tremendous growth following the introduction of DSM-III in 198
1940	Hathaway and McKinley publish MMPI data		

The birth of clinical psychology was not far behind. It was in 1896 that Lightner Witmer established the first psychological clinic at the University of Pennsylvania. Many would date the real beginning of clinical psychology from this time (Misiak & Sexton, 1966).

It was also Witmer who, in 1907, founded the first journal in clinical psychology, *The Psychological Clinic*—a journal that he edited and contributed articles to until it ceased publication in 1935.

Witmer's clinic was devoted to the treatment of children who were experiencing learning problems or were disruptive in the classroom. In the very first issue of *The Psychological Clinic* Witmer wrote:

> Children from the public schools of Philadelphia and adjacent cities have been brought to the laboratory by parents or teachers; these children had made themselves conspicuous because of an inability to progress in school work as rapidly as other children, or because of moral defects which rendered them difficult to manage under ordinary discipline.
>
> When brought to the psychological clinic, such children are given a physical and mental examination; if the result of this examination shows it to be desirable, they are then sent to specialists for the eye or ear, for the nose and throat, and for nervous diseases, one or all, as each case may require. The result of this conjoint medical and psychological examination is a diagnosis of the child's mental and physical condition and the recommendation of appropriate medical and pedagogical treatment. (Witmer, 1907, p. 1)

In many ways, Witmer's influence on the field was historical rather than substantive—that is, he got the profession under way but really added little in the way of new theories or methods. It was he who named the field clinical psychology, and he was the first to teach a specific course in the subject. But the manner in

Figure 2-4
Lightner Witmer's development of the first psychological clinic began with the referral
of a boy who showed an odd spelling problem. It ended by stimulating the
establishment of a profession that was different from both education and
medicine. *Brown Brothers*

which clinical psychologists do things today may not have been influenced much
by Witmer. Nonetheless, the fact that they are doing them at all is due in no small
measure to his efforts and foresight (McReynolds, 1987).

The advent of the modern era (1900–1919). In the first decade
of the twentieth century only a very small number of psychologists could be found
employed outside the universities. In 1906 Morton Prince began publishing the
Journal of Abnormal Psychology, and in 1907 Witmer began publication of *The
Psychological Clinic* (see Figure 2-5). With two journals of their own, applied clinicians could now begin to locate their identity. This identity was further reinforced
when, in 1909, Healy established the Juvenile Psychopathic Institute in Chicago.
The Iowa Psychological Clinic had been started in 1908, the same year that Goddard began offering psychological internships at the Vineland Training School in
New Jersey. With journals, clinics, and internships, the profession of clinical psychology was beginning to take shape. Furthermore, by 1910 there were 222 APA
members. And, amazingly, the yearly dues were one dollar. But the focus of the
APA was on psychology as a science, not as a profession. This was true even
though the public schools of the day were beginning to clamor for testing services
and the universities were beginning to respond with testing courses and studies of

Vol. I, No. 1   March 15, 1907

THE PSYCHOLOGICAL CLINIC

A Journal for the Study and Treatment
of Mental Retardation and Deviation

Editor:
LIGHTNER WITMER, Ph.D.,
University of Pennsylvania.

Associate Editor:
HERBERT STOTESBURY, Ph.D.,
The Temple College,
Philadelphia.

Associate Editor:
JOSEPH COLLINS, M.D.,
Post Graduate Medical College,
New York.

CONTENTS

THE PSYCHOLOGICAL CLINIC PRESS

WEST PHILADELPHIA STATION, PHILADELPHIA, PA.

Figure 2-5
Cover of the first issue of *The Psychological Clinic.*

the feebleminded. Finally, in 1919, the first Section of Clinical Psychology was created within the APA. At the same time, an ever-increasing number of psychological clinics were being established (for example, the organization by Healy in 1917 of the Judge Baker Foundation in Boston). But World War I and the growth of the group testing movement did as much as anything to spur the development of the new profession.

Between the wars (1920–1939).   The APA had long proclaimed that its mission was to further psychology as a science. But by the close of the 1920s, clinicians were becoming uneasy and increasingly sought to gain recognition of their unique roles and interests from the APA. In 1931 the clinical section of the APA appointed a committee on training standards, and in 1935 the APA Committee on Standards of Training defined clinical psychology as "that art and technology which deals with the adjustment problems of human beings" (Reisman, 1976, p. 250). It is doubtful whether many clinicians even today would reject this definition.

In 1936 Louttit published the first clinical psychology text, and in 1937 the *Journal of Consulting Psychology* was founded. Still published today as the *Journal of Consulting and Clinical Psychology* (JCCP), it serves as a major publication outlet for the research of many clinicians. Such events signaled real growth for clinical psychology as a profession.

Another trend also attested to the development of the field. Psychological tests were beginning to become financial winners. The Psychological Corporation was founded in 1921 by James McKeen Cattell to develop and market psychological tests (particularly those of interest to industry). The proceeds were to be employed in stimulating psychological research. Thus, money began to invade the ivory tower. A $75,000 gift enabled Morton Prince to establish the Harvard Psychological Clinic in 1927. Nevertheless, the clinical psychologists of the day were quite different in terms of both activities and training from those of today.

World War II and beyond (1940–1969).   The process of absorbing large numbers of men into the U.S. military machine of the early 1940s generated many needs. For example, it created a need for large-scale screening programs to weed out those who were unfit for military service. Psychologists had already begun to develop the rudiments of a testing technology that would assist in this task, and they also had an awareness of research methods, which set them apart from their colleagues in psychiatry. Both their technology and their research attitude served them well in the establishment of a professional identity early on. Over 1700 psychologists had served in World War II, and they returned to civilian life with an increased confidence in their abilities and a determination to build a profession.

All of this was very important in affecting the federal government's response to the mental health problems facing the United States after World War II. To the Veterans Administration (VA) fell the enormous burden of providing care and rehabilitation for the thousands upon thousands of men and women who had suffered some form of emotional trauma from their military service. Without a marked increase in mental health professionals there was no way that the VA could fulfill its mission and cope with the rising tide of patients that swept into its clinics and hospitals. The VA's solution was to increase the availability of mental health professionals by providing financial support for their training.

In the case of clinical psychology, the VA provided financially attractive internships for graduate students in approved university Ph.D. programs. Although not required to do so, many of these students chose to remain with the VA after completing their training. Through its programs the VA played the chief role in upgrading the profession of clinical psychology. Its willingness to hire clinicians at salaries higher than could generally be gotten elsewhere raised the entire pay scale of the profession. Its need to deal with the psychological problems of adults resulted in a major shift in clinical psychologists' services away from a focus on children. Not only that, but clinical psychologists in the VA came to be expected to conduct individual and group psychotherapy along with their accustomed psychodiagnostic activities. They also continued to serve in their familiar capacity as the research experts on mental health teams. When in 1946 the VA initiated its program to train clinical psychologists, clinical training had secured a firm financial foundation. By 1949, the doctorate in clinical psychology was offered by 42 schools, and large numbers of students of high quality were applying. The profession had attained public visibility.

The VA was not the only federal agency to promote the rise of clinical psychology. The aftermath of the war and the general increase in governmental activity also led to an attempt to ameliorate some of the mental health problems in the nation as a whole. As a result, the U.S. Public Health Service and the National Institute of Mental Health (NIMH) initiated support of clinical psychology graduate students working toward the Ph.D. and the support of research and training programs designed to provide answers to the nation's mental health problems.

Further evidence of professional growth was marked by the first publication of the *American Psychologist* in 1946. In 1945 Connecticut became the first state to pass a certification law for psychologists. During the following two years the American Board of Examiners in Professional Psychology (ABEPP) was established to certify the professional competence of clinicians holding the Ph.D. In 1949, the Educational Testing Service was started. APA was now asserting that psychotherapy was an integral function of clinical psychologists, notwithstanding the opposition from the psychiatric profession. The APA was also assuming a more activist role. It was beginning to make recommendations for the training of clinical psychologists and also to certify clinical training programs. In 1953 it published *Ethical Standards,* a landmark achievement in the codification of ethical behavior for psychologists and a great step forward in the protection of the public. And by the beginning of the 1950s, APA could claim over 1000 members in its clinical division. In just a few years after World War II, the profession had made enormous strides.

In 1949, a truly significant event in clinical psychology took place. This was a conference on graduate education in clinical psychology that was held in Boulder, Colorado. The Boulder Conference explicated the *scientist-practitioner model* for training clinical psychologists that has served as *the* principal guideline for training ever since. In succinct terms, this model asserts: (1) clinical psychologists shall pursue their training in university departments; (2) they shall be trained as psychologists first and clinicians second; (3) they shall be required to serve a clinical internship; (4) they shall achieve competence in diagnosis, psychotherapy, and research; and (5) the culmination of their training shall be the Ph.D. degree, which involves an original research contribution to the field. By and large, this still serves as the training model, even though the scientist-practitioner model has always had its critics.

The 1950s witnessed a marked growth in the psychological profession. The membership of the APA rose from 7250 in 1950 to 16,644 in 1959—a phenomenal increase. In approximately the same period, federal research grants and contracts for psychological research rose from $11 million to over $31 million.

The growth of a profession (1970–present).   In the areas of assessment, intervention, and research, clinical psychology has become increasingly behavioral since the mid-1960s. The focus shifted from a search for the traits or internal factors that lead people into a psychopathological condition to an analysis of the situational factors that control their behavior. In the late 1960s, the road to changing undesirable behavior began swerving sharply from psychotherapy (and the insight it was designed to produce) to conditioning and altered reinforcement contingencies. Research journals were full of articles describing new objective methods of assessing behavior and novel behavioral approaches to the treatment of everything from alcoholism, sexual dysfunctions, and lack of assertiveness to obesity, smoking, and loneliness. The key to everything lay not in patients' thoughts but in their behavior.

Some, of course, began to suspect all this was an overreaction. Were traits really fictions that had no utility? Could behavioral analyses and therapeutic methods actually cure everything? Many thought not, and by the mid-1970s cognition had begun to creep back on the scene. People now began talking about "cognitive behavior methods" (Goldfried & Davison, 1976). The cognitive-behavioral orientation to treatment is now among the most common.

At the same time, the field of community psychology that had seemed poised in the 1960s to revolutionize clinical psychology began to falter. Its promise seemed to many to be unfulfilled. Then in the 1980s, the preventive focus reappeared with the development of the field of health psychology. All these concepts, methods, and trends of the past 20 years constitute the major thrusts of this book and will be covered in detail in the ensuing chapters.

The 1970s and 1980s witnessed still further growth in the profession. In 1970, there were 81 fully approved graduate training programs in clinical psychology and well over 12,000 clinicians. As for the APA itself, in 1892 there had been 42 members; by 1987 there were almost 67,000 members. This phenomenal growth is shown in Figure 2-6. By 1994, membership had grown to 77,000, and the operating budget that same year was over $54 million. Also, the Division of Clinical Psychology was the largest single unit in the APA. All 50 states, the District of Columbia, Puerto Rico, and several Canadian provinces either licensed or certified psychologists. Many clinical psychologists now have hospital privileges, and most can be reimbursed for their services by insurance and managed care companies. There has also been an increase in the number of clinical psychology graduate programs. By 1994, there were 177 doctoral training programs in clinical psychology with full APA approval.

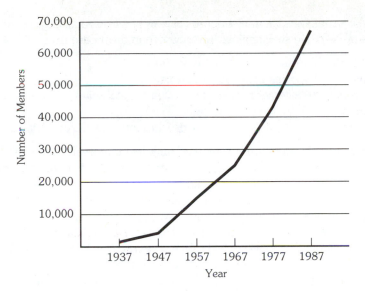

Figure 2-6

APA membership from 1937 to 1987. SOURCE: Adapted from "Report of the
Executive Vice-president," by L. D. Goodstein, *American Psychologist,* 1988,
43, 491–498. Copyright 1988 by the American Psychological Association.
Reprinted by permission.

The 1988 Schism. Within the APA there have always been conflicts, sometimes acrimonious, between clinicians and their scientific counterparts. Often, these
conflicts placed the scientist-practitioner squarely in the middle. By 1988 the
academic-scientific wing of the APA seemed to conclude that APA was under
the control of the practitioners who were using their power to promote their own
interests. Scientific interests, they said, were being replaced by goals that were essentially guild-like. The APA seemed to be preoccupied with such professional
issues as writing prescriptions, hospital privileges, reimbursement questions, licensing, legal actions against psychiatry, and so on. In short, many had come to feel
that the APA was no longer responsive to the academic-scientific needs of a significant number of its members. Indeed, former APA president Janet Spence
charged that 90% of APA Council meetings were taken up by the professional interests of practicing clinicians.

Matters seemed to come to a head when, in 1988, a plan to reorganize the APA
so as to help heal the growing schism between the clinical wing and the academic-
scientific wings failed by a two-to-one vote of the membership. The response of
those disenchanted with the APA was quite simple — form a new organization.

The American Psychological Society (APS) was founded in 1988, led by 22
former APA presidents who became founding members. The initial advisory board
of the APS read like a scientific "Who's Who." The first APS convention was held
in June 1988 and by most accounts was a resounding success. This organization
now has a newsletter, *The Observer,* a monthly *Employment Bulletin,* and two scientific journals, *Psychological Science* and *Current Directions in Psychological
Science.* By 1994, the total APS membership exceeded 15,000. Approximately

13% of APS members identify themselves as clinical, counseling, or school psychologists. The professed goals of this new organization are to:

- advance the discipline of psychology
- preserve the scientific base of psychology
- promote public understanding of psychological science and its applications
- enhance the quality of education
- encourage the "giving away" of psychology in the public interest

Many on both sides of the APA-APS split feel the break was tragic. They believe that it was unfortunate for both sides—that what the field needs is greater integration of the science of psychology and its practice. Unfortunately, the split may produce even less integration than now exists. Many believe that all this will only hasten the day when the APA unabashedly becomes a total guild organization. Of course, many in the academic-scientist group and many who are traditional scientist-practitioners now belong to both APA and APS. Many scientific psychologists are exhilarated over the quick growth of the APS. In any case, let us hope that both the APA and the APS remember their larger obligations to the public good.

Today the field of clinical psychology is challenged by a host of professional issues. In Chapter 3, we will discuss several of these in some detail. Briefly, these include the question of the optimal training model for contemporary clinical psychologists, the impact of the health care revolution and managed care on clinicians, and the current push for prescription privileges for clinical psychology. The way that these issues are resolved will greatly affect the field of clinical psychology for years to come.

As before, some of the highlights of these professional developments are noted in Table 2-4.

■ The Constant amidst Uncertainty

Clinical psychology has changed, and it will certainly change even more. Witmer would scarcely recognize it. G. Stanley Hall, APA's first president, would doubtless be amazed at the things the APA and APS are doing. However, though both training and practice are in a state of flux, certain constants remain. Clinical psychologists are still involved in assessment and treatment. They still have research contributions to make, and they are still concerned with their professional development. And the goal that binds clinical psychologists together remains the same: to apply their knowledge and skill to the mental health needs of people everywhere. In doing this, clinical psychologists must take care not to lose their soul in the marketplace (Sterling, 1982)!

■ Focus Questions

1. What theories have influenced the field of clinical psychology the most?
2. Why did personality assessment and diagnosis come back into favor?
3. How did clinical psychologists come to be so involved in the treatment of adult emotional problems?

Table 2-4
Highlights in the chronology of the profession.

1892	American Psychological Association is founded	1947	ABEPP is established to certify the competence of clinicians
1896	Witmer establishes the first psychological clinic	1949	Boulder Conference promulgates the scientist-practitioner model
1919	Section of Clinical Psychology established within APA	1953	APA publishes *Ethical Standards*
1935	APA Committee on Standards of Training defines the field	1968	First Psy.D. program is established at the University of Illinois
1936	Louttit publishes the first clinical psychology text		
1937	*Journal of Consulting Psychology* is founded	1981	Revised ethical standards are published
1945	Connecticut passes the first certification law	1988	American Psychological Society is founded
1946	VA and NIMH begin their support of clinical psychology	1992	Most recent revision of Ethical Principles of Psychologists (published in the *American Psychologist*)

4. How might clinical research inform clinical practice and clinical assessment?
5. What factors led to a splitting of the American Psychological Association membership?

■ Key Terms

American Psychological Society (APS)
behavior therapy
behavioral assessment
brief or time-effective therapy
eclectics
etiological
g
guidance clinics
health psychology
manualized treatment
measurement of intelligence
mental tests

neuropsychological assessment
objective measures
personality disorders
personality testing
play therapy
projective techniques
psychoanalysis
psychodiagnosis
psychotherapy research
radical behaviorism
scientist-practitioner model
structured diagnostic interviews
systematic desensitization

3

Current Issues in Clinical Psychology

In Chapter 2, we reviewed the history and development of the field of clinical psychology by examining important events in the areas of diagnosis and assessment, interventions and psychotherapy, research, and the profession. That review helped us to appreciate the roots of clinical psychology as well as to put current activities in the appropriate historical context.

In this chapter, we discuss a variety of contemporary issues in clinical psychology: What are the best training models for a clinical psychologist? What is the best way to ensure professional competence? What are the issues that currently face clinical psychologists who are in private practice? How can clinical psychology maintain its independence and economic viability? How should clinical psychology respond to the increasing diversity of the population it serves? How will the health care revolution affect clinical psychologists? Should clinical psychologists pursue and obtain prescription privileges? and What are contemporary ethical standards for clinical psychologists?

Of these issues, one of the most contentious has been the appropriate training models for future clinical psychologists. Let us, then, begin with this topic.

■ Models of Training in Clinical Psychology

The scientist-practitioner

The training model. Clinical psychology began in universities as a branch of scientific psychology. It arose within the structure of colleges of arts and sciences, where teaching, research, and other scholarly efforts were the rewarded activities. Practitioner concerns were grafted onto this corpus, and the graft did not always take well. The goals of professionalism were not always the goals of one's dean or even of one's peers.

In the face of such conflict, some clinical psychology professors did carry out research and did publish. But their critics (often graduate students or clinicians in the field) complained that much of the research was trivial, nonutilitarian, or just busywork whose only use was to gain financial rewards and titles. Worse, it seemed to professors that their own research detracted from their training of clinical students in the skills of the profession. Some students complained that they were learning too much about analysis of variance, theories of conditioning, or principles of physiological psychology and too little about psychotherapy and diagnostic testing.

Another problem was that the faculty did not provide clinical students with a variety of professional role models. The only models present were doing research, writing, or otherwise playing the academic game. Where were the real clinicians in academia whose forté was therapy or diagnostic testing, who got enormous pleasure from seeing patients, or who took great pride in their sensitivity in interpreting a psychological test protocol? The "true value" of clinical activities was demonstrated by assignments to teach clinical practica. Such work was led frequently by assistant professors who were often themselves but a few months out of graduate school. The tenured, the admired, and the powerful faculty always seemed to be teaching research seminars.

This, then, was the troublesome side of the Boulder *scientist-practitioner model*. These were the kinds of events that led to demands for change. But these were not the events that the architects of the Boulder model envisioned.

The Boulder model saw a profession comprised of skilled practitioners who could produce their own research as well as consume the research of others. The goal was to create a profession different from any that had gone before. The psychological clinician would practice with skill and sensitivity but would also contribute to the body of clinical knowledge by understanding how to translate experience into testable hypotheses and how, subsequently, to test those hypotheses. The Boulder vision was one of a systematic union between the art of clinical intuition and the logical empiricism of science—to separate the practitioner from the source of knowledge was to create someone who passively consumes information or buys techniques from a psychological huckster.

The scientist-practitioner model is less a quantitative breakdown of one's daily activities than it is a state of mind. No one ever intended to have all clinicians devote 50% of their activity to their clinical practice and 50% to formal research. Some will primarily be researchers and others primarily clinicians. While it is true that practicing clinicians do not do much in the way of research, this is largely because their work settings do not permit it and not because they do not wish to do it (Haynes, Lemsky, & Sexton-Radek, 1987).

Furthermore, the scientist-practitioner model is just as applicable to the clinical researcher as it is to the practicing clinician. The former can only produce solid, meaningful research if they keep their clinical sensitivity and skills honed by continuing to see patients. Just as practitioners must not forsake their research training and interests, neither must researchers ignore their clinical foundation.

The debate goes on.   A series of training conferences culminating in one at Salt Lake City, Utah, in 1987 have eroded any strict interpretation of the scientist-practitioner model. These conferences have recognized alternative routes to professional competence—specifically, they have accepted approaches that de-emphasize research experience in favor of more direct and extensive training in clinical skills.

The Boulder model has been durable, but the debate goes on. The mood of professionalism seems to grow every year. Increasingly, clinical psychologists are split into two groups: those interested primarily in clinical practice and those interested primarily in research (Peterson & Knudson, 1979). Moreover, many of those in practice show indifference to research (Barlow, 1981). Perhaps part of the problem stems from the failure to adequately implement the scientist-practitioner model. For example, Drabman (1985) describes students who arrive at their internship site without an adequate knowledge of how to administer, score, and interpret psychological tests. These students also sometimes show a surprising lack of experience with clinical populations. While knowing much about the nuts and bolts of research, they have little skill in the practical application of their knowledge. In a related vein, Goldfried (1984) has pointed out that, while research into the effectiveness of psychotherapy in real clinical settings is both exciting and needed, it is not always taught.

Many believe that the scientist-practitioner model has served us well and successfully (Marston, 1989); still others conclude that it is a poor educational model that deserves the wrath of its critics (Frank, 1984). But the prospect of totally abandoning the Boulder model is worrisome to many in the field. As Meltzoff (1984) put it:

> To train a new strain of purely applied psychologists who will be obliged to accept on faith what is handed down to them without being able to evaluate it or advance it, is the certain pathway to mediocrity. Research training conveys a mode of thought. It teaches how to be inquisitive and skeptical, how to think logically, how to formulate hypotheses and to test them, how to gather data rather than opinion, how to analyze those data and draw inferences from them, and how to make a balanced presentation of the findings. These are skills that help . . . professional psychologists to rise above the technician level. (p. 209)

The Doctor of Psychology (Psy.D.) degree

The foregoing controversy has resulted in the emergence of the Doctor of Psychology (Psy.D.) degree. The special characteristics of this degree are an emphasis on the development of clinical skills and a de-emphasis on research competency. A master's thesis is not required, and the dissertation is usually transformed into a report on a professional subject rather than an original research contribution.

The first of these programs was developed at the University of Illinois in 1968 (Peterson, 1971), although that school has since closed its program. Subsequently, similar programs were developed at Rutgers, Baylor, and elsewhere. As Peterson (1968) envisioned them, Psy.D. programs are not sufficiently different from Ph.D. programs during the first two years of training. The real divergence begins with the third year. At that point, increasing experience in therapeutic practice and assessment becomes the rule. The fourth year continues the clinical emphasis with a series of internship assignments. More recently in Psy.D. programs there has been a tendency to compress formal course work into the first year and to elaborate clinical experience by requiring such things as five-year practica. A good description and history of Psy.D. programs has been provided by McConnell (1984). Of the 2200 doctorates awarded in 1993 in clinical psychology, 544 (24.5%) were Psy.D. degrees (ODEER, 1993).

Psy.D. programs have gained an increasing foothold in the profession. Snepp and Peterson (1988) even claim that students in Psy.D. and Ph.D. programs are essentially indistinguishable when it comes to being prepared for their internships. Research by Peterson, Eaton, Levine, & Snepp (1982) paints a portrait of Psy.D. practitioners who are satisfied with their careers and even more satisfied with their graduate training than are clinicians trained in traditional programs. They encounter few problems in becoming licensed and report that the Psy.D. degree is an advantage in competing for clinical positions. Finding academic jobs, however, is difficult for them. Further, when resources and incentives in the workplace permit, Ph.D. graduates engage in scholarly activities more often than do Psy.D. graduates (Barrom, Shadish, & Montgomery, 1988). A recent survey of graduates from Baylor University (Hershey, Kopplin, & Cornell, 1991), where one of the first Psy.D. programs was established, indicated that the majority of graduates from this program (82%) identified themselves as practitioners while few identified themselves as educators or researchers. Respondents were very satisfied with their graduate education and their career choice.

Professional schools

Although the Psy.D. model represents a clear break with tradition, an even more radical innovation is the development of *professional schools*. Many of these schools have no affiliation with universities—they are autonomous, with their own financial and organizational framework. Often referred to as "freestanding" schools, they usually offer the Ph.D., although a few confer the Psy.D. Most schools emphasize clinical functions and generally have little or no research orientation. Faculty are chiefly clinical in orientation and therefore are said to provide better role models for students. The first such freestanding professional school was the California School of Professional Psychology (Dörken, 1975). It was founded by the California State Psychological Association and offers several mental health degrees (Dörken & Cummings, 1977).

In 1987, there were 45 professional schools in operation, and only several hundred of the 3000 yearly clinical doctorates were graduated from these schools (Strickland, 1988). By contrast, in 1993, almost one-half—1107 out of 2220 (49.9%)—of the doctorates in clinical psychology were awarded by professional schools! Clearly, the proportion of doctorates in clinical psychology awarded by professional schools has increased dramatically.

Whether such schools ultimately will survive is still uncertain. One of their greatest problems is stability of funding. Many must depend on tuition as their chief source of funds, and this does not generate enough money to make such institutions very secure. In addition, they often have to depend very heavily on part-time faculty whose major employment is elsewhere. This gives a shaky foundation to the structure, making it difficult for students to have the frequent and sustained contact with their professors that is so vital to a satisfactory educational experience. Although some professional schools are fully accredited by the APA (24 in 1994), they are the exception and not the rule. This is a major handicap that such schools will have to overcome if their graduates are to find professional acceptance everywhere.

Recent conferences on training seem to suggest that both Ph.D. and Psy.D. programs have found secure niches and are here to stay. But it was also recommended that all doctoral programs be in or affiliated with regionally accredited universities (Fox & Barclay, 1989).

Clinical scientist model

Over the last decade, empirically oriented clinical psychologists have become increasingly concerned that clinical psychology as currently practiced is not grounded in science. According to this view, many of the methods that practitioners employ in their treatment have not been demonstrated to be effective in controlled clinical studies. In some cases, empirical studies of these techniques have not been completed; in other cases, research has been completed but the results did not support the continued use of the technique. Similarly, the use of assessment techniques that have not been shown to be reliable, valid, and successful in leading to positive treatment outcome have been called into question.

In 1991, a call to action for clinical scientists appeared in the form of the "Manifesto for a Science of Clinical Psychology" (McFall, 1991). In this document, McFall argued the following points:

1. Scientific clinical psychology is the only legitimate and acceptable form of clinical psychology (p. 76).
2. Psychological services should not be administered to the public (except under strict experimental control) until they have satisfied these four minimal criteria:

    (a) The exact nature of the service must be described clearly.
    (b) The claimed benefits of the service must be stated explicitly.
    (c) These claimed benefits must be validated scientifically.
    (d) Possible negative side effects that outweigh any benefits must be ruled out empirically (p. 80).

3. The primary and overriding objectives of doctoral training programs in clinical psychology must be to produce the most competent clinical scientists possible (p. 84).

Like-minded clinical psychologists were urged to help build a *science* of clinical psychology by integrating scientific principles into their own clinical work, differentiating between scientifically valid techniques and pseudoscientific ones and focusing graduate training on methods that produce *clinical scientists*—individuals who "think and function as scientists in every respect and setting in their professional lives" (McFall, 1991, p. 85).

This document has proved to be quite provocative. One outgrowth of this model of training is the newly formed *Academy of Psychological Clinical Science* (APCS). The Academy consists of graduate programs that are committed to training in empirical methods of research and the integration of this training with clinical training, and it is affiliated with the American Psychological Society (APS). As of August 1995, there were 26 member programs. The primary goals of the Academy are:

1. To foster the training of students for careers in clinical science research, who skillfully will produce and apply scientific knowledge.
2. To advance the full range of clinical science research and theory and their integration with other relevant sciences.
3. To foster the development of and access to resources and opportunities for training, research, funding, and careers in clinical science.
4. To foster the broad application of clinical science to human problems in responsible and innovative ways.
5. To foster the timely dissemination of clinical science to policy-making groups, psychologists and other scientists, practitioners, and consumers.

Essentially, a network of graduate programs that adhere to the clinical science model has developed. These programs share ideas, resources, and training innovations with each other. Further, they collaborate on projects aimed at increasing grant funding from governmental agencies, addressing state licensing requirements for the practice of psychology, and increasing the visibility of clinical science programs in undergraduate education. The ultimate success and influence of this new model of training remains to be seen.

Combined professional-scientific training programs

A final alternative training model that we will briefly discuss involves a combined specialty in counseling, clinical, or school psychology. As outlined by Beutler and Fisher (1994), this training model is based on two assumptions: (1) these specialties share a number of core areas of knowledge, and (2) the actual practices of psychologists who graduate from each of these specialties are quite similar. The curriculum in these combined training programs focuses on core areas within psychology and exposes students to each subspecialty of counseling, clinical, and school psychology.

The combined training model emphasizes breadth rather than depth of psychological knowledge. However, this feature can also been seen as a potential weakness of the model. Graduates from this type of training program may not develop a specific subspecialty or area of expertise by the end of their doctoral training (Beutler & Fisher, 1994). Further, this model of training appears to be better suited for the future practitioner rather than the future academician or clinical scientist (Beutler & Fisher, 1994).

By the end of 1994, there were five APA-accredited programs in combined professional-scientific psychology.

Graduate programs: past and future

In many ways, the changes in graduate training that we have witnessed over the last 30 years have mirrored the marketplace for clinical psychologists (Ellis, 1992). Starting in the mid-1960s, a shift from university-based academic jobs to jobs in private practice began to take place. Not surprisingly, soon thereafter, complaints about the limitations of the scientist-practitioner model of training surfaced. These complaints focused primarily on the perceived inadequacy of the Boulder model of training for future practitioners. According to the critics, training in clinical skills was deficient, and faculty were oblivious to the training needs of future practitioners.

Out of the Vail Training Conference in 1973 came an explicit endorsement of alternative training models to meet the needs of the future practitioner. The alternative Psy.D. degree and the professional school models of training can be traced to the positions adopted by those attending this conference. Clearly, these alternative training programs are becoming increasingly influential, as indicated by the number of new doctorates they graduate. In addition, arguments supporting the need to designate any clinical psychologist who practices clinical work with a Psy.D. degree have recently appeared (Shapiro & Wiggins, 1994).

However, several recent trends may affect the viability and success of the various training models we have discussed. First, some believe that there may be an oversupply of practice-oriented psychologists (Robiner, 1991). If this is true, it may ultimately affect the number of students entering and finishing graduate programs in clinical psychology. In recent years, there have been many more applicants for internship positions than slots available. The net result has been that some graduate students have not been able to secure internship positions. If the internship and job markets tighten, the programs that primarily train practitioners (for example, professional schools and schools awarding the Psy.D. degree) will likely feel the brunt of this effect. This will be especially true for professional schools whose economic viability is heavily dependent on tuition fees and large numbers of students. Second, the managed health care revolution in this country will likely affect the demand for clinical psychologists in the future as well as the curriculum in training programs. Regarding the latter, more emphasis will be placed on course work involving empirically validated brief psychological interventions and focal assessment. Training programs that do not employ faculty with expertise in these areas may produce graduates without the requisite skills to compete in the marketplace. Finally, several authors (Robiner, 1991; Schneider, 1991) have noted that there may be an "undersupply" of academic and research-oriented clinical psychologists. If true, scientist-practitioner and clinical scientist programs may be in a better position to meet this need.

■ Professional Regulation

As clinical psychology grew and the numbers of its practitioners multiplied, issues of professional competence began to arise. How is the public to know who is well trained and who is not? Many people have neither the time, the inclination, nor the sophistication to distinguish the professional from the charlatan. Professional regulation, therefore, has become a method of attempting to protect the public interest by developing explicit standards of competence for clinical psychologists.

American Board of Professional Psychology (ABPP)

Because of the failure of the individual states to take the lead, the American Board of Examiners in Professional Psychology (ABEPP) was established as a separate corporation in 1947. Its name was shortened to the *American Board of Professional Psychology (ABPP)* in 1968. ABPP offers certification of professional competence in the fields of clinical psychology, counseling psychology, industrial and organizational psychology, school psychology, clinical neuropsychology, forensic psychology, health psychology, and behavioral psychology. Oral examinations are administered, handling of cases is observed, and records of previous cases are submitted for review.

Candidates for the ABPP examinations must also have had five years' post-doctoral experience. Overall, requirements are more rigorous than those involved in licensing or certification. In essence, then, the public can be assured that a clinician with ABPP credentials is someone who has submitted to the careful scrutiny of a panel of peers.

Certification

Certification is a relatively weak form of regulation in most cases. It guarantees that people cannot call themselves psychologists while offering services to the public for a fee unless they have been certified by a state board of examiners. Such certification often involves an examination, but sometimes it consists only of a review of the applicant's training and professional experience. Certification is an attempt to protect the public by restricting the use of the title *psychologist*. Its weakness is that it does not prevent anyone—from outright quacks to the poorly trained—from offering psychological services to the public, as long as the noncertified persons who offer such services do not use the title *psychologist* or the word *psychological* to describe themselves or their services. Some cynics have alleged that certification does more to protect psychologists than it does to protect the public.

Certification laws often came about because of effective psychiatric lobbies in state legislatures. Since many psychiatrists wished to reserve psychotherapy as the special province of medicine, they resisted any law that would recognize the practice of psychotherapy by any nonmedical specialty. As a result, certification laws were the best regulation that psychologists could obtain.

Licensing

Licensing is a stronger form of legislation than is certification. It not only specifies the nature of the title and training required for licensure but also usually defines what specific professional activities may be offered to the public for a fee. With certification, for example, individuals might call themselves "therapists" and then proceed to provide "psychotherapeutic" services with impunity. Many state licensing laws would prevent this, since these laws define psychotherapy and make it the specific province of psychiatry, clinical psychology, or whatever. However, determined charlatans are difficult to contain, and such persons may be very clever in disguising the true nature of their activities.

Most states and provinces require applicants for licensure to sit for an examination. In addition, the licensing board usually examines the applicant's educational background and sometimes requires several years of supervised experience beyond the doctorate. Many states also have subsequent continuing education requirements. Furthermore, it appears that licensing boards are becoming increasingly restrictive, sometimes requiring specific courses, excluding master's candidates, and demanding degrees from APA-approved programs. They are also occasionally beginning to intrude into the activities of academic and research psychologists. To help strengthen the current system, the APA has developed a model act for the licensure of psychologists (APA, 1987a).

Licensing and certification remain topics of intense professional interest. Some continue to insist that licensing standards should not be enforced until research demonstrates their utility and positive client outcomes can be shown to relate to the licensee's competence (Bernstein & Lecomte, 1981). Others have pointed out that certification and licensing are in no way valid measures of professional competence (Koocher, 1979). However, still others suggest that licensing should be designed to ensure that the public will not be harmed rather than to regulate levels of competence (Danish & Smyer, 1981). Kane (1982) reinforces this conclusion when he argues that, at the present time, licensing examinations help provide safeguards against poor practice. Finally, some academic clinical psychologists are concerned that licensing requirements violate academic freedom because these requirements essentially dictate the course work that is offered by clinical psychology programs. These clinical psychologists argue that the faculty involved in a clinical psychology training program have a better idea of what course work is needed to produce well-trained clinical psychologists.

Despite the foregoing questions and problems, the regulation of professional practice will continue. To date, it is the only method we have, imperfect though it is, to protect the public from the poorly trained.

National Register

In recent years insurance companies have increasingly extended their coverage to include mental health services. At the same time, clinical psychologists have gained recognition as competent providers of services involving prevention, assessment, and therapy. In 1975 the *National Register Of Health Service Providers in Psychology* was first published. The *Register* was a kind of self-certification since it listed only those practitioners who were licensed or certified in their own states and who submitted their names for inclusion and paid to be listed. But, along with the increasing numbers of clinicians in private practice and their recognition as health care providers by insurance companies such as Blue Cross and Blue Shield, the *Register* is one more indication of the growing professionalization of clinical psychology.

■ Private Practice

Earlier we observed that substantial numbers of clinicians are entering private practice these days. This seems to be an ever-increasing trend, which is mirrored in the aspirations of many students in clinical training. Their goal is essentially to open an office and hang out a shingle. This suggests that the physician is now serving as a role model for these aspiring clinicians—a model that creates certain hazards.

For example, the medical profession is currently experiencing a great deal of criticism and the loss of its "good Samaritan" image because it often appears more concerned with economic privileges than with the welfare of patients. Doctors operate strong lobbies both in Congress and in state legislatures. They have gotten legislation passed that not only restricts entry by others into what they perceive as their professional arena but also protects them and their vested interests. The American Medical Association is often perceived not as the public's guardian but as the protector of the rights and advantages of the physician.

What alarms many psychologists is that clinical psychology seems to be moving in this same direction. The emphasis on restrictive legislation, diplomas, and political activism, and the de-emphasis of research, strike many as misguided. They fear that what begins as an honest and devoted attempt to improve training, provide continuing professional growth, protect the public, and improve the common good will end in a selfish posture of vested interest. Obviously, private practice is not the only place where such trends can develop. But the danger exists. A larger social question is whether training clinicians for private practice is an economical, efficient response to the nation's mental health needs. Nevertheless, private practice, with all its concern about insurance coverage, professional rivalry with psychiatry, and statutory regulation, seems here to stay.

In a thought-provoking paper, Schneider (1990) concluded that private practice will have to give way to approaches that emphasize managed systems of service delivery. If this is true, it means that we are training clinicians for obsolescence. It may even happen that, because of cost, today's Ph.D. clinicians will be replaced by tomorrow's master's-level mental health professionals! We will have more to say about the impact of managed care on the practice of clinical psychology later in this chapter.

◼ Independence and Economics

Early opposition from the psychiatric profession prevented clinicians from engaging in the independent practice of psychotherapy. Eventually, clinical psychology overcame the powerful psychiatric lobby that operated in most statehouses across the country and won the right to practice independently. Logic had finally prevailed—the psychiatric argument that psychotherapy is a form of medical intervention faded into obscurity. Psychiatrists came to accept the new legal status accorded clinicians, and clinical psychologists began rushing into private practice to fill the voids in the mental health field. Now they have become fully independent practitioners.

Indeed, today one could think of psychiatrists and clinical psychologists as competitors—and there is the rub. What once had been an ideological war turned into an economic skirmish. Just as clinicians began settling into their newly found independence, more and more private and quasi-governmental health insurance plans became operative. Psychotherapy began to be included under these plans, and practitioners became eligible for reimbursement. People who previously could not have afforded therapy or were unwilling to pay for it were now covered. Very quickly the medical profession mounted campaigns to exclude clinical psychologists from reimbursement unless patients were referred to them by physicians. The old battle over independent practice had been lost earlier. The battleground now shifted to direct reimbursement of psychologists by insurance companies without a physician's involvement.

A good case example involved Blue Shield of Virginia (BSV). For a number of years, BSV required psychologists to bill through a physician. There were repeated, futile attempts to obtain direct reimbursement of psychologists for services rendered to BSV members. Eventually, the Virginia Academy of Clinical Psychologists (VACP) brought antitrust action against BSV. The court ruled in favor of BSV. But upon appeal, a higher court reversed the decision and upheld the claim of VACP. All this court action began in 1978 and was not finally settled until 1982, when VACP was awarded over $405,000 by a federal court for attorneys' fees. This represented a significant victory for clinical psychologists in their quest to establish a fully independent profession that could compete in the marketplace on equal terms with psychiatry (Resnick, 1985).

A profession that began softly in hallowed halls of ivy now finds itself battling in the marketplace—less and less the scholar and more and more the entrepreneur.

■ Sensitivity in Mental Health Services

In a pluralistic society such as the United States, it is urgent that we develop mental health services that effectively serve the needs of cultural, racial, and ethnic minorities (Sue, 1990). One can argue the point at almost any level: ethical (for example, Pedersen & Marsella, 1982), economic, and so on. But it is essential that we develop training programs that produce therapists who have learned to consider appropriate cultural factors in their clinical work with culturally diverse clients (Allison, Crawford, Echemendia, Robinson, & Knepp, 1994; Comas-Diaz, 1992; Lopez et al., 1989; Mio & Morris, 1990). For example, we must find ways to make successful treatments more available to Hispanics—treatments that are sensitive to the characteristic features of Hispanic culture (Rogler, Malgady, Costantino, & Blumenthal, 1987). Similar comments could be made in the case of Native Americans (Willis, 1989) and African Americans (Jones, 1991). Likewise, issues of gender have become prominent in recent years (for example, Good, Borst, & Wallace, 1994). We are hearing increasing numbers of reports about sexual exploitation of clients. From the days of Freud right up to the present, we seem to have trouble training therapists who are sensitized to the special life experiences of the opposite sex (Gilbert, 1987). This is particularly true with regard to the relative lack of training many clinical psychologists (men and women alike) receive that focuses on the unique needs and experiences of women. In the future, we must train clinical psychologists to recognize and understand both gender differences and cultural *diversity* as well as how these relate to the provision of mental health services.

Finally, a group that has been especially underserved and little noticed is the country's rural population. The United States is a nation with a strong rural heritage, and in recent years the farm crisis has been particularly malignant in its effects on rural communities. Yet the federal government and the clinical profession have both been slow to respond with targeted mental health services (Keller & Podrygula, 1990; Rosmann & Delworth, 1990).

■ The Health Care Revolution

The costs of health care have grown astronomically throughout many parts of the world. For example, in the United States, these costs made up but 4.5% of the Gross National Product (GNP) in 1950. More recently, those same costs have ballooned to over 14% of the Gross Domestic Product (previously the GNP) with a total dollar cost exceeding $898 billion annually (Frank & VandenBos, 1994). A few years ago we expected a national health insurance program in the United States. What we got was a profit-driven corporate health care industry that may well revolutionize all corners of health care (Zimet, 1989). The *managed care* approach to addressing health care needs targets not only the high cost of physical health services but mental health services as well. Increasingly, insurance companies or other third-party payers are determining the amount of reimbursement for mental health services. Essentially, those that ultimately pay the bills (for example, employers) have taken economic control away from practitioners (Cummings, 1995).

Although this health care revolution has been under way for more than two decades (Broskowski, 1991), its effects are now more salient. The focus is on cost containment, expanding the size of a corporation into a kind of medical-industrial complex, and a marketplace mentality (Kiesler & Morton, 1988). Thus we can look for continued pressure on the independent practitioner.

The psychological services available to patients have become a function of what diagnostic category the patients belong to and the reimbursement schedule deemed appropriate for it. In a sense, the "ideal" treatment has been replaced by whatever treatment is affordable under insurance guidelines. Long-term therapy, for example, frequently becomes short-term therapy. In effect, a company, rather than the independent practitioner, manages a patient's health care (Cummings, 1986). Brief, time-effective interventions are preferred, and practitioners are now being asked to empirically demonstrate their effectiveness and document their efficiency in the provision of services (Cummings, 1995).

There are several models of managed care, all of which attempt to control costs and reduce utilization of services while at the same time ensuring quality of services. We will briefly mention two major managed care systems: HMOs and PPOs. The *health maintenance organization (HMO)* employs a restricted number of providers to serve those who enroll in the plan; costs for all services are fixed. *Preferred provider organizations (PPOs)* have contracts with outside providers at a discounted rate to meet the needs of their membership; in exchange for the discounted rate, the providers theoretically receive an increased number of referrals.

These relatively new systems of service delivery are changing the concept of what constitutes psychological treatment as well as the modes of practice for clinical psychologists. Cummings (1995) recently discussed some of these "essential paradigm shifts": (1) clients will be seen for a fewer number of sessions and a greater number of clients will be seen per year; (2) treatment will be brief (fewer sessions) and intermittent (that is, clients may not be seen for consecutive weeks); (3) the therapist will serve as a catalyst for clients to make changes in their lives;

(4) most changes will occur outside of treatment; (5) treatment will not be terminated ("You're cured")—rather, it will be "interrupted" after client progress is evident; (6) community resources will be used to a greater extent (Alcoholics Anonymous, Parents Without Partners, and so on); and (7) most treatment will be delivered in a group format and will involve structured psychoeducational programs (for example, stress management training). Each of these predicted changes are quite dramatic, and the net effect will be a style of psychological intervention that differs greatly from "traditional" psychotherapy.

In fact, managed care may directly impact the employment outlook for doctoral-level clinical psychologists who plan to make a career out of clinical practice (Frank & VandenBos, 1994):

> Integrated managed care delivery systems will be characterized by reliance on primary care gatekeepers, clinical integration across the continuum of services provided to each patient, and sharing of financial risk by providers (capitated payment). Physician practice will shift toward primary care, and there will be an increase in the use of physician extenders, such as advanced practice nurses and physician assistants. A similar trend is likely in the mental health area, with greater use of master's level providers of all types. (p. 852)

Master's-level practitioners and paraprofessionals are much cheaper to use for the same services, and, therefore, will be seen as more economically attractive to managed care companies (Cummings, 1995; Sleek, 1995a).

But the training of the scientist-practitioner or clinical scientist does offer some opportunities in this managed care environment. For example, clinical psychologists have an empirical orientation that emphasizes the study of outcomes, which can help circumvent professional biases; have skills different from those of physicians; can bring an emphasis on preventing mental health problems in individuals and a focus on their wellness rather than their sickness; and know about the effects of the environment on behavior (Kiesler & Morton, 1988). All of these skills can impress a profit-driven, corporate-directed system. However, the clinical profession has not to date done a particularly good job of publicizing the demonstrated effectiveness of psychological interventions (Barlow, 1994).

Some have suggested, perhaps tongue-in-cheek, that clinical psychologists may actually benefit from managed care. These "hidden" benefits include increased technical assistance and education provided by the managed care companies, increased opportunities for interdisciplinary collaboration, and "free" clinical supervision from case managers of managed care companies (Anonymous, 1995).

Broskowski (1995) highlighted a number of implications for the training and careers of psychologists that follow from trends in health care reform. First, it is likely that the marketplace for independent practitioners (that is, those in private practice) will continue to diminish. In contrast, the opportunities for clinical psychologists who specialize in health psychology will likely increase dramatically because these individuals, by virtue of their training, are better able to provide a broader range of services, including those related to medical care. Second, an increased focus on accountability and patient outcomes will open the doors for clinical psychologists who have expertise in clinical and psychometric research. These individuals will be called upon to design and evaluate studies of patient outcome, patient satisfaction, and the effectiveness of various psychological interventions. Finally, training programs in clinical psychology need to place more emphasis on cost-effective psychological interventions, provide clinical training in managed care settings, and incorporate didactic instruction in applied health services research into their curricula. It is hoped that these suggestions are heeded so that future clinical psychologists receive the training necessary to thrive in a managed care environment.

■ Prescription Privileges

A current, hotly debated issue concerns the pursuit of *prescription privileges* for clinical psychologists. The American Psychological Association recently endorsed this pursuit (Martin, 1995), as have several of its highest-ranking officials (for example, see Nickelson, 1995; Fox, 1988; DeLeon et al., 1991). On the other hand, many remain either neutral or adamantly opposed to obtaining prescription privileges (DeNelsky, 1991; Handler, 1988). The decision to pursue these privileges will have far-reaching implications for clinical psychologists in terms of their role definition, the training required, and their actual practice.

Background

As noted by Brentar and McNamara (1991), clinical psychologists in recent years have expanded their area of interest from mental health to health issues in general. This redefinition of clinical psychology as a field concerned with general health (including mental health) raises a number of interesting issues regarding how best to ensure that clinical psychologists can function autonomously and not be controlled or regulated by medical or other professions (Fox, 1982). Several have argued that obtaining prescription privileges will ensure the autonomy of clinical psychologists as health service providers and will enable a continuity of care that is missing when a psychiatrist prescribes the patient's medications and a psychologist provides the same patient's psychotherapy. Further, DeLeon (1988) has argued that it is a professional and ethical duty to improve and broaden the services offered by the clinical profession so that society's needs can be met. In this spirit, clinical psychologists with prescription privileges would be available to meet the needs of underserved populations (for example, rural residents and geriatric patients).

However, the pursuit of prescription privileges has been questioned on philosophical grounds. Handler (1988) argued that the need for professional boundaries between clinical psychology and psychiatry dictates that we should not incorporate medical interventions (that is, medications) into our treatment repertoire. Further, Handler asserted that it is clinical psychology's nonmedication orientation that identifies it as a unique health profession and that is responsible for the field's appeal. For example, DeNelsky (1991) noted that, even without prescription privileges, more and more psychologists have become providers of outpatient services whereas the opposite trend is true for psychiatry. We will highlight some of the major arguments for and against prescription privileges below.

Pros

Although a number of arguments have been made in favor of prescription privileges, we will briefly present several of the most commonly cited advantages, as outlined in a recent interview with the executive director of the Practice Directorate of the American Psychological Association (Nickelson, 1995). First, prescription privileges would enable clinical psychologists to provide a wider variety of treatments and treat a wider range of clients or patients. Treatment involving medications would now be an option, and this would lead to more involvement by clinical psychologists in the treatment of conditions in which medications are the primary form of intervention (for example, schizophrenia). A second advantage of having prescription privileges is the potential increase in efficiency and cost-effectiveness of care for those patients who need both psychological treatment as well as medication. As noted above, these individuals often enlist more than one mental health professional (for example, a psychiatrist for medications and a clinical psychologist for cognitive-behavioral treatment). However, a single mental health professional who could provide all forms of treatment might be desirable from both a practical and economic standpoint. There is also the belief that prescription privileges would give clinical psychologists a competitive advantage in the health care marketplace. The health care field is becoming increasingly competitive, and prescription privileges would provide an advantage to clinical psychologists over other health care professionals (for example, nurses and social workers). Furthermore, as we mentioned above, some view obtaining prescription privileges as a natural progression in clinical psychology's quest to become a full-fledged health care profession, rather than solely a mental health care profession.

Cons

On the other hand, several have voiced concerns about the possibility of obtaining prescription privileges (Brentar & McNamara, 1991; DeNelsky, 1991; Handler, 1988). Critics point out that prescription privileges may lead to a deemphasis on "psychological" forms of treatment because medications are often faster-acting and potentially more profitable than psychotherapy. Further, many fear that a conceptual shift may occur such that biological explanations of emotional conditions take precedence over psychological ones. In addition, the pursuit of prescription privileges may damage clinical psychology's relationship with psychiatry and general medicine. Such a conflict is likely to be expensive because of lawsuits and legal fees necessary to modify current licensing laws for psychology. Finally, the granting of prescription privileges would lead to dramatic increases in malpractice liability costs. These new financial burdens would come at the expense of existing programs that are currently supported—in short, it may not be worth it.

Implications for training

If clinical psychologists gain prescription privileges, it will greatly impact the training of future clinical psychologists. Recently, the Ad Hoc Task Force on Psychopharmacology of the American Psychological Association published its recommendations on the competence criteria necessary for training psychologists to provide services to individuals who receive psychotropic medication (Smyer et al., 1993). Essentially, this task force outlined three levels of competence and training in psychopharmacology. These are presented in order of increasing levels of skill and training.

1. *Level 1: Basic Pharmacology Training.* Competence at this level would include a knowledge of the biological basis of neuropsychopharmacology and a mastery of the classes of medication used for treatment, as well as knowledge of substances that are abused (for example, alcohol and cocaine). To achieve this level of training, a one-semester survey course in psychopharmacology is recommended.

2. *Level 2: Collaborative Practice.* Competence at this level, essentially enabling one to serve as a psychopharmacology consultant, would involve more in-depth knowledge of psychopharmacology and drugs of abuse; competence in diagnostic assessment, physical assessment, drug interactions, and drug side effects; and practical, hands-on training in psychopharmacology. Specifically, the committee recommended course work in the areas listed above as well as supervised practical experience.

3. *Level 3: Prescription Privileges.* Competence must be demonstrated at this level in order to practice independently as a prescribing psychologist. The committee recommended a strong undergraduate background in biological sciences (for example, multiple courses in biology, chemistry, mathematics, and pharmacology), two years of graduate training in psychopharmacology (26 credit hours), and a postdoctoral psychopharmacology residency.

If implemented, these recommendations will impact graduate training in clinical psychology in a number of ways. First, because of additional course requirements (for Levels 2 and 3), it will take longer to complete graduate school. Second, additional faculty would need to be hired in many cases to teach these new required courses, as most of them are not currently offered in clinical psychology graduate programs. And finally, the undergraduate course background of applicants to clinical psychology graduate programs would likely be scrutinized more carefully to ensure that the applicant has a strong background in the biological sciences.

■ Ethical Standards

One yardstick by which to measure the maturity of a profession is its commitment to a set of *ethical standards.* The field of psychology led the way among the mental health professions in establishing a formal code of ethics. As early as 1951 the APA published a tentative code, and in 1953, the *Ethical Standards of Psychologists* (APA, 1953) was formally published. Revisions of these standards appeared in 1958, 1963, 1968, 1977, 1979, 1981, 1990, and 1992. In addition, a casebook of ethical standards has been published (APA, 1987b), and a statement of ethical principles involving psychological research with human subjects has also been formulated (APA, 1982). Early on, standards for testing materials were developed (APA, 1966) and later updated (APA, 1985). Finally, a wide array of ethical issues are discussed by Keith-Spiegel and Koocher (1985); Eyde, et al. (1993); and Bersoff (1995).

The 1992 publication of the *Ethical Principles of Psychologists and Conduct* (APA, 1992) presents six general principles as well as specific ethical standards relevant to various activities of clinical psychologists (for example, assessment, intervention, therapy, forensic activities, and so on. The general principles are:

- Competence
- Integrity
- Professional and Scientific Responsibility
- Respect for People's Rights and Dignity
- Concern for the Welfare of Others
- Social Responsibility

Although they are not technically enforceable rules, these principles serve to guide psychologists' actions. On the other hand, the specific ethical standards that are presented below are enforceable rules of conduct. Acceptance of membership in the APA commits the member to adherence to the Ethics Code. Of course, actual clinical practice and its day-to-day demands can generate ethical decisions and dilemmas that would tax the judgment of the wisest in the field. Also, changes in our culture over time can provide a shifting ground that challenges a clinical psychologist's ability to make appropriate assessments. Take, for instance, the example in Box 3-1.

In the following sections, we will single out several of the ethical standards for discussion.

Competence

There are several important aspects with regard to issues of *competence* (Pipes & Davenport, 1990). First, clinicians must always accurately represent their training. Thus, subdoctoral clinicians must never lead anyone to believe they possess the Ph.D. Simply ignoring the fact that someone keeps referring to such a person as "Doctor" will not suffice. If clinicians are trained as counseling psychologists, that is how they must be presented—not as clinical psychologists. Clinicians have an obligation to actively present themselves correctly in terms of both their training and all aspects of competency. This also means that clinicians should not attempt treatment or assessment procedures when they have neither specific knowledge nor past supervision in the procedures. Whenever there may be doubts about specific competencies, it is wise to seek out supervision from more experienced clinicians.

It is equally important to be sensitive to treatment or assessment issues that could be influenced by a patient's gender, ethnic or racial background, age, or sexual preference. In addition, to the extent that clinicians have personal problems or sensitive spots in their own personality that could affect performance, they must guard against allowing these problems to adversely influence encounters with patients. All aspects of competence are important, whether they involve knowledge, clinical skill, clinical judgment, or interpersonal skill (Overholser & Fine, 1990).

Confidentiality

Clinicians have a clear ethical duty to respect and protect the *confidentiality* of client information. This is vital, since confidentiality is central to the client-

Box 3-1
Clinicians Who Appear on Radio Psychology Call-In Shows or TV Talk Shows:
Are They Ethical?

In 1953, the *Ethical Standards of Psychologists* (APA, 1953) stated:

> Principle 2.64-1. It is unethical to offer psychological services for the pur-
> pose of individual diagnosis, treatment, or advisement, either directly or in-
> directly, by means of public lectures or demonstrations, newspaper or mag-
> azine articles, radio or television programs, or similar media.

In 1953, this idea was pretty clear and seemed to make good sense.
Professional advice is an individual thing. It must be tailored to the individual and there is no way a clinician can do this on the basis of a three-
minute conversation with a radio caller. But in 1953 there were relatively
few radio call-in shows hosted by clinicians. By 1982 there were roughly
50 radio call-in shows hosted by mental health professionals (Levy, 1989).
Now, there are surely many, many more. As in all professions, some
hosts are flip, comedic, and, in general, poor clinicians. Others seem quite
skilled, concerned, and sincere while advising strongly that the caller seek
professional help.

Aside from strong media ratings, there are probably valid reasons for
having good call-in shows. For many distressed or disadvantaged people,
these shows may be their only route to help or support. The shows can
also sensitize and educate other listeners while helping prevent problems
from developing or getting worse. For still others, these shows may provide the caller with that extra courage or understanding necessary to seek
out professional services. In any case, the 1992 APA revision of ethical
standards reflects these points by now permitting advice — as opposed to
therapy — on the air. Psychologists are allowed to provide advice or comment via radio or television programs as long as "they take reasonable
precautions to ensure that (1) statements are based on appropriate psychological literature and practice, (2) the statements are otherwise consistent with this Ethics Code, and (3) the recipients of the information are
not encouraged to infer that a relationship has been established with them
personally" (APA, 1992, p. 1604).

What does research tell us about the phenomena of call-in programs?
In one study, 368 patrons of shopping malls were surveyed and another
122 persons who called one New York program were interviewed before
and after they talked with the show's therapist (Bouhoutsos, Goodchilds,
& Huddy, 1986). Half of the entire sample admitted to having listened to
call-in shows and these listeners considered the programs helpful and informative. Even those listeners who thought such programs could be
harmful were generally enthusiastic about them. Although subject to several interpretations, callers reported feeling better after they called in.
Many of the callers were people who had been in therapy, so these shows
do not seem to be a simple substitute for "real" therapy. Most listeners

regarded advice given as helpful or educational. In another study done in Israel, subjects who received help from a clinic did have more favorable attitudes toward help received than did subjects who called in to a radio counseling show (Raviv, Raviv, & Yunovitz, 1989). Levy (1989) has found that responses of hosts to call-in shows are at least marginally helpful to the callers and provide a moderate amount of support both for callers and for listeners.

Recent evidence, then, suggests that these shows can be helpful to some people under some conditions. But, again, do they fall within ethical guidelines? This is a difficult question because evidence suggests that the distinction between personal advice and therapeutic services dissolves when we analyze the verbal interactions on these programs (Henricks & Stiles, 1989). Further, some feel that the professional reputation of psychology is damaged when psychologists go on one of the many sensationalistic television talk shows (Sleek, 1995b).

psychologist relationship. When information is released without the client's consent, the trusting relationship can be irreparably harmed. Clinicians should be clear and open about matters of confidentiality and the conditions under which they could be breached. In today's climate, not all information is deemed privileged. For example, third parties (such as insurance companies) may be paying for a client's therapy and they may demand periodic access to records for purposes of review. Sometimes school records that involve assessment data may be accessible to others outside the school system under certain conditions (for example, when they are subpoenaed by a court). More and more, clinicians are less certain of their ability to promise absolute confidentiality.

Another question is whether all information *should* be confidential. Take, for example, the famous 1976 *Tarasoff case*. The events leading up to this case began when a client at a university counseling center told his therapist that he planned to kill his girlfriend. The therapist informed the campus police of the client's intentions, and they promptly took the client into custody. But since the girlfriend was away on vacation, the police decided to release the client. Subsequently, the client did indeed kill his girlfriend. Later, the woman's parents sued the therapist, the police, and the university, arguing that these three parties were negligent in not informing them of the threat. The California Supreme Court eventually ruled in favor of the parents and stated that the therapist was legally remiss in not informing all appropriate persons so that the violence could have been avoided. Such a decision surely raises issues that would tax the judgment of nearly every clinician. What makes all this even more ambiguous is that the legal precedents differ in various states. Not only must clinicians decide when and whom to inform and under what circumstances, they must also try to determine whether the *Tarasoff* decision applies in their state. Despite the number of years since the *Tarasoff* case was adjudicated, there is still confusion and uncertainty among clinicians about when to break confidentiality and activate one's "duty to warn" (Fulero, 1988).

There are so many complications in the realm of confidentiality. For example, what about working with children? Sometimes, adherence to strict rules of confidentiality could mean that parents cannot be integrated into the treatment plan in a helpful way (Taylor & Adelman, 1989). Related issues of confidentiality can arise when clinicians are treating AIDS patients (Lamb, Clark, Drumheller, Frizzell, & Surrey, 1989; Knapp & VandeCreek, 1990; Morrison, 1989; Scott & Borodovsky, 1990; Totten, Lamb, & Reeder, 1990).

Apparently, the lay public believes in the principle and importance of confidentiality. But they also understand that confidences may be broken in the cases of child abuse, potential suicide or murder, and other potentially threatening situations (Rubanowitz, 1987). Most clinicians agree; however, only in situations where they have felt the need to consult with a colleague or have had a potentially dangerous client are most willing to consider disclosure without client consent (Baird & Rupert, 1987).

Client welfare

Dual relationships pose many ethical questions. Sexual activities with clients, employing a client, selling a product to a client, or even becoming friends with a client after the termination of therapy are all behaviors that can easily lead to exploitation and harm to the client. While not perhaps terribly common, such events are clearly troublesome to the profession (Borys & Pope, 1989). Sexual liaisons can be equally damaging in supervisory relationships (Bartell & Rubin, 1990).

The worst of these dual relationships are sexual intimacies between client and psychologist. Make no mistake, ethical principles condemn such behavior in no uncertain terms. What is alarming here is the dramatic increase in the number of complaints filed against psychologists for sexual improprieties (Gottlieb, Sell, & Schoenfeld, 1988). A recent survey revealed that nearly 45% of clinicians felt that intimate relations with clients were unethical. But what is frightening is that over 31% said they felt that such relationships were neither ethical nor unethical, and almost 24% regarded intimacies as only somewhat unethical (Akamatsu, 1988)! These statistics are disturbing and indicate the need for more emphasis in training programs on the harm produced by engaging in intimate relations with clients.

Another aspect of *client welfare* involves the clinician's willingness to terminate therapy when it is no longer helping the client. In one case referred to an ethics committee, a clinical psychologist had been treating a child continuously for over two years and had informed the parent that two more years of therapy would be necessary. A review committee decided that the treatment was not consistent with the diagnosis and that there was no evidence of reasonable progress (APA, 1981).

Although such ethical principles do not explicitly require that clients be informed of their rights, this issue has received much attention recently (Pope, 1990). At least nine aspects of clients' rights are relevant (Talbert & Pipes, 1988) and include:

- The right to change therapists
- Possibilities of referral to other psychologists
- Mention of community services as another option

- Right to end therapy
- Risk of experiencing unpleasant emotions during therapy
- Risk of changes in personal relationships (for example, with a spouse)
- Limits of confidentiality
- Other risks, rights, and information

We shall return to this topic again in later chapters when we begin our discussion of therapy.

What types of ethical dilemmas do psychologists most frequently face? This question was addressed in a recent study by Pope and Vetter (1992). To assess the most commonly encountered "ethically troubling incidents," the authors surveyed a randomly selected sample of American Psychological Association members. Approximately 80% of the respondents indicated that they had encountered at least one such incident in the last one or two years. The most frequently reported type of ethical dilemma involved confidentiality (for example, breaching confidentiality because of actual or potential risks to third parties, suspected child abuse, and so on). Incidents involving blurred, dual, or conflictual relationships were the second most frequently reported problem (for example, maintaining therapeutic boundaries with clients and personal versus professional relationships with clients). The third most frequently cited category of ethically troubling incidents involved payment sources, plans, settings, and methods (for example, inadequate insurance coverage for clients with urgent needs). Other categories of ethically troubling incidents were in the areas of: training and teaching dilemmas, forensic psychology, research, conduct of colleagues, sexual issues, assessment, questionable or harmful interventions, and competence.

Psychologists, whether laboratory researchers or practicing clinicians, are being increasingly scrutinized for evidence of ethical violations. Ethical issues in research or in practice are not always easy to resolve nor are violations easy to monitor. But if clinical psychology is going to survive as a profession, it must find ways of ensuring adherence to the highest possible standards of conduct.

■ Focus Questions

1. What are the advantages and disadvantages of various models of training for clinical psychologists? Why is a firm grounding in psychological science important for future clinical psychologists?
2. What obstacles face clinical psychologists who specialize in private practice?
3. How will managed care affect the practice of clinical psychology? What advantages might clinical psychologists have in a managed care environment?
4. What are the advantages and disadvantages of obtaining prescription privileges? How might this pursuit affect graduate training?
5. What important diversity and ethical issues guide the practice of clinical psychology?

■ Key Terms

Academy of Psychological
   Clinical Science
American Board of Professional
   Psychology (ABPP)
certification
client welfare
clinical scientists
combined professional-
   scientific training program
competence
confidentiality
diversity
Doctor of Psychology
   (Psy.D.) degree

ethical standards
health maintenance organization
   (HMO)
licensing
managed care
preferred provider organizations
   (PPOs)
prescription privileges
professional schools
scientist-practitioner model
Tarasoff case

4

Research Methods in Clinical Psychology

The scientist-practitioner model has long been the preeminent philosophy in training clinical psychologists. This model is responsible for stimulating the kind of training that has allowed clinicians to become the research experts on so many mental health teams. Regardless of whether clinicians become active researchers or active consumers of research, methods of research are still pivotal concerns of both groups. In this chapter, we will present a brief overview of some of the chief methods, strategies, and issues in clinical research. Specific research questions (for example, therapy outcome studies) will be addressed at appropriate points later in the book. More comprehensive and technical discussions of research methods in clinical psychology may be found elsewhere (for example, Kazdin, 1992; Kendall & Butcher, 1982; Sher & Trull, 1996).

■ Introduction to Research

Someone once remarked that a major portion of clinical training consists of erasing students' misconceptions about the reasons people behave in the ways they do. For example, is it true that:

(1) if patients talk about suicide this means that they will not try it?
(2) ridding patients of symptoms without providing insight dictates that those symptoms will return later in another guise?
(3) male homosexuality is always traceable to a close-binding, intimate mother and a detached father?
(4) projective tests prevent patients from successfully managing the impressions they wish to convey?
(5) all one needs in order to become a good therapist is a caring, empathic attitude?

All of the above are common beliefs once held or, for that matter, still held by some people — clinicians and laypeople alike. Are they true? Probably not, but research that employs the methods described in this chapter can shed light on these issues.

Human behavior is terribly complex — so complex that theories to explain it abound. So many factors affect a given behavior at a given time and a given place that we must be skeptical about explanations that appear simple or inevitable. In fact, a healthy skepticism is a directing force behind the scientist's quest for knowledge or the clinician's search for increasingly effective ways of serving their clients.

Because easy, simple, or traditional explanations are so often wrong or incomplete, increasingly sophisticated methods of generating satisfactory explanations for behavior have evolved. We now employ better methods of making the kind of systematic observations about behavior that can be publicly verified. These methods have changed over the years and will continue to change in the future. Consequently, there are no inevitable or perfect scientific methods. But somehow, ideas, hypotheses, or hunches must be stated clearly and precisely so that they can be tested by other observers. Only ideas that are stated in a manner that offers a clear opportunity for disproof are satisfactory ones.

Research has several purposes. First of all, it allows us to escape the realm of pure speculation or appeal to authority. For example, we do not just argue whether cognitive-behavior therapy works; we conduct the kind of research that will *demonstrate* its effectiveness or lack thereof. Questions are settled in the forum of publicly verifiable and objective observation. Over the long haul, such procedures are better vehicles for settling issues than simple appeals to reason. These research procedures enable us to accumulate facts, establish the existence of relationships, identify causes and effects, and generate the principles behind the facts and relationships.

Research also helps us extend and modify our theories as well as establish their efficiency and utility. There is an intimate relationship between theory and research in that theory both stimulates and guides the research we do. But theories are also modified by the outcomes of research. For example, Aaron Beck, a pioneer in the study of depression, observed many years ago that depressed patients often exhibit personality features that could be categorized into one of two types: *sociotropic* (excessively socially dependent) and *autonomous* (excessively achievement-oriented). Initially, Beck proposed that extreme sociotropy or extreme autonomy traits predisposed one to depression. However, subsequent research did not support these propositions. Investigators found that there were individuals who presented with rather extreme sociotropy or extreme autonomy, but who were not currently depressed. These results challenged Beck's initial theory and led to a reformulation of how personality and depression may be related. The revised theory, labeled the *congruency hypothesis,* proposes that it is the interaction between personality style (sociotropic or autonomous) and the experience of thematically related negative life events that leads to depression (Beck, 1983). Specifically, this theory predicts that a highly sociotropic person who experiences relationship failures (that is, negative events quite salient to a highly dependent person) will become depressed, whereas this is not necessarily true for highly autonomous individuals because negative events of this kind are less relevant to their primary needs. In other words, negative life events must be *congruent* with one's personality style in order for depression to develop. In general, results have been more supportive of Beck's revised theory (for example, Bartelstone & Trull, 1995; Robins, 1990).

This example serves to illustrate how research can inform theories in a type of feedback-loop system. Of course, the ultimate reason for research is to enhance the ability of clinical psychologists to predict and understand the behavior, feelings, and thoughts of their clients. In the final analysis, only better research will enable clinicians to intervene wisely and effectively on their behalf.

■ Methods

As noted earlier, there are many methods of research and each has distinct advantages and limitations. Therefore, no method by itself will ever answer every question definitively. But together, a variety of methods can significantly extend the ability to understand and predict.

Observation

The most basic and pervasive of all research methods is observation. Experimental, case study, and naturalistic approaches all involve the act of observing what someone is doing or has done.

Unsystematic observation. Casual observation does little by itself to establish a strong base of knowledge. However, it is through such observation that we develop hypotheses that can eventually be subjected to test. For example, suppose a clinician notes on several different occasions that when a patient struggles or has difficulty with a specific item on an achievement test, the effect seems to carry over to the next item and adversely affect performance. This observation leads the clinician to formulate the hypothesis that performance might be enhanced by making sure each failure item is followed by an easy item on which the patient will likely succeed. This should help build the patient's confidence and thus improve performance. The clinician might then administer an experimental version of the achievement test, in which difficult items are followed by easy items, to test this prediction. As this example illustrates, it would be relatively easy to develop a study that would test this hypothesis in a representative sample of clients.

Naturalistic observation. Here, observations are more systematic and rigorous. Such observations are carried out in real-life settings but they are neither casual nor freewheeling — they are carefully planned in advance. However, there is no real control exerted by the observer who is pretty much at the mercy of freely flowing events. Frequently, observations are limited to a relatively few individuals or situations. Thus, it can be uncertain how far one can generalize either to other people or to other situations. In some cases, it is even possible that in the midst of observing or recording responses, the observer may unwittingly interfere with or influence the events under study.

An example of a study using the *naturalistic observation* method might involve an investigation of patient behavior in a psychiatric hospital. Perhaps a particular unit in this hospital is composed of patients who are that day scheduled to undergo electroconvulsive therapy (ECT). A clinician's job is to focus on ten patients and observe each one for two minutes every half hour. This might yield interesting data about the reactions of patients prior to ECT. But with only ten patients from this particular hospital, can wide generalizations be made? Are these patients' reactions similar to those in other hospitals or other units where the over-all atmosphere may be very different? Or were the patients aware of the observer's presence, and could they have altered their customary reactions in order to some-how impress the observer?

Investigators committed to more rigorous experimental methods sometimes condemn naturalistic observation as too uncontrolled. But this often seems a harsh judgment. As in the case of unsystematic observation, this method can serve as a rich source of hypotheses that can be subjected to careful scrutiny later. Naturalis-tic observations do get investigators closer to the real phenomena that interest them. Such observations avoid the artificiality and contrived nature of many ex-perimental settings. And then there is Freud. Regardless of one's allegiance or lack thereof to psychodynamic theory, his clinical observation skills were quite impres-sive. Freud used his own powers of observation to construct one of the most in-fluential and sweeping theories in the history of clinical psychology. It is equally important to recall that Freud had available no objective tests, no computer print-outs, and no sophisticated experimental methods. What he did possess was the ability to observe, interpret, and generalize in a most astounding fashion.

Controlled observation.   To deal in part with the foregoing criticisms of unsystematic and naturalistic observations, some clinical investigators employ *controlled observations.* While the research may be carried out in the field or in relatively natural settings, the investigator continues to exert some degree of con-trol over the events. Controlled observation has a long history in clinical psychol-ogy. For example, it is one thing to have patients tell their clinicians about their fears or to check off items on a questionnaire. However, Bernstein and Nietzel (1973) studied the nature of snake phobias by placing study participants in the presence of real snakes and then varying the distance between participant and snake. This enabled them to gain some real insight into the nature of the partici-pants' reactions. Mathews and Canon (1975) studied helping behavior as it is af-fected by noise. But they did so not in a sterile psychological laboratory but in a real neighborhood. As a potential participant strolled down the sidewalk, a con-federate of the experimenter either operated a very noisy lawn mower or just bent over it silently. At the same time, another confederate dropped a stack of books all over the sidewalk. As it happened, 50% of the subjects helped pick up the books when there was no noise, but only 12.5% helped when the mower was running.

Case studies.   The *case study method* involves the intensive study of a client or patient who is in treatment. Under the heading of case studies we have material from interviews, test responses, or treatment accounts. There could also be biographical and autobiographical data, letters, diaries, life-course informa-tion, medical histories, and so on. Case studies, then, involve the intensive study and description of one person. Such studies have long been prominent methods in the study of abnormal behavior and in the description of treatment methods. Their great value resides in their richness as potential sources of understanding and as hypothesis generators. They can serve as excellent preludes to scientific investigation (see Box 4-1). No matter how important experiments, computer

■

Box 4-1
What case studies can tell us about phobias and early trauma

1. Specific phobias are unreasonable fears that are out of proportion to any real danger to the individual. Many learning theorists believe specific phobias are acquired through classical conditioning. As a prototypic experiment, these theorists often cite the classic Watson and Rayner (1920) study of Little Albert. Albert was conditioned to fear white rats by discovering that each time he began to play with one, a loud and unpleasant noise occurred. Over trials, Albert developed what appeared to be a full-blown phobia of rats and similar furry objects.

However, Davison and Neale (1996) have noted that despite what learning theory seems to teach us, clinical reports and histories fail to support the Little Albert model. While some specific phobias could develop in that manner, they usually occur without any prior frightening experiences in the situation. Individuals who fear elevators, snakes, or high places rarely report an early bad experience with such places or things. It is not clear that laboratory research on specific phobias is carried out in real enough settings that researchers can say that the laboratory mimics real life.

2. Everybody "knows" that early childhood trauma is likely to predispose us to unhappiness and failure. Take the following example:

> A girl who is plain and lacks grace; whose mother favors her two younger brothers; whose mother nagged her, creating constant feelings of shame and estrangement; whose father left home when she was young; whose mother died when the girl was only 9, leaving her in the care of a grandmother; whose grandmother kept her away from other children and deprived her of most of her childhood; who was so lonely that her only pursuits were reading, daydreaming, and walking.

Such a person must be ripe for failure, emotional problems, or perhaps destined to become a social misfit (White, 1976). But as White asks wryly, who is it we are describing? It is none other than Eleanor Roosevelt, depicted by White as "the champion of the poor and the oppressed; ultimately [becoming] chairman [sic] of the committee which drew up the United Nations Declaration of Human Rights" (White, 1976, p. 522).

■

printouts, or statistical norms may be, we should never neglect to consider actual treatment cases.

Over the years, many case studies have been influential in establishing our understanding of clinical phenomena. Some of the more famous and classic examples include:

The Case of Dora (Freud, 1905/1953b): taught us about the concept of resistance in therapy.

The Case of Little Hans (Freud, 1909/1955): extended our understanding of the psychodynamics of phobias.

The Three Faces of Eve (Thigpen & Cleckley, 1957): outlined the anatomy of multiple personalities.

The Mask of Sanity (Cleckley, 1964): provided detailed accounts of the lives of psychopaths.

Case Studies in Behavior Modification (Ullman & Krasner, 1965): demonstrated the efficacy of behavioral treatments with single cases.

Nothing will ever likely supplant the case study as a way of helping clinicians to understand that unique patient who sits there before them. As Allport (1961) so compellingly argued, individuals must be studied individually. But there is, of course, a downside to case study methods. For example, using individual cases to develop universal laws or behavioral principles that apply to everyone is difficult. Likewise, one case study can not lead to cause-effect conclusions because clinicians are not able to control important variables that have operated in that case. One patient may benefit enormously from psychodynamic therapy, for example, but this may have less to do with the therapy method than with the personality characteristics of that patient. Only subsequent controlled research can pin down the exact causes of—or factors influencing—change.

We can conclude this discussion by agreeing with Davison and Neale (1996), who assert that case studies have been especially useful for: providing descriptions of rare or unusual phenomena or novel, distinctive methods of interviewing, assessing, or treating patients; disconfirming "universally known" or accepted information; and generating testable hypotheses (see Box 4-2).

Epidemiological research

Epidemiology refers to the study of the incidence, prevalence, and distribution of illness or disease in a given population. Several terms are commonly used in epidemiology. *Incidence* refers to the rate of new cases of illness that develop within a given period of time, while *prevalence* refers to the overall rate of cases—old or new—within a given period of time. Incidence gives us some sense of whether the rate of new cases of the illness or disorder is on the increase (for example, is the rate of newly diagnosed AIDS cases increasing this year compared to last year?). Prevalence rates, on the other hand, estimate what percentage of the target population is affected by the illness or disorder. For example, the lifetime prevalence rate of schizophrenia is estimated at 1%, suggesting that members of the general population have a 1 in 100 chance of developing this disorder in their lifetime.

Historically, epidemiology has been most closely associated with medical research designed to understand and control the major epidemic diseases, such as cholera and yellow fever. Central to this research method is the simple counting of cases. The expectation is that analyzing the distribution of cases in a community or region and uncovering the distinguishing characteristics of the affected individuals or groups will teach us something about the causes of a particular disease

Box 4-2
Generating hypotheses from therapy

The case of Karl S. was first described by Phares (1976). Karl was an unmarried veteran referred to a Veterans Administration outpatient clinic. It did not take long for the therapist to realize that Karl's problems were not of the typical neurotic variety. No well-defined, classic neurotic symptoms were present. Karl was a bit anxious or at times depressed, but his main problem seemed to be a near total lack of interpersonal and social skills. He had no job, and he lived off his small government pension along with whatever support his mother could provide. Aside from his mother with whom he lived, he rarely interacted with anyone except perhaps to buy cigarettes or get change from a disinterested bus driver. He certainly had no friends.

Therapy, then, became not an insight-oriented uncovering process but a teaching process. The goal became one of teaching Karl to find work, to attend night school to learn a trade, and to inculcate at least a few basic social skills. The focus was on how to find a job, keep a job, and talk with a woman and gain her interest. Hour after hour was spent on these tasks during the therapy, but progress was slow.

It was not that Karl failed to understand or was totally disinterested or even loath to try out newly learned skills—the difficulty was that, even when Karl attempted a new behavior and was successful, that success seemed to have little effect on his subsequent behavior. This was strange indeed. Psychologists learn early that, given similar conditions, reinforcement strengthens the potential for the occurrence of the reinforced behavior in the future. But not so with Karl. The occurrence of reinforcement seemed to do little to raise his expectancies that the behavior would work again. Karl almost seemed to want to be the singular exception to a prime rule of learning theory—that reinforcement enhances habit strength!

The therapist and his consultants puzzled over this for months. For example, after applying for a job and getting it, Karl's confidence did not increase at all. Instead, he attributed his success to luck, not to his own efforts. Several other similar episodes followed. After much urging by the therapist, Karl asked a female coworker for a date. She accepted. But, again, Karl merely remarked on his good luck.

Eventually, the therapist decided that perhaps Karl believed that the occurrence of reinforcement was outside his personal control. If so, the inability of success to increase his confidence began to make sense. He was not responding in defiance of learning theory. Instead, the therapist's conceptualization had been incomplete—a reinforcement will stamp in a behavior but only when that behavior is seen as causally related to the subsequent reinforcement. Karl believed chance was operative rather than personal skill; and under chance conditions, when one is reinforced, there are no implications for the future. Thus, the riddle of Karl's behavior seemed to have been solved. Or, at the very least, an important hypothesis had been formulated.

In fact, a great deal of empirical study lay ahead. Only after several years of research could the utility of the chance-versus-skill hypothesis be verified. This general research field came to be referred to as *internal-external control* (Rotter, 1966), or *locus of control*.

and the methods by which it spreads. In addition, epidemiological methods can be quite important in identifying groups of individuals who are at risk.

A well-known example of epidemiological research is the study *Smoking and Health* (Surgeon General, 1964). That study linked cigarette smoking with lung cancer by the simple methods of counting and correlating. Although there was great debate as to whether smoking *caused* lung cancer, there were definite relationships and associations between smoking and lung cancer (for example, about 90% of lung cancer in males was associated with cigarette smoking, and the amount and duration of smoking were positively correlated with the probability of cancer). It is true that epidemiological research frequently suggests the possibility of multiple causation (that is, several factors must be present before the disease occurs, or, the greater the number of associated factors that are present, the greater the risk of the disease). It is equally true that obtained correlations suggest causes rather than definitively prove causation. However, the entire story of causation need not be known before preventive steps can be undertaken. Thus, we may not be sure that smoking causes lung cancer, or we may believe that some inherited predisposition interacts with smoking to produce cancer. Nevertheless, we know that groups of males who quit smoking reduce their risk of lung cancer.

As another example, a number of studies in the field of mental illness have pointed out the relationship between schizophrenia and either socioeconomic class or factors of social disorganization (Faris & Dunham, 1939; Hollingshead & Redlich, 1958). Again, though such results hardly convey the essence of schizophrenia, they do tell us about major demographic factors that are associated with its prevalence. Armed with this information, clinicians can identify people whose potential vulnerability to schizophrenia is high and can establish special programs that will provide early diagnostic evidence of its onset in such people, or treatment programs can be established that will be readily available to potential schizophrenic patients.

Much epidemiological research is based on surveys or interviews, but these data can be subject to problems of reliability and validity—that is, how shall we define a mental health problem, and having done so, where do we locate cases for counting? Checking only clinics and hospitals means ignoring other possible locales. These difficulties are magnified when we become interested in milder forms of dysfunction. In effect, we need objective methods of defining and measuring a problem. Then we need survey procedures that will enable us to estimate the problem's true incidence or prevalence and not just to locate those cases that are already under treatment or that have identified themselves by seeking treatment. We need to sample residences, block by block or area by area, and not just clinics, hospitals, and agencies.

Another potential problem with survey data is that respondents may get caught up in the need to say the right thing. They may want to report only socially desirable things and deny other, less socially desirable experiences. For example, a respondent may be unwilling to admit to the experience of serious symptoms of psychopathology (such as auditory hallucinations) because of being embarrassed.

In addition, some respondents may be asked to remember things from several years ago. Such *retrospective data* can be subject to all sorts of distortions, omissions, or embellishments. For example, a recent study (Henry, Moffitt, Caspi, Langley, & Silva, 1994) found that 18-year-olds who had been assessed on a regular basis from birth were not particularly accurate in their retrospective reports of certain types of childhood experiences (for example, family conflicts, their own depressive or anxious symptoms, or their own level of hyperactivity). These findings are noteworthy because clinical psychologists often request this type of retrospective information from clients or research participants. The point here is that we should attempt to assess our clients and research participants *at the time of interest* and not rely exclusively on retrospective reports.

Recently, several large-scale, methodologically sound epidemiological studies of mental disorder have been conducted. For example, Kessler et al. (1994) administered a structured diagnostic interview to a national probability sample in the United States in order to obtain estimates of the 12-month and lifetime prevalence of a variety of mental disorders. Some of these results appear in Table 4-1. What is of interest are the differences in lifetime prevalence rates between men and women for some but not all disorders. Men are more likely than women to receive a substance use disorder or antisocial personality disorder diagnosis, whereas mood and anxiety disorder diagnoses are more prevalent in women. From these data, one can conclude that men appear to have a greater risk for a variety of substance use disorders than women. Therefore, being a man is a *risk factor* for these disorders. Risk factors need not be limited to gender but can involve other sociodemographic features as well (for example, socioeconomic status, age, urban versus rural residence, and so forth).

Correlational methods

We just saw that epidemiology often relies on *correlational methods* because this field assesses the correlates—that is, risk factors—of illness or disorder. We now focus more specifically on these methods. Correlational techniques enable us to determine whether variable x is related to variable y. For example, is a certain pattern of scores on an intelligence test related to specific psychiatric diagnostic categories? Are particular patient characteristics related to therapy outcomes? Is depression related to gender?

The technique.   In order to correlate two variables, we first obtain two sets of observations. Suppose that we administer two tests to ten study participants. One test measures anxiety and the other a belief in personal control. These hypothetical data are shown in Table 4-2. When the data are correlated the result is a

Table 4-1

Lifetime prevalence rates for selected DSM-III-R mental disorders.

Disorder	Male %	Female %	Total %
Mood Disorders			
Major Depressive Episode	12.7	21.3	17.1
Manic Episode	1.6	1.7	1.6
Dysthymia	4.8	8.0	6.4
ANY Mood Disorder	14.7	23.9	19.3
Anxiety Disorders			
Panic Disorder	2.0	5.0	3.5
Agoraphobia without Panic Disorder	3.5	7.0	5.3
Social Phobia	11.1	15.5	13.3
Simple Phobia	6.7	15.7	11.3
Generalized Anxiety Disorder	3.6	6.6	5.1
ANY Anxiety Disorder	19.2	30.5	24.9
Substance Use Disorders			
Alcohol Abuse without Dependence	12.5	6.4	9.4
Alcohol Dependence	20.1	8.2	14.1
Drug Abuse without Dependence	5.4	3.5	4.4
Drug Dependence	9.2	5.9	7.5
ANY Substance Abuse/Dependence	35.4	17.9	26.6
Other Disorders			
Antisocial Personality	5.8	1.2	3.5
Non-Mood Psychosis	0.6	0.8	0.7
ANY DISORDER	48.7	47.3	48.0

SOURCE: From "Lifetime and 12-month Prevalence of DSM-III-R Psychiatric Disorders in the United States: Results from the *National Comorbidity Survey*," by R. C. Kessler, et al., 1994, *Archives of General Psychiatry, 51,* 8–19. Copyright © 1994 by the American Medical Association. Adapted by permission.

Table 4-2

Hypothetical data for the correlation between anxiety and control.

Subject	Anxiety score	Control score
Ann	26	22
Jane	24	28
Tom	20	22
George	20	14
Esther	16	18
Nancy	12	22
Robert	12	6
Kevin	10	14
Lisa	6	12
Ralph	4	2

correlation coefficient, which in this case is +.76, indicating a strong positive re-lationship. As anxiety scores increase, so do scores on belief in external control, which means that anxiety and feelings of lack of control are positively related.

The *Pearson product-moment coefficient* is a commonly used index to de-termine the degree of relationship between two variables. This is symbolized by *r,* which may vary anywhere from −1.00 to +1.00. An *r* of +1.00 denotes that the two variables are perfectly and positively related—an *r* of −1.00 indicates a per-fect negative relationship. The *r* of +.76 from the data of Table 4-2 signifies a high but less-than-perfect relationship. A *scatter plot* of the data points for the two variables from Table 4-2 are shown in Figure 4-1. Each data point corresponds to one participant's scores on both anxiety and control. Thus, the data point nearest the lower left corner is Ralph's data (anxiety = 4; control = 2). Figure 4-2 presents scatter plots for several correlations.

The more nearly perfect a relationship, the closer to a straight line the data points will be. As *r* approaches zero (no relationship), the data points are scattered in a nearly random fashion around a straight line.

Statistical versus practical significance.   After a correlation coefficient has been calculated, it can be determined whether the obtained num-ber is significant. Traditionally, if it is found that the obtained correlation (or a more extreme value) could be expected to occur by chance alone less than 5 times out of 100, it is deemed statistically significant. Such a correlation is said to be significant at the .05 level, usually written as *p*<.05. The larger the corre-lation, of course, the more likely it is to be significant. But when large numbers of participants are involved, even relatively small correlations can be significant—that is, with 180 participants, a correlation of .19 is considered significant; when

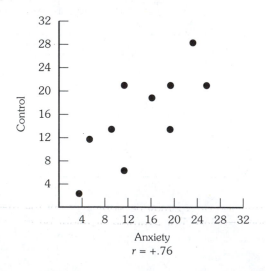

Figure 4-1
Scatter plot of data from Table 4-2.

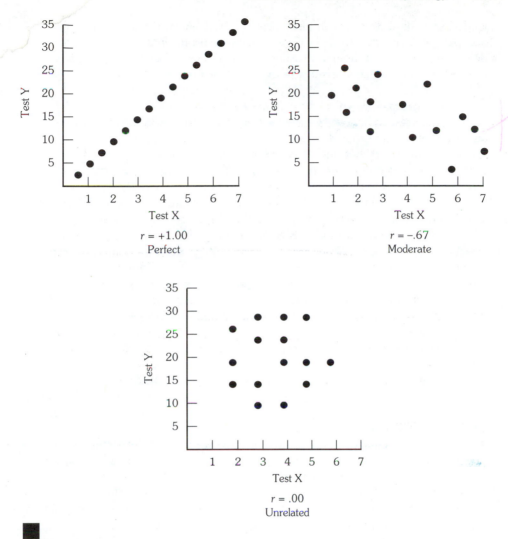

Figure 4-2
Scatter plots showing several different magnitudes of relationships.

only 30 participants are involved, however, a correlation of .30 would fail to be significant.

Therefore, it is important to distinguish between *practical* and *statistical significance*. The correlation of .19 may be significant but the magnitude of the relationship is still quite modest. For example, it might be true that in a study involving 5000 second-year graduate students in clinical psychology across the nation, there is a correlation of .15 between their GRE scores and their faculty ratings of academic competence. Even though the relationship is not a chance one, the actual importance is rather small. Most of the variance in faculty ratings is due to factors other than GRE scores. In some cases, a correlation of .15 may be judged important, but in many instances it is not. Also, we must remember that accepting significance levels of .05 as nonchance represents a kind of scientific tradition; it is not sacred, however. Other information may persuade some, in certain cases, that significance levels of .07 or .09 should be taken seriously.

The question of causality.   As noted previously in the case of epidemiological research, correlational methods can founder on the question of cause and effect. No matter how logical it may appear, we cannot on the basis of a correlation alone assert that one variable has caused another. For example, suppose that an investigator discovers there is a correlation between being diagnosed with schizophrenia and having elevated levels of the neurotransmitter dopamine in the central nervous system. Does this mean that schizophrenia is caused by excessive levels of dopamine or, alternatively, that the experience of an episode of schizophrenia results in changes in levels of dopamine? Maybe the real culprit is a third variable. For example, many patients with schizophrenia have a long history of taking psychoactive drugs (for example, long-term use of amphetamines). Such long-term use could conceivably affect neurotransmitter levels; therefore, the investigator must avoid assuming that one variable causes the other since there is always the possibility that a third, unmeasured variable is involved.

A classic example of the *third variable problem* is the observation that crime rates are significantly correlated with the number of churches and synagogues in a community. Does this mean that religion causes crime? No. The third variable that has been neglected in this example is the population rate. Both the crime rate as well as the number of churches and synagogues are positively correlated with the population rate, and they are correlated with each other because both increase as the population increases.

Of course, correlational methods can demonstrate that a cause-effect hypothesis is invalid. If the expectation is that variable *a* causes variable *b,* we should at least be able to show they are correlated. Failure to find a significant relationship most certainly contradicts the hypothesis. While causal inferences are not possible from correlation coefficients, this is not to say that cause-effect relationships do not exist in a given case, but such relationships must be demonstrated through additional experimental methods (to be discussed later). There are research methods that can help vitiate the causation problem—for example, matching participants on other variables that might be contributing to the obtained relationship or by longitudinal methods that study variables before a given disorder develops. But these are often cumbersome and expensive procedures and, thus, are less frequently employed.

Sometimes we are forced to use correlational methods because we cannot either ethically or practically manipulate certain variables such as age, sex, marital status, or birth order. For example, we cannot ethically train someone to commit a homicide in order to study the effects of personality on violence. Certain things can *only* be studied by observing their occurrences—creating them is not an acceptable alternative.

Factor analysis.   This method derives from the correlational strategy. *Factor analysis* is a way of examining the interrelationships among a number of variables at the same time. It is a statistical method that utilizes many separate correlations in order to determine which variables change in concert and thus can be considered functionally related. The idea is that when variables change together, they must have some element in common that underlies their relationship.

Consider the following example (Phares, 1991). Suppose we are trying to identify the basic elements of what is called "clinical skill." First, we ask a panel of judges to select 100 clinicians who are known to have excellent records in providing skilled services. Then, we administer a large number of tests that are believed to assess a variety of clinical skills and achievements. Next, we correlate each of those tests with every other test. This gives us a correlation matrix in which the correlations between all possible pairs of tests are displayed. Such a matrix with hypothetical correlations entered is shown in Table 4-3. Let us suppose that only seven tests were used as follows:

A = IQ test
B = Mathematical achievement test
C = Test of spatial reasoning
D = Test of analytical reasoning
E = Measure of empathy
F = Measure of personal adjustment
G = Measure of altruism

Looking at the correlation matrix, an interesting pattern emerges. Measures A, B, C, and D all show a strong positive relationship (correlations range from .70 to .80). At the same time, E, F, and G also correlate highly with each other (correlations range from .75 to .85). But there is virtually no relationship between the group E, F, G and the group A, B, C, D (for example, the correlation between A and E = .15, between B and F = .10, and between D and G = .12). These patterns indicate that A, B, C, and D appear to be measuring a similar underlying dimension, or *factor*. Similarly, E, F, and G belong together, suggesting a second underlying dimension. In effect, factor analysis does statistically with large correlation

Table 4-3
Hypothetical correlation matrix for seven tests.

Test	A	B	C	D	E	F	G
A		.70	.80	.75	.15	.20	.10
B			.75	.70	.12	.10	.10
C				.70	.18	.15	.11
D					.12	.14	.12
E						.80	.85
F							.75
G							

SOURCE: From *Introduction to Personality*, 3rd Ed., by E. J. Phares. Copyright © 1991 by HarperCollins. Reprinted by permission.

matrices what was done here by inspection with correlations from seven measures. Were we to have had 200 measures, simple inspection would have been an impossible task.

From the previous example, it would appear that two factors or dimensions are involved. Let us call them X (derived from the correlations among A, B, C, and D) and Y (derived from E, F, and G). Together, these two factors account for the significant relationships in the matrix. Usually, these factors are then named. This is often a highly inferential decision that can sometimes lead to communication problems, as the names that are chosen sometimes convey information that is different from what was intended. However, in our example, where factor X involves A, B, C, and D, perhaps we could choose the name "intellectual ability." Factor Y is more difficult to name since it involves measures of empathy, adjustment, and altruism. Perhaps "healthy altruism" would be appropriate.

Factor analysis is an especially good way of helping to organize in a coherent fashion the relationships that emerge from large arrays of data. For identifying the basic elements of clinical skill (as in the example) or those of personality, however, factor analysis is not the ultimate answer. After all, what emerges from a factor analysis is determined by the nature of the measures included in the first place. What was not included in the sample battery of tests to study clinical skill could hardly be expected to turn up as factors!

Longitudinal versus cross-sectional approaches

In fields such as gerontology there have long been two major approaches to research. *Cross-sectional designs* are those that compare different age groups at the same point in time. *Longitudinal designs* follow the same subjects over time. The basic format of these two approaches is shown in Figure 4-3. In this example, row *a* illustrates the longitudinal design and column *b* the cross-sectional design.

Cross-sectional approaches are correlational since the investigator cannot manipulate age nor can participants be assigned to different age groups. Since there are different participants in each age group, one cannot assume that the outcome of the study reflects age changes; it only reflects differences among the age groups employed. These differences could be due to the eras in which participants were raised rather than age per se. For example, a group of 65-year-olds might show up as more frugal than a group of 35-year-olds. Does this mean that advancing age promotes frugality? Perhaps. But it might indicate only that the 65-year-olds were raised during the Great Depression when money was very hard to come by.

Longitudinal studies are those in which we collect data on the same people over time. Such designs allow us to gain insight into how behavior changes with age. In the interpretive sense, longitudinal studies enable investigators to better speculate about time-order relationships among factors that vary together. They also help eliminate the third variable factor that so often can be a problem in correlational studies. For example, suppose we know that states of depression come and go over the years. If this condition is then responsible for the fact that significant losses of weight and decreasing levels of self-confidence are correlated, then both weight loss and decline in self-confidence should vary along with depressive states.

Birthdate	Age				
1890	65	70	75 [b]	80	85
1895	60	65	70	75	80
1900	55	60	65	70	75
1905	50	55	60	65	70
1910	[a] 45	50	55	60	65
1915	40	45	50	55	60
1920	35	40	45	50	55
1925	30	35	40	45	50
Time of measurement	1955	1960	1965	1970	1975

Figure 4-3
Cross-sectional and longitudinal research designs. SOURCE: Diana Woodruff-Pak, *Psychology and Aging,* © 1988, p. 32. Reprinted by permission of Prentice Hall, Englewood Cliffs, New Jersey.

There are, of course, many variations in cross-sectional and longitudinal designs (Kausler, 1991). In the case of longitudinal studies, however, the main problems are practical ones. Such studies are costly to carry out and they require great patience and continuity of leadership in the research program. Sometimes, too, one must live with design mistakes made years earlier or put up with outmoded research and assessment methods. Because longitudinal research is expensive in terms of both time and money, it is not employed as often as it should be. For these reasons, research in the developmental aspects of psychopathology has long suffered (Rotter, 1990; Wierson & Forehand, 1994). Still, it is hoped that there will be a return to those strategies that deal with psychopathology, treatment, or personality over extended periods of time and with a variety of measures (Phares, 1991). Too often, clinical psychologists have been captives of a cross-sectional methodology that sometimes seems to have focused exclusively on 50-minute experiments. Such strategies have promoted a snapshot view that has done little to help us understand the coherence and organization of human behavior and personality.

The Experimental Method

To determine cause-effect relationships among events, we must employ *experimental methods.* Consider the following study in which personal responsibility was studied in relation to several indicants of well-being (Langer & Rodin, 1976). Although this study was conducted some time ago, the design of the research nicely illustrates important features of the experimental method.

The study was carried out in a Connecticut nursing home where participants' ages ranged from 65 to 90. The *experimental group* contained 47 subjects who were told that they would be encouraged to make a number of decisions. For example, rather than looking to the staff, they could decide on their own room arrangement, where they wished to meet visitors, how they wanted to spend their spare time, and so on. They were even encouraged to report their complaints to the staff. In addition, each was expected to personally care for a plant. The *control group* consisted of 44 participants who were left with the distinct impression that all the foregoing matters would be decided by the staff. They were told how eager the staff was to care not only for them but even for their plants! The two groups were otherwise matched initially (one week before the instructions were given) on several variables, including health status, prior socio-economic level, and psychological adjustment. Despite this matching, three weeks later the two groups differed significantly on a variety of measures—alertness, happiness, general well-being, frequency of attendance at movies, and engagement in group activities. Figure 4-4 shows the findings for self-reports of happiness before and after the instructions.

This example illustrates several features of a typical experimental study; the *experimental hypothesis*, the *independent variable*, and the *dependent variable*. The experimental hypothesis—that elderly subjects would benefit from a sense of

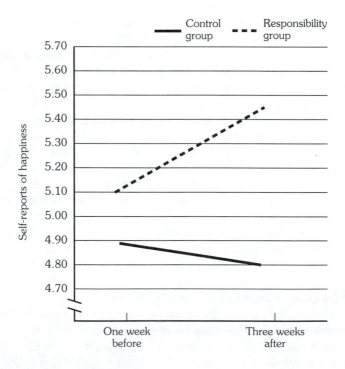

Figure 4-4

Self-reports of happiness before and after experimental intervention. SOURCE: Based on data from Langer & Rodin (1976).

personal responsibility — is developed both from observation of similar populations and from prior published research. The independent variable — in this case, personal responsibility — is supposed to be under the control of the investigator and is expected to have a causal effect on participants' behavior. The dependent variable — the participants' response (for example, reports of happiness) to perceived responsibility or lack thereof — is a reaction to changes in the independent variable.

Good experimental procedure is also followed by *matching* subjects on important variables that might have affected the outcome of the research (such as health status and adjustment). Sometimes, when matching is difficult, participants are assigned randomly to experimental and control groups. In any case, the idea is that the only significant feature different for the two groups was the induced sense of personal responsibility. Hence, the higher happiness scores in the experimental group must have been *caused* by the instructions.

Between- and within-group designs

In *between-group designs* we have two separate sets of participants where each receives a different kind of treatment. Take, for example, a study of therapy effectiveness. In its simplest form an experimental group (receiving some form of treatment) is compared to a control group (receiving no treatment at all). Ideally, patients would be randomly assigned to each group. Some set of measures — for example, level of anxiety, interview impressions, or test data — is taken from all patients in both groups prior to treatment (or no treatment), after treatment, and perhaps at a follow-up period six months or a year after treatment is concluded. Any differences between the two groups at either the conclusion of treatment or during the follow-up are assumed to be a function of the treatment that was received by the experimental group.

In the case of *within-group designs,* comparisons might be made on the same patient at different points in time. To illustrate how this procedure works, suppose we are interested in the effects (for example, level of distress) of being on a waiting list. We might decide to place every patient on a six-week waiting list, but we carry out a variety of assessment procedures before doing so (point A). Six weeks later, these patients would be reassessed just prior to beginning treatment (point B). At the conclusion of treatment (point C), the patients would be assessed a third time, and there might also be follow-up later, perhaps at point D. Any changes taking place between points A and B (while on the waiting list) could be compared to the changes that take place between point B and point C or D. These more complex analyses of changes would give us a better view of the efficacy of treatment relative to being on a waiting list.

There are many variations of within-group design. However, a major advantage is that it requires fewer participants. Indeed, as we shall see later in the case of single-subject designs, we can determine whether or not a specific intervention has an effect merely by observing one participant.

Internal validity

Sometimes it happens that an experiment is not *internally valid* — that is, we are not sure that the obtained outcome is really attributable to our manipulation of the independent variable. Some studies do not even include a control group for comparison with an experimental group. As a result, any observed changes could be the result of some other variable. For example, suppose in the nursing home experiment that Langer and Rodin did not have a control group. Even though the experimental group showed increases in happiness, perhaps this was not at all due to feelings of responsibility. Maybe it was due to a new nursing home administrator hired in the midst of the study. Or maybe it was due to a change in dieticians that occurred over the course of the study. Without a control group that also experienced the latter events, one can never be sure. In short, when extraneous variables are not controlled or cannot be shown to exist equally in experimental and control groups, the results may have been *confounded* by such variables.

We shall see later that, sometimes in studies of therapy effectiveness, one group of patients receives a new form of therapy. A second group of patients is either matched with the therapy group, or else patients are randomly assigned to both groups, and then assigned to a waiting list. The assumption is that the only difference between the waiting-list subjects and the therapy subjects is that the latter received therapy and the former did not. Therefore, the study is internally valid. But is it really? Experience has shown that subjects who go on a waiting list do not always fail to receive help. Instead, they often seek help from a minister, wise counsel from a friend, or some other form of assistance from someone else. Thus, any improvement shown by the therapy group may be confounded by the extratherapy help received informally by subjects on the waiting list. Therefore, the fact that the therapy group improved no more than did the waiting-list group hardly means that the therapy intervention was ineffective — it may only mean that both groups received some form of intervention.

Another factor that detracts from internal validity involves *expectations*. When either the investigator or the participant expects a certain outcome, that very outcome may be produced. It is not the experimental manipulation that causes the outcome but the expectations that are responsible. When this happens, it is called a *placebo effect*. For example, some people have been known to behave in a drunken manner when they believe that the situation calls for such behavior, despite the fact that they were not drinking alcohol but only thought they were. Similarly, patients have reported that therapy has helped them when objectively they were not any better. Since the therapist has devoted so much time to them, they feel they must be better!

In other cases, the experimenters have been known to unwittingly produce the very responses they expected to get. Perhaps they behaved in subtle ways that encouraged their patients to behave in the "proper" fashion. This is especially likely to happen when the experimenter knows who are experimental subjects and who are control subjects. Clinicians on occasion have been guilty of unconsciously giving a patient a little extra time on a test item simply because they expected the patient to do well.

To avoid the effects of experimenter or participant expectations, the *double-blind procedure* is commonly used. Here, neither participant nor experimenter knows what treatment or procedure is being employed. For example, if an investigator is interested in studying the effects of two drugs, the person dispensing the drug does not know which is which. Nor can the participant tell either because the two kinds of pills are identical in size, shape, color, weight, texture, taste, and so on. But double-blind studies are not always as "blind" as we think they are (see Margraf et al., 1991).

In summary, then, methods such as matching, random assignment of participants to experimental and control groups, use of control groups, and the employment of double-blind procedures all help to ensure that experiments will display internal validity.

External validity

When it is discovered that the results of an experiment cannot be generalized beyond the narrow and exact conditions of the experiment, the research does not show *external validity*. If the Langer and Rodin results applied only to that specific nursing home, they have a problem. In fact, most experimental research is done with the hope of generalizing the results beyond the confines of the immediate setting. Actually, it can be very difficult to determine the external validity of a given study. All too often results produced in the laboratory cannot be reproduced in real-life settings. The worst mistake is merely to assume that because certain results were produced in situation A, they will automatically occur in situation B. While laboratory experimental research usually allows better control of variables, its artificial nature may often prevent wide generalizations.

Analogue research

The question of generalization of results is particularly salient for *analogue studies*—those that are conducted in the laboratory where control is easier to exert and where conditions are said to be "analogous" to real life. Most often these studies are employed to highlight the nature of psychopathology or therapy.

There are many examples of analogue procedures. When Watson and Rayner (1920) tried to show how Little Albert could learn to be phobic for white rats, they were constructing an analogue of the way they thought real-life phobias were acquired (see Box 4-1). As another example, some researchers study the correlates and effects of depression by inducing depressive mood in nondepressed participants through the use of traditional mood induction techniques (for example, reading text that has been shown to increase levels of dysphoria) or through the use of slides and music that induce certain mood states (for example, Goodwin & Sher, 1993). These techniques presumably create a depressive state analogous to that seen in clinical depression.

In one sense, almost all experimental studies are analogue studies to some extent or other. But when severe practical or ethical constraints prevent us from creating real-life conditions, we must turn to analogue situations. The advantage of analogue studies is that better internal validity is possible because of the superior control we can exert in the laboratory; but the Achilles heel of the method is the degree of similarity between the analogue and the real thing. For example, suppose we decide to study the role of failure in creating depression. We do not want to study real depressives for several reasons. First, it is difficult to get a large enough sample of participants who have similar backgrounds and who are equally depressed. Second, would it really be ethical to subject such people to a strong, significant failure experience and thereby risk plunging them even deeper into depression? This, by the way, illustrates a real dilemma with analogue research. If our experimental manipulations are effective, they might be harmful—and therefore unethical. If they are mild, the research becomes trivial and has little external validity (Suomi, 1982). Nevertheless, the fact that analogue conditions will allow the experimenter to control the degree and kind of failure, the nature of the participants, and so on makes the use of analogue studies an attractive alternative.

When clinical psychologists employ analogue procedures, however, they may pay a price. For example, in the previous hypothetical experiment, how do we know that our participants are really the same as participants professionally diagnosed as depressed? Perhaps they are participants recruited from general psychology classes whose only claim to being depressed is a score above some cutting point on a questionnaire that purports to measure depression. These are not, then, clinical cases of depression. In addition, the clinician has no assurance that an experience of failure on a problem in a laboratory setting is at all the same as failure in a depressive's everyday life.

Some have urged the use of animals in analogue studies because they do not present some of the methodological problems that exist in research with humans. With animals, experimenters can exert nearly perfect control—over their diets, their living conditions, and even their genetic background. They can be much more intrusive in the lives of animals; and since animals have shorter life spans, phenomena that may take years to study in humans can be studied in a few months with, say, rats. Further, there are a number of naturally occurring behavior disorders (for example, aggression, mood disorders, hyperactivity, and eating disorders) commonly seen in veterinary practice that appear to be relevant to the field of psychopathology (Stein, Dodman, Borchelt, & Hollander, 1994). But again, exactly how similar is animal behavior to human behavior? Perhaps similar enough in certain instances, but in others, not at all. In the final analysis, analogue research is important and can be quite enlightening. But experimenters can never afford to completely relinquish their skepticism when they employ it.

A closing note

In closing this section on experimental methods, it should be noted that not everyone is enamored with these traditional approaches. For example, many years ago Cattell (1965) critiqued the so-called bivariate research strategy. This is a hallowed method going all the way back to Pavlov and Wundt in which only two variables are studied at once. The investigator manipulates an independent variable and then observes its effects on the dependent variable. For example, the experimenter induces the belief in participants that they lack personal control over the onset of electric shock (independent variable). The question is, what happens to the participants' anxiety level as measured by the galvanic skin response (dependent variable)? If the focus is on anxiety, it may become necessary to carry out thousands of such bivariate studies to determine how people become anxious. The experimenters must vary measures of anxiety, the nature of the stimulus, and the presence of preexisting personality traits that may affect the nature of the participants' responses. If the experimenters vary one condition at a time in study after study, they are left with a piecemeal view of the human being. Putting the results of all these bivariate studies together can be worse than trying to put Humpty Dumpty together again. And because the study is looking at anxiety in isolation from other variables such as competency and adjustment, the results offer no sense of how these variables might affect anxiety.

As a consequence, some have advocated the use of a multivariate strategy. Here, the experimenters employ a variety of measures on the same person but do not exert much in the way of control. They can use questionnaires, life records, observation, and so on—data that can be correlated and factor-analyzed. Because the method can focus on naturally occurring phenomena and can deal with many variables simultaneously, many regard it as a superior strategy. However, this method, like other correlational approaches, has its limitations as well (see Phares, 1991).

■ Single-Case Designs

Single-case designs are an outgrowth of behavioral and operant approaches. They bear similarities to both experimental and case study methods. For example, an experimenter measures a subject's behavior under several conditions and, in this sense, is employing a method akin to experimental techniques. But the focus is on the responses of one participant only. Such research usually begins by establishing a baseline. Here, a record is made of the participant's behavior prior to any intervention—for example, the number of anxiety attacks per week. After a reliable baseline has been established, an intervention is introduced. The effects of this intervention are then determined by comparing the baseline level of behavior with the postintervention level.

Single-case designs allow the experimenter to establish cause-effect relationships. They have often been applied to studies in which the effectiveness of a therapeutic method is being examined, because they provide a method of studying clinical behavior, especially therapy methods, that does not require the withholding of treatment by assigning certain participants to control groups or waiting lists. Some have argued that the latter procedures, although representing good science, are essentially unethical because they may deprive people of hope for relief. Even though the therapy to be used may be unproved or even though some assert that, in the interests of the ultimate good of many people, science must deprive a few of the possibility of improvement, the specter of ethics still lurks in the background.

Other practical reasons for using single-case designs include the fact that it is often extremely difficult in clinical settings to find enough participants for matching or random assignment to control groups. Single-case studies reduce the numbers needed. Also, some have argued that most research—personality and clinical alike—generalizes findings based on mean scores. Consequently, the results may not really apply to or characterize any one case (Lamiell, 1987). Single-case designs sidestep this problem.

The ABAB design

The *ABAB design* permits measurement of a treatment's effectiveness by observing systematic changes in the participant's behavior as treatment and no-treatment conditions alternate. It is called the ABAB design because the initial baseline period (A) is followed by a treatment period (B), a return to the baseline (A), and then a second treatment period (B).

A good illustration of the single-case approach is the study of Robbie (Hall, Lund, & Jackson, 1968). Robbie was a third-grader who was very disruptive in the classroom. About 75% of his time was spent laughing, throwing things, and being a general nuisance. The rest of the time (25%), he studied. This behavior pattern is shown in Figure 4-5 as baseline period (A). During reinforcement period I (B), the teacher paid a lot of attention to Robbie and his study behavior increased accordingly. During the reversal period (A), the teacher returned to her former level of attention to Robbie and his study behavior reverted to about its baseline level. When attention was again introduced—reinforcement period II (B)—his behavior once again improved. The reversal period was inserted between the two reinforcement periods to enable the investigators to demonstrate a causal relationship between the teacher's behavior and Robbie's behavior.

One difficulty with the ABAB procedure is that withdrawing treatment could pose some ethical problems. However, the seriousness of this issue depends upon the specific circumstances involved.

Multiple baseline designs

In some cases, it is impossible to employ a reversal period. There may be ethical constraints as we noted. Also, in clinical research settings, therapists might be unwilling to have their clients reexperience situations that could reinstate the very behaviors they are seeking to eradicate. In such cases, investigators have em-

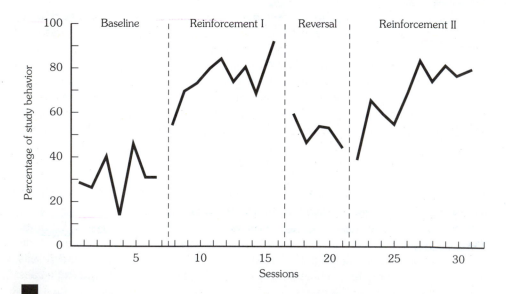

Figure 4-5

Robbie: The giving and withdrawal of reinforcement. SOURCE: From "Effects of Teacher Attention on Study Behavior," by R. V. Hall, D. Lund, and D. Jackson, *Journal of Applied Behavior Analysis,* 1968, 1, 1–12. Copyright 1968 by the Society for the Experimental Analysis of Behavior. Reprinted by permission.

ployed what are called *multiple baseline designs.* Here, two or more behaviors are chosen for analysis. For example, perhaps an institutionalized patient has severe problems in behaving in a responsible manner. He does not take care of his room, fails to follow good personal hygiene, and does not show up on time for work assignments. Baseline data are collected for his behavior in both personal and work settings. Next, immediate rewards are introduced whenever he behaves responsibly in personal settings but not in work settings. Then, after a prescribed period of time, measurements of behavior in both settings are once again collected. The last phase would involve rewards for responsible behavior in both settings. If responsible behavior increased in the personal setting following reward, but not in the work setting when there was no reward, it might be possible that some unknown and uncontrolled factor other than reward was operative. But if reward in the work setting also enhanced responsible behavior, it seems very unlikely that any factors other than reward were involved. Utilization of dual baselines gives investigators increased confidence in their manipulations.

Of course, all these single-subject designs by definition deal with one person. Can experimenters generalize what has been shown to be true of one person to an entire population? Like case study methods, the external validity of the results or attempts to generalize about them can be problematic. But as long as investigators are interested in one specific person or are seeking evidence that will encourage them to later initiate a full-blown traditional experimental study, the method has great merit.

Mixed designs

When experimental and correlational techniques are combined, the resulting approach is known as the *mixed design.* Here, participants who can be divided into specific populations (for example, schizophrenic versus normal) are assigned as groups to each experimental condition. Variables such as psychosis or normality are not manipulated or induced by the investigator — instead, they are correlated with the experimental condition.

Davison and Neale (1996) provide an excellent hypothetical example of how mixed designs work. Suppose we decide to investigate the efficacy of three forms of therapy (the experimental manipulation). We do this by identifying psychiatric patients who can be divided into two groups on the basis of the severity of their illness (the so-called classificatory variable). Does effectiveness of treatment vary with severity of illness? The results of our research are shown in Figure 4-6. The (b) section of that figure presents data obtained when the patients were divided into two groups according to the severity of their illness. The (a) section of Figure 4-6 shows how confused we could become had patients not been divided into two groups. When all patients are combined, treatment 3 produces the largest improvement, thus mistakenly encouraging us to believe that this treatment is the best. But when we analyze according to the severity of patients' illness, as in section (b), treatment 3 is not the preferred one for either group of patients. Instead, for patients with less severe problems, treatment 1 is desirable, and for those with more severe problems, treatment 2 would be preferable.

Later in this book, it will become apparent that there is no "best" therapy — there are only treatments that vary in their effectiveness for different kinds of

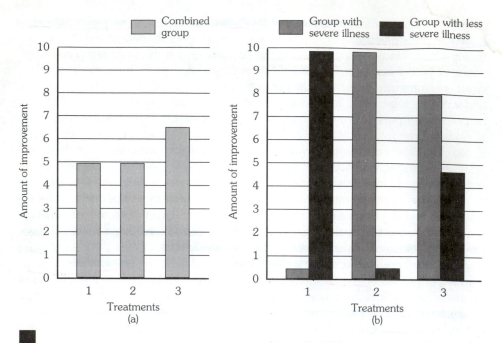

Figure 4-6

Effects of three treatments on patients whose problems vary in degree of severity. In
(a), when the severity of the illness is not known and the patients are grouped
together, treatment number 3 appears to be best. In (b), the same data as in (a)
are reanalyzed, dividing patients by severity. Now, treatment 3 is no longer best
for any patients. SOURCE: From *Abnormal Psychology,* 6th ed., revised by
G. C. Davison and J. M. Neale, p. 124. Copyright © 1996 by John Wiley &
Sons, Inc.

psychological problems and different kinds of people. Mixed designs can help us
discern what is best for whom. Of course, we must not forget that, in mixed designs, one of the factors is not manipulated (for example, severity of illness), and
this raises the kinds of problems discussed earlier in the case of correlational methods (Davison & Neale, 1996).

■ Research and Ethics

In Chapter 3 we discussed some of the ethical issues that involve the practice of clinical psychology. There are also important ethical considerations involving research. Just like patients, research participants have rights and investigators
have responsibilities to them.

A 1992 update of ethical standards for research with human participants
was published by the American Psychological Association (APA, 1992). This section of the ethical standards was greatly expanded in the latest revision, and we offer a brief overview here. These standards require that investigators:

1. plan research according to recognized standards of scientific competence and ethical principles
2. implement safeguards for the welfare of participants, others that may be affected by the research, and animal subjects
3. retain responsibility for ensuring ethical practices in research
4. comply with pertinent federal and state law and regulations
5. gain appropriate approval from host institutions or organizations prior to conducting research
6. establish clear and fair agreements with their research participants so that the rights and obligations of each party are clarified
7. use language that is easily understandable to research participants in the process of obtaining informed consent (informed consent should be documented)
8. take great care in offering inducements for research participation such that the nature of the compensation (for example, professional services) is made clear; financial or other types of inducements should not be so excessive as to coerce participation
9. employ deception as part of their procedures only when it is not possible to use alternative methods
10. protect participants from mental and physical discomfort, harm, and danger that might arise during the research
11. inform research participants of the anticipated use of the data and of the possibility of sharing the data with other investigators or any unanticipated future uses
12. minimize the invasiveness of research procedures
13. provide participants with information at the close of the research to erase any misconceptions that may have arisen
14. treat animal subjects humanely and in accordance with federal, state, and local laws as well as in keeping with professional standards

We elaborate on several of these points in the discussion below.

Informed consent

Good ethical practice as well as legal requirements demand that participants give their formal *informed consent,* usually in writing, prior to their participation in research. Researchers inform the participants of any risks, discomforts, or limitations on confidentiality and of any compensation for their participation. In addition, the researcher agrees to guarantee the participant's privacy, safety, and freedom to withdraw from the study. Box 4-3 presents an example of a consent form that was recently used in one of the author's research projects. Other consent forms from other investigators and other institutions will likely vary in the language that is used and, possibly, the points that are emphasized. However, most consent forms would be expected to contain the basic features in this example.

Confidentiality

Participants' individual data and responses should be confidential and guarded from public scrutiny. Instead of names, code numbers are typically used

Box 4-3
Example of a consent form.

Development of Personality Features
Consent Form

Code _____

CONSENT TO SERVE AS A PARTICIPANT IN RESEARCH STUDY ENTRY

I consent to participate in the study "Development of Personality Features" sponsored by the Psychology Department at the University of Missouri and conducted under the direction of Timothy J. Trull, Ph.D. This research project is aimed at assessing how personality features develop in young adults.

I understand that the study will involve the following procedures: (1) At Time 1 (study entry), I will be asked a number of questions, some of which may be extremely sensitive or upsetting, concerning various personal problems that I might have experienced as well as personal problems my biological parents may have experienced (for example, depression, suicidal feelings, child abuse). I understand that I will also complete a computerized interview and will be given two interview questionnaires that allow the researcher to develop a psychological profile. I understand that these interviews will be audiotaped. Only project staff will have access to these audiotapes, and these tapes will be erased at the end of the project.

For my participation at Time 1, which should take a total of about four hours, I will be compensated $35.00 for my time and efforts. (2) At Time 2 (two years later), I will be asked a number of questions, some of which may be extremely sensitive or upsetting, concerning various personal problems that I might have experienced as well as personal problems my biological parents may have experienced. I understand that I will also complete a computerized interview and will be given two interview questionnaires that allow the researcher to develop a psychological profile. For my participation at Time 2, which should take a total of about four hours, I will be compensated $35.00 for my time and efforts. Therefore, if I participate in all aspects of this study (that is, at Time 1 and at Time 2) I will receive a total of $70.00. I also understand that I may be contacted at some point in the future and asked to provide follow-up information. I understand that I am under no obligation to participate at that time and I may at any time withdraw and request that I not be asked to participate in the future.

I give the project director permission to gain access to the following information from the University of Missouri-Columbia Office of Admissions and Registrar: High school rank and percentile, ACT scores, GPA at MU, standardized test scores at MU, and possibly some other information related to academic performance.

I also understand that all possible steps have been taken to assure my privacy. I understand that the project staff will code the results of this research in such a manner that my identity will not be attached physically to the information I contribute. The key listing my identity and participant code number will be kept separate from the information in a locked file accessible only to the project staff. This key will be destroyed at the conclusion of the research project. Although the researchers do not know at this point when additional follow-ups may be attempted, the project will be concluded within fifteen years time. I also understand that these identifiers will be preserved for the duration of the project unless I request otherwise. I understand that I may contact the project director at any time and request that all identifiers which link my identity to the information I have contributed be destroyed. If requested, all data I have contributed and all identifying information will be destroyed by the project director (Dr. Trull).

Also, I realize that the purpose of this project is to examine the relations between certain variables in groups of individuals and not to evaluate the responses of a particular individual. I also understand that responding to some of the questions about personal problems, feelings, and behavior as well as about problems my biological parents may have experienced may cause discomfort because of their sensitive nature.

I understand that in the unlikely event that I am found to be suicidal or an imminent threat to someone else, the appropriate authorities will be contacted. Also, if I divulge information indicating that I am aware of possible ongoing child abuse or information raising the suspicion of ongoing child abuse, appropriate authorities will have to be notified. I understand that, although remote, it is possible that the information I contribute may be subject to subpoena.

I understand that participation is voluntary, that there is no penalty for refusal to participate, and that I am free to withdraw my consent and discontinue my participation before I complete the session. I also understand that I may refuse to answer any individual questions without penalty. In the event that I elect to discontinue participation, I understand that I will not receive any compensation and that any information I have contributed at any time to the study that is linked to me individually in any way will be destroyed. My name or any other identifiers also will be removed completely from the records.

If at any time I have questions about any procedures in this project, I understand that I may contact the project director, Timothy J. Trull, Ph.D., at 123-456-7890.

Name (Print) _____

Signature _____

Student Number _____

Date _____

to protect anonymity. While the results of the research are usually open to the public, it is presented so that no one can identify a specific participant's data. Further, clinical psychologists must obtain consent before disclosing any confidential or personally identifiable information in the psychologist's writings, lectures, or presentations in some other public medium (for example, television interview).

Deception

Sometimes the purpose of the research or meaning of a participant's responses is withheld. Obviously, *deception* should be used only when the research is important and there is no alternative to this method—in other words, when veridical information would compromise the participants' data. Deception should never be employed lightly. When it is used, extreme care must be taken so that participants do not leave the research setting feeling exploited or disillusioned. It is important that careful debriefing be undertaken so that participants are told exactly why deception was necessary. Investigators must take precautions to keep the participants' levels of interpersonal trust from being shaken. And, clearly, it is very important how they obtain informed consent when deception is employed.

An example of the need for deception in a study might be an experiment where it is predicted that the viewing of gun magazines or other materials associated with potential violence may lead to increased scores on a questionnaire measuring hostility. All participants are told that the experiment is one focusing on short-term memory, and they will be completing a memory task on two occasions separated by a 15-minute waiting period, during which they will be reading magazine articles. All participants first complete baseline measures, including the hostility questionnaire. Next, all participants complete a computer-administered memory task. During the waiting period, the experimental group is told to read selections from a gun magazine that are made available in the lab; the control group is told to read selections from a nature magazine (neutral with regard to violent imagery). All participants later complete the computer-administered memory task again. Finally, all participants complete the battery of self-report instruments a second time.

The point of describing the experiment outlined above is to demonstrate the need for deception in some experiments. As you can see, to tell the participants the real purpose of the experiment would likely influence their responses to the questionnaires—especially to the one measuring hostility. Therefore, the investigator might need to introduce the experiment as one that is focusing on short-term memory.

Debriefing

Because participants have a right to know why researchers are interested in studying their behavior, a *debriefing* at the end of the research is mandatory. It should be explained to them why the research is being carried out, why it is important, and what the results have been. In some cases, it is not possible to do the latter since the research is still in progress. But subjects can be told what kind of results are expected and that they may return at a later date for a complete briefing if they wish.

Fraudulent data

It hardly seems necessary to mention that investigators are under the strictest standards of honesty in reporting their data. Under no circumstances may they alter obtained data in any way. To do so can bring charges of *fraud* and create enormous legal, professional, and ethical problems for the investigator. While the frequency of fraud in psychological research has so far been minimal, the profession must be on guard. There is no quicker way to lose the trust of the public than through fraudulent practices.

As noted at the close of Chapter 3, if clinical psychology is going to survive as a profession, both researchers and practitioners must ensure adherence to the very highest standards of conduct.

■ Focus Questions

1. What are the advantages and limitations of the case study method?
2. What are the advantages and limitations of the correlational method?
3. What are the advantages and limitations of longitudinal studies?
4. What are the basic components of the experimental method?
5. What are the major ethical issues to consider when conducting clinical research?

■ Key Terms

ABAB design
analogue studies
between-group designs
case study method
confidentiality
confounded
control group
controlled observations
correlation coefficient
correlation matrix
correlational methods
cross-sectional designs
debriefing
deception
dependent variable
double-blind procedure
epidemiology
expectations
experimental group
experimental hypothesis
experimental methods
external validity

factor
factor analysis
fraud
incidence
independent variable
informed consent
internally valid
longitudinal designs
matching
mixed design
multiple baseline designs
naturalistic observation
placebo effect
prevalence
retrospective data
risk factor
scatter plot
single-case designs
statistical significance
third variable problem
within-group designs

5

Abnormal Behavior and Psychopathology

Clinical psychology is usually thought of as an applied field—one in which attempts are made to apply empirically supported psychological principles to problems of adjustment and abnormal behavior. Typically, this involves finding successful ways of changing the behavior, thoughts, and feelings of clients. In this way, clinical psychologists lessen their clients' maladjustment or dysfunction or increase their levels of adjustment. But before clinicians can apply their principles, they must first assess their clients' symptoms of psychopathology and levels of maladjustment. Interestingly, the precise definitions of these and related terms can be elusive. Further, the manner in which the terms are applied to clients is sometimes quite unsystematic.

To a large extent, clinical psychology has moved beyond the primitive views that defined mental illness as possession by demons or spirits, and maladjustment is no longer considered a state of sin. The eighteenth and nineteenth centuries ushered in the notion that so-called insane individuals are sick and require humane treatment. Even then, however, mental health practices could be bizarre, to say the least (see Figure 5-1). Clearly, clinical psychologists' contemporary views are considerably more sophisticated than those of their forebears. Yet many view current treatments like electroconvulsive therapy (ECT) with some skepticism and concern. Still others might see the popularity of treatments using *psychotropics*—antipsychotic, antidepressant, antimanic, or antianxiety medications—as less than enlightened. Finally, there are many forms of psychological treatment (for example, primal scream therapy, age regression therapy) that are questionable at best. All of these treatment approaches and views are linked to the ways clinical psychologists decide who needs assessment, treatment, or intervention, as well as the rationale for providing these services. These judgments are influenced by the labels or diagnoses often applied to people. Therefore, in this chapter, we will take a critical look at some of clinical psychology's definitions and labels. In this way, perhaps we can clarify some of the issues involved in their use.

To give you a better idea of the activities of clinical psychologists who specialize in abnormal behavior or psychopathology, we present a specific example in

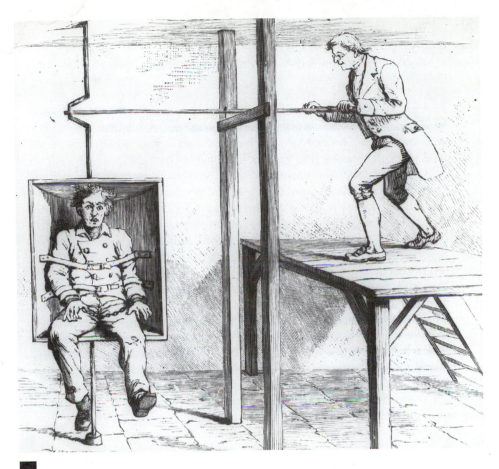

Figure 5-1
In the nineteenth century, people were treated for depression by spinning them in a
rotating chair. *The Bettmann Archive*

Box 5-1. It describes the work of a *psychopathologist* —a scientist who studies the
causes of mental disorders as well as the factors that influence their development.

What Is Abnormal Behavior?

Ask ten different people for a definition of abnormal behavior and you may
get ten different answers. Abnormal behavior is difficult to define for several reasons: (1) no single descriptive feature is shared by all forms of abnormal behavior,
(2) no one criterion for abnormality is sufficient, and (3) no discrete boundary
exists between normal and abnormal behavior. Many myths about abnormal behavior survive and flourish even in this age of enlightenment. For example, many

Box 5-1
Psychopathology: A specialty area of clinical psychology

A psychopathologist is a scientist who studies the development of mental disorders as well as their causes, or *etiology.* A relatively small, but very productive, proportion of clinical psychologists who conduct research call themselves psychopathologists.

Kenneth J. Sher is a prominent psychopathologist whose research focuses on the etiology and development of alcohol use disorders. Dr. Sher's empirical work has evaluated many theories of alcohol use (for example, tension reduction and self-awareness) as well as factors that influence the development of alcohol use disorders in at-risk subjects (that is, biological offspring of fathers diagnosed with alcoholism). Dr. Sher is currently conducting a major prospective study that assesses at-risk subjects at regular intervals during their collegiate and young adult years. For example, one of the studies from this large project indicated that children of alcoholics reported a greater number of alcohol and drug problems, stronger alcohol expectancies, greater behavioral undercontrol, and lower academic achievement than control subjects who did not have a family history of alcoholism (Sher, Walitzer, Wood, & Brent, 1991). Data from the prospective phase of Dr. Sher's study will be used to evaluate a variety of theoretical models for how alcohol problems and other forms of psychopathology develop in children of alcoholics.

individuals still equate abnormal behavior with bizarre behavior, dangerous behavior, shameful behavior.

In this section, we will examine in some detail several definitions of abnormal behavior that have been proposed, and we will discuss the pros and cons of each definition. Three definitions of abnormal behavior are examined: (1) *conformity to norms,* (2) *subjective distress,* and (3) *disability or dysfunction.* Although each of these three definitions highlights an important part of our understanding of abnormal behavior, each definition by itself is incomplete.

Conformity to norms: statistical infrequency or violation of social norms

When a person's behavior tends to conform to prevailing social norms or when this particular behavior is frequently observed in other people, the individual is not likely to come to the attention of mental health professionals. But when behavior becomes patently deviant, outrageous, or otherwise nonconforming, then an individual is more likely to be categorized as abnormal. Let us consider some examples.

The Case of Billy A.

Billy is now in the second grade. He is of average height and weight and manifests no physical problems. He is somewhat aggressive and tends to bully children smaller than himself. His birth was a normal one, and although he was a bit slow in learning to walk and talk, the deficit was not marked. The first grade was difficult for Billy, and his progress was slow—by the end of the school year he was considerably behind the rest of the class. However, the school authorities decided to pass him anyway. They reasoned that he was merely a bit slow in maturing and would come around shortly. They noted that his status as an only child, his doting parents, his short attention span, and his aggressiveness were all factors that combined to produce his poor school performance.

At the beginning of the second grade, Billy was administered a routine achievement test on which he did very poorly. As a matter of school policy, he was referred to the school psychologist for individual testing and evaluation. Based upon the results of the Stanford-Binet Intelligence Scale, the Draw-a-Person Test, school records, and a social history taken from the parents, it was concluded that Billy was mentally retarded. His IQ was 64 on the Stanford-Binet and was estimated to be 61 based on the Draw-a-Person Test. Further, a social maturity index derived from parental reports of his social behavior was quite low.

The Case of Martha L.

Martha seemed to have a normal childhood. She made adequate progress in school and caused few problems for her teachers or parents. Although she never made friends easily, she could not be described as withdrawn. Her medical history was negative. When Martha entered high school, changes began—she combed her hair in a very severe, plain style; she chose clothing that was ill-fitting and almost like that worn 50 years ago; she wore neither makeup nor jewelry of any kind. Where before she would have been hard to distinguish from the other girls in her class, now she easily stood out.

Martha's schoolwork began to slip. She spent hours alone in her room reading the Bible. She also began slipping notes to other girls that commented on their immorality when she observed them holding hands with boys, giggling, dancing, and so on. She attended religious services constantly—sometimes on Sundays she went to services at five or six separate churches. She fasted frequently and decorated her walls at home with countless pictures of Christ, religious quotations, and crucifixes.

When Martha told her parents that she was going to join an obscure religious sect and travel about the country, in a state of poverty, to deliver Christ's message, they took her to a psychiatrist. Shortly afterward, she was institutionalized. Her diagnosis varied, but it included such terms as schizophrenia, paranoid type; schizoid personality; and schizophrenia, simple type.

Both of these cases are examples of individuals commonly seen by clinical psychologists for evaluation or treatment. The feature that immediately characterizes both cases is that Billy's and Martha's behavior violates norms. Billy may be considered abnormal because his IQ and school performance depart considerably from the mean. This aspect of deviance from the norm is very clear in Billy's case because it can be described statistically and with numbers. Once this numerical categorization is accomplished, Billy's assignment to the deviant category is assured. Martha comes to people's attention because she is different — her clothes, appearance, and interests do not conform to the norms typical of females in her culture.

Advantages of this definition.   (1) *Cutoff points:* The statistical infrequency approach is appealing because *cutoff points are established that are quantitative in nature.* If the cutoff point on a scale is 80 and an individual scores a 75, the decision to label that individual's behavior as abnormal is relatively straightforward. This principle of statistical deviance is also frequently employed in the interpretation of psychological test scores. A cutoff point is presented by test authors in the manual for the test, often based on statistical deviance from the mean score obtained by a "normal" sample of test-takers, and scores at or beyond the cutoff are considered clinically significant — that is, abnormal or deviant.

(2) *Intuitive appeal:* It may seem quite clear to us that those behaviors we ourselves consider abnormal would be evaluated similarly by others. The struggle to define exactly what abnormal behavior is does not tend to bother us because, as a Supreme Court justice once said about pornography, we believe that we know it when we see it.

Problems with this definition.   Conformity criteria seem to play a subtle yet important role in making judgments of others. However, although clinicians must systematically seek the determinants of the individual's nonconformity or deviance, they should resist the reflexive tendency to categorize every nonconformist behavior as evidence of mental health problems. There are a number of problems with conformity criteria, as the following paragraphs will illustrate.

(1) *Choice of cutoff points:* Conformity-oriented definitions are limited by the difficulty in establishing agreed-upon cutoff points. As mentioned above, a cutoff is very easy to use once it is established. However, very few guidelines are available for choosing a cutoff point. For example, in the case of Billy, is there something magical about an IQ of 64? Traditional practice sets the cutoff point at 70. Get an IQ below 70 and you may be labeled as mentally retarded. But is a score of 69 all that different from a score of 72? Rationally justifying such arbitrary IQ cutoff points is difficult. This problem is equally salient in Martha's case. Are five crucifixes on the wall too many, or is attendance at three church services per week acceptable?

(2) *The number of deviations:* Another difficulty with nonconformity standards is the number of behaviors that one must evidence to be considered deviant. Was it just the crucifixes in Martha's case, or was it the total behavioral configuration: crucifixes + clothes + makeup + withdrawal + fasting and so on? Had Martha

manifested only three classes of unusual behavior, would she have escaped the label "deviant"?

(3) *Cultural relativity:* Martha's case in particular illustrates an additional point. Her behavior was not deviant in some absolute sense. Had she been a member of an exceptionally religious family that subscribed to radical religious beliefs and practices, she might never have been classified as maladjusted. In short, what is deviant for one group is not necessarily so for another. Thus, the notion of *cultural relativity* is important. Likewise, judgments can vary, depending upon whether family, school authorities, or peers are making them. Such variability may contribute to considerable diagnostic unreliability since it is undoubtedly true that even clinicians' judgments may be relative to those of the group or groups to which they belong.

Two other points about cultural relativity are also relevant. First, carrying cultural relativity notions to the extreme can place nearly every reference group beyond reproach. Cultures can be reduced to subcultures and subcultures to minicultures. If we are not careful, this reduction process can result in our judging nearly every behavior as healthy. Second, the elevation of conformity to a position of preeminence can be alarming. One is reminded that many of the most beneficial social contributions have been made by so-called nonconformists.

It can also become very easy to remove those whose different or unusual behavior bothers society. Some years ago in Russia, political dissidents were often placed in mental hospitals. In the United States, it sometimes happens that the family of 70-year-old Uncle Arthur is successful in hospitalizing him largely to obtain his power of attorney. His deviation is that, at age 70, he is spending too much of the money that will eventually be inherited by the family. And if these points are not enough, here is one more to note: *excessive* conformity has sometimes been the basis for judging persons abnormal as well.

Subjective distress

We now shift the focus from the perceptions of the observer to the perceptions of the affected individual. Here the basic data are not the observable deviations of behavior so much as they are the subjective feelings and the sense of well-being of the individual. Whether a person feels happy or sad, tranquil or troubled, and fulfilled or barren are the crucial considerations. If the person is anxiety-ridden, then he or she is maladjusted, regardless of whether the anxiety seems to produce overt behaviors that are deviant in some way.

The Case of Cynthia S.

Cynthia has been married for 23 years. Her husband is a highly successful civil engineer. They have two children, one in high school and the other in college. There is nothing in Cynthia's history to suggest psychological problems. She is above average in intelligence, and she completed two years of college before marrying. Her friends all characterize her as devoted to her family. Of all her features, those that seem to describe her best include her strong sense of responsibility and a capacity to get things done. She has always been a "coper," continuing to function effectively despite a great deal of personal stress and anxiety. She is a warm person, yet not one to wear her feelings or her troubles on her sleeve.

She recently enrolled in a night course at the local community college. In that course, the students were asked to write an existential account of their innermost selves. The psychologist who taught the course was surprised to find the following excerpts in Cynthia's account:

"In the morning, I often feel as if I cannot make it through the day. I frequently experience headaches and feel that I am getting sick. I am terribly frightened when I have to meet new people or serve as a hostess at a party. At times I feel a tremendous sense of sadness; whether this is because of my lack of personal identity, I don't know."

What surprised the instructor was that none of these expressed feelings were apparent from Cynthia's overt behavior. She appeared confident, reasonably assertive, competent, in good spirits, and outgoing.

The Case of Robert G.

In the course of a routine screening report for a promotion, Robert was interviewed by the personnel analyst in the accounting company for which he worked. A number of Robert's peers in the office were also questioned about him. In the course of these interviews, several things were established.

Robert was a very self-confident person. He seemed very sure of his goals and of what he needed to do to achieve them. Although hardly a happy-go-lucky person, he was certainly content with his progress so far. He never expressed the anxieties and uncertainty that seemed typical of so many of his peers. There was nothing to suggest any internal distress. Even his enemies conceded that Robert really "had it together."

These enemies began to be quite visible as the screening process moved along. Not many people in the office liked Robert. He tended to use people and was not above stepping on them now and then to keep his career moving. He was usually inconsiderate and frequently downright cruel and particularly insensitive to those below him. He loved ethnic humor and seemed to revel in his prejudices toward minority groups and those women who intruded into a "man's world." Even at home, his wife and son could have reported that they were kept in a constant turmoil because of his insensitive demands for their attention and services.

Cynthia and Robert are obviously two very different kinds of people. Cynthia's behavior is, in a sense, quite conforming. Her ability to cope would be cause for admiration by many. Yet she is unhappy and conflicted, and she experiences much anxiety. A clinical psychologist might not be surprised if she turned up in the consulting room. Her friends, however, would likely be shocked were they to learn that she had sought psychological assistance.

In contrast, many of Robert's friends, associates, and family would be gratified if he were to seek help, since most of them have at one time or another described him as sick. But Robert is not at odds with himself—he sees nothing wrong with himself and would probably react negatively to any suggestion that he should seek therapy. Furthermore, his lack of motivation for therapy would probably make it an unprofitable venture.

Advantages of this definition. Defining abnormal behavior in terms of subjective distress has some appeal. It seems reasonable to expect that individuals can assess whether they are experiencing emotional or behavioral problems and can share this information when asked to do so. Indeed, many methods of clinical assessment (for example, self-report inventories and clinical interviews) assume that the respondents are aware of their internal state and will respond to inquiries about personal distress in an honest manner. In some ways, this relieves the clinician of the burden of making an absolute judgment as to the question of the respondents' maladjustment.

Problems with this definition. The question is whether Cynthia, Robert, or both are maladjusted—the judgment will depend upon one's criteria or values. From a strict standpoint of subjective report, Cynthia qualifies but Robert does not. This illustrates that labeling someone maladjusted is not very meaningful unless the basis for the judgment is specified and the behavioral manifestations are stated.

Not everyone that is diagnosed as disordered reports subjective distress. For example, clinicians sometimes encounter individuals who may have little contact with reality yet profess inner tranquillity—however, these individuals are institutionalized. Such examples remind us that subjective reports must yield at times to other criteria.

Another problem concerns the amount of subjective distress necessary to be considered abnormal. All of us become aware of our own anxieties from time to time so that the total absence of such feelings cannot be the sole criterion of adjustment. If not, then how much anxiety is allowed, and for how long, before we acquire a label? Many would assert that the very fact of being alive and in an environment that can never wholly satisfy us will inevitably bring anxieties. Thus, as in the case of other criteria, using phenomenological reports is subject to limitations. Although there is a certain charm to the idea that if clinicians want to know whether a person is maladjusted then they should ask that person, there are obvious pitfalls in doing so.

Disability or dysfunction

A third definition of abnormal behavior invokes the concept of disability or dysfunction. For behavior to be considered abnormal, it must create some degree of social (that is, interpersonal) or occupational problems for the individual. Dysfunction in these two spheres is often quite apparent to both the individual as well as the clinician. For example, a lack of friendships or relationships because of a lack of interpersonal contact would be considered indicative of social dysfunction, while the loss of one's job due to emotional problems (for example, depression) would suggest occupational dysfunction.

The Case of Richard Z.

Richard was convinced by his wife to consult with a clinical psychologist. Previous contacts with psychiatrists had on one occasion resulted in a diagnosis of "hypochondriacal neurosis" and on another a diagnosis of "passive aggressive personality." Richard has not worked in several years even though he possesses a bachelor's degree in library science. He claims that he is unable to find employment because of his health. He reports a variety of physical symptoms, including dizziness, breathlessness, weakness, and "funny" sensations in the abdominal area. Going the rounds from physician to physician has enabled him to build an impressive stock of pills, which he takes incessantly. None of his physicians, however, has been able to find anything physically wrong with him.

As a child, Richard was the apple of his mother's eye. She doted on him, praised him constantly, and generally reinforced the notion that he was someone special. His father disappeared about 18 months after Richard was born. His mother died six years ago, and he married shortly after that. Since then, his wife has supported both of them, thus enabling him to finish college. Only recently has she begun to accept the fact that something is wrong with Richard.

The Case of Phyllis H.

Phyllis is a college student. She is in her sixth year of undergraduate study but has not yet obtained a degree. She has changed majors at least four times and has also had to withdraw from school on four occasions.

Her withdrawals from school have been associated with her drug habit. In two instances her family placed her in a mental hospital, and on two other occasions she served short jail sentences following convictions on shoplifting charges. From time to time, Phyllis engages in prostitution to support her drug habit. Usually she can secure the money from her parents, who seem to have an uncanny knack for accepting her outrageous justifications. She has been diagnosed with "antisocial personality disorder" and with "drug dependence" (cocaine).

According to the disability/dysfunction definition, both of these cases would suggest the presence of abnormal behavior. Richard is completely dependent on his wife (social dysfunction), and this, coupled with his litany of somatic complaints and his inability to cope with stress, has left him unemployed (occupational dysfunction). And Phyllis's drug habit has interfered with her occupational functioning — in this case, attending school.

   Advantages of this definition.   Perhaps the greatest advantage to adopting this definition of abnormal behavior is that relatively little inference is required, and problems in both the social and occupational spheres often prompt individuals to seek out treatment. It is often the case that individuals come to realize the extent of their emotional problems when these problems impact their family or social relationships as well as significantly affect their performance at work or school.

   Problems with this definition.   Who should establish the standards for social or occupational dysfunction — the patient, the therapist, friends, or the employer? In some ways, judgments regarding both social and occupational functioning are relative — not absolute — and involve a value-oriented standard. Although most of us may agree that having relationships and contributing to society as an employee or student are valuable characteristics, it is harder to agree upon what specifically constitutes an adequate level of functioning in these spheres. In short, achieving a reliable consensus about the nature of an individual's social relationships and contributions as a worker or student may be difficult. Recognizing this problem, psychopathologists have developed self-report inventories and special interviews to assess social and occupational functioning in a systematic and reliable way (see Goldman, Skodol, & Lave, 1992, for a review of these instruments).

Where does this leave us?

   To summarize, there are several criteria that are used to define abnormal behavior. Each criterion has its advantages and disadvantages, and no one criterion can be used as a gold standard — some subjectivity is involved. As one of the authors has stated elsewhere:

> The inevitable conclusion . . . is that a definition of abnormality (maladjustment, pathology, etc.) is possible only with reference to a set of value judgments. To characterize someone as abnormal is to assert that he [sic] needs treatment. In short, someone has decided that the patient needs help in changing his behaviors — a relative, a court, or perhaps the patient himself. . . . Once someone decides that the patient needs treatment, then our psychiatrist or psychologist can deliver an opinion on how best to effect the desired changes. But the decision for treatment as a function of abnormality must be based on someone's value system — it does not reside in psychiatry or psychology. (Phares, 1967, p. 501)

   As the discussion above points out, all definitions of abnormal behavior have their strengths and weaknesses. These definitions can readily incorporate certain examples of abnormal behavior, but exceptions that do not fit these definitions are easy to provide. For example, all of us can think of an "abnormal behavior" that would not be classified as such if we adopted the subjective distress criterion (for example, spending sprees during a manic episode); we can also think of a behavior that might be incorrectly classified as abnormal if we adopted the violation of norms definition (for example, an NFL all-star's athletic prowess).

It is important to note that *abnormal behavior does not necessarily indicate mental illness.* Rather, the term *mental illness* refers to a large class of frequently observed syndromes that are comprised of certain abnormal behaviors or features. These abnormalities tend to covary or occur together such that they often are present in the same individual. For example, major depression is a widely recognized mental illness whose features — depressed mood, sleep disturbance, appetite disturbance, suicidal ideation — tend to co-occur in the same individual. However, an individual who manifests only one or two of these features of major depression would not receive this diagnosis and might not be considered mentally ill. One can manifest a wide variety of abnormal behaviors (as judged by any definition) and yet not receive a mental disorder diagnosis.

■ Mental Illness

Like abnormal behavior, mental illness or disorder is also difficult to define. For any definition, exceptions come to mind. Nevertheless, it seems important to actually define mental illness rather than to assume that we all share the same implicit idea of what mental illness is.

The fourth edition of the *Diagnostic and Statistical Manual of Mental Disorders* (DSM-IV), published by the American Psychiatric Association (1994), states that a *mental disorder:*

> . . . is conceptualized as a clinically significant behavioral or psychological syndrome or pattern that occurs in an individual and that is associated with present distress (e.g., a painful symptom) or disability (i.e., impairment in one or more important areas of functioning) or with a significantly increased risk of suffering, death, pain, disability, or an important loss of freedom. In addition, this syndrome or pattern must not be merely an expectable and culturally sanctioned response to a particular event, for example, the death of a loved one. Whatever its original cause, it must currently be considered a manifestation of a behavioral, psychological, or biological dysfunction in the individual. Neither deviant behavior (e.g., religious, political, or sexual) nor conflicts that are primarily between the individual and society are mental disorders unless the deviance or conflict is a symptom of the dysfunction in the individual as described above. (pp. xxi–xxii)

Several aspects of this definition are important to note: (1) the *syndrome,* or cluster of abnormal behaviors, must be associated with distress, disability, or increased risk of problems; (2) a mental disorder is considered to represent a dysfunction *within an individual;* and (3) not all deviant behaviors or conflicts with society are signs of mental disorder.

The astute reader probably noticed that the DSM-IV definition of mental disorder incorporates the three definitions of abnormal behavior presented earlier in this chapter. On the one hand, the DSM-IV definition is more comprehensive than any one of the three individual definitions of abnormal behavior that were previously presented. However, at the same time, the DSM-IV definition is more restrictive because it focuses on syndromes or clusters of abnormal behavior that are associated with distress, disability, or an increased risk for problems.

The importance of diagnosis

Categorization is essential to our survival because it allows critical distinctions to be made (for example, a mild cold versus viral pneumonia, a malignant versus a benign tumor). Diagnosis is a type of expert-level categorization. It is used by mental health professionals to enable them to make important distinctions (for example, schizophrenia versus bipolar disorder with psychotic features).

Before uncritically accepting the DSM-IV definition of mental illness or taking for granted the utility of diagnosing and classifying individuals, however, the question needs to be asked, "Why should mental disorder diagnoses be used?" There are at least four major advantages of diagnosis, which are outlined below.

First, and perhaps most importantly, a primary function of diagnosis is communication. A wealth of information can be conveyed in a single diagnostic term. For example, a patient with a diagnosis of paranoid schizophrenia was referred to one of the authors by a colleague in New York City. Immediately, without knowing anything else about the patient, a symptom pattern came to mind (for example, delusions, auditory hallucinations, severe social or occupational dysfunction, and continuous signs of the illness for at least six months). Therefore, diagnosis can be thought of as a verbal shorthand for representing features of a particular mental disorder. Using standardized diagnostic criteria like those that appear in the DSM-IV ensures some degree of comparability with regard to mental disorder features between patients diagnosed in Missouri, Manhattan (N.Y.), and Manhattan, Kansas.

Diagnostic systems for mental disorders have survived for many reasons. The major reason is that these classificatory systems are largely descriptive — that is, behaviors and symptoms that are characteristic of the various disorders are presented without any reference to theories regarding the causes of these features. As a result, a diagnostician of nearly any theoretical persuasion can use them. If every psychologist used a different theoretically based system of classification, however, a great number of communication problems would likely result.

Second, the use of diagnoses enables and promotes empirical research in psychopathology. Clinical psychologists define experimental groups in terms of individuals' diagnostic features, thus allowing comparisons between groups with regard to personality features, psychological test performance, or performance on an experimental task. Further, the way diagnostic constructs are defined and described will stimulate research on the disorders' individual criteria, on alternative criteria sets, and on the comorbidity (co-occurrence) between disorders.

Third, and in a related vein, research into the etiology (that is, causes) of abnormal behavior would be almost impossible to conduct without a standardized diagnostic system. In order to investigate the importance of potential *etiological factors* for a given psychopathological syndrome, the experimenter must first assign participants to groups whose members share diagnostic features. For example, several years ago, it was hypothesized that the experience of childhood sexual abuse may predispose individuals to develop features of borderline personality disorder (BPD). The first empirical attempts to evaluate the veracity of this hypothesis involved assessing the prevalence rate of childhood sexual abuse in well-defined groups of study participants with borderline personality disorder as well as in non-borderline psychiatric controls. These initial studies have indicated that childhood sexual abuse does occur quite frequently in BPD individuals and that these rates are significantly higher than those found in patients with other (non-BPD) mental disorder diagnoses. Before investigators could reach these types of conclusions, there had to be a reliable and systematic method of assigning subjects to the BPD category.

Finally, diagnoses are important because, at least in theory, they may suggest which mode of treatment is most likely to be effective. Indeed, this is a general goal of a classification system for mental disorders, as stated by Blashfield and Draguns (1976): "The final decision on the value of a psychiatric classification for prediction rests on an empirical evaluation of the utility of classification for treatment decisions" (p. 148). For example, a diagnosis of schizophrenia suggests to us that the administration of an antipsychotic medication is more likely to be effective than is a course of psychoanalytic psychotherapy. However, it is important to note one thing in passing—although in theory the linkage between diagnosis and treatment would seem to justify the time involved in diagnostic assessment, often several treatments appear to be equally effective for an individual disorder.

In summary, diagnosis and classification of psychopathology serve many useful functions. Whether they are researchers or practitioners, contemporary clinical psychologists use some form of diagnostic scheme in their work. At this point, we turn to a brief description of classification systems that have been used to diagnose mental disorders over the years, and then we examine in more detail the features of the diagnostic classification system that is used most frequently in the United States—the DSM-IV.

Early classification systems

Classification systems for mental disorders have proliferated for many years. For example, the earliest reference to a depressive syndrome appeared as far back as 2600 B.C. (Menninger, 1963). Since that time, both the number and breadth of classification systems have increased. To bring some measure of order out of this chaos, the Congress of Mental Science adopted a single classification system in Paris in 1889. A more recent attempt can be traced to the World Health Organization and its 1948 *International Statistical Classification of Diseases, Injuries, and Causes of Death,* which included a classification of abnormal behavior.

In 1952, the American Psychiatric Association published its own classification system in the *Diagnostic and Statistical Manual* (DSM-I), which contained a glossary describing each of the diagnostic categories that were included. This first edition of the DSM was followed by revisions in 1968 (DSM-II), 1980 (DSM-III), and 1987 (DSM-III-R). Presently, the most widely used classification system is the American Psychiatric Association's *Diagnostic and Statistical Manual of Mental Disorders,* or DSM-IV, which appeared in 1994. All of these manuals are embodiments of Emil Kraepelin's efforts in the late nineteenth century. To illustrate how things have changed over the past 40 years, compare the British system in use in the late 1940s (Table 5-1) with the DSM-IV system (Table 5-2).

Table 5-1

Classifications of mental disorders in use by the Royal Medico-Psychological Association in the late 1940s.

A. Oligophrenia (amentia, mental deficiency):
    (a) Idiocy
    (b) Imbecility
    (c) Feeblemindedness (moron)
    (d) Moral deficiency
B. Neuroses and psychoneuroses:
    (a) Exhaustion states (including neurasthenia)
    (b) Anxiety states
    (c) Compulsions, obsessions, and phobias
    (d) Hysteria
    (e) Mixed and other forms
C. Schizophrenic psychoses:
    (a) Dementia praecox
        i. Simple
        ii. Hebephrenic
        iii. Catatonic
        iv. Paranoid
    (b) Paraphrenia
    (c) Other forms
D. Psychopathic constitution (including paranoia)
E. Affective psychoses:
    (a) Manic-depressive psychosis (cyclothymia)
        i. Elation
        ii. Depression
        iii. Stupor
    (b) Involutional melancholia
F. Confusional states
G. Epileptic psychoses
H. General paralysis
 I. Other psychoses associated with organic brain disease
J. Dementia
K. Indeterminate types

SOURCE: Adapted from Henderson & Gillespie (1950, pp. 20–21).

From the 1950s to the early 1960s, the enthusiasm for psychiatric diagnosis waned (Robins & Helzer, 1986). Diagnosis was said to be dehumanizing and to ignore individual variation. But diagnosis in psychiatry and psychology has staged a comeback. The most revolutionary changes in the diagnostic system were introduced in DSM-III, published in 1980. These included: the use of explicit diagnostic criteria for mental disorders, a multiaxial system of diagnosis, a descriptive approach to diagnosis that attempted to be neutral with regard to theories of etiology, and a greater emphasis on the clinical utility of the diagnostic system. Because these innovations were retained in subsequent editions of the DSM (that is, DSM-III-R and DSM-IV), they will be described below.

■

Figure 5-2
Emil Kraepelin is generally regarded as the father of modern systems of psychiatric
diagnosis and classification. *Culver Pictures, Inc.*

■ DSM-IV

In 1994, the fourth edition of the *Diagnostic and Statistical Manual of Mental Disorders* (American Psychiatric Association) was published. Revisions to the previous diagnostic manual, DSM-III-R, were guided by a three-stage empirical process. First, 150 comprehensive reviews of the literature on important diagnostic issues were conducted. These literature reviews were both systematic and thorough. Results from these reviews led to recommendations for revisions and served to document the rationale and empirical support for the changes made in DSM-IV. Second, 40 major reanalyses of existing data sets were completed in cases where the literature reviews could not adequately resolve the targeted diagnostic issue. Third, 12 DSM-IV field trials were conducted in order to assess the clinical utility and predictive power of alternative criteria sets for selected disorders (for example, antisocial personality disorder). In summary, the changes made in DSM-IV were based on empirical data to a much greater extent than was true in previous editions of the DSM. A condensed version of the DSM-IV appears in Table 5-2.

A complete DSM-IV diagnostic evaluation is a *multiaxial assessment:* clients or patients are evaluated along five axes, or domains, of information. Each of these axes should aid in treatment planning and prediction of outcome. *Axis I* is used to indicate the presence of any of the clinical disorders or other relevant conditions, with the exception of the personality disorders and mental retardation. These latter two classes of diagnoses are coded on *Axis II. Axis III* is used to highlight any current medical condition that may be relevant to the conceptualization or treatment of

Table 5-2
A condensed version of the DSM-IV.

Axis I: *Clinical Disorders or Other Conditions That May Be a Focus of Clinical Attention*
- Disorders usually first diagnosed in infancy, childhood, or adolescence (for example, pervasive developmental disorders)
- Delirium, dementia, and amnestic and other cognitive disorders
- Mental disorders due to a general medical condition
- Substance-related disorders (for example, alcohol abuse, cocaine dependence)
- Schizophrenia and other psychotic disorders
- Mood disorders (for example, major depression, bipolar disorder)
- Anxiety disorders (for example, agoraphobia, post-traumatic stress disorder)
- Somatoform disorders (for example, hypochondriasis)
- Factitious disorders
- Dissociative disorders (for example, dissociative identity disorder)
- Sexual and gender identity disorders (for example, vaginismus, fetishism)
- Eating disorders (for example, anorexia nervosa)
- Sleep disorders (for example, narcolepsy)
- Impulse control disorders (for example, kleptomania)
- Adjustment disorders
- Other conditions that may be a focus of clinical attention (for example, bereavement)

Axis II: *Personality Disorders and Mental Retardation*
- Personality disorders (for example, borderline, antisocial, dependent, paranoid)
- Mental retardation

Axis III: *General Medical Conditions That Are Potentially Relevant to the Understanding or Management of the Individual's Mental Disorder*

Axis IV: *Psychosocial and Enviornmental Problems*
- Problems with primary support group
- Problems related to the social environment
- Educational problems
- Occupational problems
- Housing problems
- Economic problems
- Problems with access to health care services
- Problems related to interaction with the legal system and crime
- Other psychosocial and environmental problems

Axis V: *Global Assessment of Functioning (GAF) Scale***

Code	Description
91 to 100	Superior functioning in a wide range of activities.
81 to 90	Absent or minimal symptoms (for example, mild anxiety before an exam), good functioning in all areas, interested and involved in a wide range of activities, socially effective, generally satisfied with life, no more than everyday problems or concerns (for example, occasional argument).
71 to 80	If symptoms are present, they are transient, expectable reactions to psychosocial stressors.

(continued)

Table 5-2 continued

Code	Description
61 to 70	Some mild symptoms.
51 to 60	Moderate symptoms.
41 to 50	Serious symptoms (for example, suicidal ideation, severe obsessional rituals, frequent shoplifting) or any serious impairment in social, occupational, or school functioning (for example, no friends, unable to keep a job).
31 to 40	Some impairment in reality testing or communication.
21 to 30	Behavior is considerably influenced by delusions or hallucinations.
11 to 20	Some danger of hurting self or others.
1 to 10	Persistent danger of severely hurting self or others (for example, recurrent violence) or persistent inability to maintain minimal personal hygiene or serious suicidal act with clear expectation of death.
0	Inadequate information.

*Full descriptions are provided here only for Codes 81–90, 41–50, and 1–10.

SOURCE: From American Psychiatric Association (1994). *Diagnostic and Statistical Manual of Mental Disorders* (4th ed.). Reprinted by permission

an individual's Axis I or II clinical disorder. Psychosocial and environmental problems relevant to diagnosis, treatment, and prognosis are indicated on *Axis IV.* Finally, a quantitative estimate (1 to 100; see Table 5-2) of an individual's overall level of functioning is provided on *Axis V.* Each of the five axes contributes important information about the patient, and together they provide a fairly comprehensive description of the patient's major problems, stressors, and level of functioning.

The Case of Michelle M.

Michelle M. was a 23-year-old woman who was admitted to an inpatient unit at a hospital following her sixth suicide attempt in the last two years. She told her ex-boyfriend (who had broken up with her a week earlier) that she had swallowed a bottle of aspirin, and he rushed her to the local emergency room. Michelle had a five-year history of multiple depressive symptoms that never abated; however, these had not been severe enough to necessitate hospitalization or treatment. The symptoms included dysphoric mood, poor appetite, low self-esteem, poor concentration, and feelings of hopelessness. In addition, Michelle had a history of a number of rather severe problems that had been present since her teenage years. First, she had great difficulty controlling her emotions—she was prone to become intensely dysphoric, irritable, or anxious almost at a moment's notice. These intense negative affect states were often unpredictable and, although frequent, rarely lasted more than four or five hours. Michelle also reported a long history of impulsive behaviors, including polysubstance abuse, excessive promiscuity (an average of about 30 different sexual partners a year), and binge eating. Her anger was unpredictable and quite intense. For example, she once used a hammer to literally smash a wall to pieces following a bad grade on a test.

Michelle's relationships with her friends, boyfriends, and parents were rather intense and unstable. People who spent time with her frequently complained that she would often be quite angry at them and devalue them for no apparent reason. She also constantly reported an intense fear that others, including her parents, might abandon her. For example, she once clutched a friend's leg and was dragged out the door to her friend's car while trying to convince her friend to stay for dinner. In addition, she had attempted to leave home and attend college in nearby cities on four occasions. Each time, she returned home within a few weeks. Prior to her hospital admission, her words to her ex-boyfriend over the telephone were, "I want to end it all. No one loves me."

Here is the DSM-IV diagnostic evaluation for Michelle:

Axis I:	Dysthymic disorder, early onset
	Alcohol abuse
	Cannabis abuse
	Cocaine abuse
	Hallucinogen abuse
Axis II:	Borderline personality disorder (Principal diagnosis)
Axis III:	None
Axis IV:	Problems with primary support group
	Educational problems
Axis V:	GAF=20 (Current)

Several features of this diagnostic formulation are noteworthy. First, Michelle has received *multiple diagnoses* on Axis I. This is allowed, and even encouraged, in the DSM-IV system because the goal is to describe the client's problems comprehensively. Second, note that her borderline personality disorder (BPD) diagnosis on Axis II is considered to be the *principal diagnosis*. This means that this condition is chiefly responsible for her admission to the hospital and may be the focus of treatment. Finally, her *Global Assessment of Functioning* (GAF) score on Axis V indicates serious impairment, in this case a high degree of risk for hurting herself.

■ General Issues in Classification

The DSM-IV has been briefly described to give the reader a general idea of what psychiatric classification entails. However, it is important to examine a number of broad issues related to classification in general and to DSM-IV specifically. Table 5-3 presents a summary of the eight major issues that we discuss below.

Table 5-3
General issues in classification.

Categories versus dimensions
Is the categorical model adopted in the DSM-IV (that is, the disorder is either present or absent) really appropriate? Is a dimensional model preferable?

Bases of categorization
Should there be multiple ways of making diagnostic judgments? Does this create too much heterogeneity within a diagnostic category?

Pragmatics of classification
How do we decide whether a condition is included in the diagnostic manual?

Description
Are the features of the diagnostic categories adequately described? Are the diagnostic criteria specific and objective?

Reliability
Are diagnostic judgments reliable? Can different diagnosticians agree on the classification of an individual?

Validity
Can we make meaningful predictions based on our knowledge of an individual's diagnosis?

Bias
Are the features of the disorders in the DSM-IV biased against particular individuals because of their gender, race, or socioeconomic status/background? Are diagnosticians biased in their interpretation or application of the diagnostic criteria?

Coverage
Do the DSM-IV diagnoses apply to the people who present for psychological or psychiatric treatment? Is the DSM-IV too narrow in its coverage, or is it too broad?

Categories versus dimensions

Essentially, the mental disorder *categories* represent a typology. Based upon certain presenting symptoms or upon a particular history of symptoms, the patient is placed in a category. There are several potential limitations to this approach. First, in too many instances, it is easy to confuse such categorization with explanation. If one is not careful, there is a tendency to think, "This patient is experiencing obsessions because she has obsessive-compulsive disorder," or "This person is acting psychotic because he has schizophrenia." When this kind of thinking occurs, explanation has been supplanted by a circular form of description.

In addition, as noted earlier in this chapter, abnormal behavior is not qualitatively different from so-called normal behavior; rather, these are endpoints of a continuous *dimension.* The difference between normal behavior and psychotic behavior, for example, is one of degree rather than kind (Chapman & Chapman, 1985). Yet mental disorder diagnoses encourage thinking in terms of categories that imply that individuals either have the disorder in question or they do not. This promotes a kind of all-or-none thinking that in fact may be at odds with what we know about how symptoms of psychopathology are distributed in the population. For example, a categorical model of borderline personality disorder (BPD), as presented in the DSM-IV (that is, present versus absent), may not be appropriate because individuals differ only with respect to how many BPD symptoms they exhibit (a quantitative difference). In other words, it appears that the categorical model may misrepresent the true nature of the borderline construct (Trull, Widiger, & Guthrie, 1990). In fact, there may be relatively few diagnostic constructs that are truly categorical in nature.

What are the bases of categorization?

In order to classify psychiatric patients, one must utilize a wide assortment of methods and principles. In some cases, patients are classified almost solely on the basis of their current behavior or presenting symptoms. In other cases, the judgment is made almost entirely on the basis of history. In the case of major depression, for example, an individual may be diagnosed on the basis of a diagnostic interview conducted by a clinician, whereas another individual may be classified because of a laboratory result (for example, a positive dexamethasone suppression test, or DST), and still another individual may be diagnosed as a result of scores on a self-report measure of depression.

Laboratory results provide the basis for some diagnoses of cognitive disorders (for example, vascular dementia), whereas other cognitive disorder diagnoses (for example, delirium) are determined solely by behavioral observation. Therefore, the diagnostic enterprise may be quite complicated for the clinician, requiring both knowledge of and access to a wide variety of diagnostic techniques. A major implication is that membership in any one diagnostic category is likely to be heterogeneous because there are multiple bases for a diagnosis.

The pragmatics of classification

Psychiatric classification has always been accompanied by a certain degree of appeal to medical authority. But there is a concurrent democratic aspect to the system that is quite puzzling. For example, psychiatry for many years regarded homosexuality as a disease to be cured through psychiatric intervention. As a result of society's changing attitudes and other valid psychological reasons, homosexuality was dropped from the DSM system and is now regarded as an alternate lifestyle (see Spitzer, 1981). Only when homosexual individuals are disturbed by their sexual orientation or wish to change it do we encounter homosexuality in the DSM-IV (as an example under the category "sexual disorder not otherwise specified"). The issue here is not whether this decision was valid but rather, how it was made. In fact, the decision to drop homosexuality as a disease entity occurred through a vote of the psychiatric membership.

This example also serves as a reminder that classification systems such as the DSM are crafted by committees. The members of such committees represent varying scientific, theoretical, professional, and even economic constituencies. Consequently, the final classification product adopted may represent a political document that reflects compromises that will make it acceptable to a heterogeneous professional clientele.

Description

Without doubt, the DSM-IV provides thorough descriptions of the diagnostic categories. For Axis I and II disorders, a detailed description of the symptoms of each diagnostic category is presented. As an example, Table 5-4 presents the DSM-IV diagnostic criteria for the eating disorder bulimia nervosa. Additional information for each diagnosis is provided as well, including: the age of onset, course, prevalence, complications, family patterns, cultural considerations, associated descriptive features and mental disorders, and associated laboratory findings. All this descriptive detail should enhance the system's reliability and validity.

Is the classification system reliable?

A scheme that cannot establish its reliability has serious problems. In this context, *reliability* refers to the consistency of diagnostic judgments across raters. One of the major changes seen in DSM-III (APA, 1980)—the inclusion of specific and objective criteria for each disorder—reflected an attempt to increase the reliability of the diagnostic system. If psychologist A and psychologist B both observe

Table 5-4
DSM-IV criteria for Bulimia Nervosa.

A. Recurrent episodes of binge eating. An episode of binge eating is characterized by both of the following:

    (1) eating, in a discrete period of time (e.g., within any 2-hour period), an amount of food that is definitely larger than most people would eat during a similar period of time and under similar circumstances.

    (2) a sense of lack of control of eating during the episode (e.g., a feeling that one cannot stop eating or control what or how much one is eating).

B. Recurrent inappropriate compensatory behavior in order to prevent weight gain, such as self-induced vomiting; misuse of laxatives, diuretics, enemas, or other medications; fasting; or excessive exercise.

C. The binge eating and inappropriate compensatory behaviors both occur, on average, at least twice a week for 3 months.

D. Self-evaluation is unduly influenced by body shape and weight.

E. The disturbance does not occur exclusively during episodes of Anorexia Nervosa.

Specify type:

    Purging Type: during the current episode of Bulimia Nervosa, the person has regularly engaged in self-induced vomiting or the misuse of laxatives, diuretics, or enemas.

    Nonpurging Type: during the current episode of Bulimia Nervosa, the person has used other inappropriate compensatory behaviors, such as fasting or excessive exercise, but has not regularly engaged in self-induced vomiting or the misuse of laxatives, diuretics, or enemas.

SOURCE: Reprinted from DSM-IV (APA, 1994). Reprinted with permission.

---

the same patient but cannot agree on the diagnosis, then both their diagnoses are useless because we do not know which to accept. This is the very situation that plagued the U.S. diagnostic systems for many years. For example, an early study illustrating the unreliability of previous diagnostic systems was carried out by Beck, Ward, Mendelson, Mock, and Erbaugh (1962). Two different psychiatrists each interviewed the same 153 newly admitted psychiatric patients. Overall agreement among these psychiatrists was only 54%. Some of the disagreements in diagnosis seemed to stem from inconsistencies in the information patients presented to the psychiatrists. For example, patient A may have been relatively open with psychiatrist F, but less so with psychiatrist G. But much of the unreliability problem seemed to lie with the diagnosticians and the diagnostic system itself.

There are some pragmatic factors that can also reduce reliability among diagnosticians. Sometimes it happens that a given institution will not admit patients who carry a certain diagnosis, yet a mental health professional may feel strongly that the patient could benefit from admission (or perhaps has nowhere else to go). What should be done? The humanitarian choice may be to alter a diagnosis or at least to "fudge" a bit. The patient with alcohol dependence, then suddenly is diagnosed with something else. Similarly, an insurance company may reimburse a clinic for the treatment of patients with one diagnosis but not another. Or perhaps one diagnosis permits six therapy visits but another allows as many as fifteen. Therefore, a diagnosis may be intentionally or unintentionally manipulated.

These examples may lead us to believe that diagnostic unreliability is the rule and not the exception. However, Meehl (1977), for example, feels that psychiatric diagnosis is not nearly as unreliable as it is made out to be. Specifically, Meehl argues that if mental health professionals confine themselves to major diagnostic categories, require adequate clinical exposure to the patient, and study well-trained clinicians who take diagnosis seriously, then interclinician agreement will reach acceptable levels.

The field of psychopathology has begun to address concerns about reliability by developing *structured diagnostic interviews* that essentially force diagnosticians to assess individuals for the specific DSM criteria that appear in the diagnostic manual. For example, there are now several structured interviews that assess features of Axis I disorders, and a number of structured interviews for Axis II disorders exist as well. Interestingly, the overall level of diagnostic reliability reported in empirical studies has greatly increased following the introduction of these structured interviews. It is clear that adhering to the structure and format of these interviews has led to a significant increase in diagnostic reliability. Table 5-5 presents a brief section from a structured interview. We will discuss this topic in more detail in Chapter 6.

However, even with the use of structured interviews, reliability is not equally good across all categories. The presence or absence of some disorders (for example, generalized anxiety disorder) may be particularly difficult to judge. Further, there is some question as to whether or not busy clinicians will devote the time and effort necessary to systematically evaluate the relevant diagnostic criteria. Reliability coefficients never seem to be as high in routine, everyday work settings as they are in structured research studies.

Table 5-5
SIDP-IV questions used to assess a dependent personality disorder criterion.

CRITERION 1: HAS DIFFICULTY MAKING EVERYDAY DECISIONS WITHOUT AN EXCESSIVE AMOUNT OF ADVICE AND REASSURANCE FROM OTHERS.

Questions to ask:

Some people enjoy making decisions and other people prefer to have someone they trust tell them what to do. Which do you prefer?

Do you often turn to others for advice about everyday decisions like what to have for lunch or what clothes to buy?

Scoring:

> 0 = not present
> 1 = subthreshold
> 2 = present
> 3 = strongly present

SOURCE: From *Structured Interview for DSM-IV Personality*, by B. Pfohl, N. Blum, and M. Zimmerman. Copyright 1994. Reprinted by permission.

Is the classification system valid?

Reliability will directly impact the *validity* of a diagnostic system. As long as diagnosticians fail to agree upon the proper classification of patients, we cannot demonstrate that the classification system has meaningful correlates—that is, validity. Important correlates include prognosis, treatment outcome, ward management, etiology, and so on. And without predictive validity, classification becomes an intellectual exercise devoid of any really important utility. However, if we could demonstrate that categorization accurately indicates etiology, course of illness, or preferred kinds of treatment, then a valid basis for its use would be established.

The predominant method for establishing the validity of a diagnostic construct was outlined in a classic article by Robins and Guze (1970). They proposed that establishing the diagnostic validity of a syndrome is a five-stage process: (1) *clinical description,* to describe the characteristic features beyond the disorder's symptoms (for example, demographic features); (2) *laboratory studies,* including psychological tests, to identify meaningful correlates of the diagnosis; (3) *delimitation from other disorders* to ensure some degree of homogeneity among diagnostic members; (4) *follow-up studies* to assess the test-retest reliability of a diagnosis; and (5) *family studies* to demonstrate that the proposed disorder tends to run in families, suggesting a hereditary component. This particular five-stage method for establishing diagnostic validity remains quite influential even today. In fact, most contemporary research in psychopathology represents one or more of the validation stages outlined by Robins and Guze.

Is the classification system biased?

Ideally, a classification system would not be biased with respect to how diagnoses are assigned to individuals who have different backgrounds (for example, different gender, race, or SES). For instance, the validity and utility of a classification system would be called into question if the same cluster of behaviors resulted in a diagnosis for one individual but not for another. The two areas of potential bias that have received the most attention are sex bias (see Widiger & Spitzer, 1991) and racial bias (see Pavkov, Lewis, & Lyons, 1989).

Some have attacked the DSM system as a male-centered device that overestimates pathology in women (Kaplan, 1983) while others deny this charge (Kass, Spitzer, & Williams, 1983). A useful conceptual analysis of what constitutes *sex bias* in a diagnostic system was presented by Widiger and Spitzer (1991). The authors argue that previous attempts to demonstrate diagnostic sex bias have been both conceptually and methodologically flawed. Further, some of the findings of earlier studies (for example, Broverman, Broverman, Clarkson, Rosenkrantz, & Vogel, 1970) have been grossly misinterpreted and misunderstood (see Widiger & Settle, 1987, for a demonstration of the flaws in the Broverman et al. study).

Widiger and Spitzer note that differential sex prevalence for a disorder does not in and of itself demonstrate diagnostic sex bias because, for example, it is conceivable that biological or cultural factors may make it more likely that men (or women) exhibit the criteria for a certain diagnosis. For example, antisocial personality disorder is diagnosed much more frequently in men versus women, but this may be the result of biological differences (for example, testosterone) or other factors that influence the two genders differentially (for example, societal expectations for aggressiveness in men). Widiger and Spitzer did, however, present evidence suggesting that clinicians may be biased in the way they *apply* diagnoses to men versus women, even in cases where the symptoms presented by men and women were exactly the same! However, this only suggests that there may be some bias in the way clinicians interpret the diagnostic criteria—that is, clinicians may exhibit sex bias but that does not indicate sex bias within the diagnostic criteria. These results suggest the need for better training of diagnosticians rather than an overhaul of the diagnostic criteria sets.

Coverage of the classification system

With close to 400 possible diagnoses, DSM-IV cannot be faulted for being too limited in its coverage of possible diagnostic conditions. It is likely that most conditions that bring individuals in for psychiatric or psychological treatment could be classified within the DSM-IV system. However, some may feel that DSM-IV errs in the opposite direction: it is too broad in its scope. For example, a host of childhood developmental disorders are included as mental disorders. The child who is dyslexic, has speech problems such as stuttering, or has great difficulties with arithmetic is given a DSM-IV diagnosis. Many question the appropriateness and benefit of labeling these conditions as mental disorders.

Another example of the possible over-inclusiveness of the DSM-IV is the inclusion of premenstrual dysphoric disorder as a proposed diagnostic category. This

diagnosis and its criteria appear in the appendix containing diagnostic criteria provided for further study. Many women objected strenuously to this diagnosis when
it was first proposed because they argued that such a category could easily be used
to discriminate against women in many arenas, including employment. Controversial diagnoses like this one cause some to wonder whether the architects of the
DSM have gone too far.

Some additional concerns

Although the previously described difficulties are real and fairly obvious, a
number of indirect or subtle problems arise through the acceptance and use of diagnostic classification systems. For example, classifications tend to create the feeling that mental disorders exist per se. Such terms as *disorders, symptoms, conditions,* and *suffering from* suggest that the patient is the victim of a disease
process. The language of the system can lead even astute observers toward a view
that interprets learned reactions as disease processes.

In addition, if clinicians are not careful they may come to feel that classifying
people is more satisfying than trying to relieve their problems. As we shall see
later, therapy can be an uncertain, time-consuming process that is often fraught
with failure. But pigeonholing can be immediately rewarding: it provides a sense
of closure to the classifier. Like solving crossword puzzles, it may relieve tension
without having any long-term positive social significance.

The system likewise caters to the public's desire to regard problems in living as
medical entities that can be dealt with simply and easily by a pill, an injection, or a
knife. Unfortunately, however, learning to solve psychological problems is hard
work. The easier approach is to adopt a passive, dependent posture in which the patient is relieved of psychological pain by an omniscient doctor. Although such a view
may be serviceable in dealing with strictly medical problems (but see Engel, 1977),
its value is dubious at best in confronting the psychosocial problems of living.

A final indirect problem lies in the fact that diagnosis can be harmful or even
stigmatizing to the person that is labeled. In our society, diagnosis may close doors
rather than open them for patients and ex-patients alike. Too often diagnosis
seems to obscure the real person—observers see labels but not the real people
behind them. Thus, labels can damage relationships, prevent people from being
hired or promoted, and, in extreme cases, even result in a loss of civil rights. Furthermore, labels can even encourage some people to capitulate and assume the
role of a "sick" person.

Other classification systems

A variety of attempts have been made to improve psychiatric classification.
Many have employed multivariate statistical methods such as cluster analysis to
generate homogeneous categories. For example, Overall and Gorham (1962),
working within the traditional psychiatric framework, developed the Brief Psychiatric Rating Scale (BPRS). It allows for the evaluation of symptoms in 16 relatively
independent factor areas. Overall and Hollister (1982) have used cluster analysis
and related numerical taxonomy methods to identify eight distinct phenomenological types in terms of BPRS profiles.

Other systems have focused on psychotic behavior. For example, Lorr (1986) has helped in the development of a research-oriented interview procedure for assigning patients quantitative values on 12 dimensions (for example, paranoid projection, hostile belligerence). McReynolds (1989) has reviewed several other alternatives to the DSM classification system.

A relatively new alternative to the traditional diagnostic system for Axis II personality disorders is the *Five-Factor Model of personality* (FFM). The FFM includes the personality dimensions of neuroticism, extraversion, openness to experience, agreeableness, and conscientiousness (Costa & McCrae, 1992). As Digman (1990) noted, a growing consensus regarding these five trait dimensions as a fairly comprehensive representation of adult personality has been evident in the psychological literature (see McCrae & John, 1992).

If, however, the FFM is to be seen as a comprehensive account of normal and abnormal personality, then we would expect this model to be relevant to the personality disorders that are coded on Axis II. Personality disorders by definition involve inflexible and maladaptive personality traits. Studies that have explored the relationship between the FFM and Axis II disorders have obtained encouraging results (Costa & McCrae, 1990; Soldz, Budman, Demby, & Merry, 1993; Trull, 1992; Wiggins & Pincus, 1989). For example, Trull (1992) found that the FFM dimensions of neuroticism, extraversion, and agreeableness were most apparent in the DSM-III-R conceptualizations of personality disorders in his clinical sample of outpatients.

Based on these and other findings, some have called for the use of the FFM as an alternative to DSM-IV's categorical classification system (Costa & Widiger, 1994). However, a number of issues must be addressed before converting to a dimensional system like the FFM. These issues include: How is the maladaptivity of a personality trait assessed in these FFM personality measures? How are cutoff points determined on a dimensional personality scale to decide the presence or absence of personality disorder? and How can investigators take into account the context in which the maladaptive personality traits occur? (Costa & Widiger, 1994). Finally, there is the practical issue of training clinicians to use the FFM. To date, these issues have not been resolved, but it is likely that future research will shed some light on the viability of the FFM as a model of personality pathology. The interested reader might consider consulting McCrae and John (1992) for a good overview of the FFM, as well as Widiger (1991) for a survey of additional dimensional models of personality that were proposed for inclusion in the DSM-IV.

■ Causes of Abnormal Behavior and Mental Illness

Up to this point, we have discussed issues regarding the description and definition of abnormal behavior as well as the implications of diagnosing and classifying individuals. However, very little has been said about what factors may cause abnormal behavior and mental illness. Although we will discuss various *etiological models of psychopathology* in the chapters on intervention, it is useful to briefly present these models here in order to give the reader some idea of the predominant viewpoints.

Table 5-6 presents a brief overview of major models of psychopathology, as well as the explanation of abnormal behavior offered by each. As can be seen, some of the etiological models are quite different in their perspective on abnormal behavior. This certainly has implications for how a clinician adhering to one of these viewpoints will conduct assessment and treatment. For example, a clinical psychologist subscribing to a cognitive theory of depression will probably use cognitively based assessment instruments to identify maladaptive cognitions as well as cognitive-behavioral interventions to treat depression.

A more general model of etiology that can accommodate a variety of theoretical viewpoints (like those in Table 5-6) is the *diathesis-stress model of psychopathology* (see Davison & Neale, 1996). The diathesis-stress model is not wedded to one school of thought and can incorporate biological, psychological, and environmental factors. A *diathesis* refers to a vulnerability or predisposition to developing the disorder in question. A diathesis can be biological (for example, a genetic predisposition, a deficit or excess in neurotransmitters) or psychological (for example, maladaptive cognitive schema, maladaptive personality style). A diathesis is necessary but not sufficient to produce a mental disorder — rather, what is required in addition to a diathesis is sufficient *environmental stress*. Stressors can also be biological (for example, poor nutrition) or psychological (for example, malignant family environment, traumatic life event). Both the diathesis and

Table 5-6
Brief description of several models of psychopathology.

Model	Explanation of Abnormal Behavior	Example
Biological	Processes in central nervous system have gone awry	Schizophrenia is caused by an excess of dopaminergic activity
Psychodynamic	Intrapsychic conflict	Specific phobia is due to the displacement of an intrapsychic conflict onto an external object that can then be avoided
Learning	Learned the same way normal behavior is learned	Specific phobia is learned via classical conditioning
Cognitive	Due to maladaptive cognitions	Depression results from negative views about oneself, the world, and the future
Humanistic	Relative neglect of one's own self-view and overreliance on the appraisals of others when the two are incongruous	Generalized anxiety disorder reflects this overreliance and incongruity

the stress are necessary to produce the disorder in question. Possessing the diathesis simply increases the likelihood of developing the disorder but does not guarantee that outcome. Further, as may be apparent, the exact nature of the diathesis and the stress necessary for developing a specific disorder is likely to vary from disorder to disorder; the interaction between the diathesis and the stress is also likely to be disorder-specific (see Monroe & Simons, 1991).

◾ Conclusion

Classification systems are necessary—otherwise, our experience and our consciousness become a chaotic array of events. By abstracting the similarities and the differences among the events of people's experience, clinicians can establish categories of varying width and purpose that allow them to generalize and predict.

Clinical psychology is very much concerned with the diagnosis, classification, and treatment of mental illness. The DSM-IV system, although clearly not perfect, will continue to be used by contemporary clinical psychologists in their research, consultation, and practice. There has been and will continue to be some disagreement about the DSM-IV or any other diagnostic system for that matter. Diagnostic systems have their advantages and disadvantages, and the criteria for individual mental disorders are fallible (Widiger & Trull, 1991). The DSM-IV, like its predecessors, has been said to be more useful for clinical research than for clinical practice. This is probably why clinicians often fail to use the diagnostic manual (Jampala, Sierles, & Taylor, 1988; Morey & Ochoa, 1989). However, we hope that the reader is convinced that diagnostic formulations are important because of their communication value, their potential treatment implications, and their facilitation of psychopathology research.

◾ Focus Questions

1. What are the advantages and disadvantages of the three major definitions of abnormal behavior?
2. What is mental illness or mental disorder? Why are mental disorder diagnoses important?
3. How was the DSM-IV developed? Describe the five diagnostic axes used for a DSM-IV diagnostic formulation.
4. How are diagnostic classification systems evaluated?
5. What is the diathesis-stress model of psychopathology?

◾ Key Terms

Axis I	Axis IV	conformity to norms
Axis II	Axis V	cultural relativity
Axis III	categories	cutoff points

diathesis
dimension
disability or
  dysfunction
DSM-III
DSM-IV
environmental stress
etiological factors
etiological models of
  psychopathology

Five-Factor Model of
  personality
Global Assessment
  of Functioning
mental disorder
mental illness
multiaxial assessment
principal diagnosis
psychopathologist
reliability

sex bias
structured diagnostic
  interviews
subjective distress
syndrome
validity

II

CLINICAL ASSESSMENT

6

The Assessment Interview

Assessment has long been an important activity of clinical psychologists. In the previous chapter we touched on assessment in our discussion of the diagnosis of mental disorders. In this chapter the focus will be on interviewing. Subsequent chapters will deal with the assessment of intelligence, personality, and behavior, along with the process of clinical judgment. Before we plunge into the specifics of interviewing, however, let us make a few general comments about assessment.

■ Assessment in Clinical Psychology

There are, perhaps, many ways to formally define psychological assessment. *Clinical assessment* involves an evaluation of an individual's strengths and weaknesses, a conceptualization of the problem at hand (as well as possible etiological factors), and some prescription for alleviating the problem, all of which lead to a better understanding of the patient. Assessment is not something that is done once and then is forever finished. In many cases, it is an ongoing process—even an everyday process, as in psychotherapy. Whether the clinician is making decisions or solving problems, clinical assessment is the means to the end.

The purpose of diagnosis or assessment is fairly straightforward. Before physicians can prescribe a treatment, they must first understand the nature of the illness. Before plumbers can begin banging on pipes, they must first determine the character and location of the difficulty. And what is true in medicine and plumbing is equally true in clinical psychology. Aside from a few cases involving pure luck, a capacity to solve clinical problems is directly related to the skill of defining them. Most of us can remember our parents' stern admonition: "Think before you act!" In a sense, this is the essence of the assessment or diagnostic process. To illustrate this idea, consider the following case.

The case of Billy G.

Billy was in the third grade and having trouble. His teacher found him to be a real behavior problem in class. He was loud, talkative, and easily distracted. He was aggressive, and sometimes he struck the other children. His behavior was impulsive, erratic, and obviously hyperactive. He had become a totally disruptive force in the classroom.

Several conferences with the teacher finally convinced Billy's parents that the problem was not completely the school's responsibility. Indeed, much of Billy's behavior was mirrored at home, where he was equally difficult to control. His grades had plummeted in recent months, but his parents could not believe there was an intellectual problem. Therefore, it seemed to them that the explanation must lie in either physical or emotional factors.

Their first decision was to take Billy to their family physician. However, she could find nothing wrong physically and suggested that they have Billy see a neurologist. After a full neurological examination, including an electroencephalogram and an exhaustive behavioral and medical history, the neurologist could not arrive at a definitive diagnosis. There was no history of birth trauma, head injury, encephalitis, or risk factors for neurological disease. At the same time, a behavioral history compiled from teachers' reports, parental observations, and the neurologist's own observations confirmed the existence of a definite problem. The neurologist was leaning toward a diagnosis of attention-deficit/hyperactivity disorder (ADHD).

However, the neurologist was psychologically minded, and he felt that he detected a strained relationship between the parents. There almost appeared to be a hostile aura. In the course of his conversations with the parents, he also learned that the husband was rarely home and seemed totally absorbed in his ambitions to advance in his job. The mother seemed to be reacting to her perceived neglect by becoming extremely active in community service and social functions. When Billy came home from school, she was almost always playing bridge, attending fundraising activities, or shopping. It certainly seemed that neither parent had much time for Billy. In fact, only since Billy's problems had come to a head in school had the parents seemed aware of him at all.

Thus, the neurologist faced a diagnostic dilemma. Since stimulant medication (for example, Ritalin) has often been effective with such cases, this might be the way to go. On the other hand, there certainly seemed to be a pattern of parental rejection that might have produced resentment in Billy. Therefore, the hyperactivity could be construed as an attempt to gain attention from the parents and parental surrogates (teachers). Such a formulation seemed to imply a recommendation of psychotherapy for the parents and for Billy as well.

The neurologist was concerned about making the wrong diagnosis. Medication has its side effects and might even exacerbate the problem. Further, if the problem were not ADHD, then Billy's behavioral reactions might become more established during the time wasted and psychotherapy might be more difficult. A diagnosis of ADHD might also create a greater unwillingness in the parents to accept their role in Billy's behavioral difficulties. On the other hand, suppose that the family went the psychotherapeutic route only to learn later that the problem was treatable with medication. Then precious time would have been wasted, and perhaps avoidable physical harm would have occurred.

Clearly, then, the assessment question became that of choosing between a behavioral or biological explanation for Billy's problems—each of which had very distinct treatment implications. Faced with this quandary, the neurologist decided to refer the parents to a clinical child psychologist who could be expected to interview the parents more thoroughly, to administer a variety of intelligence and personality tests to Billy, and to observe Billy under a variety of conditions. The neurologist hoped that a psychological report, coupled with his own neurological findings, would allow him to arrive at a more informed diagnostic and treatment decision.

The influence of theory

The kinds of information sought out by clinicians are often heavily influenced by their own theoretical commitments. For example, a psychodynamic clinician may be more likely to ask about early childhood experiences than a behavioral clinician. In other cases, the information obtained may be similar, but clinicians will make different inferences from it. For instance, frequent headaches may suggest the presence of underlying hostility to a psychodynamic clinician and merely evidence of job stress to a behavioral clinician. For some clinicians, case-history data are important because they aid in helping the client develop an anxiety hierarchy; for others they are a way of confirming hypotheses about the client's needs and expectations. Assessment, then, is not a completely standardized set of procedures—all clients are not given the same tests or asked the same questions. The purpose of assessment is not to discover the true psychic essence of the client but to describe that client in a useful way—a way that will lead to the solution of a problem. Of course, this hardly means that one description is as good as another for a particular case. One clinician's cognitive-behavioral formulation of a case may involve a poor understanding of cognitive-behavioral theory. There are even instances when certain cases seem to lend themselves more to a psychodynamic description than to a behavioral description. Because of the complexity of the subject matter and the incomplete state of the knowledge base, there is sometimes more than one good road to Rome.

The referral

The assessment process begins with a referral. Someone—a parent, a teacher, a psychiatrist, a judge, or perhaps a psychologist—poses a question about the patient. "Why is Johnny disobedient?" "Why can't Alice learn to read like the other children?" "Is the patient's impoverished behavioral repertoire a function of poor learning opportunities, or does this constriction represent an effort to avoid close relationships with other people who might be threatening?"

Clinicians begin with this *referral question*. It is important that they take pains to understand precisely what the question is or what the referral source is seeking. In some instances the question may be impossible to answer, whereas in other instances the clinician may decide that a direct answer is inappropriate or that the question needs rephrasing. For example, the clinician may decide that the question "Is this patient capable of murder?" is unanswerable unless there is more information about the situation. Thus, the question might be rephrased to include probabilities with respect to certain kinds of situations. If parents want their child tested for the sole, often narcissistic, purpose of determining the child's IQ, the clinician might decide that providing such information would eventually do the child more harm than good. Most parents are unequipped to understand what the numerical IQ estimate means and are quite likely to misinterpret it. Thus, before accepting the referral in an instance of this kind, the clinical psychologist would be well advised to discuss the matter with the parents.

Assessment: the current scene

As we mentioned in Chapter 2, psychological assessment as an area of emphasis has seen its ups and downs. Abeles (1990) commented on the recent rediscovery of assessment. He observed that during the 1960s and 1970s there seemed to be a decline in interest in psychological assessment. Therapy was a more glamorous enterprise and assessment almost seemed to be somehow "unfair" to clients. It appeared that clinical psychology's historical commitment to assessment was waning. The prevailing attitude about assessment was, "Let the technicians do it!" But in the 1980s something else began to happen. Students began to show an interest in specialization. They discovered forensic psychology (the application of psychology to legal issues), or they became intrigued by pediatric psychology, geriatrics, or even neuropsychology. But to become a specialist in such areas, you need to know a great deal about assessment. You cannot answer a lawyer's questions about the competence of a defendant unless you have thoroughly assessed that individual through tests, interviews, or observations (Matarazzo, 1990). You cannot decide on issues of neurological insult versus mental disorder until you have assessed that client. The questions raised earlier in the case of Billy G. could only be answered through assessment. As Abeles (1990) stated:

> It is my contention that one of the unique contributions of the clinical psychologist is the ability to provide assessment data. Providing assessments is again becoming a highly valued and respected part of clinical psychology and in my opinion is coequal with intervention and psychotherapy as a vital activity of clinical psychology. Let us continue to rediscover assessment! (p. 4)

■ The Interview: Characteristics and Varieties

Almost all professions count interviewing as a chief technique for gathering data and making decisions. For politicians, consumers, psychiatrists, employers, or people in general, interviewing has become a major tool. As with any activity that is engaged in frequently, people sometimes take interviewing for granted or believe that it involves no special skills; they can all too easily overestimate their understanding of the interview process. Although many people seem awed by the mystique of projective tests or impressed by the psychometric intricacies of objective tests, there is an easy yet deceptive familiarity to interviewing.

Nevertheless, the *assessment interview* is at once the most basic and the most serviceable technique employed by the clinician. In the hands of a skilled mental health professional, its wide range of application and adaptability make it a major instrument for clinical decision making, understanding, and prediction. But for all this, it must be remembered that the clinical utility of the interview can be no greater than the skill and sensitivity of the clinician who employs it. In this section, we will discuss some basic features of the clinical interview, interviewing skills and techniques that must be mastered, and different types of interviews that are employed by clinical psychologists.

General characteristics of interviews

An interaction.   An interview is an interaction between at least two persons. Each participant contributes to the process, and each influences the responses of the other. But this characterization falls short of defining the process. Ordinary conversation is interactional, but surely interviewing goes beyond that. Interviewing, like conversation, involves face-to-face verbal encounters or exchanges. However, unlike conversation, the clinical interview is initiated with a goal or set of goals in mind. The interviewer approaches the interaction purposefully, bearing the responsibility for keeping the interview on track and moving toward the goal. Thus, the easy informality that often characterizes ordinary conversation is less evident. A good interview is one that is carefully planned, deliberately and skillfully executed, and goal-oriented throughout.

There are clearly many forms of interviewing—from fact-finding to emotional release to cross-examination. But all forms of professionally executed interviews are devoid of one feature that often characterizes normal conversation: interviewers are not using the interchange to achieve either personal satisfaction or enhanced prestige. They are using it to elicit data, information, beliefs, or attitudes in the most skilled fashion possible.

Interviews versus tests.   In a sense, interviews occupy a position somewhere between ordinary conversation and tests. Interviews are more purposeful and organized than conversation, but sometimes less formalized or standardized than psychological tests. The exceptions are the structured diagnostic interviews that we will discuss later in this chapter. Structured interviews in some ways resemble standardized psychological tests. The hallmark of psychological testing is the collection of data under standardized conditions by means of explicit procedures. Most interviews, however, make provision for at least some flexibility. Thus, a unique characteristic of the interview method is the wider opportunity it provides for an individualized approach that will be effective in eliciting data from a particular person or patient. This flexibility represents both the strength and the weakness of many interviewing techniques—although one can seek information in the way that seems most appropriate for patient X, there is also a distinct potential for unreliability and error. We'll have more to say about threats to the reliability and validity of interview data later.

Art versus science. Interviewing has often been regarded as an art. Except in the most structured, formal interviews, there is a degree of freedom to exercise a skill and a resourcefulness that is generally absent from other assessment procedures. When to probe, when to be silent, and when to be indirect or subtle are decisions that test the ability of the interviewer. With experience, an interviewer learns to respond to interviewee cues in a progressively more sensitive fashion that ultimately serves the purposes of the interview.

A considerable amount of research on interviewing has been carried out, and, consequently, there is a solid foundation of scientific research on the subject. Practically, this means that novices do not need to rely solely on the slow and sometimes painful accumulation of experience in order to polish their skill. They can profit from the study of a considerable body of research on interviewing that provides a scientific foundation for their art (Wiens, 1983).

■ Interviewing Essentials and Techniques

Many factors influence the productivity and utility of data obtained from assessment interviews. Some involve the physical setting; others are related to the nature of the patient. A mute or uncommunicative patient may not cooperate regardless of interviewer skills or characteristics — thus, interviewers should not stake their self-esteem on being effective with every patient.

Several factors or skills can help make interviews more productive. Training and supervised experience in interviewing are very important — however, techniques that work well for one interviewer can be notably less effective for another. There is a crucial interaction between technique and interviewer. This is why gaining experience in a supervised setting is so important: it enables the interviewer to achieve some awareness of the nature of this interaction. Training, then, involves not just a simple memorization of rules but, rather, a growing knowledge of the relationships among rules, the concrete situation being confronted, and the interviewer's own impact in interview situations.

The physical arrangements

An interview can be conducted anywhere that two people can meet and interact. Interviews of one sort or another have been conducted in hallways, on the sidewalk, on buses, or even during cocktail parties. Often this happens by chance — an encounter with a patient on the street, for example. Usually, the clinician does not choose such a setting. But the needs of the patient, the emergency nature of the situation, or even, in some instances, sheer coincidence may make an interview of sorts inevitable.

The setting.   Obviously, certain physical arrangements are especially desirable for an interview. Two are privacy and protection from interruptions. Nothing is more damaging to the continuity of an interview than a jangling phone, a secretary's query, or an imperative knock on the door. Such interruptions are destructive and disruptive. But even more important is the message they subtly convey: that the patient and the patient's problems are of secondary importance. After all, secretaries do not knock on the door or put through a call unless they have been instructed to do so.

Since lack of privacy can have many deleterious outcomes, soundproofing is also very important. If noise from a hallway or an adjacent office intrudes, patients will probably assume that their own voices may also be heard outside. Few patients are likely to be open and responsive under such conditions.

The office or its furnishings can be as distracting as loud noises and external clamor. There are few rules in this area, and much depends on individual taste. However, the preferences of many clinicians are for offices that are fairly neutral yet tasteful. Consequently, they play down wild, splashy paintings or carpeting that reaches up to the ankles. In short, an office with furnishings that demand attention or seem to cry out for comment are not ideal. The therapist-golfer need not turn the office into a shrine for those who chase par; the therapist with a penchant for antique cars would do well not to litter the desk with scale models of 1928 Fords. Somehow, there must be a middle ground between an office that is cold and forbidding through its very neutrality and one that is littered with obtrusive and distracting objects.

Note-taking and recording.   Again, there are few absolutes. In general, it would seem desirable to take occasional notes during an interview. A few key phrases jotted down will help the clinician's recall. Most clinicians have had the experience of feeling that the material in an interview is so important that there is no need to take notes—that the material will easily be remembered. However, after having seen a few additional patients, the clinician may not be able to recall a single element from such an interview. Therefore, a moderate, controlled degree of note-taking seems worthwhile. Most patients will not be troubled by it, and if one should be, the note-taking can be stopped. Occasionally, a patient may comment that what is said must be really important since the interviewer is writing it down. Occasionally, too, a patient may request that the clinician not take notes while a certain topic is being discussed. In any event, most patients probably expect a certain amount of note-taking.

However, any attempt at taking verbatim notes should be avoided, except when administering a structured interview. One danger in taking verbatim notes is that this practice may prevent the clinician from fully attending to the essence of the patient's verbalizations. An overriding compulsion to get it all down can develop, and this may detract from a genuine understanding of the nuances and significance of the patient's remarks. In addition, excessive note-taking tends to prevent the clinician from observing the patient and from detecting subtle changes of expression or slight changes in muscular movements. Furthermore, it should be remembered that a fully transcribed interview must be read in full later. The clinician must then plow through 50 minutes of notes in order to extract the really important material, which may have taken up only 15 minutes.

With today's technology, it is easy to audiotape or videotape interviews—under no circumstances, however, should this be done without the patient's fully informed consent. In the vast majority of cases, a few minutes' explanation of the desirability of taping, with an accompanying assurance to the patient that the tape will be kept confidential (or released only to persons authorized by the patient), will result in complete cooperation. Since today's world is awash with tape recording, most patients are unlikely to object to it. By and large, patients are not even upset by a microphone and recorder that is in plain view. There may be a few passing moments of self-consciousness, but these quickly fade. Indeed, it may turn out that the clinician is more threatened by the recording than the patient, especially if the interview is likely to be examined or evaluated by superiors or consultants.

In some instances, it may even be desirable to videotape certain interviews. In the interests of research, of training interviewers or therapists, or of feedback to the patient as part of the therapeutic process, such taping sometimes has value. Like tape recording, videotaping should be done openly, unobtrusively, and with the patient's informed consent.

Rapport

Perhaps the most essential ingredient of a good interview is a relationship between the clinician and the patient. The quality and nature of that relationship will, of course, vary depending on the purpose of the interview. These differences will undoubtedly affect the kind of relationship that develops during the contact.

Definition and functions.   *Rapport* is the word often used to characterize this clinical relationship. There is often an ineffable or intuitive quality to the word. However, rapport involves a comfortable atmosphere and a mutual understanding of the purpose of the interview. Good rapport can be a primary instrument by which the clinician achieves the purposes of the interview. A cold, hostile, or adversarial relationship is not likely to be constructive. Although a positive atmosphere is certainly not the sole ingredient for a productive interview (a warm, yet ill-prepared or slow-witted interviewer will not generate the best of interviews), it is usually a necessary one. Whatever skills the interviewer possesses will surely be rendered more effective in proportion to the interviewer's capacity to stimulate a positive relationship.

Patients approach most interviews with some degree of anxiety. They may be anxious lest they are discovered to be "crazy"; they may be fearful that what they state in the interview will be passed along to employers. Whatever the specific nature of these concerns, their presence is enough to reduce the interviewer's potential for effectiveness.

Characteristics.   There are many ways to achieve good rapport—perhaps as many as there are clinicians. However, no bag of rapport tricks is likely to substitute for an attitude of acceptance, understanding, and respect for the integrity of the patient (Tyler, 1969). Such an attitude does not require that the clinician like *every* patient. It does not require the clinician to befriend every patient. It does not require the clinician to master an agreed-upon set of behaviors guaranteed to produce instant rapport. It *does* require that patients not be prejudged based on the problems for which they are seeking help. In addition, attitudes of understanding, sincerity, acceptance, and empathy are not techniques—to regard them as such is to miss their true import. To ask to be taught the appearances of sincerity, acceptance, and empathy is to confess their absence. When patients realize that the clinician is striving to understand their problems in order to help them, then a broad range of interviewer behavior becomes possible. Probing, confrontation, even a certain amount of interviewer aggression, may be acceptable when rapport has been established. If the patient accepts the clinician's ultimate goal of helping, a state of mutual liking is not necessary. The patient will recognize that the clinician is not seeking personal satisfaction in the interview. Rapport is not, as is often thought by beginning students, a state wherein the clinician is always liked or regarded as a great person—it is neither a prize bestowed by an awed client nor a popularity contest to be won by the clinician. It is, rather, a relationship founded upon respect, mutual confidence, trust, and a certain degree of permissiveness.

Some patients have had past experiences that will not easily permit them to accept even genuine overtures for a professional relationship. But in most cases, if the clinician perseveres in the proper role and maintains an attitude of respect and a quest for understanding, the relationship will develop. A common mistake of beginning interviewers is to say, "There, there, don't worry; I know exactly what you're feeling." Such comments may actually convince the client that the interviewer does not really know how they feel. (After all, how could this stranger possibly know how I feel?) Rapport will come, but it will come through quiet attitudes of respect, acceptance, and competence rather than through quick fixes.

Communication

In any interview, there must be communication. Whether we are helping persons in distress or assisting patients in realizing their potential, communication is our vehicle. The real challenge is to identify those skills or techniques that will ensure maximum communication.

Beginning a session. It is often useful to begin an assessment session with a casual conversation. A brief comment or question about difficulties in finding a parking space or even a banal comment on the weather may help establish the clinician as a real person and allay any fears the patient may have about relating to a "shrink." Whatever its specific content, a brief conversation designed to relax things before plunging into the patient's reasons for coming will usually facilitate a good interview.

Language. Of extreme importance is the use of language that the patient can understand. Some initial estimate of the patient's background, educational level, or general sophistication should be made. The kind of language employed should then reflect that judgment. It is offensive to speak to a 40-year-old woman with a master's degree in history as if she were an eighth grader. It is not necessary to infantilize people seeking help—the act of asking for help need not imply a diminished capacity to understand.

At the same time, it may be necessary to abandon psychological jargon in order to be understood by some patients. And it may well be that the depth of their understanding is questionable if clinicians cannot communicate without resorting to a four-syllable jargon. If they find themselves unwittingly using grandiose language to extort admiration from patients, then something is really amiss. Similarly, clinicians who try to use "teenage" language when interviewing a 15-year-old may wind up not only alienating the client but looking foolish in the process. In short, if their respect for the patient is intact, interviewers generally need not reach for shallower techniques.

In a related vein, it is important to use words that will be interpreted by the patient as the interviewer means them to be. Very often, for example, asking a mother how her son behaves is likely to prompt the response, "Oh, he's a good boy—he does just what I tell him." Sometimes psychologists become so enamored of the words "behave" and "behavior" that they forget that for many people these words have connotations quite different from the ones they have in mind.

It is also important to clarify the intended meaning of a word or term that is used by a client if there is any uncertainty or alternative interpretations. For example, a clinician should not assume he or she knows what a client means by the statement, "She's abusive." It may indicate that the individual does not treat others particularly well, or it may indicate that the individual is physically abusive, warranting immediate intervention.

Silence.   Perhaps nothing is more disturbing to a beginning interviewer than silence. But silences need not signify interviewer inadequacy. The important thing is to assess the meaning and function of silence in the context of the specific interview. The clinician's response to silence should be reasoned and responsive to the goals of the interview rather than to personal needs or insecurities. Perhaps the patient is organizing a thought or deciding which topic to discuss next. Perhaps the silence is indicative of some resistance. But it is as inappropriate to jump in and fill every momentary silence with chatter as it is to wait out the patient every time, regardless of the length of the silence. Whether the clinician ends a lengthy silence with a comment about the silence or decides to introduce a new line of inquiry, the response should facilitate communication and understanding and not be a desperate solution to an awkward moment.

Listening.   If therapists are to communicate effectively in the clinical role, their communication must reflect understanding and acceptance. They cannot hope to do this if they have not been listening—for it is by listening that they come to appreciate the information and emotions that the patient is conveying. If they are concerned about impressing the patient, or insecure in their role, or guided by motivations other than the need to understand and accept, then they are not likely to be effective listeners. Many people, for example, when introduced to someone, cannot recall the name two minutes later. The most common reason for this is their failure to listen. They were distracted, preoccupied, or perhaps so concerned about their own appearance that they never really heard the name. It sometimes happens that therapists are so sure of an impression about the patient that they stop listening and thereby ignore important new data. The skilled clinician is one who has learned how and when to be an active listener.

Gratification of self.   The clinical interview is not the time nor place for clinicians to work out their own problems. Sometimes a clinician is professionally insecure or inexperienced. Sometimes the patient's problems, experiences, or conversation remind clinicians of their own problems or threaten their own values, attitudes, or adjustment. In one way or another, however, clinicians must resist the temptation to shift the focus inward. Rather, their concentration must remain on the patient. This is obviously a matter of degree. No one is so self-controlled that their thoughts never wander or their concentration never falters. But it is critical to keep in mind that the clinician-patient roles are definite and should not be confused.

In some instances, the patient will ask personal questions of the clinician. In general, clinicians should avoid discussing their personal lives or opinions — however, this advice must be tempered by awareness of the reasons for the question. Thus, a breezy opening question such as, "Say, what did you think of that basketball game last night?" does not have the same significance as the question, "Do you think Freud was correct in his assessment of the importance of penis envy in women?" When a question seems to suggest something of importance about the patient's problems, it is usually best for interviewers to deflect it or to turn it around in a way that allows them to pursue their clinical hypothesis. But if a question is trivial, innocent, or otherwise basically inconsequential, a failure to respond directly will probably be perceived as the worst kind of evasion.

The impact of the clinician.   Some years ago, one of the authors worked in a clinic with several therapists. One therapist was a fiftyish matronly psychiatrist with a marked affinity for print housedresses. Another was a clinical psychologist — male, very youthful in appearance, quite thin, carefully dressed, and seemingly quite unsure of himself. It was inevitable that these two therapists would be perceived differently by their patients. The point is that each of us has a characteristic impact on others, both socially and professionally. As a result, the same behavior in different clinicians is unlikely to provoke the same response from a patient. The tall, well-muscled, athletic therapist may intimidate certain kinds of patients somewhat. The very feminine female interviewer may elicit responses in a client very different from those elicited by her male counterpart. Therefore, it behooves all clinicians to cultivate a degree of self-insight or at least a mental set to consider the possible effects of their own impact before attaching meaning to the behavior of their patients.

The clinician's values and background.   Nearly everyone accepts the notion that their own values, background, and biases will affect their perceptions. Unfortunately, we are usually more skilled in validating this notion in others than in ourselves. Therefore, clinicians must examine their own experiences and seek the bases for their own assumptions before making clinical judgments of others. What to the clinician may appear to be evidence of severe pathology may actually reflect the patient's culture. Take the following example:

A 48-year-old ethnic Chinese woman had been receiving antipsychotic and antidepressant medication for psychotic depression. On this regimen, the patient had lost even more weight and more hope and had become more immobilized. A critical element in this diagnosis of psychosis was the woman's belief that her deceased mother, who had appeared in her dreams, had traveled from the place of the dead to induce the patient's own death and to bring her to the next world. We interpreted this symptom not as a delusional belief but as a culturally consistent belief in a depressed woman who had recently begun to see her deceased mother in her dreams (a common harbinger of death in the dreams of some Asian patients). This patient responded well after the antipsychotic medication was discontinued, the antidepressant medication was reduced in dosage, and weekly psychotherapy was instituted. (Westermeyer, 1987, pp. 471–472)

This case illustrates how all the behavioral cues that clinicians typically rely upon may lose their meaning when applied to a patient from another culture. It is important to realize how much a clinician's ability to make sense of a patient's verbalizations is dependent upon a shared background. For example, some midwestern clinicians listening to Asian American patients may suddenly feel as if they have lost their own frame of reference. But in dealing with midwestern patients, how many times will those same clinicians mistakenly assume that their frames of reference are identical to those of their patients?

In other cases, gender differences can sometimes produce nearly the same effects. When gender-related factors interact with a clinician's values and background, everything from sheer ignorance to gender stereotypes can result, thus reducing the validity of the assessment interview. The answer seems to lie in making assessors more gender-aware (Brown, 1990; Good, Gilbert, & Scher, 1990). How does that happen? An expert in gender issues makes the following suggestions:

> Clinicians seeking to enhance their gender awareness might focus on three areas—their knowledge, attitudes, and behaviors. Knowledge is typically increased by reading (e.g., research and conceptual articles/books) or attending a course or seminar on gender issues. Attitudes are enhanced through experiences with people holding conceptions of gender which differ from one's own (e.g., from differing cultures, religions, or sexual orientations) which serve to broaden our understanding of gender issues. Behaviors are improved through practice and feedback (i.e., with a supervisor that has expertise in gender-related issues). (G. Good, personal communication)

The use of questions

Maloney and Ward (1976) observed that the clinician's questions may become progressively more structured as the interview proceeds. They distinguish among several forms of questions including *open-ended, facilitative, clarifying, confronting,* and *direct* questions. Each is designed in its own way to promote communication. And each is useful for a specific purpose or patient. Table 6-1 illustrates these forms of questions.

The patient's frame of reference

If the clinician is going to be effective in achieving the goals of the interview, it is essential to have an idea of how the patient views the first meeting. Only with such awareness can the patient's verbalizations and behaviors be placed in their proper context. By the same token, the establishment of rapport will be more difficult if the clinician is not sensitive to the patient's initial perceptions and expectations. A patient may have an entirely distorted notion of the clinic and even be ashamed of having to seek help.

Patients have often been pressured into seeking help. A spouse has finally said, "Do it or we're through!" A sorority lays down an ultimatum that a member

Table 6-1
Five forms of interview questions.

Type	Importance	Example
Open-ended	Gives patient responsibility and latitude for responding	"Would you tell me about your experiences in the Army?"
Facilitative	Encourages patient's flow of conversation	"Can you tell me a little more about that?"
Clarifying	Encourages clarity or amplification	"I guess this means you felt like . . . ?"
Confronting	Challenges inconsistencies or contradictions	"Before when you said . . . ?"
Direct	Once rapport has been established and patient is taking responsibility for conversation, such questions can be efficient and useful	"What did you say to your father when he criticized your choice?"

SOURCE: Based on data from Maloney & Ward (1976).

either "get therapy" or be dropped from the house. Some patients present themselves at the clinic in order to placate employers. Whatever the reason for the patient's presence, it will inevitably color the nature of interview behavior.

For many individuals, going to see a clinical psychologist arouses feelings of inadequacy. Some individuals will respond to this by clamming up. Others will display a kind of bravura that says, "See, I'm not weak at all!" Still others may become competitive and imply that psychology is not all it's cracked up to be or suggest that it is really unlikely that the clinician has much to offer.

In contrast, there are patients who start with a view of the clinician as a kind of savior. Although it is often quite reinforcing to be viewed as a miracle worker or a great healer, remember that the patient will probably reconsider this evaluation later. Some individuals also seek help so that they will have someone to intercede on their behalf. They can thus have a "go-between" to help fight their battles with spouse, employer, police, and so on. For example, one of the authors' first patients was an alcoholic who had been hospitalized off and on for over twenty years and was quite charming and highly articulate. His major motivation was to manipulate the author into interceding with the ward psychiatrist to get him open-ward privileges and an occasional visit to town.

The clinician's frame of reference

In a sense, the general dictum here, as in any endeavor, is "Be prepared." This implies that the clinician should have carefully gone over any existing records on the patient, checked the information provided by the person who arranged the appointment, and so on. Such a posture will ensure that the clinician knows as much as can be known at that point about the patient. It will also avoid the necessity of going over material during the interview that the patient may have already covered with other clinic staff.

In addition, the clinician should be perfectly clear about the purpose of the interview. Is it to evaluate the patient for hospitalization? Is the patient seeking information? If the interview is being conducted on a referral basis, the clinician should be quite sure about what information is being requested by the referring person. It is always disconcerting, as a clinician, to discover after the fact that you entirely misinterpreted the reason for the interview.

Through it all, the clinician must remain objective. However, objectivity need not imply coldness or aloofness—rather, it suggests that the clinician must be secure enough to maintain composure and not lose sight of the purposes of the interview. For example, if a patient should become very angry and attack the clinician's ability, training, or good intentions, the clinician must remember that the first obligation is to understand. The clinician should be secure enough to distinguish between reality and the forces that drive the patient.

Depending on the purpose of the interview, the clinician should also be prepared to provide some closure for the patient at the conclusion of the interview. As the interview progresses, the clinician will be formulating hypotheses and recommendations. A confident but enigmatic smile at the close of the interview, coupled with a "We'll be in touch," will not suffice. The clinician should be prepared to make a referral, set up another appointment, provide some feedback, and so on.

■ Varieties of Interviews

Up to this point, we have reviewed various interviewing essentials and techniques that are relevant to the interviewing process, regardless of the type of interview that is administered. In this section, we will discuss several of the more common types of interviews that are conducted by clinical psychologists. It is important to note, however, that more than one of these interviews may be administered to the same client or patient. For example, the same patient may complete an intake-admission interview when admitted to a hospital, a case-history and mental status examination interview once on the hospital unit, and, later, a structured diagnostic interview by the treating clinician. With this in mind, let us now turn to a survey of some of the more commonly employed types of interviews.

There are many varieties of interviews; however, there are two primary distinguishing factors. First, interviews differ with regard to their *purpose*. For example, the purpose of one interview may be to evaluate a client who is presenting to an outpatient clinic for the first time (intake-admission interview), whereas the purpose of another interview may be to arrive at a DSM-IV diagnostic formulation (diagnostic interview). The second major distinguishing factor is whether an interview is structured or unstructured (often labeled a clinical interview). In *structured interviews,* clinicians are required to ask verbatim a set of standardized questions in a specific sequence. In contrast, *unstructured interviews* allow the clinician to ask any questions that come to mind in any order. We will have much more to say about structured versus unstructured interviews later in this chapter.

Regardless of the purpose or type of interview, the same kinds of skills are required. Rapport, good communication skills, appropriate questions, and good observational skills are all necessary, even when administering a structured interview. Also, it is well to bear in mind that any assessment interview may have strong therapeutic overtones — after all, patients' perceptions of the clinic, their motivation, and their expectations for help may all be shaped to a significant extent by their experiences in intake interviews or in diagnostic screening sessions. We will organize our presentation in this section by the purpose of the interview, but it is important to keep in mind that structured and unstructured versions of these interviews exist.

The intake-admission interview

An *intake-admission interview* generally has two purposes: (1) to determine why the patient has come to the clinic or hospital and (2) to judge whether the agency's facilities, policies, and focus of competence will meet the needs and expectations of the patient. Many times, a psychiatric social worker conducts such interviews, often face-to-face but increasingly by telephone contact prior to the initial interview. A skilled, sensitive telephone interviewer can obtain much of the information that has traditionally been gathered at the clinic. Under some conditions or in particular clinics, the intake interview may be conducted by the same person who later does the diagnostic interview or the test workup. An advantage of this procedure is that patients do not get shoved from pillar to post as they make the rounds from one type of interview to the next.

Another function of the initial interview is to apprise the patient of such matters as the clinic's functions, fees, policies, procedures, and personnel. Patients are consumers and have every right to information regarding services and charges. Such concrete details can certainly influence patients' motivation for therapy and can often dispel some myths that might decrease their expectations for help.

Box 6-1 presents an example of an intake report based on an interview with a prospective client in a community-based outpatient clinic (the names are fictitious).

The case-history interview

In a *case-history interview,* as complete a personal and social history of the patient as possible is taken. There is interest both in concrete facts, dates, and events and in the patient's feelings about them. It is also important to note that a relentless pursuit of dates and names can sometimes obscure important data and create in the patient a set to respond in concrete terms, sometimes impeding progress in later interviews.

Basically, the purpose of a case history is to provide a broad background and context in which both the patient and the problem can be placed. Diagnostic and therapeutic technology is not yet so well advanced that specific behaviors, problems, or thoughts can always be understood in exactly the same way in every person. It is therefore essential that the patient's problems be placed in a proper historical-developmental context so that their diagnostic significance and their therapeutic implications can be more reliably determined.

The range of material covered in personal-social histories is quite broad. It covers both childhood and adulthood, and it includes educational, sexual, medical,

Box 6-1
Sample Intake Report

Name: MORTON, Charles
Age: 22
Sex: Male
Occupation: Student
Date of Interview: June 1, 1995
Therapist: Luke Baldry, Ph.D.

Identifying Information: The client is a 22-year-old white male who is presently a full-time student at a large midwestern university. Currently, he lives alone in an apartment and works part-time at a local grocery store.

Chief Complaint: The client presents to the clinic today complaining of "depression" that reportedly has become worse over the last two weeks.

History of Presenting Problem: The client reports that he has experienced symptoms of depression "off and on" for the last year. These symptoms include: depressed mood ("feeling sad"), appetite disturbance but no significant weight loss, sleep disturbance (early morning awakening), fatigue, feelings of worthlessness, and difficulty concentrating. All of these symptoms have been present nearly every day over the last two weeks.

About one year ago, the client reports, a long-standing romantic relationship of four years ended. Following this break-up, the client reports that he became increasingly withdrawn and, in addition to some of the symptoms noted above, experienced several crying spells. Although his adjustment to this event became better as time progressed, the client reports that the break-up "shook" his confidence and led to a decrease in the number of social activities he engaged in. Further, he reports that he has not dated since.

Last semester (winter 1995), the client transferred to this university from a community college in another midwestern location. He reports that the move was difficult both emotionally and academically. Specifically, being away from his hometown, family, and friends has led him to feel more isolated and dysphoric. Further, his grades last semester reportedly suffered. He reports that his grades dropped from A's in his previous school to C's at this university. Toward the end of last semester (once his grades in his classes became apparent), he developed an increasing number of depressive symptoms.

Past Treatment History: The client reports that he has not previously sought out psychological or psychiatric treatment.

Medical History: No significant medical history was reported.

Substance Use/Abuse: The client denies any current symptoms of substance abuse or dependence. He has "tried" marijuana on three occasions in the past but denies current use. He reports drinking on average 3 to 4 cans of beer per week.

Medication: The client reports that he is not currently taking any medication.

Family History: Both of the client's biological parents are living, and he has one brother (age 20) and one sister (age 26). The client reports that his mother suffers from depression and has received outpatient treatment on numerous occasions. Further, he reports that his maternal grandfather was diagnosed with depression. No substance use problems among family members were noted.

Suicidal/Homicidal Ideation: The client denied any current or past suicidal or homicidal ideation, intent, or action.

Mental Status: The client was well-groomed, cooperative, and dressed appropriately. He was alert and oriented in all spheres. His mood and affect were dysphoric. His speech was clear, coherent, and goal-directed. Some attention and concentration difficulties were noted. Further, his immediate memory was mildly impaired. No evidence of formal thought disorder, delusions, hallucinations, or suicidal/homicidal ideation was found. His insight and judgment appear to be fair.

Diagnostic Impression:

Axis I:	296.22, Major Depressive Disorder, Single Episode
Axis II:	V71.09, No Diagnosis
Axis III:	None
Axis IV:	Problems related to the social environment
	Educational problems
Axis V:	GAF = 55 (current)

Recommendations: Individual psychotherapy. Cognitive-behavioral treatment for depression.

Luke Baldry, Ph.D.
Licensed Clinical Psychologist

parental-environmental, religious, and psychopathological matters. Although, as noted above, much of this material will be factual, it is extremely important to indicate how the patient presents the material — the mode of verbalization, the emotional reactions to the material, evasiveness or openness, and so on.

Although most patients, particularly competent adults, provide their own personal-social history, other knowledgeable adults can often furnish invaluable data and impressions. A spouse, an employer, a teacher, or a friend can be rich sources of information. Clinicians have never made as much use of such sources as they might, perhaps because such additional interviews are costly in time and effort. In addition, there are issues of confidentiality and trust. And even when the patient gives consent and helps recruit the informants, many clinicians fear that using them can impede the subsequent therapeutic relationship. Still, outside sources can often provide a picture of the patient that cannot be achieved in any other fashion. In the case of young children, persons who are mentally retarded, and persons who are incompetent, there are, of course, fewer barriers to the use of such sources.

In Table 6-2, a typical case-history outline is presented.

Mental status examination interview

The *mental status examination* is typically conducted to assess the presence of cognitive, emotional, or behavioral problems. The general areas covered in mental status examination interviews, as well as excerpts from the ensuing report, are shown in Table 6-3.

For many years, a major limitation of mental status interviews was their unreliability since they are often highly unstructured in their execution. To address this problem, structured mental status examination interviews were devised. Here, specific questions are asked to assess behavior in a variety of areas. As noted by Rogers (1995), it is important for clinical psychologists to be familiar with the mental status examination because these interviews are one of the primary modes of clinical assessment for a variety of mental health professionals (for example, psychiatrists).

The crisis interview

Increasingly, clinicians have been functioning in novel settings, including storefront clinics and all-night telephone stations specializing in advice or comfort to drug users, to parents fearful of abusing their children, or to persons who are just lonely. Many of the usual rules of interviewing or the usual neat categorizations of interviews are blurred in these instances. However, the basic principles remain. Take the example of a mother who, during the absence of her husband, became terrified that she would abuse her small son. The following telephone conversation ensued:

> *Mother:* My God, help me. Is this the place . . . that . . . I mean, I need somebody. Tell me.
> *Volunteer:* Yes, it is. Tell me what it is. Go ahead and talk.
> *Mother:* I'm so nervous. I feel like I'll bust. Danny is crying, and my husband isn't here, and I've got to stop him. I can't stand it any longer.
> *Volunteer:* OK, I think I understand. Are you alone?
> *Mother:* Yes, but I can't handle it.

Table 6-2
A typical case-history outline.

---

1. *Identifying data,* including name, sex, occupation, address, date and place of birth, religion, and education.
2. *Reason for coming* to the agency and expectations for service.
3. *Present situation,* such as description of daily behavior and any recent or impending changes.
4. *Family constellation* (family of orientation), including descriptions of mother, father, and other family members and respondent's role in the family in which he or she grew up.
5. *Early recollections,* descriptions of earliest clear events and their surroundings.
6. *Birth and development,* including ages of walking and talking, problems compared with other children, and the person's view of his or her early experiences.
7. *Health,* including childhood and later diseases and injuries, problems with drugs or alcohol, and comparison of one's body with others.
8. *Education and training,* including subjects of special interest and achievement.
9. *Work record,* including reasons for changing jobs and attitudes toward work.
10. *Recreation and interests,* including volunteer work, reading, and the respondent's report of adequacy of self-expression and pleasures.
11. *Sexual development,* covering first awareness, kinds of sexual activities, and view of the adequacy of sexual expressions.
12. *Marital and family data,* covering major events and what led to them and comparison of present family of birth and orientation.
13. *Self-description,* including strengths, weaknesses, and ideals.
14. *Choices and turning points in life,* a review of the respondents's most important decisions and changes, including the single most important happening.
15. *View of the future,* including what the subject would like to see happen next year and in five or ten years, and what is necessary for these events to happen.
16. *Any further material* the respondent may see as omitted from the history.

SOURCE: Norman D. Sundberg, *Assessment of Persons,* © 1977, pp. 97–98. Reprinted by permission of Prentice Hall, Englewood Cliffs, New Jersey.

Volunteer: I know. And you're very upset. But I think we can talk it over. Where are you? What's your address?

Mother: I'm at home at 308 Park Place. I wish John would come home. I feel better when he's here. I just can't handle it. Nobody thought I should get married.

Volunteer: What do you think is wrong? Are you afraid of hurting Danny?

Mother: He won't stop crying. He's always crying. John doesn't know what it's like. I suppose he blames me — I know Mother does. (Starts crying uncontrollably.)

Volunteer: Look, that's all right. Take it easy. Where is John?

Table 6-3

Example of a mental status examination interview of a 24-year-old man diagnosed with schizophrenia.

General Outline of Mental Status Examination
  I. General Presentation: Appearance, Behavior, Attitude
 II. State of Consciousness: Alert, Hyperalert, Lethargic
III. Attention and Concentration
 IV. Speech: Clarity, Goal-directedness, Language deficits
  V. Orientation: To Person, Place, Time
 VI. Mood and Affect
VII. Form of Thought; Formal Thought Disorder
VIII. Thought Content: Preoccupations, Obsessions, Delusions
 IX. Ability to Think Abstractly
  X. Perceptions: Hallucinations
 XI. Memory: Immediate, Recent, Remote
XII. Intellectual Functioning
XIII. Insight and Judgment

     The patient appeared disheveled and exhibited "odd" behavior throughout the interview. Although he appeared alert, some impairment in his attention and concentration was noted. Specifically, he experienced difficulty repeating a series of digits and performing simple calculations without the aid of pencil and paper. No language deficits were noted, although the patient's speech was at times difficult to understand and did not appear to be goal-directed (that is, did not respond to the question posed). He was oriented to person and place, but was not oriented to time. Specifically, he was unsure of the month and day. He reported his mood as "fine"; his affect appeared to be blunted. He demonstrated some signs of formal thought disorder: tangentiality and loose associations. He denied suicidal ideation but did report his belief that he was being "framed by the FBI" for a crime he did not commit. When confronted with the fact that he was in a psychiatric hospital, not a prison, he stated that this was all part of an FBI "cover-up," so that he could be made to look "crazy." Although he denied hallucinations, his behavior suggested that on occasion he was responding to auditory hallucinations. For example, he stared off into space and began whispering on several occasions. His ability to abstract appeared to be impaired. For example, when asked how a baseball and an orange are alike, he responded "They both are alive." The patient's immediate and recent memory were slightly impaired although his remote memory was intact. It is estimated that he is of average intelligence. Currently his insight and judgment appear to be poor.

Mother: He's . . . he drives a truck. He won't be back till Thursday.
Volunteer: I think I understand . . . and I know this is hard for you. Have you talked with anybody about your feelings on these things?
Mother: No. Well, with Marge next door a little bit. She said she felt like that a few times. But . . . I don't know.

The volunteer in this situation kept on reinforcing the notion that she understood. The calm yet confident manner of the volunteer seemed to reassure the mother, who agreed to come in the next afternoon and to bring her son along with her.

    Obviously, the purpose of *crisis interviews* is to meet problems as they occur and to provide an immediate resource. Their intention is to deflect the potential for disaster and to encourage callers to enter into a relationship with the clinic or make a referral so that a longer-term solution can be worked out. Such interviewing requires training, sensitivity, and judgment. Asking the wrong question in a case-history interview may only result in a piece of misinformation — but a caller who is asked a wrong question on the telephone may hang up. As clinical services begin to transcend the boundaries of the conventional clinic, there is a chance that they will be diluted by having to operate in situations that offer less opportunity for control. But the problems seem to be outweighed by the opportunity to intervene during real crises.

The diagnostic interview

As mentioned in Chapter 5, clinical psychologists evaluate patients according to DSM-IV criteria. Insurance companies, research protocols, or even court proceedings may require a diagnostic evaluation. How clinicians arrive at such a formulation, however, is for the most part left up to them. Historically, a clinical interview has been employed — a free-form, unstructured interview whose content varies greatly from clinician to clinician. As might be expected, this interviewing method often results in unreliable ratings because two clinicians evaluating the same patient may arrive at different diagnostic formulations. Research on the reliability of diagnoses using unstructured clinical interviews has not supported this approach (Matarazzo, 1983; Ward, Beck, Mendelson, Mock, & Erbauch, 1962).

Fortunately, things have changed. Researchers have developed structured diagnostic interviews that can be used by clinical psychologists in their research or clinical work. A *structured diagnostic interview* consists of a standard set of questions and follow-up probes that are asked in a specified sequence. The use of structured diagnostic interviews ensures that all patients or subjects are asked the same questions, thereby making it more likely that two clinicians who evaluate the same patient would arrive at the same diagnostic formulation (that is, high interrater reliability). We'll have more to say about the reliability and validity of interviews later in this chapter.

Several structured diagnostic interviews are available to clinical psychologists. Figure 6-1 presents a portion of the *Structured Clinical Interview for Axis I DSM-IV Disorders,* or SCID-I (First, Spitzer, Gibbon, & Williams, 1995). This section of the SCID-I assesses the presence of the DSM-IV criteria for Specific Phobia. The questions the interviewer asks appear in the left-hand column, and the actual DSM-IV criteria for this disorder appear in the middle column.

Computer interviewing

In recent years, use of *computer interviewing* has been growing. Computers have been used to take psychiatric histories, cover assessment of specific problems, do behavioral assessments, and assist in the diagnosis of mental disorders. Such uses of the computer are said to have several advantages (Erdman, Klein, & Greist, 1985). For example, the computer always asks all the questions assigned, reliability is 100%, and, for some patients at least, it is less uncomfortable and embarrassing to deal with an inanimate object than a live clinician.

At the same time, computers are impersonal and, some might even say, dehumanizing. Then, too, only structured interviews can be employed, thus precluding interviewer flexibility — for example, it is not possible to ask additional

SPECIFIC PHOBIA   **SPECIFIC PHOBIA CRITERIA**   SCREEN Q #7

| | YES | NO |

IF SCREENING QUESTION #7 ANSWERED "NO,"
SKIP TO *OBSESSIVE COMPULSIVE DISORDER*.

IF NO: GO TO
*OBSESSIVE COM-
PULSIVE DISORDER*

IF QUESTION #7
ANSWERED "YES": You've
said that there are other
things that you've been
especially afraid of, like flying,
seeing blood, getting a shot,
heights, closed places, or
certain kinds of animals or
insects . . .

IF SCREENER NOT USED:
Are there any other things
that you have been especially
afraid of, like flying, seeing
blood, getting a shot, heights,
closed places, or certain kinds
of animals of insects?

A. Marked and persistent fear
that is excessive or unreasonable,
cued by the presence or anticipation of a specific object or situation
(e.g., flying, heights, animals, receiving an injection, seeing blood).

? 1 2 3   F67

GO TO
*OBSES-
SIVE
COMPUL-
SIVE
DIS-
ORDER*

Tell me about that.

What were you afraid would
happen when (CONFRONTED
WITH PHOBIC STIMULUS)?

Did you always feel frightened
when you (CONFRONTED
PHOBIC STIMULUS)?

B. Exposure to the phobic
stimulus almost invariably provokes
an immediate anxiety response,
which may take the form of a situationally bound or situationally
predisposed panic attack. Note: in
children, the anxiety may be
expressed by crying, tantrums,
freezing, or clinging.

? 1 2 3   F68

GO TO
*OBSES-
SIVE
COMPUL-
SIVE
DIS-
ORDER*

Did you think that you were more
afraid of (PHOBIC STIMULUS)
than you should have been (or
than made sense)?

C. The person recognizes that the
fear is excessive or unreasonable.
Note: in children, this feature may
be absent.

? 1 2 3   F69

GO TO
*OBSES-
SIVE
COMPUL-
SIVE
DIS-
ORDER*

? = inadequate information   1 = absent or false   2 = subthreshold   3 = threshold or true

Figure 6-1
Specific Phobia section of the Structured Clinical Interview for DSM-IV Axis I Disorders,
    or SCID-I. SOURCE: From *Structured Clinical Interview for DSM-IV Axis I
    Disorder,* by M. B. First, R. L. Spitzer, M. Gibbon, and J. B. W. Williams,
    pp F16–F19. Copyright 1996 Biometrics Research. Reprinted by permission.

| | | ? | 1 | 2 | 3 | F70 |

Did you go out of your way to avoid (PHOBIC STIMULUS)?

(Are there things you didn't do because of this fear, that you would otherwise have done?)

    IF NO: How hard (is/was) it for you to (CONFRONT PHOBIC STIMULUS)?

D. The phobic situation(s) is avoided or else endured with intense anxiety or distress.

?   1   2   3   F70

GO TO *OBSESSIVE COMPULSIVE DISORDER*

IF UNCLEAR WHETHER FEAR WAS CLINICALLY SIGNIFICANT: How much did (PHOBIA) interfere with your life?

(Is there anything you've avoided because of being afraid of (PHOBIC STIMULUS)?

    IF DOES NOT INTERFERE WITH LIFE: How much has the fact that you were afraid of (PHOBIC STIMULUS) bothered you?

E. The avoidance, anxious anticipation, or distress in the feared situation interferes significantly with the person's normal routine, occupational (academic) functioning, or with social activities or relationships with others, or there is marked distress about having the phobia.

?   1   2   3   F71

GO TO *OBSESSIVE COMPULSIVE DISORDER*

IF YOUNGER THAN AGE 18: How long have you had these fears?

F. For individuals under age 18 years, the duration is at least 6 months.

?   1   2   3   F72

GO TO *OBSESSIVE COMPULSIVE DISORDER*

IF NOT ALREADY CLEAR: RETURN TO THIS ITEM AFTER COMPLETING SECTION ON PTSD AND OBSESSIVE-COMPULSIVE DISORDER.

G. The anxiety, panic attacks, or phobic avoidance associated with the specific object or situation are not better accounted for by another mental disorder, such as Obsessive-Compulsive Disorder (for example, fear of contamination), Posttraumatic Stress Disorder (for example, avoidance of stimuli associated with a severe stressor), Separation Anxiety Disorder (for example, avoidance of school), Social Phobia (for example, avoidance of social situations because of fear of embarrassment), Panic Disorder with Agoraphobia, or Agoraphobia without History of Panic Disorder.

?   1   2   3   F73

GO TO *OBSESSIVE COMPULSIVE DISORDER*

? = inadequate information   1 = absent or false   2 = subthreshold   3 = threshold or true

Figure 6-1 *(continued)*

SPECIFIC PHOBIA CRITERIA   1   3 | F74
A, B, C, D, E, F, AND G | |
ARE CODED "3"

GO TO	SPE-
*OBSESSIVE	CIFIC
COMPULSIVE	PHO-
DISORDERS	BIA

INDICATE TYPE:
(Check all that apply)

___ Animal Type (includes insects)   F75

___ Natural Environment Type (includes storms,   F76
    heights, water)

___ Blood/Injection/Injury Type (includes   F77
    seeing blood or injury or receiving an
    injection or other invasive procedure)

___ Situational Type (includes public trans-   F78
    portation, tunnels, bridges, elevators,
    flying, driving, or enclosed places)

___ Other Type (for example, fear of situations   F79
    that might lead to choking, vomiting, or
    contracting an illness)
    Specify: _____

SPECIFIC PHOBIA CHRONOLOGY

IF UNCLEAR: During the past   Has met criteria for Specific   ?   1   3 | F80
month have you been bothered by   Phobia during past month
(SPECIFIC PHOBIA)?

INDICATE CURRENT SEVERITY: | F81
1 – Mild: Few, if any, symptoms in excess of those required to make the diagnosis
    are present, and symptoms result in no more than minor impairments in social
    or occupational functioning.
2 – Moderate: Symptoms or functional impairment between "mild" and "severe"
    are present.
3 – Severe: Many symptoms in excess of those required to make the diagnosis or
    several symptoms that are particularly severe are present, or the symptoms re-
    sult in marked impairment in social or occupational functioning.

CONTINUE WITH *AGE AT ONSET*, BELOW.

? = inadequate information   1 = absent or false   2 = subthreshold   3 = threshold or true

Figure 6-1 *(continued)*

IF CURRENT CRITERIA NOT FULLY MET (OR NOT AT ALL):

4 – In Partial Remission: The full criteria for the disorder were previously met but currently only some of the symptoms or signs of the disorder remain.

5 – In Full Remission: There are no longer any symptoms or signs of the disorder but it is still clinically relevant to note the disorder—for example, in an individual with previous episodes of Specific Phobia who has been symptom-free on an antianxiety agent for the past three years.

6 – Prior History: There is a history of the criteria having been met for the disorder but the individual is considered to have recovered from it.

F82

When did you last have (ANY SX OF SPECIFIC PHOBIA)?	Number of months prior to interview when last had a symptom of Specific Phobia

F83

AGE AT ONSET

IF UNKNOWN: How old were you when you first started having (SXS OF SPECIFIC PHOBIA)?   Age at onset of Specific Phobia (CODE 99 IF UNKNOWN)   __ __   F84

GO TO
*OBSESSIVE
COMPULSIVE
DISORDER*

? = inadequate information   1 = absent or false   2 = subthreshold   3 = threshold or true

Figure 6-1 (continued)

questions aimed at clarification when an interviewee's response is unclear. Also, the wording and order of questions cannot be tailored to meet the special needs of individual patients.

Still, computer interviews have been shown to be useful in identifying target symptoms in clients (Farrell, Complair, & McCullough, 1987). There are computerized versions of diagnostic interviews as well—the *Computerized Diagnostic Interview Schedule Revised,* or CDISR (Blouin, 1991), can be administered by a personal computer, and it assesses the presence and severity of symptoms related to over 30 Axis I mental disorder diagnoses (for example, major depression, alcohol dependence, and panic disorder). Studies comparing computer-administered and interviewer-administered versions of the DIS have been supportive of the computerized approach (Blouin, Perez, & Blouin, 1988; Griest et al., 1987).

Finally, it is interesting to note that the use of computer-assisted interviews has been taken a step further. Recently, Baer et al. (1995) reported preliminary data on a fully automated telephone screening system that uses computerized digital voice recordings and touch-tone responses to assess community residents for symptoms of depression. In this study, a screening test was offered to residents who called a toll-free number to hear a series of questions about a variety of depressive symptoms. The questions were narrated by a professional actress and actor, and there was an option to have the questions repeated. Callers answered the questions by selecting specified numbers on the telephone keypad. Immediate feedback regarding the level of depression (no depression, minimal or mild depression, severe or extreme depression) was provided to each caller, and toll-free telephone numbers of selected health care professionals were provided to those whose responses indicated at least minimal levels of depression.

■ Reliability and Validity of Interviews

As with any form of psychological assessment, it is important to evaluate the reliability and validity of interviews. The reliability of an interview is typically evaluated in terms of the level of agreement between at least two raters who evaluated the same patient or client. By agreement, we mean consensus on diagnoses assigned, on ratings of levels of personality traits, or on any other type of summary information derived from an interview. This is often referred to as *interrater reliability*. A number of measures can be used to quantify interrater reliability, including the kappa coefficient (Cohen, 1960) and the intraclass correlation coefficient (Shrout & Fleiss, 1979).

The validity of an interview concerns how well the interview measures what it intends to measure. For example, a demonstration that scores from a depression interview correlate highly with scores from a well-respected self-report measure of depression would suggest there is some level of validity in the use of this interview to assess depression. Evidence for an interview's *predictive validity* would be demonstrated if scores from this measure were significantly correlated with (and therefore "predicted") future events believed to be relevant to that construct. For instance, if scores from the depression interview were highly correlated with poorer academic performance over the next two months, then this might be considered as evidence supporting the predictive validity of the interview.

As should be apparent, both the reliability and validity of a measure like an interview are a matter of degree. Interviews, like psychological tests, are not perfectly reliable or perfectly valid. But the higher the reliability and validity, the more confident clinicians can be in their conclusions. Let us turn now to a closer look at reliability and validity issues for interviews.

Reliability

Standardized, or structured, interviews with clear scoring instructions will be more reliable than unstructured interviews. The reason is that structured interviews reduce both information variance and criterion variance. *Information variance* refers to the variation in the questions that clinicians ask, the observations that are made during the interview, and the method of integrating the information that is obtained (Rogers, 1995). *Criterion variance* refers to the variation in scoring thresholds among clinicians (Rogers, 1995). Clear-cut scoring guidelines make it more likely that two clinicians will score the same interviewee response in a similar way.

Because most of the research on the psychometric properties of interviews has focused on structured diagnostic interviews, we will discuss these in some detail. For many years, diagnostic interviews were considered quite unreliable (Matarazzo, 1983; Ward, Beck, Mendelson, Mock, & Erbauch, 1962). However, several things changed. First, with the introduction of DSM-III (APA, 1980), operational criteria were developed for most of the mental disorder diagnoses. This made it much easier to know what specific features to assess in order to rule in or rule out a particular mental disorder diagnosis. Second, and perhaps more important, several groups of investigators developed structured interviews to systematically assess the various DSM criteria for mental disorders. Clearly, the reliability of the diagnostic information derived from structured interviews exceeds that obtained via unstructured interviews (Rogers, 1995).

As previously mentioned, interrater reliability is the most common type of reliability assessed and reported for structured diagnostic interviews. Another type of reliability that is examined in structured diagnostic and other interviews is *test-retest reliability,* which refers to the consistency of scores or diagnoses across time. The expectation is that individuals should in general receive similar scores or diagnoses when an interview is readministered. For example, a male patient assigned a diagnosis of major depressive disorder based on a structured interview would be expected to receive the same diagnosis if reinterviewed (using the same structured interview) the next day.

The test-retest reliability of an interview should be quite high when the intervening time period between the initial testing and the retest is short (for example, hours or a few days). However, when the intervening time period is quite large (months or years), test-retest reliability typically suffers. One reason for this is the possibility that the psychological status of the patient has changed. This is especially relevant when assessing current mental disorder diagnoses. As an example, the fact that a patient does not receive a major depressive disorder diagnosis again at a six-month retest is not necessarily an indictment of the structured interview. Because major depressive episodes can be of relatively short duration, the interview may be quite accurate in revealing no diagnosis at retest.

The point is that the level of test-retest reliability that is obtained must be interpreted in the context of the nature of the variable (for example, a brief state or temporary syndrome versus a long-standing personality trait) as well as the length of the intervening time period between test and retest. When test-retest reliability is low, it can be due to a host of factors, including subjects' tendency to report fewer symptoms at retest, subjects' boredom or fatigue at retest, or the effect of variations in mood on the report of symptoms (Sher & Trull, 1996). Table 6-4 describes reliability indices for structured interviews.

Table 6-5 presents a hypothetical data set from a study assessing the reliability of alcoholism diagnoses derived from a structured interview. In this example we are focusing on interrater reliability, but the calculations would be the same if one wanted to assess the test-retest reliability of diagnoses. In this latter case, data for Rater 2 would be substituted with data for Testing 2 (Retest).

As can be seen, the two raters evaluated the same 100 patients for the presence or absence of an alcoholism diagnosis using a structured interview. These two raters agreed in 90% of the cases [(30 + 60)/100]. Agreement here refers to coming to the same conclusion—not just agreeing that the diagnosis is present, but also that the diagnosis is absent. Table 6-5 also presents the calculation for kappa. The *kappa coefficient* is an index of chance-corrected agreement, which will typically

Table 6-4

Common types of reliability that are assessed in order to evaluate interviews.

Type of Reliability	Definition	Statistical Index
Interrater or interjudge reliability	Index of the degree of agreement between two or more raters or judges as to the level of a trait that is present or the presence or absence of a feature or diagnosis	Pearson's r Intraclass correlation Kappa
Test-retest reliability	Index of the consistency of interview scores across some period of time	Pearson's r Intraclass correlation

Table 6-5

Diagnostic agreement between two raters.

		Rater 2	
		Present	Absent
Rater 1	Present	30 a	5 b
	Absent	5 c	60 d

N = 100

Overall Agreement = a + d/N = .90

$$\text{Kappa} = \frac{(a+d/N) - ((a+b)(a+c) + (c+d)(b+d))/N^2}{1 - ((a+b)(a+c) + (c+d)(b+d))/N^2}$$

$$= \frac{ad - bc}{ad - bc + N(b + c)/2}$$

$$= \frac{1775}{2275}$$

$$= .78$$

be lower than overall agreement. The reason for this is that raters will agree on the basis of chance alone in situations where the prevalence rate for a diagnosis is relatively high or, alternatively, relatively low. In the example presented in Table 6-5, we see that the diagnosis of alcoholism is relatively infrequent. Because of this, a rater who *always* judged the disorder to be absent would be correct — and likely to agree with another rater — in many cases. This is what agreement based on chance alone refers to. The kappa coefficient takes this into account and adjusts the agreement index downward accordingly. In general, a kappa value between .75 and 1.00 is considered to reflect excellent interrater agreement beyond chance (Cicchetti, 1994).

Validity

Validity of any type of psychological measure can take on many forms. *Content validity* refers to the measure's comprehensiveness in assessing the variable of interest. In other words, does it do a good job of adequately measuring all important aspects of the construct of interest? For example, if an interview is designed to measure depression, then it should contain multiple questions assessing various emotional, cognitive, and physiological aspects of depression. *Criterion-related validity* refers to the ability of a measure to predict (that is, correlate with) scores on other relevant measures. These measures may be administered concurrently with the interview or at some point in the future. For instance, an interview assessing conduct disorder in childhood might be said to have criterion-related validity to the extent that its scores correlated with measures of peer rejection and aggressive behavior. *Discriminant validity* focuses on the *absence* of correlation of an assessment instrument with measures that are not theoretically related to the construct being measured. For example, there is no theoretical reason why Generalized Anxiety Disorder (GAD) should be correlated with level of intelligence. Therefore, a demonstration that the two measures are not significantly correlated would indicate the GAD interview's discriminant validity. Finally, it should be noted that the term *construct validity* is used to refer to all of the aspects of validity noted above. Thus, many researchers describe the process of developing and validating a measure as a process of construct validation. Table 6-6 describes these and related validity indices.

In the case of structured diagnostic interviews, content validity is usually assumed because these interviews were developed to measure the DSM criteria for specific mental disorders. That leaves the need for validation efforts aimed at establishing an interview's criterion-related, discriminant, and construct validity. Although some studies on validation have been conducted, many more are needed. Let us take a popular structured diagnostic interview, the SCID, as an example. As noted by Rogers (1995), relatively few studies have been conducted that attempted to demonstrate the criterion-related or discriminant validity of the SCID. Specifically, not many studies have compared SCID diagnoses and scores to clinical diagnoses, to scores from self-report inventories, or to those obtained from other diagnostic interviews.

Why is this the case? Robins (1985) has noted several of the difficulties associated with validating a structured diagnostic interview. First, laboratory tests that validate mental disorder diagnoses are not available. Therefore, there is no "gold

Table 6-6
Common types of validity that are assessed in order to evaluate interviews.

Type of Validity	Definition
Content Validity	The degree to which the interview items adequately measure the various aspects of the variable or construct.
Predictive Validity	The degree to which interview scores can predict (that is, correlate with) behavior or test scores that are observed or obtained at some point in the future.
Concurrent Validity	The extent to which interview scores are correlated with a related, but independent, set of test and interview scores or behaviors.
Construct Validity	The extent to which interview scores are correlated with other measures or behaviors in a logical and theoretically consistent way. (This will involve a demonstration of both convergent and discriminant validity.)

Note: Predictive and concurrent validity are both subtypes of criterion-related validity.

standard" to use as a comparison. Further, structured diagnostic interviews were developed at least partially because of a dissatisfaction with self-report inventories. In that light, it does not seem appropriate or desirable to use a self-report inventory as a standard. Any lack of agreement between a structured diagnostic interview and a self-report inventory may be more of an indictment against the validity of the self-report inventory than it is against the validity of the structured diagnostic interview. The same problem exists with using a clinical impression, based on an unstructured clinical interview, as a comparison. Second, some investigators have used a test-retest design to address the validity issue; however, this speaks more to the stability or reliability of interview scores than to the validity of the measure. Of course, a valid measure should also be reliable. But the test-retest design does not directly address the validity question.

These points are well taken — no infallible criterion measure exists for comparison purposes. In these situations, clinicians should conduct multiple validity studies using a variety of criterion measures. Confidence in the validity of the structured interview will increase as a function of the number of times that scores from this interview are highly associated with scores from alternative measures of the same or similar constructs *and* are not significantly related to scores from measures of constructs that theoretically should be unrelated to the diagnosis in question.

Suggestions for improving reliability and validity
The suggestions listed below summarize the main points of the previous discussion. Following them should help improve both the reliability and validity of interviews.

1. *Whenever possible, use a structured interview.* A wide variety of structured interviews exist for conducting intake-admission, case-history, mental status examination, crisis, and diagnostic interviews.
2. *If a structured interview does not exist for your purpose, consider developing one.* Generate a standard set of questions to be used, develop a set of guidelines to score respondents' answers, administer this interview to a representative sample of subjects, and use the feedback from subjects and interviewers to modify the interview. If nothing else, completing this process will help you better understand what it is that you are attempting to assess and will help you become a better interviewer.
3. *Whether you are using a structured interview or not, certain interviewing skills are essential:* establishing rapport, being an effective communicator, being a good listener, knowing when and how to ask additional questions, and being a good observer of nonverbal behavior.
4. *Be aware of the patient's motives and expectancies with regard to the interview.* For example, how strong are his or her needs for approval or social desirability?
5. *Be aware of your own expectations, biases, and cultural values.* Periodically, have someone else assess the reliability of the interviews you administer and score.

The art and science of interviewing

Becoming a skilled interviewer requires practice. Without the opportunity to conduct real interviews, to make mistakes, or to discuss techniques and strategies with more experienced interviewers, a simple awareness of scientific investigations of interviewing will not confer great skill. What, then, are the functions of research on interviewing? A major one is to make clinicians more humble. Research suggests, for example, that prior expectancies can color the interviewer's observations, that implicit theories of personality and psychopathology can influence the focus of an interview, and that the match or mismatch of interviewer and interviewee in terms of race, age, and gender may influence the course and outcome of the interview. Thus, a number of influences on the interview process have been identified.

Furthermore, if clinicians never test their hypotheses, if they never assess the validity of their diagnoses, if they never check their reliability against someone else, or if they never measure the efficacy of a specific interview tactic, they can easily develop an ill-placed confidence that will ultimately be hard on their patients. It may be true, as some cynics argue, that ten studies all purporting to show that "mm-hmm" is no more effective than a nod of the head in expressing interviewer interest still fail to disprove that in one specific or unique clinical interaction there may indeed be a difference. But such studies and many others like them will surely give pause to conscientious interviewers and encourage them to question their assumptions.

Though no single interview study will offer an unambiguous solution to an interview problem, such studies have a cumulative effect. Research can offer suggestions about improving the validity of clinicians' observations and tactics, while at the same time shattering some timeworn illusions and splintering a few clichés. By the sheer cumulative weight of its controlled, scientific approach, research can make interviewers more sensitive and effective. A clinician steeped in both the art and the science of interviewing will be more effective (though hardly more comfortable) than one who is conscious of only one of these dual aspects of interviewing.

■ Focus Questions

1. What are the major issues to consider when conducting an assessment interview?
2. What are the common types of assessment interviews that are conducted? Briefly describe each type.
3. What are the similarities and differences between structured and unstructured interviews?
4. What types of reliability and validity are relevant to an evaluation of a structured interview?
5. Why is the validity of a structured diagnostic interview difficult to assess?

■ Key Terms

assessment interview
case-history interview
clinical assessment
computer interviewing
construct validity
content validity
crisis interviews
criterion-related validity
discriminant validity
intake-admission interview

interrater reliability
kappa coefficient
mental status examination
predictive validity
rapport
referral question
structured diagnostic interview
structured interviews
test-retest reliability
unstructured interviews

7

The Assessment of Intelligence

The history of clinical psychology is inextricably tied to the assessment of intelligence. Without the success in this and related assessment enterprises, there may not have been a field of clinical psychology. As the years passed, however, clinicians became increasingly interested in the more "glamorous" aspects of the profession, such as therapy. Consequently, assessment began to take a backseat and technicians started to become the assessors as they had been prior to World War II (Tyler, 1976). But, as noted in the last chapter, all this is beginning to change (Abeles, 1990). Not only is the value of assessment being rediscovered, but, in particular, intelligence tests remain prominent in the clinician's arsenal of assessment devices (Craig & Horowitz, 1990).

■ Yesterday and Today

Alfred Binet and his collaborator, Theodore Simon, became leaders in the intelligence testing movement when they devised the Binet-Simon test to identify individual differences in mental functioning (see Chapter 2). Like others of the day, they regarded intelligence as a "faculty" that was inherited, although they also spoke of it as affected by training and opportunity. With the interest in quantifying intellectual performance and with the rise of compulsory education in Europe and North America, intelligence testing became firmly entrenched (Tyler, 1976).

Institutions like schools, industries, military forces, and governments were, by their nature, quite interested in individual differences (for example, levels of intelligence) that might affect performance in these various settings; therefore, intelligence testing prospered (Herrnstein & Murray, 1994). For many years, the critical importance and widespread use of intelligence tests went largely unchallenged. But by the end of the 1960s, everyone from minority psychologists to Ralph Nader seemed to be attacking the validity of these tests. Basically, the argument was that such tests discriminate through the inclusion of unfair items (see, for example, Cronbach, 1975; Tyler, 1972). Because of a lengthy civil rights suit (*Larry P.* v. *Wilson Riles*) begun in 1971, the California State Board of Education imposed a

Figure 7-1
Alfred Binet developed the first widely accepted test of intelligence. The test eventually
    became the Stanford-Binet and has undergone numerous revisions over the years.
    The Bettmann Archive

moratorium on the use of intelligence tests in 1975. It was decided by the court
that IQ testing is prejudicial to African American children and tends to place them,
without real justification, in allegedly stigmatizing programs for mentally retarded
individuals. Others (for example, Lambert, 1981) have disputed the court's judgment, however. Some African Americans contemplated a court challenge of the
ruling, claiming it assumed that African Americans would do poorly on the tests.
Still others argued that IQ testing is not a social evil but the principal means by
which we can right the wrongs imposed upon minorities by a devastating environment (Hebb, 1978).

Stephen Gould's popular book *The Mismeasure of Man* (1981) was a scathing critique of the intelligence testing movement as well as of the "reification" of
the notion of intelligence. Essentially, Gould argued that theorists like Spearman
(see below) mistakenly accorded general intelligence, or *g*, the status of a true entity because of their misunderstanding of factor analytic techniques. Further, Gould
contended that those arguing for the heritability of intelligence were in some cases
mistaken and in other cases guilty of fraud. Gould's book was a huge success and
further intensified the attack on intelligence testing.

This rather heated debate has recently resurfaced with the publication of *The
Bell Curve* (Herrnstein & Murray, 1994). In this book, Herrnstein and Murray review the concept of intelligence, recount the history of intelligence testing, respond
to many of the critiques offered by Gould (1981), and delve into public policy is-

Box 7-1
The Bell Curve

Perhaps no other book in recent times has generated as much con-troversy as Herrnstein and Murray's *The Bell Curve* (1994). Briefly, Herrnstein and Murray argue that, over the last 30 years, the United States has increasingly become more divided based on the cognitive or in-tellectual ability of its citizens. What has emerged is a class labeled "the cognitive elite," primarily concentrated in a small group of occupations (for example, doctors, lawyers, professors), who essentially screen for high IQ. Although intelligence is a product of both genetic and environmental fac-tors, our country's attempt to "equalize" the environment for all (that is, give everyone the same opportunities to succeed) ironically leads to a situ-ation in which the genes we inherit are the primary source of individual dif-ferences. In a sense, Herrnstein and Murray contend, this will only serve to widen the gap between the have's and the have-not's in coming gener-ations. The authors also present evidence supporting their position that cognitive ability/intelligence is the most important predictor of outcomes like financial stability, success in college, welfare dependency, producing "illegitimate" children, and criminal behavior. They also review the data on ethnic and racial differences in IQ and argue that efforts to raise IQ scores via educational programs or programs like Head Start have not produced positive, long-term effects. Finally, Herrnstein and Murray provide a num-ber of prescriptions for remedying the current disparity, including over-hauling affirmative action policies for education and the workplace, as well as returning decision-making power to local governing bodies.

Most of the negative reaction to this book appears to be based on dis-agreement with the authors' prescriptions for social policy and, at times, seems to take the form of ad hominum arguments. In addition, some have taken issue with the methodology, analysis, and interpretation of some of the empirical studies cited and discussed in the book. On the other hand, a group of experts in the field of intelligence recently pub-lished a brief article in the *Wall Street Journal* (Arvey et al., 1994) that outlined "mainstream" conclusions among researchers on intelligence. Many of the points made in *The Bell Curve* are consistent with these. The experts, however, stopped short of prescribing social policy based on these conclusions.

sues like poverty, crime, welfare, and affirmative action. Box 7-1 briefly presents some of the more controversial aspects of this book. Whatever the outcome of all this, it does illustrate that assessment is no longer an obscure academic activity— it is right there in the midst of contemporary social and public policy issues.

There is little question that intelligence tests have been misused at times in ways that have penalized minorities. There is also little doubt that some tests have contained certain items that have handicapped the performance of some minorities. Every effort should be made, therefore, to develop better tests and to administer and interpret them in a sensitive fashion. But banning tests seems an unlikely cure because it might ultimately harm the very people who need help.

■ The Concept of Intelligence

The two issues that have, from the beginning, plagued psychologists are still not resolved. First, exactly what is meant by the term *intelligence?* Second, how do we develop valid instruments for measuring it? In this section we will address both questions. But before we address these issues, it is necessary to review the psychometric concepts of reliability and validity.

Reliability and validity

As we mentioned in the last chapter, all interviews and tests must demonstrate both reliability and validity in order to be useful. Tables 7-1 and 7-2 present brief definitions of the most common forms of reliability and validity that are used to evaluate psychological tests.

Reliability.
With regard to psychological tests, reliability refers to the consistency with which individuals respond to test stimuli. There are several ways of evaluating reliability. First, there is *test-retest reliability*—the extent to which an individual makes similar responses to the same test stimuli on repeated occasions. Clearly, the test data will not be very useful if each time we test a person we get different responses. In some instances, patients may remember on the second occasion their responses from the first time. Or perhaps patients may simply have developed a kind of test-wiseness from the first test so that their scores the second time around are more influenced by this than they are by the variable being measured. In still other cases, patients might rehearse between testing occasions or show practice effects. For all these reasons, another gauge of reliability is sometimes used—*equivalent-forms reliability*. Here, equivalent or parallel forms of a test are developed to avoid these problems. However, sometimes it is too expensive (in time or money) to develop an equivalent form, or it is difficult or impossible to be sure the forms are really equivalent. Under such circumstances, or when retesting is not practical, assessing *split-half reliability* is a possibility. This means that a test is divided into halves (usually odd-numbered items versus even-numbered items) and participants' scores on each half are compared. Split-half reliability also serves as one possible index of a test's internal consistency. When the focus is on the internal consistency of a test, the investigator is interested in estimating whether or not the test items appear to be measuring the same thing (that is, whether the items are highly correlated with each other). The preferred method of assessing *internal consistency reliability* involves computing the average of all possible split-half correlations for a given test.

Table 7-1
Common types of reliability that are assessed in order to evaluate psychological tests.

Type of Reliability	Definition	Statistical Index
Test-retest reliability	Index of the consistency of test scores across some period of time	Pearson's *r* Intraclass correlation
Equivalent-forms reliability	Index of the consistency of test scores across time; this index is not vulnerable to a practice effect (that is, completing the same test twice)	Pearson's *r*
Split-half reliability	Index of the internal consistency of the test (do the items seem to be measuring the same variable or construct?)	Pearson's *r*
Internal consistency reliability	Preferred index of internal consistency in which the average of all possible split-half correlations is computed	Cronbach's *alpha* Kuder-Richardson-20
Interrater or Interjudge reliability	Index of the degree of agreement between two or more raters or judges as to the level of a trait that is present or the presence or absence of a feature or diagnosis	Pearson's *r* Intraclass correlation *Kappa*

Table 7-2
Common types of validity that are assessed in order to evaluate psychological tests.

Type of Validity	Definition
Content Validity	The degree to which the test items adequately measure the various aspects of the variable or construct.
Predictive Validity	The degree to which test scores can predict (that is, correlate with) behavior or test scores that are observed or obtained at some point in the future.
Concurrent Validity	The extent to which test scores are correlated with a related, but independent, set of test scores or behaviors.
Construct Validity	The extent to which test scores are correlated with other measures or behaviors in a logical and theoretically consistent way. This involves a demonstration of both convergent and discriminant validity.

Note: Predictive and concurrent validity are both subtypes of criterion-related validity.

Another aspect of reliability is called *interrater* or *interjudge reliability*. We discussed this in the last chapter in the context of interview assessment. The goal of this method is to demonstrate that independent observers can agree about their ratings or judgments of some particular aspect of the person's behavior.

Regardless of the particular kind of reliability in question, the goal is to show consistency in the data. A test must be able to provide evidence that the scores it yields are consistent over time and over examiners or are otherwise reliable (for example, split-half or equivalent-forms reliability). Without reliability, consistency, or stability of measurement, a test cannot be valid. However, the evidence of a test's reliability does not automatically imply validity. For example, a test involving the ability to discriminate among weights may produce scores that are highly reliable over time but still may not be a valid measure of intelligence.

Validity.   In general, *validity* refers to the extent to which an assessment technique measures what it is supposed to measure. Like reliability, there are several forms of validity. *Content validity* indicates the degree to which a group of test items actually covers the various aspects of the variable under study. For example, a test that purports to measure overall adjustment but which contains only items dealing with adjustment at work would not have content validity since it fails to include items dealing with adjustment at home, with friends, and adjustment in other contexts. *Predictive validity* is shown when test scores accurately predict some behavior or event in the future. A test designed to predict school success is valid if scores today reflect the school achievement behavior of children two years hence. *Concurrent validity* involves relating today's test scores to a concurrent criterion (for example, teachers' judgments of school success). Finally, there is *construct validity*. Here, validity is shown when test scores relate to other measures or behaviors in a logical, theoretically expected fashion. For example, suppose we have a test for alienation. Given the nature of alienation, a valid test of it might be expected to correlate with lack of vigor or even depression. If our test does that, our confidence in its construct validity is increased.

■ Definitions of Intelligence

Before dealing specifically with intelligence, we should distinguish among *ability, aptitude,* and *achievement*. As Sundberg (1977) states: "Ability is the currently available power to perform something and aptitude is the potential for performance after training. Both concepts have similarities with achievement, which is a measure of successful performance in the past" (p. 228). There can be considerable conceptual overlap between achievement and intelligence as measured on tests of intelligence. In one sense, intelligence tests are achievement tests, since they measure what one has learned (Anastasi, 1988). How the tests are used or how inferences are made from them determines whether they are tapping achievement or intelligence.

There is no universally accepted definition of intelligence. However, over the years, most have fallen into one of three classes:

1. Definitions that emphasize *adjustment or adaptation to the environment* — adaptability to new situations or the capacity to deal with a range of situations.
2. Definitions that focus on the *ability to learn* — on educability in the broad sense of the term.
3. Definitions that emphasize *abstract thinking* — the ability to use a wide range of concepts and both verbal and numerical symbols.

To illustrate a little of the long-standing diversity of definitions, consider the following examples:

> [Intelligence is] the aggregate or global capacity of the individual to act purposefully, to think rationally, and to deal effectively with his [sic] environment. (Wechsler, 1939, p. 3)
>
> As a concept, intelligence refers to the whole class of cognitive behaviors which reflect an individual's capacity to solve problems with insight, to adapt himself [sic] to new situations, to think abstractly, and to profit from his experience. (Robinson & Robinson, 1965, p. 15)
>
> . . . intelligence is expressed in terms of adaptive, goal-directed behavior. The subset of such behavior that is labeled "intelligent" seems to be determined in large part by cultural or societal norms. (Sternberg & Salter, 1982, p. 24)
>
> Intelligence is a very general mental capability that, among other things, involves the ability to reason, plan, solve problems, think abstractly, comprehend complex ideas, learn quickly and learn from experience. It is not merely book learning, a narrow academic skill, or test-taking smarts. Rather, it reflects a broader and deeper capability for comprehending our surroundings — "catching on," "making sense" of things, or "figuring out" what to do. (Arvey et al., 1994).

Certainly none of the foregoing classes or specific definitions of intelligence are mutually exclusive. Furthermore, several of the definitions given above contain distinct overtones of both social values and motivational elements. Beyond this, however, many definitions of intelligence are so broad or general as to be nearly useless. In many ways there is an overall sameness to tests of intelligence that belies their origins in diverse definitions. Thus, one begins to wonder whether definitions really make all that much difference or whether constructing IQ tests is just an atheoretical, pragmatic enterprise in which we generate items that we hope will correlate with some external criterion (such as school grades).

For some, the answer to all this ambiguity lies in prototype definitions. As Neisser (1979) put it:

> Our confidence that a *person* deserves to be called "intelligent" depends on that person's overall similarity to an imagined prototype, just as our confidence that some object is to be called "chair" depends on its similarity to prototypical chairs. There are no definitive criteria of intelligence, just as there are none for chairness; it is a fuzzy-edged concept to which many features are relevant. Two people may both be quite intelligent and yet have very few traits in common — they resemble the prototype along different dimensions. Thus, there is no such thing as chairness — resemblance is an external fact and not an internal essence. There can be no process-based definition of intelligence, because it is not a unitary quality. It is a resemblance between two individuals, one real and the other prototypical. (p. 185)

■ Theories of Intelligence

There have been many theoretical approaches to the understanding of intelligence, including psychometric theories, developmental theories, neuropsychological theories, and information processing theories (Kamphaus, 1993). Over the years there has been no dearth of either theories or controversies (Weinberg, 1989). We present only a brief overview of several leading theories here.

Historical views

Spearman (1927), the father of factor analysis, posited the existence of a g factor (general intelligence) and s factors (specific intelligence). The elements that tests have in common are represented by g, whereas the elements unique to a given test are s factors. Basically, however, Spearman's message, buttressed by factor analytic evidence, was that intelligence is a broad, generalized entity. However, Thurstone (1938) presented evidence (based on factor analysis of 57 separate tests administered to 240 participants) that there were really group factors at work rather than the almighty g factor. He described seven group factors that he labeled number, word fluency, verbal meaning, perceptual speed, space, reasoning, and memory (Thurstone's *Primary Mental Abilities*). Unfortunately, Spearman and Thurstone were using different methods of factor extraction (principal components versus principal factors, respectively) and rotation, which often result in different solutions even when applied to the same data set (Gould, 1981). Further, both men appeared to be guilty of reifying the factor(s) "discovered" by their respective analyses. The end result was an ongoing, and often acrimonious, debate between Spearman, Thurstone, and their followers.

Cattell's theory.   The work of Cattell (1987) emphasizes the centrality of g. At the same time, Cattell has offered a tentative list of 17 primary ability concepts. He has described two important second-order factors which seem to represent a partitioning of Spearman's g into two components. These are *fluid ability* (a person's genetically based intellectual capacity) and *crystallized ability* (the capacities tapped by the usual standardized intelligence test or the capacities that can be attributed to culture-based learning). Essentially, Cattell's approach might be described as a hierarchical model of intelligence. An example of this sort of model is shown schematically in Figure 7-2.

Guilford's theory.   The views of Guilford (1967) were quite different from those of Cattell, Spearman, Thurstone, and of most other psychometricians. Guilford proposed a *Structure of the Intellect model* and then employed a variety of statistical and factor analytic techniques to test it. Where other psychometric approaches generally attempted to infer the model from the data, Guilford used the model as a guide in generating data.

Guilford reasoned that the components of intelligence could be organized into three dimensions: operations, contents, and products. The *operations* are cognition, memory, divergent production (constructing logical alternatives), convergent

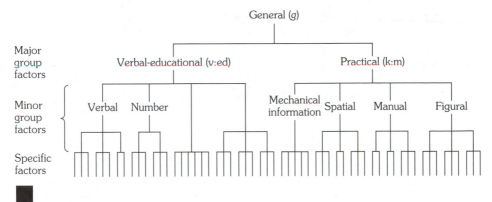

Figure 7-2
Model of a hierarchical organization of abilities.
SOURCE: Adapted from *The Structure of Human Abilities,* rev. ed., by P. E. Vernon, p. 22. Copyright © 1960 by Methuen & Co., Ltd. Reprinted by permission.

production (constructing logic-tight arguments), and evaluation. The *content* dimension involves the areas of information in which the operations are performed: figural, symbolic, semantic, and behavioral. When a particular mental operation is applied to a specific type of content, there are six possible *products:* units, classes, systems, relations, transformations, and implications. If all possible combinations are contemplated, the investigator arrives at 120 separate intellectual abilities. Perhaps the most widely held reservation about Guilford's approach is that it is a taxonomy or classification rather than a theory.

Recent developments

Traditionally, intelligence tests have been constructed to assess what we know or can do. Recent approaches, however, have begun to take on a highly cognitive or information-processing look. For example, some researchers try to describe a person's moment-by-moment attempts to solve a problem—from the moment a stimulus registers to the person's verbal or motor response. This is a more dynamic view of intelligence than the older theories of mental components. Some of these researchers have focused on speed of information processing and others on strategies of processing. Thus far, a number of levels of processing have been studied, including speed of processing, speed in making choices in response to stimuli, and speed with which individuals can extract various aspects of language from their long-term memory. But there are problems. As Gardner (1983) asks, is there a central processing mechanism for information? How do the processing elements change as the person develops? Are there general problem-solving skills or merely skills specific to certain ability areas? Perhaps time will tell.

Sternberg (1985; 1991) has proposed a *triarchic theory of intelligence.* He maintains that people function on the basis of three aspects of intelligence: componential, experiential, and contextual. This approach de-emphasizes speed and accuracy of performance. Instead, the emphasis is on planning responses and monitoring them. The *componential* aspect refers to analytical thinking; high scores would characterize the person who is a good test-taker. The *experiential* aspect relates to creative thinking and characterizes the person who can take separate elements of experience and combine them insightfully. Finally, the *contextual* aspect is seen in the person who is street-smart: one who knows how to play the game and can successfully manipulate the environment. According to Sternberg, a person's performance is governed by these three aspects of intelligence. Other investigators are particularly interested in social competence as an important aspect of intelligence (Sternberg & Wagner, 1986). But whether all the foregoing accounts for individual differences or is just a theory of cognition is debatable.

Gardner (1983) has described a *theory of multiple intelligences*. Human intellectual competence involves a set of problem-solving skills that enable the person to resolve problems or difficulties that sometimes result in the potential for acquiring new information. Gardner suggests that there is a family of six intelligences: linguistic, musical, logical-mathematical, spatial, bodily kinesthetic, and personal. For example, the personal refers both to access to one's own feeling life and the ability to notice and make distinctions among other individuals.

Although Spearman, Thurstone, and others may seem to have given way to Cattell, Guilford, or Gardner, clinicians' day-to-day use of tests suggests that they have not really outgrown the *g* factor of Spearman or the group factors of Thurstone. The whole notion of a single IQ score that will represent the individual's intelligence strongly implies that we are trying to discover how much *g* the person has. At the same time, however, most current intelligence tests are composed of subtests, so that the total IQ represents some average of subtest scores. This implies that, to some extent at least, clinicians have also accepted Thurstone's group factors. They seem to want to identify and quantify how much intelligence the person has, yet they cannot escape the belief that intelligence is somehow patterned — that two people may have the same overall IQ score and still differ in specific abilities. Thus, it would appear that practicing clinicians think more in line with Spearman or Thurstone and are as yet little affected by the recent information-processing developments.

■ The IQ and Its Meaning

How is intelligence quantified? The two indices employed most frequently over the years have been the ratio IQ and the deviation IQ.

Ratio IQ

Binet regarded the *mental age* (MA) as an index of mental performance. Each item successfully passed on a Binet test signified so many months' credit. At the conclusion of the test, the items passed were added up and the MA emerged. Thus, there was nothing magical about an MA — all it meant was that *X* number of items had been passed. Subsequently, Stern (1938) developed the concept of *intelligence quotient* (IQ) to circumvent several problems that had arisen in using the difference between the *chronological age* (CA) and the MA to express deviance. At first glance, two children, one with an MA of 4 years and a CA of 5 years and another with an MA of 14 years and a CA of 15 years, would seem to be equally deficient. However, this is not the case, since intellectual growth is much more rapid at younger age levels. Therefore, even though there is only a one-year discrepancy between the MA and the CA of both children, the younger child is actually more deviant than the older one. The IQ notion, however, enables us to perform the following computation:

$$IQ = MA/CA \times 100$$

As a result, we find that our 15-year-old has an IQ of 93, whereas the 5-year-old has an IQ of 80. This better reflects the reality of more rapid intellectual growth at younger ages.

Another point worth noting is that measurement of intelligence suffers from the fact that clinicians cannot really be sure that they are dealing with equal-interval measurement. They cannot be sure that an IQ of 50 is really twice as much as an IQ of 25 or that their scale has an absolute zero point. They cannot add and subtract IQs. All they can do is state that a person with an IQ of 50 is brighter than a person with an IQ of 25. This should serve as a reminder that IQs and MAs are merely scores—nothing more.

Deviation IQ

Although initially appealing, the ratio IQ is significantly limited in its application to older age groups. The reason is that a consistent mental age (MA) score (even if it is very high) accompanied by an increasing chronological age (CA) score will result in a lower IQ. Therefore, there may be the appearance that IQ has *decreased* over time when, in fact, the person's intellectual ability has been maintained over time.

Wechsler introduced the concept of *deviation IQ* to deal with this problem. A deviation IQ assumes that intelligence is normally distributed throughout the population, and it involves the comparison of an individual's performance on an IQ test with that of members of the same age group. Thus, the same IQ score means similar things for two individuals even though they may be markedly different in age (for example, a 22-year-old versus an 80-year-old). In both cases, an IQ of 100 indicates an average level of intellectual ability for that age group.

Correlates of the IQ

Whether or not intelligence tests are valid depends on how we define intelligence. If we are looking for some global entity that transcends school success or related achievements, the answer is probably no. But if we define intelligence mainly as a predictor of success in school, then the answer is likely to be yes.

An important thing to remember is that, whether we define intelligence in terms of *g,* separate abilities, or hierarchical relationships among factors, society ultimately decides which abilities will be valued, rewarded, and nurtured. Perhaps this is why all intelligence tests seem so much alike: they are designed to predict what society values. In this society, the skills that have value are verbal ability, reasoning, reading, information acquisition, analytic ability, and so on.

School success. In general, IQs have been shown to relate substantially both to success in school and to achievement tests that measure what has been learned (Herrnstein & Murray, 1994; Kamphaus, 1993). It does seem apparent that success in school is related to a host of variables—motivation, teacher expectations, cultural background, and attitudes of parents, to name a few. Clinicians are then confronted with the very difficult task of sorting out those variables. When success or failure in school occurs, is this because of intelligence, motivation, cultural background, or what? Any behavior is complexly determined by many variables other than just general or specific intelligence. But the relationship between IQ scores and achievement is so high that many have suggested that intelligence tests might be best interpreted as a type of achievement test (Anastasi, 1988; Kaufman, 1990).

Occupational status and success. Since level of education would seem to be, in general, a strong determinant of the kind of job a person can obtain, it will come as no surprise to learn that IQ and occupational status are related. This seems to be true whether occupational status is defined in terms of income, rated prestige, or social prestige (Brody & Brody, 1976). Interestingly, however, intelligence scores appear to be strong predictors of job performance (Hunter & Hunter, 1984); IQ scores outperform predictors like biographical data, reference checks, education, and college grades. However, once entry to a profession has been gained, the degree of intelligence may not separate the more eminent from the less eminent (Matarazzo, 1972; Roe, 1953). The apparent reason for this is that some minimum level of ability is necessary in order to achieve entry to or minimal performance in a given occupation (though this may be debatable). Once an individual gains entry, however, the degree of subsequent success may be more a function of nonintellectual factors.

Heritability of intelligence

In contrast to the situation 30 or 40 years ago, almost all psychologists now acknowledge that intelligence is influenced, at least in part, by genetic factors (Snyderman & Rothman, 1990). The reason for this reversal of opinion is the large body of empirical evidence provided by *behavioral genetics* studies over the last several decades (McGue, Bouchard, Iacono, & Lykken, 1993). Box 7-2 presents a brief overview of the methods of behavioral genetics.

A landmark review (Bouchard & McGue, 1981) summarizes many of these behavioral genetics studies of intelligence. Table 7-3 presents some of these data. As can be seen, similarity in intelligence appears to be a function of the amount of genetic material shared (that is, monozygotic twins are more similar in intelligence than dizygotic twins or siblings). Further, it is notable that this pattern holds true in reared-apart biological relatives. As McGue, Bouchard, Iacono, and Lykken (1993) note:

> When taken in aggregate, twin, family, and adoption studies of IQ provide a demonstration of the existence of genetic influences on IQ as good as can be achieved in the behavioral sciences with nonexperimental methods. Without positing the existence of genetic influences, it simply is not possible to give a credible account for the

Box 7-2
Behavioral genetics

Behavioral genetics refers to a research specialty in which both genetic and environmental influences on the development of behavior are evaluated. Proteins are produced and regulated by genetic codes, and proteins interact with physiological intermediaries (for example, hormones, neurotransmitters, and structural properties of the nervous system) to produce behavior (Plomin, DeFries, & McClearn, 1990). The genetic makeup of an individual, passed down from biological parents, is referred to as *genotype,* and this is fixed at birth. In contrast, *phenotype* refers to observable characteristics of an individual, and this can change. For example, intelligence or mental disorders refer to phenotypic characteristics that may change over time. The phenotype is a product of the genotype and the environment.

One of the most powerful designs (in the explanatory sense) that is employed in behavioral genetics is the twin method. Here, both *monozygotic (MZ),* or genetically identical, twins and *dizygotic (DZ)* twins (those who share about 50% of their genetic material) are compared on the behavior or characteristic of interest. The similarity among twin pairs is typically presented in the form of a *concordance rate,* or similarity index. In its simplest form, a concordance rate is the percentage of instances across all twin pairs in which both twins exhibit similar behaviors or characteristics. Because MZ twins are genetically identical and DZ twins share only about 50% of their genetic material, a concordance rate or similarity index for the MZ twin sample that is significantly greater than that for the DZ twin sample suggests that genetic influences play an important role in the development of that set of behaviors or features.

Because MZ twins are identical, however, and if reared together may be treated more similarly than DZ twins, one could argue that the higher concordance rate for MZ twins may have as much to do with environmental influences as genetic influences. Therefore, an even more informative method used in behavioral genetic studies involves sampling *MZ twins reared together* (MZT); *MZ twins reared apart* (MZA), separated from each other shortly after birth; *DZ twins reared together* (DZT); and *DZ twins reared apart* (DZA). In this way, it is easier to tease apart genetic and environmental influences. For example, the following findings would suggest genetic influences in the manifestation of the behaviors or features under study: (1) the concordance rates for MZT and MZA twins are significantly greater than those for DZT and DZA twins, respectively; (2) the concordance rate for MZA twins approaches that of MZT twins; and (3) the concordance rate of DZA twins approaches that of DZT twins. These findings would suggest that genetics play an important role because similarity-concordance is a function of the amount of genetic material shared and that being raised in different environments does not have an appreciable effect on similarity.

We have presented only a brief and rather simplistic overview of behavioral genetics. Interest in this field has waxed and waned over the years, and, at times, the field has been the target of attacks from a variety of groups (Plomin et al., 1990). However, it is important to keep in mind several things. First, concordance rates or similarity indices of less than 100% (or 1.00) necessarily implicate environmental influences. Therefore, behavioral genetics methods are tools for identifying and quantifying environmental as well as genetic factors in behavior. Second, finding that a behavior or characteristic is genetically influenced does not mean that it is immutable or unchangeable—genetics and the environment interact in complex ways to produce behavior.

Table 7-3
Average familial IQ correlations.

Relationship	Weighted Average Correlation	Number of Pairs
Reared-together biological relatives		
MZ twins	0.86	4,672
DZ twins	0.60	5,546
Siblings	0.47	26,473
Parent offspring	0.42	8,433
Half-siblings	0.31	200
Cousins	0.15	1,176
Reared-apart biological relatives		
MZ twins	0.72	65
Siblings	0.24	203
Parent offspring	0.22	814
Reared-together nonbiological relatives		
Siblings	0.32	714
Adoptive parent offspring	0.19	1,397

Note: MZ = monozygotic; DZ = dizygotic. Weighted average correlation was determined using sample-sized weighted average of *z* transformations.

SOURCE: From "Familial Studies of Intelligence: A Review" by T. J. Bouchard, Jr., and M. McGue, 1981, *Science, 250*, p. 1056. Copyright © 1981 by the American Association for the Advancement of Science. Reprinted by permission.

consistently greater IQ similarity among monozygotic (MZ) twins than among like-sex dizygotic (DZ) twins, the significant IQ correlations among biological relatives even when they are reared apart, and the strong association between the magnitude of familial IQ correlation and the degree of genetic relatedness. (p. 60)

Recent estimates of the percentage of IQ variance associated with genetic factors range from 51% (Chipeur, Rovine, & Plomin, 1990) to 81% (Pederson, Plomin, Nesselroade, & McClearn, 1992). In general, it appears that IQ heritability estimates vary as a function of the age of the sample; these estimates are maximal in older age groups (McGue et al., 1993).

Given the evidence that intelligence scores are influenced by genetic factors, does this mean that IQ is not malleable? No. This is the source of much confusion and controversy. Recall that heritability estimates are *not* 100%, which suggests that the environment plays some role in the development of intelligence. As McGue et al. (1993) state, behavioral genetics studies of IQ "strongly implicate the existence of environmental influences: The correlation among reared-together MZ twins is less than unity; biological relatives who were reared together are more similar than biological relatives who were reared apart; and there is a significant correlation between the IQs of nonbiologically related but reared-together relatives" (p. 60-61).

Even if heritability estimates were 100%, this does not rule out the possibility that IQ scores may change. Some "genetically determined" traits like height can be influenced by environmental circumstances, and genetic disorders can be controlled or even cured by environmental intervention (Kamphaus, 1993). Although some short-term gains or changes have been noted, in general the research examining the efficacy of psychosocial interventions for improving IQ scores has been mixed (Kamphaus, 1993). Despite these sometimes disappointing results, the general notion that favorable environments should be provided so as to allow individuals to realize their "innate potential" seems both a plausible and a worthy goal (see Box 7-3).

It is worth reiterating that genetic versus environmental influences are not either-or choices. Clearly, both play some role in the development and expression of intelligence. Behavioral geneticists *do not* claim that environment plays no role in IQ — rather, their data clearly implicate environmental factors and should serve as a stimulus for more research on the nature and effect of these factors on the development of intelligence.

Stability of IQ scores

As indicated above, one method of assessing the reliability of a measure is by computing a test-retest correlation. This gives us a sense of how stable scores are over time. As noted by Schuerger and Witt (1989), IQ scores tend to be less stable for young children and more stable for adults. Further, and not too surprisingly, a longer test-retest interval (for example, one year versus ten years) results in lower reliability-stability estimates. Figure 7-3 depicts the stability of IQ scores as a function of age.

The implication of these findings is clear. Clinicians cannot assume that a single IQ test score will accurately characterize an individual's level of intelligence

■

Box 7-3
The concept of heritability

The evergreens in A vary in height. The degree to which they vary from each other is called the variance. What produces this variance? Some is probably due to genetics. To find out how much, we equate environmental conditions such as soil, water, and sunlight (indicated by different shadings of the ground). We now take a random group of seedlings chosen from A. We plant them in this equated environment (B) and wait patiently until they mature. We note that the size variation in B is less than it was in A. This reflects the fact that environmental conditions in B are equal for all the trees so that any environmental sources of variance have been eliminated. The remaining variance in B is entirely produced by genetic factors. Therefore, the heritability of height for A is the variance in B (the variation attributable to genetic factors) divided by the variance in A (the total variation in the population).

SOURCE: Adapted from *Psychology* by Henry Gleitman, by permission of W. W. Norton & Company, Inc. Copyright © 1981 by W. W. Norton & Company, Inc.

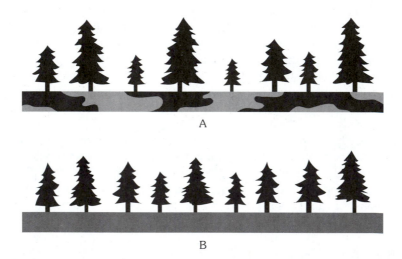

A

B

throughout his or her life span. IQ scores do tend to change, and this is especially true for young children. For this reason, clinicians often describe the individual's "present level of intellectual functioning" in their test reports. A variety of influences (for example, illness, motivational and emotional changes, and so on) may affect an individual's score.

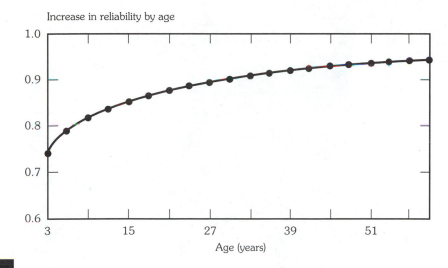

Increase in reliability by age

Figure 7-3

Graph depicting the relationship between age and stability. SOURCE: From "The Temporal Stability of Individually Tested Intelligence," by J. M. Schuerger and A. C. Witt, 1989, *Journal of Clinical Psychology, 45,* p. 300. Copyright © 1989 by Clinical Psychology Publishing Co., Inc. Reprinted by permission.

The Clinical Assessment of Intelligence

In this section, we will briefly describe several of the most frequently employed intelligence tests for children and adults.

The Stanford-Binet scales

For many years, the Binet scales were the preferred tests. They underwent many revisions after Binet's work in 1905. There was Terman's revision in 1916 and then the 1937 revised Stanford-Binet (Terman & Merrill, 1937). The 1960 version of the Stanford-Binet (Terman & Merrill, 1960) gave way to a 1972 test kit with revised norms. Recently, a major revision of the scale appeared, the *Stanford-Binet Fourth Edition* (Thorndike, Hagen, & Sattler, 1986).

Description. Until this latest revision, the Stanford-Binet was notable for being an age scale. It had 20 age levels beginning at Year II and proceeding through Superior Adult Level III. There were six items at each level. Each item passed was converted into one or two months of mental age credit (depending upon whether it was located before or after Year Level V).

The 1986 version, however, is radically different. It is based on a hierarchical model of intelligence. The *Stanford-Binet Fourth Edition* (SB-4) contains four general classes of items, and each class consists of several kinds of subtests:

Figure 7-4
The Stanford-Binet Intelligence Scale. *Photograph by courtesy of the Riverside Publishing Company, Chicago, IL*

1. *Verbal reasoning:* vocabulary, comprehension, absurdities, verbal relations
2. *Quantitative reasoning:* quantitative, number series, equation building
3. *Abstract and visual reasoning:* pattern analysis, copying, matrices, paper folding and cutting
4. *Short-term memory:* bead memory, memory for sentences, memory for digits, memory for objects

Each subtest is composed of items at varying levels of difficulty from age two to adulthood. This revision uses an adaptive testing procedure called *multistage testing*. This means that the examiner first gives the vocabulary test to determine the entry point (that is, which item to start with) for each remaining subtest. This initial estimate of ability will enable a more appropriate entry or starting point on subsequent subtests and is likely to result in a more efficient testing versus relying exclusively on chronological age as a guide for a starting point. Thus, not all examinees of the same age are given the same items. Short forms or abbreviated versions of the SB-4 are discussed in the manual; however, more research on the equivalency of the full SB-4 and the abbreviated versions is needed (Kamphaus, 1993).

Standardization. Final standardization of the SB-4 included 5013 participants sampled according to geographic region, community size, ethnic group, age group, and gender using 1980 U.S. Census figures. Socioeconomic status was considered as well.

Items for testing were selected according to how well they seemed to measure the four listed classes. Those items that led to unreliable scoring, showed ethnic or gender bias, or were not appropriate for a wide range of age groups were dropped.

Reliability and validity.   The SB-4 manual (Thorndike et al., 1986) indicates general support for the reliability of the composite score and subtest scores. Internal consistency reliabilities were basically in the .80s and .90s. Test-retest reliabilities for intervals of two to eight months were (for preschoolers) mostly in the .70s, with a few in the .80s and .90s; but a few correlations for specific subtests were disappointingly low.

As for the validity of SB-4 composite scores, a variety of supportive evidence has been obtained (Laurent, Swerdlik, & Ryburn, 1992; Thorndike et al., 1986). For example, the correlation between SB-4 scores and scores on the 1972 Stanford-Binet were .81. Correlations between the SB-4 and several Wechsler scales (described next) were .83 for children, .80 for preschoolers, and .91 for adults. Correlations among subtests of the SB-4 and the Wechsler scales were also substantial. Therefore, using the criterion of relationship to other accepted tests of intelligence, the validity of the new Stanford-Binet is supported.

Finally, it was determined that the IQ scores of gifted children were significantly above the means of the standardization sample. Further, learning disabled and mentally retarded participants produced scores significantly below those of the standardization sample. All in all, the validity of the SB-4 looks promising. However, it should be noted that there has been only mixed support for the four factors originally proposed by the test authors that underlie SB-4 scores (Laurent, Swerdlik, & Ryburn, 1992).

The Wechsler scales

Earlier versions of the Stanford-Binet had a number of disadvantages that led David Wechsler in 1939 to develop the Wechsler-Bellevue Intelligence Scale. This was a test designed for adults—one that would offer items whose content was more appropriate for and more motivating to adults than the school-oriented Binet. In contrast to the Stanford-Binet, whose items were arranged in age levels, the Wechsler-Bellevue Intelligence Scale grouped its items into subtests. For example, all arithmetic items were put into one subtest and arranged in order of increasing difficulty. In addition, there was a Performance scale and a Verbal scale (consisting of five and six subtests, respectively). A separate IQ for each scale could be calculated, along with a Full-Scale IQ. This systematic inclusion of performance items helped remedy the overemphasis on verbal skills that limited the utility of the earlier Stanford-Binet with special populations.

Wechsler employed the deviation IQ concept. As described earlier, this approach assumes that intelligence is normally distributed and dictates that diagnosticians compare individuals with their age peers. In effect, this method compares the performance of a 15-year-old with that of other 15-year-olds, which statistically establishes an IQ of 100 as the mean for each age group. As a result, an IQ of 100 for any person means the same thing, regardless of the age group involved.

Figure 7-5
David Wechsler published the Wechsler-Bellevue Intelligence Scale in 1939. The adult
and children's versions of this test have become the most widely used techniques
to assess intellectual functioning. *Stock Montage, Inc., Chicago*

The WAIS-R

Description.   In 1955, a revision of the Wechsler-Bellevue appeared—
the *Wechsler Adult Intelligent Scale* (WAIS). In 1981, a further revision appeared—the *WAIS-R*. The first six subtests listed below constitute the Verbal
scale, whereas subtests seven through eleven make up the Performance scale.

1. *Information.* There are 29 items that tap knowledge an individual would be expected to have acquired as a result of everyday living and cultural interactions.
2. *Comprehension.* The 16 items of this subtest require the examinee to explain why certain procedures are followed, to interpret proverbs, and to determine what should be done in a given situation. The items measure common sense and practical judgment in solving a problem.
3. *Arithmetic.* Here there are 14 items similar to arithmetic problems that appear in most elementary-school textbooks. The items are administered orally.
4. *Similarities.* This subtest consists of 14 items for which the examinee must
   explain how two objects are alike. These items require the basic ability to form
   abstractions and develop concepts.
5. *Digit Span.* This subtest is a measure of short-term memory and attention.
   Two sets of digits are read aloud by the examiner. For the first list, the ex-

aminee must repeat the digits in the order that they were read. For the second list, the digits must be repeated backward.

6. *Vocabulary.* Here the examinee must define 35 words that increase in difficulty. This is, perhaps, the best single verbal subtest. It correlates highly with Full-Scale IQs, and some feel that it comes close to measuring what is usually termed *g*.

7. *Digit Symbol.* This is a code-substitution task that requires the examinee to fill in the blanks under a long series of numbers with the help of a key. The subtest requires the examinee to work in a direct, single-minded fashion.

8. *Picture Completion.* There are 20 cards in this subtest, each with a picture that has a part missing. The examinee must identify the missing part. This requires concentration and the ability to note details and incongruities.

9. *Block Design.* The examinee must assemble blocks to match the designs on a set of cards. The task involves visual-motor coordination and analytic synthesizing ability.

10. *Picture Arrangement.* Several sets of cartoons must be arranged in a proper sequence so they tell a coherent story. This subtest measures the ability to judge, anticipate, and plan ahead.

11. *Object Assembly.* Here four puzzles must be assembled. The ability to visualize a whole from its parts and to plan ahead is required, along with a certain degree of visual-motor coordination.

Over the years, many abbreviated Wechsler scales have been described. Some consist of two subtests; others involve three to seven. The seven-subtest short form has garnered the most empirical support (Benedict, Schretlen, & Bobholz, 1992). The use of these short forms is legitimate for research purposes or when a rough index or quick check of IQ is needed (Silverstein, 1990). However, if important decisions hinge on the testing outcome, short forms are definitely not the best choice.

Figure 7-6
Simulated item from the WAIS-R Picture Completion subtest. SOURCE: Reproduced by permission of The Psychological Corporation.

Standardization.   Based upon U.S. Census data, the WAIS-R was re-standardized using a sample of 1880 adults. There were equal numbers of men and women in each of nine age groups ranging from age 16 to 74 years old, and the sample was stratified according to age, sex, race, geographic region, occupation, education, and rural-urban residence. All testing was carried out between 1976 and 1980. Recently, further standardization has been completed for people 75 years and older (Ryan, Paolo, & Brungardt, 1990).

Reliability and validity.   Full-Scale, Performance, and Verbal IQ odd-even (split-half) reliability coefficients range from .93 to .97, thus demonstrating good internal consistency. Test-retest reliabilities over intervals of two to seven weeks range from .72 to .94 for the various subtests. No new validity data are offered in the WAIS-R manual, but the validity data on the older WAIS are largely summarized by Matarazzo (1972). For example, white-collar workers tend to achieve higher verbal scores than performance scores, whereas for skilled workers this is reversed. Correlations as high as .50 have been reported between Verbal IQs and college grades. The WAIS correlates well with many other intelligence tests, including the old Stanford-Binet — sometimes the correlation is as high as .80 when the samples are heterogeneous. Although factor analyses of the WAIS are somewhat variable in their conclusions (Anastasi, 1988), the subtests have enough in common to suggest the existence of a single general factor. In addition, there appear to be three group factors: verbal comprehension, perceptual organization, and freedom from distractibility (Burton, Ryan, Paolo, & Mittenberg, 1994). Finally, Parker, Hanson, and Hunsley (1988), in a meta-analytic review of research on the WAIS, note that it shows acceptable stability, reliability, and validity.

A Brief Case Report: Intellectual Evaluation

The following brief excerpt is from a report prepared by a clinical psychology intern. It was written in response to a referral by a psychiatrist who requested that his patient be evaluated for the presence of a learning disability and for the presence of a substance-induced cognitive disorder. Here we will focus primarily on the WAIS-R test results and interpretation.

Patient: Smith, Brad (Fictitious name)

Age: 17 years

Grade: 11th

Dates Tested: 5/11/95, 5/12/95

Test Behavior: The patient was cooperative with all aspects of the testing, working diligently on all tasks that were presented. The patient reported that he believed his school work had been adversely affected by his polysubstance abuse over the last year. He reported that he had not used any substances in the last two months.

Intellectual Functioning: Based on his WAIS-R scores, the patient is currently functioning in the Average range of intelligence with a Full-Scale IQ of 109. There was a significant discrepancy between his Verbal IQ (97) and his Performance IQ (128), placing him in the Average and Superior ranges, respectively. There was variability both between and within individual subtests. His scores on the various subtests ranged from the Below Average to the Superior levels, with scaled scores as indicated below:

Verbal		*Performance*	
Information	6	Picture Completion	17
Digit Span	10	Picture Arrangement	12
Vocabulary	7	Block Design	12
Arithmetic	7	Object Assembly	13
Comprehension	8	Digit Symbol	9
Similarities	10		

Verbal IQ   = 97
Performance IQ = 128
Full-Scale IQ   = 109

In general, the patient's verbal skills appear weaker than his visual-spatial skills. His pattern of scores indicates relative weaknesses in general fund of information, vocabulary, and mental arithmetic. These weaknesses are notable because they are consistent with reports of his academic difficulties.

The WISC-III

The *Wechsler Intelligence Scale for Children* (WISC) was first developed in 1949, revised in 1974 (WISC-R), and revised again in 1991 (Wechsler, 1991). This most recent revision, known as the *WISC-III*, is appropriate for children ages 6 through 16 years. It consists of ten mandatory and three supplementary subtests. As with its predecessors, the WISC-III in many ways is a downward extension of the WAIS-R.

Description.   As in the WAIS-R, the WISC-III contains both Verbal and Performance subscales. The Verbal subtests include: information, similarities, arithmetic, vocabulary, and comprehension; digit span is the supplementary Verbal subtest. The Performance subtests include: picture completion, picture arrangement, block design, object assembly, and coding; mazes and symbol search are the two supplementary Performance subtests. Verbal and Performance IQs are calculated, as is an overall Full-Scale IQ.

Several new *WISC-III* features are noteworthy: the Symbol Search optional subtest is new, Picture Completion is now the first subtest to be administered to examinees, and improvements in subtest content, administration, and scoring have been developed (Wechsler, 1991).

Standardization.   Normative data for the WISC-III were obtained from a standardization sample of 2200 cases that was representative of the United States population of children. Using the 1988 U. S. Census data, cases were selected to represent (proportionally) the U. S. population of children according to race and ethnicity, geographic region, and parent education. The sample included 200 children (100 girls and 100 boys) in each of 11 age groups (that is, ages 6 to 16 years).

Reliability and validity. Wechsler (1991) reported that the average (across age groups) split-half reliabilities for the Verbal, Performance, and Full-Scale of the WISC-III were .95, .91, and .96, respectively. Further, the average split-half reliabilities for the individual subtests ranged from .69 to .87. The test-retest reliabilities (median interval between testings = 23 days) across three different age groups were fairly high, with the exception of the Mazes subtest (Wechsler, 1991). Examiners should keep in mind that this subtest's scores are likely to be unstable over time. As for validity, WISC-III scores are highly correlated with scores from other measures of intelligence (for example, the WISC-R, WAIS-R, and SB-4). Further, scores from the WISC-R, and presumably the WISC-III, have been shown to be predictive of academic achievement.

Finally, several factor analytic studies have been conducted using WISC-III scores. Previous factor analyses of WISC-R scores have suggested a three-factor structure: verbal comprehension, perceptual organization, and freedom from distractibility. However, results supporting this third factor have been mixed (Wechsler, 1991). Interestingly, factor analyses reported in the WISC-III manual suggest a *four*-factor solution for WISC-III scores: verbal comprehension, perceptual organization, freedom from distractibility, and processing speed. The latter two are quite different from the factors identified using the WISC-R. To date, the validity and utility of these latter two factors remains to be demonstrated (Kamphaus, 1993).

■ The Clinical Use of Intelligence Tests

In the preceding sections we have described several of the more commonly employed intelligence tests. Now it is time to take a closer look at how such tests are employed in the clinical setting.

The estimation of general intellectual level

The most obvious use of an intelligence test is as a means for arriving at an estimate of the patient's general intellectual level. Often the goal is the determination of how much general intelligence (*g*) a given person possesses. Frequently, the question is stated a bit differently—for example, What is the patient's intellectual potential? Posing the question in this way suggests that perhaps the person is not functioning as well as his or her potential would indicate. The potential can form a baseline against which to measure current achievements, thus providing information about the patient's current level of functioning.

Many pitfalls and fallacies are associated with the pursuit of these goals. The following is an example.

The Case of Harold

Harold was being routinely evaluated prior to transfer to a special class for advanced junior high school students. Rather surprisingly, his Full-Scale WISC-III IQ turned out to be 107. This score was in the average range but below the cutting point for admission to the class. It was also considerably below what his teachers had estimated, based on his classroom performance. A closer look at his subtest scores revealed that his performances on block design, coding, and object assembly were significantly below those on the other subtests. A follow-up interview with Harold was quite revealing. Since early childhood he had suffered from muscular weakness in both arms and hands. This weakness prevented him from making fine, quick motor responses. However, he had developed a number of clever compensations to prevent others from guessing his limitation. For example, what had appeared to be slow, deliberate, even confused responses on block design were really not that at all. He was feigning confusion in order to mask his difficulty with fine motor functions. Clearly, then, Harold's IQ score had been unduly affected by a motor weakness that had nothing to do with his ability to perform intellectually.

This example is but the tip of the iceberg. It does suggest, however, that obtaining an IQ is not the end of a clinician's task. It is but the beginning. The IQ score must be interpreted — only by knowledge of the patient's learning history and by observations made during the testing situation can that score be placed in an appropriate interpretive context and adequately evaluated (Oakland & Glutting, 1990).

Prediction of academic success
As mentioned previously, there are data that demonstrate a relationship between intelligence test scores and school success (Kamphaus, 1993). To the extent that intelligence should logically reflect the capacity to do well in school, we are justified in expecting intelligence tests to predict school success. Not everyone, of course, would equate intelligence with scholastic aptitude; however, the fact remains that a major function of intelligence tests is to predict school performance. At the same time, it is important to remember that intelligence and academic success are not conceptually identical.

The appraisal of style
As we noted above, what is significant is not only whether the client succeeds or fails on particular test items but also how that success or failure occurs. One of the major values of individual intelligence tests is that they permit the observation of the client or patient at work. Such observations can help greatly in interpreting an IQ. For example, did this child do as well as possible? Was there failure avoidance? Did the child struggle with most items, or was there easy success? Was the child unmotivated, and could this have detracted from the child's performance? Such questions and the ensuing interpretations breathe life into an otherwise inert IQ score.

The following simulated questions from the WAIS-R and a hypothetical patient's responses to them are examples of the data that can be obtained beyond the sheer correctness or incorrectness of a response:

Query: Who wrote *Paradise Lost?* (Information subtest)
Answer: Probably a Catholic. But since the Pope began changing things around, they retitled it.

Query: What is the advantage of keeping money in a bank? (Comprehension subtest)

Answer: There isn't. There's so damn many crooks. But they'll get theirs someday.

Query: In what ways are a lion and a tiger alike? (Similarities subtest)

Answer: Well, now, that's a long story. Do they look alike? They really can't breed together, you know.

(These simulated items were provided courtesy of The Psychological Corporation, New York. The answers are based upon responses to actual items.)

Clinicians have in fact ventured considerably beyond making a few limited personality inferences that would inject some added meaning into IQs. They sometimes have based mental disorder diagnoses on the Binet and Wechsler scales. By examining patterns of scores (so-called intertest scatter), it was believed that diagnostic labels could be applied to patients (for example, schizophrenia, depression, and so on). But over the years, rarely could the results of a given study purporting to show the validity of these interpretations of intertest scatter be replicated. Diagnoses then, cannot be reliably inferred from patterns of test performance (Piedmont, Sokolove, & Fleming, 1989).

Some final observations and conclusions

In the preceding pages we have discussed many facets of the assessment of intelligence. Definitions and theories of intelligence, descriptions of intelligence tests, and a brief discussion of the uses of intelligence tests have all been taken up. We can now make some general concluding statements.

An abstraction. Since the IQ does not signify that a person will perform in all situations at a constant level, clinicians speak of "present functioning" rather than innate potential. Many would argue that intelligence, like an attitude, is not a thing; rather, it is an abstraction that may enable clinicians to accurately predict certain behaviors. If a clinician observes that Charles gets A's in class, is highly regarded by his instructors, and solves problems faster than his peers, he or she will probably conclude that Charles is intelligent. The clinician will have abstracted a common element of Charles's behavior in several situations in order to reach that conclusion. The clinician can now employ that abstraction to predict that Charles will again be successful in related future situations. However, despite the notion that intelligence is an abstraction rather than an entity located in a specific region of the brain, and despite the difficulties in distinguishing between what people cannot do and what they choose not to do, most tend to believe that a true IQ exists and that intelligence tests are the best way to assess this.

The role of the situation. Over the years, research has demonstrated the role of situational factors and examiner effects on vulnerable groups such as patients, young children, minorities, and others (for example, Masling, 1960; Sattler, 1970). The age, socioeconomic status, professional level, and even appearance of the examiner can play a role as can similar qualities in the person being tested (Babad, Mann, & Mar-Hayim, 1975). Some have also claimed that African American children get lower IQs when tested by white examiners (Sattler,

1970), whereas other research seems less clear about this point (for example, Sattler & Gwynne, 1982). The examiner's expectations about a person's abilities can also have an effect—the so-called self-fulfilling prophecy (Rosenthal, 1966). And then coaching, practice, and the overall test sophistication of the examinee may affect scores (Anastasi, 1988).

As Flaugher (1978) argues, however, it is a mistake to believe that a test that is unbiased or free of situational effects will automatically result in the same performance level for all groups. A child from a background where standard English is not used may well have trouble coping with the highly verbal nature of the Binet. Such children may show lower test scores than will other children. Although clinicians should be wary of inferring too much about native ability from such scores, the fact remains that the scores may reflect what will later happen in school. The less verbal children may achieve lower grades just as they received lower IQ scores, and for the same reasons. As Green (1978) indicates, with regard to ethnic differences in average test scores, the culprit is not so much test bias as it is a reflection of different cultural backgrounds. We'll have more to say about the issue of test bias in Chapter 8.

Generality versus specificity of measurement. Given all the caveats, qualifications, and disclaimers, the reader may wonder why clinical psychologists use general tests of intelligence at all. In many ways, this question can be reduced to cost-benefit terms. If clinicians are especially pressed for time, or if the diagnostic issues do not particularly revolve around intellectual matters, then they would probably be better advised to either skip such general tests or to employ a short form.

But it is important to recognize exactly what a general test of intellectual functioning such as a Binet or a Wechsler can do. It can provide a broad, general index of intellectual functioning across a range of situations. Because the Full-Scale IQ is a general index, it may predict moderately well for many diverse situations that depend significantly upon intellectual skills. But it may not predict to any specific situation at an acceptable level. Thus, if the goal is solely to predict scholastic success in situation Y, then clinicians would be better advised to use a more specific measure than a Wechsler test or at least to use a Wechsler test whose subtests contain elements similar to the performance they hope to predict. Often, however, goals may be somewhat different. The clinician may need a basis for choosing remedial or therapeutic options. By using standardized procedures, the clinical psychologist can compare the patient with similar persons who have performed in the same situation.

■ Focus Questions

1. What is intelligence, and what are some of the problems we face in measuring this construct?
2. What is the relationship between intelligence and school success as well as between intelligence and occupational status and success?
3. What do studies suggest regarding the genetic versus environmental influence on intelligence?

4. How are the Stanford-Binet Fourth Edition (SB-4) and Wechsler scales (WAIS-R, WISC-III) similar? How are they different?
5. How are intelligence tests used in a clinical situation? What are some of the limitations regarding their use in these situations?

■ Key Terms

behavioral genetics

chronological age

concordance rate

concurrent validity

construct validity

content validity

crystallized ability

deviation IQ

dizygotic (DZ) twins

equivalent-forms reliability

fluid ability

g

genotype

intelligence

intelligence quotient

internal consistency reliability

interrater or interjudge reliability

mental age

monozygotic (MZ) twins

phenotype

predictive validity

Primary Mental Abilities

split-half reliability

stability of IQ scores

Stanford-Binet Fourth Edition (SB-4)

Structure of the Intellect model

test-retest reliability

theory of multiple intelligences

triarchic theory of intelligence

twins reared apart

twins reared together

validity

Wechsler Adult Intelligence Scale-Revised (WAIS-R)

Wechsler Intelligence Scale for Children-Third Edition (WISC-III)

8

Personality Assessment

For years it has been popular to bemoan the sorry state of psychological testing. Supposedly, no one uses such tests any longer. Many academics argue that testing in general and projective testing in particular is invalid. Except for perhaps the Minnesota Multiphasic Personality Inventory (MMPI), they say, objective tests are also out of style. Others advise that textbooks such as this one should drastically reduce the coverage of personality assessment.

There is only one thing wrong with the foregoing claims and advice: they do not reflect the real world of clinical practice. In fact, psychological assessment continues to be a high-profile activity of today's practicing clinician (see Butcher, 1995). A recent survey of directors of training at clinical practicum sites reinforces the conclusion that projective tests, the Wechsler scales, and the MMPI continue to be highly popular (Craig & Horowitz, 1990). Without question, there is still widespread dependence on psychological tests by many clinicians (Lubin, Larsen, & Matarazzo, 1984; Piotrowski, Sherry, & Keller, 1985; Watkins, Campbell, Nieberding, & Hallmark, 1995). As we shall see later in Part 4 of this book, testing in such specialty areas as forensic psychology, pediatric psychology, neuropsychological assessment, and health psychology actually seems to be on the upswing. Even in the case of projective testing (the favorite whipping boy of many who claim that testing is a dying field), usage trends are strong.

Perhaps, then, the reports of the demise of personality assessment are a bit exaggerated (Exner, 1995). To give the reader an idea of the kinds of tests in use today and the frequency of their use, an examination of Table 8-1 would be helpful. This table presents a rank-ordering of the top 20 assessment procedures used by a randomly selected sample of clinical psychologists (Watkins et al., 1995).

But there are other important considerations besides frequency of usage. Personality assessment measures must show high levels of reliability and validity in order to be useful to clinical psychologists. A long history of relatively uncritical use of certain personality measures does not justify their use today. Therefore, in this chapter, we will not only describe some of the more popular objective and projective personality measures but we will critically evaluate their psychometric properties as well.

Table 8-1
Top twenty assessment procedures used by clinical psychologists.

Test or Procedure	Percentage of Use*
Clinical interview	95
Wechsler Adult Intelligence Scale-Revised (WAIS-R)	93
Minnesota Multiphasic Personality Inventory-2 (MMPI-2)	85
Sentence completion methods	84
Thematic Apperception Test (TAT)	82
Rorschach	82
Bender-Gestalt	80
Projective drawings	80
Beck Depression Inventory	71
Wechsler Intelligence Scale for Children-III (WISC-III)	69
Wide Range Achievement Test-Revised (WRAT-R)	68
Wechsler Memory Scale-Revised	65
Peabody Picture Vocabulary Test-Revised (PPVT-R)	50
Million Clinical Multiaxial Inventory-II (MCMI-II)	49
Wechsler Preschool and Primary Scale of Intelligence — Revised	44
Children's Apperception Test	42
Vineland Social Maturity Scale	42
Million Adolescent Personality Inventory	40
Strong Interest Inventory	39
Stanford-Binet Intelligence Scale	38

*Percentage of clinical psychologists who indicated that they at least "occasionally" used test or procedure.

SOURCE: From "Contemporary Practice of Psychological Assessment by Clinical Psychologists," by C. E. Watkins, V. L. Campbell, R. Nieberding, and R. Hallmark, 1995, *Professional Psychology: Research and Practice, 26,* p 57. Copyright © 1995 by American Psychological Association. Reprinted by permission.

■ Objective Tests

We will begin our survey of personality assessment with an examination of objective tests. *Objective personality measures* involve the administration of a standard set of questions or statements to which the examinee responds using a fixed set of options. For example, many objective tests use a true-false or yes-no response format, whereas others may provide a dimensional scale (for example, 0 = strongly disagree; 1 = disagree; 2 = neutral; 3 = agree; 4 = strongly agree). Objective tests have both advantages and disadvantages, as we indicate below.

Some advantages
Objective tests of personality or self-report inventories have had a central role in the historical development of clinical psychology (Goldberg, 1971; Watson, 1959). The historical role of inventories as well as their current prominence are in large part due to their obvious advantages. First of all, they are economical. After only brief instructions, large groups can be tested simultaneously, or a single pa-

tient can complete an inventory alone. Even computer scoring and interpretation of these tests are possible. Second, scoring and administration are relatively simple and objective. This, in turn, tends to make interpretation easier and seems to require less interpretive skill on the part of the clinician. Often a simple score along a single dimension (for example, adjustment-maladjustment) or on a single trait (for example, dependency or psychopathy) is possible. This apparent simplicity obviously attracts many clinicians. However, as we shall illustrate, rarely does such simple interpretation culminate in the validity claimed for it. In fact, this apparent simplicity can frequently lead to rather widespread misuse by ill-trained testers. A final attraction of self-report inventories, particularly for clinicians who are disenchanted with the problems inherent in projective tests, is their apparent objectivity and reliability.

Of course, as is so often the case, in the process of achieving the foregoing advantages and economies, clinical psychology seems to have traded one set of problems for another. Whether the trade-off is worthwhile is ultimately determined by the individual clinician's values and theoretical orientation.

Some disadvantages

The items of many inventories are often behavioral in nature—that is, the questions or statements concern behaviors that may or may not characterize the respondent. Those interested in identifying motives or dynamics may glean little understanding through such items. For example, although two individuals may endorse the same behavioral item (such as, "I have trouble getting to sleep"), they may do so for entirely different reasons. Of course, for clinicians who tend to eschew mediating variables, like motives or cognitions, this is a virtue rather than a defect.

Some inventories contain a mixture of items dealing with behaviors, cognitions, and needs. Yet inventories often provide a single, overall score—one that reflects various combinations of these behaviors, cognitions, and needs. Therefore, two individuals who achieve the same score may actually be quite different, even in reference to the personality trait or construct in question. Also, this means that the same score on a measure may have several alternative interpretations.

Other difficulties involve the transparent meaning of some inventory's questions, which can obviously facilitate faking on the part of some patients. Some tests tend to depend heavily upon the patient's self-knowledge. In addition, the forced-choice approach prevents individuals from qualifying or elaborating their responses, so that some additional information may be lost or distorted. In other instances, the limited understanding or even the limited literacy of certain individuals may lead them to misinterpret questions—a misinterpretation not necessarily attributable to personality determinants.

Methods of test construction for objective tests

Now that we have outlined some of the advantages and limitations of objective tests, it is instructive to focus on the various methods of test construction employed in developing these tests. Over the years a variety of strategies for constructing self-report inventories have been proposed, and we discuss several of these methods below.

Content validation.   The most straightforward approach to measurement is for clinicians to decide what it is they wish to assess and then simply to ask the patient for that information. For example, the Woodworth Personal Data Sheet used in World War I was a kind of standardized psychiatric interview. Content was determined by surveying the psychiatric literature to identify the major manifestations of "neuroses" and "psychoses." Items were then constructed that would tap those manifestations. Consequently, if the domain of neurosis or psychosis (as defined by the psychiatric literature) were adequately sampled, then the test could be assumed to be valid. "Do you sleep well at night?" "Do you get angry easily?" and "Are you easily insulted?" were considered good items if they related to what prevailing psychiatric opinion regarded as maladjustment.

Ensuring content validity, however, involves much more than simply deciding what you want to assess and then making up some items that appear to do the job. More sophisticated content validation methods involve: (1) carefully defining all relevant aspects of the variable you are attempting to measure; (2) consulting experts before generating items; (3) employing judges to assess each potential item's relevance to the variable of interest; and (4) using psychometric analyses to evaluate each item before you include it in your measure (Haynes, Richard, & Kubany, 1995; Nunnally & Bernstein, 1994).

However, as Wiggins (1973) observes, several potential problems are inherent in the content validity approach to test construction. First, can clinicians assume that every patient interprets a given item in exactly the same way? Second, can patients accurately report their own behavior or emotions? Third, will patients be honest, or will they attempt to place themselves in a good light (or even a bad light at times)? Fourth, can clinicians assume that the "experts" can be counted on to define the essence of the concept they are trying to measure? At the same time, it should be noted that most of these issues seem to be general problems for the majority of inventories, regardless of whether they depend on content sampling to establish their validity.

Empirical criterion keying.   In an attempt to help remedy the foregoing difficulties, the empirical criterion keying approach was developed. The most prominent example of this general method is the original Minnesota Multiphasic Personality Inventory (MMPI). In this approach, no assumptions are made as to whether a patient is telling the truth or whether the response really corresponds to behavior or feelings. What is important is that certain patients describe themselves in certain ways. As Meehl (1945) put it: "Thus if a hypochondriac says that he [sic] has 'many headaches' the fact of interest is that he says this" (p. 9).

The important assumption inherent to this approach is that members of a particular group will tend to respond in the same way. Consequently, it is not necessary to select test items in a rational, theoretical fashion. All that is required is to show on an empirical basis that the members of a given group respond to a given item in a similar fashion. For example, if, in contrast to nonclinical respondents, most individuals diagnosed with psychopathy agree with the item "I grew up in a house that had three steps on the front porch," then that item is a good one because it is endorsed by members of the psychopathic group. Thus, independent of an item's surface content, the test response becomes a sign of one's diagnostic status. In this way the utility of an item is solely determined by the extent to which it discriminates among known groups. The test response, however, is not necessarily a sample of behavior because the content of the item may not be directly associated with the symptoms that characterize members of that diagnostic group.

Of course, the criterion keying method has its problems. Foremost is the difficulty of interpreting the meaning of a score. For example, suppose that some patients diagnosed with schizophrenia are answering items intended to place them somewhere along the adjusted-maladjusted dimension. Suppose also that most of these patients happen to come from more poorly educated families than do the participants in a comparison group. When these patients with schizophrenia endorse the item "I almost never read books," that endorsement may reflect their poor educational background rather than their psychopathology. Although demonstrating that the test can discriminate among various patient groups is one aspect of establishing the validity of a test, the sole use of the empirical criterion keying method to *select items* for a test is not recommended (Clark & Watson, 1995).

Factor analysis.   These days, the majority of test developers use a factor analytic (or internal consistency) approach to test construction (Clark & Watson, 1995; Floyd & Widaman, 1995). The Guilford Inventories (Guilford, 1959) are excellent historical examples of a factor analytic approach. Here, the idea is to examine the intercorrelations among the individual items from many existing personality inventories. Succeeding factor analyses will then reduce or "purify" scales thought to reflect basic dimensions of personality.

The *exploratory* factor analytic approach is atheoretical. One begins by capturing a universe of items and then proceeds to reduce them to basic elements — personality, adjustment, diagnostic affiliation, or whatever — hoping to arrive at the core traits and dimensions of personality. In contrast, *confirmatory* factor analytic approaches are more theory driven because one seeks to confirm a hypothesized factor structure, based on theoretical predictions, for the test items (Floyd & Widaman, 1995). Although a detailed explanation of confirmatory factor analysis procedures is beyond the scope of this book, we anticipate that an increasing number of clinical psychologists will employ confirmatory factor analysis in the development and evaluation of objective assessment measures.

The strength of the factor analytic approach to test construction is its emphasis on empirically demonstrating that items purporting to measure a variable or dimension of personality are highly related to each other. However, a limitation of this approach is that it does not in and of itself demonstrate that these items actually are measuring the variable of interest; it only shows that the items tend to be measuring the same "thing."

Construct validity approach.   This approach combines many aspects of the content validity, empirical criterion keying, and factor analytic approaches (Clark & Watson, 1995). In this method, scales are developed to measure specific concepts from a given theory. In the case of personality assessment, the intent is to develop measures anchored in a theory of personality. Validation

Table 8-2
Strategies for determining validity of inventory item "I wish I could be happier."

Strategy	Items Is Valid If:
Content validity	"authorities" assert that the item is representative of the trait or dimension being measured.
Empirical criterion keying	it discriminates between contrasting groups.
Factor analysis	it has been shown through factor analysis to be a member of a homogeneous and independent cluster of items.
Construct validity	it measures the construct as theoretically defined.

is achieved when it can be said that a given scale measures the theoretical construct in question. The selection of items is based upon the extent to which they reflect the theoretical construct under study. Item analysis, factor analysis, and other procedures are utilized to ensure that a homogeneous scale is developed. Construct validity for the scale is then determined by demonstrating that those who achieve certain scores on the scale behave in nontest situations in a fashion that could be predicted from their scale score.

Because of its comprehensiveness, the construct validity approach to test construction is both the most desirable and the most labor-intensive. In fact, establishing the construct validity of a test is a never-ending process; one uses empirical feedback to refine both the theory *and* the personality measure (Smith & McCarthy, 1995).

To summarize and oversimplify a bit, Table 8-2 outlines the validity of an item according to each of the four strategies just discussed. We will turn now to a discussion of several of the major objective personality measures available to clinical psychologists.

■ The MMPI and the MMPI-2

The MMPI was long the best example of the empirical keying approach to test construction. Over 50 years after its publication by Hathaway and McKinley in 1943, it is still considered the preeminent self-report inventory. The MMPI has been used for virtually every predictive purpose imaginable, from likelihood of schizophrenic episodes to marriage suitability. What is even more staggering, Graham (1990) estimates that more than 10,000 studies on the MMPI have been published. With all its success, nonetheless, it was decided that the MMPI needed updating and restandardization. The result was the new *MMPI-2* (Butcher, Dahlstrom, Graham, Tellegen, & Kaemmer, 1989).

Description—MMPI

When Hathaway and McKinley developed the MMPI, their basic purpose was to fit psychiatric labels to individuals. Items were assembled from previously published tests of personality, from case histories, and from clinical experience. This pool of items was administered to nonclinical individuals (over 700 visitors to University of Minnesota hospitals) and psychiatric patients (over 800). The psychiatric categories used were: hypochondriasis (Hs), depression (D), hysteria (Hy), psychopathic deviate (Pd), paranoia (Pa), psychasthenia (Pt), schizophrenia (Sc), and hypomania (Ma). Two additional scales, masculinity-femininity (Mf) and social introversion (Si), were added later. It is important to note that these scale names reflect a diagnostic classification system that is antiquated. To translate all these diagnostic labels into more meaningful terms, the reader should refer to Table 8-3.

The MMPI is composed of 550 items to which the patient answers "True," "False," or "Cannot Say." Only those items that differentiated a given clinical group from a nonclinical group were included. For example, items were retained if they distinguished individuals with depression from nonclinical individuals, or individuals with schizophrenia from nonclinical individuals, or individuals with psychopathic features from nonclinical individuals. No attempt was made to select items that differentiated one diagnostic category from another. As a result, some items tend to be highly correlated with each other, and the same item may appear in several different scales.

There is an individual form of the test in which the items are printed on cards; here the individual separates the cards according to the True/False/Cannot Say categories. There is also a group form with items printed in a test booklet; here the answers are marked on an answer sheet. Although the test was originally designed for people 16 years and older, the MMPI has actually been used with individuals considerably younger. The test can be machine-scored or hand-scored. Indeed, it is possible to completely administer, score, and interpret the MMPI by computer (Dunn, Lushene, & O'Neil, 1972). Supervision is necessary only for extremely disturbed patients.

Description—MMPI-2

The original MMPI standardization sample had been criticized for many years as unrepresentative of the general U.S. population. Participants came largely from the Minneapolis area—all were white, had an average of eight years' education, and were typically 35 years old, married, and small-town residents. The test language was a particular problem: much of the terminology had become obsolete, and items often contained sexist language. In addition, some items made inappropriate references to Christian religious beliefs and sometimes seemed to overemphasize sexual, bowel, and bladder functions. Even the grammar and punctuation in some instances was poor! Finally, many clinicians felt the items did not adequately address such behaviors as suicide or drug use. All in all, the time seemed ripe for revision (Graham, 1990).

During the restandardization process, all 550 original items were retained—of those, 82 were rewritten to make the language more contemporary. In addition, 154 new items were added to the pool, bringing the total to 704. After some

Table 8-3
Simulated MMPI items.

Clinical Scales	Simulated Items (Answered True)
Hypochondriasis (Hs) (Excessive concern with bodily functions)	"At times I get strong cramps in my intestines."
Depression (D) (Pessimism, hopelessness, slowing of action and thought	"I am often very tense on the job."
Hysteria (Hy) (Unconscious use of physical and mental problems to avoid conflicts or responsiblity)	"Sometimes there is a feeling like something is pressing in on my head."
Psychopathic Deviate (Pd) (Disregard of social custom, shallow emotions, inability to profit from experience)	"I wish I could do over some of the things I have done."
Masculinity-Femininity (Mf) (Items differentiating between traditional sex roles)	"I used to like to do the dances in gym class."
Paranoia (Pa) (Abnormal suspiciousness, delusions of grandeur or persecution)	"It distresses me that people have the wrong ideas about me."
Psychasthenia (Pt) (Obsessions, compulsiveness, fears, guilt, indecisiveness)	"The things that run through my head sometimes are horrible."
Schizophrenia (Sc) (Bizarre, unusual thoughts or behavior, withdrawal, hallucinations, delusions)	"There are those out there who want to get me."
Hypomania (Ma) (Emotional excitement, flight of ideas, overactivity)	"Sometimes I think so fast I can't keep up."
Social Introversion (Si) (Shyness, disinterest in others, insecurity)	"I give up too easily when discussing things with others."

final adjustments, the MMPI-2 now includes 567 items. However, when only the traditional validity and clinical scales are of interest, just the first 370 items in the test booklet are administered.

Participants for the restandardization sample came from Minnesota, Ohio, North Carolina, Washington, Pennsylvania, Virginia, and California and were based upon U.S. Census data from 1980. The final sample contained 1138 men and 1462 women. The racial composition was as follows: White, 81%; African American, 12%; Hispanic, 3%; American Indian, 3%; and Asian American, 1%. Participants ranged in age from 18 to 85 years and in formal education from 3 to 20 + years. About 3% of the men and 6% of the women reported being in treatment for mental health problems at the time of testing.

The authors of the MMPI-2 state that it can be used with individuals who are at least 13 years old or can read at an eighth-grade level. It can be administered individually or in groups. Unlike the MMPI, the MMPI-2 has only one booklet form. It can be computer-scored, and non-English language versions of the test are available. There is also an adolescent version of the MMPI-2, known as the MMPI-A (Butcher et al., 1992).

Test-taking attitude

A potential problem with self-report inventories is their susceptibility to distortion through various test-taking attitudes or response sets. For example, some respondents may wish to place themselves in a favorable light; others may "fake bad" so they can increase the probability of receiving aid, sympathy, or perhaps a discharge from military service; still others have a seeming need to agree with almost any item regardless of its content. Obviously, if the clinician is not aware of these response styles in a given patient, the test interpretation can be in gross error.

To help detect malingering, other response sets or test-taking attitudes, and carelessness or misunderstanding, the MMPI-2 continues to incorporate the traditional four *validity scales* that were included in the original MMPI. They are as follows:

1. *? (Cannot Say) Scale.* This is the number of items left unanswered.
2. *F (Infrequency) Scale.* These are 60 items that were seldom answered in the scored direction by the standardization group. A high F score may suggest deviant response sets, markedly aberrant behavior, or other hypotheses about extratest characteristics or behaviors.
3. *L (Lie) Scale.* This includes 15 items whose endorsement places the respondent in a very positive light. However, in reality it is unlikely that they would be truthfully so endorsed. For example, "I like everyone I meet."
4. *K (Defensiveness) Scale.* These are 30 items that suggest defensiveness in admitting certain problems. These items purportedly detect "faking good," but they are more subtle than either L or F items. For example, "Criticism from others never bothers me."

In addition, three "new" validity scales can be scored from the MMPI-2. They are:

5. *F_b (Back-page Infrequency) Scale.* These are 40 items occurring near the end of the MMPI-2 that are infrequently endorsed.
6. *VRIN (Variable Response Inconsistency) Scale.* This includes 67 pairs of items with either similar or opposite content. High VRIN scores suggest random responding to MMPI-2 items.
7. *TRIN (True Response Inconsistency) Scale.* These 23 item pairs are opposite in content. Higher TRIN scores suggest a tendency to give True responses

indiscriminately, whereas lower TRIN scores suggest a tendency to give False responses indiscriminately.

These seven MMPI-2 validity scales provide a means for understanding the test respondent's motivations and test-taking attitudes. For example, attempts to present oneself in an overly favorable light will likely be detected by the L (Lie) or K (Defensiveness) scale (Baer, Wetter, & Berry, 1992), whereas the tendency to exaggerate one's problems or symptoms usually results in elevations on the F (Infrequency) and F_b (Back-page Infrequency) scales (Berry, Baer, & Harris, 1991; Rogers, Bagby, & Chakraborty, 1993; Wetter, Baer, Berry, Smith, & Larsen, 1992; Wetter, Baer, Berry, Robison, & Sumpter, 1993). Finally, the VRIN and TRIN scales are useful indicators of random responding and mostly true (or mostly false) responding, respectively (Berry, Wetter, Baer, Larsen, Clark, & Monroe, 1992; Tellegen & Ben-Porath, 1992).

Short forms

Over the years, a variety of short forms of the MMPI have appeared. Such scales typically shorten the MMPI to considerably less than the traditional 550 items. Although economies in screening or rapid classification may be achieved by their use, some loss in interpretive power can also be expected. Controversies such as those between Butcher, Kendall, and Hoffman (1980), who urge caution in the use of MMPI short forms, and Newmark, Woody, Finch, and Ziff (1980), who press for the utility of certain short forms, are still unresolved. As for the MMPI-2, the use of short forms has been called into question as well (Butcher, Dahlstrom, Graham, Tellegen, & Kaemmer, 1989; Butcher, Graham, & Ben-Porath, 1995).

Interpretation through patterns

Since the original scales were developed to predict psychiatric categorization, the initial use of the MMPI depended upon simple interpretations based on elevated scale scores. That is, if an Sc scale score was significantly elevated, this suggested a diagnosis of schizophrenia. However, clinical experience quickly taught that such compartmentalized interpretations were gross oversimplifications. Some nonclinical respondents achieve high Sc scores, and so do other diagnostic groups.

Interpretation has now shifted to an examination of patterns, or profiles, of scores. For example, individuals who produce elevations on the first three clinical scales (Hs, D, Hy) tend to present with somatic complaints and depressive symptoms and often receive somatoform, anxiety, or depressive disorder diagnoses. Elevations on scales 6 (Pa) and 8 (Sc) suggest extreme suspiciousness and potential psychotic thought processes; these characteristics are found among individuals diagnosed with paranoid schizophrenia.

Interpretation through content

Lest the reader conclude that only diagnostic labels can result from the analysis of a profile, consider the following excerpt from a pretherapy workup based on the MMPI-2 profile shown in Figure 8-1 (Butcher, 1990):

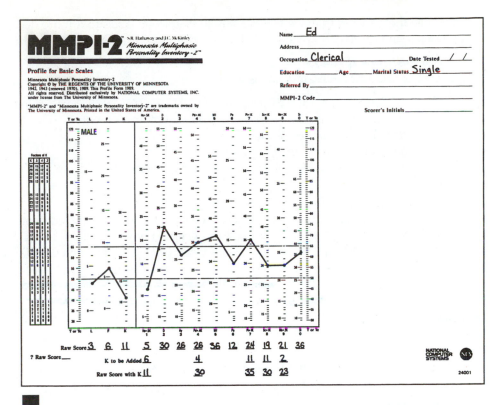

Figure 8-1
The case of Ed: A pretreatment MMPI-2 clinical profile.

Ed approached the testing in a frank and open manner, producing a valid MMPI-2 profile. . . . He related a number of psychological adjustment problems and seemingly was seeking help in overcoming them. The MMPI-2 clinical profile highlights a number of problems and symptoms that Ed was experiencing at the time of his first treatment session. He reported being depressed and anxious about his situation and related feeling tense, lonely, and insecure. He appeared to be having great difficulty concentrating on his work and was indecisive. He had no zest for life and was preoccupied with his inability to accomplish personal goals. The relatively high score on the psychopathic deviate scale (Pd) reflects rebellious attitudes and family conflict (the Harris-Lingoes Family Problems Scale, Pd1, was T = 69). He appeared to be a somewhat passive young man who reported being shy and isolated. (p. 12)

Thus, a major change and improvement in the clinical use of the MMPI and MMPI-2 has been the shift away from differential psychiatric diagnosis based upon the evaluation of a single score to a more sophisticated profile analysis of scale scores considered as measures of personality traits.

For the MMPI-2, a variety of *content scales* have been identified (Butcher, Graham, Williams, & Ben-Porath, 1990). For example, certain items can help identify fears, health concerns, cynicism, the Type A personality, and so on. Such scales enable the clinician to move beyond simple diagnostic labels to a more dynamic level of interpretation. Take the following example from Graham (1990):

Family problems (FAM)

High scores on the FAM indicate persons who:

1. describe considerable discord in their current families and/or families of origin
2. describe their families as lacking in love, understanding, and support
3. resent the demands and advice of their families
4. feel angry and hostile toward their families
5. see marital relationships as involving unhappiness and lack of affection (p. 137)

Supplementary scales

In addition to the standard validity scales, the clinical scales, and the content scales, the MMPI-2 item pool has been used to develop numerous other scales. Many years ago, Dahlstrom, Welsh, and Dahlstrom (1972, 1975) noted 450 MMPI supplementary scales ranging from dominance and suspiciousness to success in basketball! For the MMPI-2, 12 supplemental scales have been developed so far. A few examples are: anxiety, repression, ego strength, dominance, and social responsibility. It is likely that many more supplemental scales will be developed in the future (Butcher, Graham, & Ben-Porath, 1995).

A summary evaluation of the MMPI and MMPI-2

Screening. Many clinicians are attracted to the MMPI-2 because of its screening capabilities. When information about the severity of a patient's problems is needed, and when the clinician must generate hypotheses about a patient's diagnostic status, the MMPI-2 can be a valuable asset. Therefore, when groups of patients are being screened, it can be both useful and efficient as an aid to mental disorder diagnosis or as a hypothesis generator. The MMPI-2, however, is quite long, and for many screening purposes, such a time-intensive self-report inventory may be unnecessary. For example, if a clinician simply wants to screen new clients for depression, a much shorter inventory than the MMPI-2 might be more desirable. The MMPI-2 items measure a wide range of symptoms, only a minority of which are related to depression. The comprehensiveness of the MMPI-2, then, is both a strength and a weakness.

The question of personality dynamics. The MMPI-2 is atheoretical (Butcher, 1995; Helmes & Reddon, 1993). For those clinicians who are psychodynamically oriented or who seek an understanding of their patients through the subtle interplay of general personality characteristics and situational determinants, the MMPI may not be the instrument of choice. The MMPI-2 is primarily a measure of various symptoms of psychopathology. Although the features tapped by MMPI-2 items may suggest certain personality traits or styles, it was not developed with personality constructs in mind. But does it help with personality description, psychotherapy planning, or the host of other predictions that the clinician must confront in day-to-day interactions with the patient? Many would question the MMPI's contribution to ongoing clinical decisions once the initial diagnostic category has been selected. However, Butcher (1990; 1995) would object and argue that both the MMPI and MMPI-2 are valuable aids in planning and evaluating the effects of treatment.

Reliability and validity. As noted earlier, there have been over 10,000 published studies of the MMPI. Given this fact, the authors of this textbook do not have the temerity to "briefly" summarize all this research (aside from the comments already made). Perhaps, though, something of the flavor of MMPI research is contained in the following remarks.

When the MMPI "is used in the manner for which it was designed and validated, its psychometric properties are likely to be adequate for either clinical or research purposes" (Parker, Hanson, & Hunsley, 1988, p. 373). There may, however, be some debate about those exact purposes. In any case, Parker, Hanson, and Hunsley's survey pronounced the reliability, stability, and validity of the MMPI to be acceptable. Its validity seems adequate according to the survey, particularly when there is a theoretical or empirical rationale for the MMPI. The ultimate question, then, is still not whether the MMPI-2 is valid — rather, for what specific purposes is it valid?

There are many instances when specific scales do not seem to work all that well. For example, research on the original MMPI MacAndrew Scale (a scale designed to classify individuals with alcohol problems) was surveyed by Gottesman and Prescott (1989). The data were so weak that Gottesman and Prescott called for a suspension of the use of the scale.

Two other issues related to the validity of MMPI-2 scores are important as well. Although presented in the context of developing new MMPI-2 supplemental scales, Butcher, Graham, and Ben-Porath (1995) noted the necessity of establishing the *incremental validity* of a scale as well as the *validity of cutoff scores (thresholds)*. Incremental validity is supported if scale scores provide unique information about a person's behavior, personality features, or psychopathology features that is not provided by other measures. Regarding the MMPI-2, the question is, "Do MMPI-2 scores convey information relevant to psychopathology or personality that cannot be provided by other measures?" The issue of incremental validity tends to be neglected for all psychological tests, including the MMPI-2. As for the validity of cutoff scores, it is important to keep in mind that the optimal cutoff score (in terms of maximizing correct decisions as to which patient has the disorder or trait in question given his or her score on the measure) will vary depending on the nature of the population of patients sampled. The cutoff scores provided in test manuals were derived for a certain population, which may or may not be similar to the population of patients a clinician is working with. MMPI-2 cutoffs (*T* score of 65 or greater) were derived using the distribution of scores from the normative sample. Therefore, these cutoffs may or may not be appropriate in certain clinical contexts.

Social trust. Recent developments in our society have also created problems for the MMPI-2. Lack of trust in our social institutions and the concerns of minorities have each been reflected in criticisms of the test. For example, the

MMPI-2 has often been lauded for its empirical criterion keying approach, which works well for those who understand it. But what about people who know nothing of criterion keying or psychometrics but want to work for corporation X? Suppose that these individuals fail to get a job after taking an MMPI-2. What is the answer when they demand to know what the following items have to do with hiring: "I used to keep a diary" or "My sex life is satisfactory"? For the person who is seeking therapy, a test such as the MMPI-2 may be acceptable. However, for one who takes the test in a personnel setting, it may be regarded as an invasion of privacy (Butcher, 1971).

Given the nature of the original sample on which the MMPI was validated, questions have been raised as to whether or not the instrument may be biased against certain ethnic and racial groups. This has been a rather contentious debate over the years (see Gynther, 1972; Gynther & Green, 1980; Pritchard & Rosenblatt, 1980). Some studies have found significant differences in scores between racial groups, whereas others have not. It is important to keep in mind, however, that a significant difference between mean scores does not in and of itself indicate test bias. Rather, *test bias* refers to the situation where different decisions or predictions are made for members of two groups even when they obtain the same score (Anastasi, 1988). We will return to the general issue of test bias later in this chapter. To our knowledge, there have been very few published studies that evaluate the possibility of test bias for the MMPI-2. It is encouraging that, to date, studies have not found evidence suggesting that the use of the MMPI-2 for certain purposes results in bias against certain ethnic or racial groups (for example, Timbrook & Graham, 1994).

The MMPI-2.   The reasons that prompted the revision of the MMPI were, in the main, laudable. However, it is still too early to know how successful the revision has been. Without doubt, though, some clinicians seem to be nervous about the MMPI-2. Perhaps these jitters will disappear as they become more familiar with the revision. There are some, nevertheless, who are adamantly opposed and say that they will continue to use the old version. Here is a sample of the complaints and reservations heard about the MMPI-2:

1. The normative sample, compared to U.S. Census data, is too highly educated. Only 5% of MMPI-2 normative respondents have less than a college education and 45% of the normal respondents in the sample are college educated. Schooling can account for much of the variance in the scores of psychiatric patients.
2. It is questionable whether all the old MMPI research is applicable to the new MMPI-2.
3. Unnecessary revisions seem to have been made.
4. Criteria for the inclusion of "normal" respondents are puzzling.
5. Some respondents who are administered both versions of the test show problems on the one version but not the other.
6. Scores are generally lower on the MMPI-2 compared to the MMPI.
7. Validity of the new content scales is unclear.
8. Many scales on the MMPI-2 are somewhat unrealiable over time.
9. Internal consistency of several MMPI-2 scales is quite low.

10. There remains too much item overlap among the scales, making study results hard to interpret.

In summary, the MMPI and MMPI-2 are the benchmarks for self-report inventories measuring psychopathology or personality. It is likely that the MMPI-2 will enjoy the same success as its predecessor. However, it is important that clinical psychologists appreciate the potential limitations as well as the strengths of this instrument.

■ The Revised NEO-Personality Inventory

A relatively new personality inventory, the NEO-PI-R, has received a great deal of attention from clinical psychologists in recent years. Unlike the MMPI, the NEO-PI-R was not developed specifically to assess various forms of psychopathology. In this section, we describe the NEO-PI-R, evaluate its psychometric properties, and comment on its potential clinical utility.

Description

The Revised NEO-Personality Inventory, or *NEO-PI-R* (Costa & McCrae, 1992), is a self-report measure of personality features that make up an influential model of personality known as the *Five-Factor Model (FFM)*. The FFM of personality has evolved over the last four decades (Digman, 1990) and has roots in both the lexical tradition (that is, the analysis of trait adjectives found in English and other languages) as well as the factor analytic tradition in personality research. As operationalized by the NEO-PI-R, the five factors or *domains* are: *Neuroticism, Extraversion, Openness to Experience, Agreeableness,* and *Conscientiousness.* In addition, six subscales or *facets* are provided for each domain. These facets are personality traits that represent various aspects for each domain. Table 8-4 presents the facets that represent each domain.

Table 8-4

Domains and facets of personality measured by the NEO-PI-R.

Domain	Facets
Neuroticism	Anxiety, hostility, depression, self-consciousness, impulsiveness, vulnerability
Extraversion	Warmth, gregariousness, assertiveness, activity, excitement seeking, positive emotions
Openness to Experience	Fantasy, aesthetics, feelings, actions, ideas, values
Agreeableness	Trust, straightforwardness, altruism, compliance, modesty, tender-mindedness
Conscientiousness	Competence, order, dutifulness, achievement, striving, self-discipline, deliberation.

The NEO-PI-R consists of 240 items (8 items for each of the 30 facets, or, alternatively, 48 items for each of the 5 domains). Individuals rate each of the 240 statements on a five-point scale (strongly disagree, disagree, neutral, agree, strongly agree). Research that led to development of the NEO-PI-R began in the 1970s. At that time, there was no clear consensus regarding which personality model or system provided the most useful and comprehensive description of personality features. Costa and McCrae (1992) became convinced that there was more agreement among the various competing personality models regarding higher-order dimensions (for example, Neuroticism and Extraversion) than there was for the lower-level traits of which they are composed (for example, the facets of each dimension). For this reason, they adopted a top-down approach in constructing their inventory—they selected those higher-order factors or dimensions of personality believed to be of most import and utility (based on reviews of the literature as well as their own empirical research). They then identified those traits or facets that constituted each major dimension. The original version of their instrument assessed only three of the five factors (Neuroticism, Extraversion, and Openness), whereas the NEO-PI-R assesses all five domains of the FFM and includes facet scales for each.

The NEO-PI-R was developed using a rational-empirical test construction strategy that emphasized construct validity. Each personality trait to be included was identified, defined, and then analyzed such that items measuring various aspects of the trait could be generated. Final item selection was based on empirical performance (that is, the most reliable and valid items were retained). Further, factor analyses were performed to ensure that items loaded on their respective factors.

Approximately half of the NEO-PI-R items are reverse-scored, whereby lower scores are *more* indicative of the trait in question. This was done in order to address a potential acquiescence (or, alternatively, a potential nay-saying) bias that may present problems for inventories in which all items or the majority of items are keyed in the same direction. In this latter instance, high scores may be due either to acquiescence *or* to the actual level of the trait in question, making the interpretation of a high score problematic.

One of the more controversial aspects of the NEO-PI-R is its lack of a validity scale (or set of scales) to evaluate respondents' test-taking approaches. Instead, the NEO-PI-R has three individual items that assess the validity of responses. One item asks respondents to indicate if they have responded to the items in an honest and accurate manner, another asks if the respondent has answered all items, and the last assesses whether responses have been placed in the correct spaces.

Norms.   Adult norms are based on a total of 500 men and 500 women drawn from several samples of community residents. The normative sample closely approximates U.S. Census projections for 1995 in the distribution of age and racial groups. In addition, the NEO-PI-R manual presents normative data for college students as well.

Reliability and stability   NEO-PI-R scores evidence excellent levels of both internal consistency as well as test-retest reliability. Internal consistency coefficients range from .86 to .92 for the domain scales and from .56 to .81 for the facet scales. As for test-retest reliability, these have been impressively high over time periods as long as six years. Further, a recent study of clinical outpatients reported six-month test-retest reliability coefficients that ranged from .76 to .84 for the domain scores (Trull, Useda, Costa, & McCrae, 1995).

Factor structure. Factor analyses have, in general, supported the hypothesized five-factor structure of the NEO-PI-R. This is true whether individual item scores or facet scores were employed in the analyses (Costa & McCrae, 1992).

Validity. The NEO-PI-R manual (Costa & McCrae, 1992) presents a variety of evidence attesting to the validity of the instrument's scores. Domain and facet scores from the NEO-PI-R have been shown to relate in predictable ways to personality trait scores from a variety of personality measures, peer reports, and adjective checklists.

Clinical applications. Although the NEO-PI-R was developed from a model of "normal" personality, investigators have begun to assess this instrument's usefulness in clinical samples. Because Axis II personality disorders involve, by definition, maladaptive personality traits (that is, extreme variants of personality traits common in all individuals), these disorders represent an obvious application for FFM instruments like the NEO-PI-R. Several studies have supported the utility of NEO-PI in characterizing personality disorders (for example, Schroeder, Wormworth, & Livesley, 1992; Trull, 1992; Trull, Useda, Costa, & McCrae, 1995). Further, investigators are now beginning to evaluate the utility of FFM instruments like the NEO-PI-R in assessing personality characteristics of individuals with Axis I mood, anxiety, and substance use disorders (Trull & Sher, 1994). Taken together, these studies suggest that the NEO-PI-R and related instruments hold some promise in the area of clinical assessment.

Alternate forms. A 60-item short form of the NEO-PI-R exists and is called the *NEO–Five Factor Inventory* (NEO-FFI). It may be useful in situations where a relatively short measure of the five major personality dimensions is desired, as it does not contain facet scales. Another version of the NEO-PI-R is also noteworthy. *Form R* is used for observer ratings. It contains the 240 items of the self-report version, yet these are reworded to reflect the gender of the target person being rated. Form R scores can be used to validate or supplement self-report scores (Costa & McCrae, 1992).

Case study. Bruehl (1994) presents a case study of a 45-year-old, white, divorced woman who received an Axis I diagnosis of major depressive disorder and an Axis II diagnosis of borderline personality disorder. "Betty" presented for treatment because of her concerns over parenting her daughter, who had recently been arrested for drug possession and suspended from high school. Betty had a history of sexual abuse in childhood, of poor family and peer relationships, of physical abuse in adulthood, and of intense and labile emotions. Table 8-5 presents the results of her NEO-PI-R administration.

Table 8-5
The Revised NEO-Personality Inventory personality profile for "Betty."

Scale	Range	Clinical Implications
Neuroticism	Very high	
Anxiety	High	Nervous/ruminative
Angry hostility	Very high	Rageful/bitter
Depression	Very high	Gloomy/despondent
Self-consciousness	High	Insecure/ashamed
Impulsiveness	High	Spontaneous/unpredictable
Vulnerability	High	Overwhelmed/defenseless
Extraversion	Low	
Warmth	Low	Cold
Gregariousness	Low	Shy/withdrawn
Assertiveness	Average	
Activity	Average	
Excitement seeking	High	Adventurous
Positive emotions	Low	Placid/disinterested
Openness	High	
Fantasy	Very high	Imaginative/dissociative
Aesthetics	Average	
Feelings	Average	
Actions	Average	
Ideas	High	Cognitively flexible
Values	High	Open-minded
Agreeableness	Low	
Trust	Low	Cynical/suspicious
Straightforwardness	Low	Deceptive/manipulative
Altruism	Average	
Compliance	Low	Aggressive/oppositional
Modesty	Average	
Tender-mindedness	Average	
Conscientiousness	Average	
Competence	High	Perfectionistic
Order	Average	
Dutifulness	Low	Unreliable/irresponsible
Achievement striving	High	Driven
Self-discipline	Average	
Deliberation	Low	Hasty

SOURCE: From "A Case of Borderline Personality Disorder," by S. Bruehl in *Personality Disorders and the Five-Factor Model of Personality* edited by P. T. Costa, Jr. and T. A. Widiger, pp. 189–198. Copyright © 1994 by American Psychological Association. Reprinted by permission.

As can be seen, she produced elevations on all Neuroticism facets, scored in the low range on several Extraversion and Agreeableness facets, and produced several elevations on Openness facets. Several interpretative statements regarding Betty's NEO-PI-R scores illustrate how these scores can be useful in understanding a client and in treatment planning.

- Betty's elevated Neuroticism and low Agreeableness were consistent with what would be expected based on the DSM-III-R criteria for BDL [Borderline Personality Disorder]. . . .
- The strength of the psychotherapeutic relationship was slow to develop because of Betty's low levels of Warmth and Trust. . . .
- The transference issues observed in therapy related primarily to Betty's low Trust and High Hostility. As might be expected given her low Straightforwardness, she expressed her anger and lack of trust passively. . . .
- Betty's low Compliance suggested that it was important to watch for control issues in therapy. On the few occasions when therapeutic "homework" assignments were attempted and agreed on, Betty failed to complete them. . . .
- Her low Compliance seemed to interact with her low Trust and High Hostility to cause interpersonal difficulties in therapy. These same issues were responsible for her problems in previous intimate relationships with close friends, family members, and husbands. . . .
- Information provided by the NEO-PI-R also suggested strengths that improved treatment progress. Betty's high level of Openness to Ideas did reflect in part pathological aspects, but it also reflected an ability to be more cognitively flexible. . . . She was very open to looking at her problems in different ways and considering alternative ways for understanding and addressing these problems. (Bruehl, 1994, pp. 195–196)

Limitations of the NEO-PI-R

Recently, several authors have suggested limitations of the NEO-PI-R in clinical assessment (Ben-Porath & Waller, 1992; Block, 1995; Tellegen, 1993). First, the NEO-PI-R has been criticized for its relative lack of validity items. In contrast to the MMPI-2 and other self-report measures, the NEO-PI-R does not devote a number of test items to assess response styles that may influence interpretations of the obtained scores. Second, the use of the NEO-PI-R for clinical diagnostic purposes remains to be demonstrated. Although the initial studies that have shown associations between NEO-PI-R scores and mental disorder diagnoses are encouraging, the NEO-PI-R may not be especially well suited for the general purpose of clinical diagnosis because its development was guided by a model of "normal" personality. Third, too little research has been conducted on the use of the NEO-PI-R in treatment planning to warrant the routine use of this measure in clinical settings at this time. Finally, several psychometric criticisms have been leveled at the NEO-PI-R, including the intercorrelation among certain domain scores as well as the placements of certain facets within particular domains (for example, the placement of Impulsiveness and Hostility within the Neuroticism domain).

◼ Projective Tests

Projective techniques have a long and rich history. William Shakespeare wrote about the projective qualities of clouds, and William Stern used clouds as test stimuli before Rorschach and his inkblots. Sir Francis Galton (1879) suggested word-association methods, and Kraepelin made use of them. Binet and Henri (1896) experimented with pictures as projective devices, and Alfred Adler asked patients to recall their first memory, another kind of projective approach.

However, the real impetus for projective techniques was created by Hermann Rorschach's classic monograph in 1921, in which he described the use of inkblots as a method for the differential diagnosis of psychopathology. Later in the 1920s, David Levy brought the inkblot test to America, and it was not long before Beck, Klopfer, and Hertz all began giving Rorschach courses. In 1935, Morgan and Murray introduced the Thematic Apperception Test (TAT), and in 1938 Murray carefully described the process of projection. The term projective really came into popular use following Frank's widely discussed 1939 paper on projective methods.

The nature of projective tests

For some, the definition of a projective test resides in Freudian notions regarding the nature of ego defenses and unconscious processes. But these do not seem to be essential characteristics. Over the years, there have been many definitions offered (Anderson & Anderson, 1951; Lindzey, 1961; Murstein, 1963; Zubin, Eron, & Schumer, 1965; Wiggins, 1973; Semenoff, 1976). Perhaps the easiest solution is a pragmatic one that comes from consulting the English and English psychological dictionary (1958)—a projective technique is "a procedure for discovering a person's characteristic modes of behavior by observing his behavior in response to a situation that does not elicit or compel a particular response."

Characteristics.   Projective techniques tend to have several characteristics that, when taken as a whole, can be distinguishing (Rotter, 1954).

1. In response to an unstructured or ambiguous stimulus, examinees are *forced to impose their own structure,* and in so doing they reveal something of themselves (for example, needs, wishes, or conflicts).

2. The stimulus material is *unstructured.* This is a very tenuous criterion, even though it is widely assumed to reflect the essence of projective techniques. For example, if 70% of all examinees perceive card V on the Rorschach as a bat, then we can hardly say that the stimulus is unstructured. Thus, whether a test is projective or not depends on the kinds of responses that the individual is encouraged to give and on how those responses are utilized. The instructions are the important element. If a patient is asked to classify the people in a set of TAT cards as men or women, then there is a great deal of structure—the test is far from ambiguous. But if the patient is asked what the people on the card are saying, the task has suddenly become quite ambiguous indeed.

3. The method is *indirect.* To some degree or other, examinees are not aware of the purposes of the test; at least, the purposes are disguised. Although patients may know that the test has something to do with adjustment-maladjustment, they are not usually aware in detail of the significance of their responses. There is no attempt to ask patients directly about their needs or troubles; the route is indirect, and the hope is that this very indirectness will make it more difficult for patients to censor the data they provide.

4. There is *freedom of response*. Where questionnaire methods may allow only for a yes or a no, projectives permit a nearly infinite range of responses.

5. Response interpretation deals with *more variables*. Since the range of possible responses is so broad, the clinician can make interpretations along multiple dimensions (needs, adjustment, diagnostic category, ego defenses, and so on). Many objective tests, in contrast, provide but a single score (for example, degree of psychological distress) or scores on a fixed number of dimensions or scales.

The agony: measurement and standardization

The contrasts between objective tests and projective tests are striking. The former, by their very nature, lend themselves to an actuarial interpretive approach. Norms, reliability, and even validity seem easier to manage. The projectives, by their very nature, seem to resist psychometric manipulation and evaluation. Indeed, some clinicians reject even the suggestion that a test such as the Rorschach should be subjected to the indignities of psychometrics; they would see this as an assault upon their intuitive art.

Standardization.   Should, then, projective techniques be standardized? There are surely many reasons for doing so. Such standardization would facilitate communication and would also serve as a check against the biases and the interpretive zeal of some clinicians. Furthermore, the enthusiastic proponents of projectives usually act as if they have norms (implicit though these may be), so that there seems to be no good reason *not* to attempt the standardization of those norms. Of course, research problems with projectives can be formidable.

The dissenters argue that interpretations from projectives cannot be standardized: every person is unique, and any normative descriptions will inevitably be misleading. There are so many interacting variables that standardized interpretive approaches would surely destroy the holistic nature of projective tests. After all, they say, interpretation is an art.

Reliability.   Even the determination of reliability turns out not to be so simple after all. For example, it is surely too much to expect an individual to produce, word for word, exactly the same TAT story on two different occasions. Yet how many differences between two stories are permissible? Of course, one can bypass test responses altogether and deal only with the reliability of the personality interpretations made by clinicians. But this may confound the reliability of the test with the reliability of the judge. Also, test-retest reliability may be affected by psychological changes in the individual—particularly when dealing with patient populations. It is true that clinicians can opt for establishing reliability through the use of alternate forms. But how do they decide that alternate forms for TAT cards or inkblots are equivalent? Even split-half reliability is difficult to attain because there is difficulty demonstrating the equivalence of the two halves of each test.

Validity.   Because projectives have been used for such a multiplicity of purposes, there is little point in asking such questions as, Is the TAT valid? or Is the Rorschach a good personality test? The questions must be more specific: Does the TAT predict aggression in situation X? Does score X from the Rorschach correlate with clinical judgments of anxiety?

With these issues in mind, we turn now to a discussion of several of the more popular projective tests.

■ The Rorschach

Although the origins of the Rorschach lie in Europe, its subsequent development and elaboration occurred in the United States (Exner, 1993). Disenchantment with objective inventories probably facilitated this development (Shneidman, 1965), but the general rise of the psychodynamic-psychoanalytic movement and the emigration of many of its adherents from Europe to the United States in the 1930s were also important.

What has confused Rorschach development and perhaps interfered with the demonstration of adequate validity is the fact that there are several different general Rorschach approaches. For example, in the past, Klopfer, Beck, Hertz, Piotrowski, and Rapaport each offered their own versions of Rorschach systems (Exner, 1993). Their systems differ in the manner in which they score, administer, and interpret the results of the test, and they also differ in the instructions they provide to examinees. This has created many problems in interpreting the results of research studies and in generalizing from one study to another. In addition, Exner and Exner (1972) discovered that 22% of the clinicians they surveyed did not formally score the Rorschach at all and that 75% reported that, when they did use a scoring scheme, it was a highly idiosyncratic one. However, it is now virtually a requirement for research publication that Rorschach protocols be scored in a systematic fashion and that adequate interscorer agreement be demonstrated (Weiner, 1991). At a minimum, it is expected that Rorschach responses should be scored similarly by independent raters.

Description
The *Rorschach* consists of ten cards on which are printed inkblots that are symmetrical from right to left. Five of the ten cards are black and white (with shades of gray), and the other five are colored. A simulated Rorschach card is shown in Figure 8-2.

Administration.   There are various techniques for administering the Rorschach. However, for many clinicians, the process goes something like this. The clinician hands the patient the first card and says, "Tell me what you see— what it might be for you. There are no right or wrong answers. Just tell me what it looks like to you." All of the subsequent cards are administered in order. The clinician takes down verbatim everything the patient says. Some clinicians also record the length of time it takes the patient to make the first response to each card as well as the total time spent on each card. Some patients produce many responses per card, others very few. The clinician also notes the position of the card as each response is given (for example, right side up, upside down, and so on). All spontaneous remarks or exclamations are also recorded.

Figure 8-2
Inkblot similar to those employed by Rorschach.

Following this phase, the clinician moves to what is called "the inquiry." Here the patient is reminded of all previous responses, one by one, and asked what it was that prompted each response. The patient is also asked to indicate for each card the exact location of the various responses. This is also a time when the patient may elaborate or clarify responses.

Scoring. Although Rorschach scoring schemes vary, most employ three major determinants. *Location* refers to the area of the card to which the patient responded—the whole blot, a large detail, a small detail, white space, and so on. *Content* refers to the nature of the object seen (an animal, a person, a rock, fog, clothing, and so on). *Determinants* refer to those aspects of the card that prompted the patient's response (the form of the blot, its color, texture, apparent movement, shading, and so on). Some systems also score *popular* responses and *original* responses (often based upon the relative frequency of certain responses in the general population). Currently, Exner's Comprehensive System of scoring is the most frequently employed (Exner, 1974, 1993). Although the specifics of this scoring system are beyond the scope of this chapter (there are 54 indices calculated in

Exner's Structural Summary alone), a number of resources are available that provide details on the Comprehensive System (for example, Exner, 1991, 1993).

The actual scoring of the Rorschach involves such things as the compilation of the number of various determinants, computing their percentages based upon the total number of responses, computing the ratio of one set of responses to another set (for example, computing the total number of movement responses divided by the number of color responses), and so on. Indeed, the layperson is often surprised to learn that orthodox scoring of the Rorschach is much more concerned with the formal determinants than with the actual content of the responses. However, many contemporary clinicians do not bother with formal scoring at all, preferring to rely on the informal notation of determinants. Furthermore, these clinicians tend to make heavy use of content in their interpretations. The following brief examples may help provide an idea of what is involved in the administration and scoring of a Rorschach:

Case Illustration 1

The examinee is an 18-year-old "normal" male college student.

	Response	Inquiry	Scoring
Card I	Looks like a crab or a sea animal of some kind	Claws make it look like a crab.	D F + A (large detail, good form, animal object)
Card VIII	A flower of some kind. Possibly an iris	The petals have that shape. And the colors of it, I guess.	W FC P1 (whole card, form predominant over color, plant)

Case Illustration 2

The following unscored set of responses was provided by a 42-year-old woman who was diagnosed by a psychiatrist as "anxiety reaction, chronic, severe" following a traumatic accident in her home. It is important to note that this diagnosis was arrived at by an examination of all the data available and not by use of the Rorschach alone.

Card I.   Bat. (Anything else?) It's on a web.
Card II.   A couple of bears.
Card III. I don't know. (See anything at all?) A couple of little birds.
Card IV.   Looks like a bearskin of some kind stretched out.
Card V.   A butterfly.
Card VI.   The middle looks like a lampstand or a pipestand.

Card VII.   Looks like an island. (Anything else?) A ship in port. A vessel of some kind.

Card VIII.   A couple bears climbing a tree. (Anything else?) No.

Card IX.   I don't know what that looks like.

Card X.   Looks like something I've seen in the bottom of the ocean. A crawfish.

An excerpt from the clinician's report observed: "On the Rorschach, the patient's performance was constricted and conforming. Her responses seemed to be influenced by anxiety factors. There was a noticeable tendency for her to avoid the threatening aspects of the test (lack of structure) by giving only a few responses and then making them into popular or conforming ones. Her tendency to respond to the test in terms of animals or inanimate objects suggests some disturbance in social relationships or else a potential for withdrawal."

As we observed earlier, Rorschach interpretation can be a complex process. For example, a patient's overuse of form may suggest conformity. Poor form, coupled with unusual responses, may hint at psychosis. Color is said to relate to emotionality, and if it is not accompanied by good form it may often indicate impulsivity. Extensive use of white spaces has been interpreted as indicative of oppositional or even psychopathic qualities. Use of the whole blot points to a tendency to be concerned with integration and to be well organized. Extensive use of details is thought to be correlated with compulsivity or obsessional tendencies. But content is also important. Seeing small animals might mean passivity. Responses of blood, claws, teeth, and the like could suggest hostility and aggression. Even turning a card over and examining the back might lead to an interpretation of suspiciousness. However, it is important that the reader treat these as examples of potential interpretations or hypotheses and not as successfully validated facts!

As previously mentioned, the most contemporary approach to scoring has been developed by Exner (1974; 1993), whose system incorporates elements from the scoring systems of other clinicians. Exner and his associates have offered a substantial amount of psychometric data, evidence of stable retest reliability, and construct validity studies. It is a promising, research-based approach that warrants careful attention of clinicians who choose to use the Rorschach. However, it is also important to note that, recently, many of the reliability and validity studies cited by Exner have been challenged (Wood, Nezworski, & Stejskal, 1996).

A summary evaluation of the Rorschach

We will conclude our discussion of the Rorschach with some general evaluative comments.

Reliability and validity.   Lack of demonstrated reliability is a real problem. We briefly discussed interscorer reliability in Chapter 7, but here we are concerned with the consistency of an individual's scores across time or test conditions as well as the reliability of interpretations of scores. Although Weiner (1995) argues that frequent retests (even on a daily basis) are possible because "the basic structure and thematic focus of their Rorschach data tends to remain the same" (p. 335), we are not aware of a body of empirical studies that support the stability of summary scores. Further, the consistency of scores is often questionable because of the rarity with which certain response categories occur. Of crucial importance, however, is the reliability of clinicians' interpretations. It is quite probable that two clinicians trained together over several years can achieve reliability in their interpretations. But what about two clinicians with no common training? The proliferation of formal scoring schemes, coupled with the tendency of so many clinicians to use freewheeling interpretive approaches, makes the establishment of reliability an elusive goal.

As for validity, there have been many testimonials over the years. And when skilled, experienced clinicians speak highly of an instrument, those in the field must listen. But at some point these testimonials must give way to hard evidence. For many years, a procedure involving interpretation of a Rorschach with almost no other information about the patient was employed to assess Rorschach validity. Even when Rorschach response protocols are submitted for analysis in this manner, however, identifying cues are often present. For example, the Rorschach protocols of 10-year-olds may be combined in one study with those of 60-year-olds. Sometimes the protocols are sent to former teachers or to friends, so that there may be a higher level of agreement than usual. Just knowing that the protocols came from hospital X may provide important cues about the nature of the patients.

Other studies have used a matching technique to assess the validity of Rorschach interpretations, specifically the matching of Rorschach protocols with case histories. However, there are also problems with these studies. Correct matching may be a function of one or two strikingly deviant variables. Consequently, what has really been validated? There have even been instances in which the person who had administered the Rorschach was subsequently asked to match it with the correct case history. Thus, a correct match may have been determined by the recall of patient characteristics observed during the testing.

Despite the questions raised about its validity, however, several surveys have placed the Rorschach in a favorable light (for example, Atkinson, 1986; Parker, 1983). Further, Parker, Hanson, and Hunsley (1988) in a broad survey of Rorschach studies found the average validity coefficient across a variety of Rorschach scales to be .42. Also, both interjudge reliability and test-retest reliability were in the middle .80s. Although these results may surprise some, they seem to suggest that when an adequate theoretical or empirical basis exists for making specific predictions, the Rorschach may be a useful instrument. Still, many remain critical of the quality of the individual studies that have been cited as supportive of the validity of Rorschach scores (for example, Wood et al., 1996).

From the vast Rorschach literature, it is apparent that the test is not equally valid for all purposes. In a very real sense, the problem is not one of determining whether the Rorschach is valid but of differentiating the conditions under which it is useful from those under which it is not.

Fantasy and symbolism.   Interpreting Rorschach responses in terms of their fantasy content or in terms of what they symbolize has long been a popular approach. Indeed, such an approach is one of the reasons why it appears important to disguise the meaning of test stimuli. Since inkblots seem far removed from what the patient thinks is being measured, such test stimuli should be very useful in circumventing the patient's defenses and unmasking psychodynamic determinants of behavior. Obviously, clinicians who are psychoanalytically oriented will find these aspects of Rorschach stimuli particularly attractive. However, it is important to bear in mind that, as test stimuli become farther and farther removed from culturally defined meanings or from the situations to which clinicians are predicting, the potential for errors in prediction rises dramatically.

    Rorschach inkblot "method."   Recently, Weiner (1994) argued that the Rorschach is best conceptualized as a method of data collection, not a test.

> . . . the Rorschach is not a test because it does not test anything. A test is intended to measure whether something is present or not and in what quantity . . . But with the Rorschach, which has traditionally been classified as a test of personality, we do not measure whether people have a personality or how much personality they have. (p. 499)

Several implications follow. First, Weiner argues that data generated from the Rorschach method can be interpreted from a variety of theoretical positions. These data suggest how the respondent typically solves problems or makes decisions (that is, cognitive structuring processes) as well as the meanings that are assigned to these perceptions (that is, associational processes). Weiner calls this an "integrationist" view of the Rorschach because the method provides data relevant to both the structure of personality as well as to the dynamics of personality. According to Weiner, a second, practical implication is that viewing the Rorschach as a method allows one to fully use all aspects of the data that are generated, resulting in a more thorough diagnostic evaluation.

    As before, empirical data supporting the utility and incremental validity of data generated by the Rorschach inkblot "method" are necessary before its routine use in clinical settings can be advocated.

■ The Thematic Apperception Test

    The *Thematic Apperception Test (TAT)* was introduced by Morgan and Murray in 1935. It purports to reveal patients' basic personality characteristics through the interpretation of their imaginative productions in response to a series of pictures. Although the test is designed to reveal central conflicts, attitudes, goals, and repressed material, it actually produces material that is a collage of these characteristics coupled with situational influences, cultural stereotypes, trivia, and so on. The clinician's job is to separate the wheat from the chaff.

    Most clinicians use the TAT as a method of inferring psychological needs (for example, achievement, affiliation, dependency, power, sex, and so on) and of disclosing how the patient interacts with the environment. In contrast to the Rorschach, the TAT is used to infer the content of personality and the mode of social interactions. With a TAT, clinicians are likely to make specific judgments, such as "This patient is hostile toward authority figures, yet seeks their affection and approval." The TAT is less likely to be used to assess the degree of maladjustment than to reveal the locus of problems, the nature of needs, or the quality of interpersonal relationships.

Description
There are 31 TAT cards in all. Most depict people in a variety of situations, but a few contain only objects; one is blank. Some cards are said to be useful for boys and men, some for girls and women, and some for both genders. Murray suggested that 20 of the 31 cards be selected for a given examinee. As a test, the TAT does not appear to be as ambiguous or unstructured as the Rorschach. However, though the figures in the pictures may clearly be people, it is not always clear what their gender is, exactly who they are, what they are doing, or what they are thinking. Figure 8-3 illustrates one of the TAT cards.

Administration.   In practice, clinicians typically select somewhere between 6 and 12 cards for administration to a given patient. Although the exact instructions used will vary from clinician to clinician, they go something like this: "Now, I want you to make up a story about each of these pictures. Tell me who the people are, what they are doing, and what they are thinking or feeling, what led up to the scene, and how it will turn out. OK?" The patient's productions are transcribed verbatim by the clinician (or sometimes tape-recorded). In some instances, patients may be asked to write out their stories, but this can result in shorter-than-normal stories.

Scoring.   Many scoring schemes have been proposed over the years (Exner, 1983; Shneidman, 1951, 1965). It seems that most clinicians have chosen to accept the judgment that quantified scoring schemes cause clinically useful evidence to be distorted or lost and therefore use such schemes only for research purposes. Interestingly, the TAT has never been as soundly criticized as has the Rorschach. Perhaps this is partially due to the fact that there has never been much interest or emphasis on scoring the TAT—it is hard to carry out empirical studies that fail to support underutilized scoring schemes.

The following examples illustrate several TAT themes and the interpretations or analyses made from them. They are verbatim responses from the same 42-year-old woman described in Case Illustration 2 of the Rorschach section.

Case Illustration 3

Card 3BM. Looks like a little boy crying for something he can't have. (Why is he crying?) Probably because he can't go somewhere. (How will it turn out?) Probably sit there and sob hisself [sic] to sleep.
Card 3GF. Looks like her boyfriend might have let her down. She hurt his feelings. He's closed the door on her. (What did he say?) I don't know.
Card 9GF. Girl looks like somebody's run off and left her. She's ready for a dance. Maid is watching to see where she goes. (Why run off?) Probably because she wasn't ready in time.

Figure 8-3
Card 12F of the TAT. SOURCE: Reprinted by permission of the publishers from
Thematic Apperception Test by H. A. Murray, Cambridge, Mass.: Harvard
University Press, Copyright © 1943 by the President and Fellows of Harvard
College (renewed 1974 by Henry A. Murray).

> *Card 10.* Looks like there's sorrow here. Grieving about something. (About
>   what?) Looks like maybe one of the children's passed away.
> *Card 13MF.* Looks like his wife might have passed away and he feels
>   there's nothing more to do.

Card 20. Looks like a man that's ready to rob something. Hiding behind a high fence of some kind. Has his hand in his pocket with a gun ready to shoot if anybody comes out.

An excerpt from the clinician's report offers this analysis. "The TAT produced responses that were uniformly indicative of unhappiness, threat, misfortune, or lack of control over environmental forces. None of the test responses were indicative of satisfaction, happy endings, and so on. In this test, as in the Rorschach, impoverished and constricted responses are evident which probably indicate anxiety and depression. . . . In summary, the test results point to an individual who is anxious and, at the same time, depressed. Feelings of insecurity, inadequacy, and lack of control over environmental forces are apparent, as are unhappiness and apprehension. These factors result in a constriction of performance that is largely oriented toward avoiding threat and that hampers sufficient mobilization of energy to perform at an optimal level."

Lindzey, Bradford, Tejessy, and Davids (1959) have compiled a dictionary of interpretive generalizations that might be made from TAT stories. It covers nearly 200 publications, and the sheer volume of possible TAT interpretations from the various story cues is tremendous. This highlights the difficulties that are encountered when one raises questions about TAT validity—the inevitable rejoinder must be, Valid with respect to what? A few of the interpretive generalizations culled from the literature by Lindzey et al. are listed below:

Paranoid symptomatology indicated by: Stereotyped phrases perseverating throughout a record. (Rapaport, 1946, p. 449)

Anxiety indicated by: . . . plots emphasizing sudden physical accidents and emotional trauma, such as loss of wife, mother, sweetheart, job, a house burning down, or a stock crash. (Rotter, 1946, p. 88)

Dependency in adolescents indicated by . . . three or more references to one or more members of the family. (Symonds, 1949, p. 87)

Patients with sexual problems may: . . . avoid the picture on the wall in Picture #4 or refuse to discuss the nude female in Picture #13. (Stein, 1948, p. 42)

Unfortunately, these propositions have received relatively little research attention. Further, we are not aware of any research suggesting that information obtained from the TAT is significantly related to treatment outcome. Given the TAT's purported ability to identify interpersonal styles that might influence choices regarding the therapists' treatment approach, this is somewhat surprising.

A summary evaluation of the TAT

As with the Rorschach, let us conclude this section with a summary evaluation of the TAT.

Reliability and validity.

It is very difficult to evaluate the reliability and validity of the TAT in any formal sense. There are many variations in instructions, methods of administration, number of cards used, and type of scoring scheme (if any) so that hard conclusions are virtually impossible. The same methodological issues arise when studying reliability. For example, personality changes may obscure any conclusions about test-retest reliability, or there may be uncertainty about equivalent forms when trying to assess equivalent-forms reliability. It is possible to investigate theme reliability, but since clinicians cannot expect word-for-word similarity from one occasion to the next, they are therefore usually studying the reliability of judges' interpretations. When there is an explicit, theoretically derived set of scoring instructions (for example, Fitzgerald, 1958), interjudge agreement can reach acceptable proportions. Interjudge reliability can also be achieved when quantitative ratings are involved (Harrison, 1965). But broad, global interpretations can present problems.

Some attempts have been made to establish the validity of the TAT. These include (1) comparison of TAT interpretations with case data or with therapist evaluations of the patient, (2) matching techniques and analyses of protocols with no additional knowledge about the patient, (3) comparisons between clinical diagnoses derived from the TAT and psychiatrists' judgments, and (4) establishment of the validity of certain general principles of interpretation (for example, the tendency of the person to identify with the hero of the story, the probability that unusual themes are more significant than common ones, and so on).

The typical clinical use of the TAT suggests that it remains basically a subjective instrument. Although it is possible to identify general principles of interpretation, these can serve only as guides—not as exact prescriptions for interpretation. Adequate interpretation depends upon some knowledge of the patient's background. As the clinician examines the test protocol, attention must be paid to the frequency with which thematic elements occur, the unusualness of stories, the manner in which plots are developed, the occurrence of misrecognitions, the choice of words, the identifications with plot characters, and so on. The clinician will want to look closely at the nature of the TAT heroes or heroines and at their needs and goals. The environmental presses are also important, as is the general emotional ambience of the themes.

■ Completion Techniques

A very durable and serviceable, yet simple, testing technique is the *sentence completion method*. The most widely used and best known of the many versions of this test is the Rotter Incomplete Sentences Blank (Rotter & Rafferty, 1950; Rotter, 1954). The Rotter *Incomplete Sentences Blank (ISB)* consists of 40 sentence stems, for example: "I like . . ."; "What annoys me . . ."; "I wish . . ."; and "Most girls. . . ." Each of the completions can be scored along a seven-point scale to provide a general index of adjustment-maladjustment (see Jessor, Liverant, & Opochinsky, 1963). The ISB has great versatility, and scoring schemes for a variety of variables have been developed (for example, Fitzgerald, 1958).

The ISB has several advantages. The scoring is objective and reliable, due in part to extensive scoring examples provided in the manual. The ISB can be easily and economically employed, and it appears to be a good screening device. Although it can be scored objectively, it also allows considerable freedom of response.

Thus, the ISB falls somewhere between the extremes of the objective-projective dimension. It represents a fairly direct approach to measurement that does not require the degree of training that is necessary to score the Rorschach, for example. Some clinicians may be disturbed by the ISB's relative lack of disguise. Perhaps because of this, the ISB does not typically provide information that could not be gleaned from a reasonably extensive interview. In many ways, then, the ISB provides a cognitive and behavioral picture of the patient rather than a deep, psychodynamic picture.

■ Illusory Correlation

The interpretation of projective test responses depends heavily on the psychodiagnostician's experience. Observations of certain test responses that supposedly occur in connection with certain personality characteristics are observed over time. As a result, the clinician learns to associate these test responses with specific personality characteristics—they become "signs" or indicators.

However, a great deal of research evidence fails to support the meaningfulness of many of these diagnostic signs. Little and Shneidman (1959) found, for example, that eminent clinicians performed only slightly better than chance in making valid statements about patients on the basis of their test responses. Chapman and Chapman (1969) believe that one reason for this poor performance lies in the tendency to rely on *illusory correlations* between test responses and personality characteristics. Chapman and Chapman found that, in the case of the Rorschach, clinicians tended to focus on test responses that have a high associative value with male homosexuality. Thus, when they observed such test responses of males as, "This looks like a man bending over," or "This is an anal opening," they quickly but mistakenly assumed they had evidence for the presence of homosexual tendencies. Just as quickly, they overlooked valid signs that had low associative strength, such as threatening animals or animals that are humanized (for example, a headless monster or a woman with butterfly wings). Although the "diagnosis" of homosexuality is not relevant to the practice of contemporary clinical psychology because homosexuality is no longer considered a mental disorder, the important point is that illusory correlation based on associative strength can introduce a powerful source of error.

■ Incremental Utility

As mentioned in the discussion of the MMPI-2, *incremental validity* refers to the degree to which a procedure adds to the prediction obtainable from other sources (Meehl & Rosen, 1955; Sechrest, 1963).

For an assessment procedure to be of real value, it must tell clinicians something of importance that they cannot get from merely inspecting the *base rates,* or prevalence rates, for the population of interest. For the clinician in a state school for the mentally retarded to report via the WISC-III that a given patient is mentally retarded hardly comes as a surprise, since we already know that 98% of the institutional populace is retarded. If, however, the test can tell the clinician something about the patient's patterning of abilities that will assist in planning vocational training, then some incremental validity may be attached to the testing procedure. Discovering from a Rorschach that a 70-year-old widower "seems to be grappling with intense feelings of loneliness" hardly represents a breakthrough in incremental validity, even though the statement may be entirely true. Asserting that the TAT themes of a patient with schizophrenia reveal adjustment difficulties or that the Rorschach responses of a patient known to be depressed are suggestive of dysphoria and sadness adds little if anything to existing knowledge, even though it may appear that something correct and profound has been said. Finally, it should be noted that a given assessment instrument must demonstrate incremental validity over other more economical measures (for example, short, self-report inventories) in order to justify its use. Otherwise, the extra effort for the same information wastes the clinician's and the patient's time.

■ The Use and Abuse of Testing

Ours has long been a test-oriented society. Whether the question concerns personnel selection, intellectual assessment, or measuring the "real me," many, it seems, turn to tests. People sometimes consult popular magazines for these tests, other times skilled clinicians, but the abiding curiosity and the inflated set of expectations seem constant. And, quite often, high expectations lead to abuse.

Testing is big business. Psychological, educational, and personnel corporations sell many thousands of tests each year. So many of our lives are touched in so many ways by assessment procedures that we have become accustomed to them and hardly notice them. College admission, employment, military discharge, imprisonment, adoption, therapeutic planning, computer dating, and special classes all may depend upon test performance. Any enterprise that becomes this large and affects such a vast number of people in so many different arenas invites careful scrutiny.

Protections

The ethical standards of psychologists (APA, 1992) require that they employ only techniques or procedures that lie within their competence. These ethical standards, along with the growth of state certification and licensing boards and the certification of professional competence offered by the American Board of Professional Psychology, all combine to increase the probability that the public's interests will be protected.

In addition, the purchase of testing materials is generally restricted by the publisher to individuals or institutions that can demonstrate their competence in administering, scoring, and interpreting tests. In effect, then, the sale of tests is not open but is dependent upon the user's qualifications. However, neither professional ethics nor publishers' restrictions are totally successful. Tests still sometimes find their way into the hands of unscrupulous individuals. And ethical standards are not always sufficient either.

An additional protection involves the responsibility of the marketers of tests for their careful standardization. Normative data and instructions for administration and scoring should be included in every test manual. All in all, enough data should be included to enable the user to evaluate the reliability and validity of the test.

The question of privacy

Most people assume that they have the right to reveal as little or as much as they like about their attitudes, feelings, fears, or aspirations. Of course, with subtle or indirect assessment procedures, an examinee cannot always judge with complete certainty whether a given response is desirable. But whatever the nature of a test, the individual has the right to a full explanation of its purposes and of the use to which the results will be put.

The examinee must be given only tests relevant to the purposes of the evaluation. If an MMPI-2 or a Rorschach is included in a personnel selection battery, it is the psychologist's responsibility to explain the relevancy of the test to the individual. Informed consent to the entire assessment process should be obtained, and individuals should be fully informed of their options. This applies even to those who have initiated the contact by voluntarily seeking clinical services.

The question of confidentiality

Issues of trust and confidentiality loom large in our society. The proliferation of computer processing facilities and huge data banks makes it very easy for one government agency to gain access to personal records that are in the files of another agency or company. Credit card agencies, the FBI, the CIA, the IRS, all create a climate in which no one's records or past seems to be confidential or inviolable. Although information revealed to psychiatrists and clinical psychologists is typically regarded as privileged, there are continuing assaults on the right to withhold such information. For example, the *Tarasoff* decision of the California Supreme Court makes it clear that information provided by a patient in the course of therapy cannot remain privileged if that information indicates that the patient may be dangerous. If the sanctity of the therapy room is less than unassailable, it is certain that personnel records, school records, and other test repositories are even more vulnerable. Clinical psychologists employed in industrial settings are also unable to ensure absolutely the privacy of test results. Clinicians can become caught in the middle of tugs-of-war between union and management over grievance claims. In addition, it sometimes happens that when people are treated under insurance or medical assistance programs, their diagnoses are entered into computer records to which many companies may obtain access.

When an individual is tested, every effort should be made to explain the purposes and use of the testing and to provide information about the people or institutions that will have access to the results. If the individual gives informed consent, the testing can proceed. If, however, it subsequently becomes desirable to release the results to someone else, the individual's consent must be obtained. It is clear that not all clients wish to have their mental health records released, and even when they sign consent forms they often seem to do so either out of a fear that they will be denied services or out of sheer obedience to authority (Rosen, 1977).

The question of discrimination

Since the rise of the civil rights movement, most people have become increasingly aware of the ways in which society has both knowingly and unknowingly discriminated against minorities. Within psychology, attacks have recently centered on the ways in which tests discriminate against minorities. For example, the original standardization of the Stanford-Binet contained no African American samples. Since then, many tests have been published whose attempts to include racially unbiased samples were questioned. It is often charged that most psychological tests are really designed for white middle-class populations and that other groups are handicapped by being tested with devices that are really inappropriate for them. Anastasi (1988), Lanyon and Goodstein (1982), and Sundberg (1977) have all commented on these problems.

Very often, the minority group member's lack of experience with tests and test situations is a major source of the problem. Such inexperience, inadequate motivation, and discomfort in the presence of an examiner from another race all may affect test performance. Often, too, test materials are prepared or embedded in a racially unfair context—for example, the TAT cards may all depict white characters or the items on an intelligence test may not be familiar to an African American child. What is wrong here is that the test items themselves, the manner in which they are presented, or the circumstances surrounding the test may work to the disadvantage of the minority individual.

Test bias

It is important to remember, however, that significant differences between mean scores on a test for different groups do not in and of themselves indicate test bias or discrimination. Rather, test bias or discrimination is a validity issue. That is, if it can be demonstrated that the validity of a test (for example, in predicting criterion characteristics or performance) varies significantly across groups, then a case can be made that the test is biased for that purpose. In other words, a test is biased to the extent that it predicts more accurately for one group than for another group.

An example can illustrate these considerations. Let us assume that one of the authors developed a personality inventory to measure hostility. As part of the standardization project for this test, the author discovered that men scored significantly higher than women on this test. Doe this indicate that the test is biased? Not necessarily. The author found, in a series of validity studies, that the relationship (correlation) between hostility inventory scores and the number of verbal fights over the succeeding two months was quite similar for both men and women. In other words, the predictive validity coefficients for the two groups were comparable; similar hostility scores meant the same thing (that is, predicted a comparable number of verbal fights) for men and women. On the other hand, it is quite possible the strength of the correlation between hostility scores and physical fights over the next two months is significantly greater for men than women. In this latter case, the use of the test to predict physical aggression in women would be biased if these predictions were based on the known association between hostility scores and physical fights found in men.

Several general points should be clear. First, differences in mean scores do not necessarily indicate test bias. In the example above, there may be good reasons why men score higher on average than women on a measure of hostility (for example, hormonal differences or other biological differences may lead to higher levels of hostility for men). In fact, to find no difference in mean scores might call into question the validity of the test in this case. Second, the pronouncement of a test as "valid," although frequently seen in the clinical psychology literature, is incorrect. Tests may be valid (and not biased) for some purposes but not for others. Finally, the clinician can overcome test bias by using different (and more appropriate) prediction equations for different groups. In other words, bias comes into play when the clinical psychologist makes predictions based on empirical associations that are characteristic of another group (for example, men) but not of members of the group of interest (women). The goal is to investigate the possibility of differential validity, and, if found, to employ the appropriate prediction equation for that group.

Computer assessment

Computers have been used for years to score tests and to generate psychological profiles. Now they are also used to administer and interpret responses to clinical interviews, IQ tests, self-report inventories, and even projective tests. The reasons for such use are said to involve cost cutting, enhancing clients' attention and motivation, and standardizing procedures across clinicians. Clearly, computers have great potential, but they also contain the seeds of definite problems (Burke & Normand, 1987). To begin with, there needs to be greater acceptance of computer assessment by professionals. Beyond that, more attention must be devoted to the feelings and reactions of clients upon whom these computerized procedures are imposed. Important issues of reliability and validity (see Gottesman & Prescott, 1989) as well as proper feedback to clients have yet to be settled. And finally, the field needs better overall professional standards for such testing. It is important to remember that computer systems can easily be misused, either by those who are poorly trained or by those who endow computers with a sagacity that transcends the quality and utility of the information programmed into them.

In recent years, a number of abuses of computer analyses of tests in general and the MMPI in particular have arisen. The attorney general in one state was asked by that state's psychological association to review such abuses. For example, psychologically untrained medical personnel employed computer interpretations of a self-report inventory whose norms had been outdated for years. In other cases, companies selling computer services advertise how economical these services are compared to conventional interpretation methods. Yet there is little evidence that these economies are being passed along to patients, who are the real consumers.

Recently, guidelines have been proposed as to how best to evaluate the reliability and validity of *computer-based test interpretations,* or *CBTIs* (Moreland, 1985; Snyder, Widiger, & Hoover, 1990), as well as how best to utilize CBTIs in clinical work (Butcher, 1995). For example, Butcher (1995, p. 82) outlined seven steps for providing MMPI-2 feedback to clients:

1. Provide historical information about the MMPI-2.
2. Briefly describe how the MMPI-2 scales were developed as well as the vastness of the empirical literature on the MMPI and MMPI-2.
3. Briefly describe the validity scales and how they indicate the client's approach to the testing.
4. Describe the clinical hypotheses that have been generated based on the MMPI-2 profile, couching this in terms of how clients presented themselves and how they are viewing their problems (if any) at this time.
5. Discuss any significant elevations on the content scales because what these items measure is intuitively apparent.
6. Invite clients to ask questions about their scores and clarify any confusing issues.
7. Discuss how clients feel the test results fit or do not fit their experience.

Interestingly, results from a recent study (Finn & Tonsager, 1992) suggest that MMPI-2 test feedback may actually serve as a type of clinical intervention. In this study, one group of student clients at a university counseling center received MMPI-2 test feedback while they were on a waiting list at the clinic, and a second group did not take the MMPI-2. The first group showed improvement on measures of both psychopathology symptoms and self-esteem whereas the control group did not. Although it is possible that the "therapeutic effect" observed may be attributable to just taking the MMPI-2, and not necessarily to getting the feedback, future research in this area seems warranted. This study is laudable because it attempts to demonstrate the clinical utility of the MMPI-2.

As for computer assessment and the MMPI specifically, numerous efforts to computerize its scoring and interpretation have been made (Honaker, 1988; Kleinmuntz, 1972; Dahlstrom, Welsh, & Dahlstrom, 1972). The approaches are mainly descriptive and useful most often for screening, but programs exist for highly interpretive statements to be generated as well (for example, Dahlstrom, Welsh, & Dahlstrom, 1972). Certainly, though, not everyone believes that computerized and conventional usage of the MMPI yield comparable results (Buros, 1972; Honaker, 1988).

The use of computer-based test interpretations is a contentious issue that continues to generate considerable debate among professionals (see Bloom, 1992; Fowler & Butcher, 1986; Matarazzo, 1986). Ultimately, however, the success of *any* clinical assessment instrument depends on whether the information provided by the test is useful for planning, conducting, and evaluating treatment.

■ Focus Questions

1. What are the advantages and disadvantages of objective tests?
2. What are the major strategies of test construction? Briefly describe each of these.
3. What are the similarities and differences between objective and projective measures?
4. Why is the reliability and validity of projective measures so difficult to assess?
5. What does and what does *not* constitute evidence for test bias?

■ Key Terms

base rates
computer assessment
computer-based test
  interpretations (CBTIs)
construct validity approach
content validation
empirical criterion keying
factor analysis
Five-Factor Model (FFM)
illusory correlations
Incomplete Sentences Blank
  (ISB)
incremental validity

MMPI-2
NEO-PI-R
objective personality measures
projective techniques
Rorschach
sentence completion method
test bias
Thematic Apperception Test
  (TAT)
validity of cutoff scores
  (thresholds)
validity scales

9

Behavioral Assessment

In the traditional view, personality is a system of constructs that mediates behavior. Whether the construct is ego, expectancy, trait, paranoia, or growth potential, this view is concerned with relatively stable personal characteristics that contribute to behavior. It follows, then, that if one is going to understand or predict behavior one must assess those underlying variables. This is, of course, an oversimplification that masks a good deal of disagreement, since the underlying constructs that are important to a psychoanalytic clinician are likely to be quite different from those that are important to a social learning theorist.

Behavior therapists and assessors, however, do not look at personality in the traditional fashion. They see personality more in terms of behavioral tendencies in specific situations. Their focus shifts from a search for underlying personality characteristics to one that looks for the interaction between behaviors and situations. This kind of conceptualization leads some clinicians to view personality much like a set of abilities (Wallace, 1966). For such people, personality becomes a set of abilities or skills rather than a constellation of predispositions (for example, needs, traits) that convey the essence of the person. Aggression and dependency are seen as skills, much like riding a bicycle. The focus turns to adjectival properties rather than to nouns—for example, behavior therapists are interested in aggressive behavior, not aggression.

■ The Behavioral Tradition

Before we examine specific methods of behavioral assessment, let us consider three broad ways in which it differs from traditional assessment.

Sample versus sign
In *traditional assessment,* a description of the situation is much less important than the identification of the more enduring personality characteristics. In *behavioral assessment,* the paramount issue is how well the assessment device samples the behaviors and situations in which the clinician is interested. How well the

test is disguised or how deeply into the recesses of personality it reaches become irrelevant questions. Years ago, Goldfried (1976) described the relevance of a *sign* and a *sample* orientation to testing as follows:

> When test responses are viewed as a sample, one assumes that they parallel the way in which a person is likely to behave in a nontest situation. Thus, if a person responds aggressively on a test, one assumes that this aggression also occurs in other situations as well. When test responses are viewed as signs, an inference is made that the performance is an indirect or symbolic manifestation of some other characteristic. An example is a predominance of Vista responses on the Rorschach, in which the individual reports that his [sic] percepts are viewed as if they were seen from a distance. In interpreting such a response, one does not typically conclude that the individual is in great need of optometric care, but rather that such responses presumably indicate the person's ability for self-evaluation and insight. For the most part, traditional assessment has employed a sign as opposed to sample approach to test interpretation. In the case of behavioral assessment only the sample approach makes sense. (pp. 283–284)

Functional analysis

Another central feature of behavioral assessment is traceable to Skinner's (1953) notion of *functional analysis*. This means that exact analyses are made of the stimuli that precede a behavior and the consequences that follow it. By assessing the manner in which variations in stimulus conditions and outcomes are related to behavior changes, a more precise understanding of the causes of behavior is possible (Haynes & O'Brien, 1990). The major thesis is that behaviors are learned and maintained because of the consequences that follow them. Thus, to change an undesirable behavior, the clinician must (1) identify the stimulus conditions that precipitate it, and (2) determine the reinforcements that follow. Once these two sets of factors are assessed, the clinician is in a position to modify the behavior by manipulating the stimuli and reinforcements involved.

Crucial to a functional analysis is careful and precise description. The behavior of concern must be described in observable, measurable terms so that its rate of occurrence can be recorded reliably. With equal precision, the conditions that control it must also be specified. Both *antecedent conditions* and *consequent events* are thus carefully elaborated. Such events as time, place, and people present when the behavior occurs are determined, along with the specific outcomes that follow the behavior of concern.

Suppose, for example, that a child is aggressively disruptive in the classroom. Traditional assessment might well be directed toward analyzing the needs that the child is trying to satisfy, with the hope that once they are identified they can be modified. This, in turn, would eliminate the undesirable behavior. A behavioral assessment, however, would ignore such hypothesized internal determinants as needs and focus instead on the target—aggressive behavior. It might be discovered that the child usually takes objects (for example, a pencil) from another child (that is, behaves aggressively) when the teacher is paying attention to others in the classroom. Moreover, when the aggressiveness occurs, the teacher almost invariably turns her attention to the disruptive child. A functional analysis, then, reveals that lack of attention (stimulus) is followed by taking a pencil from another child (behavior), which, in turn, is followed by attention (consequence). Once this pattern of relationships is established, steps can be taken to change it and thereby modify the undesirable behavior. As an example, the child might be put in a room alone following the disruptive behavior. This treatment would be expected to alter the behavior, since it is no longer followed by consequences that the child finds reinforcing. This scenario may not seem much different from what many parents would do intuitively. The difference, however, resides in the care and precision with which relationships are identified and in the exact specification of the target behaviors. Table 9-1 summarizes a variety of differences between traditional and behavioral approaches to assessment.

Most behavioral therapists have broadened the method of functional analysis to include "organismic" variables as well. *Organismic variables* include physical, physiological, or cognitive characteristics of the individual that are important for both the conceptualization of the client's problem and the ultimate treatment that is administered. For example, attitudes and beliefs that are characteristic of individuals who are prone to experience depressive episodes may be quite important to assess because of their purported relationship to depression and their suitability as targets for intervention. A useful model for conceptualizing a clinical problem from a behavioral perspective is the *SORC model* (Kanfer & Phillips, 1970):

S = stimulus or antecedent conditions that bring on the problematic behavior
O = organismic variables related to the problematic behavior
R = response or problematic behavior
C = consequences of the problematic behavior

Behavioral clinicians use this model to guide and inform them about both the information needed to fully describe the problem and, ultimately, the interventions that may be prescribed.

Behavioral assessment as an ongoing process

As pointed out by Peterson and Sobell (1994), behavioral assessment in a clinical context is not a one-shot evaluation performed before treatment is initiated. Rather, it is an ongoing process that occurs before, during, and after treatment. Behavioral assessment is important because it informs the initial selection of treatment strategies, provides a means of feedback regarding the efficacy of treatment strategies as they are enacted in the treatment process, allows an evaluation of the overall effectiveness of treatment once completed, and highlights situational factors that may lead to the recurrence of problematic behavior.

Figure 9-1 illustrates behavioral assessment at various stages of treatment (Peterson & Sobell, 1994). First, *diagnostic formulations* can be useful to the behavioral clinician because these include descriptions of maladaptive behaviors or potential targets for intervention. Second, the patient's *context or environment* (for example, his or her social support system, physical environment) is important to assess because of the relevance to treatment planning and the setting of realistic treatment goals. An evaluation of *client resources* like skills, level of motivation, beliefs, and expectations is important as well. As noted by Peterson and Sobell (1994), the initial assessments of diagnosis/maladaptive behaviors, treatment

Table 9-1
Differences between behavioral and traditional approaches to assessment.

	Behavioral	Traditional
I. Assumptions		
1. Conception of personality	Personality constructs mainly employed to summarize specific behavior patterns, if at all	Personality as a reflection of enduring underlying states or traits
2. Causes of behavior	Maintaining conditions sought in current environment	Intrapsychic (within the individual)
II. Implications		
1. Role of behavior	Important as a sample of person's repertoire in specific situation	Behavior assumes importance only insofar as it indexes underlying causes
2. Role of history	Relatively unimportant, except, for example, to provide a retrospective baseline	Crucial in that present conditions seen as a product of the past
3. Consistency of behavior	Behavior thought to be specific to the situation	Behavior expected to be consistent across time and settings
III. Uses of data	To describe target behaviors and maintaining conditions	To describe personality functioning and etiology
	To select the appropriate treatment	To disgnose or classify
	To evaluate and revise treatment	To make prognosis; to predict
IV. Other characteristics		
1. Level of inferences	Low	Medium to high
2. Comparison	More emphasis on intraindividual or idiographic	More emphasis on interindividual or nomothetic
3. Methods of assessment	More emphasis on direct methods (for example, observations of behavior in natural environment)	More emphasis on indirect methods (for example, interviews and self-report)
4. Timing of assessment	Ongoing—prior, during, and after treatment	Pre- and perhaps post-treatment, or strictly to diagnose
5. Scope of assessment	Specific measures and of more variables (for example, of target behaviors in various situations, of side effects, context, strengths as well as deficiencies)	More global measures (for example, of cure or improvement) but only of the individual

SOURCE: From "Some Relationships Between Behavioral and Traditional Assessment," by D. P. Hartmann, B. L. Roper, and D. C. Bradford, 1979, *Journal of Behavioral Assessment, 1,* 4. Copyright © 1979 by Plenum Publishing Corporation. Reprinted by permission.

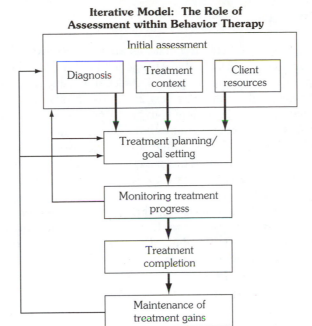

Figure 9-1
Model of the role of behavioral assessment within behavior therapy. SOURCE: From
"Introduction to the State-of-the-Art Review Series: Research Contributions to
Clinical Assessment," by L. Peterson and L. C. Sobell, *Behavior Therapy, 25,*
523–531. Copyright © 1994 by the Association for Advancement of Behavior
Therapy. Reprinted with permission.

context, and client resources will naturally lead to a data-based initial *treatment
plan.* This plan involves collaborative goal setting between the patient and the
therapist as well as mutually agreed upon criteria to indicate improvement. Formal
assessments of treatment progress serve as ongoing feedback as well as avenues
for building the patient's self-efficacy as progress is being made. Assessment of the
patient following completion of treatment provides objective data regarding his or
her "end-state functioning," and this can be compared to data from the pretreatment assessment. Finally, thorough assessment throughout the foregoing stages
will provide information regarding the likelihood of symptom recurrence as well as
high-risk environments that may lead to relapse.

Peterson and Sobell (1994) argue that this model of behavioral assessment
has great potential to bridge the often wide gap between behavioral research and
actual clinical practice. As we shall discuss in Chapter 14, the field of behavior
therapy is unique in its emphasis on data-based decision making throughout all
phases of treatment. Therefore, behavioral assessment is not a luxury but, rather,
a necessity.

With these notions in mind we can now turn to an examination of some of
the more typical behavioral assessment methods.

■ Interviews

Obviously, one cannot begin a functional analysis or develop a program of behavioral treatment before having at least a general notion of what the problem is. To develop such notions, the behavioral clinician is likely to turn to that old standby, the interview—the clinician's best and most durable friend. During *behavioral interviews,* the clinician attempts to gain a general impression of the presenting problem and of the variables that seem to be maintaining that problem behavior (Goldfried & Davison, 1994). Other information sought includes relevant historical data and an assessment of the patient's strengths and of past attempts to cope with the problem. Also of interest are the patient's expectations regarding therapy. Finally, when feasible, some initial establishment and communication of therapeutic goals by the clinician can be quite helpful. However, the basic goal of the interview is to identify specific problem behaviors, situational factors that maintain the problem behavior, and the consequences that result from the problem behavior. It should also be noted that the use of *structured diagnostic interviews* (see Chapter 6) is increasing among behavioral clinicians because the symptoms of the mental disorders are viewed as problematic behaviors targeted for intervention (Morrison, 1988).

■ Observational Methods

Behavioral clinicians employ a variety of observational methods during the assessment process, all of which involve the direct observation of behavior. In these methods, the observations are made by the clinicians, trained observers, peers, or the clients themselves.

Naturalistic observation

To assess and understand behavior, clinicians first have to know what they are dealing with. It comes as no surprise, then, that behavioral assessment employs *observation* as a primary technique. A clinician can try to understand a phobic's fear of heights, a student's avoidance of evaluation settings, or anyone's tendencies to overeat. These people could be interviewed, probed with projectives, or examined with self-report inventories. But many clinicians would argue that, unless those people are directly observed in their natural environments, true understanding will be incomplete. To determine the frequency, strength, and pervasiveness of the problem behavior or the factors that are maintaining it, behavioral clinicians would advise turning to direct observation.

Of course, all this is easier said than done. Practically speaking, it is difficult and expensive to maintain trained observers and have them available. This is especially true in the case of adults who are being treated on an outpatient basis. It is relatively easier to accomplish with children, those with mental retardation, and other similar groups, or to make observations in a sheltered or institutional setting. In some cases, it is possible to utilize observers who are characteristically part of the person's environment (for example, spouse, parents, teachers, friends, nurses, and so on). In certain instances, as we shall see later, it is even possible to have the client do some self-observation. Naturally, there is the ever-present question of ethics: clinical psychologists must take pains to make sure that people are not observed without their knowledge or that friends and associates of the client are not unwittingly drawn into the observational net in a fashion that compromises their dignity and right to privacy.

Perhaps because of these reasons, naturalistic observation has never been used in clinical practice as much as it might be. Indeed, observation is still more prominent in research than in clinical practice. But one need not be a diehard proponent of the behavioral approach to concede the importance of observational data. It is not unlikely that clinicians of many different persuasions have arrived at incomplete pictures of their clients—after all, they may never see them except during the 50-minute therapy session or through the prisms of objective or projective test data. But because of the cumbersome nature of many observational procedures, for years most clinicians have opted for the simpler and seemingly more efficient methods of traditional assessment.

It should be noted, of course, that naturalistic observation is hardly a new idea. McReynolds (1975) traced the roots of naturalistic observation to the ancient civilizations of Greece and China. Over 40 years ago, Barker and Wright (1951) described their systematic and detailed recordings of the behavior of a 7-year-old over one day (a major effort that took an entire book). Beyond this, all of us recognize instantly that our own informal assessments of friends and associates are heavily influenced by observations of their naturally occurring behavior. But observation, like testing, is useful only when steps are taken to ensure its reliability and validity. As we pursue these topics, the reader may notice that a number of the factors that affect the reliability and validity of observations are basically the same as those discussed in connection with the interview (see Chapter 6).

Examples of naturalistic observation

Many forms of naturalistic observation have been employed over the years for specific settings, such as classrooms, playgrounds, general and psychiatric hospitals, home environments, institutions for those with mental retardation, therapy encounters in outpatient clinics, and more. Again, it is important to note that many of the systems employed in these settings have been most widely used for research purposes, but most of them are adaptable for clinical use as well.

Home observation. Since experiences in the family or home have such pervasive effects on adjustment, it is not surprising that a number of assessment procedures have been developed for behaviors occurring there. One of the best-known systems for this purpose is the Behavioral Coding System (BCS), which was developed by Patterson (1977) and his colleagues (Jones, Reid, & Patterson, 1975). This observational system was designed for use in the homes of predelinquent boys who exhibited problems in the areas of aggressiveness and noncompliance. Under the BCS method, trained observers spend one or two hours in the homes of such boys, observing and recording family interactions. Usually the observations are made immediately before or during dinner. Observers

BLANK SAMPLE CODING SHEET FOR THE BCS

Family Number _____

ID Number _____

BEHAVIOR CODING SHEET

Phase _____

Subject _____ Observer _____ Date _____ No. _____

AP	Approval	HU	Humiliate	PP	Positive physical
AT	Attention	IG	Ignore		contact
CM	Command	LA	Laugh	RC	Receive
CN	Command	NC	Noncompliance	SS	Self-stimulation
	(negative)	NE	Negativism	TA	Talk
CO	Compliance	NO	Normative	TE	Tease
CR	Cry	NR	No response	TH	Touching,
DI	Disapproval	PL	Play		handling
DP	Dependency	PN	Negative physical	WH	Whine
DS	Destructiveness		contact	WK	Work
HR	High rate			YE	Yell

1				
2				
• • •				
10				

Description _____

Figure 9-2

A blank sample coding sheet for the BCS. SOURCE: From "Naturalistic Observation in Clinical Assessment," by R. R. Jones, J. B. Reid, and G. R. Patterson. In P. McReynolds (ed.), *Advances in Psychological Assessment,* Vol. 3, p. 56. Copyright © 1975 by Jossey-Bass, Inc. Reprinted by permission.

are not allowed to interact with family members (although occasionally they may talk with them before or after the observations to elicit better acceptance of the procedure). Each family member is observed for two 5-minute periods during each observational occasion. Observations are made of behaviors in 28 categories, and every 6 seconds during the period a given family member is being observed, the observer notes whether these behaviors have or have not occurred. Figure 9-2 shows a sample BCS coding sheet. The 6-second subintervals are shown within each row of the sheet, and each row represents a 30-second interval. Examples of the 28 rated categories are:

HU (Humiliate): Makes fun of, shames, or embarrasses the individual intentionally.

CO (Compliance): A person immediately does what is asked of him or her.
WH (Whine): A person states something in a slurring, nasal, high-pitched, falsetto voice.

Similar methods have been used by Mash, Terdal, and Anderson (1973) and by Lewinsohn and Shaffer (1971). Another example comes from the work of Hops et al. (1987). They coded family interactions observed in the homes of depressed women and found a number of behavioral and interactional effects related to their depression.

School observation.   Clinical child psychologists very often must deal with behavior problems that take place in the school setting; children are disruptive in class, overly aggressive on the playground, generally fearful, cling to the teacher, will not concentrate, and so on. While the verbal reports of parents and teachers are useful, the most direct assessment procedure is actually to observe the problem behavior in its natural habitat. A variety of coding systems have been developed over the years for use in school settings (for example, Bijou, Peterson, & Ault, 1968; Kent, Miner, & Ray, 1974; O'Leary & Becker, 1967).

An example of how such systems are employed is found in a study by Madsen and Becker (1968). They focused on inappropriate behaviors in elementary-school children. Observers were given extensive training to establish the reliability of their ratings. While observing in the classroom they were instructed not to respond to the children, but to "fade into the background." Target children were observed 20 minutes per day, 3 days per week. Each observer was equipped with a clipboard, stopwatch, and rating sheet. Observers watched for 10 seconds and then recorded the occurrence of behaviors. In each minute, ratings were made in five consecutive 10-second intervals with the final 10 seconds used for recording comments. Each behavior category could be rated only once per 10-second interval. Of major interest was the percentage of intervals in which an inappropriate behavior took place. Table 9-2 shows the behavioral coding categories employed for inappropriate behaviors.

Hospital observation.   Observation techniques have long been used in such settings as psychiatric hospitals or institutions for those with mental retardation. The sheltered characteristics of these settings have made careful observation of behavior much more feasible than in more open, uncontrolled environments. One of the most widely used devices has been the Wittenborn Psychiatric Rating Scales (Wittenborn, 1955). This device is composed of 52 scales, each containing several descriptive statements that characterize the patient. Hospital staff observe the patient and then choose the statement that best fits (for example, refuses to eat, definitely avoids people, acute insomnia, and so on). The scores associated with each statement are added, and a profile can be constructed that will indicate the patient's standing with regard to various psychiatric categories as anxiety, schizophrenia, and the like.

The Wittenborn scale and others similar to it suffer from one limitation that many strict behaviorists find quite disconcerting. These scales require that the observer often make inferences from the behavior observed. For example, rather

Table 9-2
Behavioral coding categories for inappropriate behaviors.

Inappropriate Behaviors

Gross Motor
Getting out of seat, standing up, running, hopping, skipping, jumping, walking around, moving chair, and so on.

Object Noise
Tapping pencil or other objects, clapping, tapping feet, rattling or tearing paper, throwing book on desk, slamming desk. (Be conservative: only rate if you can hear the noise when eyes are closed. Do not include accidental dropping of objects.)

Disturbance of Others's Property
Grabbing objects or work, knocking neighbors' books off desk, destroying another's property, pushing with desk (only rate if someone is there). Throwing objects at another person without hitting him or her.

Contact (high or low intensity)
Hitting, kicking, shoving, pinching, slapping, striking with object, throwing object which hits another person, poking with object, biting, pulling hair, touching, patting, and so on. (Any physical contact is rated.)

Verbalization
Carrying on conversations with other children when it is not permitted. Answering teacher without raising hand or without being called on; making comments or calling out remarks when no questions have been asked; calling teacher's name to get her attention; crying, screamng, singing, whistling, laughing, coughing, or blowing loudly. These responses may be directed to teacher or children.

Turning Around
Turning head or head and body to look at another person, showing objects to another child, attending to another child. (Must be of 4-second duration, or more than 90 degrees using desk as a reference. Not rated unless seated. If this response overlaps two time intervals and cannot be rated in the first because it is less than 4-second duration, then rate in the interval in which the end of the response occurs.)

Other Inappropriate Behavior
Ignores teacher's question or command. Does something different from that directed to do, including minor motor behavior such as playing with pencil or eraser when supposed to be writing, coloring while the record is on, doing spelling during arithmetic lesson, playing with object. The child is involved in a task that is not appropriate. (Not rated when other Inappropriate Behaviors are rated. Must be time off task.)

Mouthing Objects
Bringing thumb, fingers, pencils, or any object in contact with the mouth.

Isolate Play
Limited to kindergarten free-play period. Child must be farther than three feet from any person, neither initiates nor responds to verbalizations with other people, engages in no interaction of a nonverbal nature with other children for the entire 10-second period.

(continued)

■

Table 9-2 (continued)

Appropriate Behavior

Time on Task
Answers questions, listens, raises hand, works on assignment. Must include whole 10-second interval except for Turning Around responses of less than 4-second duration.

SOURCE: Adapted from "Rules, Praise and Ignoring: Elements of Elementary Classroom Control," by C. H. Madsen, Jr., and W. C. Becker, 1968, *Journal of Applied Behavior Analysis, 1,* 42. Copyright © 1968 by the Society for the Experimental Analysis of Behavior, Inc. Reprinted by permission.

---

than note that a patient walks away from an attendant, the Wittenborn requires that the observer select the statement that best fits the patient's behavior (for example, fluctuating attitude). The strict recording of objective bits of behavior is replaced by what the observer interprets the behavior to be. In many instances, too, the ratings are based on sequences of observations that may have occurred several hours or days earlier.

Another example of a hospital observational device is the Time-Sample Behavioral Checklist (TSBC), developed by Gordon Paul and his associates (Mariotto & Paul, 1974). This checklist can be used with chronic psychiatric patients. The term *time-sample* refers to observations that are made at regular intervals for a given patient. In the case of the TSBC, observers make one 2-second observation of the patient once every waking hour. From these observations, a daily behavioral profile can be constructed on each patient. Interobserver reliability for this checklist has typically been reported in the .90s. Scales such as the TSBC are helpful in providing a comprehensive behavioral picture of the patient. Such information can be quite useful in the subsequent formulation of appropriate treatment strategies.

Controlled observation

Naturalistic observation has a great deal of intuitive appeal—it provides a picture of how individuals actually behave that is unfiltered by self-reports, inferences, or other potentially contaminating variables. But this is easier said than done. Sometimes the specific kind of behavior in which clinicians are interested does not occur naturally very often. Therefore, they could waste much time and resources waiting for the right behavior or situation to happen. The assessment of responsibility taking, for example, might require day after day of expensive observation before the right situation arises. Then, just as the clinician is about to start recording, some unexpected "other" figure in the environment could step in to spoil the situation by subtly changing its whole character. Furthermore, in free-flowing, spontaneous situations, the client might move away so that conversations cannot be overheard, or the entire scene might move down the hall too quickly to be followed. In short, naturalistic settings often put clinicians at the mercy of events that can sometimes overwhelm opportunities for careful, objective assessment. As a way of handling these problems, observation is sometimes carried out in controlled situations.

For many years, researchers have used *controlled observation* techniques to elicit samples of behavior from patients (Lanyon & Goodstein, 1982). These are really *situational tests* that put individuals in situations more or less similar to those of real life, and direct observations are then made of how the individuals react. In a sense, this is a kind of work-sample approach, in which the behavioral test situation and the criterion behavior to be predicted are quite similar. This method is designed to reduce errors in prediction, as contrasted, for example, to psychological tests whose stimuli are far removed from predictive situations.

Studies in deceit.   Early arrivals on this scene were the studies of Hartshorne and May and their associates (1928, 1929, 1930). Although Hartshorne and May were oriented principally toward research, the approaches they employed have found direct application in the assessment field. Since Hartshorne and May viewed personality or character in habit-response terms, they attempted to measure it by directly sampling behavior. For example, if a clinician wishes to assess children's honesty, why not do so by confronting them with situations where cheating is possible and then observing their responses? This is exactly what Hartshorne and May did in assessing such behaviors as cheating, lying, and stealing. Using a series of ingenious natural settings, they were able to execute their research under disguised, yet highly controlled, conditions. Of particular interest were data that suggested that the deceitful behavior of children was highly situation-specific and should not be construed as reflecting a generalized trait.

Response to stress.   During World War II, the urgent demand for highly trained and resourceful military intelligence personnel led to the development of a series of situational stress tests. Instead of using personality tests to assess the manner in which the individual might handle disruptive or emotionally stressful situations, the U.S. Office of Strategic Services used assigned tasks (OSS Assessment Staff, 1948). Through both objective records and qualitative observation by trained staff, the assessment of reaction to stress was undertaken. Although the demands of war did not provide very many good opportunities for the strict validation of OSS assessment techniques, they did provide an excellent model of what is possible in assessment. The following is a description of an OSS task:

> A large cube had to be constructed out of pegs, poles, and blocks. Since the job could not be done by one person alone, two helpers were provided—but the task had to be completed in ten minutes. The helpers were actually stooges who interfered, were passive, made impractical suggestions, and the like. They ridiculed the candidate and generally frustrated him terribly. In fact, no candidate was ever successful in assembling the cube.

Somewhat related techniques were utilized in selecting candidates for the British Civil Service (Vernon, 1950). Although stress was not incorporated into the British procedures, the tasks on which candidates worked prior to their selection were based on careful job analyses. In another study, Gordon (1967) evaluated several work-sample approaches to assessment used in predicting the performance of Peace Corps trainees.

Leaderless group discussion. In this technique, which originated from German and British military assessment programs (Ansbacher, 1951), small groups of candidates are directed to discuss a specific problem or area of interest. The group members are typically strangers. Without specific directions or procedures, there is much ambiguity in the situation. Observations and ratings of behaviors, such as leading, following, the expression of social poise, the facilitation of group goals, and so on, are possible. Formal techniques for categorizing the observed behavior, such as the Bales Interaction Check List (Bales, 1950), are also available.

For the strict behaviorist, of course, the preceding techniques represent a mixture of observation and inference. When ratings of leadership, stress level, or ingenuity are made, what is really happening is that observers are inferring something from behavior. They are not just compiling lists of behaviors or checking off occurrences.

Controlled performance techniques

As seen in the OSS assessment studies, contrived situations allow the clinician to observe behavior under conditions that offer potential for control and standardization. A more exotic example is the case in which Lazarus (1961) assessed claustrophobic behavior by placing a patient in a closed room which was made progressively smaller by moving a screen. Similarly, Bandura (1969) has used films to expose people to a graduated series of anxiety-provoking stimuli.

A series of assessment procedures to study chronic snake phobias illustrates several approaches to *controlled performance techniques* (Bandura, Adams, & Beyer, 1977):

> *Behavioral avoidance.* The test of avoidance behavior consisted of a series of 29 performance tasks requiring increasingly more threatening interactions with a red-tailed boa constrictor. Subjects were instructed to approach a glass cage containing the snake, to look down at it, to touch and hold the snake with gloved and then bare hands, to let it loose in the room and then return it to the cage, to hold it within 12 cm of their faces, and finally to tolerate the snake crawling in their laps while they held their hands passively at their sides. . . . Those who could not enter the room containing the snake received a score of 0; subjects who did enter were asked to perform the various tasks in the graded series. To control for any possible influence of expressive cues from the tester, she stood behind the subject and read aloud the tasks to be performed. . . . The avoidance score was the number of snake-interaction tasks the subject performed successfully.
>
> *Fear arousal accompanying approach responses.* In addition to the measurement of performance capabilities, the degree of fear aroused by each approach response was assessed. During the behavioral test, subjects rated orally, on a 10-interval scale, the intensity of fear they experienced when each snake approach task was described to them and again while they were performing the corresponding behavior. (pp. 127–128)

It is especially important when working with this kind of measurement that the demand characteristics of the situation be carefully examined. Behavior under these conditions may not be at all typical of a patient's real-life behavior. The presence of the clinician, combined with a trusting attitude that such a clinician would not permit harm to come to the patient, may significantly distort the reality of the situation.

In some cases, controlled performance techniques make use of psychophysiological assessments to carry out studies in both clinical and research settings (Sturgis & Gramling, 1988). For example, techniques to measure penile volume may be used to assess the sexual arousal of paraphiliacs in response to erotic stimuli (Barlow, 1977). Paul (1966) has used both heart rate and sweating measures to assess levels of anxiety in individuals fearful of speaking in public. These and many other methods of assessing anxiety have been reviewed by Nietzel, Bernstein, & Russell (1988).

Self-monitoring

In the previous discussion of naturalistic observation, the observational procedures were designed for use by trained staff: clinicians, research assistants, teachers, nurses, ward attendants, and others. But such procedures are often expensive in both time and money. Furthermore, it is necessary in most cases to rely on time-sampling or otherwise limit the extent of the observations. Also, when dealing with individual clients, it is often impractical or too expensive to observe them as they move freely about in their daily activities. Therefore, clinicians have been increasingly relying on *self-monitoring,* in which individuals observe and record their own behaviors, thoughts, and emotions (Ciminero, Calhoun, & Adams, 1986; Mahoney, 1977a).

In effect, clients are asked to maintain behavioral logs or diaries over some predetermined time period. The log can provide a running record of the frequency, intensity, and duration of certain target behaviors, along with the stimulus conditions that accompanied them and the consequences that followed. Such data are especially useful in telling both clinician and client how often the behavior in question occurs. In addition, it can serve as an index of change as a result of therapy (for example, comparison of baseline frequency with frequency after six weeks of therapy). It can also help focus the client's attention on undesirable behavior and thus aid in reducing it. Finally, clients can come to realize the connections between environmental stimuli, the consequences of their behavior, and the behavior itself.

Of course, there are problems with self-monitoring. Sometimes clients are inaccurate or may purposely distort their observations or recordings for various reasons. Others may simply resist the whole procedure. Despite these obvious difficulties, self-monitoring has become a useful and efficient technique that can provide a great deal of information at very low cost. However, self-monitoring is usually effective as a change agent only in conjunction with a larger program of therapeutic intervention.

Over the years, a variety of self-monitoring aids have been developed. Some clients are provided with small counters or stopwatches, depending upon what is to be monitored. Small file-sized or wallet-sized cards have been devised upon

Table 9-3

A behavioral diary for the assessment of assertive behavior.

Date	Time	Place	Situation	Preceding Event	Outcome	Subsequent Thoughts-Reactions
March 14	4:00 P.M.	Office	Asking Tom for ride home; he owes me a favor	Car broke down; need ride home	Too inhibited to ask	Felt stupid and inadequate
March 15	9:00 A.M.	Office	Mr. C. asked me to work late tonight	Fifth time this month	I agreed	Mad at Mr. C.; mad at me; mad at everyone
March 16	7:00 P.M.	Home	Telephone solicitor	None	Listened to her entire pitch; could hardly say no	Angry at myself for being wishy-washy

which clients can quickly and unobtrusively record their data. At a more informal level, some clients are simply encouraged to make entries in a diary. Such aids are especially useful when assessing or treating problems like obesity, smoking, lack of assertiveness, and alcoholism. These aids can help reinforce the notion that the client's problems can be reduced to specific behaviors. Thus, a client who started with global complaints of an ephemeral nature can begin to see that "not feeling good about myself" really involves the inability to stand up for one's rights in specific circumstances, speaking without thinking, or whatever. An example of a self-monitoring diary is illustrated in Table 9-3.

Variables affecting reliability of observations

Whether they are discussing interviewing, testing, or observation, clinicians must be assured that their data are reliable. In the case of observers this means that the clinicians have confidence that different observers will produce basically the same ratings and scores. For example, when an observer of interactions in the home returns with ratings of a spouse's behavior as "low in empathy," what assurance does the clinician have that someone else rating the same behavior in the same circumstances would have made the same report? There are, of course, many factors that can affect the reliability of observations. The following is a good sample of them.

Complexity of target behavior. Obviously, the more complex the behavior to be observed, the greater the opportunity for unreliability. Observations about what a person eats for breakfast are likely to be more reliable than those centering on interpersonal behavior. This applies to self-monitoring as well. Unless specific, agreed upon behaviors are designated, the observer has an enormous range of behavior on which to concentrate. Thus, to identify an instance of interpersonal aggression, one observer might react to sarcasm, whereas another would fail to include it and focus instead on clear physical acts.

Training observers.   There is no substitute for the careful and systematic training of observers (Foster, Bell-Dolan, & Burge, 1988). Observers who, for example, are sent into psychiatric hospitals to study patient behaviors and then make diagnostic ratings must be carefully prepared in advance. It is necessary to brief them extensively on just what the definition of, say, depression is, what specific behaviors represent depression, and so on. Their goal should not be one of pleasing their supervisor by coming up (consciously or unconsciously) with data helpful to the project. Nor should they protect one another by talking over their ratings and then "agreeing to agree." It even happens that, occasionally, there are instances of what has come to be called *observer drift* —when observers work closely together and subtly, without awareness, begin to drift away from other observers in their ratings. Although reliability among the drifting observers may be acceptable, it is only so because they have, over time, begun to shift their definitions of target behaviors (Kent & Foster, 1977). Occasionally, too, observers are not as careful in their observations when they feel they are on their own as when they expect to be monitored or checked (Reid, 1970). In order to guard against observer drift, regularly scheduled reliability checks should be conducted by an independent rater and feedback then provided to the observers.

Variables affecting validity of observations
At this point, it seems unnecessary to reiterate the importance of validity. We have encountered the concept before in our discussions of both interviewing and testing, and it is no less critical in the case of observation. But here, issues of validity can be deceptive. It seems obvious in interviewing that what patients tell the interviewer may not correspond to their actual behavior in noninterview settings. Or in the case of projective tests, there may be validity questions about inferring aggression from Rorschach responses that involve vicious animals, blood, or large teeth. After all, percepts are not the same as real behavior. But in the case of observation, things seem much clearer. When a child is observed to bully his peers unmercifully and these observations are corroborated by reports from teachers, there would seem to be little question of the validity of the observers' data. Aggression is aggression! However, things are not always so simple, as the following discussion will illustrate.

Content validity.   A behavioral observation schema should include the behaviors that are deemed important for the research or clinical purposes at hand. Usually the investigator or clinician who develops the system also determines whether or not the system shows content validity. But this is almost circular in the sense that a system is valid if the clinician decides that it is valid. Jones et al. (1975) circumvented this problem when they developed the Behavioral Coding System (BCS). Their method was to organize several categories of noxious behaviors in children and then to submit them to mothers for ratings. By using mothers' ratings, they were able to confirm their own a priori clinical judgments as to whether or not certain deviant behaviors were in fact noxious or aversive.

Concurrent validity.   Another way to approach the validity of observations is to ask whether the observer's obtained observational ratings correspond to what others (for example, teachers, spouse, friends, and so on) are observing in the same time frame. For example, do observational ratings of children's aggression on the playground made by trained observers agree with the ratings made by the children's peers? In short, do the children perceive each other's aggression in the same way that observers do?

Construct validity.   Observational systems are usually derived from some implicit or explicit theoretical framework. Such an observational system for rating behavior as the previously noted BCS was derived from a social learning framework that described aggression as the result of learning in the family. When the rewards for aggression are substantial, aggression will occur. When such rewards are no longer contingent on the behavior, aggression should subside. Therefore, the construct validity of the BCS could be demonstrated by showing that aggressive behavior declines from a baseline point after clinical treatment of children—clinical treatment being defined as rearranging the social contingencies in the family that, in turn, should reduce the incidence of observed aggression.

Mechanics of rating.   With observational systems, it is important that a *unit of analysis* be chosen. This refers to the length of time observations will be made and the type and number of responses that will be considered. For example, it might be decided that every physical movement or gesture will be recorded for 1 minute at 4-minute intervals. The total observational time might consist of a 20-minute recess period for kindergarten children. This means that every 4 minutes the child would be observed for 1 minute and all physical movements recorded. These movements would then be coded or rated for the variable under study (for example, aggression, problem solving, dependency).

In addition to the units of analysis chosen, the specific form that the ratings will take must also be decided. Thus, one could decide to record along a dimension of intensity (How strong was the aggressive behavior?) as well as duration (How long did the behavior last?). In other cases, a simple frequency count might be employed (How many times in a designated period did the behavior under study occur?).

Beyond this, a scoring procedure must be developed. Such procedures can range from making check marks on a sheet of paper attached to a clipboard to the use of counters, stopwatches, timers, and even laptop computers. All raters, of course, must employ the same procedure.

Observer error.   No one is perfect, and observers must be monitored from time to time to ensure the accuracy of their reports. Sometimes they simply miss things or else believe they have observed things that never really happened. A child's yell may be accidentally attributed to the wrong child. Or perhaps the yell is coded as verbal aggression when actually it really represented a kind of camaraderie. In other cases, it may not be error so much as bias. An observer may not, for some reason, like a person in a family being observed. The observer, then, may be more prone to provide a less than flattering rating for that person whenever the opportunity arises. It sometimes happens, further, that a person being observed does something early in the observational sequence that the observer reacts to—perhaps a problem is quickly solved or an intelligent remark is made—that serves as a kind of halo, so that later the observer responds with more favorable ratings of that person. Whatever the nature of the potential bias or error, it is important that careful training sessions for observers be held in advance, along with periodic review sessions, to help keep these sources of trouble in check.

Reactivity.   Another factor affecting the validity of observations is called *reactivity*. Patients or study participants sometimes react to the fact that they are being observed by changing the way they behave. The talkative person suddenly becomes quiet. The complaining spouse suddenly becomes the epitome of self-sacrifice. Sometimes an individual may feel it is even necessary to apologize for the dog by saying, "He never does that when he is alone with us." In any case, reactivity can severely hamper the validity of observations because it makes the observed behavior unrepresentative of what normally occurs. The real danger of reactivity is that the observer may not recognize its presence. As Wolff and Merrens (1974) point out, observed behavior may not be a true sample, and this affects the extent to which one can generalize from this instance of behavior. Unfortunately, too, observers may unwittingly interfere with or influence the very behavior they are sent to observe (Goldfried, 1976). In the case of sexual dysfunction, Conte (1986) noted that behavioral ratings are so intrusive that clinicians usually have to rely on self-report methods.

Ecological validity.   One of the biggest problems in psychology (and one that has never been fully resolved) is what Brunswik (1947) referred to many years ago as *ecological validity*. The basic question is whether or not clinicians very often obtain genuinely representative samples of behavior. Is the client's behavior today typical, or is it the product of some uncharacteristic stimulus? Such a question goes beyond simple reactivity—it asks whether or not observers have a large enough sample to assure that their observations will be truly representative. It is doubtful that any one piece of behavior will be typical of a given client; this being so, is the sample of four or ten or twenty instances the proper number? All areas of psychology have long grappled with this problem. Is one experiment on altruism a good enough sample of all possible situations to allow psychologists to make generalizations about it? Are responses to three TAT cards enough of a sample to permit sweeping generalizations about the client's need structure? Are observations of hospitalized patients about to undergo surgery general enough to suggest how these patients might react to other stressful situations?

Suggestions for improving reliability and validity of observations

The following suggestions are offered as ways to improve the reliability and validity of observational procedures. Like similar suggestions made for interviews (see Chapter 6), they often cannot be fully implemented in clinical situations. Nevertheless, an awareness of these points may help focus the clinician's attention in directions that will improve the validity of observations.

1. Decide on target behaviors that are both relevant and comprehensive. Specify direct and observable behaviors that can be defined objectively.
2. In specifying these behaviors, work as much as possible from an explicit theoretical framework that will help define the behaviors of interest.
3. Employ trained observers whose reliability has been established and who are familiar with the objective, standardized observational format to be used.
4. The observational format should be strictly specified in terms of the units of analysis to be used, the form in which observers' ratings will be made, the exact observational procedures to be employed, the scoring scheme designated, and the observational schedule to be followed.
5. Be aware of such potential sources of error in the observations as bias, fluctuations in concentration, and others.
6. Consider the possibilities for reactivity on the part of those being observed and the general influence of awareness that one is being observed may create.
7. Give careful consideration to issues of how representative the observations really are and how much one can generalize from them to behavior in other settings.

■ Role-Playing Methods

Role playing is another technique that has been utilized in behavioral assessment for many years. Rotter and Wickens (1948) suggested this procedure for behavioral assessment many years ago. Goldfried (1976) catalogs several instances in which role playing has been employed, particularly in the area of assertiveness training. Goldfried and Davison (1994) also discuss role playing, or *behavioral rehearsal,* as a means of training new response patterns. Although role playing is an old clinical technique, behavioral assessors have carried out few systematic studies on the methodological problems inherent in the technique as a means of assessment (for example, demand characteristics, standardization of procedures, rater halo effects, sampling problems involved in role selections, and so on).

The use of role playing has been widely employed in the assessment of social skills and assertiveness. For example, in a study of social skills in shy men, Twentyman and McFall (1975) developed six social behavior situations that required the individual to play a role. Participants were instructed to respond aloud as they would were they actually in the situation described to them. For example:

> You are on a break at your job. You see a girl who is about your age at the canteen. She works in another part of the store, and consequently you don't know her very well. You would like to talk to her. What would you say? (p. 386)

Once the individual began speaking, a trained female assistant responded to his efforts. The conversation continued until the participant terminated the conversation or 3 minutes had gone by.

McFall and Lillesand (1971) have also used role-playing in assessing assertiveness. Individuals were asked to respond aloud to nine prerecorded stimuli — for example:

> *Narrator:* A person you do not know very well is going home for the weekend. He, or she, has some books which are due at the library and asks if you would take them back so they won't be overdue. From where you live it is a twenty-five minute walk to the library, the books are heavy, and you hadn't planned on going near the library that weekend. What do you say? (Subject responds aloud.) (p. 315)

Obviously, role-playing techniques are not new; they have been employed as therapeutic devices for many years (for example, Kelly, 1955; Moreno, 1946). However, the behaviorally oriented clinician is interested in role-playing techniques because they provide a simple, efficient means of sampling the client's behavioral skills and deficits. Nonetheless, it must always be remembered that one cannot *assume* that the behavioral skills developed in the therapy room are consistently practiced in the real world.

■ Inventories and Checklists

Behavioral clinicians use a variety of *self-report techniques* to identify behaviors, emotional responses, and perceptions of the environment. One widely used technique is the Fear Survey Schedule (Geer, 1965; Lang & Lazovik, 1963), consisting of 51 potentially fear-arousing situations that the patient rates as to the degree of fear each situation provokes. Other self-report inventories often used include the Stimulus-Response Inventory of Anxiousness (Endler & Okada, 1975), the Rathus Assertiveness Schedule (Rathus, 1973), the Beck Depression Inventory (Beck, 1972) and the Marital Conflict Form (Weiss & Margolin, 1977).

Notably absent from the brief and partial listing of inventories above are instruments that have a psychiatric diagnostic orientation. This has been a conscious omission of the behavioral assessors because, in the past, they generally found little merit in psychiatric classification (Follette & Hayes, 1992). Consequently, their tests were more oriented toward the assessment of specific behavioral deficits, behavioral inappropriateness, and behavioral assets (Sundberg, 1977). The focus of behavioral inventories, then, is *behavior.* Clients are asked about specific actions, feelings, or thoughts that minimize the necessity for them to make inferences about what their own behavior really means.

It is also worth noting that inventories have been developed to assess a person's perception of the social environment (Insel & Moos, 1974). The scales that Moos and his colleagues have devised attempt to assess environments in terms of the opportunities they provide for relationships, personal growth, and systems maintenance and change. There are separate scales for several environments, including work, family, classrooms, wards, and so on.

■ Cognitive-Behavioral Assessment

As we shall see in later chapters, behavioral approaches have become increasingly oriented toward the *cognitive* (Goldfried & Davison, 1994; Meichenbaum, 1977). This means that cognitions, along with behaviors, are becoming the subject of intense study as they relate to the development of a pathological situation, its maintenance, and the changes in it (Kendall & Hollon, 1981). Central to the *cognitive-behavioral assessment* emphasis is the notion that the client's cognitions and thoughts (from self-images to self-statements) play an important role in behavior (Brewin, 1988). Indeed, Meichenbaum (1977) advocates a *cognitive-functional approach.* In essence, this means that a functional analysis of the client's thinking processes must be made in order to plan an intervention strategy. A careful inventory of cognitive strategies must be undertaken to determine which cognitions (or lack thereof) are aiding or interfering with adequate performance and under what circumstances this is occurring.

As Parks and Hollon (1988) note, a number of methods and procedures are available for assessing cognitive functioning. For example, clients can be instructed to "think aloud," or verbalize immediate thoughts; clients can report their thoughts and feelings about prerecorded conversations of various types (for example, stressful, social-evaluative situations); clients can complete rating scales whose items target adaptive and maladaptive cognitions that may have occurred in the past; and clients can list thoughts that occur in reaction to specific stimuli (for example, topics, problems) that are presented to them.

A good example comes from the work of Schwartz and Gottman (1976), in which a task analysis of assertive behavior was made. Cognitive self-statements as they related to assertion situations were assessed by means of the Assertiveness Self-Statement Test (ASST). This is a 34-item questionnaire with 17 positive self-statements that would make it easier to refuse a request and 17 negative self-statements that would make it harder. For example:

> *Positive:* I was thinking that I am perfectly free to say no; I was thinking that this request is an unreasonable one.
> *Negative:* I was worried about what the other person would think of me if I refused; I was thinking that the other person might be hurt or insulted if I refused. (Schwartz & Gottman, 1976, p. 913)

Through such assessment, it becomes clearer exactly what role is being played by self-statements in the maintenance of such problems as lack of assertiveness. Similar procedures can be applied to other problems such as overeating, depression, and shyness or, as another example, to the assessment of agoraphobics' fear of fear. In this regard, Chambless, Caputo, Bright, and Gallagher (1984) have developed a scale composed of thoughts about negative consequences as one experiences anxiety.

Davison, Robins, and Johnson (1983) have used a method in which participants listen to an audiotape that presents several problem situations. Every 10 or 15 seconds, the tape pauses so that the participants can report whatever is in their minds at that point. Results from numerous studies suggest that this method uncovers how people think about both difficult and innocuous situations (Davison & Neale, 1996).

Yet another example of cognitive assessment comes from the work of Seligman et al. (1988). Using the Attributional Style Questionnaire, they found that healthier explanations for events occurred in depressive patients following a course of cognitive therapy. Finally, a number of cognitive devices for assessing social anxiety have been reviewed by Arnkoff and Glass (1989).

■ Concluding Comments

The field of behavioral assessment's use of more systematic and precise methods of evaluation is laudable. Behavioral assessors operationalize the clinical problem by specifying the behaviors targeted for intervention. Further, multiple assessments of these behaviors are conducted before, during, and following treatment. Then, assessment results are used to inform or modify treatment. This is in contrast to "traditional" assessment in which, too often, assessment occurs only once, either before or in the beginning stages of treatment. In addition, it is often unclear how these assessment results impact or influence the mode of treatment that is ultimately prescribed.

The precision and comprehensiveness of behavioral assessment methods, however, appear to be both a strength and a weakness. Many of these techniques have proved to be impractical in clinical settings. For example, some of the natural observation methods as well as the psychophysiological methods of assessment are quite time-intensive and expensive. Therefore, behavioral clinicians have begun to incorporate less time-intensive methods and measures into their assessments. For example, it is now quite common to administer some type of self-report inventory as part of the behavioral assessment battery. Granted, these inventories contain items of a more cognitive or behavioral nature than those found in traditional self-report inventories, but all these measures assume that a patient's self-report conveys an accurate representation of behavior and cognitive processes. Early behaviorists placed little faith in these types of self-report inventories.

Another interesting development in this field is the seeming acceptance of the *Diagnostic and Statistical Manual of Mental Disorders* (DSM) diagnostic classification scheme. Behavioral assessors in general now concede that such a diagnostic formulation may be useful as one component of the overall assessment, but they are quick to add that diagnoses must be supplemented with data from more traditional behavioral methods. It was not that long ago, however, when behavioral clinicians not only ignored mental disorder diagnostic information but they attacked the legitimacy and utility of this source of information. Of course, there are still some radical behaviorists who maintain this rather anachronistic perspective on mental disorder diagnoses. Even so, they are in the minority.

Why the change of heart for most behaviorists? A multitude of explanations are plausible, but several possibilities stand out. First, the criteria for the various mental disorders have increasingly become more objective and behavioral. Second, and relatedly, behavioral clinicians have discovered some degree of utility in using diagnostic labels. These diagnoses describe constellations of maladaptive behaviors that can be targeted for intervention and may also help the clinician anticipate which other symptoms (that is, other than the target behaviors) may change as a result of treatment. These predictions are based on the established covariation patterns among the disorder's symptoms. For example, increasing the amount of social interaction engaged in by a depressed patient may also result in fewer reports of depressed mood. Although more research is needed regarding the covariation among problematic behaviors (Kazdin, 1985), the criteria sets or symptom lists for mental disorders at least give us some initial hypotheses about which behaviors may or may not change as the result of treatment.

Finally, it is noteworthy that cognitive phenomena and processes are now considered to be more legitimate subjects for behavioral assessment and behavioral intervention. In behavioral assessment, not only are behaviors, antecedent-stimulus conditions, and consequences sampled, but so are organismic variables (Goldfried & Davison, 1994). The organismic variables may include a variety of physiological factors, but many cognitive variables are assessed as well. In particular, client *expectations* are regarded as quite important. The client's expectations concerning the nature and meaning of the presenting problem, the minimal standards of success that the client sets, and the client's expectations from behavior therapy are just a few of the variables that are assessed in contemporary behavioral assessment. Behavior therapists appear to have found that an overly rigid adherence to learning models that does not incorporate organismic variables is too constraining.

This does not, however, leave the door wide open for any kind of physiological or cognitive measure—rather, these measures and methods must satisfy the same rigorous standards set forth for the more traditional behavioral methods. Validity must be demonstrated, not assumed. For example, a cognitive measure purported to be related to panic disorder (for example, beliefs of uncontrollability) must be correlated with other behavioral measures of panic disorder symptoms, and changes in these beliefs should result in some improvement in other panic disorder symptoms and lead to better outcome in the future. Through these and other procedures, the concurrent and predictive validity of a measure, as well as its treatment utility, can be established (Hayes, Nelson, & Jarrett, 1987; Kazdin, 1985).

■ Focus Questions

1. Why is behavioral assessment an ongoing process?
2. What are the major differences between behavioral assessment and traditional assessment?
3. What factors affect the reliability and validity of observations?
4. What is the SORC model, and how is it applied to clinical problems?
5. What is the importance of cognitive variables in behavioral assessment?

■ Key Terms

antecedent conditions
behavioral assessment
behavioral interviews
behavioral rehearsal
cognitive-behavioral assessment
cognitive-functional approach
consequent events
controlled observation
controlled performance techniques
ecological validity
functional analysis
home observation
hospital observation

observation
observer drift
organismic variables
reactivity
role playing
sample
school observation
self-monitoring
sign
situational tests
SORC model
unit of analysis

10

Clinical Judgment

As scientific and objective as clinical psychology has tried to become, it is still virtually impossible to evaluate its diagnostic and assessment techniques apart from the clinician involved. The very title of this chapter, "Clinical Judgment," is enough to suggest that clinicians utilize inferential processes that are often far from objective. The process, accuracy, and communication of clinical judgment are still very often extremely personalized phenomena.

In this chapter we shall examine some of the means by which the clinician puts together assessment data and arrives at particular conclusions. In addition, we shall discuss the accuracy of clinical judgments and impressions. Finally, we shall examine briefly the method by which the results of assessment are typically communicated—the clinical report.

■ Process and Accuracy

Our discussion of clinical judgment will begin with its basic element—interpretation.

Interpretation

It is hard to disagree with Levy (1963) when he said, "Interpretation is the most important single activity engaged in by the clinician" (p. viii). Interpretation is an inferential process (Nisbett & Ross, 1980) that takes up where assessment leaves off. The interviews have been completed, the psychological tests have been administered—now what does it all mean and what decisions are to be made? (Peterson & Fishman, 1987). To quote Levy further:

> Without interpretation, the clinician must take the data furnished him [sic] at face value; without interpretation, the clinician is not much further ahead in understanding his patient's behavior than is the patient himself [sic], without interpretation, the clinician is at best a technician who must record whatever is presented him and then hope that some of the data will appear in actuarial tables or cookbooks so that he can find out what to do next. (Levy, 1963, p. viii)

At the very least, *clinical interpretation* or judgment is a complex process. It involves a stimulus (an MMPI-2 profile, an IQ score, a gesture, a sound) and a response by the clinician ("Is this patient psychotic?" "Is the patient's behavior expressive of a low expectancy for success?" "What is the patient like?"). It also involves the characteristics of clinicians — their cognitive structures and theoretical orientations. In addition, situational variables enter into the process. These can include everything from the type and range of patients to the constraints that the demands of the setting place on predictions. For example, a clinician in a university mental health center may make a range of judgments — from hospitalization, to psychotherapy, to just dropping out of school — whereas a clinician in a prison setting may be limited to many fewer options.

The theoretical framework. As we have mentioned throughout this book, clinical psychologists strive to discover the etiology or origins of psychological problems and to understand patients so that they can be helped. There are a variety of ways to conceptualize clinical problems (for example, psychodynamic, behavioral, cognitive, and so on). The kinds of interpretations made by a Freudian are vastly different from those made by a behavioral clinician. Two clinicians may each observe that a child persistently attempts to sleep in his mother's bed. For the Freudian, this becomes a sign of an unresolved Oedipus complex. For the behaviorist, the interpretation may be in terms of reinforcement. Indeed, one way in which clinicians can evaluate interpretations is by examining their consistency with the theory from which they are derived. Also, the number of interpretations that can be made from a set of observations, interview responses, or test data is both awesome and bewildering. A preferred theoretical framework can help reduce this number to reasonable proportions (Bieri et al., 1966).

Samples, signs, and correlates. As noted in Chapter 9, patient data can be viewed in several ways. First, the clinician can view such data as *samples*. Observations, test scores, test responses, or other data are seen as samples of a larger pool of information that could be obtained outside the consulting room. For example, when a patient does poorly on the Wechsler Memory Scale, this could be regarded as a sample of nontest behavior (memory problems).

A second way in which patient data could be interpreted is as *signs* of some underlying state, condition, or determinant. Aside from radical behaviorists, many clinicians will seek to infer from observations of the patient's behavior and test responses a variety of underlying determinants. For some clinicians, the underlying determinant might be anxiety; for others, ego strength; and for still others, expectancies. But in every case the observation is utilized as something that signifies underlying determinants. For example, poor form quality in Rorschach responses is often interpreted as a sign of poor reality testing (that is, psychosis) in a patient.

A third view of patient data emphasizes their status as *correlates* of other things. Once the anxious behavior, the flat affect, the inability to concentrate have been noted in a depressed patient, the clinician might predict an associated decline in sexual activity, social relationships, willingness to seek employment, and so on. In effect, then, assessment data can be interpreted to suggest behavioral, attitudinal, or emotional correlates.

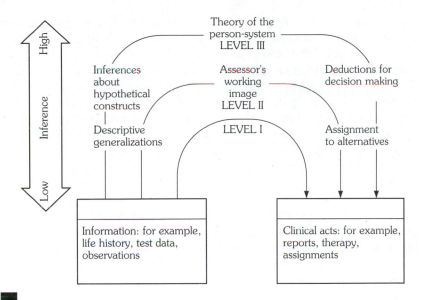

Figure 10-1
Levels of interpretation. SOURCE: From *Clinical Psychology: Expanding Horizons,* 2nd ed., p. 143, by N. D. Sundberg, L. E. Tyler, and J. R. Taplin. Copyright © 1973. Reprinted by permission of Prentice Hall, Englewood Cliffs, NJ.

> ***Levels of interpretation.***   Whether clinicians view clinical data as signs, samples, or correlates, they are making inferences that will enable them to go from those clinical data to recommendations, reports, or predictions. Sundberg, Tyler, and Taplin (1973) have described three levels of inferences or interpretations, as shown in Figure 10-1.

> *Level I interpretations* generally involve little in the way of inference and certainly nothing in the way of a sign approach. From input to output, there are practically no intervening steps. For example, if it is known on the basis of past experience that students who sit in the front row of a class almost always get A's or B's, then clinicians can go directly from seat number to grade prediction without any necessity for intervening attributions of intelligence scores, previous courses, and so on. This is a simple yet efficient approach that can dispense with high-level clinicians who make exotic inferences prior to their predictions. Technicians, computers, or machines can be employed instead. Level I interpretations can often be used with large populations if the prime purpose is screening and if predicting the outcome for a specific person is relatively unimportant. A college entrance exam is a case in point. Here a single test score may predict with considerable accuracy the academic performance of 1000 freshmen. Although that single score may be erroneous as a predictor for student X, a certain degree of error can easily be tolerated if all one is interested in is the number who are likely to graduate.

> *Level II interpretations* involve two kinds of inferences. The clinician may observe a patient and then conclude that the observed behavior generally characterizes

the patient. Sundberg et al. (1973) call this first kind of inference *descriptive generalization*. In effect, the clinician goes from a few behavioral instances to a broader generalization — still at the descriptive level. Thus, for a patient who fidgets, smokes three cigarettes during the interview, and stammers, the clinician may make a descriptive generalization: interview tension. If it turns out later that the patient has trouble relaxing at home, cannot sit through meetings at the office, and is very worried about paying off the mortgage, the clinician may go to a broader descriptive generalization. The second kind of inference is a *hypothetical construct* that suggests an inner state and takes the clinician a bit beyond descriptive generalizations. When clinicians begin to make generalizations and, particularly, to impute inner determinants to the patient, they are moving directly into clinical interpretation as it is often employed.

Finally, *Level III interpretations* take clinicians beyond Level II primarily by being more inclusive and better integrated. At this level they attempt to achieve a consistent, broad understanding of the "individual in situation." Clinicians will draw an integrated picture of the patient's developmental, social, and physiological determinants that involves a highly articulated theoretical system of hypotheses and deductions. For example, a preponderance of "blood" responses on the Rorschach might be interpreted as a sign of underlying aggression that may lead to future impulsive outbursts or loss of control (Rapaport, 1946).

Theory and interpretation

Currently, clinicians may be assigned to three very broad interpretive classes. First, there are the *behavioral* clinicians. As we have seen, the strict behaviorist avoids making inferences about underlying states and instead concentrates on the behavior of the patient. The behavioral clinician seeks patient data based upon personal observation or direct reports from the patient or other observers. These data are regarded as samples. Interpretation is largely at Levels I and II, although more recently some behavioral clinicians have begun to show an interest in Level III interpretation.

A second group of clinicians pride themselves upon being empirical and objective. In particular, these clinicians are likely to use objective tests in order to predict to relatively specific criteria. For example, will scores from tests A, B, and C predict success in college, therapy outcome, aggressive outbursts, and so on? This *psychometric* approach to interpretation, as we shall discuss a bit later, is especially useful when the criteria one is predicting are crisp and well articulated. In general, this approach utilizes data as correlates of something else — for example, a score at the 95th percentile on test X may be related to recidivism in prisoners. The psychometrically oriented clinician is immersed in tests and their norms, regression equations, and actuarial tables and tends to employ Level I and II interpretations.

A third group of clinicians is more comfortable with a *psychodynamic* approach. This has long been a popular mode of operation in clinical psychology, and, although current clinicians often seem to opt for a more objective behavioral or psychometric approach, there is still more of the psychodynamicist in many of them than they might like to admit. The psychodynamic approach strives to identify inner states or determinants. Data from projective tests, unstructured clinical interviews, and other sources are viewed as signs of an underlying state. Interpretation tends to be pitched at Level III. A broad, often highly impressionistic picture of the patient is drawn, although in many instances subtle normative assertions are made. Sundberg et al. (1973) feel that most theories of personality are very difficult to apply consistently and that Level III understanding is therefore difficult to achieve with a given patient.

Quantitative versus subjective approaches

Quietly embedded in the preceding discussion are two distinct approaches to clinical judgment and interpretation. First, there is the *quantitative or statistical approach,* which emphasizes objectivity and is presumably free from fuzzy thinking. Second, there is the *subjective or clinical approach,* which adherents claim is the only method to offer truly useful interpretations and predictions.

The quantitative, statistical approach. Perhaps the simplest form of quantitative prediction that clinicians can employ involves the assignment of scores to the various characteristics of their patients. This enables them to determine the correlation between any two characteristics. For example, suppose that after several years of practice a clinician begins to feel that a direct relationship exists between the early termination of therapy cases and patients' needs for independence. The clinician might attempt to verify this hypothesis by correlating "need for independence" scores from the TAT with the length of time that patients remain in therapy. Should the correlation turn out to be substantially above .50, the clinician could use the TAT to make interpretations and predictions regarding the duration of therapy.

Of course, more often than not, clinicians cannot base highly useful predictions upon a single score or attribute. The conclusion of therapy is more often a complex event that has a number of determinants. Consequently, the clinician might want to employ several other scores: ego strength, the experience of the therapist, marital satisfaction, interpersonal trust, and others. Then a multiple correlation could be carried out. A particular caution to bear in mind, however, is that, even though a multiple correlation may turn out to be quite high, there is a real danger that it will shrink when applied to a new sample. The sample on which the initial study is carried out may not be representative of therapy patients in general. What is true in Kansas may not be true in California; what is true for psychoanalytic therapy may not be true for behavior therapy. Therefore, clinicians have to be sure that they have correctly weighted various predictor scores before they can generalize very far. They must cross-validate any studies on other samples.

These statistical techniques permit a mechanical application that does not involve clinical decision making at all, once the formulas have been established. The feature that distinguishes statistical approaches from clinical approaches is that the former (no matter what their complex mathematical development), once established, can be routinely applied by a clerk or a machine (Gough, 1962).

The quantitative, statistical approach, then, requires that the clinician keep careful records of test data, observations, and related material to enable the quantification of clinical interpretations and judgments. Such careful record keeping permits the clinician to go beyond informal impressions based upon previous experience; with adequate records of large enough samples, a host of variables can be interrelated. Whether clinicians are evaluating their own performance or the performance of an entire clinic, or are relating certain patient characteristics to various diagnostic or therapeutic outcomes, quantified data can play a facilitating role. Such data, then, enable clinicians to evaluate their judgment, interpretations, and performance.

The subjective, clinical approach. The clinical approach is much more subjective, experiential, and intuitive. Here, the emphasis is on the application of judgment to the individual case, and subjective weights based on experience have to suffice. The classical notion is that there exists a kind of clinical intuition that is not readily amenable to analysis and quantification. If so, it must be a private process in which clinicians themselves are sometimes unable to identify the cues in a patient's test responses or verbalizations that led them to a given conclusion or judgment.

Once, for example, in the course of a Rorschach administration a patient said, "This looks like a Christmas tree." What did this mean? Perhaps nothing. Or perhaps it indicated a career in forestry. Or perhaps it suggested an underlying sadness or depression in a person with few friends or family with whom to enjoy the approaching holiday season. In this case, the last interpretation was later supported by the patient during a discussion of his family background. The clinical student who had made the correct interpretation in a training exercise explained her reasoning as follows: "It was near the Christmas season; there were several references in the TAT to remote family figures; I remembered how I always seem to become a little sad during Christmas; it suddenly popped into my head, and I just knew with complete certainty that it was true—it simply felt right!"

This example illustrates several things about clinical interpretation. First, such interpretation involves a sensitive capacity to integrate material. The astute clinical psychologist pays attention to the wide range of events that characterize patient behavior, history, test responses, and so on. A clinician must function a bit like the detective who takes in everything at the scene of the crime and then makes a series of inductive or deductive generalizations that link these observations together. In addition, there is often a willingness in clinicians to see a bit of themselves in the patient—a kind of assumed similarity that enables clinicians to utilize their own experience in interpreting the behavior and feelings of another.

Unfortunately, the presentation of this example has been one-sided. Little has been made of the clinical student who believed that the Christmas tree suggested an interest in forestry. Therefore, we may make two additional observations. First, there are individual differences in clinical sensitivity. Second, for every instance in which there has been a brilliant and sensitive clinical inference, there is probably lurking in the unrecalled recesses of memory an equally impressive misinterpretation.

Clinical interpretation, then, involves the sensitive integration of many sources of data into a coherent picture of the patient. It also fulfills a hypothesis-generating function that is best served by guidance from a well-articulated theory of personality. But it behooves responsible clinicians to make every effort to articulate the cues involved in their judgments and to explicate the manner in which they make the leap from cues to conclusions. It is not enough to be good clinicians. There is also a responsibility to pass on these skills to others.

The case for a statistical approach

A quantitative, statistical approach to clinical judgment is particularly effective when the outcome or event to be predicted is known and specific. Indeed, in such cases additional clinical data of an impressionistic nature usually add little. This is especially true when dealing with fairly large numbers of persons and when the percentage of correct predictions is more important than the correct prediction of the performance of any one of the individuals. As noted earlier, were the task solely one of predicting the grades of an incoming class of college freshmen, the clinician would be well advised to use the objective data of high school grades and ability test scores. Since good grades in college may generally be predicted from ability and its previous effective use, more ubiquitous and subtle personality factors may add little.

Many of the failings in purely subjective, clinical approaches result from the tendency to depend upon vague criteria. Too often a clinician will make the following judgment: the patient, based upon projective test data, will benefit from psychotherapy. This vague statement contains no explicit referents. What constitutes benefit? Will the conclusion that the patient has or has not benefited from therapy be based on the patient's own assertions or on the therapist's judgment? The loose conceptualization of the foregoing judgment precludes an actuarial approach. But suppose that the clinician explicitly defines the outcome as, say, remaining in rational-emotive therapy for 12 months coupled with a therapy success rating of 7 or higher (on a 10-point scale) by an outside observer? Then it might be possible to develop a formula based upon objective interview or test criteria that would successfully predict to a defined universe of therapists.

Clinical terms are often used loosely and without explicit meaning. For example, long ago, Grayson and Tolman (1950) showed that marked variations in meaning are ascribed to such concepts as aggression and compulsion by psychologists and psychiatrists. An objective, statistical approach would force greater specification of meaning that should eventually lead to more specific predictions that could be developed from formulas. This would erase much of the unreliability of judgment inherent in more intuitive approaches.

There is another reason for moving toward a statistical position: so many clinical descriptions seem applicable to everyone. As noted in Chapter 8, personality descriptions should show *incremental utility*—they must reveal something beyond what everyone knew before the assessment began. More precisely, clinicians must develop descriptions of their patients that are meaningful and that lead to explicit predictions. This, in turn, would prevent clinicians from making interpretations that seem valid but in actuality characterize everybody. This is the so-called *Barnum effect*—a notion that goes back to a report distributed by D. G. Paterson

■

Box 10-1

An example of the Barnum effect: Purported characteristics of adult
    children of alcoholics (ACOAs)

Logue, Sher, and Frensch (1992) recently examined whether the apparent widespread acceptance of personality descriptions of ACOAs was
due, at least in part, to a Barnum effect. Barnum-like statements apply to
most everyone, and therefore appear to be self-descriptive. In reality,
however, they are descriptive of people in general and lack both discriminative ability and clinical utility. Authors of several popular books on
ACOAs have proposed that parental alcoholism produces negative effects
on the family, leading to a host of problems in children of alcoholics once
they become adults. These include: feelings of guilt, shame, insecurity,
low self-esteem, and powerlessness, as well as problems coping with emotions and intimate relationships. Logue et al. hypothesized that these descriptors have gained popularity because they not only describe ACOAs
but also tend to be descriptive of people in general. Two groups of undergraduates (ACOAs and non-ACOAs) rated personality profiles as to
how self-descriptive they were. These profiles consisted of six personality
statements (for example, "In times of crisis, you need to take care of others."). There were two personality profile types: (1) the ACOA personality
profile, consisting of personality statements drawn from ACOA literature;
and (2) the Barnum personality profile, consisting of personality statements drawn from several existing personality inventories and used in previous Barnum research. These two profile types were matched on overall
level of social desirability (assessed through an independent sample).
Briefly, the results of the Logue et al. study indicated that ACOA profiles
were rated highly self-descriptive by both ACOA and non-ACOA participants. The authors concluded that these popular personality descriptors
appear to have a Barnum-like quality and, therefore, lack validity as specific descriptors of ACOA individuals.

■

and later cited by Meehl (1956). Thus, who would deny the personal relevance of
the following statements:

At times I am unsure of my sexual maturity.
I am not always as confident as most people think I am.
Often I keep my real feelings to myself unless I am around people I like.

Box 10-1 discusses the Barnum effect in more detail.

By moving toward quantification, the statistical approach could eliminate
much of the unreliability in clinical judgment. Objectively derived formulas, explicit norms, weighted predictors and regression equations, and carefully stated

descriptions and predictions could combine to replace the fallibilities of clinical judgment with a mechanical procedure that would minimize errors.

On the other hand, there are probably many reasons why some people find statistical approaches distasteful. Dawes (1979) describes three. For example, take a situation in which a student is denied admittance to graduate school because of the application of such empirical criteria as GPAs and low test scores. As Dawes notes, some argue with such criteria on technical grounds: they are short-term and rather unprofound. The plea "I just know I could succeed if they would only give me a chance" is less an argument than an expression of hope. Also, the antistatistical argument often claims that there are expert judges "out there somewhere" who could do as well or better than formulas. But, somehow, they never seem to be produced. Others reject the statistical approach on psychological grounds: many persons easily remember those instances when their intuition was right but forget those when it was wrong. Sometimes, too, clinicians may unconsciously work harder with a client for whom they have predicted success in therapy. This outcome will then prove that their clinical hunch was right! And, finally, there are still other sources of resistance on ethical grounds: some people have the idea that reducing an applicant to a set of numbers is unfair or dehumanizing. Dawes (1979) discusses this argument:

> No matter how psychologically uncompelling or distasteful we may find their results to be, no matter how ethically uncomfortable we may feel at "reducing people to mere numbers," the fact remains that our clients are people who deserve to be treated in the best manner possible. If that means—as it appears at present—that selection, diagnosis, and prognosis should be based on nothing more than the addition of a few numbers representing values or important attributes, so be it. To do otherwise is cheating the people we serve. (p. 581)

The case for a clinical approach

The difficulty with a statistical approach that relies upon regression equations is that clinical psychologists would need a multitude of them were they to function at all as clinicians. The field currently does not have well-established, cross-validated formulas to predict therapy outcomes, to make interpretations during the course of a therapy session, or to recommend a special class rather than institutionalization. Should the clinician suggest bibliotherapy, a hobby, a marriage counselor, a trial separation, or what? The busy, harried clinician does not have available a regression equation for even important decisions, let alone the pedestrian judgments that must continually be made. It was Meehl (1957) who long ago said, "Mostly we will use our heads, because there just aren't any formulas" (p. 273). Unfortunately, the situation has not changed much over the last 40 years. In a review that extends beyond the realm of clinical judgment, Kleinmuntz (1990) reinforces Meehl's conclusion.

Of course, when specific outcomes are to be predicted and the clinician has enough time to develop good formulas, the clinician can easily be outperformed by those formulas. We will review this evidence shortly. However, even here, the clinician's judgment can add something in some instances—especially when the sample is quite homogeneous. Suppose, for instance, that the formula for selecting students for graduate training depends solely upon Graduate Record Examination

scores and undergraduate grades. The formula would probably do quite well in selecting from an initial heterogeneous sample of applicants those who will do well.
However, from that point on, clinical judgments regarding motivation or personality
features may be quite helpful in further discriminating among those selected. In other
words, the final sample is so selective that previous grades and test scores will not
be very discriminating. Therefore, clinical inferences may become useful after the initial screening since they provide extra data that relate to success in training. Make
no mistake, however, holding large amounts of data in our heads and integrating
them are not what we humans excel at (Dawes, 1979). Clinicians, then, should use
computers and formulas for that and save their own mental powers for what they
do excel at—selecting what to look at and deciding what to do with the results.

Another important contribution of the clinical approach involves the clinician's function as a data gatherer. For example, it may be important to know about
certain patient characteristics for purposes of prediction, but it may not be possible to uncover those characteristics without extensive interviewing or some in-
depth interpretation based on test results. As a further example, several facets of
a patient's life history data may suggest to a sensitive clinician that the patient
could be prone toward making violent sexual assaults on women. Although clinical psychology does not have a reliable regression equation to predict such assaults, the data uncovered by an astute clinician could be important. Thus, at present, certain data may be discoverable only through extensive clinical investigation.
It should also be noted that predictive formulas work best when test data are available, but sometimes tests of the right sort simply do not exist. When dealing with
rare events (such as suicide), the frequency of occurrence is so low that clinicians
cannot develop adequate equations for them. Rare or not, however, such events
are important and must be dealt with by clinical judgment.

Furthermore, there are many who would argue that the power to predict
specific outcomes is not the only goal of science: understanding and describing
phenomena are the overriding goals. Although there is perhaps some validity to
this argument, all too frequently it can become a rationalization for employing
vague terminology and applying equally vague criteria, as noted above. Thus, the
counterargument would assert that, when description and understanding are
couched in explicit terms with clear-cut referents and criteria, prediction will be a
natural by-product.

The efficiency of clinical versus actuarial approaches

Over the years, many studies have compared the relative efficacy of clinical
and actuarial methods. Let us examine some of that work now.

Some evidence.   Sarbin (1943) contrasted the prediction of academic
success for college freshmen made by a clerk employing a regression equation
with the predictions made by several counselors. The regression equation predictors were aptitude test scores and high school rank. The counselors had available
to them the two preceding sources of data (but without their mathematical weight-
ing), vocational interest scores, interview data, and biographical data. The upshot
of this study was that the counselors were no better than the regression equation
in their predictions, even though they had the benefit of much more information.

Figure 10-2
Paul Meehl is widely recognized as a major proponent of the actuarial approach to
    prediction. *Courtesy of Paul Meehl*

Meehl (1954) surveyed a number of the studies available on clinical versus
statistical prediction and concluded that in "all but one . . . the predictions made
actuarially [statistically] were either approximately equal or superior to those
made by a clinician" (p. 119). In a later survey of additional research, Meehl (1965)
reaffirmed his earlier conclusions. Furthermore, Meehl (1954) also observed that,
in several studies statistical predictions were made on the same data from which
the regression equations were developed—in short, the formulas were not cross-
validated. As noted earlier, such formulas frequently show a marked reduction in
efficiency when they are applied to samples different from those used in their
derivation.

Sawyer (1966) regarded data collected by interview or observation as clinical data. He viewed inventory, biographical, or clerically obtained data as statistical
or mechanical. Having considered the methodological problems and the equivocal
results of the studies he examined, Sawyer concluded that, in combining data, the
mechanical mode is superior to the clinical mode. However, he also affirmed that
the clinical method is useful in the data collection process, as it gives an assessment of characteristics that would not normally be provided by more mechanical
techniques of data collection. But once the data (from whatever source) are collected, they can best be combined by statistical approaches.

An example of an individual study comparing clinical and statistical prediction may help further illustrate the nature of this controversy. This study, reported

by Goldberg (1965), is one of the most frequently cited concerning clinical versus statistical prediction. It involved 13 Ph.D.-level staff members and 16 predoctoral trainees who were asked to make judgments regarding the diagnostic status of over 800 patients based on their MMPI scores. These judgments were made without any contact with, or additional information on, the patient. That is, each judge simply examined the MMPI profile (scores) for each patient and then predicted whether the patient was "psychotic" or "neurotic." These judgments constituted clinical predictions because it was left up to each judge as to how to use the MMPI information for formulating a diagnosis. In contrast, statistical predictions involved the application of a variety of algorithms in which MMPI scale scores were combined (added or subtracted) in some manner and previously established cutoff scores for psychosis versus neurosis were employed. In addition, some statistical predictions involved the application of specified decision rules based on MMPI high-point codes or other psychometric signs. A total of 65 different quantitatively based rules were considered.

What were these clinical and statistical predictions compared to in order to assess their accuracy? In this study, the criterion diagnosis was the psychotic versus neurotic diagnosis provided for each patient by their respective hospitals or clinics. Thus, the accuracy of each clinician's and each statistical algorithm's prediction was determined by assessing the agreement between predictions and the actual criterion diagnoses across all cases.

Table 10-1 presents selected results from this study. Not all of the statistical indices employed are presented in this table, but this should give the reader a general impression of the findings. First, on average, judges (clinical prediction) were correct in 62% of the cases. (It is noteworthy that the trainees' accuracy rate was comparable to that of doctoral-level clinicians with more years of clinical experience.) Second, 14 of the statistical indices (statistical prediction) were comparable to or outperformed the judges with regard to overall accuracy of prediction. Several diagnostic decision rules based on simple linear combinations of MMPI scale scores (for example, $Pt - Sc$) also outperformed the clinicians.

A variety of additional updated reviews of the studies pitting clinical versus statistical prediction have uniformly demonstrated the superiority of statistical procedures (for example, Dawes, 1979, 1994; Dawes, Faust, & Meehl, 1989; Goldberg, 1991; Kleinmuntz, 1990; Meehl, 1986; Wiggins, 1973). As stated by Meehl (1986):

> There is no controversy in social science which shows such a large body of qualitatively diverse studies coming out so uniformly in the same direction as this one. When you are pushing 90 investigations [Note: this number is dramatically higher as of 1995], predicting everything from the outcome of football games to the diagnosis of liver disease and when you can hardly come up with a half dozen studies showing even a weak tendency in favor of the clinician, it is time to draw a practical conclusion. (pp. 373–374)

Objections to these findings.   Recently, Dawes (1994) outlined several of the major objections to the large body of evidence supporting the superiority of statistical prediction as well as his responses to each objection. First, crit-

Table 10-1
Accuracy of clinical versus statistical predictions in the Goldberg study (1965).

Source of Prediction	*Average Accuracy Percentage*
Clinicians	
13 Ph.D.-level staff	62 (range = 59 to 65)
16 Trainees	61 (range = 55 to 67)
29 Total judges	62 (range = 55 to 67)
Statistical Indices	
$(L + Pa + Sc) - (Hy + Pt)$	70
Two-point code rules	67
$Sc - (Hs + D + Hy)$	67
$(Pt - Sc)$	65
High-point code rules	66
$(Hy - Pa)$	61
$Pa - (Hs + D + Hy)$	62
$(Hs - Sc)$	61
$(Pd + Pa) - (Hs + Hy)$	63

SOURCE: From "Diagnosticians versus Diagnostic Signs: The Diagnosis of Psychosis versus Neurosis from the MMPI," by L. R. Goldberg, 1965, *Psychological Monographs, 79* (9, Whole No. 602). Copyright © 1965 by the American Psychological Association. Reprinted by permission.

ics argue that several of the individual studies contained research design flaws that may have affected the findings. Dawes refers to this as an "argument from a vacuum"—a possibility is raised, but there is no empirical demonstration supporting the possibility. Although every study has its limitations, it is difficult to imagine that the opposite conclusion (that is, clinical prediction is superior) is warranted when practically all of the studies support statistical prediction. The second objection concerns the expertise of the judges/clinicians in these studies. Perhaps they were not true experts, and a study employing expert clinicians would demonstrate the superiority of clinical judgment. Although a wide variety of judges/clinicians were used in these studies, a number of studies employed recognized experts—clinicians with many years of experience performing the predictive task in question. There were a few instances in which an individual clinician performed as well as the statistical formula, but this was more the exception than the rule. Thus, there is no compelling empirical evidence that expert clinicians are superior. A third objection is that the predictive tasks were not representative (that is, not ecologically valid) of prediction situations facing clinicians. For example, clinicians may not make a diagnosis only from the MMPI-2 but also from patient interviews. Dawes argues, however, that the predictive tasks are components of what may go on in clinical practice—clinicians purportedly use the MMPI-2 information to make predictions. Further, several of the studies demonstrate that additional information (for example, interview material) obtained and used in the judge's clinical prediction may actually result in less accurate predictions than would be the case if the clinician had simply stuck with the statistical formula that was available.

Dawes goes on to suggest that much of the negative reaction to the findings is a function of the human need to believe in a high degree of predictability in the world. This appears to be both a cognitive and an emotional need. There is a built-in tendency to both seek and see order in the world, and a lack of predictability would likely result in some degree of emotional distress. Unfortunately, however, the *need* for predictability does not prove its existence.

Bias.   Clinical judgment suffers when bias of any kind intrudes into the decision-making process. Such bias can run the gamut from racial bias to that based on socioeconomic status (Lopez, 1989). To help overcome the role of bias, Arkes (1981) suggests that clinicians work at considering alternative hypotheses, increase their attention to data that is too often ignored, and decrease their reliance on memory. But clinicians must do more than exhort each other to do these things. Students must be trained in these techniques and in principles of inferential reasoning (Dumont & Lecomte, 1987).

Experience and training.   Faust (1986) made the following observation:

> To whom do these studies of low judgment performance apply? The answer is not that they apply to hacks or novices alone. There is limited evidence—in fact, almost none that experts or those with exhaustive experience perform significantly better than "regulars" or "relative beginners." (p. 420)

To date, empirical evidence does not support the position that increased clinical experience results in increased accuracy in prediction (Dawes, 1994; Garb, 1989). This seems to fly in the face of conventional wisdom: Why is it that we do not see evidence for the effect of clinical experience in the field of clinical psychology and other mental health fields? There are several possibilities (Dawes, 1994). First, the accuracy of predictions is limited by the available measures and methods that are employed as aids in the prediction process. If scores from psychological tests, for example, are not strongly correlated with the criterion of interest (that is, highly valid), then it is unlikely one could ever observe an effect for clinical experience. The accuracy of predictions will remain modest at best and will not depend on how clinically experienced the clinician is. Second, we often cannot precisely define what we are trying to predict (for example, "abusive personality"), and no gold standards for criteria exist such that clinicians can objectively assess the accuracy of their predictions. Because of this, true feedback is impossible, and diagnosticians are not able to profit from experience. Third, clinicians tend to remember their accurate predictions and forget their inaccurate ones. Therefore, more experience in the prediction process does not necessarily lead to increased accuracy because the feedback that is incorporated is incomplete.

As for the virtue of receiving specific types of professional training, there is not much evidence to suggest that one profession is superior to another in making accurate diagnostic judgments. For example, even in differentiating medical disorders masquerading with psychological symptoms from those without underlying medical disorders, medical and nonmedical practitioners did not differ in their accuracy (Sánchez & Kahn, 1991).

All of this research is somewhat sobering for the field of clinical psychology. However, it is a professional responsibility for clinicians to be aware of the limits of their predictive ability and to avoid promoting the "myth of experience." One thing is sure. Clinicians will continue to make decisions — they have no choice. The important thing is to ensure that clinical psychologists are as well prepared as they can be and to train clinical psychologists to use the best available measures and techniques for a given prediction situation.

Conclusions

Given the current state of affairs, the following conclusions regarding the relative strengths of clinical and actuarial methods seem warranted.

The clinical approach is especially valuable when:

- *information is needed about areas or events for which no adequate tests are available.* In this case, the research fails to offer any evidence that the data-gathering function of the clinician can be replaced by a machine.
- *rare, unusual events of a highly individualized nature are to be predicted or judged.* Regression equations or other formulas cannot be developed to handle such events, and clinical judgment is the only recourse.
- *the clinical judgments involve instances for which no statistical equations have been developed.* In effect, this refers to the vast majority of instances. The day-to-day decisions of the clinician are such that encountering a useful equation would itself be a rare and unusual event.
- *the role of unforeseen circumstances could negate the efficiency of a formula.* For example, a formula might very easily outstrip the performance of a clinician in predicting suitability for hospital discharge. In the role of data gatherer, however, the clinician might unearth important data from a patient that would negate an otherwise perfectly logical statistical prediction.

The statistical approach is especially valuable when:

- *the outcome to be predicted is objective and specific.* For example, the statistical approach will be especially effective in predicting grades, successful discharge, vocational success, and similar objective outcomes.
- *the outcomes for large, heterogeneous samples are involved, and interest in the individual case is minimal.* Having a statistical formula to predict how many of 50,000 men will receive dishonorable discharges from the Army will be highly useful to the Army, though less so for the clinician who is dealing with Private Smith.
- *there is reason to be particularly concerned about human judgmental error or bias.* Fatigue, boredom, bias, and a host of other human failings can be responsible for clinical error. Often, such effects are random and unpredictable. Formulas, equations, and computers never become tired, bored, or biased.

Much of the controversy over clinical versus statistical methods has been heated. Each camp seems to scorn the other. If a formula appears to do better than intuition, clinicians become threatened and react defensively. Similarly, some researchers view all clinicians as nothing but second-rate adding machines when it comes to making predictions. Such reactions do little to resolve anything but, instead, freeze both factions into positions that prevent either from accepting the strengths of the other.

The most useful position would seem to be one that integrates the two approaches. The sensible clinician will employ every regression equation, objective test score, or statistical method that shows promise of working for a specific task. Such a clinician will fully understand that clinical data gathering and hypothesis formation and even intuition will never be totally supplanted by a formula.

By the same token, the clinician can take comfort from the fact that even regression equations must spring from somewhere. Just as someone must program a computer, so, too, must someone decide which kinds of data should be quantified so that the data can be submitted for statistical analysis. Someone must initially select the tests and the test items. Although formulas can be applied mechanically, their initial development depends on the clinical psychologist.

◾ Improving Judgment and Interpretation

In this chapter and in preceding chapters on interviewing and assessment, we have discussed a variety of factors that can reduce the efficiency and validity of clinical predictions and interpretation. We cannot presume to lay down a series of prescriptions that will lead inevitably to perfect performance, but let us call attention to several factors that are important to keep in mind as one moves from data to interpretation to prediction. As Faust (1986) points out, although the performance of clinicians has not been good, there are ways of making improvements.

Information processing

As clinicians process assessment information, they are often bombarded with tremendous amounts of data. In many instances, this information can be difficult to integrate because of its amount and complexity, and clinicians must guard against the tendency to oversimplify. It can be easy for them to overreact to a few outstanding bits of information and to ignore other data that do not fit into the picture they are trying to paint. Whether the pressure comes from an overload of information or from a need to be consistent in inferences about the patient, clinicians must be able to tolerate the ambiguity and complexity that arise from patients, who are inherently complex.

The reading-in syndrome

We have commented previously that clinicians sometimes tend to overinterpret. They often inject meaning into remarks and actions that are best regarded as something less than deeply meaningful. Because they are set to make such observations, it can be very easy to react to minimal cues as evidence of psychopathology. What is really amazing is that the world gets along with so many "sick" people out there! It is so easy to emphasize the negative rather than the positive that clinicians can readily make dire predictions or interpretations that fail to take the person's assets into account.

Validation and records

Too often, clinicians make interpretations or predictions without following them up. If clinicians fail to record their interpretations and predictions, it can become too easy to remember only the correct ones. Taking pains to compare the clinician's view with that of professional colleagues, relatives, or others who know the patient can also help to refine interpretive skills. Strasburg and Jackson (1977) carried out a study to determine the kinds of information that lead to increased accuracy of clinical judgments. One of their conclusions was that a feedback-learning paradigm in research on clinical inference would be highly useful.

Vague reports, concepts, and criteria

One of the most pervasive obstacles to valid clinical judgment is the tendency to employ vague concepts and poorly defined criteria. This, of course, culminates in psychological reports that are equally vague. Under these conditions, it can be very difficult to determine whether clinicians' predictions and judgments are correct. (Perhaps that is why some of them use such shadowy terminology.)

The effects of predictions

Sometimes predictions turn out to be in error not because they were based upon faulty inferences but because the predictions themselves influenced the behavioral situation. For example, a prediction that a patient would have difficulty in adjusting at home after release from the hospital may have been correct. However, the patient's relatives may have accepted the prediction as a challenge and thereupon provided an environment that was more conducive to the patient's adjustment than it would have been in the absence of the prediction. Thus, the very act of having made a judgment may serve to alter the clinician's own behavior or that of others.

Prediction to unknown situations

Clinical inferences and predictions are likely to be in error when clinicians are not clear about the situations to which they are predicting. Inferring aggression from the TAT is one thing—relating it to specific situations is another. Furthermore, no matter how careful and correct clinicians are, an extraneous event can erase an otherwise perfectly valid prediction. Take the following example from the OSS assessment program:

> One high-ranking OSS officer, while operating abroad, received a letter from a friend of his in America informing him that his wife had run off with the local garage man, leaving no message or address. As a result the officer's morale, which had formerly been high, dropped to zero. The assessment staff could predict that a small percentage of men would have to cope with a profoundly depressing or disquieting event of this sort, but, again, it was not possible to guess which of the assessees would be thus afflicted. (OSS Assessment Staff, 1948, p. 454)

Common sense should suggest that, in order to accurately predict a person's behavior, the clinician must consider the environment in which that behavior will take place. And yet, clinicians are frequently asked to make predictions based on only imprecise and vague information about their patient's environmental situation.

In a hospital setting, a clinician may be requested to provide a prerelease workup on a given psychiatric patient. But the information available to the clinician too often covers largely only general background with supplementary descriptions of individual differences. Unfortunately, however, investigators such as Chase (1975), Ekehammar (1974), Megargee (1970), Mischel (1968), and Moos (1975) all agree that such data are subject to a ceiling effect that will allow correlations of no better than .30 to .40 between the data and the subsequent behavior. To say the least, correlations of that magnitude leave a great deal to be desired. As might be expected, Fairweather (1967) has shown that predicting posthospital adjustment is much better when information is available about the environment in which the patient will live; personality data alone are insufficient.

Fallacious prediction principles

In some instances, intuitive predictions can lead clinicians into error because they ignore the logic of statistical prediction. Intuitive predictions often ignore base rates, fail to consider regression effects, and assume that highly correlated predictors will yield higher validity (Kahneman & Tversky, 1973). For example, suppose that a clinician is assessing a patient by collecting samples of behavior in a variety of situations. Even though observations reveal an extremely aggressive person, the clinician should not be surprised to learn that eventually the person behaves in a very passive fashion. Regression concepts should lead the clinician to expect that exceptionally tall parents will have a shorter child, that brilliant students sometimes do poorly, and so on.

In addition, the clinician's own confidence can sometimes be quite misleading. For example, Kahneman and Tversky (1973) showed that individuals are more confident when they are predicting from correlated tests. More specifically, although clinicians are often more confident of their inferences when they stem from a combination of the Rorschach, the TAT, and the MMPI rather than from a single test, Golden (1964) could find no evidence to support this confidence. The reliability and validity of clinical interpretations did not increase as a function of increasing amounts of test data. Therefore, even though clinicians should always seek to corroborate their inferences, it is a mistake to believe that the validity of inferences is inevitably correlated with the size of the test battery.

The influence of stereotyped beliefs

Sometimes clinicians seem to interpret data in terms of *stereotyped beliefs* (Chapman & Chapman, 1967). For example, Golding and Rorer (1972) found that certain clinicians believed that anal responses on the Rorschach indicated homosexuality, and they were extremely resistant to changing their preconceptions even in the face of intensive training to the contrary. Such research is a reminder that clinicians must constantly be on guard against any tendency to believe that certain diagnostic signs are inevitably valid indicators of certain characteristics.

Another example comes from a survey of the effects of clients' socioeconomic status on clinicians' judgments (Sutton & Kessler, 1986). A sample of 242 respondents read case histories identical in all respects, except that the client was placed in various socioeconomic classes. When the client was described as an unemployed welfare recipient with a seventh-grade education, clinicians attributed a poorer prognosis and were less likely to recommend insight therapy.

■ "Why I Do Not Attend Case Conferences"

In an engaging paper explaining why he gave up attending case conferences, Meehl (1977) lists a variety of reasons. He catalogs a number of fallacies that often crop up at such meetings. Most of them are entirely relevant to the interpretive process generally. The following synopsis of a few of the simpler ones provides something of their general flavor:

- *Sick-sick fallacy:* the tendency to perceive people very unlike ourselves as being sick. There is a tendency to interpret behavior unlike our own as maladjusted, and it is easier to see pathology in such clients.
- *Me too fallacy:* denying the diagnostic significance of an event in the patient's life because it also happened to us. Some of us are narcissistic or defensive enough to believe we are all right. Therefore, the more our patients are like ourselves the less likely we are to detect problems.
- *Uncle George's pancakes fallacy:* "There is nothing wrong with that; my Uncle George did not like to throw away leftover pancakes either." This is, perhaps, an extension of the previous fallacy. Things that we do (and by extension, things that those close to us do) could not be maladjusted. Therefore, those like us cannot be maladjusted either.
- *Multiple Napoleons fallacy:* There was only one Napoleon, despite how strongly a psychotic patient may feel that he or she is also Napoleon. An objection to interpreting such a patient's belief as pathological is buttressed by the remark, "Well, it may not be real to us, but it's real to him (or her)!" Further, "Everything is real to the person doing the perceiving. In fact, our percepts are our reality." If this argument were invoked consistently, nothing could possibly be pathological. Even the male patient with paranoid schizophrenia who believes aliens are living in his nasal passages would be normal since, after all, this is reality for him.
- *Understanding-it-makes-it-normal fallacy:* the idea that understanding a patient's beliefs or behaviors strips them of their significance. This trap is very easy for clinicians to fall into. Even the most deviant and curious behavior can somehow begin to seem acceptable once we convince ourselves that we know the reasons for its occurrence. This may not be unlike the tendency of those who excuse the criminal's behavior because they understand the motives and poor childhood experiences involved.

■ Communication: The Clinical Report

The clinician has completed the interview, administered the tests, and read the case history. The tests have been scored, and hypotheses and impressions have been developed. The time has come to write the report. This is the communication phase of the assessment process.

Appelbaum (1970) has characterized the role of the assessor as sociologist, politician, diplomat, group dynamicist, salesperson, artist, and yes, even psychologist. As a sociologist, the assessor must assay the local mores to aid in the acceptance of the report and to direct the report to those most likely to implement it. In some instances, this may mean directly interacting with hospital personnel in order to convince them of the validity of the report and to encourage them to act on it. This could involve ward attendants, nurses, psychiatrists, and so on. Such persuasion may at times seem more suitable for a politician or a diplomat than for a clinician. However, there are certainly times when reports will have to serve the function of convincing reluctant others. Not everyone is willing to regard the clinician as a purveyor of wisdom and unadulterated truth. Ideally, of course, the evidence for clinicians' conclusions and the tightness of their arguments will be reasons enough for accepting their descriptions and recommendations.

There is, of course, no single best format for a report. The nature of the referral, the audience to which the report is directed, the kinds of assessment procedures used, and the theoretical persuasion of the clinician are just a few of the considerations that could affect the presentation of a clinical report (Tallent, 1983). What one says to a psychiatrist is likely to be couched in language different from that directed to a school official. The feedback one provides to the parents of a child with mental retardation must be presented differently from the feedback that one gives to a professional colleague. Nevertheless, any written assessment should include certain fundamental elements. In Table 10-2, we present a sample outline of the basic criteria for a psychological test report (Beutler, 1995).

The referral source

The major responsibility of the report is to address the *referral questions*. The test report should carefully and explicitly answer the questions that prompted the assessment in the first place. If the referral questions cannot be answered or if they are somehow inappropriate, this should be stated in the report and the reasons given. In some instances (perhaps in most instances), contradictions will be inherent in the assessment data. Although the clinician must make every effort to resolve such contradictions and present a unified view of the patient, there are instances in which such resolution is not possible. In those instances, the contradictions should be described. Distortion in the service of consistency is not a desirable alternative.

Although the primary report is sent to the referring person (a psychiatrist, another clinician, or an agency), a secondary reader (an agency administrator, a program evaluator, or a research psychologist) may also be receiving the information. In specific circumstances, it may be necessary or even desirable to prepare a

Table 10-2
Sample outline of a psychological report.

I. Identifying information
   A. Name of patient
   B. Sex
   C. Age
   D. Ethnicity
   E. Date of evaluation
   F. Referring clinician
II. Referral question
III. Assessment procedures
IV. Background
   A. Information relevant to clarifying the referral question
   B. A statement of the probable reliability and validity of conclusions
V. Summary of impressions and findings
   A. Cognitive level
     1. Current intellectual and cognitive functioning (for example, ideation, intelligence, memory, perception)
     2. Degree (amount of) impairment compared to premorbid level
     3. Probable cause of impairment
     (By end of this subsection, referrer should know whether the patient has a thought disorder, mental retardation, or organicity.)
   B. Affective and mood levels
     1. Mood, affect at present—compare this with premorbid levels
     2. Degree of disturbance (mild, moderate, severe)
     3. Chronic versus acute nature of disturbance
     4. Lability—how well can the person modulate, control affect with his or her cognitive resources?
     (By end of this subsection, referrer should know whether there is a mood disturbance, what the patient's affects are, and how well controlled emotions are.)
   C. Interpersonal-intrapersonal level
     1. Primary interpersonal and intrapersonal conflicts and their significance
     2. Interpersonal and intrapersonal coping strategies (including major defenses)
     3. Formulation of personality
VI. Diagnostic impressions
   A. Series of impressions about cognitive and affective functioning, *or*
   B. The most probable diagnoses
VII. Recommendations
   A. Assessment of risk, need for confinement, medication
   B. Duration, modality, frequency of treatment

SOURCE: From "Integrating and Communicating Findings," by L. E. Beutler in *Integrative Assessment of Adult Personality* edited by L. E. Beutler and M. R. Berren, p. 36. Copyright © 1995 by Guilford Publications, Inc. Reprinted by permission.

special report for such people. In any event, a clinical report does not always serve an exclusively clinical or direct helping function. It can also be useful in assisting an agency to evaluate the effect of its programs. It can likewise be useful from the standpoint of psychological research. Information in clinical reports can often be helpful in validating tests or the interpretations and predictions made from tests. Such data can sometimes provide a baseline against which to compare subsequent change in the patient as a function of various forms of intervention.

Aids to communication

The primary function of a report is *communication.* The following are some suggestions for enhancing that function.

Language.   One should not resort to jargon or to a boring and minute test-by-test account of patient responses. Again, it is important to recall the nature of the referral source. In general, it is probably best to write in a style and language that can be understood by the intelligent layperson. Of course, what is jargon or excessively technical is partly in the eye of the beholder. A considerable amount of technical language can be tolerated in a report sent to a professional colleague whom one knows. On the other hand, technical jargon has no place in a report that is going to a parent. The terms *intertest scatter* and *Erlebnistypus* may be all right for another clinician, but they should not appear in a report sent to a junior high school counselor.

Individualized reports.   We observed earlier in this chapter the importance of avoiding the Barnum effect, and it is well to repeat the point here. The distinctive—be it current characteristics, development, or learning history— is preferred over the general. To say that Jack is insecure hardly distinguishes him from 90% of all psychotherapy patients. To say that Jack's insecurity stems from a history of living with several different relatives as a child and that it will become particularly acute whenever he must make a decision that will take him away (even temporarily) from his wife and home is considerably more meaningful. In this case, a general characteristic has been distinctly qualified by both antecedent and subsequent conditions.

The level of detail.   The question of how detailed a report ought to be often arises. Again, this depends largely upon one's audience. In general, however, it seems desirable to include a mix of abstract generalities, specific behavioral illustrations, and some testing detail. For example, in reporting depressive tendencies, a few illustrations of the test responses that led to the inference would be quite in order. A few of the relevant behavioral observations that were made during testing could also be quite helpful. A certain amount of detail can give readers the feeling that they can evaluate the clinician's conclusions and interpretations, whereas the exclusive use of abstract generalities places the reader at the mercy of the author's inferential processes.

■ A Case Illustration

To illustrate several of the points that this chapter has made regarding clinical judgment and communication, let us consider a specific clinical case report (Corbishley & Yost, 1995, pp. 322–340).

Identifying information
Name: Antonio Ramirez
Date of birth: 7/4/62
Sex: Male
Dates of examination: 8/22/94, 8/23/94

Referral question
Antonio Ramirez, a 32-year-old Latino male, is a sergeant with the Detroit, Michigan, Police Department, currently working as a narcotics officer. In the past few weeks, he has exhibited signs of stress but has refused to take sick leave, claiming that there is nothing wrong. He was referred by his commanding officer for psychological assessment to determine the extent to which recent events in Mr. Ramirez's life may have affected his ability to continue with his present duties.

Assessment procedures
Mr. Ramirez's personnel file and the referring physician's report were reviewed, and Mr. Ramirez reluctantly agreed to allow his wife, Donna, to be interviewed. On August 22, 1994, Mrs. Ramirez was interviewed for 1 hour while her husband took the Minnesota Multiphasic Personality Inventory-2 (MMPI-2). He complained of headache and blurred vision, which he claimed prevented further assessment that day. He returned the next day for a 1-hour interview, after which he completed the Rorschach and the Wechsler Adult Intelligence Scale-Revised (WAIS-R).

Background
Information Relevant to Referral Question
Mr. Ramirez is currently living with his wife of 8 years, a 6-year-old daughter, and a 4-year-old son. He has been employed by the Detroit Police Department since 1984 and has a satisfactory record. In general his health is good, and he expresses satisfaction with his job and marriage. His social life is limited, which he attributes to the fact that as a police officer he is viewed with unease by potential friends, and also to the unpredictable hours he must work.

He has good relationships with his siblings but sees them rarely, as they all live in distant parts of the country. He has no hobbies and spends his limited spare time at home, occasionally playing with his children, but primarily maintaining his house and yard. His relationship with his wife is by his report close, but he says they rarely discuss feelings and he would not burden her with his worries. His wife describes him as a good husband, faithful, even-tempered, and a loving father, but she says he takes life too seriously, and would like him to learn to have more fun.

Mr. Ramirez was raised by his mother in considerable poverty, his father having died in an industrial accident when Antonio was 8 years old. He remembers his father as "stern, but you knew he loved you." He describes his mother as "always worn out, always sad." At the time of his father's death, there were three younger children, ages 5 years, 3 years, and 6 months. Mr. Ramirez early took on the role of family supporter, working after school and on weekends to add to the family income, and helping to discipline his younger siblings. He remembers his development years as "not much fun, a lot of struggling to survive."

At school he was an isolate because of his work schedule and also because he was determined to complete his education, and thus had no time for "fooling with the guys." He learned to fight in self-defense when necessary, to pursue his own course, and to persist at whatever he tried. His sexual development was unremarkable. Since his mother seemed already to be burdened and since he had no close friends, he learned to keep problems and feelings to himself. After 2 years of college he entered the police academy, attracted by the discipline and structure of the organization and the opportunity to defend the public. On the police force he acquired a reputation for being fair, even-tempered, tough, and completely dependable, but not an easy person to get close to—indeed, almost frightening in his self-sufficiency.

In the last 3 months, he has experienced a number of disturbing events. His partner was wounded during a raid; Mr. Ramirez himself was shot at, though not injured, while making a routine traffic check; his wife was attacked, though not raped or physically harmed, on the way home from work one evening; and he was the first on the scene to discover two children under the age of 5 beaten to death in a "crack" house.

This accumulation of violence appears to have affected Mr. Ramirez in several ways. He has had several uncharacteristic outbursts of temper at minor frustrations; on one occasion, to the distress of his fellow officers, he fired his police weapon with insufficient provocation. Somatic symptoms include a 15-pound weight loss over the past 2 months, and (according to his wife) restless sleep and nightmares several times a week. In addition, he has become irrationally overprotective of his family, refusing to let the children visit friends' houses, and angrily demanding that his wife stop work. At work he appears jumpy and distractible, to an extent that has become a concern to his fellow officers. When doing work requiring close attention, he has, on several occasions, developed a headache. Several of his written reports, usually meticulously completed, have contained careless errors and omissions. He has refused to discuss any of these incidents or their impact with his partner, his immediate supervisor, or the police-appointed physician.

When asked about these unusual behaviors, Mr. Ramirez denied that he had changed and claimed that people were exaggerating. On probing, he admitted that sometimes, when he is involved in unrelated daily activities, he gets flashbacks (especially to the scene with the dead children), but claimed that they neither upset him nor made him lose concentration. He attributed his weight loss and restless sleep to the hot summer weather, and insisted throughout the assessment process that he is "fine," that the events of the past months are just part of his job and of life, and that he is capable of continuing to work as before.

Reliability and Validity of Conclusions

At various points in the evaluation, Mr. Ramirez became agitated and appeared irritated; he jokingly accused the examiner of trying to make him remember "things best forgotten." In unstructured situations (i.e., the Rorschach), he produced fewer responses as the test proceeded. It is likely that his high level of arousal affected the validity of his responses to unstructured materials. He had fewer complaints regarding structured materials (i.e., the MMPI-2), but indices of validity indicate an effort to present himself in a favorable light and to deny pathology. During intellectually challenging tasks (i.e., the WAIS-R), he appeared to try hard and was minimally distracted.

All external evidence indicates that Mr. Ramirez's behavior over the past few weeks represents a considerable departure from premorbid levels of functioning, despite his denials. The results of procedures should therefore be interpreted in the light of objective information from external sources.

Summary of impressions and findings

On both days of assessment, Mr. Ramirez arrived punctually, in full uniform and meticulously groomed. Whether standing or sitting, he held himself rigidly and made little movement, as if at attention. He made eye contact infrequently and briefly, and spoke in a clear, quite loud, monotone voice, often pausing before speaking, and rarely expanding upon his answers without prompting. Even when he spoke of his inner experiences, he gave the impression of a person making a formal report to a superior. Only while he was responding to unstructured material was there a sense that his responses were spontaneous.

Intellectually, this man is functioning within the "bright normal" range of intelligence, but at a considerably lower level than previous assessment has indicated. In normal circumstances, he thinks carefully and logically (though unimaginatively), and is capable of sustained intellectual efforts. At the present time, he is easily distracted by intense inner experiences. Strong affect and mental images of unpleasant recent events appear to intrude on his problem-solving efforts and reduce his cognitive efficiency. Thus, his concentration and memory are somewhat impaired; recognizing this, he makes halting and ineffective efforts to overcome and compensate. These efforts produce increased physical tension, which may account for his somatic symptoms. It is likely that his reality testing is somewhat impaired under conditions of high stress, especially the stress of perceived threats to his sense of competence or to the welfare of others; under these conditions, his cognitive controls may be insufficient to prevent his becoming overwhelmed by internal or external stimuli. There is no evidence of a thought disorder, and it is likely that he can return to premorbid levels of functioning if he receives appropriate treatment.

Mr. Ramirez's mood is normally bland, almost stoic, with mild expression of emotions appropriate to the situation. He rarely exhibits anger, and, indeed, generally manages his affective experiences so as to avoid arousing strong feelings in himself. He is, however, capable of great emotional intensity, the expression of which he views as weakness, both in himself and in others. His greatest fear is the loss of self-control, since he believes such control to be the prime means of attaining satisfaction in life. Typically, he maintains control over his emotions by avoidance, withdrawal, and denial — even at home, where he feels less need to protect himself. He attempts to prevent both his wife and his children from expressing intense or prolonged affect, both positive and negative. He is experienced by others as emotionally insulated, but not cold or threatening.

Currently, he is reacting with unusual intensity to mild stimuli, and there are indications that he is experiencing acute dysphoria, with barely suppressed rage and frustration. It is apparent that his normal controls over affect are becoming less effective, though he continues to deny either the existence of strong emotion or his own inability to contain it. Since, as a police officer, he must work in daily contact with situations that are bound to elicit unpleasant emotions, and since he will never be able to completely protect his family from all harm, it is likely that his emotions will intensify and that his control will weaken further. A breakdown of control may manifest itself in more severe somatic complaints or in hostile and aggressive action, or in both. It is clear that Mr. Ramirez's current method of dealing with recently encountered stresses is increasingly ineffective.

Mr. Ramirez is generally conforming and conventional, with a need for structure and a strong sense of morality, loyalty, and responsibility to others. He performs best, and experiences a strong sense of competence and self-confidence, in situations where both role and task are clear. He has a need to be — and to be seen as — strong, effective, and in control. To this end, he is planful, vigilant, persistent, and determined, setting goals for himself and pursuing them in an organized manner. When difficulties arise, he tackles them immediately, directly, and actively, and is impatient with ambiguous resolutions to problems. On the other hand, he demonstrates a lack of flexibility and a tendency to be dogmatic and domineering, especially with those he views as inferior or in need of his protection. Because of his confidence and competence, others tend to trust, rely on, and respect him, but they find him emotionally distant and hard to know. Because of these attitudes and behaviors, Mr. Ramirez is, in general, a highly competent police officer.

In his personal life, both his single-minded pursuit of goals and his refusal to acknowledge intense affect make for a rather joyless and dogged existence. His need to avoid appearing vulnerable and his tendency to enjoy solitary pursuits keep him from an active social life, and he experiences considerable discomfort in what appear to him to be purposeless social occasions. Only in his most intimate relationships is he able to relax to some degree—for example, when playing with his children. He has a strong sense of the importance of family, and generally adheres to a traditional view of the male's role as provider and protector. Thus, the recent attack on his wife was experienced by Mr. Ramirez as a severe and multifaceted threat, calling for immediate action. Because he had no control over the situation and has no way to control future, similar situations, Mr. Ramirez feels helpless and vulnerable to a degree that is extremely difficult for him to tolerate.

Diagnostic impressions

This man's premorbid functioning is likely to have been characterized by mild social phobia, a tendency to restrict affective experiences and expression, and a somewhat rigid personality structure. However, it is likely that he was generally effective in daily living, with stable work and personal relationships. Recent changes in his affect, behavior, and cognitive functioning appear directly related to several severe psychosocial stressors. He re-experiences these events; avoids stimuli associated with the events; and suffers from loss of interest in significant activities, poor concentration, exaggerated startle response, and intense irritability. These symptoms having persisted for at least 1 month, a diagnosis of Post-Traumatic Stress Disorder is warranted.

Axis I	309.89, Post-Traumatic Stress Disorder
Axis II	No diagnosis on Axis II
Axis III	None
Axis IV	Psychosocial stressors: Injury of partner; wife attacked; discovery of dead children in "crack" house Severity: 4-5 (acute events)
Axis V	Global Assessment of Functioning (GAF): Current, 53; highest past year, 75

Recommendations

Mr. Ramirez's responses to his environment are increasingly atypical and therefore unpredictable. His current assignment requires self-discipline and cool judgment, which he may no longer be able to produce reliably at premorbid levels. Furthermore, he has apparently almost no insight into his condition, is experiencing anger, and is capable of acting aggressively. It is recommended, therefore, that he be relieved of those duties that involve direct confrontation with violence or danger to himself or to others, with return to active duty contingent upon psychological change.

It is further recommended that Mr. Ramirez seek behavioral psychotherapy—in a group, if possible—that takes a self-management approach. His defensiveness, self-sufficiency, assumption of a conventional male role, and resistance to psychological material indicate that he is unlikely to be a good candidate for insight-oriented psychotherapy, which he would be likely to see as evidence of personal failure. However, it is essential that he learn to modify his need to control every aspect of life, especially if he wishes to continue his present career path. The behavioral/self-management approach seems most likely to present the process of self-examination and change in an acceptable light.

Some comments on the Antonio Ramirez report

As stated previously, the primary function of a report is communication—it should not be an ego trip for the writer. In general, the report on Antonio Ramirez could be read and understood by a layperson, using little language of a technical nature. However, some of the language (for example, "intense inner experiences," "reality testing") may only be familiar to other mental health professionals.

Another positive feature of this report involves the level of detail. The report began with some background material, along with references to the patient's accounts of his behavior and feelings. It also included some behavioral observations by the clinician. It then moved to a discussion of test responses and some inferences from them. Following that, several integrative statements were made.

At the same time, occasional examples of Barnum statements were apparent in the report, for example, "It is likely that his reality testing is somewhat impaired under conditions of high stress." There were also occasional predictions or statements that were somewhat vague. For example, how would one validate the prediction "it is likely that he can return to premorbid levels of functioning if he receives appropriate treatment"? Further, in many cases it is unclear what test data were used to support an interpretation or make a prediction. Were these based on MMPI-2, WAIS-R, or Rorschach results? What specific test scores from any or all of these measures were employed as the basis for these statements?

Although we have provided a few critical comments regarding this test report, we want to emphasize that this report has many more strengths than it has limitations. Reports will vary with regard to structure, style, and language. What is most important, however, is that the test report contributes to an increased understanding of the patient so that the appropriate course of action or treatment can be undertaken. After all, that is the primary goal of psychological assessment.

■ Focus Questions

1. What are the advantages and disadvantages of the clinical approach to prediction?
2. What are the advantages and disadvantages of the statistical approach to prediction?
3. How can clinical judgment be improved?
4. What are the major obstacles in implementing statistical prediction procedures?
5. What are the major considerations when preparing a psychological report?

■ Key Terms

Barnum effect
clinical interpretation
correlates
quantitative or statistical approach
referral questions

samples
signs
stereotyped beliefs
subjective or clinical approach

III

CLINICAL INTERVENTIONS

11

Psychological Interventions

Therapy. Some call it the greatest vehicle yet invented for curing society's psychic ills and achieving unparalleled levels of personal growth. Others say that it is just an indoor sport invented for a pampered middle class that has little to worry about save self-awareness, now that Western technology has rescued it from the daily problems of physical survival. A more tempered evaluation would characterize it as a tool that is imperfect at best—a tool that is limited both by the complexity of the tasks to which it is applied and by the skill and knowledge of the practitioners who employ it. Because therapy is imperfect, it is unlikely to achieve the more grandiose claims that have been made for it. But it is equally unlikely that therapy will become the diabolical twister of minds and human values that some of its detractors claim it can be.

In this chapter we will provide a general description of therapy, explain its major features, discuss issues about its effectiveness, and present an introduction to psychotherapy research. Our focus will also be on a broad overview of some of the main features shared by different methods of clinical intervention. These interventions go by many different names: psychoanalysis, cognitive therapy, group therapy, family therapy, behavior therapy, existential therapy, and on and on. In some ways, each has a set of unique defining characteristics or is directed toward specific kinds of problems. In subsequent chapters we shall focus on these defining characteristics. Here, however, our attention will be directed toward shared features rather than differences.

■ General Description

In a most general way, *psychological intervention* is a method of inducing changes in a person's behavior, thoughts, or feelings. While the same might also be said for a TV commercial or the efforts of teachers and close friends, therapy involves intervention in the context of a professional relationship—a relationship sought by the client or the client's guardians. In some cases, therapy is undertaken

293

to solve a specific problem or to improve the individual's capacity to deal with existing behaviors, feelings, or thoughts that are debilitating. In other cases, the focus may be more on the prevention of problems than on remedying an existing condition. In still other instances, the focus is less on solving or preventing problems than it is on increasing the person's ability to take pleasure in life or to achieve some latent potential.

Over the years, many definitions of the intervention process have been offered. As often as not, the terms intervention and psychotherapy have been used interchangeably. A rather typical general definition of psychotherapy was provided by Wolberg years ago:

> Psychotherapy is a form of treatment for problems of an emotional nature in which a trained person deliberately establishes a professional relationship with a patient with the object of removing, modifying or retarding existing symptoms, of mediating disturbed patterns of behavior, and of promoting positive personality growth and development. (Wolberg, 1967, p. 3)

Wolberg's definition includes such words as *symptoms* and *treatment,* and his subsequent elaboration of the definition gives it a distinctly medical flavor. Yet, overall, the definition is not much different from one offered by a more psychologically oriented clinician: "Psychotherapy . . . is planned activity of the psychologist, the purpose of which is to accomplish changes in the individual that make his [sic] life adjustment potentially happier, more constructive, or both" (Rotter, 1971b, p. 79). Frank elaborates this general theme as follows:

> Psychotherapy is a planned, emotionally charged, confiding interaction between a trained, socially sanctioned healer and a sufferer. During this interaction the healer seeks to relieve the sufferer's distress and disability through symbolic communications, primarily words but also sometimes bodily activities. The healer may or may not involve the patient's relatives and others in the healing rituals. Psychotherapy also often includes helping the patient to accept and endure suffering as an inevitable aspect of life that can be used as an opportunity for personal growth. (Frank, 1982, p. 10)

Granted, such definitions are rather broad. Practitioners of such specific approaches as psychoanalysis, rational-emotive therapy, client-centered counseling, cognitive therapy, gestalt therapy, and other forms of psychological treatment will rightly note that these definitions hardly convey the essence of their unique brand of therapy.

Does psychotherapy help?

Before we describe in more detail the goals and features of psychotherapy, a general question needs to be addressed: Does psychotherapy work? Both advocates (for example, Lambert & Bergin, 1994) and critics (for example, Dawes, 1994) agree that empirical evidence supports the efficacy of psychotherapy. Of course, this does not mean that everyone benefits from psychotherapy—rather, on average, individuals who seek out and receive psychotherapy achieve some degree of relief. For example, a frequently cited meta-analytic review of over 475 psychotherapy outcome studies reported that the average person receiving psychological treatment is functioning better than 80% of those not receiving treatment (Smith, Glass, & Miller, 1980). We will discuss this study and other reviews of psychotherapy outcomes in a later section on psychotherapy research methods.

At this point, however, a recent large-scale survey on the benefits of psychotherapy deserves mention. The November 1995 issue of *Consumer Reports* summarized the results of a survey of 4000 readers who had sought treatment for a psychological problem from a mental health professional, family doctor, or self-help group during the years 1991–1994. Most of the respondents were well-educated, their median age was 46 years, and about half the sample were women. Forty-three percent described their emotional state at the time that treatment was sought as "very poor" ("I barely managed to deal with things") or "fairly poor" ("Life was usually pretty tough"). The 4000 respondents presented for treatment of a wide range of problems, including depression, anxiety, panic, phobias, marital or sexual problems, alcohol or drug problems, and problems with children. The major findings were:

1. Psychotherapy resulted in some improvement for the majority of respondents. Those who felt the worst before treatment began reported the most improvement.
2. As for which types of mental health professionals were most helpful, psychiatrists, psychologists, and social workers all received high marks. All appeared to be equally effective even after controlling for the severity of and type of psychological problem.
3. Respondents who received psychotherapy alone improved as much as those who received psychotherapy and medication as part of their treatment.
4. In this survey, longer treatment (that is, more sessions) was related to more improvement.

These findings are both interesting and provocative. This survey, however, is limited in a number of respects such that we must be cautious in our generalizations. For example, few respondents reported severe psychopathology (such as schizophrenia), and reports were both retrospective and based solely on the clients' self-report. Despite these limitations, the *Consumer Reports* survey provides further support for the contention that psychotherapy works. Further, it represents the largest study to date that assessed "the effectiveness of psychotherapy as it is actually performed in the field with the population that actually seeks it, and it is the most extensive, carefully done study to do this" (Seligman, 1995, p. 971).

What problems are amenable to change?

Are all concerns, worries, problematic behaviors, and psychopathological symptoms responsive to psychological interventions? Probably not. Despite the proliferation of pop psychology antidotes and charlatanesque claims to the contrary, it appears that some conditions clients present with are difficult to change, whereas other conditions are quite amenable to change. In an intriguing guide to self-improvement, Seligman (1994) reviewed the empirical research on the treatment of a wide variety of "problems" in order to compile a list of "what you can change and what you can't." Table 11-1 summarizes some of his findings.

Why are some problems amenable to change whereas others are not? Seligman (1994) invokes the concept of *depth of a problem* to explain the

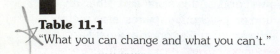

Table 11-1
"What you can change and what you can't."

Problem/Condition	Changeability
Panic disorder	Curable
Specific phobias	Almost curable
Sexual dysfunctions	Marked relief possible
Social phobia	Moderate relief possible
Agoraphobia	Moderate relief possible
Depression	Moderate relief possible
Obsessive-compulsive disorder	Moderate/mild relief possible
Anger	Mild/moderate relief possible
Everyday anxiety	Mild/moderate relief possible
Alcoholism	Mild relief possible
Overweight	Temporary change only
Posttraumatic stress disorder	Marginal relief only

SOURCE: From *What You Can Change and What You Can't,* by Martin E. P. Seligman, PhD. Copyright © 1994 by Martin E. P. Seligman. Reprinted by permission of Alfred A. Knopf, Inc.

"changeability" of a variety of conditions or behaviors. The level of depth of a problem depends on whether it is innate (biologically determined), whether it is difficult to disconfirm the belief underlying it, and whether the belief underlying the problem is "powerful" in the sense that it is quite general and can explain many of the facts of the world. For example, transsexuality is probably unchangeable (that is, "deep") because "it is biologically laid down in gestation. It is virtually undisconfirmable and pervades all of life" (Seligman, 1994, p. 247). On the other hand, a specific phobia of spiders is not deep because spider phobias per se are not inherited, they can be disconfirmed, and the underlying belief (spiders are dangerous) is not powerful because it explains only spiders.

Seligman's (1994) review, analysis, and theory help us to make some sense out of why certain psychological problems seem relatively intractable whereas others can be alleviated with appropriate treatment. An additional attractive feature of this book is Seligman's critical, empirically based evaluation of various popular treatments for specific disorders. This is an issue we will return to in later chapters.

Features common to many therapies

There are literally hundreds of "brands" of psychotherapy that have been identified over the years. Some are effective, whereas others probably are not. Unfortunately, not all of these forms of psychological intervention have been subjected to empirical scrutiny. And of those that have received research attention, there is only limited evidence that one approach or technique is more effective than others.

Often lost in the apparent diversity among psychotherapies, however, are the marked similarities among them. This is due in part to the fact that the purveyor of a new brand of psychotherapy must emphasize the special features of the new product; bringing forth a minor variation of an old therapeutic theme would be unlikely to capture anyone's interest. Yet most psychotherapies have a great deal in common—a commonality that in many respects outweighs the diversity.

As Lambert and Bergin (1994) note, one implication of therapeutic equivalence is that a set of *common factors* that cuts across various theoretical and therapeutic boundaries may actually be the source of the positive changes effected by psychological treatment. They provide a list of common factors categorized according to a sequential process that they believe is associated with positive outcome. Briefly, they propose that *support factors* (for example, positive relationship, trust) lay the groundwork for changes in clients' beliefs and attitudes (that is, *learning factors* such as cognitive learning and insight), which then lead to client *action* or behavioral change (for example, mastery efforts and taking risks). Although a detailed discussion of each of the common factors listed in Table 11-2 is beyond the scope of this book, it may be instructive to briefly discuss some of them.

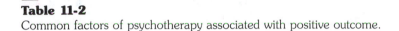

Table 11-2
Common factors of psychotherapy associated with positive outcome.

Support Factors	Learning Factors	Action Factors
Catharsis	Advice	Behavioral regulation
Identification with therapist	Affective experiencing	Cognitive mastery
Mitigation of isolation	Assimilation of problematic experiences	Encouragement of facing fears
Positive relationship	Changing expectations for personal effectiveness	Taking risks
Reassurance	Cognitive learning	Mastery efforts
Release of tension	Corrective emotional experience	Modeling
Structure	Exploration of internal frame of reference	Practice
Therapeutic alliance	Feedback	Reality testing
Therapist/client active participation	Insight	Success experience
Therapist expertness	Rationale	Working through
Therapist warmth, respect, empathy, acceptance, genuineness		
Trust		

SOURCE: From "The Effectiveness of Psychotherapy," by M. J. Lambert and A. E. Bergin in *Handbook of Psychotherapy and Behavior Change,* 4/e, edited by A. E. Bergin and S. L. Garfield, pp. 143–189. Copyright © 1994 by John Wiley & Sons, Inc. Reprinted by permission.

The expert role.   It is assumed that the therapist brings to the therapy situation something more than acceptance, warmth, respect, and interest. These are not sufficient for certification as a psychotherapist. Conventional wisdom seems to suggest that all one needs in order to conduct psychotherapy is an unflagging interest in others. But this is not enough.

In all forms of psychotherapy, patients have a right to expect that not only are they seeing a warm human being but a competent one as well; and competence can only come from a long, arduous period of training. Some may be quick to assert that the assumption of an expert role introduces an authoritarian element into the relationship, implying that the patient and the therapist are not equal and thus destroying the mutual respect that should exist between them. However, mutual understanding and mutual acceptance of the different roles to be played would seem sufficient to guarantee the maintenance of mutual respect. Therapists are, of course, no better than patients, and they cannot lay claim to any superior consideration in the cosmic scheme of things. But this kind of equality need not deny the importance of training, knowledge, and experience that assists therapists in their efforts to resolve the patient's problems.

The release of emotions/catharsis.   Some have stated that psychotherapy without anger, anxiety, or tears is no psychotherapy at all. Psychotherapy is an emotional experience. The conviction of most psychotherapists is so strong on this point that they would seriously question whether a patient who, session after session, maintains a calm, cool, detached, or intellectual demeanor is really benefiting. The problems that bring a person to psychotherapy are typically important ones. Consequently, they are likely to have important antecedents.

Therefore, the release of emotions, or *catharsis* as it is sometimes termed, is a vital part of most psychotherapies. Its depth and intensity will vary, depending on the nature and severity of the problem and on the particular stage in therapy. But the psychotherapist must be prepared to deal with emotional expression and to use it to bring about change. Although some forms of psychotherapy certainly place more reliance upon emotional expression than do others, a new brand of therapy is likely to be criticized if it seems to neglect this important facet.

Relationship/therapeutic alliance.   For some, the nature of the relationship between patient and therapist is the single element most responsible for the success of psychotherapy. Although not all therapists would elevate the relationship to the status of the primary curative agent, almost all therapists would attest to the unique importance of the relationship. For example, where else can patients find an accepting, nonjudgmental atmosphere in which to discuss their innermost urges, secrets, and disappointments? Discussions of this kind with a friend or a relative always seem to contain an implicit evaluational aura and often lead to unforeseen complications because the other person has a personal stake in the matters discussed. Friends can easily be threatened by such discussions because the content of the discussions has the potential to disturb the basis for the relationship. Can a husband discuss his dependency anxieties with his wife, whose perception of her role may be disturbed by such revelations? Can a son reveal his fear of failure to a father who has been boastful of the son's achievements? Can a daughter tell her mother that she wishes to give up her role as housewife in favor of a career without seeming to question her mother's values?

In psychotherapy all of this is possible. The effective therapist is someone who can be accepting, nonjudgmental, objective, insightful, and professional all at the same time. These lavish adjectives scarcely fit all therapists all of the time. Nevertheless, the general ability of therapists to rise above their personal needs and to respond with professional skill in a nonjudgmental atmosphere of confidentiality, understanding, and warmth is probably a major reason for the success and persistence of psychotherapy in our society.

Anxiety reduction/release of tension.   Initially, it is important that the anxiety accompanying the patient's problems be reduced enough to permit examination of the factors responsible for the problems. The essential conditions of psychotherapy, including the nature of the relationship, the qualifications of the therapist, and confidentiality and privacy, combine to provide a reassurance and a sense of security that can lower anxiety and permit patients to contemplate their experiences systematically.

In instances in which the anxiety level is extremely high, some patients may require, on medical advice, antianxiety medications to help deal with the situation. However, it is important that such medications be regarded as a temporary tool rather than as a permanent solution.

Interpretation/insight.   Many nonprofessionals erroneously view psychotherapy as a rather straightforward process in which a person presents a problem, the therapist asks the person to describe his or her childhood experiences, a series of interpretations as to the real meaning of those childhood experiences is made by the therapist, and the person then achieves *insight*. With the sudden, explosive force of revelation, this insight strikes home. A brief period of wonderment follows as the problem falls away like melting snow. In the end, the patient walks away from the consulting room, framed in the light from the setting sun, assured that relief and everlasting joy have been attained. This, of course, is a scenario from a bad movie or from the fantasies of a beginning therapist.

There is, however, a small amount of reality in the foregoing. A broad band of psychotherapies does attach importance to patients' childhood experiences, though such psychotherapies vary in the degree of importance they attach to them, the amount of related information they seek, and their view of the effects generated by the experiences. Similarly, *interpretation* is a very common component of psychotherapy. But again, the extent of its use, the kinds and the timing of the interpretations, and the importance attributed to them, vary with the school of psychotherapy. Regardless of terminology, however, an important element in many forms of psychotherapy is the attempt to get the patient to view past experience in a different light.

The importance that therapists attach to insight has eroded over the years. Once it was naively thought that insight into the nature and origin of problems would somehow automatically propel the patient into a higher level of adjustment. Most psychotherapists no longer cling to this simple belief. Insight is still viewed as important, but it is recognized that significant behavioral change can be brought about by other means. Insight may be seen as a facilitator of psychological growth and improvement, but not as something that by itself will inevitably bring about such changes. Indeed, waiting for insight to free one from problems can be a delaying tactic used by some patients to avoid taking the responsibility for initiating changes in their lives.

Building competence/mastery.   In one sense, a goal of most therapies is to make the client a more competent and effective human being. All of the foregoing features will, of course, facilitate the achievement of greater effectiveness and satisfaction. But beyond such elements as the therapeutic relationship or anxiety reduction there are other features in some forms of therapy that are also applicable here. For example, therapy can be a setting in which the client learns new things and corrects faulty ways of thinking. At times, some forms of therapy will take on distinct teaching overtones. The client is "tutored" on more effective ways to find a job, or perhaps sexual information is provided to help alleviate past sexual difficulties and promote a better sexual adjustment in the future. Therapy, then, can be more than just exorcising old psychological demons — it can also be a learning experience in the direct sense of the word. In recent years, Bandura (1989) has emphasized the importance of feelings of self-efficacy in promoting a higher performance level in the individual. In short, those persons who feel confident, expect to do well, or just feel good about themselves are more likely to function in an effective fashion.

Nonspecific factors.   Call it faith, hope, or expectations for increased competence, successful therapy tends to be associated with such factors (Kazdin, 1979). Numerous factors can conspire to promote these expectancies. First of all, there is often a mystique to therapy — at least in the eyes of the general public. Patients often come to therapy fully expecting to participate in a process almost guaranteed to promote mental health. Then, too, therapists often encourage such beliefs, knowing full well that a believing, motivated client is more likely to show progress than a cynical, recalcitrant one. Finally, nearly every therapist is committed to a theory of therapeutic change. Whether it be an operant theory, a theory of the unconscious, or a belief in growth potential, its ubiquitous presence in the therapist's explanations of how therapy works can ignite a confidence that helps alleviate the client's feelings of despair. Although successful therapy may almost always be characterized as having rekindled the patient's hope, faith, and morale (Frank, 1973), it seems unlikely that therapy can be reduced to nothing more than what some have disparagingly referred to as a placebo. The expectations of the client help make even more effective the specific techniques applied in therapy, and the successes of such techniques then act to further increase the client's expectations.

In Frank's description of psychotherapy (1982), he notes that therapy involves a rationale, a conceptual scheme, or a myth that provides a plausible explanation for the patient's difficulties and also prescribes a ritual for restoring equilibrium. Such explanations and rituals can, as Frank adds, provide the patient with a face-saving reason to abandon a symptom when ready to do so. To cease complaining or give up a cherished symptom without a good reason would imply that it was trivial. So, whatever we call it—nonspecific factor, placebo effect, or just plain faith—it becomes an important element in the therapy process.

■ Nature of Specific Therapeutic Variables

It would be pleasant if psychotherapy were an easy routine in which the therapist could make a diagnosis, convey it to the patient, give a lecture or two, and presto—the patient would be cured. Unfortunately, things do not work that way. Indeed, it is often necessary for therapists to spend a considerable amount of time correcting patients' expectations that they will be given a simple psychological prescription. Because psychotherapy is an active, dynamic process, passivity and lack of motivation are tangible obstacles. On the other hand, a number of factors involving the nature of the patient, the therapist, and the patient-therapist interaction affect the process of therapy in important ways, often transcending the specific mode of therapy employed.

The patient or client

Are there specific or general patient characteristics that influence the outcomes of therapy? Such a deceptively simple question really has no answer other than "It depends." The reason it depends is that the outcomes of therapy are exceedingly complex events that are not shaped by patient characteristics alone—they are also determined by therapist qualities and skills, the kinds of therapeutic procedures employed, the circumstances and environment of the patient, and so on. Eventually, the field will have to specifically identify which kinds of patients benefit from which procedures, under which circumstances, and by which therapists (Kiesler, 1966; Paul, 1967).

With the foregoing caveat firmly in mind, we can proceed to discuss some of the more prominent patient variables that have been related to outcomes in traditional therapies.

The degree of the patient's distress.

A broad generalization often made by clinicians is that the persons who need therapy the least are the persons who will receive the greatest benefit from it. A more sophisticated version of this relationship is reflected in Truax and Carkhuff's distinction (1967) between patients' feelings of disturbance and their overt behavioral disturbance. This distinction implies to many clinicians that a good prognosis may be expected for a patient who is experiencing distress or anxiety but is functioning well behaviorally.

At best, however, the research data are contradictory and inconsistent (which, again, probably only reflects the impossibility of coming to a simple conclusion without considering the nature of the therapy involved, other patient-therapist characteristics, and so on). For example, one group of studies finds that greater initial distress is associated with greater improvement (see Stone, Frank, Nash, & Imber, 1961). Another group of studies (for example, Barron, 1953) finds exactly the reverse. Adding a further complication are Miller and Gross (1973), who contend that the relationship between improvement and the initial disturbance is curvilinear—that is, patients with little disturbance or extreme disturbance show poorer outcomes than do moderately disturbed patients. Summarizing research in this area, Garfield (1994) stated that, while mixed findings across studies temper the degree of confidence in general conclusions, more recent studies seem to consistently find that individuals who are more severely disturbed have poorer outcomes.

Intelligence.   In general, psychotherapy requires a reasonable level of intelligence (Garfield, 1994). This is not to say that persons who are mentally retarded do not under certain conditions benefit from counseling or from the opportunity to talk about their difficulties. Nevertheless, other things being equal, brighter individuals seem better able to handle the demands of psychotherapy.

This is so for several reasons. First, psychotherapy is a verbal process—it requires patients to articulate their problems, to frame them in words. Second, psychotherapy calls for patients to establish connections among events. Patients must have the capacity to see relationships between prior events and current problems, and ultimately they must be able to connect their current feelings with a variety of events whose relationship to those feelings may at first seem improbable. Finally, to enable connections among events to be made, psychotherapy also takes a degree of introspection. Since traditional psychotherapy has always emphasized the inner determinants of behavior, it follows that a patient who finds it difficult to look inward may have problems in adjusting to the process.

At the same time, it is well to note that behavioral forms of therapy have often been used for considerable success for individuals suffering from mental retardation. A variety of behavior modification approaches are quite feasible, especially when goals involve specific behavioral changes rather than insight. In such populations, improved social abilities, self-care skills, and other capacities can be developed with a focus on behavior rather than cognition. As a generalization, when behavioral deficits are the problem, behavioral techniques are frequently the preferred ones.

Age.   Other things being equal, younger patients have long been considered the best bets for therapy. Younger patients are presumably more plastic or less set in their ways. Perhaps younger patients are better able to make the appropriate connections because they are closer to their childhood years. Or perhaps they have been reinforced for negative behaviors less often than their older counterparts. In any event, the notion that younger persons do better in therapy is quite prevalent among clinicians. Research evidence supporting the contention that older clients have a poorer prognosis, however, is weak at best (Smith, Glass, & Miller, 1980; Garfield, 1994).

It is best to consider not age alone but, rather, the specific characteristics of the prospective patient. It often happens that a 55-year-old will be an active, open, introspective person who can really benefit from therapy. In short, denial of therapy to an elderly person can be construed as a form of ageism in some instances. Further, research supports the efficacy of various forms of both cognitive-behavioral and psychodynamic treatment with older adults (Gallagher-Thompson & Thompson, 1995; Scogin & McElreath, 1994).

Motivation.   Psychotherapy is sometimes a lengthy process. It demands much from a patient, and it can be fraught with anxiety, setbacks, and long periods of a seeming absence of progress. If psychotherapy is to be successful, it will force the patient to examine corners of the mind that have long remained unscrutinized. It may demand that the patient engage in new behaviors that will provoke anxiety. As was noted previously, psychotherapy is not a passive process in which insights are fed to the patient—instead, the patient must actively seek insights. Typically, the search is not easy. For these and other reasons, successful psychotherapy seems to require motivation. At some level, the patient must want psychotherapy (though there are times during psychotherapy when even highly motivated patients want out). It follows, then, that psychotherapy is a voluntary process: one cannot be forced into it. When people are forced—either openly or subtly—to become patients, they rarely profit from the experience. Therapy is not likely to be of much benefit to the prisoner who seeks it in order to impress a parole board, to the college student whom, following a marijuana charge, the court gives the option of reporting to a counseling center or facing the prospect of jail, or to the person who undergoes it in order to protect an insurance claim.

Despite the conventional wisdom in citing client motivation as a necessary condition for positive change, though, research support is mixed (Garfield, 1994). One procedural problem concerns how best to assess and measure client motivation, and studies vary widely in their methodologies. For example, Yoken and Berman (1987) used client payment for services as an index of client motivation. Given the relative lack of difference in outcome between those clients who paid the standard fees for services and those whose fees were waived, Yoken and Berman concluded that motivation appeared to be unrelated to outcome. The lack of definitive findings on this issue however, may say more about the difficulty researchers have experienced in defining and measuring client motivation than it does about the impact of motivation on the therapeutic process.

Openness.   Most therapists intuitively attach a better prognosis to patients who seem to show some respect for and optimism about the utility of psychotherapy. They are relieved when patients are willing to see their problems in psychological rather than medical terms. Such persons can be more easily "taught" to be "good psychotherapy patients," in contrast to those who view their difficulties as symptoms to be cured by an omniscient, authoritative therapist while they passively await the outcome. Thus, a kind of "openness" to the therapeutic process (Strupp & Bergin, 1969) appears to make the patient a better candidate for therapy.

Gender bias.   In the present climate, there are several prominent issues related to gender. One is the relationship between the outcome of therapy and the gender of the patient. Research does not support the view that the biological sex of the client is significantly related to outcome in psychotherapy (Garfield, 1994).

The second, and more volatile, issue is whether sexism operates in therapy and whether, for example, male therapists exploit female patients. Stricker (1977) suggests that the latter issue has so far served as a platform for extremists of both sides: those at the feminist end of the spectrum claim exploitation, and the male chauvinists deny all claims. Research into the question of whether therapists and counselors are guilty of gender bias and stereotyping is highly inconsistent (Barak & Fisher, 1989). Many, however, are confident in suggesting that clinical psychologists should do a better job of educating clinical students regarding gender issues (for example, Gilbert, 1987). Good, Gilbert, and Scher (1990) have even recommended a brand of psychotherapy called *gender-aware therapy* (GAT). GAT integrates both feminist psychotherapy and a knowledge of gender into a treatment approach for both men and women. This approach focuses on an exploration of unique gender-related experiences and may be appropriate for a variety of issues faced by women (for example, career development, eating disorders) and men (for example, depression, sexual dysfunction).

Finally, although the sex of the client has not been reliably linked to outcome, it is probably true that the sex or gender of the therapist may be especially important to consider in certain cases. For example, women rape victims may feel much more comfortable talking to women psychotherapists than men psychotherapists.

Feminist therapy.   For many years, therapy was a male-dominated enterprise. The special problems facing women were poorly addressed and perhaps, even more, poorly understood by male therapists. New treatment models that dealt with the disorders prevalent among women were necessary (Hare-Mustin, 1983). What was needed, many felt, was a *feminist therapy*—an approach that would recognize the manner in which women have been oppressed by society over the ages (Ballou & Gabalac, 1985; Rosewater & Walker, 1985).

Feminist therapy grew out of the women's movement and has been quite visible since the early 1970s. It developed because of the failure of the psychiatric and psychological establishment to see the oppression of women as a prime factor in their development of personal distress. The feminist approach acknowledges that many of the personal problems of women arise out of the social position they have traditionally been forced to adopt. It is a method in which clinical psychologists view the relationship between therapist and patient in terms of equality rather than power versus subordination. Feminists, in short, do not take kindly to the "power of expertise." This form of therapy also requires a frank admission of the values of both therapist and client and the development of specific contracts as regards the therapy process itself.

Feminist therapists tend to be especially attuned to specific emotional problems experienced by women: anger and its expression, learned helplessness and depression, autonomy and dependency, and sexuality. Also important are concrete issues such as work, finances, and family choices. Particularly critical are questions of personal freedom and choice and a willingness to consider life alternatives that depart from traditional sex-role expectations (Brody, 1987; Sturdivant, 1980).

Race, ethnicity, and social class.   For years, debate has raged over the effectiveness of therapy for ethnic minority patients—especially when they are treated by white therapists. And it does appear that many of the therapeutic techniques have been designed and developed for white middle- and upper-class patients. Too few procedures seem to have evolved that take into account the particular cultural background and expectations of patients. Banks (1972) has suggested that greater rapport and self-exploration may occur when both therapist and patient are of the same race. The same conclusion has been reached by others regarding social class, background, values, and experience. Still, two decades of research have seemingly failed to show conclusively that ethnic minorities achieve differential treatment outcomes (Sue, 1988; Sue, Zane, & Young, 1994).

It was Schofield (1964) who described the psychotherapist's belief in the ideal patient as the YAVIS syndrome (young, attractive, verbal, intelligent, and successful). However, numerous reviews of existing research arrive at the same conclusion: there appears to be virtually no relationship between social class and outcome (Garfield, 1994). What has not been examined in great detail is whether patients and therapists should be matched according to social class or whether some forms of psychotherapy are more effective for patients from lower socioeconomic levels. When there is a significant difference between the social class or the values of the patient and those of the therapist, some researchers have found that the patient's willingness to remain in therapy may suffer (Pettit, Pettit, & Welkowitz, 1974). Others (Hunt, 1960; Lorion, 1974; Magaro, 1969) have suggested that traditional forms of therapy are inappropriate for patients from lower socioeconomic levels. Still others (Orne & Wender, 1968; Terestman, Miller, & Weber, 1974), however, continue to feel that special efforts to build a therapeutic relationship can overcome the difficulties encountered when there are therapist-patient differences in background. Heitler (1976) has reviewed not only the difficulties encountered in offering traditional therapy to unsophisticated patients but also the methods devised to prepare such patients for so-called expressive psychotherapy. As an example of the latter, Goldstein (1973) has described a "psychotherapy for the poor." In it, he adapts the language and the methods of psychotherapy to these patients while making heavy use of such techniques as modeling, role playing, and related behavioral procedures.

Few would disagree, however, that cultural sensitivity on the part of the therapist is very important. The field needs to develop culturally sensitive mental health services (Rogler, Malgady, Constantino, & Blumenthal, 1987; Sue et al., 1994). Clinicians also need to cultivate a kind of cognitive empathy, or what Scott and Borodovsky (1990) have referred to as "cultural role taking," in their work with ethnic minorities. In the final analysis, it is imperative that clinical psychology develop culturally sensitive therapists who can work effectively with culturally diverse populations (Lopez et al., 1989).

The patient's stimulus value. In the best of all worlds, it would not make any difference whether or not the patient was an engaging person who elicited positive responses from others. A therapist should be able to work with elegant effectiveness regardless of any given patient's positive or negative stimulus value. As we saw earlier, however, therapists are far from perfect creatures; they are indeed affected by the personal qualities of other persons. Fortunately, the understanding and self-control of therapists in their professional relations with patients exceed the understanding and self-control of many laypersons in their social and interpersonal relationships. Nevertheless, there is some evidence to suggest that patients who receive higher global ratings of attractiveness (for example, Nash et al., 1965) or to whom the therapist can relate better (for example, Isaacs & Haggard, 1966) are associated with better outcomes in therapy (Garfield, 1994). Also, in at least one study, therapists were less inclined to treat hypothetical patients whom they did not like as compared to those whom they did like (Lehman & Salovey, 1990).

The therapist

It will hardly come as a shock to learn that certain therapist characteristics may affect the process of therapy. Merely possessing a specific theoretical or therapeutic orientation does not override the role of personality, warmth, or sensitivity. Freud very early recognized the potential effects of the psychoanalyst's personality on the process of psychoanalysis. To "prevent" such personal factors from affecting the process, he recommended that analysts undergo periodic analyses to learn to recognize and control the influence of their own personality traits. In a sense, Rogers turned to the other side of the same coin and made therapist qualities such as acceptance and warmth the cornerstones of therapy. Although Freud may have emphasized the negative and Rogers the positive, they both set the stage for an understanding of the role of therapist variables in the process of therapy. Unfortunately, although nearly everyone agrees that therapist variables are important, there is much less agreement on specifics. How therapist characteristics contribute to therapy outcome has become an important area of research (Beutler, Machado, & Neufeldt, 1994).

Sex, age, and ethnicity. In a recent comprehensive review of therapist features that may influence psychotherapy outcome, Beutler et al. (1994) note that the available research evidence suggests that therapist age is not related to outcome, that female versus male therapists do not appear to produce significantly better therapeutic effects, and that patient-therapist similarity with regard to ethnicity does not necessarily result in better outcome. Beutler et al. acknowledge that these conclusions may run counter to prevailing sociopolitical opinions, but, at the same time, they assert that existing research in this area suffers from a number of methodological problems. These therapist variables may interact with client characteristics, setting for treatment, and modality of treatment. Again, the solution seems to be for therapists to become more sensitized to age, gender, and racial identity issues as they relate to themselves as well as to the patient.

Personality. In discussing therapist variables, Strupp and Bergin (1969) made two points worth noting. First, even though the evidence shows that the therapist's personality is a potent force, other factors taken as a whole largely determine outcomes in therapy. Second, research in this area has taken a backseat as behavioral therapies have gained in popularity. However, as behavior therapists attend increasingly to factors other than techniques or mechanics, it is likely that they will rediscover the importance of therapist characteristics and begin to integrate those characteristics into their research and practice.

Is there a set of personality traits that the "ideal" therapist should possess? Krasner (1963), with tongue in cheek, observed that the research literature would depict the ideal therapist as:

> mature, well-adjusted, sympathetic, tolerant, patient, kindly, tactful, nonjudgmental, accepting, permissive, non-critical, warm, likable, interested in human beings, respectful, cherishing and working for a democratic kind of interpersonal relationship with all people, free of racial and religious bigotry, having a worthwhile goal in life, friendly, encouraging, optimistic, strong, intelligent, wise, curious, creative, artistic, scientifically oriented, competent, trustworthy, a model for the patient to follow, resourceful, emotionally sensitive, self-aware, insightful of his own problems, spontaneous, having a sense of humor, feeling personally secure, mature about sex, growing and maturing with life's experiences, having a high frustration tolerance, self-confident, relaxed, objective, self-analytic, aware of his own prejudices, non-obsequious, humble, skeptical but not pessimistic or self-deprecatory . . . dependable, consistent, open, honest, frank, technically sophisticated, professionally dedicated, and charming. (pp. 16–17)

Certainly no human being, let alone a therapist, could possibly possess all of these traits—even allowing for overlap in terms. Therefore, as Goldstein, Heller, and Sechrest (1966) point out, it is doubtful whether the concept of the ideal therapist is very useful. Any study that is confined to a single trait or a small group of traits seems to make a great deal of sense; taking all the traits together makes the message much less coherent.

Beutler et al. (1994) note that the influence of therapist personality traits on outcome has not received adequate research attention. Of those traits that have been studied, the greatest amount of attention has been focused on dominance and dogmatism, locus of perceived control, and cognitive processing style. General conclusions are difficult to draw, however, because each of these variables appears to affect outcome differentially depending on client traits and type of therapy (Beutler et al., 1994). For example, Hall and Malony (1983) argued that high levels of dominance in a therapist resulted in better outcome in cases where therapist and client were culturally similar; low-dominance therapists were more effective with culturally dissimilar clients.

Empathy, warmth, and genuineness.   Swenson (1971) has suggested that a major factor that differentiates the successful therapists from the unsuccessful is their interest in people and their commitment to the patient. In a related vein, Brunink and Schroeder (1979) found that expert therapists of several different theoretical persuasions were similar in their communication of empathy.

The attention to empathy and related notions of warmth and genuineness grew out of Roger's system of client-centered therapy (1951). He described these variables as *necessary and sufficient* conditions for therapeutic change (Rogers, 1957). Some research evidence seems to point to a relationship between these three qualities and successful outcomes in therapy (Truax & Carkhuff, 1967; Truax & Mitchell, 1971). In the case of empathy, some have found that less effective therapists tend to score lower on empathy relative to their effective peers (Lafferty, Beutler, & Crago, 1989). And in recent years, these three qualities have been regarded more as trainable and learnable skills. However, in a careful review of research on therapeutic outcomes as they relate to therapist interpersonal skills of empathy, regard, and genuineness, Lambert, Dejulio, and Stein (1978) could find only modest support for the Rogerian hypothesis. Strupp and Bergin (1969), also in contrast to Rogers, regard empathy, warmth, and genuineness as *necessary but not sufficient* conditions for good therapy outcomes. As Bergin and Suinn (1975) have stated: "It is clearer now that these variables are not as prepotent as once believed; but their presence and influence is ubiquitous, even showing up strongly in behavior therapies" (p. 52).

Several researchers (Beutler et al., 1994; Gurman, 1977) argue that these three features reflect not only qualities of the therapist but also qualities of the therapeutic relationship. Viewed this way, these features can be considered indicators of the quality of the therapeutic alliance. Studies have consistently demonstrated that the nature and strength of the working relationship between therapist and patient is a major contributor to positive outcome (Beutler et al., 1994).

Freedom from personal problems.

Does personal therapy lead to greater effectiveness as a therapist? In a survey of 749 practicing therapists who were APA members, 44% responded regarding their own personal problems. Of the latter, 18% reported that they had never received any form of personal therapy at any time (Guy, Stark, & Poelstra, 1988). But over 44% reported experiencing personal distress in the past three years, and almost 37% said that it decreased the quality of patient care (Guy, Poelstra, & Stark, 1989). Further, out of 562 licensed psychologists, over a third reported high levels of both emotional exhaustion and depersonalization—what is often called burnout (Ackerley, Burnell, Holder, & Kurdek, 1988). Although therapists need not be paragons of adjustment, it is unlikely that a therapist beset with emotional problems can be as effective as one would like. It is important that therapists recognize areas in their own lives that are tender. The tendency to become angry or anxious when certain topics arise or the inability to handle a client's questions without becoming defensive is a signal that something is amiss; in short, self-awareness is an important quality in the therapist (I. B. Weiner, 1975). Therapists must be able to look at their patients with objectivity and not become entangled in their own personal dynamics.

Nor is the therapy room a place for the gratification of the therapist's emotional needs (Bugental, 1964; Singer, 1965). In some instances, therapists may find it necessary to undergo personal therapy in order to resolve emotional problems. Whether undergoing personal therapy makes the therapist more effective has long been argued—unfortunately, the actual research evidence (Beutler et al., 1994) is less than definitive. But this is not surprising, considering the complexity of the therapy process. Nevertheless, it would not seem that engagement in personal treatment for all therapists should be a qualification for conducting therapy.

Sexual exploitation.

In Chapter 3, it was noted in no uncertain terms that sexual intimacies between patient and therapist are to be condemned unequivocally. Unfortunately, there are still too many examples of victimization of women by their male therapists (Bates & Brodsky, 1989; Pope, 1990). Many questions about this kind of unethical conduct, what kinds of behaviors are appropriate on the part of the therapist, what patients should do in response, and with whom they may lodge complaints have been discussed in detail (Committee on Women in Psychology, 1989). But too often, women do not complain to the proper authorities because they lack knowledge about the complaint process (Vinson, 1987). There are, however, concrete suggestions available to help women file complaints (Gottlieb, 1990). Even the act of touching clients or other nonerotic physical contact are sensitive issues that need to be addressed in training programs and by ethics committees. It can hardly be surmised that it is the patient whose needs are being met by such contact (Holub & Lee, 1990).

Experience and professional identification.   Conventional wisdom suggests that the more experienced the psychotherapist, the greater the level of effectiveness with patients. Although this is intuitively appealing, the bulk of research evidence has not supported this position (Beutler et al., 1994; Smith, Glass, & Miller, 1980). Not only does there appear to be a lack of a consistent relationship between therapist experience and positive outcome but several studies suggest that *paraprofessionals* (that is, those not trained specifically to conduct psychotherapy) produce outcomes equivalent to, or sometimes even exceeding, those produced by trained psychotherapists (Berman & Norton, 1985; Durlak, 1981; Hattie, Sharpley, & Rogers, 1984; Weisz, Weiss, Alicke, & Klotz, 1987). Lambert and Bergin (1994) argue that the jury is still out on this issue because the studies that have been conducted to date are flawed. However, the research that is available is somewhat sobering. Like many others, Lambert and Bergin (1994) wonder why more studies supporting the superiority of experience and professional training have not appeared.

Does one profession turn out better therapists than others? Over the years, there have been many running feuds over which profession is best equipped to carry out proper therapy. For a long time, psychiatrists actively sought to prevent clinical psychologists from conducting therapy in the absence of psychiatric supervision. Their main argument was often reducible to one of medical omniscience and was never based on solid research. Clinical psychologists gradually freed themselves from this psychiatric domination. But old animosities and fights over territorial prerogatives fade slowly. Indeed, with the availability of federal funds to pay for health costs and with insurance coverage being broadened to include psychotherapy, economic competition has once again kindled these territorial fights between psychiatry and clinical psychology.

In fact, however, no real evidence supports the argument that one profession boasts superior therapists, be they clinical psychologists, psychiatric social workers, psychiatrists, or psychoanalysts. Some tangential findings may be of interest, however. In a survey of almost 4000 practicing therapists in New York, Chicago, and Los Angeles, the team of Henry, Sims, and Spray (1973) noted that two-thirds of those therapists made referrals to their colleagues on the basis of the latter's function and orientation rather than on profession (psychiatrist, clinical psychologist, and so on).

Samples of both patients and nonpatients rated the competence of psychologists, psychiatrists, nonpsychiatric physicians, and the clergy to treat various

Table 11-3

Common, but unfounded, assumptions regarding the relationship between patient/client and therapist variables and psychotherapy outcome.

Assumption	Evidence
1. Patients who are the least disturbed or distressed benefit from psychotherapy the most.	Results are inconclusive (Garfield, 1994)
2. Older patients have worse outcomes.	No strong support for this assumption (Garfield, 1994; Smith et al., 1980)
3. Only highly motivated patients achieve good outcomes.	Mixed support (Garfield, 1994)
4. Women patients achieve better outcomes.	Biological sex appears unrelated to outcome (Sue et al., 1994)
5. Ethnic minority patients achieve worse outcomes.	No support for this assumption (Sue et al., 1994)
6. Patients of high socioeconomic status achieve better outcomes.	No relationship between social class and outcome (Garfield, 1994)
7. Older therapists produce better outcomes.	No relationship between therapist age and outcome (Beutler et al., 1994)
8. Women therapists produce better outcomes.	Mixed support (Beutler et al., 1994)
9. Therapists matched with patients according to their ethnicity produce better outcomes.	Effect is equivocal (Beutler et al., 1994)
10. Therapists who have undergone their own personal therapy produce better outcomes.	Mixed results (Beutler et al., 1994)
11. More experienced therapists produce better outcomes.	No relationship between therapist experience and outcome (Beutler et al., 1994; Smith et al., 1980)

kinds of patients. Psychologists and psychiatrists were rated significantly better than the other two groups (Schindler, Berren, Hanna, Beigel, & Santiago, 1987). Still, solid empirical evidence for the efficacy of training is hard to come by (Alberts & Edelstein, 1990).

To this point, we have surveyed a variety of patient and therapist variables that are commonly assumed to be related to outcome in psychotherapy. As noted in our discussion, many of these assumptions are unfounded because psychotherapy research findings do not support these beliefs. Table 11-3 lists some common assumptions about psychotherapy outcome that currently have little or no empirical support.

■ Course of Clinical Intervention .

There are, of course, so many forms of intervention along with so many different kinds of problems that it is impossible to describe with precision a sequence of procedures that would apply equally well to every case. Nevertheless, it may be useful to examine the sequence of therapeutic progress as described by Hokanson (1983).

Initial contact

When clients first contact the clinic or enter the clinician's office they often do not know exactly what to expect. Some will be anxious; others, suspicious (Pipes & Davenport, 1990). Some do not clearly understand the differences between medical treatment and psychotherapy. Others may be embarrassed or feel inadequate because they are seeking help. The first order of business, then, is for someone to explain generally what the clinic is all about and the kind of help that can be given. This is an important step that can have a significant bearing on the client's attitude and willingness to cooperate. Whether this initial contact is made by a therapist, a social worker, a psychological technician, or whomever, it is important that the contact be handled with skill and sensitivity.

Once the client's reasons for coming have been discussed, the next step in the general sequence can be explained. It may be useful at this point to discuss several specific issues. For example, Who are the professional staff and what are their qualifications? What about the matter of fees? Are the contacts confidential, and, if not, exactly who will have access to information? If there are medical complications, how will these problems be integrated with therapy contacts? Does it seem reasonable to proceed with the client or does a referral to another agency or professional seem more appropriate? These and other questions must be dealt with up front.

Assessment

Once it has been mutually agreed upon that the client can likely profit from continued contact with the clinic, one or more appointments can be arranged for an assessment of the client's problems. As we have already seen in preceding chapters, a variety of assessment procedures may be followed, depending upon the exact nature of the client's problem, the orientation of the professional staff, and so on. Often there is an intake interview, which may consist largely of compiling a case history. Other information may be gathered by administering various psychological tests. Sometimes arrangements are made to interview a spouse, family members, or friends. In some instances, too, it may be considered desirable to have the client systematically record self-observations of behavior, thoughts, or feelings in different situations.

For some clients, consultations with other professionals may be desirable. A neurological workup may be necessary, or a medical examination may be scheduled to rule out nonpsychological factors. For some clients whose problems are related to economic difficulties or unemployment, additional consultation with social workers or job counselors may be appropriate.

After all the information has been compiled and analyzed, a preliminary integration is attempted. What is desirable here is not just a simple diagnostic label but a comprehensive construction of the client's problems in light of all the psychological, environmental, and medical data available. In this fashion an initial conceptualization of the client can be established. This, in turn, provides guidelines for the specific therapeutic interventions to be undertaken. Of course, as therapy proceeds, changes in the conceptualization of the client will likely occur. Assessment is an ongoing process that does not cease with the second or third interview — as a result, therapeutic goals and techniques may well change as conceptualization changes.

The goals of treatment

As soon as the assessment data are integrated, the therapist and client can begin to discuss more systematically the nature of the problems and what can be done about them. Some therapists describe this phase as a period of negotiation over the goals of treatment. Still others suggest that client and therapist enter into a "contract" in which the therapist agrees to alleviate a specified set of the client's problems and to do it in the most effective way possible. Naturally, no one can absolutely promise a perfect cure or resolution of all problems. Clients, in turn, will state their desires and intentions. In effect, their contract usually covers such matters as the goals of therapy, length of therapy, frequency of meetings, cost, general format of therapy, and client responsibilities.

Again, it is important to understand that various features of the contract may be modified as time goes on. Therapists must deal with clients in terms of what they are prepared to accept now. An especially anxious or defensive client may be willing to accept only a limited set of goals or procedures. As therapy proceeds, that client may become more open and comfortable and thus better able to accept an expanded set of goals. Then, too, additional information about the client may surface during therapy, with the result that some modifications may be necessary. Some clients will wish to expand their goals for treatment as they gain more confidence and trust in the therapist. Discussion of goals and methods must be handled with discretion, sensitivity, and skill. The therapist must try to take clients only where they are psychologically prepared to go. Moving too fast or setting up grandiose treatment objectives can frighten or alienate certain clients. Therefore, it is usually desirable to proceed with enough subtlety and skill so that clients feel that they are the ones who are establishing or modifying the goals.

Hokanson (1983) employs a classification of the goals of therapy into the following categories: *crisis management, behavior change, corrective emotional experience,* and *insight and change.* Table 11-4 illustrates these goals. In the most general sense, however, the goal of psychotherapy is to improve the patient's level of psychosocial adjustment and to increase the patient's capacity for achieving satisfaction from life.

Implementing treatment

After the initial goals are established, the specific form of treatment is decided upon by the therapist. It may be client-centered, cognitive, behavioral, or psychoanalytic. The treatment may be very circumscribed and deal only with a

Table 11-4

The nature of goals and therapy according to Hokanson.

Therapeutic Goal	Examples of Problems	Treatment Procedures
Crisis management	Incipient psychotic episode; poorly planned, impulsive actions; explosive acting-out behavior	Supportive therapy; emergency consultation in psychiatric hospital; crisis work in community
Behavior change	Habits and behaviors of long standing that create health problems for patient	Behavior therapy; self-regulation techniques
Corrective emotional experience	Broadly based maladaptive "way of life" stemming from persistent negative interpersonal experiences	Relationship therapy
Insight and change	Symptoms, distress, and so on for which client can find no suitable explanation	Psychoanalytic therapy; client centered therapy; existential analysis; gestalt therapies; and so on.

specific phobia, or it may involve a wider approach to the client's personality style. All of this must be carefully described to the client in terms of how the treatment relates to the client's problems, the length of time involved, and perhaps even the difficulties and trying times that may be ahead. Exactly what is expected of the client should be detailed as well: free association, "homework" assignments, self-monitoring, or whatever. Inherent in all of this is the issue of informed consent. Just as participants have a right to know what will happen in research, patients have a right to know what will happen in therapy. Box 11-1 outlines a consent form that addresses the issue of the therapy patient's right to information.

Termination, evaluation, and follow-up

Nothing lasts forever. It is certainly to be hoped that this is true of therapy. As the therapist begins to believe the client is able to handle his or her problems independently, discussions of termination are initiated. Sometimes termination is a gradual process in which meetings are reduced, for example, from once a week to once a month, and so on. As termination approaches, it is important that it be discussed in detail and the client's feelings and attitudes thoroughly aired and dealt with. Clients do sometimes terminate suddenly and, in some cases, before the therapist feels it is appropriate. Whenever possible, however, it is important to find the time to discuss at least briefly the client's feelings about leaving the support of therapy and the possibility of returning later for additional sessions if necessary. In other instances, the termination is forced because the therapist must leave the clinic, which can precipitate numerous client reactions (Penn, 1990).

Box 11-1
Information patients have a right to know

Handelsman and Galvin (1988) have prepared a consent form for prospective patients that sets forth the questions they are entitled to ask their therapists. Some research has shown that forms such as this can enhance patients' first impressions of their therapists (Handelsman, 1990).

When you come for therapy, you are buying a service. Therefore, you need information to make a good decision. Below are some questions you might want to ask. We've talked about some of them. You are entitled to ask me any of these questions, if you want to know. If you don't understand my answers, ask me again.

I. Therapy
    A. How does your kind of therapy work?
    B. What are the possible risks involved? (like divorce, depression)
    C. What percentage of clients improve? In what ways?
    D. What percentage of clients get worse?
    E. What percentage of clients improve or get worse without this therapy?
    F. About how long will it take?
    G. What should I do if I feel therapy isn't working?
    H. Will I have to take any tests? What kind?

II. Alternatives
    A. What other types of therapy or help are there? (like support groups)
    B. How often do they work?
    C. What are the risks of these other approaches?

III. Appointments
    A. How are appointments scheduled?
    B. How long are sessions? Do I have to pay more for longer ones?
    C. How can I reach you in an emergency?
    D. If you are not available, who is there I can talk to?
    E. What happens if the weather is bad, or I'm sick?

IV. Confidentiality
    A. What kind of records do you keep? Who has access to them? (insurance companies, supervisors)
    B. Under what conditions are you allowed to tell others about the things we discuss? (suicidal or homicidal threats, child abuse, court cases, insurance companies, supervisors)
    C. Do other members of my family, or of the group, have access to information?

V. Money
    A. What is your fee?

    B. How do I need to pay? At the session, monthly, etc.?

    C. Do I need to pay for missed sessions?

    D. Do I need to pay for telephone calls or letters?

    E. What are your policies about raising fees? (for example, How many times have you raised them in the past two years?)

    F. If I lose my source of income, can my fee be lowered?

    G. If I do not pay my fee, will you take me to small claims court? Do you use a collection agency or lawyer? Under what circumstances?

VI. General

    A. What is your training and experience? Are you licensed? Supervised? Board certified?

    B. Who do I talk to if I have a complaint about therapy which we can't work out? (e.g., Supervisor, State Board of Psychologist Examiners, APA ethics committee)

The contract [or brochure, or our conversation] dealt with most of these questions. I will be happy to explain them, and to answer other questions you have. This will help make your decision a good one. You can keep this information. Please read it carefully at home. We will also look this over from time to time.

It is important to evaluate with clients the progress they have made. Therapists should also compile data and make notes on progress in order to evaluate the quality of their own efforts or the agency's services and to continue to improve services to their clients. The most reliable data will, of course, come from formally designed research projects (see description below). But clinicians and individual agencies also owe it to themselves and their clients to evaluate the success of their work.

■ Psychotherapy Research

In this last section, we will briefly review the methods of psychotherapy research, the results of several major outcome studies, and the process of change itself. More extensive reviews and books on methods of psychotherapy research are available for the interested reader (for example, Bergin & Garfield, 1994; Kazdin, 1994).

For many years, the prevailing philosophy seemed to be that therapy probably benefits many patients and at the very least is not harmful to the others. So why worry? But over the years some did worry. For example, Cartwright (1956),

Box 11-2
Eysenck's Bombshell

In arriving at his conclusions about the efficacy of psychotherapy, Eysenck considered statistical outcome data from over 7000 patients. These patients included 5 psychoanalytic groups and 14 groups who had undergone "eclectic" therapy. As control data, Eysenck employed the discharge rate among hospitalized patients from New York state hospitals and the amount of improvement that occurred in individuals who were seeking insurance settlements and were receiving medical treatment from general practitioners.

Basically, Eysenck claimed that 72% of the patients who had received only custodial or medical care had improved, whereas only 44% of the patients who had received psychoanalytic treatment and only 66% of the patients who had received eclectic therapy showed improvement. Clearly, a smaller percentage of psychotherapy patients than of control patients showed improvement.

While some have argued for the validity of Eysenck's conclusions (for example, Rachman, 1973; Truax & Carkhuff, 1967), others have vehemently disagreed (for example, Bergin, 1971; deCharms, Levy, & Wertheimer, 1954). The criticisms have centered around Eysenck's failure to match participants in the treatment and control groups. In fact, there really was no control group in the classic sense and there certainly was no matching for education, social class, personality structure, expectations about therapy, and so on. Also, there was little evidence that physicians and psychiatrists were using the same standards for improvement. Finally, there is a question about how Eysenck calculated his improvement rates. For example, Bergin (1971) argued that the improvement rates of custodial and medical care groups was really 30% rather than 72% as calculated by Eysenck.

Bergin (1971), and Hadley and Strupp (1977) called attention to the likelihood of deterioration effects in some psychotherapy patients and the need, therefore, to study outcomes in therapy. While not everyone believes that therapy patients are at greater risk for psychological deterioration than similar individuals not in treatment, there still may be danger for some individuals (Bergin, 1980; Lambert & Bergin, 1994; Mays & Franks, 1985).

The work that really stood the psychotherapy establishment on its ear was Eysenck's report (1952) that declared in no uncertain terms that research evidence failed to support the claim that psychotherapy with neurotics was more effective than no therapy at all (see Box 11-2). Investigators took this and related work

(Eysenck, 1965, 1966) as a challenge. Consequently, the significance of Eysenck's work lies less in the validity of his conclusions (which many deemed flawed) and more in the attack he made on the field's complacency.

As we mentioned earlier in this chapter, now the evidence is considerably more favorable toward the therapy enterprise. Still, there is an undercurrent of suspicion about the efficacy of therapy (Dawes, 1994). To better understand the nature of therapeutic change, we shall, in the following pages, consider issues of research design and method, the results of outcome studies, and the process of change itself.

Issues in psychotherapy research

It is not enough to collect 25 patients undergoing psychoanalytic therapy, administer before-and-after measures of adjustment, determine that positive changes have occurred after six months, and then conclude that psychoanalytic treatment is effective. Would a comparable group of patients without therapy have shown improvement? Would a similar group undergoing systematic desensitization have improved as much? Was the improvement due to the psychoanalytic procedures employed, or was the crucial factor the mere presence of a warm, interested person who listened? Unfortunately, the design of the study as described above does not permit answering any of these questions, and, consequently, little can be learned from it.

As with many psychological experiments (see Chapter 4), studies that seek to investigate the effectiveness of psychotherapy typically employ an experimental and a control group of patients. The experimental group (or *treatment group*) receives the treatment that is being investigated, whereas the *control group* does not. Control groups can take many forms, including *waiting list control groups* (patients' treatment is delayed until after the study is completed) and *attention only control groups* (patients meet regularly with a clinician, but no active treatment is administered). As much as possible, patients in the treatment and control groups are matched on variables that might be related to outcome (for example, gender, age, diagnostic status, and severity of symptoms prior to study) before they are randomly assigned to groups. Assessments of *patient functioning* (for example, symptoms of psychopathology) are conducted in parallel fashion for both treatment and control participants. At the very least, assessments are obtained at the beginning of the study, at treatment completion, and possibly at some period of time after treatment is completed (that is, follow-up). This allows a comparison of the two groups at treatment completion and follow-up as well as an evaluation of the amount of change, if any, within each group.

This is but a brief presentation of aspects of a study investigating the effectiveness of psychotherapy. Below, we summarize some of the research considerations that help shape the meaning and generality of research findings on therapeutic outcomes.

1. What is the sample? Are the patients voluntary, or were they subtly or overtly coerced into therapy (for example, prisoners versus private practice patients). Were the therapists experienced, or were they neophytes? Were they psychoanalysts, or were they behaviorists? Were the patients real ones, or were they

recruited by a newspaper ad requesting paid volunteers for an analog study on the treatment of snake phobias? Undoubtedly, the answer to each of these questions (and others like them) will determine how researchers can interpret their results. There are, then, no absolute findings — only findings relative to the sample and to the conditions of the given study.

2. What relevant patient variables were controlled? Unfortunately, it is not possible to provide a control group that is exactly the same as the treatment group. This being the case, how close did the study come to controlling relevant factors? If the waiting list or attention only control group was not identical with the patient group, in what ways did it differ? Were the presenting complaints of the patient group all basically alike, or was there diversity? Was the control group similar to the treatment group with respect to demographic factors, personality, knowledge about therapy, expectations for help, and so on?

3. What were the *outcome measures?* Were they identical for *every* patient and control, or were they tailored to meet the idiosyncratic situation (goals, hopes, and expectations) of each patient? Was a single outcome measure used, or were multiple measures employed? Were the measures nonreactive or unobtrusive, or were they measures which, by their very character, might reflect things other than those they were supposed to be measuring?

4. What was the general nature of the study? There are a variety of ways to evaluate the effects of therapy. So far we have concentrated on experimental studies. But there are other methods as well, including case studies, clinical surveys, correlational studies, and analog studies. Each type has characteristic strengths and weaknesses. For example, a case study can offer a richness of detail and a fountain of hypotheses that may be far more valuable than an experimental study or an analog study. But then a case study has a sample of one, and how far can the researcher generalize from a single patient? Analog studies offer great potential for the control of relevant variables, the avoidance of ethical problems with no-treatment groups, and the collection of a satisfactory number of participants. But then how close to reality is an analog study? As we have had occasion to remark before, each method offers unique advantages and characteristic limitations. How researchers choose to proceed must be determined by what they seek to learn and by what they can tolerate in the way of limitations. Perhaps the best hope is that numerous good investigators will decide to follow diverse research paths.

Comparative studies

Therapy research has become increasingly sophisticated since Eysenck's critique. Evidence of that increased sophistication lies in the fact that more and more studies of outcomes are not just focusing on the outcome itself but also often contrast two or more techniques in terms of efficacy. However, several have questioned whether some designs are powerful enough (for example, have enough study participants) to detect differences between alternative treatments (Kazdin & Bass, 1989).

The Temple University study.   A major comparative study was conducted by Sloane, Staples, Cristol, Yorkston, and Whipple (1975a, 1975b). Over 90 outpatient neurotics were assigned to one of three groups: (1) behavior ther-

apy; (2) short-term psychoanalytically oriented therapy; or (3) a minimal-treatment waiting list. The groups were matched in terms of sex and the severity of symptoms—otherwise, assignment was random. Treatment was carried out by three behavior therapists and three analysts, all of whom were highly trained and experienced. There were before and after measurements that included psychological tests, a target symptoms technique (a measure oriented toward individualized treatment criteria), a standard interview, informants' reports (people who had known the patients for an average of 12 years), and ratings by the therapist, the patient, and an independent rater. The reader will note that these procedures correspond closely to several of the recommendations made earlier in the methodology section of this chapter.

All three groups had improved at a four-month posttesting point. However, the psychoanalytic (PT) and behavior therapy (BT) groups improved more than did the waiting list (W) group. The independent rater could find no differences with respect to improvement in target symptoms between the BT and PT groups. General estimates, such as improvement in work or social situations, also failed to discriminate between the PT and BT groups. The rater's global outcome assessment indicated that 80% of both the BT group and the PT group improved, whereas only 48% of the W group was better off. For general adjustment, 93% of the BT group and 77% of both the PT group and the W group showed improvement. Although the comparative change between the BT group and the PT group varied, depending on the specific criterion, in general there was a slight trend in favor of the BT group. There was no evidence of deterioration effects, and all three groups maintained their improvement after one year. It should be noted, however, that there was a trend for the improvement to continue and for patients in the W group to approach or equal the BT and PT groups. This could suggest that what therapy does is accelerate change (rather than produce more of it) as compared to no treatment. Greater versatility may characterize behavior therapy since psychoanalysts produced better outcomes with less disturbed patients, whereas for behavior therapists the level of patient disturbance made no difference. Perhaps this has something to do with the greater flexibility and eclecticism of the techniques employed by behavior therapists.

Meta-analyses.   In 1977, Smith and Glass published a review of nearly 400 psychotherapy outcome studies, in which they concluded that the evidence of the effectiveness of psychotherapy is convincing. What is unique about their review is their use of a method called *meta-analysis.* Using this method, they analyzed all therapy studies that dealt with at least one therapy group and one control group or with two therapy groups. The effects of therapy were averaged across all these studies. In their analysis, the size of the therapy effect (*effect size*) equals the mean difference between treated and control participants' scores on relevant outcome measures divided by the standard deviation of the control group.

Earlier, we mentioned the meta-analysis of Smith, Glass, and Miller (1980). Their survey included 475 studies involving 25,000 patients treated by some 78 therapies for an average of 16 sessions. Outcome comparisons showed effect sizes that averaged .85 standard deviations. As previously mentioned, this means that "the average person who receives therapy is better off at the end of it than

Table 11-5

Average effect size ($\overline{ES}$) and percentile equivalent for select forms of psychological intervention.

Type of Therapy	$\overline{ES}$	Percentile Equivalent
Psychodynamic	0.69	75%
Client-centered	0.62	73%
Gestalt	0.64	74%
Rational-emotive therapy (RET)	0.68	75%
Non-RET cognitive therapies	2.38	99%
Systematic desensitization	1.05	85%
Behavior modification	0.73	77%
Cognitive-behavioral therapy	1.13	87%
Undifferentiated counseling	0.28	61%
All forms of psychological intervention	0.85	80%

NOTE: *Percentile equivalent* indicates the percentage of those not receiving treatment whose outcome is exceeded by those receiving the treatment in question.

SOURCE: Adapted from *The Benefits of Psychotherapy,* by M. L. Smith, G. V. Glass, and T. I. Miller. Copyright © 1980 by Johns Hopkins University Press. Reprinted by permission.

80% of the persons who do not" (Smith et al., 1980, p. 87). Using a somewhat stricter definition of therapy and removing placebo therapy and undifferentiated counseling from the data, the average effect size increased from .85 to .93 of a standard deviation unit. This figure would be analogous to reducing an illness or death rate from 66% to 34%! Table 11-5 presents a summary of Smith et al.'s findings for several major forms of psychotherapy.

A number of investigators have supported the general utility of meta-analysis procedures and have thereby corroborated the Smith and Glass conclusions on the efficacy of psychotherapy (for example, Fiske, 1983; Landman & Dawes, 1982; Shapiro & Shapiro, 1982, 1983). There are, however, difficulties with meta-analytic studies (Parloff, London, & Wolfe, 1986). Major clinical conditions, such as depression and alcoholism, are underrepresented in these studies, while others (for example, phobias) are overrepresented. Therapists tend to be novice clinicians or psychiatric residents, and therapies are too often short-term behavioral interventions. As a result, some are skeptical of meta-analysis methods. For example, Wilson and Rachman (1983) are concerned about Smith and Glass's tendency to lump together for analysis studies that vary significantly in their quality and methodological sophistication.

On balance, it would appear that meta-analysis has served to strengthen the case for the effectiveness of psychotherapy. The danger is that some may decide that meta-analysis has solved all the problems in this area. In actuality, the real effort is yet to come. Anyone who thinks that statistical analysis can ever really substitute for carefully designed research is in for a rude shock. As Wilson and

Rachman (1983) put it, "A failure to recognize the problems with meta-analysis threatens to perpetuate the impression that statistical techniques can make acceptable poor quality data that distort therapeutic process and outcome" (p. 54).

Recent trends.   Asking whether therapy is effective is no longer a very good strategy. The question is too broad. The real question must consider specific therapies applied to specific patients in specific ways.

Recently, many studies have begun to focus on the effectiveness of treatments with specific psychiatric problems. For example, Robinson, Berman, and Neimeyer (1990) centered their study on depressives. Kazdin (1987) focused on antisocial children. And Brom, Kleber, and Defares (1989) looked at treatments for posttraumatic stress disorders. Formerly, the concern was the overall efficacy of therapy in general. Now the concern is focused on the efficacy of specific forms of therapy with particular populations (for example, Jay, Elliott, Katz, & Siegel, 1987; Scogin, Bynum, Stephens, & Calhoon, 1990) and on the study of groups with specific Axis I diagnoses (see Chapter 5) and their responsiveness to specific therapies. Some, however, have questioned whether this is the correct focus or whether studies instead should concentrate more on Axis II (personality disorder) diagnoses (Goldfried, Greenberg, & Marmar, 1990).

Another trend is research to evaluate the effects of psychotherapy versus medication. Given the increasing tendency of many psychiatrists to prescribe drugs, the unwillingness of the health care bureaucracy to pay for "interminable" therapy, and the growing interest of some clinical psychologists in prescribing drugs (see Chapter 1), such research is gaining in importance. In any event, it is important to know how the effectiveness of drugs and psychotherapy compare and how the two may interact (see Klosko, Barlow, Tassinari, & Cerny, 1990).

Finally, there is a movement among more academically oriented clinical psychologists to identify *empirically validated treatments* (EVTs)—those that have been shown to be effective in controlled research studies (Task Force on Promotion and Dissemination of Psychological Procedures, 1995). Utilizing standard criteria, this task force developed lists of what they termed as *well-established treatments* and *probably efficacious treatments.* In all likelihood, these lists will probably influence methods of future training in clinical psychology as well as issues of insurance coverage for certain forms of psychological intervention. Table 11-6 presents a list of well-established EVTs for a variety of conditions (Chambless et al., 1996). We will discuss several of these forms of psychological intervention in subsequent chapters.

Process research.   Many of the patient and therapist variables that may affect outcome were discussed earlier, and we focused on the outcomes of therapeutic intervention. Other investigators, however, are more likely to address the specific events that occur during therapy in the course of the interaction between therapist and patient. This is called *process research.* The Rogerians were pioneers in this area and commonly conducted studies relating, for example, the amount of therapist talk in a given session to client spontaneity or the effects of therapist clarifications and restatements on the client's taking responsibility for the progress in a given session.

Table 11-6
List of "well-established" empirically validated treatments (EVTs).

Anxiety and Stress Problems
Cognitive-behavior therapy for panic disorder (with and without agoraphobia)
Cognitive-behavior therapy for generalized anxiety disorder
Group cognitive-behavior therapy for social phobia
Exposure treatment for agoraphobia
Exposure treatment for social phobia
Exposure and response prevention for obsessive-compulsive disorder
Stress inoculation training for coping with stressors
Systematic desensitization for simple or specific phobia

Depression
Cognitive therapy for depression
Interpersonal therapy for depression

Health Problems
Behavior therapy for headache
Cognitive-behavior therapy for irritable bowel syndrome
Cognitive-behavior therapy for chronic pain
Cognitive-behavior therapy for bulimia
Interpersonal therapy for bulimia

Childhood Problems
Behavior modification for enuresis
Parent training programs for children with oppositional behavior

Marital Problems
Behavioral marital therapy

Sexual Dysfunction
Behavior therapy for female organismic dysfunction and male erectile disorder

Other Problems
Family education programs for schizophrenia
Behavior modification for developmentally disabled individuals
Token economy programs

SOURCE: Adapted from "An Update on Empirically Validated Therapies," by D. L. Chambless et al., 1996, *The Clinical Psychologist, 49,* 5–18. Copyright © 1996 by the American Psychological Association. Reprinted by permission.

For a long time, therapy investigators were split into two camps (Beutler, 1990): those who did process research and those who did outcome research. The latter group often felt that process research failed to show how processes internal to therapy were correlated with outcome and therefore deemed it unworthy of serious consideration. Indeed, it sometimes seemed as if the process was misleading in predicting outcomes. But others felt there ought to be relationships between outcome and the processes that occur during therapy (Strupp, 1971). An example of how to do process research is to film or tape actual therapy sessions. This kind of research has increasingly begun to show that there are substantive relationships between what happened during therapy and ultimate outcome (Garfield,

1990; Marmar, 1990). As a specific example, Windholz and Silberschatz (1988) found that by examining audiotapes they could show that active involvement in the therapy process was a significant predictor of therapy outcomes for outpatients ranging in age from 20 to 85.

A simple example of process research is provided by a study that investigated the effects of distance on anxiety and communication in an initial psychiatric interview (Lassen, 1973). Interviews between the patient and the therapist were conducted at distances of 3 feet, 6 feet, and 9 feet. Several results emerged: (1) the speech disturbance ratio (a measure of anxiety) increased with increasing distance; (2) patients reported that they were not as well understood when the distances were larger; (3) patients talked more about their anxieties and fears and reported themselves as having been more open at 6 feet. Such a study certainly does not turn the therapy field around, but carefully building many such studies one upon the other can give greater understanding of what affects what in the course of therapy.

Another example of process research is the work on communication and speech interactions (Matarazzo & Wiens, 1972). This kind of research has investigated formal properties of utterances, including their duration and frequency, as well as interruptions, the proportions of patient-therapist talk, and so on. Other research combines process and outcome features. For example, Staples, Sloane, Whipple, Cristol, and Yorkston (1976) found that patients showing greater total speech time and longer speech durations in therapy evidenced more improvement.

More recently, Hill (1990) has reviewed a variety of studies of process variables. Some of these are therapist variables such as verbal responses, facilitative behavior (for example, empathy), or items such as the tendency to give advice, provide information, or offer interpretations. Client process variables include degree of involvement, nature of client statements, presence of emotions during therapy, or the identification of "good" moments in therapy that seem to portend improvement.

■ Some General Conclusions

As more and more studies are conducted, a general affirmation of the effectiveness of psychotherapy seems to be emerging. On the other hand, there is little evidence to suggest that one specific form of therapy is in any sense uniquely effective for all problems. Indeed, Frank (1979) has suggested several overall conclusions about the state of the art, which may be summarized as follows:

1. Nearly all forms of psychotherapy are somewhat more effective than unplanned or informal help.
2. One form of therapy has typically not been shown to be more effective than another.
3. Clients who show initial improvement tend to maintain it.
4. Characteristics of the client, the therapist, and their interaction may be more important than therapeutic technique.

This last point is important since it suggests that, given the equal effectiveness of various forms of therapy, the field should turn its attention to those elements that are common to all forms of therapy. Not all agree with this conclusion, however. Telch (1981), for one, feels that the more potent the therapeutic technique being used, the less important are therapist or client characteristics. As an example of his point, Telch states that evidence strongly suggests that systematic desensitization is highly effective with phobic patients. Yet for those phobics who have trouble using mental imagery, desensitization may prove ineffective, and modeling could be the technique of choice. Lazarus (1980) also argues that specific therapies are indicated for specific problems. At the same time, however, he seems to suggest that various nonspecific factors play an important role in improvement. For example, regardless of whether the therapist is employing desensitization, modeling, or the quest for insight, the result may be an increased sense of self-efficacy on the part of the patient that, in turn, facilitates change.

Perhaps the safest course is to pursue a two-front assault. Careful research should be designed to help predict which therapy will best work for a given problem. At the same time, equal effort should be given to the investigation of factors common to all therapies and the manner in which they operate. For example, some have suggested that these common factors include development of a therapeutic alliance, opportunity for catharsis, acquisition and practice of new behaviors, and clients' positive expectancies (Grencavage & Norcross, 1990). In any case, research in this area could help in the selection and training of therapists well grounded in these nonspecific factors (Strupp, 1982). It would also suggest the need for greater attention to matching patients and therapists in terms of relevant characteristics. However, Brodsky (1982) suggests that, in the final analysis, therapist competence may be more critical than the simple matching of patients and therapists along lines of race, class, or sex.

Therapy is an intermittent process that occurs, say, once per week. This is really only a small part of a patient's ongoing life. Other concurrent experiences may be as important or even more important in determining whether or not improvement occurs. Or what happens in therapy may interact with other experiences in complex ways. Others may begin to react differently to the patient, and these changed reactions may reinforce or counteract changes induced by therapy. Changes in the patient may threaten family members who then quietly conspire to sabotage treatment. The whole process is so complex and interactive that it is difficult for research to show what factors in therapy are related to patient change or lack of it (Frank, 1982).

Possibly the greatest limitation of all is suggested by Barlow's (1981) charge that many clinical psychologists simply do not pay attention to outcome research. They continue doing what they have always done without full realization of the difficulties in making valid inferences from their experiences with single cases (Kazdin, 1981). Perhaps Chambless et al. (1996) said it best:

> Psychology is a science. Seeking to help those in need, clinical psychology draws its strength and uniqueness from the ethic of scientific validation. Whatever interventions that mysticism, authority, commercialism, politics, custom, convenience, or carelessness might dictate, clinical psychologists focus on what works. They bear a fundamental ethical responsibility to use where possible interventions that work and to subject any intervention they use to scientific scrutiny. (p. 10)

Until clinical psychologists know more about the specifics of the effectiveness of various forms of therapy and routinely implement this knowledge, policymakers and consumers alike will be uneasy (Linden & Wen, 1990).

■ Focus Questions

1. What is psychological treatment or intervention?
2. What patient or therapist variables have been shown to be related to psychotherapy outcome?
3. What are the typical phases or steps involved in clinical intervention? Describe each phase.
4. What are the major issues to consider when designing a psychotherapy research study?
5. What conclusions can be drawn from the major comparative studies of different forms of psychotherapy?

■ Key Terms

attention only control groups
behavior change
catharsis
common factors
control group
corrective emotional experience
crisis management
depth of a problem
effect size
empirically validated treatments (EVTs)
expert role
feminist therapy
gender bias

insight
interpretation
mastery
meta-analysis
nonspecific factors
outcome measures
paraprofessionals
patient functioning
process research
psychological intervention
therapeutic alliance
treatment group
waiting list control groups

12

Psychotherapy: The Psychodynamic Perspective

The psychodynamic approach to therapy utilizes unconscious motives and conflicts in the search for the roots of behavior. It likewise depends heavily on the analysis of past experience. The epitome of this perspective resides in the psychoanalytic therapy of Sigmund Freud (see Box 12-1).

Without question, psychoanalytic theory represents the single most sweeping contribution to the field of personality. What began as a halting flow of controversial ideas based on a few neurotic Viennese patients was transformed into a torrent that forever changed the face of personality theory and clinical practice. Hardly an area of modern life remains untouched by Freudian thought. It influences art, literature, and motion pictures as well as our textbooks. Such words and phrases as *ego, unconscious, death wish,* and *Freudian slip* have become a part of our everyday language.

What is true in our culture at large is no less true for therapeutic interventions. While psychoanalytic therapy is sometimes regarded as an anachronism, it is still widely practiced by clinical psychologists (Norcross, Karg-Bray, & Prochaska, 1995). In fact, almost every form of therapy that relies on verbal transactions between therapist and patient owes a large debt to psychoanalysis—both as a theory and as a therapy. Whether it be existential therapy, cognitive-behavioral therapy, or family therapy, psychoanalytic influences are clearly evident even though they are not always formally acknowledged.

We now turn to a discussion of the background of the theory that underlies psychodynamic approaches to treatment.

■ Psychoanalysis: The Beginnings

In 1885 Freud was awarded a grant to study in Paris with the famous Jean Charcot. Charcot was noted for his work on hysteria, which, at the time, was viewed as a "female" disorder most often marked by paralysis, blindness, and deafness. Such symptoms suggested a neurological basis, yet no organic cause for them could be found. Earlier, Charcot had discovered that some hysterical patients would, while under hypnosis, relinquish their symptoms and sometimes recall the traumatic experiences that had caused them. It is likely that such recall under hypnosis helped stimulate Freud's thinking about the nature of the unconscious. In any event, Freud was greatly impressed by Charcot's work and, upon his return to Vienna, explained it to his physician friends. Many were quite skeptical about the benefits of hypnosis, but Freud nevertheless began to use it in his neurological practice.

Anna O.

A few years earlier, Freud had been fascinated by Josef Breuer's work with a young "hysterical" patient called Anna O. She presented many classic hysterical symptoms, apparently precipitated by the death of her father. Breuer had been treating her using hypnosis, and during one trance she told him about the first appearance of one of her symptoms. What was extraordinary, however, was that when she came out of the trance, the symptom had disappeared! Breuer quickly realized that he had stumbled onto something very important, so he repeated the same procedures over a period of time. He was rather successful until a complication arose. Anna began to develop a strong emotional attachment to Breuer. The intensity of this reaction, coupled with a remarkable session in which Anna began showing hysterical labor pains, convinced Breuer that he should abandon the case. The jealousy of Breuer's wife may also have played a part in his decision.

Freud, of course, was familiar with all these events. They undoubtedly were instrumental in prompting his initial theories about the unconscious, the talking cure, catharsis, transference, and moral anxiety. He treated many of his patients with hypnosis; however, not all patients were very good candidates for hypnotic procedures. Others were easily hypnotized but showed the disconcerting tendency not to remember what had transpired during the trance, which of course destroyed most of the advantages of hypnosis. An example was Elisabeth, a patient Freud saw in 1892. He asked her, while she was fully awake, to concentrate on her ailment and to remember when it began. He asked her to lie on a couch as he pressed his hand against her forehead. Subsequently, Freud found that placing his hand on patients' foreheads and asking them to remember events surrounding the origin of the symptom was just as effective as hypnosis. He soon gave up placing his hand on patients' foreheads and simply asked them to talk about whatever came to their minds. This was the beginning of what came to be known as the method of free association.

The Freudian view: A brief review

A major assumption of Freudian theory, _psychic determinism,_ holds that everything we do has meaning and purpose and is goal-directed. Such a view enables the psychoanalyst to utilize an exceptionally large amount of data in searching for the roots of the patient's behavior and problems. The mundane behavior, the bizarre behavior, the dream, and the slip of the tongue all have significance and meaning.

In order to account for many aspects of human behavior, Freud also assumed the existence of *unconscious motivation*. His use of this assumption was more extensive than that of any previous theorist, and it allowed him to explain much

■

Box 12-1
A brief biography of Sigmund Freud

Sigmund Freud was born in Austria (in an area now part of Czechoslovakia) on May 6, 1856, but most of his childhood was spent in Vienna. He was the oldest of seven children. After a classical education, he began medical studies at the University of Vienna and received an M.D. degree in 1881. Following a short period in research, he began a private practice, even though such work did not greatly interest him. At least three things helped him make this decision. First, he knew that as a Jew he stood little chance of advancement in an academic research environment rife with anti-Semitic feelings. Second, his research efforts did not seem likely to produce much income. Third, he had fallen in love with Martha Bernays. Just as it does today, marriage required money and Freud had very little. Consequently, he decided to open a practice as a neurologist. His marriage to Martha produced six children, one of whom, Anna, became a famous psychoanalyst herself.

Around this time, Freud began a brief but very productive collaboration with Josef Breuer, a renowned physician in Vienna. Together they sought an explanation for Breuer's discovery of the *talking cure,* a method by which a patient's neurotic problems are alleviated just by talking about them. In 1895 Breuer and Freud published *Studies on Hysteria,* a landmark psychiatric treatise. A bit later, the two men had a falling out for reasons not completely clear. Some suggest the problem was a disagreement over money, whereas others believe it had to do with Breuer's alarm over Freud's growing emphasis on sexual factors as a cause of hysteria.

Freud's most acclaimed work, *The Interpretation of Dreams,* appeared in 1900, capping a remarkably productive decade of work. As the twentieth century dawned, his professional stature was growing and his

Photo-Researchers

work had begun to attract a dedicated band of followers. Later, however, several of these converts left the orthodox Freudian camp to develop their own psychoanalytic theories. Notable among these were Alfred Adler, Carl Jung, and Otto Rank. Freud became a truly international figure when, in 1909, he was invited to lecture at Clark University in the United States.

Many books and papers followed, but so did Nazi harassment in the 1930s. They burned his books and turned him into a choice anti-Semitic target. Eventually, he was allowed to emigrate to England. His declining years were especially unpleasant ones since he suffered from cancer of the jaw and experienced great pain, undergoing some 32 operations. A heavy cigar smoker, he periodically gave up cigars but never completely. He died in England in September of 1939.

that had previously resisted explanation. The analyst first of all assumes that healthy behavior is behavior for which the person understands the motivation, whereas the important causes of disturbed behavior reside in the unconscious. Therefore, it follows that the goal of therapy is to make the unconscious conscious.

The instincts.   The energy that makes the human machine is provided by two sets of instincts: the *life instincts (Eros)* and the *death instincts (Thanatos).* The life instincts are the basis for all the positive and constructive aspects of behavior and include such bodily urges as sex, hunger, and thirst as well as the creative components of culture, such as art, music, and literature. But all these activities can serve destructive ends as well—when this happens, the death instincts are responsible. In practice, modern analysts pay scant attention to death instincts; however, Freud found them necessary to account for the dark side of behavior (the compulsively self-destructive behavior of the neurotic, the inability to avoid war, and so on). In any event, for Freud the ultimate explanation for all behavior was an instinctual one, even though the instincts he posited are unobservable, cannot be measured, and often seem better able to explain events after they occur than before.

The structure.   Psychoanalysis views personality as composed of three basic structures: the *id,* the *ego,* and the *superego.* The id represents the deep, inaccessible portion of the personality, which is studied through the analysis of dreams and various forms of neurotic behavior. The id has no commerce with the external world—it is the true psychic reality. Within the id reside the instinctual urges, with their desire for immediate gratification. The id is without values, ethics, or logic; its essential purpose is to attain the unhampered gratification of urges whose origins reside in the somatic processes. Its goal, then, is to achieve a state free from all tension or, if that is unattainable, to keep the level as low as possible. The id is said to obey the *pleasure principle,* while utilizing a *primary process* kind of thinking—that is, it tries to discharge tension as quickly as tension reaches it. At first, it does this by expending energy immediately in motor activity (for example, a swelling of the bladder that results in immediate urination). Later, the id replaces this aspect of the primary process by another form: it manufactures a mental image to lessen the tension (for example, hunger results in a mental representation of food). Dreaming is regarded as an excellent example of this form. Of course, the primary process cannot provide real gratification (such as food) and, because of this inability, a second process develops that brings into play the second component of the personality—the ego.

The ego is the executive of the personality. It is an organized, rational system that utilizes perception, learning, memory, and the like in the service of need satisfaction and that arises out of the inadequacies of the id in serving and preserving the organism. It operates according to the *reality principle* in the sense that it defers the gratification of instinctual urges until a suitable object and mode are discovered. To do this, it employs the *secondary process*—a process that involves learning, memory, planning, judgment, and so on. In essence, the role of the ego is to mediate the demands of the id, the superego, and the real world in a manner that will provide satisfaction to the organism and at the same time prevent it from being destroyed.

The third component of the personality is the superego. It develops during childhood from the ego, and it arises specifically out of the resolution of the *Oedipus complex* (the child's sexual attraction to the parent of the opposite sex). It represents the ideals and values of society as they are conveyed to the child through the words and deeds of the parents in the form of rewards and punishments. Behavior that is punished typically becomes incorporated into one's *conscience,* whereas rewarded behavior generally becomes a part of the *ego-ideal.* Thus, within the superego, the conscience eventually serves the purpose of punishing individuals by making them feel guilty or worthless, whereas the ego-ideal's rewards are experienced as pride and a sense of worthiness. In general, the role of the superego is to block unacceptable id impulses, to pressure the ego to serve the ends of morality rather than expediency, and to generate strivings toward perfection.

The psychosexual stages. Like many other theorists, Freud considered childhood to be of paramount importance in shaping the character and personality of the individual. He felt that each person goes through a series of developmental stages, each of which is marked by the involvement of a particular erogenous zone of the body (especially during the first five years). Thus, the *oral stage*—the first stage—lasts about a year and is the period in which the mouth is the chief means of reaching satisfaction. It is followed by the *anal stage,* in which attention becomes centered on defecation and urination; this stage may span the period from 6 months to 3 years of age. Next is the *phallic stage* (from 3 to 7 years of age), during which the sexual organs become the prime source of gratification. Following these so-called pregenital stages, the child enters the *latency stage,* which is characterized by a lack of overt sexual activity and, indeed, by an almost negative orientation toward anything sexual. This stage may extend from about the age of 5 until 12 or so. Following the onset of adolescence, the *genital stage* begins. Ideally, this stage will culminate in a mature expression of sexuality, assuming that the sexual impulses have been handled successfully by the ego.

When the child experiences difficulties at any stage, they may be expressed in symptoms of maladjustment, especially when the troubles are severe. For example, either excessive frustration or overindulgence at any psychosexual stage will lead to problems. The particular stage at which excessive gratification or frustration is encountered will determine the specific nature of the symptoms. Thus, obsessive-compulsive symptoms signify that the individual failed to successfully negotiate the anal stage, whereas excessive dependency needs in an adult suggest the influence of the oral stage. Freud believed that all people manifest a particular character formation, which may not always be particularly neurotic but nonetheless does represent perpetuations of original childish impulses, either as subliminations of these impulses or as reaction formations against them. Examples include an oral character's food fads or puristic speech patterns, an anal character's prudishness or dislike of dirt, and a phallic character's excessive modesty.

Anxiety.   The circumstances that give rise to the formation of the ego, and later to the superego, produce a painful affective experience called *anxiety.* Exaggerated responses of the heart, the lungs, and other internal organs are perceived and experienced as anxiety. There are three general classes of anxiety: *reality anxiety* is based upon a real danger from the outside world; *neurotic anxiety* stems from a fear that one's id impulses will be expressed unchecked and lead to trouble from the environment; and *moral anxiety* arises from the feeling that one will not conform to the standards of the conscience. What identifies and defines these anxieties is the source, rather than the quality, of the anxiety experience. The essential function of anxiety is to serve as a warning signal to the ego that certain steps must be initiated to quell the danger and thus protect the organism.

The ego defenses.   We have already discussed how the ego utilizes the secondary process of memory, judgment, and learning to solve problems and stave off environmental threats. But such measures are less serviceable when threats arise from within the individual. When people fear the wrath of the superego or the unleashed lusts of the id, where do they turn? The answer lies in the ego's utilization of the *ego defenses,* or as they are sometimes called, *defense mechanisms.* Nowhere was the genius of Freud more evident than in his ability to abstract the defense mechanisms from the often disconnected and illogical verbalizations of his patients. These mechanisms are generally regarded as pathological because they divert psychic energy from more constructive activities and at the same time distort reality. All the defense mechanisms operate actively and involuntarily, yet without the person's awareness.

The basic ego defense is *repression.* This can be described as the banishment from consciousness of highly threatening sexual or aggressive material. In some instances, the process operates by preventing the offending impulse from reaching consciousness in the first place. *Fixation* occurs when the frustration and anxiety of the next psychosexual stage are so great that individuals remain at their present level of psychosexual development. *Regression* involves a return to a stage that earlier provided a great deal of gratification; this may occur following extensive frustration. *Reaction formation* is said to occur when an unconscious impulse is consciously expressed by its behavioral opposite. Thus, "I hate you" is expressed as "I love you." *Projection* is revealed when people's unconscious feelings are attributed not to themselves but to another. Thus, the feeling "I hate you" is transformed into "You hate me."

Figure 12-1
Freud's consulting room. *The Bettmann Archive*

From theory to practice

As mentioned earlier, Breuer's experiences with Anna had led to the discovery of the talking cure, which, in turn, became transformed into free association during Freud's work with Elisabeth. *Free association* meant simply that the patient was to say everything and anything that came to mind regardless of how irrelevant, silly, dull, or revolting it might seem. Through his observations of the Anna O. case, Freud also realized that Anna had transferred onto Breuer many of her feelings that really applied to significant males in her life. This notion of *transference* would eventually become a valuable diagnostic tool during therapy by which to understand the nature of the patient's problems — especially the unconscious ones.

With hypnosis, Freud learned that patients could relive traumatic events associated with the onset of the hysterical symptom. In some cases, this reliving served to release formerly bottled-up energy. This became known as *catharsis,* a release of energy that often has important therapeutic benefits. In his work with Elisabeth, Freud also witnessed the phenomenon of *resistance* — a general reluctance to discuss, remember, or think about events that are particularly troubling or threatening. He viewed this as a kind of defense, but later he also analyzed it as repression — the involuntary banishing of a thought or impulse to the unconscious. (The *unconscious,* of course, is the area of the mind inaccessible to conscious thought.)

The role of insight

The ultimate goal of psychoanalytic intervention is the removal of debilitating neurotic problems. Not much new in that. But the unswerving credo of the traditional psychoanalytic therapist is that, ultimately, the only final and effective way of doing this is to help the patient achieve *insight*. What does insight mean? It means total understanding of the unconscious determinants of one's irrational feelings, thoughts, or behaviors that are producing so much personal misery. Once these unconscious reasons are fully confronted and understood, the need for neurotic defenses and symptoms will disappear. All of the specific techniques described later in this chapter have as their ultimate purpose the facilitation of insight.

An analysis culminating in insight is slow, tedious, and often very lengthy — an orthodox analysis is not measured in weeks or months but years. This is so because the patient is not simply informed, for example, that unconscious feelings of hostility and competitiveness toward a long-departed father are causing present outbursts against friends, a boss, or coworkers. At an intellectual level, the patient might readily concede this interpretation. But the unconscious is not likely to be much affected by such sterile information — the patient must actually experience the unconscious hostility. This may happen through the transference process: early experiences associated with the father may be relived as competition with the therapist begins to occur. The analyst begins to seem like that father of years gone by, and all the old reactions start flooding back. As the therapist comes to stand for someone else (the father), old emotions are reexperienced and then reevaluated. From this comes a deeper insight.

The true meaning of this insight is then brought into the patient's consciousness by the *working-through process*. This refers to a careful and repeated examination of how the individual's conflicts and defenses have operated in many different areas of life; little may be accomplished by a simple interpretation that passivity and helplessness are really an unconscious form of aggression. Once the basis for the interpretation is firmly laid, it must be repeated time and time again. The patient must be confronted with the insight as it applies to relations with a spouse, a friend, or a supervisor, and, yes, even as it affects reactions to the therapist. Patients must be helped to work through all corners of their lives with this insight. It is not unlike learning a principle in a physics class: the principle only begins to take on real life and importance when one sees that it applies not just in a laboratory but everywhere — in automobile engines, house construction, baseball, and so on. So it is with insight. It comes alive when it becomes painfully clear in example after example how it has affected the person's life and relationships. It is due in part to this extensive working-through period that traditional psychoanalysis takes so long — three to five therapy sessions per week for three to five years and sometimes much longer.

■ Techniques of Psychodynamic Psychotherapy

Symptoms of neurosis are regarded by the analyst as signs of conflict among the id, the ego, the superego, and the demands of reality. Phobias, undesirable character traits, and excessive reliance on defense mechanisms are all signs of a deeper problem. The symptom, then, indicates an unconscious problem that needs resolution. Obviously, could patients resolve their problems alone they would not need therapy. But the very nature of unconscious problems and defenses makes self-healing exceedingly difficult.

To dissolve defenses and confront the unconscious in a therapeutic relationship is the whole purpose of psychoanalysis. Over the years, many variations in techniques have arisen; however, in nearly all these variations, the basic emphasis is on the dissolution of repression through the reanalysis of previous experience. The fundamental goal remains the freedom from the oppression of the unconscious through insight.

Free association

A cardinal rule in psychoanalysis is that the patient must say anything and everything that comes to mind. This is not as easy as it may appear to be at first glance. It requires the patient to stop censoring or screening thoughts that are ridiculous, aggressive, embarrassing, or sexual. All our lives we learn to exercise conscious control over such thoughts to protect both ourselves and others. According to Freud, however, if the therapist is to release patients from the tyranny of their unconscious and thereby free them from their symptoms and other undesirable behavior, then such an uncensored train of free associations is essential. From this process the patient and the therapist can begin to discover the long-hidden bases of the patient's problems.

Traditionally, the psychoanalyst sits behind the patient, who reclines on a couch to make it easier to relax and free-associate. In this fashion, the analyst is not in the patient's line of vision and will not, therefore, be as likely to hinder the associative stream; it also tends to be less fatiguing for the analyst.

In the free-association process, the psychoanalyst assumes that one association will lead to another. As it continues, the patient gets closer and closer to unconscious thoughts and urges. Any single set of associations may not be terribly clear, but, over many sessions, patterns of associations start to emerge, and the analyst can begin to make sense out of them through their repetitive themes. In one sense, free associations are not really "free" at all—they are outgrowths of unconscious forces that determine the direction of one's associations. Often, but not always, these associations lead to early childhood memories and problems. Such memories of long-forgotten experiences give the analyst clues as to the structure of personality and its development.

Analysis of dreams

A technique related to free association is the *analysis of dreams*. Dreams are thought to reveal the nature of the unconscious because they are regarded as heavily laden with unconscious wishes, albeit in symbolic form. Like free association, dreams often provide important clues to childhood wishes and feelings.

During sleep, customary defenses are relaxed and symbolic material may surface. Of course, censorship by the ego is not totally removed during sleep, or the material from the id would become so threatening that the person would quickly awaken. In a sense, then, dreams are a way for people to have their cake and eat it too—the material of the dream is important enough to provide some gratification to the id but not usually so threatening as to terrorize the ego. However, in some cases this scenario is not applicable, and traumatizing dreams do occur. The *manifest content* of a dream is that which actually happens during the dream. For example, a man dreaming that he is confronted with two large, delicious looking ice cream cones is the manifest content. *Latent content* refers to the dream's symbolic meaning. In the present example, perhaps there is a message about the need for oral gratification or a longing to return to the mother's breast.

In order to get at the latent content, the patient is often encouraged to free-associate to a dream with the hope of gaining insight into its meaning. Normally, the manifest content is an amalgam of displacement, condensation, substitution, symbolization, or lack of logic—it is not easy to cut through all this to find the latent meaning. Free association will help in this search, but the meaning of one dream alone is not always apparent. The real meaning of a dream in the life of an individual may only become apparent from the analysis of a whole series of dreams.

Another problem is that patients often distort the actual content of a dream as they retell it during the analytic session. Thus, not only does the analyst have to delve deeply to find the symbolic meaning, but there is also the added burden of the patient's waking defenses that strive to thwart the goal of understanding. For many analysts, dreams do not provide inevitable, final clues to the patient's dynamics; rather, they are clues that help the analyst formulate hypotheses that can be validated or invalidated with further information. An example of how dreams and free associations go hand in hand is shown in a brief description of Freud's self-analysis (Box 12-2).

Psychopathology of everyday life

Another important method for gaining access to the unconscious is illustrated by Freud's sensitive analysis ([1901]1960) of the "psychopathology of everyday life." In the Freudian view, everything is determined; there are no accidents. The slip of the tongue and the forgotten appointment are not simple mistakes—rather, they represent the conscious expression of an unconscious wish. These little mistakes of everyday life are like dreams in the sense that sexual and aggressive urges receive partial gratification even though they interfere with our lives in minor ways. When the patient makes such mistakes in therapy or recounts during therapy mistakes made outside the therapy room, the therapist is provided additional data by which to assess the patient's problems. In some instances, the meaning of the mistake is not readily apparent, so the patient may be asked to free-associate to the mistake. These associations, coupled with the therapist's interpretation, can help provide the patient with added insight.

Resistance

During the course of psychotherapy, the patient may attempt to ward off efforts to dissolve neurotic methods of resolving problems, a characteristic defense known as resistance. Patients are typically loathe to give up behaviors that have been working for them, even though these behaviors may cause great distress—the distress, in fact, that led them to seek help in the first place. In addition, patients may find painful subjects difficult to contemplate or discuss. For example, a male patient who has always feared his father or has felt he did not measure up

■

Box 12-2
Freud's self-analysis

> To support his notion that people are motivated by sexual wishes that go all the way back to their childhood, Freud drew upon the results of his own self-analysis.
>
> Freud's father died in 1896. This disturbed Freud a great deal even though his father had been old and ill. In fact, Freud became extremely anxious and depressed, so much so that his work was severely hampered. He became so disturbed at his own reactions that he decided to embark upon a detailed self-analysis, drawing upon his dreams, associations, and behavior.
>
> One childhood dream in particular seemed important. This was a dream Freud remembered having when he was seven or eight years old. Thirty years later he interpreted it. In his dream he saw his "beloved mother, with a peculiarly calm, sleeping countenance, carried into the room and laid on the bed by two (or three) persons with birds' beaks" (Freud, 1938, p. 522). His free associations led him to the idea of death and to an expression on his grandfather's face shortly before his death. This was a composite dream, then, combining elements of both his mother and grandfather. From here, his associations took him to the idea of a dying father. To his dismay, Freud then realized that as a child he had unconsciously harbored hostile wishes toward his father. Additional associations (for example, the German slang word for sexual intercourse was derived from the German word for bird) inevitably led him to the conclusion that his childhood sexual urges were directed toward his mother. So it was that the unconscious oedipal strivings he had interpreted so often in his patients were equally true for him.

■

to his father's standards may not wish to discuss or even recall matters related to his father. Although a certain amount of resistance is to be expected from most patients, when the resistance becomes sufficient to retard the progress of therapy, it must be recognized and dealt with by the therapist.

There are numerous forms of resistance. Patients may begin to talk less, to pause longer, or to report that their minds are blank. Lengthy silences are also frequent. Sometimes a patient may repeatedly talk around a point or endlessly repeat the same material. At other times there may be a tendency to omit or censor certain information. Therapy may become an arena to discuss such problems as unemployment or taxes—weighty issues, but hardly the ones that brought the patient to therapy. Some patients may frequently intellectualize about the relative merits of primal screaming versus nude marathons or even the effect of Freud's boyhood on his subsequent development of psychoanalysis. If the patient knows that the therapist has a penchant for dreams, then the therapist may be deluged with dream material. In some instances, the patient's feelings or ideas about the therapist may even begin to dominate the sessions. This can be very flattering until the therapist realizes that this interest is just a way of avoiding the real problems.

Resistance is also evidenced when a patient repeatedly comes late, cancels appointments without good reason, forgets meetings, and so on. The therapist may also begin to notice that a variety of "real" events in the patient's life seem to be conspiring against the sessions. For example, the patient may start to miss sessions because of a succession of physical illnesses or may constantly ask to change appointment times in order to meet one daily crisis or another.

Nearly anything can become a form of resistance. As the patient's defenses are addressed, there is sometimes an intensification of symptoms. But the opposite can also occur, so that an actual "flight into health" occurs—the patient gets better. It is almost as if in the first instance the patient is saying, "Don't make me confront these things, I'm getting worse," and in the second instance the patient is saying, "See, I don't need to deal with these matters, I'm getting better."

Another method of resistance is acting-out. Here the patient attempts to escape the anxiety generated in therapy by indulging in irrational acts or engaging in potentially dangerous behavior. For example, a patient suddenly takes up mountain climbing or begins to use cocaine or heroin. Still other patients flee into intellectualization: experiences or memories become stripped of their emotional content and dissected calmly and rationally. Everything becomes cold and detached. Losing one's job becomes an occasion for an elaborate, intellectual discussion of economic conditions or the shift to high technology. Feelings are ignored, and the experience is handled by a flight into rationality.

In one form or another, resistance goes on throughout the course of therapy. In one sense it is an impediment to the swift resolution of neurotic conflicts. But in another sense it is the central task in therapy—the resistance that goes on in therapy probably mirrors what has happened in real life. If resistance during therapy can be analyzed and the patient made to understand its true function, then such defenses will not be as likely to operate outside the therapist's office. The following is an example of how one therapist met the problem of resistance.

A Case Illustration

The wife of a minister has been seen for several months. In the previous session, a series of interpretations has been made regarding her tendency to see her husband rather than herself as completely responsible for their unsatisfactory sexual adjustment.

Therapist: You don't seem very responsive today.
Patient: I don't have much on my mind.

Therapist: You seem almost impatient.
Patient: I was just thinking what a stupid little office this is. It's so oppressive.
Therapist: That's strange. You never commented on it till now.
Patient: I never thought about it until now.

There is a long silence during which the patient glances at her watch twice. Finally, the therapist breaks the silence.

Therapist: I wonder if all this has anything to do with what we discussed last time.
Patient: I just knew you were going to say that. Well, I don't think so because I can't recall what it was we talked about.
Therapist: Is that right? (Smiling)
Patient: Well . . . as a matter of fact . . . well, I think it is my husband's fault. He can be so aggressive. With other people he seems so patient and understanding, but . . .

The session continues, and further exploration into the patient's sexual attitudes is made.

Transference

A key phenomenon in psychoanalytic therapy is *transference*. To one degree or another, transference is operative in most individual forms of verbal psychotherapy and in the form of both positive and negative feelings. Transference occurs when the patient reacts to the therapist as if the latter represented some important figure out of childhood—in short, conflicts and problems that originated in childhood are reinstated in the therapy room. This provides not only important clues as to the nature of the patient's problems but also an opportunity for the therapist to interpret the transference in an immediate and vital situation. It is important to recognize that many characteristics of the psychoanalytic session (for example, patient seated on a couch facing away from analyst, analyst does not give advice, analyst does not reveal personal information) serve to encourage the establishment of transference.

Positive transference is often responsible for what appears to be rapid improvement at the beginning stages of therapy. Being in a safe, secure relationship with a knowledgeable authority can produce rapid but superficial improvement. Later, as the patient's defenses are challenged, this improvement is likely to fade and marked negative transference is likely to intrude.

Transference can take many forms. It may be reflected in comments about the therapist's clothing or office furnishings. It may take the form of direct comments of admiration, dislike, love, or anger. It may assume the guise of an attack on the efficacy of psychotherapy or of a helpless, dependent posture. The important point to recall, however, is that these reactions do not reflect current realities but have their roots in childhood. It is all too easy to view every reaction of the patient as a manifestation of transference; the truly sensitive therapist is one who can separate reactions that have some support in reality from reactions that are neurotic in character.

Basically, both positive and negative transferences are forms of resistance. Through interpretation the patient is assisted in recognizing the irrational nature and origins of transference feelings. With repeated interpretation and analysis, the patient can begin to gain control over such reactions in the therapy room and can learn to generalize such control to the real world as well.

Interpretation

Interpretation is the cornerstone of nearly every form of dynamic psychotherapy. Although the content may vary significantly (depending upon the therapist's theoretical affiliation), the act of interpreting is perhaps the most common technique among all forms of psychotherapy. From the psychoanalyst's perspective, interpretation is the method by which the unconscious meaning of thoughts and behavior is revealed. In a broader sense, however, interpretation is a process by which the patient can be induced to view thoughts, behavior, feelings, or wishes in a different manner. It is a method calculated to free the patient from the shackles of old ways of viewing things—ways that have led to the patient's current problems in living.

Interpretation is a prime method for bringing about insight. Of course, significant insight or behavioral change rarely comes from a single interpretation; rather, it is a slow, repetitive process in which the essential meaning behind certain behaviors, thoughts, and feelings is repeatedly pointed out to the patient in one context after another. The following excerpt illustrates the interpretive process.

A Case Illustration

This exchange occurred during the 15th session of psychotherapy with the 27-year-old wife of a college professor. In previous sessions, she had described how inadequate their sexual relationship had been. In more recent sessions, she had also begun to discuss how much she and her husband shared the belief that theirs was a frank, open, and communicative relationship. Sometime before the present session, the patient had taken a two-day trip to attend a convention at a neighboring city. On the first day she met a man at the convention and promptly went to bed with him. Afterward she was several days late with her period. This convinced her that she was pregnant. Suspecting that emotional factors might have delayed her period, her therapist suggested that she hold off telling her husband until she was sure. She disregarded this suggestion and proceeded to tell her husband everything. The very next day her period began.

Patient: Well, I told Dick everything. God, was I upset.

Therapist: Then what happened?

Patient: He took it better than I thought he would. He was really understanding. Not so much forgiving, just calm and understanding. And now I'm not even pregnant. Can you beat that? But I think it really solidified our relationship and we can go on from here.

Therapist: Did you expect Dick to be so understanding?

Patient: I'm not sure I knew what to expect. I suppose I thought he would be upset as hell, but what else could I do? I know the episode at the convention was silly. But I just had to find out whether it was still possible to really enjoy sex.

Therapist: Was it?

Patient: Yes, it really was. Now I know it, and in a way I feel great.

Therapist: And now Dick knows it, and in a way he doesn't feel so great. That could well be the reason you were so eager to tell him everything.

In this example, the therapist used his final remarks to encourage understanding on the part of the patient. By calling attention to the possibility that the patient's behavior might have been a way of hurting her husband, the therapist was seeking to get the patient to reexamine her views of herself, her relationship with her husband, and her motives. His interpretation was directed to a central part of the patient's problems. It is important to emphasize that interpretations are not sprinkled about like confetti. Rather, they are limited to important life areas — those that relate directly to the problems that the therapist is trying to resolve.

It is best to offer an interpretation when it is already close to the patient's awareness. In addition, an interpretation should be offered when it will arouse enough anxiety to engage the patient's serious contemplation but not so much anxiety that the patient will reject it. Although therapists have sometimes been known to make interpretations as shots in the dark, it is generally wise to be reasonably sure of the target before firing the salvo. Being wrong, offering an interpretation too soon, or providing an interpretation that is beyond what the patient is ready to accept is likely to be counterproductive. As Colby (1951) puts it: "Like pushing a playground swing at the height of its arc for optimum momentum, the best-timed interpretations are given when the patient, already close to it himself, requires only a nudge to help him see the hitherto unseen" (p. 91).

As a general rule, small dosages are best. Therefore, rather than prepare one grand interpretation that will subsume all the major aspects of the patient's conflicts, it is advisable to approach matters slowly over a period of time. The therapist can gradually move from questions to clarifications to interpretations, allowing the patient to integrate each step. It is also important to build on what the patient has said previously and to use the patient's own comments and descriptions when building the interpretive case.

Once a specific interpretation has been made, it is often difficult to determine whether it was effective. Sometimes the patient's response (for example, a surprised exclamation, flushing, saying "My God, I never thought of it that way!") will suggest that the target has been hit. But at other times patients may be entirely noncommittal, only to remark some sessions later how true the therapist's comment was. In any event, the real test of the utility of an interpretation is more likely to come from the subsequent course of the sessions. Even a patient's overt acceptance can sometimes be nothing more than a way of diverting the therapist or erecting a defense.

A classic psychoanalytic interpretation is designed to open up the patient to new ways of viewing things and, ultimately, to neutralize unconscious conflicts and defenses. In doing this, the therapist makes use of free associations, dream material, behavior that indicates resistance and transference, and so on. Interpretations can vary a great deal in terms of their complexity and their incisiveness. Sometimes they are designed to cut right to the heart of a patient's unconscious conflicts, and in other cases they may be little more than comments or questions designed to move the patient ever so slightly in the direction of insight. Perhaps they should be labeled as verbal interventions by the therapist rather than interpretations. But all have the potential for altering how a patient thinks or feels.

■ Psychoanalytic Alternatives

Psychoanalytic theory underwent considerable modification by Carl Jung, Otto Rank, Alfred Adler, the neo-Freudians, the ego analysts, and others. The seminal contributions of Freud remained, but the emphases often changed. Jung made much more of dreams and symbolic processes. Rank elevated the birth trauma to a preeminent position. Adler and the neo-Freudians stressed the importance of culture, learning, and social relationships at the expense of instinctual forces.

Such variations would be expected to influence methods of therapy. However, these changes often did little to alter the supreme role of insight or the critical roles of free association, dream analysis, interpretation, transference, and resistance. Insight came about through traditional psychoanalytic methods, but now it was the insight of Horney or Fromm or Sullivan. The neurotic symptom was seen as rooted not only in repressed sexual or aggressive urges; it now became the outgrowth of a fear of being alone or of the insecurity that goes along with the adult role. In most of these early variants of psychoanalysis, interpretation remained the essential therapeutic ingredient. What distinguished these variants was often the content of the interpretation—the different ways in which unconscious material was construed by the analyst.

Over the years, enough changes have been made in traditional psychoanalysis that those who no longer practice the strict Freudian techniques are often said to be practicing "psychoanalytically oriented" therapy. These changes involve many factors. In some cases the number of analytic sessions is reduced from five per week to three, and the entire treatment process may last but a year and a half (Alexander & French, 1946). The therapist no longer is inevitably seated behind the patient's couch but now often sits at a desk, with the patient seated in a facing chair. Perhaps the easiest way to characterize these and other modifications is to say that greater flexibility has been introduced. Although basic Freudian tenets are still observed, the overall context is not so rigid. For example, free association is no longer absolutely required by these psychoanalytically oriented therapists. The importance of dreams may be downplayed somewhat. Drugs and even hypnosis may be employed.

For many years, the therapy room was like an inner sanctum. The therapist talked with the patient and no one else. Now, family members or a spouse are often consulted, or sometimes therapy is conducted with the family as a unit. There tends to be much less emphasis on the past (childhood) and a more active confrontation with the present. Even the nature of the clientele has changed a bit. Clinics or institutes now provide some therapeutic services geared toward aging clients, minority group clients, and others who have not traditionally received psychoanalytic treatment. Again, none of this is meant to be a denial of Freudian principles; rather, it is a demonstration that traditional Freudian treatment procedures are not the only therapeutic techniques that can be deduced from Freudian psychoanalytic theory.

Ego analysts

The *ego-analytic movement,* originating from within the framework of traditional psychoanalysis rather than as a splinter group, held that classical psychoanalysis overemphasized the unconscious and instinctual determinants at the expense of ego processes. This group of theorists accepted the role of the ego in mediating the conflict between the id and the real world but felt the ego also performed other extremely important functions. They emphasized the adaptive, "conflict-free" functions of the ego, including memory, learning, and perception. These theorists include Hartmann (1939), Anna Freud (1946a), Kris (1950), Erikson (1956), and Rapaport (1953).

Ego-analytic psychotherapy has not departed from the usual therapy methods except in degree. In a sense, the ego analysts seem to prefer reeducative goals rather than the reconstructive goals of orthodox psychoanalysis. The exploration of infantile experience and the induction of a transference neurosis seem to be less common in ego-analytic therapy than in classical psychoanalysis. Ego-analytic therapy focuses more on contemporary problems in living than on a massive examination and reinstatement of the past. Also, the therapist must understand not only the neurotic aspects of the patient's personality but also the effective parts and how they interact with those neurotic trends.

The ego-analytic approach has also tended to emphasize the importance of building the patient's trust through "reparenting" in the therapy relationship. For example, the ego-analyst promotes growth in patients by helping them recognize their strengths, facilitating the development of more adaptive ways of coping with stress, and providing an atmosphere of support and understanding. At the same time, patients are encouraged to develop their own autonomy and identity. This approach sometimes even views transference as an impediment to therapy and works toward building more adaptive defenses in the patient (Blanck & Blanck, 1974).

Other contemporary developments

In particular, the work of Horney, Sullivan, and Adler has been important in giving a new spin to psychoanalysis. Likewise, ego psychology and theories of object relations encouraged an emphasis on the manner in which the patient relates to other people rather than on conflicts among instinctual forces. A further example is the self psychology of Kohut (1977), in which the central task of maturation is not the successful negotiation of the psychosexual stages but the development of an integrated self.

Discussions of recent changes in psychoanalytic therapies emphasize a shift in the therapeutic focus to the here and now and to the interpersonal exchanges that occur within it (Spence, 1987; Stolorow, Bandchaft, & Atwood, 1987). In the same vein, Strupp and Binder (1984) have synthesized some of the more critical developmental changes in psychoanalytic practice. They emphasize a movement away from the recovery of childhood memories and their analysis and instead focus on the corrective emotional experiences that occur through the agency of the therapeutic relationship. The transference relationship as it occurs in therapy is seen as a means for constructive changes in interpersonal relations outside the therapy room.

Brief psychotherapy

Perhaps the chief practical thrust of recent years in psychodynamic methods has been the development of *brief psychotherapy* (Goldfried, Greenberg, & Marmar, 1990; Koss, Strupp, & Butcher, 1986). Many of these brief therapies retain their psychodynamic identity even as they are employed in emergency, crisis-oriented situations. This allows the therapist to capitalize on the patient's heightened motivation and also to depend on the transference relationship (Goldfried et al., 1990).

While it would be nice to believe that theory and research considerations dictated the shift toward briefer psychotherapies, this is not entirely the case. An important driving force has been the emphasis on cost containment in health care systems (Cummings, 1986), which has resulted in a reduction of the number of visits for which insurers will reimburse therapists. This has also provided indirect competition from psychiatrists who so frequently prescribe medications these days rather than psychotherapy. The net effect? A turn to brief psychotherapy to remain economically competitive.

There are now several hundred different brands of brief therapy. In fact, the widespread availability of these treatments has diminished the exclusive role of psychiatrists and brought many nonmedical therapists into the arena. Not all of these briefer therapies could appropriately be labeled psychodynamic (as we shall discuss in later chapters), and in some cases briefer therapies are more similar to crisis intervention techniques. Furthermore, many forms of brief psychotherapy are quite eclectic in their approach (Garfield, 1989).

Although some define 25 sessions as the upper limit of brief therapy (Butcher & Koss, 1978), others indicate that the range can be from one (Bloom, 1981) to 40 or 50 sessions (Sifneos, 1972). However, the issue seems to be less the number of sessions than the rationing of time allotted to therapy (Budman & Gurman, 1983) and the state of mind in patient and therapist alike. Table 12-1 presents some of the value-attitude contrasts between long-term and short-term therapists.

Events move rapidly in crisis-oriented therapy. Thus, insight is not the leisurely process that it is in traditional forms of psychotherapy. The entire working-through process is accelerated. And the ultimate goal is not reconstruction of the personality but the development of a benign cycle of functioning and the better handling of day-to-day problems in living. Transference is encouraged, as noted above, but mainly as a means of ensuring that the therapist will be perceived as helpful, competent, and active.

Specific techniques in brief therapy are numerous. However, the maintenance of a clear and specific focus on realistic goals is important. Usually, the level of therapist activity is high, and both therapist and patient are keenly aware of the

Table 12-1
Comparative values in long-term versus short-term therapy.

Long-Term Therapist	Short-Term Therapist
1. Seeks change in basic character.	Prefers pragmatism, parsimony, and least radical intervention and does not believe in notion of "cure."
2. Believes that significant psychological change is unlikely in everyday life.	Maintains an adult-development perspective from which significant psychological change is viewed as inevitable.
3. Sees presenting problems as reflecting more basic pathology.	Emphasizes patient's strengths and resources; presenting problems are taken seriously (although not necessarily at face value).
4. Wants to "be there" as patient makes significant changes.	Accepts that many changes will occur after therapy and will not be observable to the therapist.
5. Sees therapy as having a timeless quality and is patient and willing to wait for change.	Does not accept the timelessness of some models of therapy.
6. Unconsciously recognizes the fiscal convenience of maintaining long-term patients.	Fiscal issues are often muted either by the nature of the therapist's practice or by the organizational structure for reimbursement.
7. Views psychotherapy as almost always benign and useful.	Views psychotherapy as being sometimes useful and sometimes harmful.
8. Sees patient's being in therapy as the most important part of patient's life.	Sees being in the world as more important than being in therapy.

SOURCE: Adapted from "The Practice of Brief Therapy," by S. H. Budman and A. S. Gurman, 1983, *Professional Psychology Research and Practice, 14,* 277–292. Copyright © 1983 by the American Psychological Association. Reprinted by permission.

element of time. The therapist is likely to use homework assignments for the patient and to involve relatives or significant others in the treatment plan. Supportive activities outside therapy are likely to be employed as well (for example, exercise, Overeaters Anonymous). This variety and flexibility in treatment activities takes brief therapy beyond the strict psychodynamic perspective.

Research evidence attests to the efficacy of brief forms of psychotherapy across a number of clinical conditions (Koss & Shiang, 1994), and evidence suggests that brief psychodynamic psychotherapy may be as effective as traditional time-unlimited psychoanalysis (Koss, Butcher, & Strupp, 1986). A particular form of brief therapy that is psychodynamic in flavor deserves mention because it has received a great deal of attention from psychotherapy researchers. *Interpersonal psychotherapy* or *IPT* (Klerman, Weissman, Rounsaville, & Chevron, 1984) is a brief, insight-oriented approach that has primarily been applied to depressive disorders, although it has been modified for use in the treatment of other disorders (for example, substance abuse and bulimia) as well. When used to treat depression, IPT involves thorough assessment of depressive symptoms, targeting a major problem area (for example, delayed grief, role transitions or disputes, interpersonal deficits), and alleviating depressive symptoms by improving relationships with others (for example, improving communication skills and social skills). IPT has been shown to be effective in treating acute depressive episodes and in preventing or delaying their recurrence (Weissman & Markowitz, 1994).

■ Concluding Remarks

In this section the discussion will be confined to empirical evaluations as well as some general observations about those psychotherapeutic practices that trace their origins to the psychoanalytic method.

Does psychodynamic psychotherapy work?

What evidence is there that the psychodynamic approach is effective? In the last chapter, we mentioned the widely cited meta-analytic study by Smith, Glass, and Miller (1980) that examined the effectiveness of psychotherapy. In addition to examining the effects of psychotherapy in general, these authors also reported effects separately for different types of psychological intervention. Smith et al. found that the average patient who had received psychodynamic psychotherapy was functioning better than 75% of those who received no treatment. Two recent meta-analyses of studies examining the effectiveness of *brief* psychodynamic psychotherapy, however, have produced conflicting results, with one supporting the efficacy of brief psychodynamic treatment (Crits-Christoph, 1992) and the other refuting it (Svartberg & Stiles, 1991). Based on these and other results, we offer the tentative conclusion that there appears to be at least modest support for the effectiveness of psychodynamic psychotherapy. There are, however, a number of thorny methodological issues that plague research on psychodynamic therapy (for example, appropriate outcome measures and length of treatment), and additional investigations are warranted.

Interpretation and insight

A wide range of current psychotherapies depend to a greater or lesser extent upon the patient's achievement of insight through the method of therapist interpretation. In psychoanalysis there still seems to be a total commitment to insight as the supreme means for solving problems in living. When understanding is complete enough, it is believed that the patients' symptoms will be ameliorated, and sometimes they will even disappear.

This emphasis on the pursuit of understanding has great appeal to many people. For example, although many people who are sad may seek the therapeutic goal of happiness, most of them are not content just to become happy — they also want to know why they are sad. The commitment of psychoanalysis and its psychotherapeutic heirs to insight and understanding is their greatest asset, but it also contains the seeds of their failures. Especially in the case of psychoanalysis, reconstruction of the personality through insight and understanding can lead to a nearly interminable and sometimes exhausting examination of the past and analysis of motives. Although one can hardly fault psychoanalysis for teaching the importance of the past in shaping the present, there can be too much of a good thing. At times it almost seems that the patient can use the need for understanding and the pursuit of the past as reasons not to come to grips with current problems. The endless analysis of conflicts and motives and childhood origins can easily replace the necessity for finding solutions and behavioral alternatives to problems in living. Although learning the reasons for one's difficulties may be quite important (and ultimately quite efficient if one is to attain solutions that are generalized rather than piecemeal), the failure to emphasize alternative ways of behaving can easily be a major inadequacy in traditional psychoanalysis.

A tacit assumption in psychoanalysis seems to be that more adaptive behavior will automatically occur once insight is achieved by the working-through process, that behavioral change will surely follow insight. However, the evidence for this assumption is exceedingly sparse. And it has been argued for some time that, in fact, the true course of events follows a reverse pattern—that insight is brought about by behavioral change (Alexander & French, 1946).

One of the chief methods of facilitating patient insight that is used by psychodynamic clinicians is the *interpretation of transference*. A recent review (Henry, Strupp, Schacht, & Gaston, 1994) of empirical studies that examined transference interpretation in psychodynamic psychotherapy provided the following general conclusions:

1. The frequency of interpretations made is not related to better outcome; some studies have found that a higher frequency of interpretation is related to poorer outcome.
2. Transference interpretations do not result in a greater degree of affective experience in the patient versus other types of interpretations or other types of interventions. When followed by affective responses, however, transference interpretations appear to be related to positive outcome.
3. Interpretations by the therapist are more likely to result in defensive responding on the part of the patient than are other types of interventions. Frequent transference interpretations may damage the therapeutic relationship.
4. Clinicians' accuracy of interpretations may be lower than what was previously believed.

Henry et al. (1994) go on to state: "The available findings challenge some dearly held beliefs. In short, transference interpretations do not seem uniquely effective, may pose greater process risks, and may be counter-therapeutic under certain conditions" (p. 479).

This is not to say that transference interpretations are always harmful and should be avoided. Rather, the existing research suggests that the relationship between interpretation and outcome is a complex one that is likely to depend on factors such as patient characteristics, clinician interpersonal style, timing of interpretations, accuracy of interpretations, and so on (Henry et al., 1994).

Curative factors

What, then, seems to be responsible for positive outcome following psychodynamic psychotherapy? The empirical evidence points to the quality and strength of the *therapeutic alliance* (Henry et al., 1994). Although the quality of the therapeutic alliance is related to outcome across a number of modalities (for example, client-centered, cognitive-behavioral), it is interesting to note that the importance of the clinician-patient relationship was recognized by Freud (1912). Various definitions of the therapeutic alliance have been proposed, but in general this term refers to the patient's affective bond to the therapist. A positive relationship or strong bond facilitates self-examination by the patient and permits interpretation. Presumably, then, a strong therapeutic alliance would make it less likely that a patient would react defensively to interpretations by the clinician. Research evidence suggests a direct link between alliance and outcome, whether short-term or long-term psychodynamic treatments are employed and regardless of the particular outcome measure used (Henry et al., 1994).

The lack of emphasis on behavior

Except for engaging in interpretation, the stereotypical practitioner of psychoanalytic psychotherapy plays a relatively passive role in the therapeutic process. The therapist's failure to deal with behavior, to make suggestions, or to adopt a generally more activist posture would seem to prolong psychotherapy unnecessarily. For example, it may be true that a male patient's unhappy heterosexual adjustment or lack of skills with women stems from unconscious generalizations about past unfavorable comparisons with a dominant brother. But simple insight into the childhood origins of the problem does not instantly provide the skills that are lacking. The patient's expectations for success in establishing relationships with women will continue to be low and disquieting until a heterosexual behavioral repertoire is established. An active therapist who guides the patient into new learning situations, in addition to having discussions that will lead to insight, seems more likely to achieve lasting solutions to the patient's problems than does a therapist who relies solely on insight (or solely on behavior, for that matter).

It seems clear that a major reason for the rapid rise of the behavioral therapies was the failure of so many psychotherapists to deal directly with the specific problems of the patient. The inevitable approach always seemed to be one of relegating the presenting problem to the status "symptom of something deeper." The therapist then began working with that "something deeper" while clinging to the abiding belief that, once the patient understood it, the symptom or deficit would disappear. Unfortunately, things did not work out that way often enough. In any case, more and more therapists are trying to foster both insight and behavioral alternatives in their patients.

The economics of psychotherapy

Because psychoanalysis deals with the reconstruction of the personality, it is by its very nature a long and costly procedure. Its course over three to five years and the extensive and high-priced preparation of its practitioners ensure that it will be an expensive undertaking. Consequently, it has become a therapy for the affluent—for those who have both the money and the time to pursue the resolution of their neuroses. Moreover, the procedures of psychoanalysis are such that only relatively intelligent, sophisticated, and educated groups are likely to be able to accept the therapeutic demands it makes. Because of these considerations, only a small portion of those in need of psychotherapy are likely to be reached by traditional psychoanalysis. The poor, the underrepresented groups, the undereducated, the older populations, the severely disturbed, and those beset by reality burdens of living for which they are woefully unprepared will in all likelihood not become psychoanalytic patients.

For these reasons alone, many regard psychoanalysis as a failure. It is inherently incapable of putting even a dent in the mental health problems of the nation. Yet, for persons who have the necessary personal qualities and financial resources, psychoanalysis has been helpful, particularly so for those whose problems in living can best be met through the development of understanding.

Psychoanalytic techniques seem to have helped many patients, and, as a theory of therapy, psychoanalysis undergirds many forms of psychotherapy. Yet many clinicians still question whether, after all these years, there is really much in the way of definitive research evidence for its effectiveness (Fisher & Greenberg, 1977; Kline, 1981; Luborsky & Spence, 1978). These sentiments are echoed by Wolpe (1981), who, although hardly unbiased, is particularly critical of a method that can allow patients to remain so long in therapy, often with little evidence of improvement. Wolpe cites examples offered by Schmideberg (1970). In one case, a 54-year-old man had been in psychoanalysis for 30 years without noticeable improvement. A woman who began psychoanalysis with no specific symptoms later developed agoraphobia and after 12 years of therapy was worse than when she began. Admittedly, nearly every brand of therapy contains its share of horror stories. But lengthy therapy combined with little improvement does raise questions.

■ Focus Questions

1. What are the major assumptions of Freudian theory?
2. What techniques are used in psychoanalytic treatment, and why are these employed?
3. What are the major alternative forms of psychoanalytic therapy? Describe each.
4. What evidence suggests that psychodynamic treatment works?
5. What are the advantages and disadvantages of psychodynamic forms of treatment?

■ Key Terms

anal stage	defense mechanisms
analysis of dreams	ego
brief psychotherapy	ego-analytic movement
catharsis	fixation
death instincts (Thanatos)	free association

genital stage
id
insight
interpersonal psychotherapy (IPT)
interpretation of transference
latency stage
latent content
life instincts (Eros)
manifest content
moral anxiety
neurotic anxiety
Oedipus complex
oral stage
phallic stage
pleasure principle
primary process
projection

psychic determinism
psychosexual stages
reaction formation
reality anxiety
reality principle
regression
repression
resistance
secondary process
superego
talking cure
therapeutic alliance
transference
unconscious
unconscious motivation
working-through process

13

Psychotherapy: Phenomenological and Humanistic-Existential Perspectives

Traditional psychotherapy traces its origins to a psychoanalytic point of view that regards both pathology and the inability to achieve one's potential as failures in understanding the past. Moreover, those failures are seen as rooted in the unacknowledged role of inner forces or even instincts. Through therapy one can learn to understand all this, and the ensuing insight will set one free—free from the misery of problems, symptoms, and the failure to live a productive, meaningful life.

For years the foregoing views were the dominant ones in psychotherapy. But in the early 1940s, a serious alternative to psychoanalytic psychotherapy began to appear. The idea of nondirective counseling (what was later to become known as *client-centered therapy* and what some now refer to as *person-centered therapy*) was taking shape under the guidance of Carl Rogers.

■ Client-Centered Therapy

The perspective of Carl Rogers was almost the diametric opposite of psychoanalysis; yet, the two points of view do share a few characteristics. As theories they both developed out of therapeutic encounters with people who had problems. As a result, neither perspective can be totally understood without an appreciation of the ways in which each relates to therapy.

The origins

The full extent of Rogers's contribution becomes apparent as one recalls the personality therapy world of the late 1930s. Psychoanalysis, both as theory and practice, was the dominant force. The theories of psychologists such as Gordon Allport or Kurt Lewin were attracting some attention, but the real spotlight was on those theories that had a close association with treatment. This meant psychoanalysis or at least some close derivative of it. What is more, this attention seemed to increase as many prominent psychoanalysts fled Europe and settled in the United States.

Box 13-1

A Brief Biography of Carl Rogers

Born in Oak Park, Illinois, on January 8, 1902, Carl Rogers was the fourth of six children and grew up in a financially secure family. When Rogers was 12, his father, a civil engineer-contractor, moved the family to a farm outside Chicago. His parents maintained a devout, almost dogmatic set of religious beliefs and the family became a tight little unit—perhaps in part because of those beliefs. Rogers had few friends and spent much of his time alone reading. He was an outstanding student in high school but was not really a part of the social scene.

In 1919, he went to the University of Wisconsin to major in agriculture. He was very active in campus religious affairs, especially during his first two years, even attending a religious conference in Peking, China, during this period. He was so impressed by the cultural and religious diversity he encountered on this trip that his traditionalist family and religious views were shaken. As a result, his fundamentalist orientation began to change noticeably. He graduated from the university with a degree in history in 1924.

Rogers married Helen Elliott, with whom he had two children. Moving to New York City, he attended Union Theological Seminary for two years; however, a growing religious skepticism coupled with a desire to help others more directly led him to transfer to Columbia University and pursue

Courtesy of Natalie Rogers

training in clinical psychology. He was awarded the Ph.D. in 1931 and moved on to Rochester, New York, where he became a staff psychologist in a child guidance clinic.

The beginnings of Rogers's methods are clearly visible in his book *The Clinical Treatment of the Problem Child,* which was published in 1939. When Rogers moved to Ohio State University in 1940, he began to develop his approach to psychotherapy in earnest (Rogers, 1942). In 1945, he moved to the University of Chicago and began a period of intensive research as he developed a theoretical structure to buttress his therapeutic practices. During this period, the term *client-centered* began to supplant the older "nondirective" label (Rogers, 1951). Then, in 1957, Rogers accepted a position at the University of Wisconsin in order to extend his ideas about psychotherapy to more extreme populations, such as hospitalized schizophrenics (Rogers, Gendlin, Kiesler, & Truax, 1967). From 1968 until his death in February 1987, Rogers was a resident fellow at the Center for Studies of the Person in La Jolla, California.

Rogers published numerous books (several of which are cited in the reference list). His autobiography, written in 1967, is included in *A History of Psychology in Autobiography* (Volume 5). He also published a paper in 1974 entitled "In Retrospect: Forty-Six Years," which appeared in the *American Psychologist. A Way of Being,* published in 1980, provides some insight into the changes that occurred in his thinking over the years. And a sensitive and revealing portrait of Rogers—both as a psychologist and person—has been offered by Gendlin (1988).

At about the same time, Carl Rogers was struggling with the clinical problems of disturbed children as an obscure clinical psychologist in Rochester, New York. Like most therapists of the day, Rogers had been heavily exposed to psychoanalytic thinking. After completing his Ph.D. at Columbia University, he began work at a child guidance clinic in Rochester. While there, he came in touch with the will therapy of Otto Rank and the relationship therapy of Jessie Taft. Rank felt that patients should be allowed free opportunity to exert their wills and to dominate the therapist. Taft, a social worker, brought Rank's notions to America and emphasized the relationship that exists between the therapist and the patient. Indeed, Taft regarded this relationship as more important than any intellectual explanations of the patient's problems. Consequently, the therapeutic situation was made a very permissive one.

Rogers found these views highly congenial. They were consonant both with his religious beliefs and with his democratic convictions regarding the nature of human relationships in society. A belief that no person has the right to run another person's life found subsequent expression in his therapeutic notions of permissiveness, acceptance, and the refusal to give advice.

The phenomenological world

Rogers's theory of personality developed mainly out of therapeutic encounters with patients and from certain philosophic notions about the nature of people. Furthermore, client-centered therapy anchors itself in phenomenological theory (Combs & Snygg, 1959; Rogers, 1951).

Phenomenology teaches that behavior is totally determined by the phenomenal field of the person. The phenomenal field is everything experienced by the person at any given point in time. Therefore, to understand a person's behavior, the therapist must know something about the person's phenomenal field. This means understanding what the world is like for them. A difficulty, however, is that it is necessary to make inferences about this field from the person's behavior; in turn, those inferences are used to predict or understand the behavior in question. There is a real potential here for circularity if the therapist is not careful. For example, a therapist observes that George is behaving nervously prior to a test, then assumes that George must be experiencing a threat from the test, and then proceeds to account for his nervousness by attributing it to the threat. Such an observation is both the basis for the inference and the object of the explanation.

A very important concept within phenomenological theory is the *phenomenal self*—that part of the phenomenal field which the person experiences as the "Me." Obviously, this is not an objective experience. In addition, phenomenological theory states that the basic human urge is to preserve and enhance the phenomenal self. In a sense, then, self-esteem becomes the fountainhead of behavior.

Problems in adjustment arise when the phenomenal self is threatened. But what is a threat for one person is not necessarily a threat for another. In essence, people will experience threat whenever they perceive that the phenomenal self is in danger. Thus, a man who perceives himself as being very attractive to women may become anxious if he is rejected by a woman since this represents a threat to his self-concept. Faced with such a threat, the man may adopt a variety of defensive postures—for example, he may rationalize his failure or he may narrow his perceptual field. The truly adjusted person is one who can integrate all experiences into the phenomenal field, not just the experiences that are immediately consistent with the self-concept. As an example, a well-adjusted student who fails an exam will not claim unfairness or physical illness (assuming that these claims are unjustified); rather, the student will integrate this experience by perhaps revising the self-concept: "Maybe I am not as good in biochemistry as I thought. But then again, I do quite well in other areas and I have good social skills. So clearly this doesn't diminish me as a person." Or, "I did fail, but with more effort I think I can do it. But if not, I will try other things that will bring a sense of fulfillment or contribution."

Theoretical propositions

Early on, Rogers (1951) formulated a series of propositions that set the tone for a client-centered view of personality. He stated that individuals exist in a world of experience of which they are the centers. This experience can only be known by the person. Therefore, the person is the best source of information about the self. These views have led members of the client-centered movement to rely heavily on self-reports as the premier source of information rather than on inferences from test data or related observations. Since people react to the field as it is experienced and perceived, the perceptual field is reality. This leads to the conclusion that objective knowledge about stimuli is not enough to predict behavior — the clinician must know something about the person's awareness of the stimulus. The psychology of objectivity is rejected in favor of the inner world of experience as reported by the person.

The basic human tendency is toward maintaining and enhancing the experiencing self. This is the process of self-actualization, and it is what produces the forward movement of life — a force upon which the therapist relies heavily in therapeutic contacts with the client. But this forward movement can occur only when the choices of life are clearly perceived and adequately symbolized.

Behavior is fundamentally a set of goal-directed attempts by the organism to satisfy experienced needs. All needs can ultimately be subsumed under the single urge of enhancement of the phenomenal self. All of this would seem to imply a kind of learning theory, but it is difficult to find any learning concepts in Rogers's theoretical expositions.

A crucial concept is the *self,* the awareness of one's being and functioning. The structure of the self is formed out of interactions with the environment and, in particular, out of evaluations of the person by others. The self is an organized, fluid, and yet consistent pattern of perceptions of the characteristics and relationships of the I or the Me, along with the values attached to them. During the life of the individual a variety of experiences occur. Following an experience, three possibilities present themselves: (1) the experience can be symbolized or organized into some relationship with the self; (2) the experience can be ignored because its relevance to the self is not perceived; or (3) the experience can be denied symbolization or distorted because it is inconsistent with the structure of the self.

Under certain conditions, experiences that are inconsistent with the self may be examined and perceived and the structure of the self revised to assimilate them. The principal condition is one involving the complete absence of threat to the self. This, in effect, states the rationale for the warm, accepting, permissive, and nonjudgmental atmosphere that is the cardinal condition in client-centered therapy.

Theory of therapy

As Rogers (1959) stated it, psychotherapy is the "releasing of an already existing capacity in a potentially competent individual, not the expert manipulation of a more or less passive personality" (p. 221). This is the so-called *growth potential* upon which the client-centered therapist relies so heavily. All people possess such a potential — the trick is to release it. In client-centered therapy, the release is presumably effected, thus permitting the client's self-actualizing tendencies to gain ascendance over previously internalized factors that restricted acceptance of personal worth. The three therapist characteristics that precipitate all of this are: (1) accurate empathic understanding; (2) unconditional positive regard; and (3) genuineness or congruence. These three variables were briefly discussed in Chapter 11, where it was observed that research evidence does not accord them as much power as did Rogers (see Greenberg, Elliott, & Lietaer, 1994).

Empathy.   Empathic therapists are ones who can transmit to the client a sense of being understood. The expression of *empathy* conveys a kind of sensitivity to the needs, feelings, and circumstances of the client. An exceptionally empathic therapist can assume the attitudes of clients and, as it were, even climb behind their eyeballs and see the world as they do. The client must come to know that the therapist is making every effort to understand correctly. When the client realizes this, the basis is laid for a therapeutic relationship. Empathy can never be total, of course, and a good thing, too. A measure of objective detachment must always be maintained; otherwise, the therapist would have the same problems as the client. Nevertheless, the empathic therapist can convey or communicate to clients a sense of understanding and appreciation of their needs or plight, and clients can find this attitude tremendously reassuring, more so than any words or exclamations of interest. For the attitude of empathy is not stated—it is conveyed by its very existence.

Perhaps Rogers's own words (1946) will impart something of this attitude of understanding and empathy:

> We have come to recognize that if we can provide understanding of the way the client seems to himself [sic] at this moment, he can do the rest. The therapist must lay aside his [sic] preoccupation with diagnosis and his diagnostic shrewdness, must discard his tendency to make professional evaluations, must cease his endeavors to formulate an accurate prognosis, must give up the temptation subtly to guide the individual, and must concentrate on one purpose only; that of providing deep understanding and acceptance of the attitudes consciously held at this moment by the client as he explores step by step into the dangerous areas which he has been denying to consciousness.
>
> This type of relationship can exist only if the counselor is deeply and genuinely able to adopt these attitudes. Client-centered counseling, if it is to be effective, cannot be a trick, or a tool. It is not a subtle way of guiding the client while pretending to let him guide himself. To be effective, it must be genuine. (pp. 420–421)

Unconditional positive regard.   In most relationships with parents, friends, a spouse, or others, clients have learned that approval and acceptance are conditional upon meeting certain stipulations. Parents accept children if they are obedient; an employer is accepting if employees are prompt and efficient; spouses require that their partners be interested and loving. But in therapy there must be no conditions. Acceptance is given without hidden clauses or subtle disclaimers. *Unconditional positive regard* is nothing more and nothing less than a respect for the client as a human being. The therapist must lay aside all preconceived notions and be able to care about the client, be accepting, and, very importantly, convey that here is someone who has faith and trust in the client's ability and strength to achieve that inner potential. These qualities, coupled with a complete lack of evaluative judgments on the part of the therapist, will go a long way toward creating an atmosphere in which the client is free to give up debilitating defenses and can, therefore, in the absence of threat begin to grow as a person.

Of course, exhibiting these qualities with someone the therapist finds pleasing and easy to relate to in terms of background and values is relatively simple. The true test of the therapist's unconditional positive regard comes with clients whose behaviors and attitudes really challenge the therapist's beliefs. The bigot, the un-motivated or lazy, the client who describes an incestuous experience with his niece can force a real test of the therapist's tolerance and acceptance. But, just as every citizen is entitled to vote, so is every client worthy of unconditional positive regard.

Congruence.   At first glance, congruence (or genuineness, as it is some-times called) would seem to contradict the qualities of empathy and positive re-gard. Congruent therapists are those who express the behavior, feelings, or atti-tudes that the client stimulates in them. They do not smile if they are angry. If the client's remarks are upsetting, they do not hide behind a mask of calm (Rogers, 1961). Rogers believed that, in the long run, clients would respond favorably to this honesty and congruence, knowing that here was a real person dedicated to their welfare. This can be most reassuring to clients and can stimulate within them a sense of personal worth and a desire to come to grips with their latent potential.

Attitude versus technique.   In many ways, the core of client-centered therapy seems to reside more in stated values and attitudes toward peo-ple than in any specific methods. To that extent, client-centered therapy is a state of mind rather than a set of techniques. The client-centered therapist seeks to be-come nondirective by relinquishing any procedures that point to the therapist as an expert who will diagnose the client's ills and recommend the proper measures for their alleviation.

In fact, client-centered therapists will argue that such prescriptions are un-necessary, since the release of clients' resources or potential will resolve the prob-lems in question. Given the presence of therapist congruence, unconditional pos-itive regard, and accurate empathic understanding, clients will discover their own capacity for growth and self-direction. In contrast to the psychoanalysts, Rogers saw people not as destructive but as possessed of a constructive force reaching to-ward health and self-fulfillment. In addition, the Rogerians forego an emphasis on the past in favor of an awareness of current experience. For the interpretations of the activist psychoanalytic therapist, they substitute the quiet, listening therapist whose caring facilitates the client's own discovery of inner strength and valid per-sonal experience.

There are also distinct differences between client-centered therapy and the behavioral approaches (see Chapter 14). Rogerians declare that inner experiences are the paramount data and that to ignore those experiences is to ignore the ba-sic data of the human being. Where behavioral approaches sometimes seem to fo-cus on manipulating or controlling the environment in order to effect change, the client-centered therapist relies upon change that emanates from within—upon a release of inner potential.

The therapeutic process

In some ways, it almost seems easier to describe client-centered therapy by what does not take place there. For example, there is a series of don'ts that in-clude giving information or advice, using reassurance or persuasion, asking ques-tions, offering interpretations, and making criticisms. Perhaps the major activities of the nondirective therapist are the recognition and clarification of the feelings associated with the client's statements. For example, Greenberg et al. (1994) reported that approximately 75% of all client-centered therapists' responses were "reflections" of what the client had said. Comments are also made that will convey to the client the therapist's total and unconditional acceptance. Occasionally, the therapist will find it necessary to explain the respective roles of the client and the therapist. Called *structuring*, this, too, includes the element of acceptance.

Typically, neither reassurance nor interpretation is employed in client-centered therapy. It is assumed that the recognition of feeling and the accompanying acceptance are themselves reassuring. In addition, reassurance is conveyed by the therapist's tone of voice, choice of words, facial expression, and general demeanor. Providing interpretation and giving advice or information are avoided because doing this implies that the therapist knows what is best for the client (though in some instances it may be necessary to refer the client to a source of information). In general, the idea is to place the responsibility for therapeutic progress on the client's shoulders rather than on those of the therapist. Similarly, to interpret is to tell clients why they behaved in a given fashion — it means that the therapist has preempted responsibility for progress rather than waiting for clients to arrive at their own explanations.

In the case of acceptance, this is less a technique than an all-pervasive attitude. The durable belief is that the client is capable of reaching a satisfactory solution to problems in living. Acceptance provides the atmosphere in which the client's potential for growth and self-actualization can be asserted. By responding to the client's feelings and then accepting them, the therapist provides a warmth that leads to the feeling of being understood.

The sequence of progress

Therapy sessions are usually scheduled once a week. More frequent sessions, extra sessions, and phone calls are discouraged, since these can lead to a dependency that may stifle any sense of growth.

The general sequence or process of therapy has been described by Rogers as involving a series of seven stages that the client undergoes (Meador & Rogers, 1984). A very condensed version of these stages follows.

First stage: Unwillingness to reveal self; own feelings not recognized; rigid constructs; close relationships perceived as dangerous.

Second stage: Feelings sometimes described but person is still remote from own personal experience; still externalizes heavily but begins to show some recognition that problems and conflicts exist.

Third stage: Description of past feelings as unacceptable; freer flow of expressions of self; begins to question validity of own constructs; incipient recognition that problems are inside rather than outside the individual.

Fourth stage: Free description of personal feelings as owned by the self; dim recognition that long-denied feelings may break into the present; loosening of personal constructs; some expression of self-responsibility; begins to risk relating to others on a feeling basis.

Fifth stage: Free expression of feelings and acceptance of them; previously denied feelings, although fearsome, are clearly in awareness; recognition

of conflicts between intellect and emotions; acceptance of personal responsibility for problems; a desire to be what one is.
Sixth stage: Acceptance of feelings without need for denial; a vivid, releasing sense of experience; willingness to risk being oneself in relationships
with others; trusts others to be accepting.
Seventh stage: Individual now comfortable with experiencing self; experiences
new feelings; little incongruency; ability to check validity of experience.

Diagnosis

In general, diagnosis or assessment is deemphasized or avoided in client-
centered therapy. Most Rogerians believe that formal assessment is not only unnecessary but actually detrimental. According to client-centered principles, assessment places the psychologist in a superior, authoritative role that can impede the
development of autonomy and self-actualization.

The abandonment of assessment seems to imply that client-centered therapy
is so potent and effective a method that it works on all clients, regardless of their
problems or of the particular circumstances in which they find themselves. Needless to say, the utility of this assumption has not yet been adequately demonstrated
(Greenberg et al., 1994). The following case example illustrates some of the features of client-centered counseling that we have discussed.

A Case Illustration

The client is a 20-year-old sophomore who is being seen in a university
counseling center. His initial complaint involved a generalized feeling of unworthi-
ness. As the sessions moved along, he began to focus specifically on his feelings
of intellectual inadequacy. Even though his college grade point average in a demanding curriculum was 3.3, he was constantly absorbed by a sense of inferiority.
He frequently compared himself (always unfavorably) to an older brother who had
recently completed medical school and was the source of much parental pride.
The following exchange took place in the 15th session:

Client: Well, it happened again yesterday. I got back that exam in American lit.
Therapist: I see.
Client: Just like before. I got an A all right—me and eight others. But on
the third question the instructor wrote a comment that I could have been
a little clearer or else could have given more detail. The same old crap. I
got an A all right, but it's pretty damn clear that I'm like a machine that
can generate correct answers without ever understanding. That's it. I
memorize, but there's no spark, no creativity. Boy!
Therapist: What else can you tell me about the exam?
Client: Well, it was like we talked about before. I'm doing OK, but I just don't
feel like I really measure up. I remember my brother bringing home a paper in high school. It was a C, but the instructor said John had real potential. I just don't think I've got it.

Therapist: Even though you got an A, you are not satisfied.

Client: That's right. Never satisfied. I could get 42 A+'s and never feel good. I hate myself!

Therapist: M-hm.

Client: Sometimes I'm so ridiculous.

Therapist: You feel silly because of the way you react. Is that right?

Client: I should put it aside, think about other things. But I don't, and then I feel silly when I don't.

Therapist: You're silly because you feel dissatisfied and silly because you don't just forget it.

Client: I know I should be satisfied with an A. Other guys would be. They'd be glad to get an A.

Therapist: M-hm.

Client: But I can't. No wonder the folks are so proud of John. He got decent grades, and he was satisfied — not like me. It's a wonder they don't get fed up with my moping around.

Therapist: So even with good grades your unhappiness is enough to turn people off.

Client: Sure. But somehow I've got to get rid of this defeatist attitude. I've got to think about the good side.

Therapist: M-hm.

Client: A lot of times I've tried to forget my lack of potential. Just go on and plug along.

Therapist: Yeah. I guess you really felt people put you down because of this lack of potential?

Client: Boy, did they! Especially my folks. They never really said so, but I could tell from the way they acted.

Therapist: M-hm.

Client: They'd say that John really has a head on his shoulders, or (pause) . . . he can think his way out of anything.

Therapist: And this made you feel sort of worthless — not hearing things like that about yourself.

Client: That's right.

Therapist: M-hm.

Intense feelings were expressed in this session. The client felt worthless and inferior to his brother. Despite an outstanding college record he continued to find ways to prove that he was intellectually unacceptable. The therapist did not attempt to contradict him or to prove him wrong; neither did he make reassuring comments. Rather, he accepted the client's statements and the feelings they conveyed. What is important is the feelings, not whether they are wrong or whether they stem from an earlier unhealthy home situation. The therapist accepts the feelings in a manner that transmits neither approval nor disapproval — just understanding. It is the understanding and the occasional clarifications that permit the client to move ever more closely to a careful examination of himself and of what he can do to change matters. Only in an atmosphere of acceptance can this potential for growth be cultivated and released. The foregoing excerpt also highlights the empathic statements made by the therapist. Often he summarized, almost inferentially, what the client was feeling. The therapist, then, does more than just accept the client's feelings—by rephrasing and inferring, the therapist reminds the client of what he or she must be feeling.

Like any movement, client-centered therapy has evolved and changed over the years. Modifications and extensions of both method and theory have occurred. A brief summary of a number of these developments can be found in Greenberg et al. (1994).

Other applications

The client-centered approach was developed primarily in the counseling psychotherapy context, and this remains its chief application. However, the movement has found other applications: for example, the client-centered orientation is frequently being employed in human relations training. The emphasis on relationship, acceptance, and warmth is often an integral part of training programs for those who seek work in crisis centers, for paraprofessionals who engage in counseling, and for volunteers in charitable organizations or agencies. Thus, whether workers are professionals such as physicians and nurses, psychological technicians, or Peace Corps volunteers, their training in human relationships often contains a heavy dose of the client-centered philosophy. When the client-centered construct is applied to problems outside the therapy room, it is often called the *person-centered approach.*

As we shall see in Chapter 15, small groups, encounter groups, and personal growth groups make use of the client-centered framework. Often these groups are established in order to reduce tension between factions in conflict, such as blacks and whites, labor and management, or students and faculty. In some instances, the client-centered approach is employed by institutions, such as churches, businesses, and school systems, in order to foster improved human relations or changes in institutional functioning and goals.

Some concluding remarks

The positive. The client-centered approach has had many salutary effects. It has provided a serious alternative to the traditional psychoanalytic forms of therapy and, in so doing, it offered an alternative focus on self-determination and inner directedness rather than on the biological urges and instincts of the Freudian view. The becoming, evolving person replaces the victim of personal history. Freedom to choose is substituted for a mechanistically determined set of behaviors.

Rogers demonstrated that it is not necessary to dig up the past in order to conduct psychotherapy. Emphasis was placed on the relationship between the client and the therapist, and the application of techniques became secondary. Even the word *client* suggests something of importance. The role of the passive patient in the context of the physician's demand for authority was replaced by that of the client who actively seeks to experience choice, equality, and freedom.

The general ahistorical stance of the Rogerians also led to a form of therapy much shorter than the often interminable psychoanalysis. The move away from lengthy resolutions of transference relationships, the detailed reconstruction of the past, and cathartic experiences considerably shortened the therapeutic process. In addition, the less active role played by the therapist required less training. Given the mental health needs of the nation, any therapeutic discipline that can provide personnel faster and more economically is to be seriously considered. However, it is possible that client-centered therapy has become a double-edged sword. Some feel that the client-centered, humanistic axis has produced a whole generation of pseudotherapists whose lack of training can never be fully offset by their enthusiasm and "authenticity."

A contribution of major proportions was Rogers's emphasis on research. He was responsible for the earliest concerted efforts to carry out research on the therapeutic process, being the first to employ recordings of therapy sessions to study the process and to investigate its effectiveness. The use of recordings is now a staple ingredient of training and research. Prior to Rogers, the sanctity of the therapy room was guarded with a vengeance. Rogers opened up therapy and made it an object of study rather than a subject of mystery. In making available recordings and transcripts of his own therapy sessions, he exhibited a degree of courage, though perhaps commonplace today, that was unusual for its time.

In addition to the pioneering efforts of Rogers and others in the recording and transcription of interviews, significant efforts were made to investigate the outcomes of therapy. For example, Rogers and his colleagues developed indices of therapeutic outcome based upon client ratings of their present and their ideal self-concept, along with various indicators of improvement gleaned from counseling sessions, such as the ratio of client-to-therapist talk and the responsibility for talk (for example, Cartwright, 1956; Rogers & Dymond, 1954; Rogers, Gendlin, Kiesler, & Truax, 1967; Snyder, 1961; Truax & Carkhuff, 1967; Truax & Mitchell, 1971).

As noted in Chapter 11, a meta-analysis of studies employing a client-centered treatment condition have indicated an effect size of 0.62, indicating that a client who received this form of therapy was functioning on average better than 73% of those who did not receive treatment. In order to investigate whether this finding characterized newer research (1978 to 1992) on client-centered therapy, Greenberg et al. (1994) conducted another meta-analysis. It is noteworthy that they could identify only eight studies conducted during this time period that investigated the effectiveness of client-centered therapy and also employed a control group. The average effect size across these studies was 0.88, indicating better functioning than 81% of those not receiving treatment. Greenberg et al. were also able to evaluate the *relative* effectiveness of client-centered therapy (that is, compared to other forms of psychological treatment). There were seven relevant comparisons, and in only one instance did client-centered therapy outperform another treatment (in this case, short-term dynamic therapy; Meyer, 1981). In summary, research evidence suggests that client-centered therapy is effective but no more effective than any other psychological treatment.

The negative.   In all of the above, however, there is another side of the coin. For example, client-centered therapists repeatedly argue that their efforts do not change clients. Instead, they say that the client's inner potential for growth is released. Whether this view is based on conviction or modesty, it seems to be incomplete. Therapy is a stimulus—the particular character of which is greatly affected by the therapist—that sets many reactions into motion. Whether those reactions are deemed positive, negative, or neutral, they seem in large measure to be attributable to the stimuli and the methods of the therapist.

Client-centered therapists often seem to feel that, in order to understand clients, they must climb behind their eyeballs to experience the same phenomenological world. But how does one do this? With intuition? How does the therapist ever completely shed the idiosyncratic bias of a personal framework? To many it would also appear that the tendencies to avoid assessment and to give the past short shrift actually impair the therapist's ability to understand and to enter the client's perceptual framework.

In client-centered therapy, there seems to be but one technique or, rather, one attitude—empathy, acceptance, and unconditional positive regard. Thus, every client is treated in exactly the same fashion. One need not assess in order to choose the most effective therapy or the specific technique to fit the unique characteristics of the client. Thus, a good case could be made for the contention that client-centered therapy is really technique-centered!

There is also an abiding faith that the client knows best. The movement's emphasis on democracy, freedom of choice, and the indisputable supremacy of the client's inner potential leads to a position in which any semblance of therapist "interference" through interpretation, advice, or expressed values is condemned. However, it would seem that in many cases the severity of the client's problems or the deviant quality of the client's values would dictate the use of a more active and directing set of procedures. One might well have reason to doubt the wisdom and resources of a psychopathic or schizophrenic client. Even if it were true—though this is probably not a testable proposition—that, given unlimited time or optimum circumstances, each client could make the right decisions or reach the proper conclusions, it seems inefficient to operate in this way. A related point is that client-centered therapists seem to be seeking to change the client (even though claiming not to do so) without collecting enough diagnostic and historical data to do so efficiently. Their emphasis on verbal reports by the client places them at the mercy of information that is often defensive, distorted, and incomplete.

Much of the research on the effectiveness of client-centered therapy has relied upon internal criteria. That is, clients are said to be improving when they take more responsibility for the conversation during the therapy session or talk proportionately more than the therapist. Others would argue, however, that the real criteria for improvement must come from outside the therapy room, through observation, reports by peers and spouse, and so on. Without validation from such external sources, it is possible that any client changes observed within the therapy room really represent adjustments to the demands of the situation rather than changes that will generalize beyond the confines of therapy.

Very often, descriptions of client-centered treatment philosophies and procedures are unique and involve a great deal of undefined terminology. Such words as *being, becoming, actualizing,* and *congruency* are not clearly defined or seem to carry a surplus of meaning that is difficult to communicate reliably. At other times, there is a grandiosity of language that seems out of keeping with the modesty that appears elsewhere. For example, Rogers (1951) says, "Therapy is the essence of life" (p. x).

Although some may simply chalk this up to jargon, there is nevertheless a marked tendency for Rogerians to employ language that is emotionally tinged in such a way as to almost serve a propaganda function. Such words as *nondirective* and *client-centered* not only seem to convey something distinctly positive but by implication also seem to depict other approaches as *directive* or *therapist-centered*. A language that includes an inventory of such words as *freedom, democratic, genuine, warm,* and *authentic* is likely to put advocates of other approaches at an immediate disadvantage. Before such advocates can explain what their approaches really are, they may have to answer implicit charges of being authoritarian, technique-centered, controlling, and without common humanistic values.

Finally, the client-centered approach grew and came of age on college campuses. The clients of the 1940s and 1950s were college students who were being seen at campus counseling centers. As often as not, the therapists trained in the Rogerian tradition in these centers became staff members at other college counseling centers. What has all this to do with therapy? First of all, as compared with people in the general population, college students as a group are brighter, better educated, and less severely maladjusted when they do develop problems, and they have a stronger arsenal of coping methods. The so-called nondirective, client-centered methods would probably be more effective with such a population than with, for example, those with psychosis, poor verbal skills, or a limited educational background.

■ The Humanistic-Existential Movement

The strands of phenomenology, humanism, and existentialism in psychology are inextricably woven together. In the preceding section we saw the importance that Rogers attached to immediate experience. This is basic phenomenology. At the same time, client-centered approaches stress the worth, uniqueness, and dignity of the client. This is basic *humanism.* Before we proceed to discuss existential therapies, logotherapy, and Gestalt therapy, let us pause to acknowledge the humanistic tradition that pervades those therapies.

Humanism

Although humanistic psychology is a fairly recent development, its origins extend far back into philosophy and the history of psychology. When one speaks of humanism, it brings to mind such psychologists as Allport, Goldstein, James, Murray, and Rogers. Humanism contributes a number of values to psychology, but one thing is certain: those values are not rooted in the determinism of either psychoanalysis or behaviorism. In other words, people are not products of the past, the unconscious, or the environment. Rather, they exercise free choice in the pursuit of their inner potential and self-actualization. They are not fragmented patchworks of cognitions, feelings, and aspirations—they are unified, whole, and unique beings. To understand is to appreciate those qualities and also to recognize that the clinician's most powerful tool is the realization that understanding can only be achieved by an awareness of the person's experience. So-called scientific constructs based upon norms, experiments, or data must give way to intuition and empathy. The emphasis is not on sickness, deviations, or diagnostic labels but upon positive striving, self-actualization, freedom, and naturalness. Bugental (1965), Buhler (1971), Buhler and Allen (1971), Jourard (1971), and Maslow (1962) have addressed various aspects of these values. In one form or another, humanism is expressed as a resistance to the positivistic determinism of science and as an active embrace of the essential humanity of people.

Existential therapy

Existential psychology rejects the mechanistic views of the Freudians and instead sees people as engaged in a search for meaning. At a time when so many are troubled by the massive problems of a technological society and seek to repair their alienated modes of living, existentialism has gained great popularity. It seems to promise the restoration of meaning to life, along with an increased spiritual awakening and individual growth that will bring freedom from the conventional shackles created by a conformist society (Bugental, 1978).

Hardly a unified movement that speaks with a single voice, the existential view actually turns out to be many views. Its roots lie deep in the philosophies of Kierkegaard, Heidegger, Tillich, Sartre, Jaspers, and others. When discussing the psychological applications of existentialism, such names as Binswanger, Boss, Gendlin, Frankl, May, and Laing come to mind. In some respects, existentialism springs from the same sources as does phenomenology (MacLeod, 1964; Van Kaam, 1966).

The existentialists make a number of assertions about human nature (Kobasa & Maddi, 1977; Maddi, 1989). Basic to all is a fundamental human characteristic: the search for meaning (Binswanger, 1963; Boss, 1963). Through imagination, symbolization, and judgment, that search is carried out in a matrix of participation in society.

A crucial facet of personality is decision making, which resorts to the world of both facts and possibilities. Thus, personality is not just what one is—a biological, social, and psychological being—but also what one might become. Many existentialists believe that decision making involves a set of inevitable choices. One can choose the present (the status quo), which represents lack of change and a commitment to the past. That choice will lead to guilt and remorse over missed opportunities. But one can also choose alliance with the future. That choice propels the person into the future with an anxiety that stems from the inability to predict and control the unknown. Such experiences of guilt and anxiety are not learned but are part of the essence of living. It requires courage to choose the future and suffer the inevitable anxieties that this choice entails. But a person can find that courage by having faith in self and by recognizing that choosing the past will inevitably lead to a guilt that is even more terrifying than anxiety.

The goals of therapy.   The ultimate goal of existential psychotherapy is to help the individual reach a point at which awareness and decision making can be exercised responsibly. The exercise of cognitive abilities will allow for the achievement of higher states of love, intimacy, and constructive social behavior. Through therapy, individuals must learn to accept responsibility for their own decisions and to tolerate the anxiety that accumulates as they move toward change. This involves self-trust as well as a capacity to accept those things in life that are unchangeable or inevitable.

Techniques.   Existential therapy does not emphasize techniques. Too often, techniques imply that the client is an object upon which they are applied. Instead, the emphasis is on understanding and experiencing the client as a unique essence. Therapy is an encounter that should enable the client to come closer to experience, and by experiencing self, the client in turn can learn to attach meaning and value to life. Sometimes the therapist will confront the client with questions — questions that force the client to examine the reasons for the failure to search for meaning in life. For example, a client who repeatedly complains that his job is not very fulfilling may be asked why he does not search for other employment or return to school for more training, and so on. Such questions may force the client to examine his orientation toward the past more closely, which can create feelings of guilt and emptiness. Gendlin (1969, 1981) discusses the concept of focusing as a means of reaching the preconceptual, felt sense. Focusing is achieved by having the client concentrate on the concretely felt bodily sense of that which is troubling, using silence as a means to help accomplish this. However, very few research studies that evaluate the effectiveness of focusing in treating clients have been published, and therefore its efficacy remains to be established (Greenberg et al., 1994).

Logotherapy

One of the most widely known forms of existential therapy is *logotherapy,* a technique that encourages the client to find meaning in what appears to be a callous, uncaring, and meaningless world. Viktor Frankl developed the technique of logotherapy. His early ideas were shaped by the Freudian influence, but he moved to an existential framework as he tried to find ways of dealing with experiences in Nazi concentration camps. He lost his mother, father, brother, and wife to the Nazi Holocaust and was himself driven to the brink of death (Frankl, 1963). It seemed to him that the persons who could not survive these camps were those who possessed only the conventional meanings of life to sustain them. But such conventional meanings could not come to grips with the realities of the Nazi atrocities. Therefore, what was required was a personal meaning for existence. From his wartime experiences and the existential insights that he felt permitted him to survive, Frankl developed logotherapy — the therapy of meaning. Many of his ideas are expressed in a series of books (Frankl, 1963, 1965, 1967).

Logotherapy is designed not to replace but to complement more traditional psychotherapy. However, when the essence of a particular emotional problem involves agonizing over the meaning or the futility of life, Frankl regards logotherapy as the specific therapy of choice. Logotherapy, then, strives to inculcate a sense of the client's own responsibility and obligations to life once the meaning of life has been unfolded. Frankl makes much of responsibility, regarding it as more important than historical events in the client's life. What is crucial is the meaning of the present and the outlook for the future.

In particular, two techniques described by Frankl (1960) have gained considerable exposure. *Paradoxical intention* is a popular technique in which the client is told to consciously attempt to perform the very behavior or response that is the object of anxiety and concern. Fear is thus replaced by a paradoxical wish. For example, suppose that a client complains that she is fearful of blushing when she speaks before a group. She would be instructed to try to blush on such occasions. According to Frankl, the paradoxical fact is that she will usually be unable to blush when she tries to do what she fears she will do. Typically, the therapist tries to handle all of this in a light tone. For example, in the case of a client fearful of trembling before his instructor, Frankl (1965) instructs the client to say to himself: "Oh, here is the instructor! Now I'll show him what a good trembler I am—I'll really show him how nicely I can tremble" (p. 226). This procedure resembles those of exposure therapy, which is discussed in Chapter 14, and some evidence suggests the effectiveness of these techniques (Shoham-Salomon & Rosenthal, 1987). The second technique outlined by Frankl, *de-reflection,* instructs the client to ignore a troublesome behavior or symptom. Many clients are exquisitely attuned to their own responses and bodily reactions, and de-reflection attempts to divert their attention to more constructive activities and reflections.

Frankl's views about personality and his ideas about the goals of therapy are generally quite consonant with our previous discussion of existentialism. However, it is not always clear that logotherapy techniques bear any close or rational relationship to the theory.

Gestalt therapy

In *Gestalt therapy,* the emphasis is on present experience and on the immediate awareness of emotion and action. Being in touch with one's feelings replaces the search for the origins of behavior. Existential problems expressed by a failure to find meaning in life have arisen in a technological society that separates people from themselves. The "unreality" of computers and plastic credit cards has overwhelmed the true meaning of life, which can only be found in the immediate experience of emotions. Gestalt therapy promises to restore the proper balance.

A movement of heterogeneity. Frederick (Fritz) Perls was the figure who was most closely identified with the development of the gestalt therapy movement. Perls's initial grounding was in medicine and psychoanalysis. He left Germany in 1934 after the Nazis came to power and settled in South Africa, where he established a psychoanalytic institute. As time went on, however, he began to move away from the tenets of psychoanalysis and toward the development of what was to become Gestalt therapy. In 1946, Perls emigrated to the United States, where he lived until his death in 1970.

It should be clear at the outset that Gestalt therapy is really a heterogeneous mix of techniques and ideas. Gestalt therapists do not agree among themselves, and at times they even seem to revel in their lack of agreement. Their goal does not seem to be the construction of a monolithic theory of therapy, but rather to

Figure 13-1
"Fritz" Perls, the colorful founder of Gestalt therapy as well as several Gestalt institutes in Cleveland, New York, and Los Angeles. Perls was also associated with the Esalen Institute at Big Sur, California. © *Esalen Institute/Photo by Paul Herbert*

express through their therapy their own sense of uniqueness and their interpretation of life. Even the contribution of Perls himself was hardly a model of consistency. Some of his major works—*Ego, Hunger, and Aggression* (Perls, 1947), *Gestalt Therapy* (Perls, Hefferline, & Goodman, 1951), *Gestalt Therapy Verbatim* (Perls, 1969a), and *In and Out of the Garbage Pail* (Perls, 1969b)—express a variety of notions. Adding to the confusion is the fact that Gestalt therapy does not really have very much to do with the Gestalt principles of Wertheimer, Koffka, Köhler, or Lewin. The connections are more superficial than substantive. Kempler (1973) provides an account of Gestalt therapy theory, as does Smith (1976).

Basic notions.   Central to Gestalt therapy is the conceptualization of the person as an organized whole, not as a disjointed collection of emotions, cognitions, and behaviors. Also running through accounts of Gestalt therapy is the admonition that individuals must develop an awareness not only of themselves but also of the ways in which they defeat themselves. This awareness is reached through the expression of what one is feeling *now,* on a moment-to-moment basis. That which is impeding progress toward a higher plane of adjustment must be experienced, so that it, too, becomes a part of awareness. Presumably, the person's inner potential is capable of overcoming problems in adjustment, but first there must be awareness of both the obstacles to improved adjustment and the inner potential itself.

The Gestalt therapist does not give the client reasons for the ineffective use of potential or tell the client how it all got started. Instead, the therapist serves as a catalytic agent who facilitates the client's awareness of how inner potential is being deflected from expression and who shows clients that the responsibility for more effective experiences resides within themselves. The emphasis is on momentary awareness and not on the recovery of memories or repressed impulses. However, even though Perls rejected many features of psychoanalysis, his approach is really an amalgam of existentialism and psychoanalysis. For example, he seems to readily accept the importance of traditional psychoanalytic insights regarding the nature of motivation and defense.

The now. For Perls, reality is now, behavior is now, and experience is now. To seek answers in the past is to deal with that which no longer exists. Therapy is now, and it must deal with and encourage the client's awareness of that "now." The individual's capacity for growth can only be realized by attacking anything that threatens to divert awareness from the now. As Perls (1970) put it: "To me, nothing exists except the now. Now = experience = awareness = reality. The past is no more and the future not yet. Only the *now* exists" (p. 14).

For the Gestalt therapist, anxiety is the gap between now and later—a preoccupation with what the future may bring. Being preoccupied with the past creates a host of negative emotions as well. A focus on either the past or the future, then, leads to an immobilization of the individual in the present. During therapy the patient is required to repeat, "Now I am aware. . . ." Or the therapist will frequently ask, "What are you aware of now?" The role of the therapist is one of constantly calling the patient's attention to present feelings, thoughts, and experiencing. However, the therapist does not interpret, since it is assumed the awareness of the now has its own curative powers that will enable patients to integrate the formerly disavowed aspects of their personality.

Nonverbal behavior. In order to probe the patient's defenses and expose any games being played, the therapist often pays close attention to nonverbal behavior. The patient may say one thing but suggest the opposite through various cues. Take the following example:

Therapist: How are you feeling?
Patient: I'm calm; I feel good.
Therapist: You are, really?
Patient: Oh yes.
Therapist: Why are you sitting so stiff, like a ramrod?
Patient: I'm not!
Therapist: Check yourself. See your legs, feel your back against the chair?
Patient: I see what you mean.
Therapist: Let the stiffness talk. What is it telling you?
Patient: I'm afraid to let go—I feel like I'm trying to control myself.

By paying attention to nonverbal cues, the therapist was able to cut right through to a significant experience. The therapist then used the posture cue to get to present feelings and to help the patient get in touch with those feelings.

Dreams. The psychoanalyst asks the patient to associate to various elements of dreams. The Gestalt therapist, in contrast, attempts to get the patient to relive the dream now, in the therapy room. This means even acting out the dream. According to the Gestalt therapist, interpretation leads only to an intellectualized insight; to discover the inner self, the patient must confront the dream experience directly. A dream conveys messages or even epitomizes the conflicting sides of the self. It is a kind of condensed reflection of the individual's own existence and of the ways used to avoid that existence. By playing the part of various persons or objects in the dream, that individual can learn to recognize and identify the alienated parts of the self and, then, to integrate them.

Topdog-underdog. When conflicts involve opposing aspects of the personality, the patient may be asked to take each part in a dialogue. The opposing parts are usually analogous to Freud's superego and id. The *topdog* is the superego and contains the introjected "shoulds" of the personality (parental dictates and the like). The *underdog* is similar to the id—it is primitive, evasive, and constantly disruptive of the efforts of the topdog. By playing both roles in a dialogue, the patient can integrate these two conflicting aspects of the self.

The defenses. In Gestalt therapy, the aim is to expose the games clients play and the defenses behind which they hide. As Perls explains it, neurotic behavior is explicable in terms of layers. In the first layer, the client plays games, avoids facing the self, and in general is not an authentic person. Gestalt therapy forces the client to experience and become aware of these shams. But this awareness is threatening because it leads to an experience of the very fears that the shams helped evade. Genuine behavior is threatening because such behavior could lead to terrible consequences (or so the client hypothesizes). Indeed, as environmental supports are also exposed, the client really becomes terrified, feeling that the inner capacity for growth is not equal to the relinquishing of neurotic defenses in favor of honest, independent behavior. Finally, however, the client becomes aware of the hollowness that the anxieties, phobias, or doubts are producing. Such awareness then propels the person into an experience of aliveness, wholeness, and authenticity.

Responsibility. Of great importance in Gestalt therapy is getting clients to accept responsibility for their own actions and feelings. These belong to the client, and the client cannot deny them, escape them, or blame them on something or someone else. Therefore, if one had to extract from Gestalt therapy expositions the four most descriptive words, these might well be *awareness, experience, now,* and *responsibility.*

The rules. The "rules" of Gestalt therapy (Levitsky & Perls, 1970) require that:

1. Communication be in the present tense (looking backward or forward is discouraged).
2. Communication be between equals (one talks with, not at).

3. The participants use "I" language rather than "it" language (to encourage the acceptance of responsibility).
4. The client continually focus on immediate experience (for example, the therapist will ask, "How does it feel to describe the hostility?" "Tell me what you are feeling at this moment").
5. There be no gossip (in other words, talking about someone rather than to him).
6. Questions be discouraged (since so often questions are quiet ways of stating opinions rather than seeking information).

Gestalt games.   The Gestaltists have received much attention for the so-called games they have developed (Levitsky & Perls, 1970). For example, clients are taught to add the phrase *and I take responsibility for that* when describing something about themselves; thus, "I am not a very happy person . . . and I take responsibility for that." Another game involves getting the client to repeat again and again (and louder and louder) some phrase or remark that the therapist deems important. Often, various aspects of role playing are employed. To what extent any positive effects from these games are generalized beyond the therapy room has not yet been established empirically.

Moral precepts.   The *moral precepts* of Gestalt therapy—or rules for patients to live by—are described by Naranjo (1970). They are:

1. Live now (in other words, be concerned not with the past or the future but with the present).
2. Live here (in other words, be concerned with that which is present and not with that which is absent).
3. Stop imagining (in other words, experience only the real).
4. Stop unnecessary thinking (in other words, be oriented toward hearing, seeing, smelling, tasting, and touching).
5. Express directly—do not explain, judge, or manipulate.
6. Be aware of both the pleasant and the unpleasant.
7. Reject all "shoulds" and "oughts" that are not your own.
8. Take complete responsibility for your actions, thoughts, and feelings.
9. Surrender to being what you really are.

Concluding comment.   As indicated in Chapter 11, Smith et al. (1980) reported an effect size of 0.64 for Gestalt therapies based on a large meta-analysis of relevant studies. The average client who received Gestalt therapy in these studies was functioning better than 74% of those not receiving treatment. Unfortunately, very little research on Gestalt therapy has been published since this review. Of those studies that have appeared between 1978 and 1992, none suggest that Gestalt therapy is more effective than other forms of treatment and some suggest that it may be less effective (Greenberg et al., 1994). One reason we know relatively little about the effectiveness of Gestalt therapy is that most Gestalt therapists are vehemently opposed to the idea of research. For reasons that are not always clear, evaluation research is seen almost as an antihumanistic endeavor.

Gestalt therapy took root in America in an era of social turmoil and alienation. As a result, its most suitable clientele may turn out to be young, well-educated people whose problems center on personal estrangement and alienation. Therapists who have a gestalt orientation sometimes seem to do especially well with overly intellectualized people who have college educations and who have lost touch with their feelings and immediate experience. It will certainly not be an antidote suitable for all patients—no therapy is. However, it remains to be seen whether Gestalt therapy will become more than a flashy solution and whether it will be able to successfully address itself to the problems in living that a wide range of patients bring with them to therapy. By dealing only with the present, Gestalt therapy runs the danger of becoming a short-lived solution that replaces the search for meaning with a hedonism that can be quite attractive to some whose brush with a powerful, technocratic society has left them inhibited and overcontrolled. At the same time, Gestalt therapy has already demonstrated a staying power greater than many expected.

■ Summary Evaluation of Phenomenological and Humanistic-Existential Therapies

As we have mentioned throughout this chapter, surprisingly few empirically sound studies evaluating the effectiveness of client-centered, Gestalt, and other existential therapies have been conducted. This is somewhat ironic, given that Carl Rogers was a pioneer in psychotherapy research. Although some believe that this state of affairs is changing (Greenberg et al., 1994), the relative lack of well-controlled outcome studies makes an evaluation of the effectiveness of these therapies difficult. Based on this limited database, it does appear that these therapies are modestly effective but, again, no more so than any other form of treatment. More research is clearly needed, especially studies investigating the clinical conditions for which these approaches are most appropriate. The general phenomenological and humanistic-existential therapies presented in this chapter, like all therapeutic approaches, offer a mixed bag of contributions and problems. The reader will recall that several of the following points were made earlier about Rogerian approaches specifically.

Contributions
Let us begin with an enumeration of some of the chief contributions of the phenomenological and humanistic-existential perspectives.

Experience. By stressing the importance of inner experience and awareness, these therapies have helped reaffirm the view that clinicians must rely on something more than the sheer quantification or enumeration of stimulus-environment conditions. Human experiences run the gamut from knowing to joy to agony, and clinical psychologists can ill afford to ignore them in either their theories or their therapies. The phenomenological-humanistic-existential axis has brought them in touch once more with the essential data of experience and awareness.

Choices. The phenomenological and humanistic-existential therapies also are reminders that humans are more than just concatenations of instincts, urges, and habits. We are not simply automatons that respond to stimuli—we make choices, we decide, we change, we examine ourselves, and yes, we even invent such words as *existential* and *humanistic*. Human beings are not only the objects of study; they are also the initiators of study. For perhaps too many years, psychology has tried to deny its essential human qualities by slavishly following the paths of the biologists and the physicists. Although the controversy over free will versus determinism is unlikely to be resolved soon, there does seem to be a growing recognition that a simple deterministic view of the individual can be sterile and unproductive.

The present.   By emphasizing the present, phenomenologists have helped the field to cast aside the view that positive change can only be achieved by insight into the past or by some enlightened awareness of the true nature of the unconscious. By exercising choice and responsibility, we can all mold the present and thereby escape the constrictions of the past.

The relationship.   Many of the therapies described in this chapter have attached great value to the therapeutic relationship. In these therapies, this often represents a triumph of relationship over technique. Conventional therapies had long recommended a detached therapist who exercised benign interest and cool skill. Whether the newly prescribed role is a passive yet unconditional positive regard, an acceptance, or a jumping in feet first to "have an encounter" with the patient, things have certainly changed. The nature of the therapeutic relationship is obviously of crucial importance, and indeed it may be a major contributor to the success or failure of any brand of therapy. This is now recognized, so that the relationship is no longer something that serves as a given or as an unobtrusive therapeutic backdrop. It has become a major part of the foreground, thanks, in part, to phenomenologists and to humanistic-existential therapists.

Growth.   For many years, the emphasis in therapy has been on psychopathology, sickness, or behavioral deficits; the humanists and the existentialists, however, have placed the emphasis on positive growth. They look not so much for sickness as for self-actualizing tendencies or growth potential. They seek not to contain pathology but to liberate awareness, feeling, being, peak experiences, and freedom. This is heady language that may sometimes exhilarate to the point of confusion. But it does point out an essential emphasis on the positive rather than a sometimes depressing and stultifying emphasis on the negative. Thus, the goal has become personal growth and not just the healing of psychopathology. As a result, many institutes, growth centers, encounter groups, and weekend retreats have sprung up to serve those who feel the need for experiences that will expand their awareness and heighten their authenticity as human beings.

Problems

Now we can turn to the problem side of the coin as we evaluate the phenomenological and humanistic-existential approaches.

Prejudicial language.   At times it seems that the general humanistic movement can, like the more specific client-centered approach, be accused of the prejudicial use of language. The constant use of such words as *humanistic, ac-*

ceptance, freedom, self-fulfillment, growth, and authentic seems to suggest by implication that all other approaches preach inhumanity, rejection, authoritarianism, emptiness, and phoniness. Yet nearly all of the psychoanalysts, psychiatrists, behaviorists, cognitive therapists, and eclectic psychotherapists are accepting persons who care a great deal; who are interested, involved, and permissive; and who try to do the best job possible to help their patients experience richer and more fulfilling lives. In short, not all the attributes that are said to be the core of the humanistic movement are its private domain.

Emphasis on feelings.

The reliance on subjective experience and feelings in these approaches binds the clinician to a source of data that can be unreliable, biased, or self-serving, and devoid of the most human of all qualities — reason. The real issue is whether feelings or transcendental awareness can, unleavened by sober analysis, reason, and insight, lead the individual into a durable adjustment that will increase both personal satisfactions and social contributions. It seems evident now that most individuals cannot work their way out of problems and private terrors solely by the application of cold analysis and reason. But it does not seem likely that trips into what can be a quagmire of subjectivity will enable them to do so either. Perhaps the lesson here is that any single method or route is likely to be incomplete and, therefore, less than successful. Human beings think, act, feel, experience, look to the past for guidance, and are pulled into the future by their aspirations. Any approach that focuses on behavior alone or experience alone or insight alone ignores much that is a central part of the human being. When such single-edged approaches work (at least for a while), it is probably because they confront individuals with an aspect of themselves that they had long ignored. For example, an inhibited, overintellectual, repressed patient may find great joy and happiness as he works himself through an "emotional now," guided by a sensitive therapist. But any long-term abandonment of intellect and reason is likely to lead to other problems.

Anti-intellectualism.

At times the humanistic-existential movement strikes a vigorous anti-intellectual and antiscientific pose that rejects the possibility of any meaningful contributions being made by science. To the extent that psychotherapy had become tied to a science that was too behavioral, too insight-oriented, or too rooted in a sterile scientific method, this pose has helped return many clinical psychologists to important facets of the human organism. But complete rejection of science, the past, the unconscious, the role of insight, or the modification of behavior through planned consequences seems to be a narrow and dangerous course. Although the fervor of those who urge such a course can be compelling and contagious, it seems likely that, ultimately, unchecked fervor will be no more convincing than, for example, the unbridled operationalism of psychological science.

Phenomenal field.

Another problem is that of knowing the nature of another person's subjective experience. Phenomenology instructs that behavior is determined by the individual's phenomenal field as it exists at any moment in time. This places the therapist in the position of having to know the patient's inner world of experience in order to understand or predict. Yet, how do clinicians climb into that world? How do they escape from the past experiences that have shaped their own perceptions? How do clinicians gain an unbiased appreciation of the patient's phenomenal awareness? It almost seems that the phenomenological viewpoint demands something of clinicians that, given all humans' very imperfect and biased nature, is impossible for them to achieve.

The problem is not with an empathic attempt to get close to the patient's experience or to try to put oneself in the patient's shoes—it is always useful to search one's own experience in order to better relate to the patient's feelings or predicaments (while recognizing the ever-present danger of bias). The problem lies in the clinician's exclusive reliance on an exact knowledge of the patient's inner experience in order to operate.

Assessment.   In many of the humanistic-existential approaches, there is a total disregard for assessment and diagnosis, reinforced by the belief that such methods interfere with or even destroy the empathic relationship. Assessment is seen as impinging upon the freedom and dignity of the individual. It is believed to thwart the self-actualizing potential of the patient by imposing a conceptualization from the therapist.

Many will agree that diagnosis is not always necessary in its more full-blown manifestations. Indeed, the humanistic-existential movement has rendered a real service by pointing out some of clinical psychology's diagnostic excesses and by suggesting that too often diagnostic emphasis is on pathology instead of the growth potential or strengths of patients. It is all too true that diagnosis has often become a search for weaknesses rather than strengths and assets.

But if clinical psychologists were to totally reject assessment, where would this leave them? With the patient's verbal report, perhaps—with all its potential for distortion and incompleteness. Faith in patients' abilities to solve their problems through getting in touch with their own feelings may work well with intelligent, introspective, sophisticated young persons who are not terribly disturbed; but what about the patient who is psychotic or the patient who is burdened with psychosomatic problems? And how shall one deal with the nonverbal person who has only a minimal education and has never learned to look inward? Does the clinician ignore assessment in the case of the person who is having adjustment problems and may also be retarded? No one, of course, condones diagnoses that are nothing more than mindless labeling. But the prohibition against all assessment seems to assure that therapists will remain more ignorant than they need be.

Technique-centered.   Perhaps many humanistic-existential clinicians disregard assessment in part because they treat every patient alike. Many of these clinicians seem to have an abiding faith that every troubled soul can be rescued by acceptance, positive regard, the assertion of responsibility for self, and so on. If that is so, then diagnosis does indeed become superfluous. But if this is the case, then the charge of many humanistic existentialists that psychoanalysis or behavior therapies are technique-centered can be turned against them as well. To the extent that everyone who enters the therapy room is seen as having the same basic problem—with the "cure" always the same—then, in a sense, such approaches are themselves technique-centered. Increasingly, however, clinicians seem to be recognizing the need to develop data that will allow them to select from among several treatment possibilities the one most suitable for a given patient. Such recognition should enhance the role of diagnosis in the future.

Obscure language. A final problem for many who seek to understand what it is that the humanistic-existential movement offers revolves about another aspect of the language employed. Part of this difficulty lies in the lack of cohesiveness within the movement—there are so many thematic variations that the language readily becomes vague and ill defined. But beyond this, there is often a wild, undisciplined quality to the writing that almost assures that variable meanings will be applied. The terminology is so vague that almost any interpretation is possible. It is almost as if the language has taken on a life of its own. In fact, it is possible to string together words in such a way that they sound exactly like a profound discourse in humanistic-existential psychology, even though the writer does not have the foggiest notion of what they mean. It is very like the comedian who can imitate speaking in a foreign language without ever using real words—only some characteristic sounds and emphases are necessary.

From Maslow, Perls, Bugental, Boss, Binswanger, Rogers, and others come such phrases and terms as *internal silence, from-here-to-there rhythmic awareness exercises, metaneeds, peak experiences, Dasein, authenticity, I-process, being, encounter,* and *sick point.* Granted, every theory seems to contain its share of neologisms and jargon, but the humanistic-existentialist movement seems to be especially well endowed with such terms. The language does serve to underline the movement's conscious divorce from any alliance with science; but in "humanizing" its language, the movement may have also erected barriers against the more widespread acceptance of its important contributions.

■ Focus Questions

1. What are the major features that characterize client-centered therapists?
2. How do client-centered therapists view diagnosis and psychological assessment?
3. What are the advantages and disadvantages of client-centered therapy?
4. What techniques are used by existential therapists? What techniques are used by Gestalt therapists?
5. From the research evidence that is available, how would you evaluate the effectiveness of client-centered and Gestalt therapy?

■ Key Terms

client-centered therapy	moral precepts
congruence	paradoxical intention
de-reflection	person-centered approach
empathy	phenomenal self
existential psychology	phenomenology
Gestalt games	self
growth potential	self-actualization
humanism	unconditional positive regard
logotherapy	

14

Psychotherapy: Behavioral and Cognitive-Behavioral Perspectives

Behavioral and cognitive-behavioral therapies, often together referred to as *behavior therapy* (Goldfried & Davison, 1994), have become a major force in clinical psychology. A constant flow of books appears that provide wide-ranging discussions of the theory, technique, and application for an extensive variety of these methods (for example, Eysenck & Rachman, 1980; Fishman, Rotgers, & Franks, 1988; Kazdin, 1989; Masters, Burish, Hollon, & Rimm, 1987; O'Leary & Wilson, 1987; Turner, Calhoun, & Adams, 1992). Behavior therapy has truly come of age and is now a force to be reckoned with (Wilson & Franks, 1982). In fact, it has reached the stage of maturity where it can boast not only of its successes but also admit its failures (Foa & Emmelkamp, 1983).

■ The Behavioral Approach

We will begin our discussion of behavior therapy by commenting on definitions and then moving into a brief presentation of historical matters.

Definition

The diversity of behavioral approaches to therapy makes a satisfactory definition almost impossible. Some definitions are couched largely in the terminology of operant conditioning (Skinner, 1971). Others are clothed in the style of classical conditioning (Wolpe, 1958). For still others, the emphasis is on general principles of learning (Ullman & Krasner, 1969) or may even have strikingly cognitive overtones (Meichenbaum, 1977). In light of this diversity, Goldfried and Davison (1994) were moved to comment:

> We believe that behavior therapy is more appropriately construed as reflecting a general orientation to clinical work that aligns itself philosophically with an experimental approach to the study of human behavior. The assumption basic to this particular orientation is that the problematic behaviors seen within the clinical setting can best be understood in light of those principles derived from a wide variety of psychological

experimentation, and that these principles have implications for behavior change within the clinical setting. (pp. 3–4)

Traditionally, the behavioral approach allies itself with a scientific emphasis and a deemphasis on the role of inferred variables. The behaviorists are likely to trace their origins to the "science" of Skinner or Pavlov rather than the "mentalism" of Freud. The attention is on stimuli and responses rather than variables that are presumed to mediate them. However, as we shall discuss later in this chapter, behavior therapy over the years has broadened its scope to include techniques that address cognitive and other mediational processes (Goldfried & Davison, 1994). Nevertheless, it is instructive to review behavior therapy's historical roots.

A brief history

We begin our story by citing the work of Watson and Rayner (1920), who conducted the widely quoted laboratory study of Albert and the white rat. This study was in effect a demonstration of how a neurosis can develop in a child. In the tradition of Pavlovian conditioning, Albert was given a white rat to play with. But each time that this was done, a loud noise was introduced simultaneously. After a few such trials, the white rat (previously a neutral stimulus) elicited a fearful response that also generalized to similar furry objects.

Mary Cover Jones (1924) demonstrated how such learned fears can be removed. A 3-year-old boy, Peter, was afraid of rabbits, rats, and other such objects. To eradicate the fear, Jones brought a caged rabbit closer and closer as the boy was eating. The feared object thus became associated with food, and after a few months Peter's fear of the rabbit disappeared entirely. It is important, however, to recall Jones's admonition that the fear of the rabbit must not be so intense that the child will develop an aversion to food. Watson's conditioning of fears and Jones's "reconditioning" of them were direct antecedents of the development of Wolpe's therapy by reciprocal inhibition (1958), which arrived upon the scene some 30 years later.

As the foregoing experiences of Albert and Peter suggest, the major theoretical underpinnings of the behavior therapy movement were Pavlovian conditioning and Hullian learning theory. In the 1950s, Joseph Wolpe and Arnold Lazarus in South Africa and Hans Eysenck at Maudsley Hospital in London began to apply the results of animal research to the acquisition and elimination of anxiety in humans. Wolpe began to experiment with the reduction of fears in humans by having patients imagine the situations in which their fears occurred. The patients did this, however, while in a state of heightened relaxation. Wolpe's technique of *systematic desensitization,* like Jones's reconditioning work, provided a practical demonstration of how principles of learning could be applied in the clinical setting. In his work on conditioned reflex therapy, Salter (1949) also attempted to develop a method of therapy that was derived from the Pavlovian tradition.

It is important to note that these investigators did not merely introduce new techniques—they also argued vigorously that their techniques were derived from the framework of a systematic experimental science. In addition, they took pains to point out that their demonstrations of the origins and treatment of neurotic fears proved that it was unnecessary to subscribe to the "mentalistic demonology" of Freudianism or to the "psychiatric pigeonholing" practiced by Kraepelinians.

At about the same time that Wolpe, Lazarus, and Eysenck were developing their conditioning procedures, the operant tradition was beginning to have an impact. Skinner and his colleagues (Lindsley & Skinner, 1954; Skinner, 1953) were demonstrating that the behavior of hospitalized psychotic patients could be modified by operant procedures. By establishing controlled environments to ensure that certain responses of the patient would be followed by specific consequences, significant behavioral changes were produced.

At first there was a radical quality to behavior therapy, such that the inner world of the patient was largely ignored in the rush to focus on behavior. Whether out of a reaction to the mentalism of psychoanalysis or out of an overly provincial view of what should be the subject matter of science, the early behavior therapists studiously avoided anything of a cognitive nature. However, in 1954, Julian Rotter published his book *Social Learning and Clinical Psychology*. In it he demonstrated convincingly that a motivation-reinforcement approach to psychology could be coupled with a cognitive-expectancy approach. Thus, behavior was regarded as being determined both by the value of reinforcements and by the expectancy that such reinforcements would occur following the behavior in question. What is more, Rotter's novel views were supported by a series of laboratory studies that left no doubt that one could be clinical, oriented toward both learning theory and cognitive theory, and scientifically respectable, all at the same time. Also significant in this context was the application of Albert Bandura's (1969) social learning contributions to the modification of behavior. It was theorists such as Rotter and Bandura who led the way to the current cognitive emphasis which is giving behavior therapy a more wide-ranging and serviceable character (Goldfried & Davison, 1994; Meichenbaum, 1977).

It is important to point out that the "mentalism" of psychoanalysis or other psychodynamic approaches is not the same as the "cognitive processes" concepts that are employed today. Freud's references to thinking processes were never defined operationally; they were vague notions incapable of objective measurement or poorly anchored either to antecedent conditions or consequent outcomes. More often than not, Freud viewed thinking processes as irrational and distorting rather than as problem-solving processes. In addition, for Freud, mentalism seemed to function largely in the service of the reified ego, id, and superego—little people who ran about the mind distorting, projecting, condemning, or figuring out ways of fooling one another. In contrast, current notions of cognition emphasize such concepts as expectancies or memory processes. These are concepts that can be quantified and objectively defined in ways that lead to reliable understanding among separate investigators.

■ Techniques of Behavior Therapy

Before we discuss specific behavioral techniques, let us note both the importance of the therapeutic relationship and the tendency of modern behavioral therapists to employ multiple techniques with the same patient.

The relationship

In their explanation of the success of their therapeutic methods, many behavior therapists seem to ignore the relationship as a contributing factor. Yet in Wolpe's accounts of systematic desensitization (1958), the therapist is exhorted to adopt an attitude of acceptance toward patients, to explain their difficulties to them, and to make clear to them the behavioral rationale for treatment. Furthermore, Morris and Suckerman (1974) have found that, in the case of college students with snake phobias, a warm therapeutic atmosphere significantly enhances the therapeutic value of systematic desensitization procedures. Lazarus (1971b) and Wilkins (1971) have also contended that the relationship makes an important contribution to the success of behavioral therapy. At times, behavior therapists have been said to be cold and mechanistic in their approach to patients. This is probably more myth or stereotype than fact. Indeed, Sloane, Staples, Cristol, Yorkston, and Whipple (1975a) found that behavior therapists were generally warmer and more empathic than other psychotherapists.

None of this is meant to suggest that behavior therapy can be reduced to nothing more than subtle relationship factors; what is suggested here, however, is that one can never afford to ignore aspects of the relationship as contributors to successful therapeutic intervention. After all, it is through the therapy relationship that the patient's expectations of help can be nurtured so that behavioral therapy will be accepted as a viable alternative (Goldfried & Davison, 1994). Stated another way, behavior therapy is not going to be successful if the patient expects it to fail or is otherwise antagonistic toward it.

Broad spectrum of treatment

Behavior therapists employ a variety of specific techniques—not only for different patients but for the same patient at different points in the overall treatment process. Lazarus (1971b) refers to this as *broad spectrum behavior therapy.* As specific techniques are described in the following pages, the reader must realize that each can serve a specific purpose but that, in reality, they are complementary. For example, a woman who has trouble coping with a domineering husband may undergo assertiveness training to learn specific behaviors. But when she uses these behaviors, other sets of fears about their relationship may begin to worry her. Therefore, she may also require therapeutic sessions that will help her restructure her beliefs about the marriage that are illogical and tend to perpetuate her submissive behavior. She might also participate in modeling or observational learning to help her cope.

Systematic desensitization

Systematic desensitization is typically applied when a patient has the capacity to respond adequately to a particular situation (or class of situations), yet reacts with anxiety, fear, or avoidance. Developed by Salter (1949) and Wolpe (1958), systematic desensitization is a technique to reduce anxiety, and it is based upon the apparently simple principle that one cannot simultaneously be relaxed and anxious. The idea is to teach patients to relax and then, while they are in the relaxed state, to introduce a gradually increasing series of anxiety-producing stimuli.

Eventually, the patient becomes desensitized to the feared stimuli by virtue of having experienced them in a relaxed state.

Technique and procedures.   Systematic desensitization begins with the collection of a history of the patient's problem, including information about specific precipitating conditions and developmental factors. Collecting a history may require several interviews, and it often includes the administration of questionnaires. The principle reason for all of this is to pinpoint the locus of the patient's anxiety as well as to determine whether systematic desensitization is the proper treatment. In a patient with adequate coping potential who nevertheless reacts to certain situations with severe anxiety, desensitization is often appropriate. On the other hand, if a patient lacks certain skills and then becomes anxious in situations that require those skills, desensitization could be inappropriate and counterproductive. For example, if a man becomes seriously anxious in social situations that involve dancing, it would seem more efficient to see that he learns to dance rather than desensitize him to what is, in fact, a behavioral deficit.

Next, the problem is explained to the patient. Normally this explanation might be elaborated to include examples from the patient's life and to cover the manner in which the anxieties were acquired and are now maintained. Following this, the rationale for systematic desensitization is also explained. The explanations and the illustrations should be in language that the patient will understand—free from scientific jargon—and the entire process of interviewing, assessment, and explanation should be conducted with warmth, acceptance, and understanding. In a sense, the clinician uses this phase to sell the patient on the efficacy of systematic desensitization.

The next two stages involve the establishment of an anxiety hierarchy and training in relaxation. While work is begun on the anxiety hierarchy, training in relaxation is also started, as the following section illustrates.

Relaxation.   To accomplish the relaxation-training phase of systematic desensitization, the progressive relaxation methods of Jacobson (1938) are frequently employed. According to this approach, the patient is first taught to tense and relax particular muscle groups and then to distinguish between sensations of relaxation and tensing. Generally, about six sessions are devoted to relaxation training, and the instructions can easily be taped and played at home for practice. In some instances, hypnosis may be utilized to induce relaxation; in other instances, the patient may be asked to imagine relaxing scenes; and in still other instances, breathing exercises are used to enhance relaxation.

The anxiety hierarchy.   In discussions about specific problems, the situations in which they occur, and their development, the patient and the therapist work together to construct what is known as an *anxiety hierarchy*. The recurrent themes in the patient's difficulties and anxieties are isolated and then ordered in terms of their power to induce anxiety—from situations that provoke very low levels of anxiety through situations that precipitate extreme anxiety reactions. A typical anxiety hierarchy consists of 20 to 25 items in approximately equal intervals from low to moderate to extreme. The following anxiety hierarchy is that of a 24-year-old female student who experienced severe examination anxiety (Wolpe, 1973, p. 116):

1. Four days before an examination.
2. Three days before an examination.
3. Two days before an examination.
4. One day before an examination.
5. The night before an examination.
6. The examination paper lies face down before her.
7. Awaiting the distribution of examination papers.
8. Before the unopened doors of the examination room.
9. In the process of answering an examination paper.
10. On the way to the university on the day of the examination.

This hierarchy illustrates two points: first, it is organized largely along spatial temporal lines; and, second, the items are not exactly organized in a logical fashion. One might expect item 10 (the most anxiety-provoking item) to be placed near the middle of the hierarchy. This suggests how idiosyncratic hierarchies can be—after all, it is the patient's anxiety, not the clinician's!

In the desensitization procedure, the patient is asked to imagine the weakest item in the hierarchy (the item that provokes the least anxiety) while being completely relaxed. The therapist describes the scene, and the patient imagines for about ten seconds being in the scene. The therapist moves the patient up the hierarchy gradually, between two and five items per session. However, if at any time the level of anxiety begins to increase, the patient is instructed to signal, whereupon the therapist requests that the patient stop visualizing that scene. The therapist then helps the patient to relax once more. After a few minutes, the procedure can be started up again. Over a period of several sessions the patient will, ideally, be able to imagine the highest item in the hierarchy without discomfort. A typical example of the instructions given to a male patient during desensitization is provided by Goldfried and Davison (1994):

> (*The client has been relaxing on his own in the reclining chair.*) OK, now just keep relaxing like that, nice and calm and comfortable. You may find it helpful to imagine a scene that is personally calm and relaxing, something we'll refer to as your pleasant scene . . . . Fine. Now, you recall that 0 to 100 scale we've been using in your relaxation practice, where 0 indicates complete relaxation and 100 maximum tension. Tell me approximately where you'd place yourself on that scale. . . . (*Therapist is advised to look for a rating that reflects considerable calm and relaxation, often in the range of 15 to 25.*)
>
> Fine. Soon I shall ask you to imagine a scene. After you hear the description of the situation, please imagine it as vividly as you can, through your own eyes, as if you were actually there. Try to include all the details in the scene. While you're visualizing the situation, you may continue feeling as relaxed as you are now. If so, that's good. After 5, 10, or 15 seconds, I'll ask you to stop imagining the scene and return to your pleasant image and to just relax. But if you begin to feel even the slightest increase in anxiety or tension, please signal this to me by raising your left forefinger. When you do this, I'll step in and ask you to stop imagining the situation and then will help you get relaxed once more. It's important that you indicate tension to me in this way, as we want to maximize your being exposed to fearful situations without feeling anxious. OK? Do you have any questions? . . . Fine, we'll have ample opportunity afterwards to discuss things in full. (pp. 124–125)

Figure 14-1
Joseph Wolpe has been primarily identified with the development of systematic
    desensitization as a method of reducing neurotic anxiety. *Courtesy of
    Joseph Wolpe*

A Case Illustration

In order to select the most useful hierarchy, one must determine exactly what
is prompting the patient's anxiety reactions. To illustrate the importance of selecting the appropriate hierarchy, let us consider the following example, in which
it appeared at first that the problem was essentially a simple matter of a woman's
discomfort when eating in a restaurant with her husband's business associates:

> *Therapist:* Can you tell me what it is about these business dinners which up-
>   set you? For instance, are they formal, and are you on the spot as a sort
>   of reluctant hostess having to entertain people who do not really mean
>   anything to you?
> *Patient:* I guess so.
> *Therapist:* Don't let me put words in your mouth. Think carefully. Picture
>   yourself in the situation right now. Imagine that you are at a restaurant
>   with your husband and his colleagues, and tell me what associations and
>   feelings you have.
> *Patient:* (*Closes her eyes*) It makes me angry and I don't see why I have to
>   be subjected to it.
> *Therapist:* What does your husband say?
> *Patient:* Oh, Herb says it brings in more business.
> *Therapist:* How often do these business dinners arise?

Patient: About once a month.

Therapist: How do they come about?

Patient: How do you mean?

Therapist: I mean how does Herb let you know about them?

Patient: Oh, he comes home and says, "Honey, is it all right if we take the Ryans and two other couples to the Red Goblet a week from Friday?" And I usually say, "Why bother to ask?"

Therapist: So a verbal battle ensues and by the time the dinner date is reached, you and Herb have been at each other's throats for about two weeks and a thoroughly tense atmosphere prevails.

Patient: Well, I resent it.

Therapist: Why?

Patient: What do you mean?

Therapist: You know what I mean. What is really behind all this resentment?

Patient: I simply don't like dining with the Ryans and the Millers and the rest of those money grabbers.

Therapist: Wait, let's go back. You said that you have only felt this way since Herb went into the marketing field last year.

Patient: Well, let me explain. He used to work for my dad, and when he died about two years ago, Herb took over the business.

Therapist: Let me guess. Was your father in charge of the marketing setup before he died?

Patient: What has that got to do with it?

Therapist: (*Remains silent*)

Patient: Oh for heaven's sake! You think I resent Herb because he's taken over my dad's position.

Therapist: Well?

Patient: Well, it never struck me that way before.

As the interview progressed, it became obvious that we were not dealing with a specific "sensitivity to dining in a restaurant with husband and his business associates," but to a basic resentment concerning the patient's feelings that her husband was "less of a man than her father" . . . and desensitization was directed toward a death-of-father dimension.[1]

Rationale. Although Wolpe's explanation for the success of systematic desensitization is based on the principle of *counterconditioning*—the substitution of relaxation for anxiety—others are not so sure (Davison & Wilson, 1973). For example, some have argued that the operative process is really *extinction;* that is, when the patient repeatedly visualizes anxiety-generating situations without ensuing bad experiences, the anxiety responses are eventually extinguished (Wilson & Davison, 1971). Alternatively, Mathews (1971) argues on behalf of a *habituation* hypothesis. According to this view, decreases in physiological, self-report, and behavioral measures of anxiety result from repeated exposure to fear-generating

[1]From *Behavior Therapy and Beyond,* by A. A. Lazarus, pp. 99–100. Copyright © 1971 by McGraw-Hill, Inc. Reprinted by permission.

situations, to which patients habituate. Emmelkamp (1982) has reviewed the empirical support for these and other theoretical explanations.

The standard method of desensitization is to present scenes in a graduated, ascending fashion in order to avoid premature arousal of anxiety that would disrupt the procedure. However, some have found that presenting the hierarchy in the reverse order (most anxiety-provoking items first) is also effective in reducing various phobias. Richardson and Suinn (1973) also report positive results when participants are exposed only to the three highest hierarchy scenes.

Systematic desensitization involves a number of components. For example, the instructions suggest that a positive outcome is likely—consequently, it is possible that the patient's expectations for improvement may affect the process. It may also be that the crucial element is positive reinforcement from the therapist, whether in response to reports from the patient of lessened anxiety or improvement outside the consulting room or to the patient's successful completion of anxiety hierarchies. For example, Leitenberg, Agras, Barlow, and Oliveau (1969) observed that with snake phobias the effects of systematic desensitization are best when the therapist uses reinforcing comments, such as "Good," "Excellent," and "You're doing fine," when participants (1) visualize a scene without reporting anxiety, (2) complete a hierarchy item, and (3) report progress in approaching a snake during practice. Goldfried (1971) argues that systematic desensitization is far from a passive process that is applied to patients to reduce their fears; rather, it represents the acquisition of a skill that the patient can employ to reduce fear. In that sense, Goldfried regards systematic desensitization as training in self-control. From a clearly cognitive viewpoint, Valins and Ray (1967) explain the effectiveness of systematic desensitization in terms of patients' belief that they are relaxed. Others, such as Sullivan and Denney (1977), emphasize the importance of getting the patient to expect improvement.

All of the foregoing suggests that systematic desensitization is hardly the simple mechanical or conditioning process that it was once thought to be. A number of relationship variables seem implicated, as well as beliefs or expectations on the part of the patient. In general, systematic desensitization has proven to be a moderately effective form of psychological intervention for a variety of clinical conditions (Smith et al., 1980). As might be expected, research suggests that it is most effective when used to treat anxiety disorders, particularly specific phobias and generalized anxiety disorder (Emmelkamp, 1994).

Exposure therapy

The term *exposure therapy* is used to describe a behavior therapy technique that is a refinement of a set of procedures originally termed *flooding* or *implosion*. The roots of exposure therapy can be traced to Masserman (1943), who studied anxiety reactions and avoidance behaviors in cats (Kazdin, 1978). Masserman's studies involved inducing "neurotic behaviors" in cats by administering shock under certain environmental conditions. He subsequently discovered that the avoidance behavior could be extinguished if the cats were forced to remain in the situation in which they had previously been shocked (that is, no escape or avoidance was possible). These findings were the basis for developing anxiety treatments for humans, and there is empirical support for the efficacy of exposure treatments for specific phobias, panic disorder, agoraphobia, social phobia, post-traumatic stress disorder, and obsessive-compulsive disorder (Emmelkamp, 1994).

In exposure therapy, patients expose themselves to those stimuli or situations that were previously feared and avoided. The "exposure" can be in real life (in vivo) or in fantasy (in imagino). In the latter case, patients are asked to imagine themselves in the presence of the feared stimulus (for example, a spider) or in the anxiety-provoking situation (for example, speaking in front of an audience). Several researchers suggest that certain features must be present in exposure treatments in order for the patient to achieve maximum benefit (Barlow & Cerny, 1988):

1. Exposure should be of long versus short duration.
2. Exposure should be repeated until all fear and anxiety is eliminated.
3. Exposure should be graduated, starting with low-anxiety stimuli or situations and progressing to high-anxiety stimuli or situations.
4. Patients must attend to the feared stimulus and interact with it as much as possible.
5. Exposure must provoke anxiety.

Like other behavioral therapies we describe in this chapter, exposure treatment can be used as a treatment unto itself or as one component of a multimodal treatment. For example, Barlow and Cerny (1988) describe a psychological treatment for panic disorder that includes relaxation, cognitive restructuring, *and* exposure components. What is especially ingenious about their version of exposure treatment is that they have patients expose themselves to *interoceptive cues,* or internal physiological stimuli (for example, rapid breathing, dizziness). This modification was necessary because individuals suffering from panic disorder typically report that their panic attacks are unpredictable and come "out of the blue." Therefore, no external anxiety-provoking stimulus or situation is apparent. In contrast, individuals with other (non–panic disorder) anxiety disorders report acute anxiety primarily in the face of certain external stimuli or situations.

How do clinicians convince patients that completing tasks that increase levels of anxiety will ultimately be helpful? Box 14-1 provides the introduction that is used in Barlow and Cerny's psychological treatment for panic disorder (1988), and illustrates how the rationale for exposure therapy is presented to patients suffering from panic disorder.

Behavior rehearsal

Included under this broad heading are a variety of techniques whose aim is to enlarge the patient's repertoire of coping behaviors. Clearly, behavior rehearsal is not a new concept; it has been around in one form or another for many years. For example, Moreno (1947) developed psychodrama, a form of role playing, to help solve patients' problems, and Kelly (1955) employed fixed-role therapy. However, it is important to note that such forms of role playing or behavior rehearsal have purposes that depart from behavioral goals. For Moreno, role playing provided a therapeutic release of emotions that was also diagnostic by identifying the causes of the patient's problems. For Kelly, role playing was a method of altering the patient's cognitive structure. Again, we are reminded that specific therapeutic techniques are not the exclusive province of one theoretical frame of

■

Box 14-1
Rationale for exposure therapy

As you may recall from our earlier meetings, we feel that panic attacks are essentially "false alarms" issued by the body in response to a cue or signal that you have learned to associate with danger or threat. The problem, of course, is that these panic alarms are, in fact, false. Nevertheless, the fear associated with the panic attacks is quite real. Just as false alarms are learned phenomena, the treatment for them also involves planned re-learning experiences. The term we use to describe these corrective learn-ing experiences is *exposure therapy*.

The basic logic of exposure therapy is quite simple. Exposing yourself to those situations and cues that have been associated with anxiety and panic attacks provides you with the opportunity to learn at least three things: (1) You will learn that anxiety and panic symptoms can be con-trolled using the relaxation and cognitive coping techniques that you have been learning. In fact, you will learn that you are able not only to reduce those troublesome symptoms, but also actually to bring them on at will. (2) You will learn that there is no basis for the fear associated with your panic attacks. (3) And, finally, you will learn to break the association between the cues that signal your fears and panic attacks and teach yourself new ways of responding during graduated exposure to those panic-associated cues.

At the present time, we do not fully understand the exact mechanisms that explain how this new learning takes place, but we do know that ex-posure therapy is highly effective in treating anxiety disorders. Let me em-phasize that it is the new learning that takes place during exposure trials that is the critical element in therapy. The exposure to panic-associated cues merely provides the opportunity for that learning to occur. There-fore, passive exposure to these same cues—that is, unplanned exposures during which no corrective learning takes place—is not sufficient to bring about therapeutic changes in your behavior. During the exposure trials we encourage you to deal directly with your anxiety and fear and to take an active part in the new learning process.

Because you will be exposing yourself to these anxiety-provoking cues, you should anticipate that initially you may become more anxious and perhaps notice an increase in panic attacks. However, as you know, in most cases, anxiety and panic attacks are self-limiting—that is, in most situations the anxiety and/or panic symptoms will subside. The anxiety and fear itself, of course, may be quite unpleasant.

In order to minimize the amount of unpleasantness you will have to ex-perience, we will develop together a graduated hierarchy of anxiety-provoking cues and work through that hierarchy from the least to the most anxiety-provoking situations. Nevertheless, it will be necessary for you to tolerate some anxiety, at least initially, as you learn to deal more effectively with anxiety and panic symptoms and to eliminate "false alarms," you should notice substantial reductions in the number and perhaps the intensity of your panic attacks.

There are three ways that you can expose yourself to panic-provoking cues. First, you can imagine yourself experiencing the panic-provoking situation or cues. Imaginal exposure provides not only an exposure trial under controlled and low-arousal conditions, but it also allows you rather easily to plan and practice your management skills in imagination so that you will be prepared to take advantage of in vivo exposures. Second, you can expose yourself to certain panic-provoking cues here in the office. We will explore ways to induce those bodily sensations that have come to signal the possibility of a false alarm. And, finally, you will be exposing yourself to actual situations in your daily life. Today, we will begin with imagery training and hierarchy development.

SOURCE: From *Psychological Treatment of Panic,* by D. H. Barlow and J. A. Cerny, pp. 155–156. Copyright © 1988 by Guilford Publications, Inc. Reprinted by permission.

reference. Different theorists will inevitably employ similar techniques for vastly different reasons.

According to Goldfried and Davison (1994), the use of behavior rehearsal involves four stages. The first stage is to prepare the patient by explaining the necessity for acquiring new behaviors, getting the patient to accept behavior rehearsal as a useful device, and reducing any initial anxiety over the prospect of role playing. The second stage involves the selection of target situations. At this point, many therapists will draw up a hierarchy of role playing or rehearsal situations that relates directly to those situations in which the patient has been having difficulty. A sample hierarchy of target situations (ranked in order of the increasingly complex behavioral skills required) might be as follows:

1. You ask a secretary for information about a class.
2. You ask a student in class about last week's assignment.
3. After class you approach the instructor with a question about the lecture.
4. You go to the instructor's office and engage her in conversation about a certain point.
5. You purposely engage another student, whom you know disagrees with you, in a minor debate about some issue.

The third stage is the actual behavior rehearsal. Moving up the hierarchy, the patient plays the appropriate roles, with the therapist providing both coaching and feedback regarding the adequacy of the patient's performance. Sometimes videotaped replays are employed as an aid. In other instances the therapist (or a therapeutic aide) exchanges roles with the patient in order to provide an appropriate model. When patients develop proficiency in one target situation, they move up the hierarchy.

The final stage is the patient's actual utilization of newly acquired skills in real life situations—or *in vivo,* as this is often termed. After such in vivo experiences, the patient and the therapist discuss the patient's performance and feelings about the experiences. Sometimes patients are asked to keep written records describing the situations they were in, their behavior, its consequences, and so on.

Assertiveness training.   One application of behavioral rehearsal involves *assertiveness training.* Wolpe regarded assertive responses as an example of how *reciprocal inhibition* works—that is, it is impossible to behave assertively and be simultaneously passive. Situations that once evoked anxiety will no longer do so because the assertive behavior inhibits the anxiety.

Originally, assertiveness training was designed as a treatment for persons whose anxiety seemed to stem from their timid mode of coping with situations (Wolpe, 1958; Wolpe & Lazarus, 1966). A variety of assertiveness training programs have been developed specifically for women seeking to overcome destructive passivity. But assertiveness training has also been employed in treating sexual problems (Edwards, 1972), depression (Piaget & Lazarus, 1969), and marital conflicts (Fensterheim, 1972). Even cognitive self-statements (for example, "I was thinking that I am perfectly free to say no") are thought by Schwartz and Gottman (1976) to enhance the effects of assertiveness training. In fact, many procedures can be used to increase assertiveness. Behavior rehearsal is perhaps the most obvious one.

Lack of assertiveness may stem from a variety of sources. For example, the cause may be a simple lack of information, in which case the treatment might center largely on information giving. In other instances, a kind of anticipatory anxiety may prevent persons from behaving assertively; in such cases, the treatment may involve desensitization. Yet other individuals may have unrealistic or negative expectations about what will ensue if they become assertive. Some clinicians would deal with such expectations through interpretation or rational-emotive techniques. Similar techniques might be applied to patients who feel that assertiveness is wrong. Finally, there are patients whose lack of assertiveness involves a behavioral deficit—they do not know how to behave assertively. For such patients, behavior rehearsal, modeling, and related procedures may be employed.

It is important to point out that assertiveness training is not the same as trying to teach people to be aggressive. It is really a method of training people to express how they feel without trampling on the rights of others in the process (Wolpe & Lazarus, 1966). Take the spectator at a basketball game who cannot see because the person in front constantly jumps up. To react by saying, "If you don't sit down I'm going to knock you down," is aggressive. But saying, "Please, I wish you would sit down; I just can't see anything," is an assertive response. Indeed, assertiveness training has been useful in teaching overly aggressive persons more gentle and effective ways of meeting their needs.

Contingency management
A variety of Skinnerian or operant techniques are all referred to as *contingency management* procedures. They share the common goal of controlling be-

havior by manipulating its consequences. There are many forms of contingency management (see Rimm & Masters, 1979). The following are just a few:

1. *Shaping:* Sometimes called *successive approximation.* A desired behavior is developed by first rewarding any behavior that approximates it. Gradually, by selectively reinforcing the individual only for behavior resembling the desired behavior, the final behavior is shaped.
2. *Time-out:* Undesirable behavior is extinguished by removing the person temporarily from a situation in which that behavior is reinforced. A child who disrupts the class is removed so that the disruptive behavior cannot be reinforced by the attention of others.
3. *Contingency contracting:* A formal agreement or contract is, for example, struck between therapist and patient. It specifies the consequences of certain behaviors on the part of both.
4. *Grandma's rule:* Sometimes referred to as the *Premack principle* (Premack, 1959), the basic idea is akin to Grandma's exhortation, "First you work, then you play!" It means that a desired activity is reinforced by allowing the individual the privilege of engaging in a more attractive behavior. The child, for example, is allowed to play ball after the music lesson is completed.

Token economies.   The operant approach is employed most commonly in environments in which a therapist or other institutional staff can exert significant control over the reinforcement contingencies relative to patient behavior. The principles of operant conditioning are especially apparent in *token economy* programs that are designed to modify the behavior of institutionalized populations, such as the mentally retarded or the chronically mentally ill (Kazdin, 1977; Liberman, 1972). Such programs can make an institution a more livable place that is ultimately more conducive to therapeutic gains. Further, many of the social skills that are shaped by operant techniques will facilitate a smoother transition to a noninstitutional setting.

In establishing a token economy, there are three major considerations (Krasner, 1971). First, there must be a clear and careful specification of the desirable behaviors that will be reinforced. Second, a clearly defined reinforcer or medium of exchange—for example, colored poker chips, cards, or coins—must be decided upon. Third, backup reinforcers are established. These can be special privileges or other things desired by the patient. Thus, two tokens, each worth ten points, might be exchanged for permission to watch TV an extra hour or one token worth five points might be exchanged for a small piece of candy. It goes without saying that a token economy also requires a fairly elaborate system of record keeping and a staff that is very observant and committed to the importance of the program.

It is apparent that token economies are used to promote desired behavior through the control of reinforcements. Whether the desired behavior is increased neatness, greater social participation, or improved job performance, the probability of its occurrence can be enhanced by the award of tokens of varying value. But why use tokens at all? Why not reinforce proper bedmaking immediately? The reason is essentially that the effect of reinforcement is greater if the reinforcement occurs immediately after the behavior occurs. If the reward of attending a movie occurs ten hours after a patient sweeps out his or her room, it is not likely to be nearly as effective as a token given immediately. That token will come to signify reward and will assume much of the effectiveness of the backup reward for which it may be exchanged.

Aversion therapy

One of the most controversial of all treatments is *aversion therapy*. Actually, this is not a single therapy but a series of different procedures applied to behaviors regarded as undesirable. Application is based upon the apparently simple principle that, when a response is followed by an unpleasant consequence (punishment, pain, and so on), its strength will diminish. As Wolpe (1973) put it: "Aversion therapy consists, operationally, of administering an aversive stimulus to inhibit an unwanted emotional response, thereby diminishing its habit strength" (p. 216). An unpleasant stimulus is placed in temporal contiguity with the undesirable behavior, the idea being that conditioning will take place and that in this way a permanent association between the undesirable behavior and the unpleasant stimulus will be forged.

Such techniques may appear to be recent additions to scientific and clinical repertoires, but, in fact, they have been around for eons, often in the form of such unsophisticated practices as spanking or giving orders like, "Go to your room," and "No TV tonight for you." Modern aversive therapy techniques differ from these examples in at least two important ways. First, the presentation of the aversive agent is done very systematically—the temporal contiguity is very carefully monitored. Second, the punishment is consistently applied. The punishment applied by parents is often highly inconsistent. Sometimes the undesirable behavior of the child is immediately punished; but very often, the parent forgets or is distracted, too tired, or whatever to respond. As a result, the child learns that sometimes the behavior is ignored, and thus extinction fails to occur. As formal clinical procedures, these techniques have been applied most often to help patients develop increased self-control. They have been utilized to cope with problems of obesity (Wolpe, 1973), smoking (Conway, 1977), alcoholism (Lemere & Voegtlin, 1950), and sexual deviations (Barlow & Abel, 1976).

Aversive agents.   Among the aversive agents that have been employed most frequently have been electrical stimulation and the use of drugs. For example, strong emetic drugs have been used aversively for many years (Voegtlin & Lemere, 1942), especially in the treatment of alcoholism. The patient is given a drug that produces nausea or vomiting and then takes a drink (or sometimes the drug is mixed with the drink). Soon the patient becomes quite ill. This combination of alcohol and emetic is given for a week to ten days. Eventually, just the sight of a drink is sufficient to induce nausea and discomfort.

Wolpe (1973) has described a variety of other aversive agents, including holding one's breath, stale cigarette smoke, vile-smelling solutions of asafetida, intense illumination, white noise, and shame. Clearly, the range of potential aversive agents is limited only by the imagination of resourceful therapists.

Covert sensitization.   Cautela (1967) has developed a set of procedures that rely on imagery rather than the actual use of punishment, drugs, or stimulation. With *covert sensitization,* patients are asked to imagine themselves doing the things they wish to eliminate. They are then instructed to imagine extremely aversive events once they have the undesired behaviors clearly in mind. Some of the instructions are vivid, to say the least. A rather mild example from the treatment of a case of overeating should suffice: "As you touch the fork, you can feel food particles inching up your throat. You're just about to vomit" (Cautela, 1967, p. 462). The ensuing descriptions become even more graphic.

Second thoughts.   Many clinicians have deemphasized aversion methods in their behavioral therapy approaches. For example, Lazarus (1971b) has stated that the building of better response repertoires and the reduction of anxiety produce longer-lasting results than do aversion techniques. Thus, it may turn out that, in the long run, it is more efficient to deal with a sexual fetish by reducing the patient's fear of heterosexual behaviors through behavior rehearsal than by punishing him each time he visualizes a pair of women's shoes.

The concept of dignity.   Many critics, both within and without the behavior therapy movement, have been highly critical of aversion therapy. The concentration of punishment and the use of what are sometimes terrifying stimuli often seem totally incompatible with human dignity. Whether or not patients present themselves voluntarily for treatment is beside the point. Such techniques as inducing vomiting, using a curare-like drug so that the patient will experience the sensation of suffocating, or injecting stale smoke into the nostrils seem better relegated to the status of torture than dignified as treatment.

Others, however, feel that aversive techniques employed in a sensitive fashion by reputable professionals have real merit. Most often, aversive techniques are used after everything else has failed. Furthermore, patients are not dragged kicking and screaming into the situation. Usually, the procedures are applied to people who have seriously debilitating problems (alcoholism, excessive smoking, sexual deviations) and who are in despair because nothing else has worked. Such people voluntarily take the lesser evil, aversion therapy, in the same spirit, perhaps, that one submits yearly to that terrifying torture at the hands of the friendly dentist. The debate goes on.

■ Cognitive-Behavior Therapy

Not too long ago, a chapter on behavior therapy would have been largely populated with such terms as *behavior modification, systematic desensitization, operant conditioning, shaping, token economies,* and *aversion therapy.* But this is no longer true. We now find such terms as *cognitive-behavior modification, cognitive restructuring, stress inoculation,* and *rational restructuring.* This change in terminology signifies a cognitive orientation in behavior therapy that has overtaken the field in recent years (Hollon & Beck, 1994). In the realm of *cognitive-behavior therapy,* applying a cognitive perspective to clinical problems places emphasis on the role of *thinking* in the etiology and maintenance of problems. Further, cognitive-behavioral interventions seek to modify or change patterns of thinking that are believed to contribute to a patient's problems. These techniques have a great deal of empirical support (Smith et al., 1980; Hollon & Beck, 1994) and are seen as among the most effective of all psychological interventions.

The move toward cognitive behaviorism

In reflecting upon these cognitive trends, apparent even two decades ago, Mahoney had this to say:

> Despite their long history of often bitter rivalry, behaviorists and cognitive psychologists appear to be cautiously easing into the same theoretical bed. This rather startling flirtation is not, of course, without its detractors. A few behaviorists seem to be viewing it as a softheaded fling with mentalism that they hope will pass. Likewise, some cognitive psychologists have viewed the merger with suspicion. (Mahoney, 1977b, p. 5)

But there is no mistake. Cognitions have invaded the behavioral realm (Kendall & Hollon, 1979). Some even suggest that cognition is simply an acceptable word that signals a swing back to psychodynamics; indeed, even some humanists feel that there is a developing fusion between the behavioral and humanistic traditions (Child, 1973). Others tend to feel that cognitive influences may represent a step in the wrong direction (Ledwidge, 1978), and still others are integrating psychoanalysis and behavior therapy (Wachtel, 1977).

In a sense, the present blending of behavioral and cognitive methods was stimulated by the limitations of both psychodynamics and radical behaviorism. But this blending was also facilitated by the presence of several theoretical models that incorporated cognitive variables along with the scientific and experimental rigor so precious to behaviorists.

The role of social learning theory

In particular, Rotter's social learning theory (Rotter, 1954; Rotter, Chance, & Phares, 1972) helped bridge the chasm between traditional psychodynamic clinical practice and learning theory. Rotter's theory explained behavior as a joint product of both reinforcement and expectancies—people choose to behave in the way they do because the chosen behavior is expected to lead to a goal or outcome of some value.

The presence of such a social learning theory did at least two things for the development of behavior therapy. First, it produced a number of clinicians (and influenced others) who were ready to accept newer behavioral techniques and were equipped with a theoretical point of view that could facilitate the modification of those techniques along more cognitive lines. Second, the theory, being both cognitive and motivational, was capable of blending the older psychodynamically derived therapeutic procedures with the newer behavioral and cognitive approaches. By its very presence, then, social learning theory facilitated a fusion of approaches that is still in progress. In evaluating the relevance of this theory for the practice of both traditional psychotherapy and behavior therapy, consider the following implications discussed by Rotter (1970):

1. Psychotherapy is regarded as a learning situation, and the role of the therapist is to enable the patient to achieve planned changes in observable behavior and thinking.
2. A problem-solving framework is a useful way in which to view most patients' difficulties.
3. Most often, the role of the therapist is to guide the teaming process so that not only are inadequate behaviors and attitudes weakened but more satisfying and constructive behaviors are learned.
4. It is often necessary to change unrealistic expectancies; in so doing, the therapist must realize how it was that certain behaviors and expectancies arose and how prior experience was misapplied or overgeneralized by the patient.
5. In therapy, the patient must learn to be concerned with the feelings, expectations, motives, and needs of others.
6. New experiences or different ones in real life can often be much more effective than those that occur only during the therapy situation.
7. In general, therapy is a kind of social interaction.

Another highly significant contribution that has facilitated the cognitive swing in behavior therapy has been the work of Bandura (1969). Bandura demonstrated the great importance of vicarious learning and the role of cognitive mediators in both affect and performance. Bandura's emphasis (1977) on the ways in which various treatment procedures increase the patient's sense of self-efficacy is a further step toward unifying the behavioral and cognitive realms. In his proposed model, Bandura argues that expectations of personal efficacy arise from the patient's actual accomplishments, verbal persuasion, vicarious experience, and physiological states. Various forms of therapy are seen as particularly productive in leading patients to an increased belief in their personal efficacy. Although a concept such as self-efficacy is hardly new in psychology, it does illustrate the growing cognitive swing.

Cognitive-behavioral treatments

Modeling. Bandura (1969, 1971) has advocated the use of *modeling or observational learning* — particularly with children — as a means of altering behavior patterns. Imitation, modeling, or observation are much more efficient techniques for learning than is a simple reliance on punishment for incorrect responses and reward for correct ones. A new skill or a new set of behaviors can be learned more efficiently by observing another person; seeing others perform a behavior can also help eliminate or reduce associated fears and anxieties; and, through observation, individuals can learn to employ behaviors that are already part of their behavioral repertoire.

Perhaps the most widespread use of modeling has been to eliminate unrealistic fears (Bandura, Adams, & Beyer, 1977; Bandura, Jeffrey, & Wright, 1974). Phobias, especially snake phobias, have been the principal means of both demonstrating and investigating modeling techniques. In *participant modeling,* for example, the patient observes the therapist or model holding a snake, allowing the snake to crawl over the body, and so on. Then, in *guided participation,* the patient is exhorted to try out a series of similar activities, graded according to potential for producing anxiety. Illustrative of this general approach is a study of nonorgasmic women treated by a self-administered masturbation training program over a six-week period. The general techniques were described by McMullen and Rosen (1979) as follows:

> Videotape modeling procedure. A series of six 20-minute videotape sequences were prepared specifically for the study. The tapes featured a coping model, an actress portraying a nonorgasmic woman who learns over the course of the six sessions to stimulate herself to orgasm and then to transfer her ability to sexual intercourse with her partner. Content of the tapes included self-exploration, self-stimulation, and finally, an explicit representation of reaching orgasm through intercourse with a partner.

> Written instructions. The videotaped scripts were excerpted in the form of written booklets, which pretesting indicated were of equivalent content to the videotapes. The same procedure was followed for these subjects, in that they were required to come in once a week to read the appropriate booklet over the six weeks of the training program. Booklets were also read in private, and approximately the same amount of time was spent by these subjects in the clinic. (p. 914)

Covert modeling.   In the therapy known as covert modeling, patients imagine a model engaged in the behaviors they wish to acquire (Cautela, 1971). Cautela, Flannery, and Hanley (1974) believe that covert modeling is as effective as live modeling in the case of subphobic avoidance problems. It has also been employed with problems involving a lack of assertiveness (Kazdin & Mascitelli, 1982). In this particular study, covert and overt rehearsal and homework practice were used to develop assertiveness. Clients imagined a situation in which a model engaged in assertive behaviors. In the case of clients who also overtly rehearsed situations, this imagery was followed by an enactment of the behavior with the therapist.

Rational restructuring.   Drawing upon the work of Albert Ellis (1962), Goldfried and Davison (1994) accept the notion that much maladaptive behavior is determined by the ways in which people construe their world or by the assumptions they make about it. If this is true, it follows that the behavior therapist must help patients learn to label situations more realistically so that they can ultimately attain greater satisfactions. In order to facilitate a patient's restructuring of events, the therapist may sometimes employ argument or discussion in an attempt to get that patient to see the irrationality of his or her beliefs. In addition to providing patients with a rational analysis of their problems, the therapist may attempt to teach them to "modify their internal sentences." That is, patients may be taught that, when they begin to feel upset in real situations, they should pause and ask themselves what they are telling themselves about those situations. In other instances, the therapist may have patients in the therapy room imagine particular problem situations. All of this may be combined with behavior rehearsal, in vivo assignments, modeling, and so on. Thus, rational restructuring is not a self-contained, theoretically derived procedure but an eclectic series of techniques that can be tailored to suit the particular demands of the patient's situation (see Dryden & Golden, 1987).

A good example of rational restructuring is Ellis's *rational-emotive therapy* (1962), also known as *RET*. A pioneer in what has become cognitive-behavior therapy, Ellis (1973) tried to change behavior by altering the way the patient thinks about things. Although many find it a bit difficult to classify Ellis, he is often put in the phenomenological-humanistic camp, since he begins with assumptions characteristic of those groups. Wherever RET belongs, however, it seems to have become quite popular (Ellis & Dryden, 1987; Ellis & Grieger, 1986; Grieger & Boyd, 1980; Wessler & Wessler, 1980).

Ellis begins his work from a phenomenological, humanistic posture: all behavior, whether maladjusted or otherwise, is determined not by events but by the person's interpretation of them. In the ABCs of RET, Ellis argues that it is *beliefs* (B) about *activating* events or situations (A) that determine the problematic emotional or behavioral *consequences* (C). He sees psychoanalytic therapy, with its extreme reliance on insight, as inefficient; the origins of irrational thinking are not nearly so important as the messages that people give to themselves.

In a sense, the basic goal of RET is to make people confront their own illogical thinking. Ellis tries to get the client to use common sense, and the therapist becomes an active and directive teacher in this process. Box 14-2 presents some of the more common irrational ideas believed by Ellis to influence many people. Reviews of the empirical literature suggest that RET is an effective psychological intervention (Smith et al., 1980). However, recent calls for a more detailed investigation of components of RET that lead to change in clinical status have appeared (Haaga & Davison, 1993).

Stress inoculation. Novaco (1977) has described the application of *stress inoculation* procedures to deal with the anger problems of depressed patients on acute psychiatric wards. In essence, these procedures involve cognitive preparation of such patients, acquisition and rehearsal of the necessary skills, and practice in the application of those skills. To cognitively prepare patients, instructional manuals are given to them describing the nature and functions of anxiety, including a discussion of situations in which anger is a problem, what causes anger, and how anger may be regulated. The components of this cognitive preparation include identifying persons and situations that precipitate anger, learning to differentiate between anger and aggression, discriminating between justified and unnecessary anger, and early recognition of signs of tension and arousal in a provocation sequence.

Beck's cognitive therapy. Aaron Beck has been a pioneer in the development of cognitive-behavioral treatments for a variety of clinical problems (Beck, 1991). The *cognitive therapy* model of intervention entails the use of both cognitive and behavioral techniques to modify dysfunctional thinking patterns that characterize the problem or disorder in question (Beck, 1993). For example, depressed individuals are believed to harbor negative or pessimistic beliefs about themselves, their world, and their future. Thus, a depressed 45-year-old man might be prone to be highly self-critical (and often feel guilty, even when it is not appropriate), to view the world as generally unsupportive and unfair, and to hold

Box 14-2
Common "irrational" ideas

The 12 irrational ideas that Ellis (1977) feels are very common in the thinking of many people are listed below. While most of us share this kind of thinking, extreme reliance on such beliefs could be quite debilitating.

1. The idea that you must, yes, must have sincere love and approval almost all the time from all the people you find significant.
2. The idea that you must prove yourself thoroughly competent, adequate, and achieving; or that you must at least have real competence or talent at something important.
3. The idea that people who harm you or commit misdeeds rate as generally bad, wicked, or villainous individuals, and that you should severely blame, damn, and punish them for their sins.
4. The idea that life proves awful, terrible, horrible, or catastrophic when things do not go the way you would like them to go.
5. The idea that emotional misery comes from external pressures and that you have little ability to control your feelings or rid yourself of depression and hostility.
6. The idea that if something seems dangerous or fearsome, you must become terribly occupied with and upset about it.
7. The idea that you will find it easier to avoid facing many of life's difficulties and self-responsibilities than to undertake some rewarding forms of self-discipline.
8. The idea that your past remains all-important and that, because something once strongly influenced your life, it has to keep determining your feelings and behavior today.
9. The idea that people and things should turn out better than they do; and that you have to view it as awful and horrible if you do not quickly find good solutions to life's hassles.
10. The idea that you can achieve happiness by inertia and inaction or by passively and uncommittedly "enjoying yourself."
11. The idea that you must have a high degree of order or certainty to feel comfortable; or that you need some supernatural power on which to rely.
12. The idea that you give yourself a global rating as a human and that your general worth and self-acceptance depend upon the goodness of your performance and the degree that people approve of you.

SOURCE: From "A Basic Clinical Theory of Rational-Emotive Therapy," by A. Ellis, p. 10, in *Handbook of Rational-Emotive Therapy* by A. Ellis and R. Grieger. Copyright © 1977 by Springer Publishing Company, Inc. Reprinted by permission.

little hope for things to improve in the future. Cognitive therapy techniques that might be employed in the treatment of his depression include (Beck, Rush, Shaw, & Emery, 1979):

- Scheduling activities to counteract his relative inactivity and tendency to focus on his depressive feelings.
- Increasing the rates of pleasurable activities as well as of those in which some degree of mastery is experienced.
- Cognitive rehearsal: having the patient imagine each successive step leading to the completion of an important task (for example, attending an exercise class), so that potential impediments can be identified, anticipated, and addressed.
- Assertiveness training and role playing.
- Identifying automatic thoughts that occur before or during dysphoric episodes (for example, "I can't do anything right.").
- Examining the reality or accuracy of these thoughts by gently challenging their validity (*Therapist:* "So you don't think there is *anything* you can do right?").
- Teaching the patient to reattribute the blame for negative consequences to the appropriate source. Depressed patients have a tendency to blame themselves for negative outcomes even when they are not at fault.
- Helping the patient search for alternative solutions to his problems instead of resigning himself to their insolubility.

This is an abbreviated but, we hope, illustrative sample of the techniques employed in Beck's cognitive therapy of depression. Cognitive therapy has proven to be one of the most effective techniques available for treating depression (Dobson, 1989; Hollon & Beck, 1994). Over the last decade, it has been adapted for use with patients suffering from anxiety disorders (Beck & Emery, 1985), eating disorders (Fairburn et al., 1991), and personality disorders (Beck, Freeman, & Associates, 1990), to cite but a few examples. Empirical studies suggest that it may be an especially effective form of intervention for a broad range of clinical problems (Hollon & Beck, 1994; Smith et al., 1980)

■ Behavior Therapy: Evaluation and Conclusions

Proponents of behavior therapy see their progress as tangible evidence of what can be accomplished when the mentalistic, subjective, and nonscientific "mumbo jumbo" of psychodynamics or phenomenology is cast aside. Critics, on the other hand, see behavior therapy as superficial, pretentiously scientific, and even dehumanizing in its mechanistic attempts to change human behavior. Indeed, these criticisms reflect many of the "myths" about behavior therapy (Goldfried & Davison, 1994).

We will now examine some of the strengths and limitations of the behavioral and cognitive-behavioral approaches.

The positive features

Effectiveness.   As mentioned throughout this chapter, there is ample evidence that a wide variety of behavioral and cognitive-behavioral therapies are effective (Emmelkamp, 1994; Hollon & Beck, 1994; Smith et al., 1980). The reader may recall the results of the Smith et al. (1980) meta-analysis presented in Chapter 11 (see Table 11-5). The separate effect sizes calculated for RET, non-RET cognitive therapies, systematic desensitization, behavior modification, and cognitive-behavioral therapy indicate that, on average, a client who received any of these forms of behavior therapy was functioning better than at least 75% of those who did not receive any treatment. More recent meta-analyses have reached similar conclusions across a range of disorders. Further, the majority of meta-analytic studies that compared the effectiveness of behavioral or cognitive-behavioral techniques to that of other forms of psychotherapy (for example, psychodynamic or client-centered) found a small but consistent superiority for behavioral and cognitive-behavioral methods (Dobson, 1989; Dush, Hirt, & Schroeder, 1983; Nicholson & Berman, 1983; Robinson, Berman, & Neimeyer, 1990; Shapiro & Shapiro, 1982; Svartberg & Stiles, 1991). Clearly, these are important treatment techniques for a clinician to master.

Efficiency.   It is also important to note that the behavior therapy movement brought with it a series of techniques that were shorter and apparently more efficient. The interminable number of 50-minute psychotherapy sessions was replaced by a much shorter series of consultations that focused on the patient's specific complaints. A series of equally specific procedures was applied, and the entire process terminated when the patient's complaints no longer existed. Gone was the everlasting rooting out of underlying pathology, the exhaustive sorting out of the patient's history, and the lengthy quest for insight. In their place came an emphasis on the present and a pragmatism that was signaled by the use of specific techniques for specific problems. Because of its efficiency, behavior therapy may be especially well suited for the managed care environment.

An array of techniques.   Behavior therapy has evolved into a broad array of techniques from systematic desensitization to cognitive restructuring. Unless a behavior therapist is unalterably committed to but one set of procedures, this broad spectrum demands that choices be made. In order to increase the probability of making the correct one, the therapist is likely to gather information that will best match technique with patient (Peterson & Sobell, 1994). Therefore, if assessment eventually recaptures its position of prominence in the list of the clinician's preferred activities, it will be due in no small measure to the behavior therapist's desire for information to guide the therapeutic decision-making process.

A technology.   Behavior therapy is a very active collection of procedures. It involves assessment, planning, decisions, and, techniques, and, in some ways, it may be construed as a complex technology. A technology cannot be passively allowed to happen to a patient—it is something that must be guided with care and foresight and great attention to detail. Therefore, the therapist cannot play everything by ear or wait until the patient shows up on Thursday before thinking about the case. If a therapist is using aversion procedures, the time relationship between the onset of the stimulus and the onset of punishment may need strict supervision. Similarly, token economies are not haphazard regimens that can be left to creative, on-the-spot decision making. Everything must be worked out carefully in advance. It is important to decide whether the patient possesses a behavioral deficit rather than a pure anxiety problem, since the therapeutic implications are vastly different in each case.

None of this is meant to imply that every psychodynamically oriented psychotherapist fails to think about cases between therapy sessions or always makes up strategy spontaneously along the way. Yet the nature of traditional psychotherapy renders it vulnerable to such problems of passivity. It is even possible that, to some extent, the active, vigorous quality of behavioral methods and the analogous attitude that this forces upon the therapist may be responsible for a measure of patient improvement beyond that caused by the specific procedures employed. An active therapist may be reassuring, exciting, or encouraging to some patients — in contrast to a passive, contemplative, noncommittal psychotherapist who often has little to say or suggest.

Symptom substitution.   As much as anything, behavior therapies will have a secure and valued position in the history of psychology because they helped lay to rest the hallowed notion of *symptom substitution*. They not only demonstrated that there are alternatives to the psychodynamic views of pathology but they also effectively attacked the medical model of pathology and its cherished notions of illnesses and symptoms. After years of research and clinical experience, it is now clear that not every patient's complaint can be labeled as a symptom of some underlying psychic illness — an illness that will surely return in the form of another symptom if the present one is removed without attending to the underlying pathology. Attacking a patient's anxieties directly will not necessarily force the anxieties to return in another guise. This demonstration not only lent credibility to the behavioral movement; it also chipped away at the credibility of those psychiatric and psychodynamic orientations which had so stoutly defended the symptom substitution notion. As a result, the avenue was opened for the development of specific techniques for dealing with specific patient complaints. However, it is necessary to temper these remarks by recognizing that direct onslaughts on the patient's stated problem may not always be the most efficient route. As we noted earlier in this chapter in illustrating anxiety hierarchies, it may turn out that a specific anxiety is being sustained by something not immediately obvious (Lazarus, 1971b).

Breadth of application.   A contribution of major proportions has been the extension of the range of applicability of therapy. Traditional psychotherapy had been reserved for the middle and upper classes who had the time and money to devote to their psychological woes and for articulate, relatively sophisticated college students with well-developed repertoires of coping behaviors who were attending colleges or universities that made counseling services available to them at little, if any, cost. Behavior therapy has changed all that.

Now, even financially strapped individuals with mental retardation or chronic mental illness can be aided by therapy. Such persons may not be raised to the level of independent functioning, but with the advent of operant procedures and token economies, their institutional adjustment can often be improved significantly.

Not only the institutionalized have benefited from behavioral techniques; patients at lower socioeconomic levels with limited sophistication and verbal skills can also experience anxieties and phobias or lack necessary problem-solving skills. Where lengthy verbal psychotherapies that were highly dependent upon insight, symbolism, or the release of some inner potential were likely to fail, a broad band of behavior therapies seems to offer real hope.

Scientist-practitioner and clinical scientist. For those who support the scientist-practitioner or clinical scientist models for clinical psychology, behavior therapy is a field that seems to encourage a blending of the two roles. The behavioral tradition springs from a heritage that is experimental and oriented toward research, with many of the specific techniques having developed directly from the experimental laboratory. More often than not, even the language of behavioral therapy is straight out of the experimental research journals. In behavior therapy, there is an easy communication between the researcher and the clinician, and very often the same person alternates comfortably between the two roles. Such rapport increases the likelihood that advances in the laboratory will be reflected in new therapeutic techniques and, conversely, that clinical experience will serve a vital role in determining the kind of research and evaluation that is carried out.

Personnel. Some behavioral techniques can be employed by technicians who are trained to work under the supervision of a doctoral-level clinician. Thus, not every component of behavior therapy need be executed by Ph.D. personnel. Behavior therapy programs (for example, token economies) should be set up by trained professionals, but their day-to-day execution can be put in the hands of technicians, paraprofessionals, nurses, and others. This constitutes a considerable savings in mental health personnel and enables a larger patient population to be reached than can be treated by the in-depth, one-on-one procedures of an exclusively psychodynamic approach.

Some criticisms

Many of the customary criticisms of behavior therapy have lost their force since the field assumed its cognitive stance. Indeed, the changes have been so substantial that two decades ago Lazarus (1977) asked whether the term *behavior therapy* had outlived its usefulness. Others, like Goldfried and Davison (1994), use the term more broadly to include both strictly behavioral and cognitive techniques that derive from principles established empirically in the laboratory with clinical applications. However, the degree of association between laboratory-based principles and behavior therapy techniques is the subject of much debate.

Scientific respectability. For some years, the behavioral movement rode the crest of a wave of scientific respectability. Many behaviorists, especially the radical variety, seemed to be clamoring for preferred status by claiming that behavior therapy rested on the sturdy, established scientific principles of learning theory. Psychodynamic approaches, by contrast, were said to be crude extrapolations from a mentalism only slightly removed from witchcraft. At times, the sheer repetition of claims of being scientifically based or experimentally derived seemed to delude the more ardent adherents of behavior therapy into overestimating their "science." But not all behavioral methods are based on strong experimental evidence; many have grown out of clinical experience. Moreover, many things that behavioral therapists do can be equally well explained by nonbehavioral points of view (Goldfried & Davison, 1994).

Dehumanizing. Among the more durable characterizations of the behavioral movement by its critics are that it is sterile, mechanistic, and dehumanizing. To demonstrate that there is real labeling bias operating here and not just empty rhetoric, Woolfolk, Woolfolk, and Wilson (1977) asked two groups of undergraduates to view identical videotapes of a teacher using reinforcement methods. The first group was told that the tape illustrated behavior modification; for the second group, the tape was labeled as an illustration of humanistic education. A subsequent questionnaire revealed that, when the tape was described in humanistic terms, the teacher on the tape received significantly better ratings and the teaching method depicted was seen as significantly more likely to promote learning and emotional growth.

The fact that mechanistic-sounding terms such as *response, stimulus, reinforcement,* and *operant* are employed need not imply that either the therapist or the method is detached, sterile, or dehumanizing. The systematic utilization of learning principles and the examination of animal analogs to provide simple illustrations that highlight the nature of human learning should not encourage anyone to a facile inference that behavior therapists are cold, manipulating robots whose interests lie more in their learning principles than in their clients. It is to be hoped that, with the increasing cognitive orientation, such erroneous images will begin to fade.

Although nothing inherent in behavior therapy should lead to the conclusion that it is necessarily dehumanizing, its early history provided a few unfortunate episodes and a considerable stridency of rhetoric. We have already commented on the use of aversion techniques that, to many, seemed more akin to sadism than therapy. In addition, many early behaviorists were so obsessed with their principles and their technology that common sense seemed to be the chief casualty. Their sometimes naive attacks on psychodynamics and their zealous overconfidence in technology often played right into the hands of their critics and only served to make life more difficult for their successors. In the final analysis, no technology or set of principles is going to permit clinicians the luxury of giving up their clinical sensitivity.

Inner growth. Behavior therapy has also been criticized as ameliorative but not productive of any inner growth. It has been said to relieve symptoms or provide a few skills while failing to offer fulfilling creative experiences. Although it may alter behavior, it falls short of promoting understanding. It leaves out the inner person, values, responsibility, and motives. Again, though not completely off the mark, such criticisms are less appropriate for the newer cognitive emphasis in behavior therapy, an emphasis that does deal with mediating variables such as expectancies and self-concepts — as long as these variables are objectively describable and inferred from specific stimuli and responses.

   Nonspecific problems.   For some years, critics of behavior therapy have complained that it does not adequately address problems that are vague or existential in character. For example, a good, crisp snake phobia can readily be handled by relaxation, systematic desensitization, or modeling. But what about the depressed, unfulfilled housewife who faces an empty home now that her children are grown? And what about a vague, ill-defined sense of anxiety or depression? In short, do the techniques that handle specific anxieties or behavioral deficits also resolve moral dilemmas or a sense of meaninglessness? The answer is not clear. As early as 1964, Grossberg recognized this limitation of behavior therapy when he commented: "A review of this literature revealed that behavior therapies have been applied to many neurotic and psychotic disorders, and have been most successful with disorders involving specific maladaptive behaviors" (p. 73).
   It is in part because of these limitations that behavioral therapy has begun to transform itself into a more cognitive, yes, even more psychodynamic and humanistic enterprise (Goldfried & Davison, 1994). And if it maintains its rapport with learning theory, objectivity, and scientific investigation as it moves gingerly toward this more cognitive, dynamic, and humanistic stance, it may yet have the best of all worlds.

   Mental processes.   Although few behavior therapists can be said to embrace the unconscious, only the radical behaviorists still insist on the absolute rejection of all so-called mental processes. Likewise, not many behavioral clinicians are likely to recommend an exhaustive reconstruction of the patient's past — especially the psychosexuality of childhood. But this is not to argue that past learning experiences have not led to the patient's current predicament; indeed, they have. And any sensitive behavioral clinician will devote time to understanding what those learning experiences were all about. By so doing, the clinician can better distinguish between behavioral deficits and blockages and can better understand how to structure present learning experiences so as to enable patients to better cope with their problems.

   Manipulation and control.   One of the most volatile, emotion-laden criticisms of behavior therapy centers on the issue of manipulation and control. The argument seems to be that behavior therapies represent insidious and often direct assaults upon the patient's capacity to make decisions, assume responsibility, and maintain dignity and integrity. But patients have typically sought professional assistance voluntarily and have thereby acknowledged their need for help and guidance in altering their lives. Thus, the patient does have the opportunity to accept or reject the procedures offered (though this defense may not apply as well in institutional settings). Further, many behavior therapy techniques are aimed at helping patients establish skills that will lead to greater self-direction and self-control (Goldfried & Davison, 1994).

Generalization.   A particularly damaging criticism of several forms of behavior therapy concerns their effectiveness in settings other than those in which they are executed. In other words, do the effects of behavior therapy programs generalize beyond the situations in which they are practiced? Again, in the interest of evenhandedness, it should be pointed out that most forms of psychotherapy are subject to the same question. For example, some patients show a marked improvement or adjustment in the psychotherapy situation even though this adjustment fails to generalize to nontherapy settings.

It has been the operant approaches (token economies and related behavioral management programs) that have been most suspect here. Such programs always seem to work best where a great deal of control over the life of the patient is possible. They may seem quite effective in institutions for the mentally retarded, hospitals for the chronically mentally ill, and certain classroom settings and experimental living arrangements. But this is in large measure due to the fact that trained personnel are available to observe behavior or issue tokens, making it relatively easy to maintain the appropriate contingencies between behavior and reinforcement. However, when the individual leaves such a sheltered environment, it is clear that, though certain desired behavior was maintained by the operant procedures, little was learned that would generalize to a noncontrolled setting. There are many practical problems in even establishing behavior modification programs in natural settings, let alone getting their effects to generalize beyond the institution.

Other techniques, such as aversion therapies, suffer from similar problems. For example, one of the authors once knew an alcoholic who was able to conquer his drinking problem with the help of Antabuse and a very controlled hospital environment. This patient knew full well that, with the medication in his system, he would become violently ill if he drank. However, upon his release from the hospital, he soon encountered several stressful situations. He had learned the connection between drinking and becoming ill, but, unfortunately, he had also learned that if he stopped taking the Antabuse and waited awhile he could drink with impunity—which he did.

The foregoing kinds of experiences have led many to characterize behavioral treatment techniques as superficial, simplistic, or supportive methods that produce little of lasting value. Such critics argue that the benefits of these techniques are largely confined to institutional settings in which behavioral management is important and that they do not generalize to unsupervised situations in which self-control and independence are at a premium. Indeed, some have gone so far as to contend that the use of external incentives to maintain certain desired behavior actually serves to undermine the person's real interest in the activity in question (Condry, 1977). That is, in their efforts to induce people to emit certain behaviors, therapists actually destroy whatever intrinsic motivation they might have developed for the activity. This, in turn, assures that the behavior will drop out once the extrinsic motivators have been withdrawn. Sophisticated behavior therapists are, however, not insensitive to this problem. They will often "fade" or gradually reduce the frequency of occurrence of certain reinforcers as they prepare the client for settings in which immediate reinforcement (or reinforcement at all) is not possible.

Maintenance. Another criticism of behavior therapies has been that improvements in patients' behavior do not last. In fact, this point has been made with regard to all forms of therapy at one time or another. For a long time, however, booster sessions have been advocated by behavior therapists as a maintenance strategy. A recent review of research suggests that such sessions have been at least moderately successful in maintaining treatment-induced behavior change (Whisman, 1990).

Theoretical chaos. A final problem with behavior therapy may be its potential for theoretical chaos. At present, it is an amalgam of techniques — some from the operant tradition, others from a classical conditioning base, and still others that are heavily cognitive in nature. Without an integrating theoretical framework, individual clinicians may find themselves flailing about in a morass of competing techniques, each claiming to be forms of behavior therapy. What is needed is a systematic theoretical position that will incorporate the techniques, classify them, and help the clinician decide when and under what conditions to employ one technique over another. Such a theoretical framework would be infinitely more efficient than multiple rules of thumb.

■ Focus Questions

1. What features best characterize a behavioral approach to clinical problems?
2. Describe the major features of the following forms of behavior therapy: systematic desensitization, exposure therapy, behavioral rehearsal, contingency management, and aversion therapy.
3. How have behavioral and cognitive perspectives been integrated into a cognitive-behavioral viewpoint?
4. Describe the major features of the following forms of cognitive-behavioral therapy: modeling, rational restructuring, and cognitive therapy.
5. What are the strengths and limitations of behavior therapy?

■ Key Terms

anxiety hierarchy
assertiveness training
aversion therapy
behavior rehearsal
behavioral therapy
cognitive-behavior therapy
cognitive therapy
contingency contracting
contingency management
counterconditioning
covert modeling
covert sensitization
exposure therapy
extinction

habituation
modeling
Premack principle
rational-emotive therapy (RET)
rational restructuring
relaxation
shaping
stress inoculation
successive approximation
symptom substitution
systematic desensitization
time-out
token economy

15

Group Therapy, Family Therapy, and Couples Therapy

One could argue that most of the problems that bring patients to therapy are acquired and maintained in a social context. It is very likely that current emotional and behavioral problems are influenced, to some degree, by past interpersonal dysfunction. A marital conflict, by definition, involves two people; an unassertive salesperson manifests this problem in interactions with customers. Therefore, inasmuch as the strands of human misery are woven so tightly into the fabric of social relationships, should we not consider forms of therapy that take place in a group setting?

The rise of group therapies stems from an assortment of reasons. Some maintain that it is more economical: seeing patients individually for therapy is, they argue, simply not a rational response to the mental health needs of society. Further, the economics of health care has led many insurers to demand more efficient and less costly forms of mental health treatment. Whatever the considerations, a variety of methods for treating a number of patients at one time — including group therapy, family therapy, and couples therapy — have become increasingly prevalent.

■ Group Therapy

A historical perspective

For many years, group therapy was practiced as a method of choice by only a handful of dedicated therapists. Others used it primarily because their caseload was so heavy that group therapy was the only means by which they could deal with the sheer numbers of patients. Still other therapists used group therapy as a supplementary technique. During individual therapy, for example, a therapist might work toward getting a patient to achieve insight into his need to derogate women, and then, during a group session, other members of the group might reinforce the therapist's interpretation through their reactions to the patient. Now, however, group methods have achieved considerably more visibility and respectability.

One of the earliest formal uses of group methods was represented in Joseph H. Pratt's work with tubercular patients in 1905. This was an inspirational approach that utilized lectures and group discussion to help lift the spirits of depressed patients and promote their cooperation with the medical regimen. A major figure in the group movement was J. L. Moreno, who began to develop some group methods in Vienna in the early 1900s and, in 1925, introduced psychodrama to the United States. Moreno also employed the term *group therapy*. Trigant Burrow was a psychoanalyst who used the related term *group analysis* to describe his procedures (Rosenbaum, 1965). In the 1930s, Slavson encouraged adolescent patients to work through their problems with controlled play, using procedures based on psychoanalytic concepts. These and other figures have been identified as pioneers of the group movement (American Group Psychotherapy Association, 1971; Lubin, 1976).

As was true for clinical psychology generally, it was the aftermath of World War II that really brought group methods to center stage. As we have observed before, at that time the demand for counseling and therapy increased sharply because of the large number of war veterans in need of assistance. The limitations of the existing agency and hospital facilities made it necessary to employ group methods quickly in order to cope with the demand. Once these methods had gained a foothold in the terrain of pragmatism, respectability was but a short distance away. As a result, nearly every school or approach to individual psychotherapy now has its group counterpart. There are group therapies based upon psychoanalytic principles, Gestalt therapy principles, behavior therapy principles, and many other types as well.

Approaches to group therapy

Different approaches to group therapy have emanated from different theoretical origins, and the descriptions of group therapy are couched in a variety of theoretical languages. However, as we also noted with individual psychotherapy, experienced group therapists of the same theoretical persuasion often employ quite different methods (Lieberman, Yalom, & Miles, 1973; Long, 1988). Because of this poor fit between what therapists do and where they come from theoretically, it is difficult to evaluate the similarities and the differences among approaches and, indeed, to describe in any coherent way the methods used in a particular approach. Nevertheless, the following approaches seem fairly typical of the general group therapy movement.

Psychoanalytic group therapy.

One of the best-known approaches is Slavson's *analytic group psychotherapy* (1964), which is basically psychoanalytic therapy carried out in a group setting. Although there are obvious differences from individual psychotherapy (for example, multiple transference effects, modified therapist-patient transference, and influences from one member to another), the focus is still on such phenomena as *free association, transference, interpretation of resistance, and working through*. Although one can hardly argue that group processes do not exist, their role is viewed as secondary to that of individual processes. The group becomes a vehicle through which the individual can express and eventually understand the operation of unconscious forces and defenses and thereby reach a higher level of adjustment.

Wolf (1975) has also emphasized that psychoanalysis can occur in groups as well as on the individual couch. Like Slavson, Wolf feels that the dynamics of the group are secondary to the individual analysis and that the role of the therapist is key. Wolf also argues that, in contrast to individual psychotherapy, group therapy can permit a deeper analytic experience because the individual can lean on the group and thus increase his or her anxiety tolerance. In addition, group members react to one another, to the therapist, and to relationships of authority and intimacy. By observing how others in the group communicate with one another, by participating in a situation in which the individual is not the sole object of the therapist's attention, and by both receiving help from others and giving help to them, the individual can achieve an analysis that is more effective than it might be in the individual therapy setting.

Typically, Wolf's groups consist of eight to ten members (equal numbers of men and women) who meet for 90 minutes three times a week. Sometimes the group meets once or twice a week without the therapist so as to facilitate the working through of transference relationships. Patients often free-associate to their feelings about other members, report dreams, and analyze resistance and transference feelings toward both the therapist and other group members. The following excerpts provide an illustration of psychoanalytically oriented group therapy.

A Case Illustration

This particular group consists of three men (A, B, C), three women (X, Y, Z), and the therapist (a psychoanalytically oriented psychiatrist). The meeting place is the therapist's office. He arranges chairs in a circle, seating himself behind his desk. He knows each of the members, having had them in individual treatment for from several to several hundred sessions. The group is to meet twice weekly for an hour at a time and is "closed"; that is, no new members will be permitted during the life of the group. Below, we present excerpts from the first and the tenth group sessions. The members do not know one another when the first session begins.

Session 1

Therapist: This is our first session in an experience that I hope will be helpful to each of you. None of you know each other, and I would like to introduce you. To my right is Mr. A . . . .

Now that we are through with introductions, I would like to explain how I think we should operate, and make some remarks which I hope will help us in getting the greatest value out of group psychotherapy.

Each of you has been in individual therapy with me. But we are starting here afresh. I will not reveal in the group any information that I may have about you which I have obtained prior to today. In general, the same rules will hold as in individual therapy—that is to say, you will speak about whatever may be in your mind, and I will try to tell you whatever I see in your statements. You may try to analyze one another if you wish. I expect that each of you will respect each other's confidences. While I cannot give you any guarantees about the other members, I know each of you rather well, and I have every confidence in the integrity of each of you. But at the same time you will do well to use your good judgment on what to talk about.

I don't expect to talk in the future as much as I will today in the first session, but let me continue a bit more with some further information. First, psychotherapy is psychotherapy, no matter in which mode it is found. Essentially, it is a process of self-understanding, learning what unconscious motives excite us to behavior. We want to attain insight, so that we will understand what is behind our behavior and our reactions. The goal of psychotherapy is increased satisfaction with ourselves and greater improvement in social behavior. Second, you may be somewhat suspicious about this method, and you think, as I know from talks with each of you, that it may be difficult for you to reveal yourself to others. I think you all share this feeling. However, if you will be able to defer judgment and share in the discussions, you may find that the group method will be valuable and more useful than you believe now. Third, the experience of being in the group per se may not be of value, unless you participate. As trite as this may seem, you will probably get no more out of the situation than you put in. And finally, we may experience all sorts of positive and negative attitudes about one another. These transferences are an essential part of psychotherapy, and you should not be upset if you go through these experiences.

I think that I have said enough, but let me conclude by saying that I am very optimistic about the potentialities of what we are doing, and that I have great hopes we shall all benefit. And so, let us now start.

Session 10

Therapist: Well, I guess we are all here and ought to begin. I wonder how things have been going with Miss Z? She seemed to be right in the midst of a problem when we stopped last session.

A: I was wondering about that too. I hoped that she was able to make out.

Z: Well, I thought quite a lot about what we discussed, and I am glad to say that I think I made progress. I realized that I was fighting with my mother because of resentment I had to her, and that I really did not love her as much as I thought. Then, it came to me, I was really too dependent on her and it would be much healthier if I were able to deal more realistically with her. After all, it wasn't good for her, either.

Y: Then you think you really don't love your mother?

Z: I wouldn't say that. What I think is true is that I am overly dependent on her, and that my resentment of her was really a resentment of myself because, because . . . no one really loves me. (*Begins to cry*)

X: I feel that Z is wrong. People can love her, just anybody can be loved, but in order to be loved, you have to love others.

A: Even in this group, Z seems to keep aloof and won't let others get too close to her.

Z: It is as though my mother and I formed a combination against the whole world. My father left her, and so she depended on me, and I was frightened of the world by her, and so the two of us were alone together, and I had little to do with anyone else. It is a pretty bad situation.

Therapist: Let us try to understand this. I think you are touching something of great value. Both you and your mother formed a cabal against the world. I think you resent her complete possession of you. But now you are aware that it isn't only love you have for your mother, but also hatred. However, you begin to understand how you came to depend on your mother, and also how she came to depend on you. Finally, you are able to see how you have been emotionally enslaved by her. But it must be difficult to experience such emotions, and you must feel alone.[1]

Psychodrama. Developed by Moreno (1946, 1959), *psychodrama* is a form of role playing in which patients act out roles much as if they were in a play. This acting is said to bring about a degree of catharsis and spontaneity that heightens insight and self-understanding. Patients may be asked to play themselves or another role. At times, they may be asked to switch roles in the midst of a dramatization. The drama may involve an event from the patient's past or an upcoming event toward which the patient looks with trepidation.

In general, psychodrama involves a patient, a stage on which the drama is played, a director or therapist, "auxiliary egos" (other patients, therapeutic aides, and others), and an audience. The director assigns the patient a role, and the supporting cast is made up of the auxiliary egos. The audience can provide acceptance and understanding, and may even participate contemporaneously.

Moreno contended that acting out a situation, listening to the responses of the auxiliary egos, and sensing the reactions of the audience lead to a deeper kind of catharsis and self-understanding. He felt that this is much more effective than simply talking to a therapist. Particularly for patients who are inhibited or lack social skills, psychodrama can lead to improved levels of self-expression and to the development of heightened social abilities.

Transactional analysis. Eric Berne (1961) was the developer of and the dynamic force behind *transactional analysis (TA)*. Essentially a process in which the interactions among the people in the group are analyzed, TA often focuses on three chief aspects, or ego states, of the person. Every person possesses a Child ego state, a Parent ego state, and an Adult ego state, and each state is composed of positive and negative features. For example, the positive Child is spontaneous, uninhibited, creative, and so on. The negative Child is fearful, overly emotional, or full of guilt. On the positive side, the Parent state may be characterized as supportive, loving, or understanding. The negative Parent is punishing, quick to condemn, and so on. The Adult ego state is less oriented toward feelings

---

[1]From *Methods of Group Psychotherapy*, by R. J. Corsini, pp. 160–164. Copyright © 1957 by McGraw-Hill, Inc. Reprinted by permission of the author.

and emotions and is more involved with logic, planning, or information gathering. But the Adult can be reasonable (positive) or nonspontaneous (negative).

Depending upon how individuals were raised, they will manifest various aspects of these positive and negative characteristics. A child who was oversupervised or overregulated by the parents might develop an inhibited or guilt-ridden ego state. As a result, when a person in the TA group setting discusses sex in a very pompous, authoritative way, if the inhibited person is then asked to respond, he or she may be unable to do so or may respond under great tension. The therapist might then point out how each person is playing negative roles (either Child, Adult, or Parent). One person is playing a negative Parent role by being pompous and authoritative. The other person is responding in a negative Child fashion by being inhibited and tense. Repeated analyses of the interactions among group members reveal the ego states that they typically employ and, in turn, lead the patients toward more rational, appropriate ways of thinking that are closer to the positive Adult ego state.

The units that are analyzed in this process are _transactions_ — the stimuli and responses that are active between ego states in two or more people at any given moment. The transactional analysis involves a determination of which ego states are operative in any given transaction.

Another aspect of interest in TA is the emphasis on _games_ (Berne, 1964). Games are behaviors that people frequently employ to avoid getting too close to other people; such games are orderly transactions that contain ulterior motives. In TA group therapy, much effort is devoted to discovering and analyzing how the members play games with one another. Berne tends to believe that pseudointimacy, rather than authentic intimacy, characterizes TA groups — the games members play tend to cover their real feelings and beliefs. He sees one function of the therapist as that of a teacher who, through questions, interpretation, and even confrontation, tries to bring patients to the point where they can choose between games and more satisfying behavior. In a few instances, TA principles have been employed at an institutional level. For example, Jesness (1975) describes a TA program to rehabilitate institutionalized juvenile delinquents.

TA tends to be a swift-moving, action-oriented approach. There is an emphasis on the present, a sense of grappling with immediate problems, that makes it attractive to many patients and therapists. TA has an aura of responsibility, of learning how to choose between options, and this can be a desirable alternative to more traditional forms of group therapy that often appear to lumber along at an agonizingly slow pace. There is also a conceptual simplicity to the whole scheme that seems to make it understandable and perhaps more acceptable to patient and professional alike.

Yet this very simplicity, coupled with the zeal and entrepreneurship of some TA practitioners, has led to a popularization that can be dangerous. Many feel that human problems are complex events that cannot be easily translated into games and that any gains from such procedures are therefore likely to be short-lived. Certainly there is little in the research literature to calm such fears, since TA therapists rarely produce research.

Gestalt groups. Gestalt group therapy is difficult to categorize. Like psychoanalytic group therapy, it is oriented toward the experience of the individual patient. At the same time, its emphasis on resident seminars, weekend retreats, brief workshops, and general popularization give it a distinct flavor of the encounter movement (for example, Rogers, 1970). These latter features may have stemmed in part from the strong and at times flamboyant nature of Fritz Perls, the leader of the Gestalt movement, coupled with the considerable publicity that was given the Esalen Institute in Big Sur, California.

As we saw in Chapter 13, Gestalt therapy focuses on leading the patient to an awareness of the now and an appreciation of being in the world. In group therapy this is achieved by concentrating on one member at a time. In what has been dubbed the "hot seat" approach, the therapist focuses on the patient while the remainder of the group serve as observers. Patients are asked to experience their feelings and behavior—to lose their minds and find their senses—while other group members may be called on to say how they regard the person in the hot seat. At times there are bits of role playing, the reporting of dreams, and dialogues between patients (Perls, 1973). But regardless of whether a member is an observer or in the hot seat, there tends to be intense involvement in the proceedings. As with TA methods, the popularization of the procedures, the lack of research on the results, and the emotionality involved all make it difficult to assess the effectiveness of Gestalt group therapy and to determine whether its effects generalize beyond the specific situation or weekend.

Behavior therapy groups.   Group behavior therapy seems to have grown out of considerations of efficiency rather than any feeling that the dynamics of the group interaction would be especially valuable (Lazarus, 1975; Rose, 1991). It is entirely feasible to conduct desensitization sessions, model interpersonal skills, or use cognitive restructuring interventions in a group setting (Rose, 1991). For example, it is possible to teach patients in a group setting how to relax, and it is equally possible to establish common anxiety hierarchies simultaneously with several patients. Thus, where such procedures are feasible, it is certainly efficient to use them.

Behavioral and cognitive-behavioral groups are usually time limited (for example, 12 sessions) and comprised of patients with similar problems. As in most behavior therapy treatments, these group members complete a variety of assessment instruments before, during, and after treatment in order to monitor progress. Rose (1991) provides a number of examples of how reinforcement, modeling, problem solving, and cognitive interventions are implemented in behavior therapy groups. Research has supported the efficacy of behavioral and cognitive-behavioral group interventions for the treatment of depression, social skills deficits, pain, agoraphobia, and other conditions (Rose, 1991).

One kind of group behavior therapy that was not established mainly for efficiency is assertiveness training. Here, a group approach is usually the treatment of choice. Groups provide nonassertive individuals with an excellent environment in which to confront their problems, to reduce their fear of being assertive, and to learn acceptable methods of self-expression. Such groups typically involve direct teaching whereby the therapist describes the group's goals and the problems that nonassertiveness can generate for people. Assertiveness training groups are also usually characterized by such features as cooperative problem solving, honesty, and acceptance among group members. Opportunities are provided for group members to comment and to criticize the manner in which they present themselves. New assertiveness skills are demonstrated and practiced, and homework assignments are often given, followed by group discussion of their success.

Time-limited group therapy. The final example of a group approach that we will discuss is *time-limited group therapy* (Budman & Gurman, 1988). This contemporary model is appealing because of its efficiency, and it is likely to guide group interventions in the age of managed care. These groups typically meet on a weekly basis and only for a predetermined number of sessions (for example, eight sessions for a group consisting of members who are dealing with a life crisis). As noted by Budman and Gurman (1988), there are four central features characteristic of time-limited groups:

1. *Pregroup preparation and screening.* A one-and-one-half-hour pregroup workshop is used to evaluate and screen potential group members. This screening makes it more likely that, once the actual group begins, the group can "hit the ground running" and that the group members have the requisite skills to contribute to the group and, thus, benefit.

2. Establishment and maintenance of a *working focus* in the group. The working focus is defined as a particular concern, problem or issue that is shared by all group members (for example, problems with intimacy). The focus is introduced in the first group session. For example:

   > As I've mentioned to all of you previously, this is a young adult group that will have as its central theme problems of intimacy. Members of this group have all, in one way or another, been struggling with these issues recently. Experience indicates that a short-term group like this one can be a very useful vehicle for helping people with such difficulties. Obviously, you all have other concerns as well as those related to intimacy. To the degree that it is possible, we will talk about some of these too. However, because of our limited time working together, we will need to remain focused for the most part on intimacy concerns. (Budman & Gurman, 1988, p. 269)

3. *Group cohesion.* Theorists and researchers are convinced that group cohesion (that is, the degree to which group members are involved in the process, trust each other, cooperate, focus, and express compassion) is an important determinant of outcome.

4. *Reactions to time limits.* Because these groups are time limited, group members may experience feelings related to life stage, prior losses, and frustration that more has not been accomplished in the group.

Budman and Gurman (1988) also analyze the different stages of the group (for example, starting the group, early group development, termination, and follow-up) because each stage presents the therapist with different challenges. For example, the termination stage is often characterized by the expression of sadness, and some group members may push for the therapist to extend the number of sessions. In this stage, the therapist's job is to review the positive changes in the group and in each individual in the context of the working focus and to have group members express their thoughts and feelings about what it will be like without the group. Budman and Gurman (1988) recommend a follow-up session (6 to 12 months after termination) to maintain the positive changes that took place and to demonstrate the changes group members have made on their own in the interim.

The arrangements

Because of the wide variety of group approaches that are employed by clinicians, it may be somewhat misleading to give a general description of the arrangements for group therapy. However, despite the diversity of techniques, there are some general similarities. For example, most groups consist of five to ten patients who meet with the therapist at least once a week for 90-minute to two-hour sessions. The members are often seated in a circle, so that members can all see each other. Sometimes they are seated around a table, sometimes not.

The composition of the group may vary, depending both upon the therapist's convictions and upon practical considerations. Some therapists feel strongly that a heterogeneous group is best—one having men and women clients with a variety of problems, backgrounds, and personalities. Other therapists feel that homogeneous groups are best—those composed exclusively of alcoholics, phobic patients, and so on. The latter group of therapists believes that homogeneity makes for greater efficiency, quicker understanding, and mutual acceptance (see Budman & Gurman, 1988). It is relatively easy to establish homogeneous groups in institutional settings with a large number of patients, but, in private practice, the therapist may have no alternative except to use heterogeneous groups. Most therapists agree that certain kinds of patients must generally be excluded from the group approach: those with severe cognitive limitations, those who are grossly psychotic, and those who are especially prone to disrupt the group process (for example, monopolists of the group discussions, extremely antagonistic patients, and so on).

In some instances, all group members are seen concurrently on an individual basis by the therapist—in other instances, only at group therapy meetings. At times, some therapists like to use a cotherapist (often a therapist of the opposite sex who will add another dimension to such processes as transference), and some groups meet occasionally without a therapist. In some groups there are prohibitions against extracurricular fraternizing; other therapists feel that such prohibitions are unrealistic (Yalom, 1975). Open groups admit a new member whenever someone leaves the group; closed groups admit no new members once the group has begun to function. Whatever the exact format, the role of the group leader is critical (Naar, 1982). Issues of confidentiality in group therapy can also be important (Meyer & Smith, 1977). Thus, in explaining the arrangements and rules of the group to group members, the therapist may find it necessary to state that, though it is hoped that the members will maintain the confidentiality of the sessions, no final guarantees can be offered (see the case illustration on page 407).

The curative factors

The diversity of group approaches is apparent. Yet, underlying all of them are common threads that speak to the utility of group therapy. Yalom (1975) has specified a set of *curative factors* that seems to define the essence of what these group methods offer.

1. *Imparting information.* Group members can receive advice and guidance not just from the therapist but also from other group members.
2. *Instilling hope.* Observing others who have successfully grappled with problems helps to instill hope—a necessary ingredient for any successful therapy experience.

3. *Universality.* Listening to others, group members discover that they share common problems, fears, and concerns. Knowing that one is not alone can be highly rewarding.
4. *Altruism.* In the beginning, a group member often feels useless and demoralized. As it becomes apparent that an individual can help others in the group, a feeling of greater self-value and competence emerges.
5. *Interpersonal learning.* Interacting with others in the group can teach members about interpersonal relationships, social skills, sensitivity to others, resolution of conflicts, and so on.
6. *Imitative behavior.* Watching and listening to others can lead to the modeling of more useful behaviors. Group members learn from each other.
7. *Corrective recapitulation of the primary family.* The group context can help clients understand and resolve problems related to family members. The effects of past family experiences can be dissolved by learning that maladaptive coping methods will not work in the present group situation.
8. *Catharsis.* Learning how to express feelings about others in the group in an honest, open way builds a capacity for mutual trust and understanding.
9. *Group cohesiveness.* Group members become a tightly knit little group that enhances self-esteem through group acceptance.

Does group therapy work?

Reviews of the research literature assessing the effectiveness of group psychotherapy consistently conclude that group treatment is more effective than no treatment (for example, Bednar & Kaul, 1994). However, group treatments do not appear to be any more effective than other forms of psychotherapy. The major advantage of group therapy is that it is more efficient and more economical, especially the time-limited group treatments.

Unfortunately, research on group therapy has not advanced much beyond answering the general question of overall effectiveness (Bednar & Kaul, 1994). Although theorists such as Yalom have proposed a variety of curative factors or other variables that may influence outcome in group treatment (for example, group leadership style, the necessity of pregroup training, and so on), relatively few studies have been conducted that critically examine the effects of these factors. Further, the studies that have been completed are plagued with a number of conceptual and methodological problems. Clearly, more research investigating the process of group psychotherapy and the proposed curative factors is needed in order to better understand why and how group therapy works (Bednar & Kaul, 1994; Rose, 1991).

■ Family Therapy and Couples Therapy

Generally, when a member of a family develops a problem, everyone in the family is affected. Increasingly, families are going into therapy as units in an attempt to fathom the nature of their difficulties and the means by which to deal with them. Clearly, family and couples therapy is a burgeoning field. Numerous handbooks (for example, Jacobson & Gurman, 1986; L'Abate, 1985; Piercy, Sprenkle, & Associates, 1986; Sherman & Fredman, 1986) and overviews of the field (including Barker, 1986; Glick, Clarkin, & Kessler, 1987; L'Abate, 1986; Nichols, 1988) continue to appear every year. Further evidence of this interest is the special section on the treatment of families and couples that appears frequently in clinical journals like the *Journal of Consulting and Clinical Psychology.*

Many years ago, a number of psychotherapists recognized that therapy for a child was often just an excuse to get the parents into the clinic for therapeutic interviews. For example, it was not unusual to schedule therapy for the child twice a week. During that time, the child would finger-paint, engage in expressive play, or do other things that were assumed to have cathartic, therapeutic value. But many clinicians recognized intuitively that it made little sense to work with a child for two hours a week and then send the child back to an unchanged home environment — the environment that, in all probability, was responsible for the development of the problem in the first place. Consequently, it became common practice to talk with the parents during the time that the child was in the clinic playroom. Indeed, many clinicians came to believe that those interviews were more responsible for improvements in the child's behavior than the whole of playroom experiences. Such clinical episodes paved the way for the development of the *family therapy* movement.

The development of family therapy

Fruzzetti and Jacobson (1991) trace the origins of family therapy to the nineteenth-century social work movement. However, family therapy did not immediately gain prominence. It was not until the mid-twentieth century that family therapy became a popular form of treatment. Some of the delay had to do with the dominance of psychoanalysis for so many years. The perspectives of behaviorism and humanism eventually paved the way for an alternative treatment like family therapy to become a viable option for clinicians. Using this latter approach, the problems of individuals were conceptualized in *systemic* terms, as a manifestation of some type of family dysfunction. This new perspective on clinical problems was most evident in some of the conceptualizations of severe mental disorders like schizophrenia.

In trying to understand schizophrenia, a Palo Alto research group (Bateson, Jackson, Haley, Satir, and others) approached the problem from a communication point of view. To influence one family member, the entire family system had to be dealt with (Jackson & Weakland, 1961). Thus, family therapy was the logical deduction. Also related to the idea of the family as a unit is the concept of the *double bind* (Bateson, Jackson, Haley, & Weakland, 1956). For example, a child might be told by a father, "Always stand up for your rights, no matter who, no matter what!" But that child is also told by the father, "Never question my authority; I am your father, and what I say goes!" Thus, the child is in a bind. The contradiction inherent in the two messages ensures that, no matter what the child does in relation to the father, it will be the wrong thing. According to the Bateson group, the contradiction, the father's failure to admit that there is a contradiction, and the lack of support from other family members can provide fertile soil for the development of schizophrenia. Actually, there is really very little empirical support for the double-bind theory of schizophrenia — indeed, there has been a failure even to establish such communications as reliable phenomena. But the hypothesis was a remarkably fruitful one since it nourished much of the Palo Alto family therapy work. This illustrates the point that the value of concepts and research does not reside exclusively in their rightness or wrongness. Their heuristic value — that is, the extent to which they stimulate new work, new ideas, or new procedures — is also important.

Theodore Lidz and his research team also emphasized the family in the etiology of schizophrenia (Lidz, Cornelison, Fleck, & Terry, 1957a, 1957b). Marriage partners fail to meet each other's psychological and emotional needs, and, as a result, one partner may form a pathological alliance with the child that ultimately precipitates the latter's schizophrenia. Bowen's observation (1960) of schizophrenic patients who lived together with their parents in a hospital ward for sustained periods led to the conclusion that the entire family unit was pathogenic and not just the patient. Similar conclusions were reached by Ackerman (1958, 1966). The foregoing work is being discussed here not so much because it explained the etiology of schizophrenia (it did not) but because such work and that of Satir (1967a), Haley (1971), Jackson (1957), and Bell (1961) gave impetus and direction to the family therapy movement — one rich in technique, theory, and history (Guerin, 1976).

The concept of communication

From the time of its origins in the work on schizophrenia, family therapy has placed its emphasis on *communication*. Pathology has typically been seen as a failure in communication among family members. As Foley (1974) has observed, family therapy has developed by utilizing a communication model that emphasizes feedback and information rather than insight and cure.

A part of this communication focus can be seen in what many regard as the most important concept in family therapy: *general systems theory*. According to this theory, the family is conceived of as a system, which family therapy seeks to alter in some important manner. From this point of view, the function of family therapy is to deal with the relationship between the individual family member and the family system. The emphasis is not on the overt pathological symptoms or dysfunction of a person or on the purported intrapsychic conflicts. An overactive id, for example, is not considered the cause of sexual problems. Rather, the view is that the individual experiences problems because of a lack of information. Therapy is a process of correcting this lack of information or of changing the manner of feedback. The therapist achieves positive change not from an awareness of the patient's intrapsychic conflicts but by using feedback that, in turn, alters the way in which the system functions.

Ackerman (1958, 1960, 1966) occupies a position midway between the individual or intrapsychic approach to pathology and the systems approach that characterizes the communication theorists. He feels that there is a constant interchange among the patient, the family, and society. Full understanding of the patient requires an appreciation of this interchange. Although Ackerman attaches great importance to the communication process in the family system, he also regards the content of that communication as extremely important. Others, such as Bowen (1960), see communication as something that is subsumed under a larger system of relationships.

Forms and methods

There is no clear, consensual definition of what constitutes family therapy — indeed, there is not even a consensus on who should conduct it. The general procedures of family therapy are carried out by psychologists, psychiatrists, social workers, counselors, and others. Family therapists and counselors are trained in several different programs, including clinical psychology, counseling psychology, psychiatry, social work, family and child development, and education. All of this, of course, makes for considerable confusion and some squabbling over professional credentials. Some therapists use family therapy as only one of several techniques; others are exclusively family therapists. Since there is little agreement as to who is qualified to conduct family therapy, is it any wonder that the specific techniques employed (which actually seem to have much in common) are given such distinctive titles? Thus, we have *family therapy, behavioral family therapy, conjoint family therapy, concurrent family therapy, collaborative family therapy, network family therapy, structural family therapy, multiple-family therapy,* and on and on. There are also many varieties of theoretical approaches ranging from the systemic (Campbell & Draper, 1985) to the psychodynamic (Will & Wrate, 1985) to the behavioral (Falloon, 1988) and on to those who purport to integrate various theoretical practices (Nichols & Everett, 1986).

The goals. Most family therapists share the primary goal of improving communication within the family, and, in doing so, they deemphasize the problems of the individual in favor of treating the problems of the family as a whole. However, once we get beyond such general statements, there seems to be some disarray of purposes and goals. For example, many therapists who talk about the family system still seem to view family therapy as a kind of context in which to solve an individual's problems. Seeing the family together becomes a technique (perhaps a more efficient one) for inducing changes in the individual patient. Other family therapists are devoted to the philosophy that regarding the family as a unit and working with it as such will enhance that unit. Although this may benefit the individual members, the real focus is on the family. As in most enterprises, the largest number of family therapists falls somewhere between these two extremes.

Some general characteristics. Certain aspects of family therapy differentiate it from the customary individual therapy. For example, family members have a shared frame of reference, a common history, and a shared language of connotations that may be foreign to the therapist. The therapist has to learn the family roles and something about the family's idiosyncratic subculture. This information is used in order to enhance communication or to confront family members. At the same time, the therapist must remain detached and not become overly identified with one faction of the family at the expense of another. This can be a difficult and delicate task, for often family members will attempt to use the therapist in their power struggles or in their defenses against open communication.

A history and assessment process is a typical part of family therapy. The presenting problem must be stated and understood. It may be that a son is a delinquent or that a daughter is sexually promiscuous. It is often quite interesting and diagnostically important to see how different family members construe the same problem in quite divergent ways. Usually, a family history will be taken. This, too, can have ramifications. By placing the family problem in the larger context of information about the parents' origins and their early life and marriage, improved communication and understanding can often be attained by children. By laying out the entire panorama of family history—its extended members and their goals, aspirations, fears, and frailties—deeper understanding, empathy, and tolerance are often possible. This larger context can easily promote a shared frame of reference that was not possible before. A child can begin to learn what it meant for the mother to relinquish her own aspirations in favor of the family, what it meant for the father to experience abuse from his own father. In the controlled setting of the family therapy room, the parents may, at the same time, remember (via the current experience of their children) what it was like to encounter peer pressure.

Conjoint family therapy

In *conjoint family therapy,* the entire family is seen at the same time by one therapist. In some varieties of this approach, the therapist plays a rather passive, nondirective role. In other varieties, the therapist is an active force, directing the conversation, assigning tasks to the various family members, imparting direct instruction regarding human relations, and so on.

Satir (1967a, 1967b) regarded the family therapist as a resource person who observes the family process in action and then becomes a model of communication to the family through clear, crisp communication. Thus, Satir viewed the therapist as a teacher, a resource person, and a communicator. Such a therapist illustrates to family members how they can better communicate with one another and thereby bring about more satisfying relationships.

Perhaps some of the sense of all this can be seen in the following excerpts from Satir (1967a), clarifying the interaction process for a family.

A Case Illustration

Therapist: (to husband) I notice your brow is wrinkled, Ralph. Does that mean you are angry at this moment?

Husband: I did not know that my brow was wrinkled.

Therapist: Sometimes a person looks or sounds in a way of which he is not aware. As far as you can tell, what were you thinking and feeling just now?

Husband: I was thinking over what she [his wife] said.

Therapist: What thing that she said were you thinking about?

Husband: When she said that when she was talking so loud, she wished I would tell her.

Therapist: What were you thinking about that?

Husband: I never thought about telling her. I thought she would get mad.

Therapist: Ah, then maybe that wrinkle meant you were puzzled because your wife was hoping you would do something and you did not know she had this hope? Do you suppose that by your wrinkled brow you were signaling that you were puzzled?

Husband: Yeh, I guess so.

Therapist: As far as you know, have you ever been in that same spot before, that is, where you were puzzled by something Alice said or did?

Husband: Hell, yes, lots of times.

Therapist: Have you ever told Alice you were puzzled when you were?

Wife: He never says anything.

Therapist: (*smiling, to Alice*) Just a minute, Alice, let me hear what Ralph's idea is of what he does. Ralph, how do you think you have let Alice know when you are puzzled?

Husband: I think she knows.

Therapist: Well, let's see. Suppose you ask Alice if she knows.

Husband: This is silly.

Therapist: (*smiling*) I suppose it might seem so in this situation, because Alice is right here and certainly has heard what your question is. She knows what it is. I have the suspicion, though, that neither you nor Alice are very sure about what the other expects, and I think you have not developed ways to find out. Alice, let's go back to when I commented on Ralph's wrinkled brow. Did you happen to notice it, too?

Wife: (*complaining*) Yes, he always looks like that.

Therapist: What kind of message did you get from that wrinkled brow?

Wife: He don't want to be here. He don't care. He never talks. Just looks at television or he isn't home.

Therapist: I'm curious. Do you mean that when Ralph has a wrinkled brow that you take this as Ralph's way of saying, "I don't love you, Alice. I don't care about you, Alice"?

Wife: (*exasperated and tearfully*) I don't know.

Therapist: Well, maybe the two of you have not yet worked out crystal-clear ways of giving your love and value messages to each other. Everyone needs crystal-clear ways of giving their value messages. (*to son*) What do you know, Jim, about how you give your value messages to your parents?

Son: I don't know what you mean.

Therapist: Well, how do you let your mother, for instance, know that you like her, when you are feeling that way. Everyone feels different ways at different times. When you are feeling glad your mother is around, how do you let her know?

Son: I do what she tells me to do. Work and stuff.

Therapist: I see, so when you do your work at home, you mean this for a message to your mother that you're glad she is around.

Son: Not exactly.

Therapist: You mean you are giving a different message then. Well, Alice, did you take this message from Jim to be a love message? (*to Jim*) What do you do to give your father a message that you like him?

Son: (*after a pause*) I can't think of nothing.

Therapist: Let me put it another way. What do you know crystal-clear that you could do that would bring a smile on your father's face?

Son: I could get better grades in school.

Therapist: Let's check this out and see if you are perceiving clearly. Do you, Alice, get a love message from Jim when he works around the house?

Wife: I s'pose—he doesn't do very much.

Therapist: So from where you sit, Alice, you don't get many love messages from Jim. Tell me, Alice, does Jim have any other ways that he might not now be thinking about that he has that say to you that he is glad you are around?

Wife: (*softly*) The other day he told me I looked nice.

Therapist: What about you, Ralph, does Jim perceive correctly that if he got better grades you would smile?

Husband: I don't imagine I will be smiling for some time.

Therapist: I hear that you don't think he is getting good grades, but would you smile if he did?

Husband: Sure, hell, I would be glad.

Therapist: As you think about it, how do you suppose you would show it?

Wife: You never know if you ever please him.

Therapist: We have already discovered that you and Ralph have not yet developed crystal-clear ways of showing value feelings toward one another. Maybe you, Alice, are now observing this between Jim and Ralph. What do you think, Ralph? Do you suppose it would be hard for Jim to find out when he has pleased you?[2]

In conjoint and other forms of family therapy, there are five basic modes of communication (Satir, 1975): (1) *placating* (always agreeing, no matter what is going on); (2) *blaming* (showing how much one family member can criticize another and thus throw his or her weight around); (3) *super-reasonable* (especially characteristic of teachers, whose words may sound super-reasonable but may bear no relationship to how they feel); (4) *irrelevant* (the words are completely unrelated to what is going on); and (5) *congruent* (the words relate to what is real). These modes of communication provide, in a sense, the essence of communication and feeling. They do not negate the role of cognitions, but they do place the emphasis where Satir believed it belongs.

Other varieties of family therapy

There are many versions of family therapy. The following are a sample of the more commonly encountered versions.

Concurrent family therapy. In this approach, one therapist sees all family members, but in individual sessions. The overall goals are the same as those in conjoint therapy. In some instances, the therapist may conduct traditional psychotherapy with the principal patient but also occasionally see other members of the family; as a matter of fact, it is perhaps unfortunate that this last variation is not employed more often as a part of traditional psychotherapy. Since it often happens that an individual patient's problems can be understood better and dealt

---

[2]From *Conjoint Family Therapy,* by Virginia Satir, pp. 97–100. Copyright © 1967 by Science and Behavior Books. Reprinted by permission.

with better in collaboration with significant others in the patient's life, the use of such arrangements should facilitate the therapeutic process.

Collaborative family therapy.   Here, a different therapist is used for each family member, and the therapists then get together to discuss their patients and the family as a whole. As we saw earlier, the use of this approach with child patients was one of the factors that stimulated the early growth of family therapy. In a variation of this general approach, cotherapists are sometimes assigned to work with the same family (that is, two or more therapists meet with the family unit).

Behavioral family therapy.   Some (for example, Liberman, 1970; Patterson, 1971) have viewed family relations in terms of reinforcement contingencies. The role of the therapist in this approach is to generate a behavioral analysis of family problems. This helps identify the behaviors whose frequency should be increased or decreased as well as the rewards that are maintaining undesirable behaviors or that will enhance desired behaviors. Therapy then becomes a process of inducing family members to dispense the appropriate reinforcements to each other for the desired behaviors. Indeed, some therapists (Stuart, 1969) even have family members employ tokens in this context. For example, a husband might earn four tokens if he does not watch Sunday football on TV and instead takes his wife for a drive in the country. Of course, it must be made clear in advance exactly what these tokens may be exchanged for later!

In tune with recent developments in cognitive-behavioral therapy generally, it is not surprising to find that these methods have found their way to the family therapy enterprise (see Epstein, Schlesinger, & Dryden, 1988).

Other forms.   In *network family group therapy* (Speck & Attneave, 1971), the therapist works with the entire network of important persons in the patient's life—neighbors, employers, friends, family, and so on. Obviously, such therapy requires a high degree of cooperation on the part of interested persons. *Multiple impact therapy* (MacGregor, Ritchie, Serrano, & Schuster, 1964) involves two days of very intensive work with the entire family on the part of a clinic team of professionals. Working in sessions with individual family members, the team examines the marriage, the role of authority, the views of the children regarding the family, and other things. Typically, a six-month follow-up is conducted to assess the family's progress. In *multiple-family therapy* (Strelnick, 1977), several couples or families meet as a group with a therapist. To a large degree, the notion is that sharing experiences will enable each couple or family to help the other couples or families—a sort of cross between family therapy and group therapy. Another approach is typified by the *Homebuilders Program* developed in Tacoma, Washington (Kinney, Madsen, Fleming, & Haapala, 1977). In this program, a therapist who is on call 24 hours a day will enter the home of a family in crisis to help prevent the removal of family members (via institutionalization and the like) to alternative living situations. Such a therapist can remain within the home as long as is required within a six-week period. *Structural family therapy* (Minuchin, 1974) is oriented toward the resolution of immediate problems while stressing the manner in which authority is arranged in the family. Matters concerning the development of the marriage and the family are also emphasized.

When family therapy?

There are no hard-and-fast rules as to when family therapy is appropriate and when it is not. Most often, family therapy is begun with an adolescent as the principal patient. Perhaps the patient's problems are so tied up with the family that family therapy is really the only sensible course. Perhaps the family has impeded therapeutic progress in the past or has resisted the therapist's advice; involving the entire family in the therapy network, then, may dissolve some of this resistance.

In other cases, the patient's problems (or sometimes even the patient's improvement in therapy!) have so involved or threatened the fabric of the family that it seems wise to treat the family as a whole. Sometimes, family crises, such as the death of a family member, propel the entire family unit into pathology almost as one. In some families there are conflicts over values. For example, an adolescent who begins to take drugs or becomes totally absorbed in a cult or different religion may disrupt the entire family by seeming to undermine its values. In such instances, family therapy might be a logical recourse.

Finally, significant marital or sexual problems may seem to be best resolved by a form of family therapy. It can, of course, be difficult to determine whether individual, family, or couples therapy should be undertaken as a way of working out such problems. However, family therapy or couples counseling would seem appropriate when the problems do not seem to stem from deep-seated emotional conflicts but from matters that can be dealt with educationally, including misguided attitudes, poor knowledge about sexuality, or lack of communication.

However, family therapy is not a cure-all, and it is not always appropriate. It sometimes happens that a family is so disrupted that such intervention would clearly be doomed to fail. It may also happen that one or more family members will simply refuse to cooperate. In some instances, it quickly becomes clear that a given family member is so disturbed, so uncooperative, or so disruptive that the entire process of family therapy would be poisoned by his or her presence.

Since family therapy involves several people, one must sometimes approach its possible use on a cost-benefit basis. Although family therapy might benefit the identified patient of the group, the process could have malignant possibilities for some of the other members. Like individual patients, some families simply do not possess the psychological strength or resources to cope with the threatening material that may come out in family therapy sessions. Deciding when to employ family therapy and when not to is often a difficult matter that requires careful assessment and a great deal of clinical sensitivity.

Couples therapy

Throughout this chapter, we use the term *couples therapy*. However, the reader should keep in mind that couples therapy is not limited to "married" couples, but can be provided to unmarried couples, same-sex couples, and others. There are many issues that bring couples in to consult with a clinician (Goldberg, 1985). In one sense, couples therapy can be construed as a form of family therapy. For example, when a husband and wife are seen together and the focus of treatment is on the marital relationship itself rather than on the problems of the individuals, a form of family therapy seems to be involved.

Although the couples therapy movement, like the family therapy movement, owes much to interpersonal theorists like Sullivan, Horney, and Fromm, the development of couples therapy as a discipline can be attributed to pragmatic concerns (Fruzzetti & Jacobson, 1991). Essentially, a wide variety of professionals (for example, doctors and lawyers) by necessity became more involved in attempting to resolve marital conflicts in the course of carrying out their "regular" duties. Fruzzetti and Jacobson (1991) also note the remarkable growth of couples therapy since the 1960s. Today the most popular forms of couples therapy are behavioral marital therapy, cognitive couples therapy, humanistic couples therapy, sex therapy, and insight-oriented (psychodynamic) couples therapy. To give the reader a flavor of what techniques are used in couples therapy, we will briefly describe *behavioral marital therapy,* or *BMT* (Jacobson & Margolin, 1979; Stuart, 1980; Weiss, Hops, & Patterson, 1973). Again, despite the use of the term *marital,* BMT does not require that the partners be married.

The beginnings of behavioral marital therapy are often traced to the work of Richard Stuart (1969). Stuart's treatment of marital dysfunction involved the application of reinforcement principles to couple's interactions. A major component of his treatment was a technique called *contingency contracting;* spouses were trained to modify their own behavior in order to effect a specific desired change in their mate's behavior. Over the years, BMT has broadened to include a number of additional techniques. *Support-understanding techniques* aim to increase positive behaviors emitted by partners, positive feelings in each partner, and collaboration within the couple. For example, the partners generate a list of behaviors that, if produced by their mates, will bring pleasure. Then each agrees to perform three of the behaviors from the other's list before the next session. *Problem-solving techniques* involve training couples in positive communication skills so that effective decision making and negotiating is possible. For example, couples are given a list of basic rules of positive communication skills; they then practice these skills within the session. The clinician intervenes if it seems warranted (for example, clarifying the appropriate communication skills, modeling alternative ways to communicate that are more positive, and so on). These and other BMT strategies are described in more detail in a number of sources (see Gottman, Notarius, Gonso, & Markman, 1976; Jacobson & Margolin, 1979; Stuart, 1980).

Are family therapy and couples therapy effective?

As with other forms of psychotherapy, it is important to critically evaluate the empirical evidence that speaks to the efficacy of different forms of family and couples therapy. Before presenting these data, however, it is important to note that the measurement of outcome in family and couples therapy is quite complex because of the multiple perspectives that must be considered (for example, different family members, both spouses). As in individual psychotherapy research, self-report measures, ratings by others (such as the therapist), and observational ratings are used extensively in family and couples therapy research.

Table 15-1

Average effect size ($\overline{ES}$) and percentile equivalent for select forms of family therapy and
    couples therapy.

Type of Therapy	$\overline{ES}$	Percentile Equivalent
Any type of family therapy	0.47	68%
Behavioral/psychoeducational	0.44	67%
Systemic	0.25	60%
Humanistic	0.29	61%
Eclectic	0.55	71%
Any type of couples therapy	0.60	73%
Behavioral/psychoeducational	0.74	77%
Systemic	0.62	73%
Humanistic	0.12	55%
Eclectic	0.63	74%

NOTE: *Percentile equivalent* indicates the percentage of those not receiving treatment whose outcome is
exceeded by those receiving the treatment in question.

SOURCE: From "Effects of Family and Marital Therapies: A Meta-Analysis," by W. R. Shadish, L. M.
Montgomery, P. Wilson, M. R. Wilson, I. Bright, and T. Okwumabua, 1993, *Journal of Consulting and
Clinical Psychology, 61,* 992–1002. Copyright © 1993 by the American Psychological Association.
Reprinted by permission.

Family therapy.   Despite its popularity in clinical practice, relatively few
well-controlled empirical studies evaluating the effectiveness of family therapy have
been conducted. For example, a recent meta-analysis (Shadish et al., 1993) com-
puted only 44 effect sizes from published articles and unpublished dissertations
(years 1963–1988) that evaluated the efficacy of family therapy. The average effect size for any form of family therapy was 0.47, indicating that the average
treated client was functioning better than 68% of those individuals not receiving
treatment. Shadish et al. also reported average effect sizes separately for various
types of family therapy. Eclectic (combinations of orientations) and behavioral/
psychoeductional treatments were most effective, whereas humanistic and systemic approaches were least effective. Table 15-1 presents the data from this
meta-analysis.

Couples Therapy.   Table 15-1 also presents Shadish et al.'s meta-
analytic results for couples therapy. First, it should be noted that even fewer studies and effect sizes were available to evaluate couples therapy than family therapy.
As shown in the table, the average effect size for any form of couples therapy was
0.60, somewhat higher than that found for family therapy. Shadish et al. found
great variability as to the effectiveness of different forms of couples therapy; humanistic couples therapy appeared to be much less effective than other forms.

    In summary, Shadish et al.'s review as well as other reviews of the empirical
literature (for example, Alexander, Holtzworth-Munroe, & Jameson, 1994; Hahl-

weg & Markman, 1988; Hazelrigg, Cooper, & Borduin, 1987) suggest that, in general, these treatments appear to be modestly effective. Some variation in effectiveness among types of treatment was apparent, with humanistic versions of both family and couples treatment consistently showing weaker effects.

Special problems

It would seem that family therapy poses some special problems for the therapist. For example, the expression of strong emotions, negative feelings, and hostility in the group setting could threaten the unity of the family and shake the foundations of parental authority and respect. However, it is questionable just how unique such potentialities really are. Families that seek therapy are families in trouble, and it is improbable that problems involving lack of parental respect and hostility, for example, were absent prior to therapy. When such problems arise in therapy they can be worked through by the sensitive therapist. Indeed, their resolution may be the basis on which improvement in family relations occurs. The discussion of such issues in therapy may make for some stormy sessions and some equally stormy confrontations at home. But in the long run, this may be beneficial (Fox, 1976).

Some have also pointed out that individual therapy tends to disrupt families more than does family therapy (Fitzgerald, 1973). In individual therapy, for example, patients may decide that the personal growth they have achieved makes it impossible to continue living with a spouse who has not attained comparable growth. It is sometimes true that individual therapy exposes a great deal of incompatibility of needs among family members that was not obvious before. In such instances, a family breakup may ensue. In a recent study of the effects of one partner's psychotherapy on the other partner, several findings stood out (Brody & Farber, 1989). First, the nontherapy partners believed their therapy partners were more open, empathic, and communicative as a result of the therapy. At the same time, they experienced feelings of exclusion, resentment, and inadequacy because of their partner's relationship with the therapist. Most did not appreciate the cost of their partner's therapy either. All in all, it was clear that therapy initiated a process of change in the relationship between partners. Couples therapy is known to sometimes precipitate divorce (Alexander et al., 1994). This is enough of a problem that the possibility of divorce is sometimes listed as a risk on couples therapy contracts and consent forms.

One problem that can be thorny is identifying who the real patient is. When a therapist recommends that an entire family be seen along with the patient who was originally referred individually, things are fairly clear. But, at times, another member of the family may subsequently appear to be even more disturbed than the original patient. In any case, for therapists committed to the view that the client is "the family," such situations can pose problems in communication that must be clarified. Depending upon one's theoretical orientation, seeing one person as the patient and the remainder of the family as the backdrop can prove difficult. Problem or not, however, how the therapy situation is structured must be clearly understood.

In summary, we may ask, as does Margolin (1982), "Who is the client? How is confidential information handled? Does each family member have an equal right to refuse treatment? What is the role of the therapist's values vis-à-vis conflicting values of family members?" (p. 788). Complex and controversial questions to be sure. Basically, these and other questions center around ethical issues. If family problems are the focus, then what is family health and who decides what a "good" family really is? (Huber & Baruth, 1987). Perhaps, as Constantine (1986) argues, there are many forms of normal family functioning. And what about the sexism in so many marriages and relationships that often subtly fuels the development of problems? (Goodrich, Rampage, Ellman, & Halstead, 1988). There are, then, many special issues that can arise whenever family or couples therapy is undertaken.

■ Focus Questions

1. What are the basic assumptions, arrangements and features, and purported curative factors characterizing group psychotherapy?
2. Compare and contrast time-limited group therapy with other forms of group therapy.
3. What are the major goals and features of family therapy?
4. What are the major features of marital therapy?
5. Overall, how effective are family and couples therapies?

■ Key Terms

analytic group psychotherapy
behavior therapy groups
behavioral family therapy
behavioral marital therapy (BMT)
collaborative family therapy
communication
concurrent family therapy
conjoint family therapy
contingency contracting
couples therapy
curative factors

double bind
family therapy
general systems theory
Gestalt groups
group therapy
problem-solving techniques
psychodrama
support-understanding techniques
time-limited group therapy
transactional analysis (TA)

IV

SPECIALTIES IN CLINICAL PSYCHOLOGY

16

Community Psychology

At least since the appearance of psychoanalysis, the helping professions have sought to alleviate problems by one form of therapy or another. Some approaches have emphasized insight, others have sought to change behavior more directly. Whatever the differences in approaches, their basic common focus has been on the individual who has already developed psychological problems. By and large, clinical psychology has been a psychology of the individual.

At the theoretical level, therapists have long accepted the idea that all behavior (pathological or otherwise) is a joint product of situational and personal factors. Yet in their day-to-day therapeutic efforts, the emphasis of therapists was generally on one-to-one therapy of some sort. The troubled individual engaged the help of an expert and by this act submitted to the role of a patient. The therapist treated; the patient responded. However, given the rate of mental health problems in the world today, some have questioned whether this general approach is a reasonable one. For them, a relatively newer approach, *community psychology*, shows great promise for addressing mental health problems.

■ Perspectives and History

Let us begin by trying to identify exactly what community psychology is. Then we can move to those events that gave rise to the movement. Table 16-1 presents a set of principles characterizing community psychology, including assumptions regarding the causes of problems, the variety of levels of analysis that can be used to define a problem, where community psychology is practiced, how services are planned, the emphasis on prevention, and the willingness to "give psychology away" by consulting with self-help programs and nonpsychologists. We will discuss each of these basic principles at various points throughout this chapter.

Toward a community psychology perspective

For many, community psychology is an approach to mental health that emphasizes the role of environmental forces in creating and alleviating problems (Zax

Table 16-1
Principles of community psychology.

What "causes" problems?
Problems develop due to an interaction over time between the individual, the social setting, and systems (for example, organizations); these exert a mutual influence on each other.

How are problems defined?
Problems can be defined at many levels, but particular emphasis is placed on analysis at the level of the organization and the community or neighborhood.

Where is community psychology practiced?
Community psychology is typically not practiced in clinics, but rather out in the field or in the social context of interest.

How are services planned?
Rather than planning services only for those who seek help, community psychologists proactively assess the needs and risks in a community.

What is the emphasis in community psychology interventions?
An emphasis is placed on prevention of problems rather than treatment of existing problems.

Who is qualified to intervene?
Attempts are made to share psychology with others via consultation; actual interventions are often carried out through self-help programs or through trained nonpsychologists and nonprofessionals.

SOURCE: Data from *Orford* (1992, p. 4).

& Specter, 1974). For Rappaport (1977), it is more useful to talk about community psychology in terms of a perspective than to attempt a formal definition. The major aspects of this perspective are *cultural relativity, diversity,* and *ecology* (the fit between persons and the environment).

This perspective implies several things. First, community psychologists should not be concerned exclusively with inadequate environments or persons. Rather, they should direct their attention to the fit between environments and persons—a fit that may or may not be good. Second, community psychologists should emphasize the creation of alternatives through identifying and developing the resources and strengths of people and communities. Thus, the focus is on action directed toward the competencies of persons and environments rather than their deficits. Third, the community psychologist is likely to believe that differences among people and communities are desirable. Societal resources should not, then, be allocated according to one standard of competence. The community psychologist does not become identified with a single social norm or value but instead looks to the promotion of diversity.

Rappaport (1977) feels that three sets of concerns define the community psychology perspective: human resource development, political activity, and science. In many ways, these are antagonistic elements. Political activists are often impatient and deride more traditional clinicians as bringing society too little too late. Clinicians, in turn, often criticize activists as unprofessional and overly concerned with hawking their own visions of the world. Both groups, in turn, often regard scientists as too far removed from real problems to know what is going on in the world (the "ivory tower" syndrome). Further, the scientists are appalled by activists and clinicians alike; both are seen as shockingly willing to act on the basis of unvalidated hunches and lack of data or, worst of all, without a viable theory to guide them.

Whatever else community psychology may be, it is not a field that emphasizes an individual disease or individual treatment model (Iscoe, 1982). The focus is preventive rather than curative. Further, individuals and community organizations are encouraged to take control of and master their own problems via *empowerment,* such that traditional professional intervention is not necessary (Orford, 1992).

Chronology and catalyzing events

In 1955, the U.S. Congress passed legislation creating the Joint Commission on Mental Health and Illness. Its report encouraged the development of a *community mental health* concept and also urged a reduction in the population of mental hospitals. Based on the premise that the development of mental disorders and psychological distress was influenced by adverse environmental conditions, President Kennedy called for a "bold new approach" to *prevent* mental disorder. The 1963 so-called Kennedy bill funded the construction of mental health centers. Their aims were to promote the early detection of mental health problems, treat acute disorders, and establish comprehensive delivery systems of services that would prevent the "warehousing" of chronic patients in mental hospitals (Bloom, 1973). The desirability of community residents participating in all these decisions (Smith & Hobbs, 1966) was endorsed by the American Psychological Association and helped focus attention on the concept of community approaches and participation.

A conference held in 1965 is regarded by many as the official birth of community psychology (Zax & Specter, 1974). At Swampscott, Massachusetts, a group of psychologists set out to review the status of the field and to plot a future course of development for the place of psychology in the community mental health movement.

Shortly after this conference, the Division of Community Psychology was organized within the American Psychological Association. Soon there were the *Community Mental Health Journal* and the *American Journal of Community Psychology.* Textbooks began to appear: Zax and Specter in 1974 and then Heller and Monahan (1977), Rappaport (1977), Mann (1978), and, more recently, Heller, Price, Reinharz, Riger, and Wandersman (1984), Levine and Perkins (1987), and Orford (1992). Reviews came out regularly in the *Annual Review of Psychology,* and a number of handbooks were written (Golann & Eisdorfer, 1972; Schulberg & Killilea, 1982; Rappaport & Seidman, in press). Courses in community psychology and programs of graduate training have been established, and there are even books now on the history of community mental health (for example, Levine, 1982).

To flesh out the foregoing chronology, it may be helpful to pinpoint several issues or concerns that have catalyzed the emergence of community psychology.

Treatment facilities.   Although the mental hospital population in the United States peaked at about 500,000 in the mid-1950s, socially oriented clinicians continued to press for alternatives to the costly, inefficient (and often largely custodial) hospitalization of patients. Three factors combined at about this time to markedly reduce the population of mental hospitals: the advent of psychotropic medications, a more liberal discharge philosophy, and better treatment in mental hospitals. But as more patients were being discharged (often under heavy medication), and as patients who formerly would have been hospitalized were no longer admitted, the need for better community treatment and supportive services became evident. In some ways a cause but in other ways an effect of these events, the community philosophy was beginning to gain a foothold.

Another problem with many mental hospitals was their lack of trained therapists. Regarded by laypersons as a realistic means for solving difficult emotional problems, hospitalization itself often created nearly as many problems as it alleviated. Over the years, mental hospitals—particularly those run by the states—too often became warehouses or custodial bins. Care was often marginal and sometimes downright inhumane. Professional staff was severely lacking in numbers and occasionally in quality. Indeed, many still argue (and have empirically demonstrated) that hospitalization is not an especially effective treatment strategy (for example, Kiesler, 1982a, 1982b).

Personnel shortage.   Somehow, even as more clinical psychologists and psychiatrists were trained, demands for their services outstripped their increasing numbers. Not only that but many of the newcomers were entering private practice, and others were being diverted into teaching or research. In any event, the supply of trained professionals for service in hospitals and clinics was hardly keeping pace with the demand. A variety of trends (see Albee, 1959, 1968; Arnhoff, 1968) all seemed to coalesce to produce critical shortages of hospital and clinic personnel. To grapple with these shortages, it became imperative that new sources of personnel be sought, that more effective use be made of professional time, and that new models of coping with human problems be developed. In this regard, Albee (1959, 1968) predicted that it would literally be impossible to train enough mental health professionals to meet existing and future needs; thus, prevention should be pursued as a strategy.

Questions about psychotherapy.   As we saw in Chapter 11, in the 1950s, people began to question not just the efficiency of psychotherapy but also its effectiveness. Perhaps, too, some began to think it was not only intrapsychic factors that created problems but interactions between person and society. Also, because psychotherapy was expensive and more and more clinicians and psychiatrists were going into private practice, economic factors were pushing therapy outside the reach of the poor and disadvantaged. The relationship between mental illness and social class was documented by Hollingshead and Redlich (1958). Now, it seemed, there was also a relationship between social class and the availability of psychotherapy.

Figure 16-1

President John F. Kennedy and President Lyndon B. Johnson were instrumental in
providing the political leadership to get the community psychology movement
under way. *Library of Congress*

Medical models and roles.   Throughout this book, we have commented on the widespread role of the medical model and on the discontent with it.
The 1960s ushered in a climate in which institutional prerogatives and traditionalist beliefs came under attack. That climate produced listeners who were more willing to accept attacks on traditional views about mental illness. All of this contributed
to an increased tendency to look for social and community antecedents of problems
in living rather than internal biological or psychological etiological agents.

Furthermore, the general activism of the 1960s catalyzed the long-standing
discontent of many clinicians with a role that relegated them to passively waiting
for society's casualties to walk in the door. Would not an activist role that took
mental health services to the people be more consonant with a social-community
model? If so, such a role would also provide a measure of autonomy from the dominance of the medical profession. However, we must not overstate these events—
for after all, a major current trend in clinical psychology has been a headlong rush
into private practice. Such behavior is hardly a rejection of the medical model or
an acceptance of the social-community approach.

The environment.   Another force that helped shape the community
psychology movement was a greater awareness of the importance of social
and environmental factors in determining the behavior and problems of people.
Poverty, discrimination, pollution, and crowding were being recognized as potent

factors. Providing people with choices and enhancing their well-being required that psychologists pay attention to these factors, that they go beyond a reflexive consideration of the early childhood determinants of people's personalities. The emotional problems of large numbers of people may be influenced by poverty, unemployment, job discrimination, racism, diminished educational opportunities, sexism, and so on. Such influences are hardly the ones proposed by psychoanalytic and other theories that seek answers in internal dynamics.

The tenor of the times. Perhaps as much as anything, however, the sociopolitical events that crammed the 1960s gave sustenance to the community approach. The desegregation ordered by the Supreme Court in 1954 and the rise of the civil rights movement did many things. Pointing to discrimination in all its malignant forms raised the consciousness of the entire country. For the first time, many began to understand what social repression does to the minds and emotions of its victims. At the same time, civil rights activists proved that protests, rallies, pressures, and occasionally even logic could have an effect. The lessons of this era were not lost on some of the persons who later became advocates of a community approach.

■ Key Concepts

To this point we have sketched a rough perspective for and chronology of community psychology, and we alluded to several important concepts in the process. Now we will take a closer look at these concepts.

The concept of community mental health

The 1955 Joint Commission on Mental Health and Illness made several basic recommendations that set the tone for the subsequent development of community psychology—a tone that still resonates in accord with political and financial pressures across the nation. These recommendations were: (1) more and better research into mental health phenomena; (2) a broadened definition of who may provide mental health services; (3) greater availability of mental health services in the community; (4) an awareness of the social factors (for example, ostracism, isolation) that can contribute to mental illness; and (5) financial support of these recommendations by the federal government.

In 1963, federal funds were provided to help in the construction and staffing costs of comprehensive mental health centers across the United States. To qualify for these funds, a mental health center had to provide five essential services: (1) inpatient care; (2) outpatient care; (3) partial hospitalization (the patient works during the day but returns to the hospital at night); (4) round-the-clock emergency service; and (5) consultation services to a variety of professional, educational, and service personnel in the community. Beyond these required services it was hoped that the mental health centers would also provide diagnostic services, rehabilitation services, research, training, and evaluation. But despite Hobbs's description (1964) of a "third revolution" in mental health, the medical model some-how still prevailed (perhaps because psychiatrists remained at the top of the ad-ministrative hierarchy), and there seemed to be a continuing neglect of minority patients, poverty-stricken individuals, and even children.

In a highly influential paper, Smith and Hobbs (1966) argued that commu-nity control of mental health care and services was essential. They saw the role of prevention as paramount. This implied early detection and work with schools, police departments, social service agencies, businesses, and other organizations. The idea of personal deficit was replaced by the view that the social system had failed to provide an appropriate environment. A community mental health cen-ter, then, must do everything it could to enable the system to function better; it must not merely set about remedying individual deficits. Consultation was given prominence, as was the development of new community resources. Going be-yond Smith and Hobbs, some even stressed that the center should be the cen-tral coordinator of all social systems in the community. The goal was to reach those who needed services and, in particular, those who were so often excluded from services (in other words, the poor, the indigent, minorities, and so on). New methods to meet mental health needs were encouraged (for example, crisis in-tervention and group treatment). Advocacy of social action programs to improve housing, employment, and opportunity took precedence over the one-to-one therapy session. The role of the therapist was replaced by that of the social change agent.

Many of the foregoing antecedents had an idealistic tone. Nevertheless, in the 1960s, many community centers became operational. Some approximated the hopes of Smith and Hobbs; others were more in the mold of older clinical ap-proaches even though they used a community language. Some have been smooth-running enterprises, but others have created community tensions and controversy. For many reasons (including federal cutbacks in funding beginning in 1968), the goal of establishing 2000 centers by 1975 was not realized. In fact, by 1974, only 540 centers had been established with funds from the Community Mental Health Centers Act. Despite the recommendations in 1978 from President Carter's Com-mission on Mental Health that more emphasis should be placed on "serving the underserved" (that is, children, the elderly, ethnic minorities, and rural inhabitants), fewer funds were appropriated specifically for community mental health centers over the subsequent years. Further, state and local governments did not fill the fi-nancial gaps. The end result has been a tremendous decrease in the number of community mental health centers in operation today.

The concept of prevention

The idea of *prevention* is the guiding principle that has long been at the heart of public health programs in this country. Basically, this principle asserts that, in the long run, preventive activities will be more efficient and more effec-tive than individual treatment administered after the onset of diseases or problems (Felner, Jason, Moritsugu, & Farber, 1983). That such approaches can work is graphically illustrated by Price, Cowen, Lorion, and Ramos-McKay (1988). Their book, *14 Ounces of Prevention,* presents descriptions of 14 model prevention programs for children, adolescents, and adults. Box 16-1 presents an overview of one of these programs that targets preschool children from low-income families.

Primary prevention.   The most radical departure from the traditional ways of coping with mental health problems is *primary prevention*. Perhaps the essence of the notion of primary prevention is contained in Caplan's emphasis (1964) on "counteracting harmful circumstances before they have had a chance to produce illness" (p. 26). However, it is well to note that the complexity of human problems often requires preventive strategies that depend upon social change and redistribution of power (Albee, 1986). For many in society, this is not a highly palatable prospect. Some examples of primary prevention include programs to reduce job discrimination, enhance school curricula, improve housing, teach parenting skills, and provide help to children from single-parent homes. Also grouped under this heading are genetic counseling, Head Start, prenatal care for disadvantaged women, Meals on Wheels, school lunch programs, and so on.

Secondary prevention.   Programs that promote the early diagnosis of mental disorders and prompt treatment of problems at an early stage fall under the heading of *secondary prevention*. The basic idea is to attack problems while they are still manageable, before they become resistant to intervention (Caplan, 1961; Sanford, 1965). Often, this approach suggests the screening of large numbers of people. These people are not seeking help, and they may not even appear to be at risk. Such screening is carried out by many people in the community including physicians, teachers, clergy, police, court officials, social workers, and others. Early assessment is followed by appropriate referrals, of course.

An example of secondary prevention is the early detection and treatment of those individuals with potentially damaging drinking problems (Alden, 1988). A further example is the Rochester Primary Mental Health Project pioneered by Emory Cowen, which began in 1957. The project systematically screens primary-grade children for risk of school maladjustment. The development of early detection and prevention programs in several states has been described by Cowen, Hightower, Johnson, Sarno, and Weissberg (1989).

Tertiary prevention.   Of the three strategies noted by Caplan, *tertiary prevention* is the one least associated with the community movement. The goal of tertiary prevention is to reduce the duration and negative effects of mental disorders after their occurrence.

A major focus of many tertiary programs is rehabilitation, which can range from increasing vocational competence to enhancing the client's self-concept. The methods employed may be counseling, job training, and so on. Whether the purpose of a program is to teach better independent living skills to those with mental retardation or to restore the social skills of a recently discharged patient with a diagnosis of schizophrenia, the goal is the prevention of additional problems. Although their language is a bit different, tertiary preventive programs are not too different from person-oriented programs based on a deficit philosophy. However,

Box 16-1
Prevention: The High/Scope Perry Preschool Program

The High/Scope Perry Preschool Program (HSPPP) was initiated in 1962 to help children who were deemed at risk for school failure, and its curriculum is used today by thousands of early childhood instructors (Schweinhart & Weikart, 1988). Based on the rationale that childhood poverty often leads to school failure which, in turn, results in adult poverty and social problems (for example, crime), the HSPPP targeted 3- and 4-year-olds from families of low socioeconomic status (SES) for intervention. These interventions were characterized by:

1. a developmentally appropriate curriculum, based on Piaget's views of children as active and self-initiating learners;
2. classroom enrollment limits with adequate adult supervision (at least two adults who had training in early childhood development);
3. supervisory support of staff and frequent in-service training opportunities;
4. emphasis on parental involvement in each child's education; and
5. sensitivity to the needs of the children and their families (Schweinhart & Weikart, 1988).

The 58 3- to 4-year-old children in the Perry Preschool study intervention group attended the program for two years, which included classroom instruction five mornings a week for seven months a year and home visits by the teacher once a week. Outcome data from a control group of 65 children (matched on IQ, sex, and SES) were also collected. The major findings from this study can be summarized as follows (Schweinhart & Weikart, 1988):

1. Program participants demonstrated better academic achievement throughout elementary and secondary school, were rated by teachers as more socially and emotionally mature, and endorsed more favorable attitudes toward high school.
2. Program participants as a group obtained more and better jobs and received higher wages by age 19. Further, they were more likely to be self-supporting, less likely to have dropped out of high school, less likely to be arrested, and more likely to have enrolled in college or vocational school.
3. A cost-benefit analysis of the program indicated significant benefits to society and to the taxpayer. For every dollar invested in the two-year program, three dollars in savings were returned. For example, the program resulted in a reduction of costs for special classes, welfare, and crime.

it is important to remember that *all* forms of prevention are distinguished by their attempts to reduce the rates of, or problems associated with, mental disorder on a community-wide (or population-wide) basis.

Alternative models of prevention.   Although the traditional primary-secondary-tertiary prevention model (Caplan, 1964) is the one that is most commonly cited, alternative classification frameworks have been proposed (Orford, 1992). As one example, we will briefly discuss a framework for preventing mental disorder that was proposed in the recent Institute of Medicine report, *Reducing Risks for Mental Disorders* (IOM, 1994). This model, adapting terms proposed by Gordon (1983, 1987), classifies prevention intervention into one of three types. *Universal preventive interventions* target the entire population; these interventions may be costly because they are given to everyone. *Selective preventive interventions* target individuals or subgroups of the population that have a higher than average likelihood of developing the disorder in question, either in the near or distant future. These targeted individuals are identified based on the presence of biological, psychological, or social risk factors that have been shown to be associated with disorder development. Finally, *indicated preventive interventions* target high-risk individuals, identified by their manifestation of sub-threshold symptoms of the disorder or by biological markers indicating a predisposition to develop the disorder.

The value of this model is that it places prevention, treatment of mental disorder, and maintenance on a continuum representing the full range of interventions for mental disorders—*prevention* occurs before a disorder develops, *treatment* is administered to those who meet (or are close to meeting) diagnostic criteria for a disorder, and *maintenance* involves interventions for individuals with a diagnosis of mental disorder whose illness continues to warrant attention (IOM, 1994). Figure 16-2 depicts the IOM's conceptualization of the intervention spectrum for mental disorders.

Prevention research.   Planning, developing, and evaluating prevention programs is a multistage process requiring years of community psychologists' time. To guide prevention researchers, the IOM (1994) recommended a series of steps focusing on the conceptualization, design, implementation, and evaluation of prevention intervention research programs. Figure 16-3 depicts these steps.

First, the problem or disorder that is to be addressed by the program must be clearly specified, as well as the prevalence, incidence, and costs to society. Next, risk and protective factors relevant to the problem or disorder are identified, and the existing research on the prevention or treatment of the condition is reviewed. Third, pilot studies that evaluate the efficacy of the planned intervention are designed and conducted. The fourth step involves planning and carrying out large-scale trials of the intervention program. Finally, assuming that the trials yield encouraging results, the program is implemented in the community and its effectiveness is again assessed. As can be seen from Figure 16-3, this last step does not mark the end of the process. Rather, information regarding the effectiveness of the intervention in the community (for example, does it lead to decreased inci-

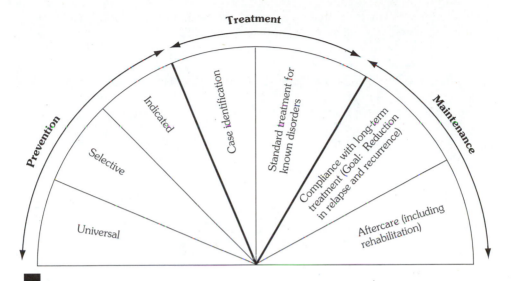

Figure 16-2
Prevention on a continuum of services addressing mental health needs. SOURCE: From *Summary: Reducing Risks for Mental Disorders,* p. 8, produced by the Institute of Medicine. Copyright © 1994 by the National Academy of Sciences. Reprinted by permission of the National Academy Press.

dence of the problem or disorder?) leads to modification of the intervention, and the steps are repeated. In this way prevention programs are refined, with the ultimate goal being the improvement of their effectiveness.

Empowerment

In their discussion of poverty, Gurin and Gurin (1970) emphasized the importance of a low expectancy of attaining valued goals and an expectancy of powerlessness. These notions are related closely to the social learning concept of locus of control (Phares, 1976; Rotter, 1966). As Rappaport (1977) says:

> What is important about this variable for community psychology is its connection to the sociological idea of power and its converse, alienation. Locus of control is one of the few variables in social science that may be shown to have a consistent relationship which ties research across levels of analysis. (p. 101)

Indeed, for Rappaport (1981), a major goal of community psychology is the prevention of feelings of powerlessness. It is not easy to accomplish this goal, and community psychologists have not been as conspicuously successful here as they would have liked (Heller, 1990). Similarly, Gesten and Jason (1987) question whether any unique methods have been developed out of the empowerment concept. Still, Rappaport (1981) initially argued that strategies to enhance peoples' sense that they control their own destinies is preferable even to prevention or treatment approaches. There are, of course, many examples of attempts

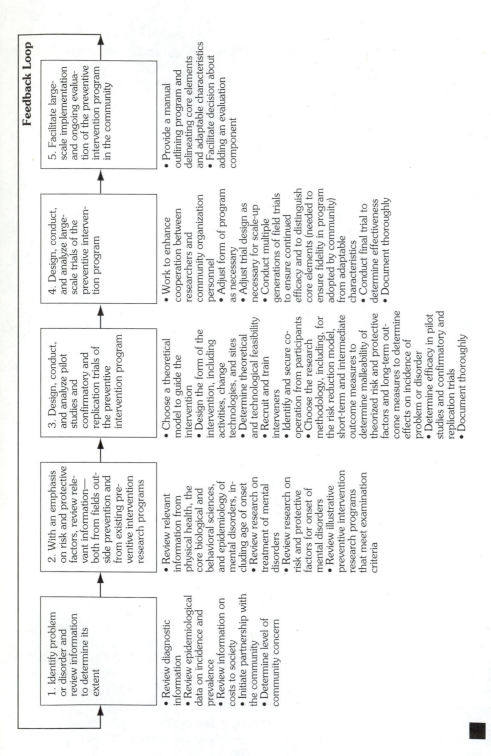

Figure 16-3

Recommended steps for designing, implementing, and evaluating prevention programs. SOURCE: IOM (1994). *Summary: Reducing Risks for Mental Disorders*, pp. 32–33, produced by the Institute of Medicine. Copyright © 1994 by the National Academy of Sciences. Reprinted by permission of the National Academy Press.

to enhance feelings of control. They range from reducing child and spouse abuse to eradicating exploitation of women, migrant workers, and the elderly and decreasing bias against the handicapped and the mentally ill.

Although he initially pitted empowerment and prevention approaches against each other, it appears that Rappaport (1987) has more recently tempered his position. He now allows for the possibility that prevention interventions may be consistent with, rather than diametrically opposed to, empowerment. However, for this to be true, preventive interventions must be collaborative and delivered in a manner that avoids a paternalistic one-up-one-down style that characterizes some traditional therapist-client interactions (Felner et al., 1983).

Social intervention concepts

The conventional strategy of intervention has always implied that people achieved good health exclusively through their own efforts, regardless of social conditions, and that when those efforts failed and ill health occurred, they visited a comprehensive mental health center for clinical help. But with community psychology, the emphasis is on restructuring societal roles and social organizations. To reduce the problems created by crime and delinquency, for example, community psychologists seek to change social institutions and organizations to make advantages and resources available to potential criminals and delinquents.

Inherent in such social intervention strategies is the idea that when individuals are given the necessary resources or alternatives, they will solve their problems themselves. Also inherent is the belief that people have competencies and strengths. When the environment is changed or when people are allowed to exert power to make their own decisions, these strengths will be evident. Thus, an emphasis on competencies rather than deficits allows the community psychologist to move toward creating a proper person-environment fit rather than changing the affected people so that they will fit the "appropriate" environment as determined by majority values.

Blaming the victim.   Particularly illustrative of the notions that have given rise to the strategy of social intervention is the contrast between blaming the victim and blaming the system. In a highly influential book, Ryan (1971) argued that society sees slum dwellers, school dropouts, drug addicts, or the unemployed as individual failures whose healing will require remedial reading programs, drug counseling, and so on. Thus, according to Ryan, society misses the real message, which is bad social environments. Their problems are not clinical—they are community-social.

The focus on intervention strategies.   One way of contrasting clinical and community orientations is by focusing on intervention strategies. Such strategies, according to Heller, Price, Reinharz, Riger, and Wandersman (1984), can vary along two dimensions: *theoretical* (deficit versus competence) and *ecological* (the individual, the organization, or the community). Table 16-2 highlights the operation of these dimensions.

Table 16-2
Strategies for change as determined by theoretical orientation and ecological levels of analysis.

Theoretical Orientation	Ecological Levels of Analysis		
	Individual	Organizational	Community
Deficit	Somatic therapies to correct biochemical or physiological imbalance	Group psycho-therapy or sensitivity training to correct interpersonal problems	Institutionalization or special facilities built for the handicapped or emotionally disturbed
	Traditional psycho-therapy to uncover and work through early traumatic events	Special education and remedial reading programs	Creating new settings and alternative programs
Competency	Most forms of behavior therapy, particularly skill training	Training and consultation to increase job competencies of organization members	Facilitating citizen participation and community organization
	Prevention programs for high-risk persons	Prevention programs to reduce organizational stress and increase coping	Community-wide prevention programs to reduce environmental stress and increase citizen competencies

SOURCE: Adapted from *Psychology and Community Change: Challenges of the Future,* by K. Heller, R. H. Price, S. Reinharz, S. Riger, and A. Wandersman. Copyright © 1984 by Kenneth Heller. Reprinted by permission of the publisher, Brooks/Cole Publishing Company, a division of Wadsworth, Inc.

■ Methods of Intervention and Change

We now shift our attention to methods of intervention. Here our stress will be on patterns of service delivery.

Consultation

What is *consultation?* Orford (1992) defines it this way:

Consultation is the process whereby an individual (the consultee) who has responsibility for providing a service to others (the clients) voluntarily consults another person (the consultant) who is believed to possess some special expertise which will help the consultee provide a better service to his or her clients. (p. 139)

In a world short of mental health personnel, the basic advantage of consultation is that its effects are multiplied like the ripples from a stone thrown into a pond. Using individual techniques of intervention, mental health specialists can reach only a very limited number of clients. But by consulting with such people as teachers, police, and ministers, they can reach many clients indirectly (O'Neill & Trickett, 1982; Orford, 1992).

Consultation may be viewed from several orientations, each springing from a somewhat different historical perspective (Brown & Schulte, 1987; Heller et al., 1984; Nietzel, Winett, MacDonald, & Davidson, 1977; Orford, 1992). First there is mental health consultation, a product of the psychoanalytic and psychodynamic tradition. Often practiced in rural or underdeveloped areas where there was a shortage of mental health personnel, consultation became a way of utilizing existing community personnel (teachers, ministers, and so on) to help solve the mental health problems of such areas. A second orientation developed out of the behavioral tradition. In order to implement the technology of behavior modification that had been so successful in laboratory settings, it was necessary to move into real-life situations. To do that, people in the patient's environment (for example, home or school) had to be trained to properly dispense reinforcements for the desired behavior. Consultation became a way of providing such training. The third orientation is an organizational one that emphasizes consultation to industry in which specialists work with management and supervisors to improve morale, job satisfaction, and productivity or to reduce inefficiency, absenteeism, and alcoholism.

Types of mental health consultation.   Approaches to mental health consultation can be classified in many ways. Perhaps the most widely accepted classification is Caplan's (1970). It includes the following categories:

1. *Client-centered case consultation.* Here the focus is on helping a specific client or patient solve a current problem. For example, a clinician might be asked to consult with a colleague on a diagnostic problem involving a specific patient.
2. *Consultee-centered case consultation.* In this instance, the aim is to help the consultee enhance the skills to deal with future cases. For example, a teacher might be advised on how to selectively reinforce behavior in order to reduce classroom disturbances.
3. *Program-centered administrative consultation.* The notion here is to assist in the administration or management of a specific program. For instance, a consultant might be hired to set up an early warning system in the schools to detect potential cases of maladjustment.
4. *Consultee-centered administrative consultation.* Here the aim is to improve the skills of administrators in the hope that this will enable them to function better in the future. For example, a sensitivity group consisting of administrators might be monitored by a consultant in order to help enhance group members' communication skills.

Techniques and phases.   Mental health consultation is an individual thing, but several general techniques will surely enhance the effectiveness of the consulting process (Altrocchi, 1972). In most cases, the consultation process will pass through several phases as outlined below:

1. *The entry or preparatory phase.* In this phase the exact nature of the consultant relationship and mutual obligations are worked out.
2. *The beginning or warming-up phase.* The establishment of the working relationship occurs here.
3. *The alternative action phase.* This phase encompasses the development of specific, alternative solutions and strategies of problem solving.
4. *Termination.* When it is mutually agreed that further consultation is unnecessary, termination follows.

Unfortunately, community mental health centers have had difficulties in providing consultation services, especially to schools and community agencies; the budgetary support has just not been there (Iscoe & Harris, 1984).

Community alternatives to hospital

As we noted earlier in this chapter, the nation's mental hospitals have long been objects of criticism. Despite the fact that there is a core of "undischargeable" patients, there are alternatives to our current hospital system—alternatives that provide environments geared to the goal of enabling patients to resume a responsible place in society.

Examples of alternatives include the community lodge (Fairweather, Sanders, Maynard, & Cressler, 1969). This is akin to a halfway house where formerly chronic, hospitalized patients can learn independent living skills. The Mendota Program (Marx, Test, & Stein, 1973) is another example of a pioneering attempt to help formerly undischargeable patients find jobs, learn cooking and shopping skills, and so on. Finally, there is the growing popularity of day hospitals (see Penk, Charles, & Van Hoose, 1978) that are often more effective and less expensive than traditional 24-hour hospitalization.

Crisis intervention

In Chapter 6 we introduced the topic of *crisis intervention* in our discussion of interviewing. The basic goal of crisis intervention is to reach people in an acute state of stress and to provide them with enough support to prevent them from becoming the chronically mentally ill of the future (Slaikeu, 1984). Persons in crisis are often in a uniquely reachable state that can pave the way for future long-term interventions. As much as anything, crisis intervention requires the relinquishing of traditional procedures and prerogatives. For example, crisis intervention centers must be close to the communities they serve. Clients should not have to travel 20 miles to reach an office or wade through 15 secretaries once they reach it. There must obviously be immediate service. Walk-in centers or phone services must be available all day and all night, and appointments should not be required. Staff members must be prepared to leave their offices—to go with police or to visit homes.

Crises tend to obliterate customary professional roles, pecking orders, and prerogatives. There is typically no time for a medical opinion, a discussion of whether a paraprofessional received an A or a B in abnormal psychology, or a visit from an expert consultant. This is not to suggest that training has no place — however, crisis intervention requires a versatility and flexibility that is not often found in traditional clinics or hospitals.

Early crisis programs were often built largely around telephone answering services. However, it soon became apparent that such services would be too slow. Consequently, the emphasis is now on 24-hour services staffed by workers who personally take calls. Current interventions emphasize follow-up both to check on the well-being of the client and to assess the adequacy of the services provided by the agency to which the client was referred. Current intervention procedures also encourage face-to-face contact rather than the earlier overreliance on the telephone. Emerging interventions even include temporary shelter (for example, for battered women and their children), transportation, and follow-up services and consultation to survivors of suicides.

One of the earliest applications of the crisis philosophy was the establishment of suicide prevention centers (Shneidman & Farberow, 1965). The general notions here are illustrated by McGee's development (1974) of the Suicide and Crisis Intervention Service (SCIS) in Gainesville, Florida. The policy of SCIS was simply "to respond to every request to participate in the solution of any human problem whenever and wherever it occurs" (McGee, 1974, p. 181 [italics deleted]). The attitude of the SCIS was that people in crisis were neither sick nor mentally ill. Thus, the service was not necessarily either a medical one or a mental health one. People in crisis were to be given immediate, active, and aggressive services. Of special importance, SCIS regarded people in crisis as the responsibilities of the community and felt that, as citizens, they had a right to expect such a community service. Contrary to many community health organizations that are often at least subtly immersed in intrapsychic concepts, the SCIS-type crisis center is organized with the idea of community control. It is staffed largely by neighborhood volunteers, and it is geared toward the specific characteristics of the immediate community.

But are these interventions really helpful? There is no definitive answer as yet. Surely, much depends on the questions asked. For example, Decker and Stubblebine (1972) found that psychiatric hospitalizations were reduced when crisis intervention procedures were employed. Yet, when Gottschalk, Fox, and Bates (1973) compared crisis patients with patients who had been randomly assigned to a waiting list, they could find no differences in several indices of psychiatric improvement. Other reports (Getz, Fujita, & Allen, 1975; Huessy, 1972; Maris & Connor, 1973) are much more optimistic. There are obviously many problems in obtaining controls in crisis intervention research. Thus, little can be said with certainty at this point. Not all research shows the efficacy of crisis intervention (Kelly, Snowden, & Munoz, 1977); however, others argue that additional preventive measures could well reduce the number of deaths from suicide (Dew, Bromet, Brent, & Greenhouse, 1987).

Clearly, crisis interventions can help reduce distress. For example, when a teacher commits suicide, interventions must be undertaken to at least try to reduce students' shock (Kneisel & Richards, 1988). When a school bus collides with a train, the survivors must be helped to cope (Klingman, 1987). Under such circumstances the community cannot wait for the ideal study to demonstrate the utility of an intervention!

Intervention in early childhood

Public health and mental health workers have long been aware of the educational disadvantages experienced by the poor. Of great concern is the fear that early deprivation in crucial developmental periods will mark children for life. Impoverished preschool environments and experiences may almost guarantee that children will do poorly in school and thus become vulnerable to a wide variety of mental health, criminal, and social problems. But if successful preschool interventions can be developed, then a truly preventive course of action will have been taken.

Head start programs. In the middle 1960s, President Johnson created the Office of Economic Opportunity (OEO). *Head Start* was one of the programs that was developed under the auspices of the OEO. Targeted specifically for disadvantaged children, Head Start was designed to prepare preschool children from disadvantaged backgrounds for elementary school. Head Start programs were controlled locally but were required to conform to general federal guidelines. Local programs varied in number of hours of attendance, number of months (summer versus the entire year), backgrounds of teachers, and so on. The specific techniques employed also varied, but basic learning skills of the child were usually stressed. Physical and medical needs were also dealt with, as were general school preparation and adjustment.

Other interventions. We have already discussed the High/Scope Perry Preschool Program (see Box 16-1). In addition, we will mention one other program as an example of intervention in early childhood. Bereiter and Engleman (1966) have described the Direct Instruction Program, an approach analogous to programmed learning procedures wherein curriculum is broken down into small units or steps. The emphasis here is not on adjustment but on providing disadvantaged children with the academic work they need to catch up with regular classes. Many of the interventions reported have been with African American children; however, Plant and Southern (1972) carried out a ten-week project with disadvantaged prekindergarten Hispanic American children that emphasized perceptual-motor skills, concept formation, and language.

Self-help

Not all help comes from professionals—informal groups of helpers can provide valuable support that may stave off the need for professional intervention. What is more, nonprofessional, *self-help groups* such as Alcoholics Anonymous, Parents without Partners, Le Leche League, Al-Anon, and many others can be incorporated as an effective part of treatment by a referring professional (Rudolfa & Hungerford, 1982).

What needs do self-help groups meet? Orford (1992) discussed eight primary functions of self-help groups: (1) they provide emotional support to members; (2) they furnish role models, individuals who have faced and conquered problems that group members are dealing with; (3) they provide ways of understanding members' problems; (4) they make available important and relevant information; (5) they provide new ideas about how to cope with existing problems; (6) they afford members the opportunity to help other members; (7) they provide social companionship; and (8) they give members an increased sense of mastery and control over their problems.

Clearly, self-help groups serve several important functions for group members. However, in order for the groups to be maximally effective, research suggests that professionals should be available to serve as consultants to these groups. Clearly, professionals should not *control* the group, but a total lack of involvement on the part of a community psychologist does not appear to be helpful either (Orford, 1992). Certain organizational features appear to be correlated with the appraisal of group success (for example, a certain degree of order and rules to govern the group and a capability and knowledge on the part of group leaders; Maton, 1988), and a community psychologist can play an invaluable, yet indirect, role in the group by serving as a consultant to group leaders.

Paraprofessionals

One of the more visible features of the community movement is its utilization of *paraprofessionals,* laypersons who have received no formal clinical training as therapists. The use of paraprofessionals in the mental health field has been growing, but this trend has generated controversy. In reviewing 42 studies, Durlak (1979) concluded that professional education, training, and experience are not prerequisites for becoming an effective helping person. However, Nietzel and Fisher (1981) took issue with this conclusion and urged caution in interpreting the results of many of the studies reviewed by Durlak. They argued that many of the studies included in the Durlak review were methodologically flawed, and they objected to Durlak's definitions of "professional" and "paraprofessional." With these and other criticisms in mind, Hattie, Sharpley, and Rogers (1984) reanalyzed the studies included in the Durlak review. Results from their meta-analysis concurred with those of Durlak. The overall results favor paraprofessionals. More recent summaries have also argued that the available evidence suggests that paraprofessionals may be as effective (and in some cases more effective) than professionals (see Christensen & Jacobson, 1994).

Besides effectiveness, there is also the issue of access to those who can provide help. Like it or not, most individuals who are in need of mental health services do not seek out mental health professionals. Instead, informal therapy takes place in many contexts and is provided by a variety of laypersons. For example, in an interesting and provocative set of studies, Cowen (1982) investigated the "helping behavior" of hairdressers and bartenders. Results indicated that a small but significant proportion of their customers raised moderate to serious personal problems, and both hairdressers and bartenders attempted a range of interventions (just listening, trying to be supportive and sympathetic, presenting alternatives). Many community psychologists view these and other studies as evidence supporting the idea that consultation programs might be aimed at laypersons who naturally come into contact with individuals with mental health needs; these needs may not otherwise be addressed because of the tendency to avoid seeking help from a mental health professional.

Although it hardly seems wise at this point to argue that professionally trained clinical psychologists are unnecessary, it appears that there is certainly a vital role for paraprofessionals in the mental health field today. Clinical psychologists are needed, at the very least, to serve as consultants. Further, research may ultimately indicate that certain types of mental health problems respond better to services provided by a mental health professional. To date, however, the research questions addressed (for example, are paraprofessionals effective overall?) have been too broad to shed light on this issue.

■ Concluding Comments

In a relatively short time, the community emphasis has become a force that has led clinical psychologists to reexamine many of their old assumptions. But there are important questions that must be confronted as we conclude our discussion of this field.

Questions of effectiveness
Years ago, Cowen (1967, 1973, 1978) raised the question of how much the community movement has accomplished beyond that of the more traditional mental health approaches. The question was whether excitement and rhetoric had masked what was really very little substantive change. For example, Cowen (1973) could find relatively few research reports in the *Community Mental Health Journal* that provided concrete data. The papers also notably failed to address issues of prevention—a notion central to the community approach. Rappaport (1977) stated that no evidence really existed to show that U.S. communities have improved mental health. He even went so far as to suggest that the community mental health movement's greatest accomplishment may have been that it opened up new careers for persons who were formerly not part of the movement.

Although for years there was more rhetoric than implementation with regard to prevention programs (Iscoe & Harris, 1984), intervention was and is one of the cornerstones of the community movement. The question remains, however, whether the field really knows enough about the causes of mental health problems to mount large-scale, successful preventive programs. Fortunately, recent reports evaluating the effectiveness of a wide range of prevention programs lead us to a state of cautious optimism (for example, Felner, DuBois, & Adan, 1991; IOM, 1994). Whereas many early reports regarding the efficacy of prevention programs were disappointing, community psychologists were able to learn from these failures and incorporate changes into new programs of intervention (Felner et al., 1991). As an example, increased focus was placed on modifying psychological processes underlying various mental disorders, and interventions were designed to be more intensive and extended over longer periods of time. The recent Institute of Medicine (IOM, 1994) report on preventing mental illness presented a group of

39 exemplary intervention programs with demonstrated effectiveness that targeted infants, preschoolers, elementary-age children, adolescents, adults, and the elderly.

Issues remain, to be sure—there are questions regarding how intervention programs should be disseminated and by whom, how the programs are to be maintained over time (for example, funding issues), and the need to train more researchers who are qualified to design, implement, and evaluate preventive interventions (IOM, 1994; Orford, 1992). Regarding this latter point, the IOM report estimates that only about ten new prevention experts are produced a year; training programs and financial support are needed to increase this woefully low number.

Values, power, and civil rights

Clearly, the community movement seeks to bring about social change and the reorganization of social institutions. The goal of such changes is undoubtedly laudable—better mental health for all. In case the reader had not noticed, this last statement almost sounds as if it might have been made by a candidate for public office. Indeed, some have argued that if community professionals wish to bring about social change they should run for political office. Those who take this position say that social change (especially when it is accomplished by public funds) is a political phenomenon and should be mandated by the public.

Obviously, there is much to be said on both sides. There is danger in adopting the narrow role of the patient's advocate rather than the broader role of advocate of the larger community. Adopting the narrow role may cause the real bases of patients' problems to be ignored. But there is also great danger in becoming a political advocate. It is hoped that the individual practitioner and the community-oriented advocate will each carefully examine the potential for both harm and good that is inherent in their positions.

The training of community psychologists

At present, many have difficulty understanding exactly what a community psychologist is. Perhaps because of its multidisciplinary orientation, community psychology has yet to develop an adequate or identifiable theoretical framework apart from those of other disciplines. This, at times, makes for role confusion. The community psychologist is part sociologist, part political scientist, part psychotherapist, part intermediary, but lacks a specific identity. Given this ambiguity, it becomes difficult to design appropriate training programs.

Fortunately, there are some guidelines for training. The recent IOM report (1994) recommends that future *prevention research specialists* should have a solid background in a relevant discipline (for example, nursing, sociology, social work, public health, epidemiology, medicine, or clinical-community psychology); further, training in the design of interventions and the empirical evaluations of interventions is necessary. Finally, practicum or internshiplike training in prevention is also recommended. On the other hand, educational requirements for *prevention field specialists*—those who actually carry out the interventions—are less stringent. Often only a bachelor's degree in a relevant field (for example, a bachelor of arts in psychology) is required.

Given the increasing cultural and ethnic diversity in the United States, it is also important for community psychologists to receive training in how diversity issues may impact their work. For example, a knowledge of and sensitivity to cultural and ethnic differences will inform the following activities and roles of a prevention researcher (IOM, 1994):

1. developing relationships with community leaders and organizations;
2. conceptualizing and identifying potential risk factors, mechanisms, and antecedents of problems or disorders;
3. developing interventions that will have maximum effect and deciding how these should be disseminated and delivered to the target population; and
4. determining the content and format of evaluation instruments.

In order to achieve "cultural competence" (Cross, Bazron, Dennis, & Isaacs, 1989; Isaacs & Benjamin, 1991), community psychologists need to garner relevant professional experience with a variety of cultural and ethnic populations and to receive supervision from those who have expertise in designing, implementing, and evaluating interventions for individuals from these cultural and ethnic groups (IOM, 1994).

The age of managed care

With its emphasis on prevention of mental health problems as well as initial reports indicating the cost-effectiveness of prevention efforts (see Box 16-1), community psychology is likely to play a primary role in designing and implementing interventions that will be recommended and financially supported by managed care companies.

However, the level of financial support for prevention efforts from the managed care industry will be related to the field's ability to continue to document the cost-effectiveness of these forms of intervention. In general, several factors influence cost-effectiveness: the cost of the intervention, the frequency of intervention necessary for the "effect," personnel costs, the length of time necessary for an adequate trial, and the ability of prevention specialists to efficiently and accurately identify and enlist at-risk individuals (IOM, 1994). These are complex considerations that can only be addressed by systematic, and often time-consuming, prevention studies.

In addition to prevention programs, several other programs often associated with community psychology may be employed in order to reduce the costs of mental health services. These include crisis intervention, community alternatives to hospitalization, and self-help groups. Finally, it is likely that community psychologists will be called upon as consultants in order to tap their expertise in planning and implementing interventions.

The future of prevention

Given the compelling rationale of prevention, and, more recently, the documented effectiveness of preventive efforts, it may seem puzzling that more resources are not dedicated to these forms of interventions. In a classic, but still highly relevant, article, Cowen (1983) described a number of barriers and resistances to the preventive movement. To cite just a few examples, those outside the field may remain skeptical because (1) the future-orientation of prevention creates the illusion that interventions can be delayed; (2) the social and environmental focus of preventive interventions differs philosophically from the traditional focus on individual variables practiced by many clinical psychologists; (3) prevention in a sense must compete with more established forms of intervention (for example, one-on-one psychotherapy); and (4) preventive programs may appear to be impractical and too costly (Cowen, 1983; Davison & Neale, 1996). In addition, the prevention field itself has served as an "enemy from within" (Cowen, 1983) by being less than precise with its terminology, being slow to document the effectiveness of preventive interventions, and neglecting to coordinate efforts across programs (see Hawkins & Catalano, 1992).

It is hoped that these issues can be adequately addressed in the future such that interventions characteristic of community psychology are employed more widely. Perhaps the focus in the future should be as much on *psychological wellness and health* as on psychopathology and treatment of mental disorders (Cowen, 1991). If this is the case, clinical psychologists will grasp the importance of such concepts as competence, resilience, prevention, modification of social systems, and empowerment.

■ Focus Questions

1. What is unique about a community psychology perspective?
2. What historical factors contributed to the community psychology movement?
3. Discuss the various types of prevention. How is prevention research conducted?
4. What are the major forms of intervention employed by community psychologists?
5. What issues are likely to confront the field of community psychology in the future?

■ Key Terms

client-centered case consultation
community mental health
community psychology
consultation
consultee-centered administrative
   consultation
consultee-centered case consultation
crisis intervention
empowerment
Head Start
indicated preventive interventions

paraprofessionals
prevention
primary prevention
program-centered administrative
   consultation
secondary prevention
selective preventive interventions
self-help groups
tertiary prevention
universal preventive interventions

17

Health Psychology and Behavioral Medicine

It seems that everyone realizes now that lifestyle affects our health and sense of well-being. Most health problems in the United States are related to chronic diseases (for example, heart disease, cancer, stroke), and these diseases are often associated with behavior or lifestyle choices (smoking, overeating, and so on) made by individuals (Brannon & Feist, 1997). Unfortunately, the costs of medical care have skyrocketed to over 14% of the gross domestic product (GDP) or over $898 billion annually (Frank & VandenBos, 1994). The potential financial burden associated with health problems has led many to reevaluate their lifestyles and behavior. There has also been a shift in perception in that health has become associated with positive well-being rather than simply absence of disease (Brannon & Feist, 1997). These trends, as well as others, have led Americans to focus much more intensely on behaviors and lifestyles that promote health and prevent disease. Not surprisingly, *health psychology* has become a buzzword (Rodin & Salovey, 1989).

Psychology, as a science of behavior, has much to contribute to the field of health, and health psychology has become a fast-growing specialty in clinical psychology. One clue that an emerging field has indeed emerged is the appearance of textbooks and handbooks detailing that field. For example, general textbooks on health psychology are prevalent (for example, Brannon & Feist, 1997; Feuerstein, Labbé, & Kuczmierczyk, 1986; Gatchel, Baum, & Krantz, 1989; Sarafino, 1990; Snyder, 1989), as are specialized textbooks on clinical health psychology (Belar, Deardorff, & Kelly, 1987), women and health (Travis, 1988), and pediatric health psychology (Peterson & Harbeck, 1988). Finally, several specialty journals (for example, *Health Psychology, Journal of Behavioral Medicine*) have been developed to report on research in these fields.

■ History and Perspectives

Although a variety of overlapping subdisciplines deal with health-related issues (for example, health psychology, behavioral medicine, behavioral health), we will focus primarily on two areas of psychology: *behavioral medicine* and *health psychology*. Recognition that mind and body are inextricably linked has been around since at least early Greek civilization. However, it was not until the late 1970s that definitions of behavioral medicine and health psychology began to crystallize.

Definitions

A variety of definitions of behavioral medicine have been offered over the years (see Miller, 1983; Schwartz & Weiss, 1977). Basically, it refers to the integration of the behavioral sciences with the practice and science of medicine (Gatchel, Baum, & Krantz, 1989). Matarazzo (1980) uses the term to refer to the broad interdisciplinary field of scientific investigation, education, and practice that is concerned with health, illness, and related physiological dysfunctions.

Health psychology is a specialty area within psychology. It is a more discipline-specific term referring to psychology's primary role as a science and profession in behavioral medicine (Gatchel, Baum, & Krantz, 1989). Health psychology includes health-related practice, research, and teaching by many kinds of psychologists — social, industrial, physiological, and so on. It has been specifically defined as follows:

> *Health psychology* is the aggregate of the specific educational, scientific, and professional contributions of the discipline of psychology to the promotion and maintenance of health, the prevention and treatment of illness, and the identification of etiologic and diagnostic correlates of health, illness and related dysfunction. (Matarazzo, 1980, p. 815)

This definition was later amended to include psychologists' roles as formulators of health care policy and contributors to the health care system (see DeLeon, Frank, & Wedding, 1995). A recent definition of health psychology that incorporates these new roles was offered by Brannon and Feist (1997). According to these authors, health psychology

> . . . includes psychology's contributions to the enhancement of health, the prevention and treatment of illness, the identification of health risk factors, the improvement of the health care system, and the shaping of public opinion with regard to health. (p. 14)

History

Suls and Rittenhouse (1987) have noted a variety of historical markers stretching all the way back to Aristotle. The idea was pretty clear even then that certain psychological processes might culminate in physical illness. By the 1940s this broad generalization had coalesced into the field of *psychosomatic medicine*. More specifically, researchers (for example, Alexander, 1950) identified several "psychosomatic" diseases such as peptic ulcers, essential hypertension, and bronchial asthma. Illnesses were divided into those caused by organic factors and those caused by psychological factors. Furthermore, it was believed that each psychosomatic illness had a different, specific underlying unconscious conflict predisposing the person to that disorder — for example, repressed hostility could result in rheumatoid arthritis. But these ideas began to founder (and with it the field of psychosomatic medicine) as it was realized that such very specific psychogenic factors were not terribly predictive; most empirical studies did not support the theories, so more general factors began to be considered instead. The fact is that psychosocial factors are involved in *all* diseases.

Psychosomatic medicine was largely the province of psychiatrists and physicians, but behavioral psychologists began to extend the range of their therapy methods to so-called medical disorders—problems such as obesity and smoking came under their scrutiny as well. Then there came the rapid increase in the use of biofeedback (to be discussed later in this chapter) to help patients control or modify certain physiological responses.

Another set of factors was slow to develop but ultimately had a strong impact. Since the major infectious diseases had been conquered by the 1960s, the helping professions began to turn their attention to two of the biggest killers: cardiovascular diseases and cancer. Many behaviors, such as overeating, smoking, and drinking, were increasingly identified as major correlates of these diseases. The spotlight began to shine not just on the disease process itself but also on the associated behaviors whose reduction or elimination might reduce individuals' vulnerability to disease.

Many other factors have been important in the development of the health psychology field. One of those factors is the tremendous cost of health care, much of which is directly traceable to faulty human behaviors and lifestyles resulting in injuries, accidents, poisonings, or violence. Then there are alcohol and drug abuse, smoking, and dietary-nutritional problems that contribute to these costs as well.

In the late 1960s, the role of stressful life events began to be implicated specifically as a risk factor for illness (see Holmes & Rahe, 1967). In the same decade came the interest in the Type A pattern, a complex of personality and behavioral predispositions said to make one prone to coronary complications.

The foregoing are just a few of the more prominent factors that were keys in the development of the health psychology field. We now turn to a discussion of the link between lifestyle and illness.

Linking lifestyle, behavior, and disease

What are the processes by which behavior influences health and disease? There are several influences.

Stress and health. Many psychosocial stimuli may generate stress, which can then directly affect the hormonal system, the autonomic system, and the immune system (Krantz, Grunberg, & Baum, 1985). Even thinking of future stressful events can precipitate physiological responses that are present during the actual event (Mason, 1971). Hormones such as catecholamines—neurotransmitters in the brain that help regulate blood pressure, heart rate, and blood glucose levels—are significant here. For example, chronically high levels of catecholamines may damage the cardiovascular system (Frankenhaeuser, 1980).

In addition, stress affects the immune system so that it cannot effectively destroy viruses, bacteria, tumors, and irregular cells. Two decades ago, Ader and Cohen (1975) presented evidence suggesting that the nervous system and the immune system interact and are interdependent by demonstrating that immune system responses in rats could be classically conditioned. This initial report eventually led to a number of studies investigating the relationship between physiological factors (for example, reactions to stress) and immune system response (Brannon & Feist, 1997). Currently it remains unclear whether immunosuppression is a direct effect of stress or whether it reflects and is part of the body's response to stressful events (Brannon & Feist, 1997). In any case, stress does appear to be an important (but not sole) influence on health and illness.

Behavior and health.   Behaviors, habits, and lifestyles can also affect both health and disease. Everything from smoking, excessive drinking, or poor diet to deficient hygiene practices have been implicated. Such behaviors are often deeply rooted in cultural values or personal needs and expectations. In any event, they are not easily changed.

Still another problem arises from the ways in which some people respond to illness. Often they are unable or unwilling to appreciate the severity of their illness and fail to seek timely medical help. And then, when they do get medical advice, they fail to heed it. All of these factors can to some degree foster unpleasant outcomes.

Personality factors.   There are many ways personality characteristics can affect health and illness, both directly and indirectly. Friedman and Booth-Kewley (1987) outlined five of them:

1. personality features might *result* from disease processes;
2. personality features might lead to unhealthy behaviors;
3. personality could directly affect disease through physiological mechanisms;
4. a third underlying biological variable might relate to both personality and disease; and
5. several causes and feedback loops might affect the relationship between personality and disease.

Certainly many personality traits have been said to relate to disease (although many times it is unclear how really different from one another they all are).

Range of applications

A full description of all the problems to which health psychology has addressed itself is beyond the scope of this chapter. A partial list culled from recent accounts would include:

Smoking	Chronic vomiting	Psoriasis
Alcohol abuse	Encopresis-fecal	Prurigo nodularis
Obesity	incontinence	Hyperhidrosis
Type A personality	Ulcers	Chronic pain
Hypertension	Irritable bowel syndrome	Headaches
Cardiac arrhythmia	Spasmodic torticollis	Insomnia
Raynaud's disease	Tics	Diabetes
Alzheimer's disease	Cerebral palsy	Dysmenorrhea
Acquired immune	Cerebrovascular	Dental disorders
deficiency syndrome	accidents	Cancer
(AIDS)	Epilepsy	Spinal cord injuries
Cystic fibrosis	Asthma	
Anorexia nervosa	Neurodermatitis	

In the pages that follow, we shall deal with several of these disorders, especially as they illustrate methods of intervention and prevention. Box 17-1, however, provides an initial flavor of issues that are within the province of health psychology and behavioral medicine, especially as they are applied to the problem of human immunodeficiency virus (HIV) infection and acquired immunodeficiency syndrome (AIDS).

■ Methods of Intervention

In essence, health psychology and behavioral medicine apply behavioral methods of assessment and treatment. It is not surprising, therefore, that much of the material in Chapters 9 and 14 is relevant here.

Respondent methods

Over time, a neutral (conditioned) stimulus that is paired with a naturally eliciting (unconditioned) stimulus may itself become capable of eliciting a particular response. This is the classic Pavlovian paradigm. Emotional reactions may, for example, become associated with formerly neutral, innocuous stimuli. This process may then produce conditioned emotional reactions that, if chronic, can produce such persistent tissue changes as ulcers, neurodermatitis, or essential hypertension.

These kinds of symptoms have been treated in various ways. In the case of respondent techniques, extinction or systematic desensitization interventions are commonly employed.

In *extinction,* a conditioned emotional reaction is eliminated by creating a situation in which the conditioned stimuli are no longer associated with the environmental stimuli that generated the behavior. For example, this approach can be used to eliminate children's fears of visiting the dentist. The child is brought to the dentist's office, familiarized with the office personnel, allowed to meet other children who have successfully negotiated the terrors of dentistry, and so on. In short, the child's emotional reactions are extinguished because they are no longer reinforced. A variation would be exposure techniques, described in Chapter 14. Instead of the gradual approach just described, the child (under professional supervision) would be forced to remain in the terrifying situation, the anxiety would peak and then rapidly diminish, and the child would thereby learn that the anxiety was needless. The result is extinction of the anxiety responses.

Systematic desensitization is a major method of counterconditioning (see Chapter 14). If the patient can be taught to relax in the face of anxiety-provoking stimuli, the anxiety diminishes. Health psychologists use the approach widely to treat such problems as accelerated heart rate and high blood pressure.

Operant methods

Operant responses are either maintained or eliminated through the consequences they bring about. *Operant conditioning* can be used in health psychology and behavioral medicine to either increase behaviors said to lead toward health or to decrease those said to produce problems in health. For example,

Box 17-1

The role of health psychology in the future: *acquired immunodeficiency syndrome* (AIDS)

Chesney (1993) recently illustrated the challenges that will likely confront the fields of health psychology and behavioral medicine in the future by using the epidemic spread of human immunodeficiency virus (HIV) infection and the subsequent lethal condition of AIDS as an example. It is estimated that over 1.5 million Americans are infected with HIV (Chesney, 1993), and projections from the World Health Organization estimate that 30 to 40 million people (adults and children) will be infected by the year 2000 (Mann, 1991). Because there currently is no cure for AIDS nor any vaccine for HIV, prevention of high-risk behavior is paramount (Chesney, 1993). Further, those who are infected with the virus and become symptomatic are in need of psychological treatment focusing on coping with AIDS. Chesney (1993) outlines five trends in medicine that are both relevant to HIV infection and AIDS as well as to other conditions that are within the province of health psychology and behavioral medicine:

1. *Early identification of those who are at risk.* With regard to HIV infection, this involves encouraging voluntary testing, counseling following the dissemination of test results, and decreasing (and hopefully stopping) high-risk behavior (for example, unprotected sex, sharing needles).
2. *Expectation of successful behavior change programs.* In order to stop the spread of HIV, behavior must be changed. In addition, "relapse" in this case (for example, engaging in unprotected sex) may potentially have lethal consequences. It is important to maintain behavior change by incorporating factors that have been shown empirically to lead to non-high-risk behavior.
3. *Growing population of those dealing with chronic disease.* Along with a trend toward the graying of America as well as the related increase in prevalence for chronic diseases that characteristically plague older adults, the number of Americans who will have AIDS in the near future will drastically increase the need for health-related services. Specifically, health psychologists will increasingly be called on to assist in teaching coping skills to patients as well as to their primary caregivers.
4. *Broadening perspectives.* Health psychologists will need to incorporate community and public health perspectives, in addition to focusing on the individual patient. For example, community-based media campaigns and community-based interventions are necessary to combat the spread of HIV and other precursors to chronic disease.
5. *Addressing health problems on a global scale.* We must keep in mind that illnesses and diseases affect people around the world, and these must be addressed in all nations.

athletically inclined patients would be permitted an hour's recreation each day that they complied with the treatment recommendations of the physician.

Modeling is another variant of operant methods. If a highly respected peer who does not smoke participates in a smoking-deterrence program, others may respond with the desired behavior of not beginning to smoke. Assertiveness training is another operant case in point. Such training may enable a patient to be more persistent in seeking information from an attending physician. This may later help the patient cooperate with the treatment regimen. Or it may induce a greater sense of personal control, which has many positive health correlates.

Finally, there is the method of _contingency contracting_. A good example is the token economy system described in Chapter 14. It is not hard to see how patients may be induced to participate more in physical therapy, take their medication, or reduce their number of somatic complaints if they are rewarded by tokens that can be exchanged for something of value to them.

The focus thus far has been on positive reinforcements. Naturally, punishment can also be applied judiciously to decrease the frequency of undesired behaviors.

Biofeedback

Biofeedback has become enormously popular and, for some, is almost synonymous with behavioral medicine itself. Indeed, it has truly become a growth industry (Roberts, 1985). By using this method under certain conditions, patients can learn to modify or control even involuntary physiological processes, such as heart rate, blood pressure, and brain waves.

Biofeedback encompasses a wide array of procedures. Basically, however, some aspect of the patient's physiological functioning (for example, heart rate, blood pressure) is monitored by the apparatus and then the information is fed back to the patient in the form of some auditory or visual signal. The idea is for the patient to then modify that signal by changing the physiological function. Thus, a patient experiencing severe headaches would have electrodes placed on the forehead. The electrodes pick up tiny muscular activity in that region of the head, which is amplified and transformed into tones. The tones vary as the muscular activity changes. The task of the patient is to voluntarily reduce or eliminate the tone, thus signifying a reduction of muscular tension and a corresponding reduction in the headache.

Schwartz and Beatty (1977), Fuller (1978), and Pinkerton, Hughes, and Wenrich (1982) have described biofeedback procedures and rationale at some length. These techniques have demonstrated the utility of biofeedback in reducing the effects of several psychosomatic problems, such as essential hypertension, Raynaud's disease, and tension headaches. Rimm and Masters (1979) regard biofeedback as useful but only for certain conditions (for example, some seizures, neuromuscular disorders, Raynaud's disease). For cardiovascular disorders, they feel the evidence is less convincing. When it comes to tension-related problems, including headaches, general anxiety, and insomnia, Rimm and Masters are more encouraged. However, even here it is not clear that biofeedback is superior to standard relaxation procedures.

Still, many remain uncomfortable about the scientific status of biofeedback. Some are suspicious because of the cultish, faddish, or evangelistic pronouncements of some of its practitioners. In some cases, biofeedback seems to operate as much as a placebo as anything else (Plotkin & Rice, 1981). There are surely many clinical reports of its efficacy, however, that serve to maintain enthusiasm. Others make the harsh judgment that "there is absolutely no convincing evidence that biofeedback is an essential or specific technique for the treatment of any condition" (Roberts, 1985, p. 940).

In all likelihood, biofeedback does not, by itself, lead to therapeutic gains. When it is effective, it usually is part of a larger package that also includes relaxation or cognitive strategies, among other things. If removed from the package it loses its effectiveness. Some, then, would regard it as a gimmick. A less harsh description is that it serves as an example to the patient that self-regulation in life is possible. Furthermore, it may be that the reason biofeedback works better in the clinic than in the research laboratory is simply that the clinic places the biofeedback machine in a larger context of an understanding clinical relationship and additional therapeutic techniques. At the very least, biofeedback appears to be a useful technique to teach patients to become more aware of their bodily signals and of what these may mean.

Relaxation

Relaxation is designed to produce a state of lowered arousal through the efforts of the individual. As a preliminary step, patients are usually taught the basic behavioral principles related to their symptoms and how therapy relates to the implementation of these principles. For example, a patient whose stressful lifestyle has led to some physical problems would be taught the relationship between lifestyle and illness by means of a fairly extensive verbal explanation (or reading material). Following this, a thorough psychophysiological assessment is conducted using recording equipment, self-ratings of tension, and the therapist's own observation (Pinkerton, Hughes, & Wenrich, 1982).

Next, the patient is taught to self-monitor. For example, there might be training in how and when to record the presence of headaches. Also recorded are data on the presence of environmental stimuli that precede the headache, how the person responds to the headache, and the consequences that follow from the symptoms.

Finally, there is specific training in relaxation. Positive expectancies for a good outcome are engendered, and the physical conditions are arranged such that relaxation will be easy to achieve (for example, assuming a comfortable position, loosening tight clothing, adjusting lighting). Regular practice in the therapist's office is followed by practice at home. (Relaxation and desensitization procedures were described in more detail in Chapter 14.)

Cognitive strategies

A variety of cognitive strategies are used by health psychologists. Sometimes these techniques are used alone, at other times in concert with other strategies, such as relaxation or biofeedback. Most of these methods have already been discussed and need not be described again (see Chapter 14). They include cognitive restructuring, stress inoculation training, and others. For example, a patient who responds to stressful situations with dizziness, heart palpitations, and nausea could be taught to identify the irrational, self-defeating thoughts that occur in stressful situations.

Self-management methods

The self-management approach is highly relevant to health psychology and behavioral medicine for one very good reason: it transfers the responsibility for health from "authorities" to oneself. The resulting sense of personal control can be beneficial all around (Strickland, 1979). As we shall see a bit later, lifestyles that include smoking or overindulging in alcohol or food greatly affect health. In the final analysis, self-management may be the critical factor in controlling these self-defeating behaviors. Very likely, many of the therapeutic techniques such as relaxation, biofeedback, and cognitive restructuring are ultimately self-management approaches.

At least five self-control or management strategies have been identified (Mahoney & Arnkoff, 1979). First, there is *self-monitoring* training noted in the section on relaxation. Second, there is training in *goal specification*—the establishment of realistic goals and the identification of the means to achieve them. Third, there is the notion of *cueing strategies*. This means that the patient gradually reduces and eliminates stimuli that, judging by past experience, are very likely to precipitate the undesirable behavior. For example, the problem drinker must learn to identify and eventually avoid those situations that tend to prompt drinking. Fourth, *incentive modification* is the process whereby patients are taught to reward themselves when their behavior meets agreed-upon criteria. Fifth, is the concept of *rehearsal*. This refers to the patient's systematically practicing those behaviors (thought, physical acts, and the like) that are consistent with the goals of self-management.

One disease in which self-management methods have been used extensively is diabetes (Brannon & Feist, 1997).

Social support

A topic attracting increased research interest is *social support* and its effects on health and well-being (Cohen & Syme, 1985). The basic idea is that interpersonal ties can actually promote health—they insulate people from harm when they encounter stress, decrease susceptibility to illness, and help people comply with and maintain treatment regimens.

Social support is, in many ways, a kind of coping assistance (Thoits, 1986). Partner behaviors, for example, can facilitate a person's quitting smoking (Cohen & Lichtenstein, 1990; Morgan, Ashenberg, & Fisher, 1988). It has also been found that high levels of spouse or partner support for the smoker's quitting and the perceived availability of general support were very important early on (Mermelstein, Cohen, Lichenstein, Baer, & Kamarck, 1986); that is, initial quitting and short-term maintenance were greatly facilitated by this support. The support was not critical, however, for long-term abstinence. In addition, there is some evidence that social support can enhance the operation of the immune function in cancer patients (Baron, Cutrona, Hicklin, Russell, & Lubaroff, 1990).

At the same time, however, it is important to note that the relationship between social support, stress, and health depends on a number of factors including race, gender, and culture. For example, Berkman (1986) reported that previous studies on social support and health consistently found that white men benefited (healthwise) the most, but results linking social support and positive health outcomes were weaker and more inconsistent for women and for those of nonwhite racial backgrounds. Clearly, the relationship between social support and health is complex.

■ Prevention

Nearly everyone agrees that a few simple behaviors, if widely practiced, would dramatically reduce the toll of human misery and the torrent of dollars pouring into the health care system. These include reduction in consumption of salt and fatty foods, driving carefully and use of seat belts, regular exercise, and reduction in stress. But giving advice and having people take it are two very different things. Therefore, psychologists, other behavioral specialists, and medical professionals have mounted research programs for the *prevention* of a variety of potentially harmful human behaviors.

Cigarette smoking

Increased awareness of the dangers of cigarette smoking has led to a steady decline in the percentage of those who are habitual smokers since the mid-1960s (Brannon & Feist, 1997). However, rates of smoking differ according to gender, level of education, and income. One disconcerting trend is that the rate of smoking in women has shown much less of a decline than that for men (Centers for Disease Control and Prevention, 1994). In fact, among white-collar workers the smoking rate for women now exceeds that for men.

Cigarette smoking has been linked to an increased risk for cardiovascular disease and cancer, the two leading causes of death in the United States. Even though smoking increases the chances of premature death from diseases such as coronary heart disease, cancers of the respiratory tract, emphysema, and bronchitis (among others), people still smoke. Why? There are many possible reasons, including tension control, social pressure, rebelliousness, the addictive nature of nicotine, and genetically influenced personality traits like extraversion (Brannon & Feist, 1997; Krantz, Grunberg, & Baum, 1985). The first two factors—tension control and social pressure—are thought to be reasons for the initiation of smoking, whereas the latter three are seen primarily as maintaining factors.

To induce people to stop smoking, a variety of techniques have been employed including educational programs, aversion therapy (for example, rapid smoking), behavioral contracts, acupuncture, cognitive therapy, group support, and so on (Brannon & Feist, 1997; Pechacek, 1979). Relapse rates are high

(70–80%), however, and research findings about which cessation approach is best are conflicting. Most smokers who do quit, do so on their own.

The best approach, then, seems to be to prevent the habit from starting in the first place. A large prevention project exemplifies the primary prevention philosophy (Farquhar et al., 1977; Meyer, Nash, McAlister, Maccoby, & Farquhar, 1980). Known as the Stanford Heart Disease Prevention Project, it involved three communities and a broad range of risk factors including smoking, fat intake, exercise, and blood pressure. One community was exposed to a mass media campaign. A second received the mass media treatment along with one-on-one behavior therapy for those identified as high-risk individuals. The third community served as a control. Just the media campaign alone resulted in some reduction in smoking at a three-year follow-up, but substantial reductions resulted when the media campaign was combined with behavior therapy.

Another encouraging prevention program aimed at children and teenagers is based on social learning principles and employs peer role models (Evans, 1976). Videotaped presentations, peer modelings, discussion groups, role playing, monitoring of smoking, and checking repeatedly on attitudes and knowledge about smoking were all used in this program involving elementary-school children. Such an approach seems superior to ones with adolescents that emphasize long-term negative effects from smoking. The trick seems to be to focus on immediate negative reinforcements (for example, from peers) rather than delayed ones (for example, emphysema). Programs similar to Evans's in Houston have been undertaken in California, Minnesota, and New York with promising results (Matarazzo & Carmody, 1983). Additional prevention programs that employ student versus adult models in order to encourage teenagers not to smoke have been successful as well (see McAlister, Perry, Killen, Slinkard, & Maccoby, 1980; Murray, Richards, Luepker, & Johnson, 1987).

Research also suggests that smoking relapses can be significantly reduced in many individuals by tailoring cessation skills for them (Stevens & Hollis, 1989). Likewise, surviving relapse crises is related to the number of coping strategies employed (Bliss, Garvey, Heinold, & Hitchcock, 1989).

Alcohol abuse and dependence

Recent statistics indicate that about 70% of men and 50% of women in the United States consume alcoholic beverages (United States Department of Health and Human Services, 1993). Although some studies have suggested positive health benefits from alcohol for light or moderate drinkers, consumption of alcohol has also been associated with a number of negative outcomes. For example, heavy alcohol use has been linked to increased risk for liver or neurological damage, certain forms of cancer, cardiovascular problems, fetal alcohol syndrome, physical aggression, suicide, motor vehicle accidents, and violence (USDHHS, 1993). This extensive list of alcohol-related problems has made the treatment and prevention of alcohol abuse and alcohol dependence (that is, alcoholism) a high priority.

Over the years, many treatment approaches have been applied to problem drinkers; most of these treatments preach total abstinence. They range from medical treatments and medications such as disulfiram (Antabuse) to traditional psychotherapy and group supportive strategies such as Alcoholics Anonymous. But alcoholism is a problem that has been extremely resistant to virtually all intervention, and the relapse rate is high. Another, more controversial, approach to the treatment of alcohol problems is *controlled drinking* (Sobell & Sobell, 1978). As the name implies, this approach has as its goals light to moderate (but controlled) drinking. Clients are taught to develop alternative coping responses in place of drinking and to closely monitor their alcohol intake. The field is divided as to the merits of this approach, but research does suggest that, for some alcoholics, controlled drinking is a viable treatment option.

Finally, it is noteworthy that some alcohol treatment programs incorporate *relapse prevention* training (Marlatt & Gordon, 1985). The majority of clients treated for alcohol problems have a relapse episode soon after treatment is terminated. Rather than see this as a failure (that is, a sign that complete relapse is imminent), clients are taught coping skills and behaviors to be employed in high-risk situations so that total relapse is less likely.

It is clear that, in general, alcohol abuse and dependence are complex problems that probably require multimodal treatment strategies. Because of the difficulties with secondary and tertiary approaches to treatment or prevention, more and more professionals have turned to primary prevention to forestall the development of problem drinking. For both drinking and drug abuse, programs similar to those to prevent adolescents from starting to smoke are being developed. Often, these programs focus on health education courses in high school or on media campaigns. School-based prevention programs typically involve one or more of the following components: *affective education* (building self-esteem, increasing decision-making skills), *life skills* (communication skills, assertiveness training), *resistance training* (learning to resist pressures to drink alcohol), and *correcting erroneous perceptions about peer norms* (USDHHS, 1993). Current research evidence suggests that programs incorporating peer resistance training and correction of misperceptions regarding peer norms show the most promise (USDHHS, 1993).

Obesity

Behavioral treatments for obesity have been more common than for any other condition. One reason for this emphasis is that obesity is associated with such medical disorders as diabetes, hypertension, cardiovascular disease, and certain cancers (Brannon & Feist, 1997). It is also a socially stigmatizing condition that impairs the self-concept and inhibits functioning in a wide array of social settings. Often, problems of weight can be traced to childhood: 10 to 25% of all children are obese, and 80% of these individuals become obese adults (Stunkard, 1979).

Although it is clear that obesity has a genetic component (Meyer & Stunkard, 1993), causes of obesity undoubtedly represent complex interactions among biological, social, and behavioral factors, and exact mechanisms are difficult to pin down. Traditional medical and dietary methods of treatment have not been very effective; obese individuals lose weight but then quickly regain it. Furthermore, the dropout rate is as high as 80% in traditional weight control programs, although a variety of behavioral treatments have shown promise (Hagen, 1981). Among these are contingency management, family support, public commitments to weight loss, and systematic programs of exercise and exercise education.

Again, however, early prevention may be the best and safest road to weight control. An excellent example of such an approach is the Stanford Adolescent Obesity Project (Coates & Thoresen, 1981). A variety of strategies were used with adolescents in the hope that control at this age would lead to prevention in adulthood. These strategies included self-observation, cue elimination, and social and family support, and they were noticeably more effective when parents were involved. Another example is the recent ten-year outcome study of a family-based behavioral treatment for childhood obesity; results suggested that early intervention in childhood can effect important and lasting changes in weight control (Epstein, Valoski, Wing, & McCurley, 1994). Also, as another early prevention strategy, the possibility of using peer group discussion is being explored by many investigators.

Stress

It has been said that stress is a state that occurs when changes in the environment place either too much or too little demand on the person and when normal adjustment responses are not available or else do not work. In short, there is a threat to the individual's security that, left unchecked, can lead to breakdown (Geen, 1976). Stress has been implicated as a contributing factor in a wide variety of illnesses and physical problems (Brannon & Feist, 1997; Gatchel & Blanchard, 1993), and it is typically linked to many sorts of events. For example, Holmes and Rahe (1967) compiled a list of events in the lives of 5000 medical patients—events that seemed to have occurred at about the time their medical problems began (for example, death of spouse, fired at work, change in financial state, start or end of school). But stress does not come about just from environmental pressure—stressors produce stress only when individuals perceive the events as threatening. Thus, the bodily responses of stress are triggered not so much by the event itself as by one's cognitions about the event. (For example, a demanding job produces stress if a person feels unable to cope with it.)

Is there such a thing as a stress-prone personality type? The notion that there may be a link between personality or coping style and adverse health consequences (specifically, coronary heart disease) was proposed by two cardiologists (Friedman & Rosenman, 1974). They identified a set of discriminating personality characteristics and behaviors and proposed that these constituted a *Type A behavior pattern*. Individuals exhibiting these characteristics have become known as "Type A's." What are these characteristics? Glass (1977) states that Type A individuals are those who tend to:

- perceive time passing rather quickly
- show a deteriorating performance on tasks that require delayed responding
- work near maximum capacity even when there is no time deadline
- arrive early for appointments
- become aggressive and hostile when frustrated

Table 17-1
Selected items from the behavior pattern interview.

- Does your job carry *heavy* responsibility?
  (a) Is there any time when you feel particularly *rushed* or under *pressure*?
  (b) When you are under *pressure,* does it bother you?
- When you get angry or upset, do people around you know about it? How do you show it?
- When you are in your automobile, and there is a car in your lane going *far too slowly* for you, what do you do about it? Would you *mutter* and *complain* to yourself? Would anyone riding with you know that you were *annoyed*?
- If you make a *date* with someone for, oh, two o'clock in the afternoon, for example, would you *be there* on *time*?
  (a) If you are kept waiting, do you *resent* it?
  (b) Would you *say* anything about it?
- Do you *eat rapidly*? Do you *walk* rapidly? After you've *finished* eating, do you like to sit around the table and chat, or do you like to *get up and get going*?
- How do you feel about waiting in lines: *bank* lines, or *supermarket* lines? *Post office* lines?

SOURCE: From "The Interview Method of Assessment of the Coronary-prone Behavior Pattern," by R. H. Rosenman, pp. 68–69. In T. M. Dembroski, S. M. Weiss, J. L. Shields, S. G. Haynes, and M. Feinleib (Eds.), *Coronary-prone Behavior.* Copyright © 1978 by Springer-Verlag. Reprinted by permission.

- report less fatigue and fewer physical symptoms
- are motivated intensely to master their physical and social environments and to maintain control

Some examples of interview questions that are used to identify Type A individuals are shown in Table 17-1.

A number of early studies suggested a relationship between Type A behavior and coronary heart disease (Rosenman et al., 1975). However, these findings were often misinterpreted as indicating that Type A individuals are likely to develop coronary heart disease (Davison & Neale, 1996). More recent studies do not show as strong a relationship between Type A behavior and heart disease as was once thought (see Matthews, 1984), and it is clear that the vast majority of Type A individuals do not develop coronary heart disease (CHD). Even so, Type A individuals are at relatively greater risk for CHD. It may turn out that the anger-hostility component of the Type A pattern does a better job of predicting coronary heart disease than the more global Type A categorization (Rodin & Salovey, 1989; Smith, 1992).

A variety of attempts have been made to modify the Type A pattern, but this can be difficult since Type A behaviors are difficult to identify clinically. What is more, society reinforces such behaviors with great regularity. Most attempts at modification involve relaxation training, guided practice, exercise, and group therapy (Suinn, 1982). Cognitive-behavioral strategies are also highly promising approaches (Meichenbaum & Jaremko, 1983). A meta-analysis of studies investigating psychological interventions aimed at modifying Type A behavior patterns indicated that modest improvements could be made, and there was some suggestion of a decreased risk for CHD following intervention (Nunes, Frank, & Kornfeld, 1987).

■ Other Applications

Preventive initiatives must also be supplemented with techniques that encourage patients to cope with medical procedures and to follow medical advice.

Coping with medical procedures

The prospect of facing surgery, a visit to the dentist, or a variety of medical examinations has been enough to strike fear into the heart of even the strongest. Faced with such procedures, many patients delay their visits or else forego them entirely. Health psychologists specializing in behavioral medicine have developed interventions to help patients deal with the stress surrounding these procedures (Peterson, 1989). Below, we provide several examples.

Medical examinations/procedures.   Some medical examinations or procedures are especially stressful. Without them, however, the patient may not be properly diagnosed and may thereby miss out on a health-saving intervention. A good example is sigmoidoscopy. This is a fairly common procedure designed to examine the mucous of the bowel in order to discover whether there are any pathological growths in the last ten inches of the colon. This, in turn, can aid in the early detection and prevention of any malignancies. For many patients, however, the procedure is very stressful. It involves inserting a scope into the colon, with some stretching of the bowel. While all of this is not very painful or dangerous, it does unnerve many people, and they perceive it as a humiliating experience. In one study, a brief intervention was contrived to help patients cope with the stress of this procedure (Kaplan, Atkins, & Lenhard, 1982). Compared to a control group, patients given brief cognitive instruction moved less during the examination and verbalized less as well. Indeed, the entire process took less time for these patients.

What kind of information is most likely to help patients cope with stressful medical procedures? Often, a distinction is made between *sensory information* (descriptions of the sensations that will be encountered) and *procedural information* (descriptions of what will occur). A recent review of studies indicated that, although procedural preparation was superior to sensory preparation in reducing negative affect, pain reports, and other distress, combined procedural-sensory preparation was the most effective method (Suls & Wan, 1989).

In addition to informational interventions, evidence also supports the use of behavioral interventions in certain situations. For example, venipuncture is common in the course of cancer treatment, and this procedure can be quite distressing to children undergoing treatment, as well as to their parents and the nurses who perform the procedure (Manne et al., 1990). Manne et al. developed a behavioral intervention to reduce the level of distress associated with venipuncture. Its components include *attentional distraction* (using a party blower during the procedure), *pacing of breathing, positive reinforcement* (for example, receiving stickers if the child cooperates), and *parent coaching.* These researchers found that this intervention package markedly reduced children's behavioral distress, parents' anxiety, and parents' ratings of child pain. Interestingly, this treatment did not significantly reduce children's self-reported pain.

Preparation for surgery.   There has been a sizable amount of research on ways to improve psychological preparation for surgery (Johnson, 1984; Olson & Elliott, 1983). Similar to those used to prepare patients for medical examinations and procedures, interventions include: (1) relaxation strategies; (2) basic information about the procedures to be employed; (3) information concerning the bodily sensations experienced during the procedures; and (4) cognitive coping skills (Olson & Elliott, 1983). Wilson (1981) carried out a well-controlled study in which intensive training in relaxation was provided. In a sample of 700 patients undergoing either cholecystectomy (removal of the gall bladder) or abdominal hysterectomy, this relaxation intervention not only reduced hospital stays but improved both self-reports and physiological data.

Another technique was used with children about to undergo surgery. It was found that a film showing a *coping model* significantly reduced the children's emotional reactions during their time in the hospital (Melamed & Siegel, 1975). Those who saw the film prior to surgery were less anxious before their operation and showed fewer behavior problems afterward.

Compliance with regimens

Despite the availability of intervention strategies, the fact remains that many individuals do not comply with program interventions or else do not maintain their new behavior over any significant period of time. For example, it is estimated that the rate of noncompliance with medical or health advice is approximately 50% (Brannon & Feist, 1997). Truly successful program strategies must generate both compliance and long-term maintenance. Both behavioral and psychosocial factors must be considered (Phillips, 1988).

In general, purported predictors of patient compliance can be broken down into four categories: *illness/disease characteristics, personal characteristics of the patient, cultural norms,* and *practitioner-patient interaction* (Brannon & Feist, 1997). Table 17-2 summarizes research findings concerning the relationship between a variety of factors and patient compliance.

As for improving compliance, educational and instructional methods have not been particularly helpful, whereas behavioral interventions have proved more successful (Brannon & Feist, 1997). For example, DiMatteo and DiNicola (1982) recommended several general strategies to improve patient compliance:

1. Use "prompts" as reminders (for example, taking medicine before each meal, telephone calls from providers).

Table 17-2
Summary of findings relating disease/illness characteristics, personal characteristics
of the patient, cultural norms, and practitioner-patient interaction factors to
adherence.

Predictions of Compliance	Findings
I. Disease Characteristics	
A. Severity of side effects	No relationship
B. Severity of illness	
(as seen by the physician)	No relationship
(as seen by the patient)	Positive relationship
C. Duration of treatment	Negative relationship
D. Complexity of treatment	Complexity leads to nonadherence, as does number of doses over 3
II. Personal Characteristics	
A. Age	
Adults	
(exercise up to 6 months)	Positive relationship
(exercise after 6 months)	No relationship
(cancer screening)	Curvilinear relationship
(diabetes)	Positive relationship
(heart disease)	Positive relationship
Adolescents	
(diabetes)	Negative relationship
B. Gender	
(exercise)	Men and Women equal
(diet)	Women more compliant
(medication)	Women more compliant
C. Social support	Positive relationship
D. Emotional support	Positive relationship
E. Personality traits	No relationship
F. Patient's beliefs	
avoidance coping	Negative relationship
personal control	Positive relationship
III. Cultural Norms	Patients' cultural beliefs predict compliance
IV. Practitioner/Patient Interaction	
A. Verbal communication	Positive relationship
B. Practitioner's personal qualities	
friendliness	Predicts compliance
gender	Women provide more information
communication skills	Positive relationship
C. Delays	
getting an appointment	Negative relationship
in the waiting room	Negative relationship

SOURCE: Brannon & Feist (1997), *Health Psychology: An Introduction to Behavior and Health*. (3rd ed),
p. 203. Pacific Grove, CA: Brooks/Cole. Reprinted by permission.

2. Tailor the treatment regimen to the patient's schedule and lifestyle.
3. Use written contracts that promise a reward to the patient for complying with treatment guidelines.

■ Health Psychology: Prospects for the Future

Health psychology is a growing field, and more psychologists are entering it every year. Therefore, it may now be time for the field to take a look at itself and decide how best to train health psychologists and to structure programs that achieve training goals. In this last section, we will discuss several health care trends, training issues for future health psychologists, and important issues for the field of health psychology to address in the future.

Health care trends

Weiner (1994) has estimated that more than 40% of all Americans will participate in managed care delivery systems by the year 2000. In managed care systems, containing costs is a high priority. In previous chapters, we noted the great impact managed care has had and will have on clinical psychologists; the impact will be even greater on health psychologists because these specialists often work in medical center or primary care settings. Health psychologists, by virtue of their training, are well suited to provide interventions that will serve to cut the costs of medical care (Friedman, Sobel, Myers, Caudill, & Benson, 1995). As business and industry realize the costs they must absorb from employees whose habits and lifestyles create absenteeism, inefficiency, and turnover, they will utilize the skills of health psychologists more often.

Although there appears to be an ever-increasing need for clinical psychologists specializing in health or behavioral medicine, it should also be noted that a surplus of mental health professionals currently exists. For example, Frank and Ross (1995) estimate that there are approximately 32.8 social workers, 22.8 psychologists, 13.1 psychiatrists, and 4.3 psychiatric nurses for every 100,000 Americans (or 73 mental health professionals per 100,000). The problem lies in the overlapping definitions of each discipline—all claim to assess and treat similar problems. Further, as the economic stakes become higher, it is likely that these disciplines' self-definitions will incorporate concepts and issues once thought to be uniquely characteristic of health psychology and behavioral medicine. Frank and Ross (1995) call for more coordination of health workforce planning at the national level. Further,

> . . . clearly defining and establishing psychology's role in health care also requires efforts at delineating psychology's unique contributions amid an increasing supply of other health-related professions. . . . efforts to establish clear professional boundaries and identities among the various health care groups should be based on dialogue, coordination, and cooperation to ensure that the health care needs of the population are met by qualified, ethical, and competent professionals. (p. 524)

Training issues

A major source of health psychologists continues to be clinical psychology programs. Matarazzo and Carmody (1983) point out that the scientist-practitioner tradition of schools with programs organized on the Boulder model enables them to train clinicians well suited for health psychology. Until recently, no other psychology specialty offered the combination of academic, scientific, professional, and hospital experiences required for work in medical settings. At the same time, Stroebe & Stroebe (1995) make a case for the background of social psychologists. Again, the roles of methodology, quantitative analysis, and research design are emphasized. But other psychology subspecialties are well represented in health psychology too. Many of the people cited in this chapter are experimental or physiological psychologists—not just clinicians or social psychologists.

For the most part, health psychology is still a kind of ad hoc appendage to many doctoral programs in psychology. The student enters a clinical, social, or experimental program and then, in addition to the core experience, does some specialized research or takes a practicum or two in a health-related topic. Perhaps this is augmented by an internship at a health care site. But, essentially, the health experiences are grafted onto an already existing program in clinical psychology or some other discipline.

However, many are now calling for health psychology to be a standard, core training component for all professional psychologists (for example, Frank & Ross, 1995). Because of the importance of health issues and the broadening of the definition of clinical and professional psychology, preparation in areas like psychopharmacology, neuropsychology, and psychoneuroimmunology is considered essential. Further, future health psychologists must be trained so that they can design and conduct studies to empirically evaluate health outcomes. Currently, some clinical psychology graduate programs offer "tracks" in health psychology or behavioral medicine, but this is the exception more than the rule. In any case, curricular recommendations for health psychology training continue to be offered (Brannon & Feist, 1997).

Other issues

Any newly emerging field has problems in defining the roles of its members, and health psychology is no exception. Taylor (1984) has identified several of these problems. One is simply role ambiguity—no one is totally prepared to say just what a health psychologist should do, especially in a practical work setting. Health psychologists may actually find themselves without psychology colleagues or role models in the health arena, which only adds to their confusion. Second, issues of status also arise. In health settings, the physician is clearly at the top of the heap. Sometimes the psychologist enjoys much less status in a medical center setting than, for example, in an academic setting. Furthermore, the psychologist and the health care professional may have competing goals. The latter may be interested only in identifying immediate ways of helping the patient, whereas the psychologist may be more tentative and contemplative in thinking about research, theoretical models, and interventions.

As one way of establishing identity and presence in settings that traditionally are dominated by physicians, health psychologists need to document the cost-effectiveness of their interventions (Friedman et al., 1995). In this era of health care reform, insurance companies and governmental agencies are scrupulously examining ways to drive down the cost of health care. Given the many successful and cost-efficient interventions performed by those specializing in health psychology and behavioral medicine, a good question is "Why haven't these interventions been integrated to a greater extent into our health care system?" (Friedman et al., 1995). Friedman et al. cite several reasons:

1. Many of the data supporting the role of health psychology are unknown to physicians.
2. Biological origins of diseases and illnesses have been emphasized, causing many to overlook the possible benefits of psychosocial explanations and behavioral interventions.
3. Patients may, in fact, be resistant to psychological interventions (and explanations).
4. Clinical health psychology and behavioral medicine are still confused with traditional, long-term psychotherapy.

Clearly, physicians, insurance companies, the federal government, and the general public need to be educated regarding the roles of health psychologists as well as the potential financial and clinical benefits of their interventions.

Another challenge for the field concerns ethnicity and health. The health profiles (for example, life expectancy, health status) of various ethnic minority populations in the U.S. appear to differ greatly from each other, and more research is needed on the health-promoting and health-damaging behaviors among members of these groups (Anderson, 1995). Informative articles reporting on the health status of African Americans, Asian Americans, and Hispanic Americans (Flack et al., 1995), behavioral risk factors related to chronic diseases in ethnic minorities (Meyers, Kagawa-Singer, Kumanyika, Lex, & Markides, 1995), and the use of health care systems by ethnic minorities (Penn, Snehendu, Kramer, Skinner, & Zambrana, 1995) appeared recently in a special issue of *Health Psychology*. These reports and others point out the need to further assess the relations between behavior and health in special populations.

It is easy to become carried away with the enthusiasm generated by an exciting new field. This has been true in virtually every area of clinical psychology so far. Inadvertently, perhaps, zealous proponents may also oversell health psychology (Elliott, 1983); there is still a gap between the field's promise and its accomplishments. And as any experienced clinician will admit, it is very hard to change human behavior over the long haul. Nevertheless, health psychology most assuredly deserves both the enthusiasm and the caution of clinical psychologists.

■ Focus Questions

1. What historical events influenced the development of the field of health psychology?

2. What are the major forms of intervention methods used by health psychologists?
3. How are prevention techniques used to address problems related to smoking, alcohol abuse and dependence, and obesity?
4. What techniques are used to help patients cope with stressful medical procedures and surgery?
5. What major influences are likely to impact the future of health psychology?

■ Key Terms

behavioral medicine
biofeedback
cognitive strategies
contingency contracting
controlled drinking
coping model
cueing strategies
extinction
goal specification
health psychology
incentive modification
operant conditioning

prevention
procedural information
psychosomatic medicine
rehearsal
relapse prevention
relaxation
self-monitoring
sensory information
social support
systematic desensitization
Type A behavior pattern

18

Neuropsychology

A very important growth area in clinical psychology over the past two decades has been the field of neuropsychology. This growth has been reflected in (1) increases in memberships in professional neuropsychological associations; (2) the number of training programs that offer neuropsychology courses; (3) the many papers, books, and journals now being published on neuropsychological topics; and (4) the increase in neuropsychology-related positions available (D'Amato, Dean, & Holloway, 1987).

■ Perspectives and History

As the term would suggest, neuropsychologists have a foot in both the psychological and neurological domains. While some have received their basic training in clinical psychology, others have been trained by neurologists.

Definitions

What is *neuropsychology?* Most simply, it can be defined as the study of the relation between brain function and behavior (Golden, Zillmer, & Spiers, 1992). It deals with the understanding, assessment, and treatment of behaviors directly related to the functioning of the brain (Golden, 1984). *Neuropsychological assessment* is a noninvasive method of describing brain functioning based on a patient's performance on standardized tests that have been shown to be accurate and sensitive indicators of brain-behavior relationships (Golden et al., 1992). The neuropsychologist

> . . . may address issues of cerebral [brain] lesion lateralizations, localization, and cerebral lesion progress. Neuropsychological evaluations have also provided useful information about the impact of a patient's limitations on educational, social, or vocational adjustment. Since many patients with neurological disorders, such as degenerative diseases, cerebrovascular accident, or multiple sclerosis, vary widely in the rate at which the illness progresses or improves, the most meaningful way to assess patients for the severity of their condition is to assess their behavior objectively *via* neuropsychological assessment procedures. (Golden et al., 1992, p. 19)

Roles of neuropsychologists

Neuropsychologists function in a number of different roles (Golden et al., 1992). First, they are often called on by neurologists or other physicians to help establish or rule out particular diagnoses. For example, a patient may present with a number of symptoms that may have either a neurological or emotional basis. Neuropsychological test results may help clarify the diagnosis in this situation. Second, because of an emphasis on functional systems of the brain (see below), neuropsychologists often can make predictions regarding prognosis for recovery. A third major role involves intervention and rehabilitation. Information provided by neuropsychologists often has important implications for treatment; test results provide guidance, for example, as to which areas of the brain are still intact and can be used to "take over" functions of the brain that have been impaired due to injury or disease. Finally, it is worth noting that neuropsychologists may be asked to evaluate patients with mental disorders in order to help predict the course of illness (based on, for example, the degree of cognitive impairment present) as well as to help tailor treatment strategies to patients' strengths and weaknesses (Keefe, 1995).

With these definitions and descriptions of the roles of neuropsychologists in mind, we now turn to a brief history of the field.

History of neuropsychology

Theories of brain functioning.   As in most areas of psychology, the historical roots of neuropsychology extend about as far back in time as we are inclined to look. Some observers look to the Upper Paleolithic period. Others suggest that it all began when Pythagoras said that human reasoning occurs in the brain. Others are partial to the second century A.D. when Galen, the Greek physician, argued that the mind was located in the brain, not in the heart as Aristotle had claimed.

However, the most significant early base for neuropsychology seems to have been laid in the nineteenth century (Hartlage, 1987). Researchers then were beginning to understand that damage to specific cortical areas was related to impaired function of certain adaptive behaviors. The earliest signs of this understanding came with Franz Gall and his now discredited *phrenology*. He believed that certain individual differences in intelligence and personality (for example, reading skills) could be measured by noting the bumps and indentations of the skull; thus, the size of a given area of the brain determined the person's corresponding psychological capacity. This was the first popularization of the notion of *localization of function*.

Localization achieved much greater believability with Paul Broca's surgical work in 1861. Observations from two autopsies of patients who had lost their powers of expressive speech convinced Broca that he had found the location of motor speech. Within the next 30 to 40 years, many books presented maps of the brain that located each major function (Golden, 1984).

Others, such as Pierre Flourens, would surgically destroy certain areas of the brains of animals and then note any consequent behavioral losses. Such work led Flourens and, later, in the early twentieth century, Karl Lashley to argue for the concept of *equipotentiality*. That is, while there certainly is localization of brain function, the cortex really functions as a whole rather than as isolated units. In particular, higher intellectual functioning is mediated by the brain as a whole, and any brain injury will impair these higher functions. Yet, there is the ability of one area of the cortex to substitute for the damaged area.

Both the localization and equipotentiality theories presented some problems, however. Localizationalists could not explain why lesions in very different parts of the brain produced the same deficit or impairment, whereas those adhering to the equipotentiality theory could not account for the observation that some patients with very small lesions manifested marked, specific behavioral deficits (Golden et al., 1992). An alternative theory that integrates these two perspectives is the *functional model*. First proposed by the neurologist Jackson and later adapted by the Soviet neuropsychologist Luria, the functional model holds that areas of the brain interact with each other to produce behavior. Further, behavior "is conceived of as being the result of several functions or systems of the brain areas, rather than the result of unitary or discrete brain areas. A disruption at any stage is sufficient to immobilize a given functional system" (Golden et al., 1992). The importance of this formulation is that it can account for many of the clinical findings that are inconsistent with previous theories. According to the functional model, the nature of the behavioral deficit depends on which functional system (for example, arousal versus perception versus planning behavior) has been affected as well as the localization of the damage within that functional system. Finally, through a process called reorganization, recovery from brain damage is sometimes possible.

Neuropsychological assessment.   Turning to the topic of specific psychological assessment instruments, we can note that, for a long time, neurology was bewitched by notions of mass action of brain functioning. These ideas tended to make localization of function a secondary goal of diagnosis. For this and other reasons, brain damage was often viewed as a unitary phenomenon. Therefore, the collection of information about specific test correlates of specific brain lesions was not accomplished very efficiently. In particular, the psychological tests used (for example, Bender-Gestalt, Benton Visual Retention Test, Graham-Kendall Memory-for-Designs Test) were oriented toward the simple assessment of the presence or absence of brain damage.

Neuropsychology as a field began to grow concurrently with World War II. This was because of (1) the large numbers of head injuries in the war; and (2) the development of the field of clinical psychology itself (Hartlage, 1987). An important development of the postwar period was the work of Ward Halstead. By observing brain-damaged people in natural settings he was able to identify certain specific characteristics of their behavior. Next, he tried to assess these characteristics by administering a variety of psychological tests to these patients. Through factor analysis, he settled on ten measures that ultimately comprised his test battery. Later, Ralph Reitan, a graduate student of Halstead's, refined the test battery by eliminating two tests and adding several others. Subsequently, Reitan and his colleagues could relate test responses to such discrete aspects of brain lesions as lateralized motor deficits. This work culminated in the Halstead-Reitan Neuropsychological Test Battery. By 1980, the Luria-Nebraska Neuropsychological Battery had been developed and is now frequently used as an alternative to the Halstead-Reitan battery. We'll have more to say about these and other neuropsychological tests in a later section.

◼ The Brain: Structure, Function, and Impairment

Before proceeding, it would be well to review some important aspects of the brain. This will, of necessity, be a brief excursion. More extensive accounts may be found elsewhere (for example, Golden et al., 1992; Kolb & Whishaw, 1985).

Structure and function

The brain consists of two hemispheres. The *left hemisphere* (or dominant hemisphere, typically) controls the right side of the body and is thought to be more involved in language functions, logical inference, and detail analysis in almost all right-handed individuals and a good many left-handers as well. The *right hemisphere* controls the left side of the body. It is more involved in visual-spatial skills, creativity, musical activities, perception of direction, and so on. But, again, note that some left-handers may reverse this hemispheric pattern. Also important is the fact that the two hemispheres communicate with one another, which helps to co-ordinate and integrate complex human behavior.

There are four lobes within each cerebral hemisphere (see Figure 18-1): the frontal, the temporal, the parietal, and the occipital. The *frontal lobes* enable us to observe and compare our behavior and the reactions of others to it in order to obtain the feedback necessary to alter our behavior to achieve valued goals. This is what Boll (1983) calls the *comparator* function; it involves appropriately deciding on goals and then selecting a course of action to attain them. The *inertia-overcoming* function (Boll, 1983)—another frontal lobe activity—is the ability to initiate and accomplish a task appropriately and with dispatch.

The *temporal lobes* mediate linguistic expression, reception, and analysis. They also are involved in auditory processing of tones, sounds, rhythms, and meanings that are nonlanguage in nature. The *parietal lobes* are related to tactile and kinesthetic perception, understanding, spatial perception, and some language understanding and processing. They are also involved in body awareness. The *occipital lobes* are mainly oriented toward visual processing and some aspects of visually mediated memory.

Antecedents or causes of brain damage

What causes brain damage? There is a large set of potential antecedent conditions.

Trauma. Traumatic head injuries affect thousands of Americans every year. Incidents producing these injuries range from automobile accidents to falls off a stepladder. The outcomes are wide-ranging. There are *concussions*—jarring of the brain—which usually result in momentary disruptions of brain function (permanent damage is uncommon unless there are repeated concussions, as in the

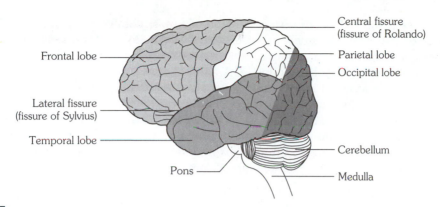

Figure 18-1
The cerebral cortex.

case of professional boxers). *Contusions* refer to cases where the brain has been shifted from its normal position and pressed against the skull. As a result, brain tissue is bruised. Outcomes often can be severe and may be followed by comas and deliriums. *Lacerations* involve actual ruptures and destruction of brain tissue. They can be caused by bullets or flying objects, for example. These lacerations are, of course, exceedingly serious forms of damage.

Vascular accidents.   Incidents classified as vascular accidents, in which blockage or rupture of cerebral blood vessels occurs, are very common forms of brain damage in adults. In *occlusions,* a blood clot blocks the vessel that feeds a particular area of the brain. This can result in *aphasia* (language impairment), *apraxia* (inability to perform certain voluntary movements), or *agnosia* (disturbed sensory perception). A typical example of an occlusion would be a stroke, most common in the elderly. In the case of a *cerebral hemorrhage,* the blood vessel ruptures and the blood escapes onto brain tissue and either damages or destroys it. The exact symptoms that ensue depend on the site of the accident and its severity. Cerebral hemorrhage can result in death; those who survive often show paralysis, speech problems, memory and judgment difficulties, and so on.

Tumors.   Brain tumors may grow outside the brain, within the brain, or result from body fluids spread from (most commonly) some other organ of the body (for example, the lung or the breast). Initial signs of brain tumors are often quite subtle and can include headaches, vision problems, gradually developing problems in judgment, and so on. As the tumor grows, so do the variety of other symptoms (poor memory, affect problems, or motor coordination). Tumors can be removed surgically, but the surgery itself can result in more brain damage. Some tumors are inoperable or located in areas too dangerous to perform an operation. In such cases, radiation treatments are often employed.

Degenerative disease. The three most common degenerative diseases of the brain are usually considered to be Alzheimer's disease, Parkinson's
disease, and Huntington's chorea. Alzheimer's disease is the most common and is
currently receiving much attention. The age of onset is typically from 45 to 65
years old. It is followed in frequency of occurrence by Parkinson's disease (age of
onset 50–60 years old) and, finally, by Huntington's chorea (age of onset 30 to
50 years old), which is quite rare. In all three cases, there is progressive cerebral
degeneration along with other symptoms in the motor areas. Eventually, patients
in these categories show severe disturbances in many behavioral areas including
motor, speech, language, memory, and judgment.

Nutritional deficiencies. Malnutrition can ultimately produce neurological and psychological disorders. Those disorders most often observed are
Korsakoff's psychosis (resulting from nutritional problems brought about by poor
eating habits common with longtime alcoholics), pellagra, and beriberi.

Toxic disorders. A variety of metals, toxins, gases, and even plants can
be absorbed through the skin. In some instances, the result is a toxic or poisonous
effect that produces brain damage. A very common symptom associated with
these disorders is *delirium* (clouding of consciousness).

Chronic alcohol abuse. Chronic exposure to alcohol often results in
tolerance for and dependence on the substance. Tolerance and dependence appear to have neurological correlates including, for example, changes in neurotransmitter sensitivity and shrinkage in brain tissue (USDHHS, 1993).

Consequences and symptoms of neurological damage

Brain injury or trauma can produce a variety of cognitive and behavioral
symptoms. Unfortunately for the diagnostician, many of these symptoms may also
occur in connection with traditional mental disorders as well. It is also true that patients' responses to their own impairment may give rise to psychological and emotional reactions. For example, a brain-damaged person may become depressed
over the inability to manage certain daily tasks; this, in turn, can easily obscure the
process of differential diagnosis. These difficulties aside, several common symptoms associated with brain damage are listed below (Bootzin, Acocella, & Alloy,
1993). However, again, be aware that all of these may occur in *every* disorder and
that there is considerable variation among patients with the same disorder.

1. *Impaired orientation:* inability, for example, to say who one is, name the day
   of the week, or know about one's surroundings.
2. *Impaired memory:* patient forgets events, especially recent ones, sometimes
   confabulates or invents memories to fill the gaps, and may show impaired ability to learn and retain new information.
3. *Impaired intellectual functions:* comprehension, speech production, calculation, and general knowledge may be affected (for example, cannot define simple words, name the president of the U.S., or add numbers).

Box 18-1
Personality changes following brain injury: a case example

A young Viet Nam veteran lost the entire right frontal portion of his brain in a land mine explosion. His mother and wife described him as having been a quietly pleasant, conscientious, and diligent sawmill worker before entering the service. When he returned home, all of his speech functions and most of his thinking abilities were intact. He was completely free of anxiety and thus without a worry in the world. He had also become very easygoing, self-indulgent, and lacking in general drive and sensitivity to others. His wife was unable to get him to share her concerns when the baby had a fever or the rent was due. Not only did she have to handle all the finances, carry all the family and home responsibilities, and do all the planning; but she also had to see that her husband went to work on time and that he didn't drink up his paycheck or spend it in a foolish spending spree before getting home on Friday night. For several years it was touch and go as to whether the wife could stand the strain of a truly carefree husband much longer. She finally left him after he had stopped working altogether and begun a pattern of monthly drinking binges that left little of his rather considerable compensation checks.

SOURCE: From *Neuropsychological Assessment,* Third Edition, by Muriel Deutsch Lezak, p. 42. Copyright © 1995 by Oxford University Press, Inc. Reprinted by permission.

4. *Impaired judgment:* patient has trouble with decisions (for example, cannot decide about lunch, when to go to bed, and so on).
5. *Shallow and labile affect:* person laughs or weeps too easily and often inappropriately; shifts from joy to tears very rapidly.
6. *Loss of emotional and mental resilience:* patient may function reasonably well under normal circumstances, but stress (for example, fatigue, mental demands, emotional upset) may result in deterioration of judgment, emotional reactions, and other similar problems.

Finally, it is also noteworthy that a group of personality characteristics can often follow the destruction of frontal-lobe tissue through surgery, tumor, or injury. Typical symptoms are: impaired impulse control, poor social judgment and planning ability, lack of concern over the consequences of one's actions, apathy and indifference, suspiciousness, and temper tantrums. Box 18-1 illustrates the personality changes that can follow injuries.

Brain-behavior relationships
Before describing specific assessment techniques, we should at least briefly review some basic ways of looking at brain-behavior relationships.

We observed earlier that in the second half of the nineteenth century, localization of function became a popular view. The idea that specific areas of the brain control specific behaviors is still an important operating principle among neuropsychologists. Such a principle means that, in assessing brain damage, a chief concern is where the injury is located in the brain. Extent of an injury is important only to the degree that larger injuries tend to involve more areas of the brain (Golden, 1984). And, indeed, some tumors may produce intracranial pressure that impairs areas located far from the tumor itself. The basic idea, however, is that same-sized lesions in different regions of the brain will produce different behavior deficits (Krech, 1962). Localization remains a critical issue today (Boll & Bryant, 1988).

According to equipotential theory, however, all areas of the brain contribute equally to overall intellectual functioning (Krech, 1962). Location of injury is secondary to the amount of brain injury. Thus, all injuries are alike except in degree. Equipotentialists tend to emphasize deficits in abstract, symbolic abilities that are thought to accompany all forms of brain damage and to produce rigid, concrete attitudes toward problem solving (see Goldstein & Scheerer, 1941). Such views have led to the development of tests that attempt to identify the basic deficits common to all cases of brain damage. Unfortunately, such tests have not worked well enough for everyday clinical use (Golden, 1981).

Many investigators, however, have been unable to accept either localization or equipotentiality completely. Thus, alternatives such as the one proposed by Hughlings Jackson (Luria, 1973) have become prominent. Although, Jackson says, very basic skills can be localized, the observable behavior is really a complex amalgamation of numerous basic skills, so the brain as a whole is involved. This, then, becomes a functional model of the brain that subsumes both localization and equipotential theory. Further, according to Luria (1973), very complex behaviors involve complex functional systems in the brain that override any simple area locations in the brain. Because our ability to abstract is a complex intellectual skill, for example, it involves many systems of the brain.

Brain damage can have many effects involving visual perception, auditory perception, kinesthetic perception, voluntary motor coordination and functioning, memory, language, conceptual behavior, attention, or emotional reactions. Often, clinicians are called upon to determine the presence of *intellectual deterioration.* This goes beyond the measurement of present functioning since it involves an implicit or explicit comparison to a prior level. Generally speaking, intellectual deterioration may be of two broad types: (1) a decline resulting from psychological factors (psychosis, lack of motivation, emotional problems, the wish to defraud an insurance company, and so on); and (2) a decline stemming from brain injuries. Of course, assessment tasks would be made a good deal easier were the clinician to have available a series of tests taken by the patient over a lengthy period of time. Such premorbid data would give a kind of baseline against which to compare present performance. Unfortunately, clinical psychologists seldom seem to have such data on the patients they most need to diagnose. They are left to infer the patient's previous level of functioning from case history material involving information on education, occupation, and other variables. Over the years, clinicians have used such "signs" of premorbid functioning in a rather intuitive fashion without much empirical evidence for their validity. Nonetheless, Leli and Filskov (1979) have shown that these signs, such as education and occupation histories, can be compared to current intellectual functioning to determine the amount of intellectual deterioration that has occurred. All these methods, however, are imperfect (Matarazzo, 1990).

■ Methods of Neuropsychological Assessment

Assessment is a complex affair that engages many issues in addition to those already discussed. Let us consider a few of the more important ones (Golden et al., 1992).

Major approaches

Should a standard test or test battery be administered to all patients referred for a neuropsychological workup or should the test(s) be chosen on the basis of clinical judgment, the nature of the referral, or the clinician's special skills and proclivities? The first approach is sometimes termed the *standard battery* approach. It has the advantages of evaluating patients for all basic neuropsychological abilities, accumulating a standard database for all patients over time, and allowing for the identification of important patterns of scores. The major disadvantages are the time and expense involved, the potential for patient fatigue, and the inflexibility of this approach such that assessments are not tailored to individual patients.

The second approach is called the *flexible approach* or the *hypothesis testing approach*. Here, each assessment is tailored to the individual patient, with the neuropsychologist choosing tests based on hypotheses about the case. Further, in some cases, a test may be altered in the way it is administered to the patient so that additional hypotheses may be tested. Some argue that the individualized approach is a sensitive one that capitalizes on the clinician's best impressions. Others suggest that if a clinician picks the wrong test(s), it may result in a poor assessment. Also, the individualized approach hampers the systematic collection of data from specific tests on specific kinds of patients. Of course, some clinicians combine these two strategies by using a standard screening device(s) and then going to other specific tests, depending on the outcome of the initial screening.

Interpretation of neuropsychological test results

Golden et al. (1992) note a number of ways neuropsychologists interpret test data. First, a patient's level of performance may be interpreted in the context of *normative data*. For example, does a patient's score fall significantly below the mean score for the appropriate reference group, suggesting some impairment in this area of functioning? Second, some calculate *difference scores* between two tests for a patient; certain levels of difference suggest impairment. Third, *pathognomonic signs* of brain damage (for example, failing to draw the left half of a picture) may be noted and interpreted. Fourth, a *pattern analysis* of scores may be undertaken; certain patterns of scores on tests have been reliably associated with specific neurological injuries or impairments. Finally, a number of statistical formulas that weight test scores differentially may be available for certain diagnostic decisions.

A final point about interpretation has to do with the desirability of making qualitative evaluations of patients' responses. Should neuropsychologists depend upon qualitative testing or quantitative methods that reduce the results to numerical values? Is the way a patient responds the important datum or is it the scored responses that are critical? Many neuropsychologists probably combine the two approaches since they need not be mutually exclusive.

Neurodiagnostic procedures

By now it may have occurred to the reader that the medical field already has a variety of neurodiagnostic procedures. They range from the traditional neurological examination performed by the neurologist and such procedures as spinal taps to X rays, electroencephalograms (EEGs), computerized axial tomography (CAT) scans, positron emission tomography (PET) scans, and the more recent nuclear magnetic resonance imaging (NMR or MRI) technique. These are, indeed, valuable means for locating the presence of damage and disease. But not all of these procedures work equally well in diagnosing impairment. Likewise, these techniques sometimes produce evidence of abnormalities in the absence of actual brain damage. Finally, some of these procedures actually pose risks for the patient. Spinal taps can be painful and sometimes harmful, and the dangers of too many X rays are well known. Still, the neurologist's diagnostic procedures search directly for evidence of brain damage, whereas the neuropsychologist searches for the connection between behavior and possible brain damage. Each approach is important, and one complements the other.

Now, then, we can consider some specific neuropsychological assessment devices and batteries.

Testing discrete areas of cognitive functioning

Many tests are available for assessing a wide range of cognitive and behavioral functioning. In this section, we discuss only a handful of the areas of functioning assessed by neuropsychologists. Further, because of space constraints (entire books on neuropsychological assessment are available), we will only give a few tests as examples.

Intellectual functioning.   A number of techniques have been employed over the years to assess levels of intellectual functioning. In order to estimate level of intellectual ability, many neuropsychologists use the WAIS-R (see Chapter 7) and subtests from a modified version of the WAIS-R, called the WAIS-R-NI (Kaplan, Fine, Morris, & Delis, 1991). The modifications include, for example, changes in administration (for example, allowing the patient to continue on a subtest despite consecutive incorrect answers) and additional subtest items. Because of these modifications, it is believed that the WAIS-R-NI provides more information regarding the patient's cognitive strategies (Anderson, 1994).

If it is not possible to administer the entire WAIS-R (or WAIS-R-NI) in order to obtain an estimate of intelligence, certain individual subtests may be used. Those most commonly employed are the information subtest, comprehension subtest, and vocabulary subtest. These subtests are believed to be least affected by brain trauma or injury, and, thus, they can also provide estimates of premorbid intelligence. This is important because often no preinjury test data are available to serve as a baseline against which to compare present functioning.

Abstract reasoning.   For many years, clinicians observed that patients diagnosed as schizophrenic or as brain damaged seemed to find it difficult to think in an abstract or conceptual fashion. Such patients seemed to approach tasks in a highly concrete manner. Some of the more commonly used tests to assess abstract reasoning abilities include the similarities subtest of the WAIS-R (see Chapter 7) and the Wisconsin Card Sorting Test, or WCST (Heaton, 1981). The similarities subtest requires the patient to produce a description of how two objects are alike. The WCST consists of decks of cards that differ according to the shapes imprinted, the colors of the shapes, and the number of shapes on each card. The patient is asked to place each card under the appropriate stimulus card according to a principle (for example, same color, same shapes, same number of shapes) deduced from the examiner's feedback ("that's right" or "that's wrong"). At various points during the test, the examiner changes principles; this can only be detected from the examiner's feedback regarding the correctness of the sorting of the next card.

Memory.   Brain damage is often marked by memory loss. To test for such loss, Wechsler (1945) developed the Wechsler Memory Scale (WMS). The scale was revised and then published after the death of Wechsler in 1981. The revised version, WMS-R (Wechsler, 1987), consists of 13 subtests covering personal and current information, orientation for time and place, counting tasks, memory for recent material, recall of digits, reproducing geometric figures, and learning paired associates, for example. Information on reliability and validity of the WMS-R as well as normative data are provided in the test manual (Wechsler, 1987).

Two additional tests also assess memory loss. But in addition to demonstrating recall, the patient must demonstrate spatial perception and perceptual-motor coordination on these tests. The Benton Visual Retention Test (Benton, 1963) is basically a test of memory for designs. Ten cards are each presented for 10 seconds. After a card is withdrawn, the patient must then draw the design from memory. There are several variants of this procedure, and scoring instructions and some normative data are available with the test (see Benton, 1974). The Memory-for-Designs Test (Graham & Kendall, 1960) requires the patient to draw from memory 15 designs that are presented for 5 seconds each; it, too, provides scoring instructions and data from cross-validation studies. This test seems to work reasonably well as a crude screening for brain damage (Kempel, 1973). Both of these tests probably work best in detecting severe brain damage—cases that can also be diagnosed by other means. To really demonstrate their utility, such tests must do a better job than the standard procedures to detect brain damage. That is, it is not overly impressive to have a given test correctly identify 82% of the patients in a

Figure 18-2
The Bender-Gestalt Test. SOURCE: Adapted from Research Monograph, p. 4,
    Plate I, from the Bender-Gestalt Test. Copyright © 1938 by the American
    Orthopsychiatric Association. Reprinted by permission. *Note:* Figures represented
    here are only about 30% of their original size.

hospital if the base rates (the percentage of brain damaged admitted) of that hospital are greater than that.

   Visual-perceptual processing.   The Bender Visual Motor Gestalt
Test (Bender, 1938) is one of the most widely used tests to screen for problems
in the area of visual-perceptual functioning. Memory is not involved since the patient reproduces nine geometric figures, one at a time, while looking at the figures (see Figure 18-2). In Figure 18-3, the reproductions of a patient with brain
damage are shown. Scoring schemes are available both for adults (Pascal &
Suttell, 1951) and children (Koppitz, 1964). In general, such errors as figure rotation, perseveration, and integration failures are considered diagnostic of visual-
perceptual impairment. Many clinicians, however, continue to utilize more subjec-

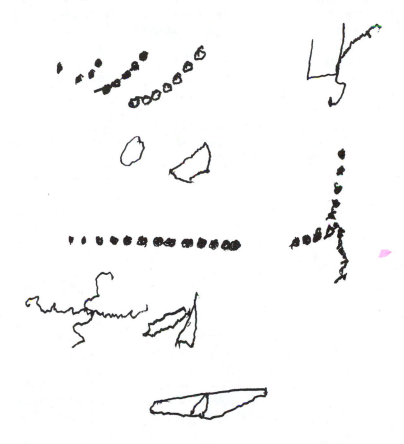

Figure 18-3

Bender-Gestalt reproductions of a patient with organic brain symptoms associated with
withdrawal from alcohol. SOURCE: From *Bender-Gestalt Screening for Brain
Dysfunction,* by P. Lacks, p. 34. Copyright © 1984 by Wiley-Interscience.
Reprinted by permission. *Note:* These figures are only about 60% of their
original size.

tive analyses based upon their own experience. The value of the Bender test lies
in its ability to serve as a rough screening device. It is brief, inexpensive to administer, and a reasonable basis for more specific referral (Lacks, 1984). However,
using the Bender as the sole evidence for the presence or exact nature of brain
damage is unwise, particularly in view of its lack of validity data (Franzen, 1989).

Language functioning.   Various forms of brain injury or trauma can affect either the production or comprehension of language. Tests that require patients to repeat words, phrases, and sentences can assess articulation difficulties and paraphasias (word substitutions); naming tests can help diagnose anomias (impaired naming). As for assessment of language comprehension, the receptive speech scale of the Luria-Nebraska (see below) may be used. This subtest requires patients to respond to verbal commands (for example, to point to named body parts or objects or to respond to simple commands).

Test batteries

Let us now examine two commonly used neuropsychological test batteries: the Halstead-Reitan and the Luria-Nebraska.

The Halstead-Reitan battery.   To counter the criticism that single tests for brain dysfunction were too limited in their scope to provide definitive answers, the Halstead-Reitan Neuropsychological Battery was developed (Halstead, 1947; Reitan & Davison, 1974). This is now undoubtedly the most widely used test battery. As generally employed, the battery consists of several measures: the Category Test, the Seashore Rhythm Test, the Finger Oscillation Test, the Speech-Sounds Perception Test, the Tactile Performance Test, the Trail-Making Test, the Strength of Grip Test, the Sensory-Perceptual Examination, the Finger Localization Test, the Fingertip Number Writing Perception Test, the Tactile Form Recognition Test, and the Aphasia Screening Test. These tests may be supplemented by the MMPI-2 and the WAIS-R. The scale can be used with people aged 15 years and older, and other versions can be employed with children aged 9 to 14 and 5 to 8.

The *Halstead-Reitan battery* is used to provide information about the probable localization of lesions and whether they appear to be of gradual or sudden onset. It also suggests something about specific psychological deficits that the therapist should note. The battery takes an entire day to administer; many clinics have trained technicians to do this work so that clinicians are not bogged down in lengthy procedures of administration and can, instead, concentrate on the complexities of interpretation.

The Halstead-Reitan battery appears to be a very promising technique (Filskov & Goldstein, 1974; Kane, Parsons, Goldstein, & Moses, 1987). Golden (1977) reports that the battery is 90% effective in differentiating between psychosis and organicity. A brief case report summary based on the Halstead-Reitan and other tests is shown in Box 18-2.

The Luria-Nebraska battery.   Another neuropsychological testing device, the *Luria-Nebraska battery,* consists of 269 separate tasks comprising 11 subtests: motor functions, rhythm functions, tactile functions, visual functions, receptive speech, expressive speech, writing functions, reading skills, arithmetical skills, memory, and intellectual processes. The battery's diagnostic validity has been reviewed by Golden, Hammeke, and Purisch (1978) and, at this point, looks promising. It appears to show substantial agreement with results obtained from the

Box 18-2
A brief neuropsychological report based on Halstead-Reitan and other
    information

Name: Mr. Y.
Date of Birth: 8/29/26
Occupation: Retired Air Force pilot-USAF
Education: 18 years (master's degree)

Referral Information
    Mr. Y. is a 57-year-old white male who is retired from the United States
Air Force. For the past several years he has noticed a decline in his perception, mechanical abilities, reaction time, driving abilities, and ability to
read and produce cursive handwriting. He reports that the symptoms have
been especially pronounced over the past two to three years. Dr. _____
requested a neuropsychological evaluation in order to evaluate the presence and/or extent of organic impairment.

Summary and Recommendations

1. Neuropsychological assessment reveals severe impairment in several
   areas of functioning, such as severe constructional difficulties and problems on all tasks requiring nonverbal and visual-spatial abilities, including memory for visual information. These areas of deficit point to a
   pathological process in the right parietal-occipital area of the brain.
   The possibility of major structural damage in this area should be investigated thoroughly.
2. Mr. Y.'s verbal abilities as well as verbal memory have been preserved
   and are, in general, in the superior range.
3. Personality assessment reveals that Mr. Y. is suffering from a moderate
   depression accompanied by worry and rumination. This appears to be
   of a rather long-standing nature rather than being an acute emotional
   reaction.
4. The patient's neuropsychological deficits cannot be attributed to his
   depression.
5. In light of our findings, a careful review of the patient's capabilities both
   at work and at home should be made with him and his wife.
6. As this information is worked through, supportive psychotherapy
   would be helpful.
7. A current neurological reevaluation is recommended.

SOURCE: From "Overview of the Halstead-Reitan Battery," by O. A. Parsons, pp. 179–180. In
T. Incagndi, G. Goldstein, and C. J. Golden (Eds.), *Clinical Application of Neuropsychological Test
Batteries.* Copyright © 1986 by Plenum Publishing Corporation. Reprinted by permission.

Halstead-Reitan method (Goldstein & Shelly, 1984; Kane, Parsons, Goldstein, & Moses, 1987; Sears, Hirt, & Hall, 1984). A children's version performs as well as the WISC-R in discriminating psychiatric and neurological cases (Carr, Sweet, & Rossini, 1986) and also seems to reliably diagnose attention deficit disorders in children (Lahey, Hynd, Stone, Piacentini, & Frick, 1989). The main advantage of the Luria-Nebraska is that it takes only approximately 2.5 hours to complete versus the 6 hours that are sometimes required to complete the Halstead-Reitan battery.

Variables that affect performance on neuropsychological tests

A variety of patient variables may influence neuropsychological test scores (Anderson, 1994; Golden et al., 1992). For example, test scores differ according to the biological sex, age, and educational level of the patients. This is why appropriate norms should be used to interpret test scores. In addition, test scores are influenced by handedness, by premorbid ability (that is, before brain trauma or injury), by the chronicity of the neurological condition, as well as by the existence of other (non-neurological) physical conditions (for example, a peripheral arm injury might affect performance on the strength of grip test of the Halstead-Reitan battery). Finally, motivational variables, such as arousal or level of cooperation, will also affect scores. For example, a patient who is taking medication that has a sedative effect will probably not be able to perform optimally.

A special case of a motivational variable that deserves additional comment is malingering. We saw earlier in Chapter 8 that to detect faking or malingering on psychological tests can be difficult for even the most astute clinician. There is controversy about how often malingering occurs in neuropsychological assessment (see Gilandas, Touyz, Beumont, & Greenberg, 1984). Recognizing that it may occur and improving clinicians' abilities to detect it are both very important, especially given the clinician's growing presence as an expert witness in court cases of various kinds (see Chapter 19).

Intervention and rehabilitation

When issues of neurological impairment arise, they usually orient themselves around two principal questions (Maloney & Ward, 1976). First, what is the nature of the deterioration or damage? (For example, is it a perceptual loss or a cognitive loss?) Second, is there, in fact, any real brain damage that can account in some way for the patient's behavior? More specifically, the neuropsychologist will be asked whether the damage is permanent or whether recovery can be expected after an acute phase; whether damage is focal or diffused throughout the brain. In general, focal damage results in more specific, limited effects on behavior, whereas diffuse damage can cause wide effects. Referral sources often need to know whether the damage will be progressive (as in diffuse brain involvement or in damage due to disease) or nonprogressive (as is often true in the case of strokes or head traumas). Answers provided by clinical psychologists significantly affect the kinds of rehabilitation programs designed for various patients.

Rehabilitation is becoming one of the major functions of neuropsychologists (Golden et al., 1992). The neuropsychologist is often thrust into the role of coordinating the cognitive and behavioral treatment of patients who have shown cognitive and behavioral impairment due to brain dysfunction or injury. First, a thorough assessment of the strengths and deficits of the patient is conducted; this may include neuropsychological test results as well as observations from other staff members (for example, nurses, physicians, physical therapists). A program of rehabilitation is then developed that will be maximally beneficial to the patient, based on the deficit assessment results, and that will be efficient in the sense of requiring a minimum amount of staff time and supervision (Golden et al., 1992).

As noted by Golden et al. (1992), rehabilitation can take place via spontaneous recovery of functioning. However, the neuropsychologist and the rehabilitation team are more likely to be involved when rehabilitation is to be accomplished by having the patient "relearn" — via developmentally older and intact functional systems, via new functional systems, or via environmental changes to ensure the best quality of life possible. In the latter case, the judgment may be that it is not possible to develop alternative or new functional systems that can significantly lessen the level of cognitive or behavioral impairment.

In the case of developing alternative or new functional systems, rehabilitation tasks are formulated in order to treat the patient's deficits. Golden et al. (1992, pp. 214–215) offer general guidelines for implementing rehabilitation tasks:

1. The task should include the impaired skill that the therapist is trying to reformulate. All other skill requirements in the task should be in areas with which the subject has little or no trouble.
2. The therapist should be able to vary the task in difficulty from a level that would be simple for the patient to a level representing normal performance.
3. The task should be quantifiable so that progress may be objectively stated.
4. The task should provide immediate feedback to the patient.
5. The number of errors made by the patient should be controlled.

Golden et al. (1992) give examples of rehabilitation programs for various cognitive and behavioral deficits. For example, verbal memory impairment might be treated by administering simple memory problems (that is, those involving one unit of information) to the patient and then, later, more complex tasks (for example, a problem requiring the memorization of six or seven units of information). The complexity of the task can be varied further by, for example, using words that are not related to each other or decreasing the time of exposure to the stimulus words.

■ Concluding Remarks

Without doubt, neuropsychology as a specialty area within clinical psychology is on the move. As noted in the beginning of this chapter, we are seeing a growing number of books in the area (Anderson, 1994; Golden et al., 1992; Lezak, 1995) and there is the recent development of the field of child neuropsychology (Hynd,

1988; Obrzut & Hynd, 1986a, 1986b; Tramontana & Hooper, 1988) as well. At the same time, however, the procedures in this subfield have become so sophisticated that specialty training is necessary.

Training

Many clinical psychologists do not feel especially comfortable doing neuropsychological assessment. Their training in such assessment was often limited and their knowledge of brain-behavior relationships sketchy at best. As Lezak (1995) has pointed out, the success of neuropsychological assessment will depend on how well examiners understand not only normal brain-behavior relationships but also the psychological effects of brain dysfunctions. Reitan and Davison (1974) some time ago remarked on the necessity for developing a new field of clinical neuropsychology. There is now some evidence that their suggestions are being implemented in clinical training programs.

Guidelines for graduate (doctoral) programs and training of future clinical neuropsychologists have been developed (International Neuropsychological Society-Division 40 Task Force, 1987); briefly, these guidelines recommend a Ph.D. from a graduate program in clinical neuropsychology or from a clinical psychology program with a specialty track in clinical neuropsychology. Recommendations regarding the coursework the program should contain include the following:

1. a generic psychology core (for example, statistics, learning, social psychology, physiological psychology, developmental psychology, history);
2. a generic clinical core (for example, psychopathology, psychometrics, assessment, intervention, ethics);
3. neurosciences and basic human and animal neuropsychology (for example, basic neurosciences, advanced physiological psychology and pharmacology, neuropsychology, research design and research practicum in neuropsychology); and
4. specific clinical neuropsychological training (for example, clinical neurology and neuropathology, specialized neuropsychological assessment techniques, specialized neuropsychological intervention techniques, assessment practicum, intervention practicum, clinical neuropsychological internship of 1800 hours).

This report also includes specific recommendations for internship training as well as postdoctoral training.

The future

Certainly, neuropsychology may hope for the development of increasingly more sophisticated individual tests and batteries. In short, better assessment devices and procedures, including enhanced provisions for planning, therapy, and rehabilitation for patients with brain dysfunction are highly desirable. Assessment obviously is designed for more than the sheer pinning of labels on people—it is meant to enable clinicians to help the patient adjust to the future (Johnstone & Frank, 1995). In particular, then, the field of neuropsychology must concern itself more with the prediction and facilitation of recovery from brain injury, and this is exactly what is beginning to happen (Meier, Benton, & Diller, 1987). Training procedures that help foster rehabilitation, tests that predict the extent and rate of re-covery, and general information on the course of debilitating injury can offer hope and structure to both patients and their families. Even bad news, offered sensitively and constructively, can facilitate adjustment.

Johnstone and Frank (1995) recently urged neuropsychologists to shift their focus to issues involving rehabilitation. Although the need for rehabilitation services has increased in recent years, relatively few neuropsychologists have received specific training in rehabilitation. Further, traditional neuropsychological tests, in general, have not been used (or adapted) to provide information that is clinically useful to rehabilitation specialists. For example, Johnstone and Frank argue that many important cognitive abilities (for example, attention, executive functions, and memory) are poorly understood and poorly measured. In their view, neuropsychological test results need to be clearly tied (via empirical research) to real-world functions. In this way rehabilitation can address deficits or impairments that, if improved, will lead to positive outcome. If heeded, the suggestions made by Johnstone and Frank will likely impact research, training, and clinical applications in the field of neuropsychology.

Changes in the way health care is delivered and reimbursed will also have a great impact on the field of neuropsychology. Recently, Adams (1996) discussed many of the ways that managed health care will affect present and future neuropsychologists. First, neuropsychological assessment may no longer be routinely conducted when brain-behavior issues are raised, nor is it likely that it will be routinely reimbursed. Rather, neuropsychological assessment is likely to be seen by managed care companies as a luxury—to be conducted only when absolutely necessary. Adams also predicts that the marketplace for neuropsychologists will likely shrink, and neuropsychologists will be called upon to document their utility. If true, this tightening of the job market will stand in sharp contrast to the wealth of job opportunities in neuropsychology that has been characteristic over the last decade. Lastly, Adams notes that there is a need to educate insurance companies, physicians, and hospital administrators as to what neuropsychologists do, how they can be helpful, and how their examination and rehabilitation procedures are cost-effective.

■ Focus Questions

1. What features distinguish the field of neuropsychology and neuropsychological assessment?
2. Compare and contrast the localization-of-function, equipotentiality, and functional models of brain function.
3. What are the basic structures of the brain as well as the functions associated with each structure?
4. What variables may affect neuropsychological test performance? How are neuropsychological test results interpreted?
5. What forms of neuropsychological assessment and intervention are likely to be emphasized in the future? Why?

■ Key Terms

agnosia

aphasia

apraxia

cerebral hemorrhage

concussions

contusions

degenerative disease

delirium

difference scores

equipotentiality

flexible approach or hypothesis
   testing approach

frontal lobes

functional model

Halstead-Reitan battery

lacerations

left hemisphere

localization of function

Luria-Nebraska battery

neuropsychological assessment

neuropsychology

occipital lobes

occlusions

parietal lobes

pathognomonic signs

pattern analysis

rehabilitation

right hemisphere

standard battery

temporal lobes

tumors

19

Forensic Psychology

Because clinical psychologists are said to be "experts" in human behavior, it is not surprising that some of them would begin to specialize in the application of psychological knowledge to the problems that face judges, attorneys, police officials, and, indeed, anyone who must face or deal with issues related to civil, criminal, or administrative justice—victims and violators alike. This domain of clinical psychology, now called *forensic psychology,* underwent a highly visible growth spurt in the 1970s. Now it has gained all the trappings of a significant subspecialty: graduate training programs, professional organizations and boards, an APA division, and journals and textbooks. Many of these entities are distinctly interdisciplinary and span the fields of both law and psychology.

■ Perspectives and History

Let us begin our description of the field by defining it, briefly tracing its history, and then discussing a few professional matters.

Definitions

Forensic psychology is typically defined as dealing "with the interface of psychology and the law, and with the application of psychology to legal issues" (Cooke, 1984, p. 29). Just how broad these applications are is briefly illustrated in Table 19-1, where several examples are given. It should be noted that a variety of kinds of clients and settings may be included. Children as well as adults may be involved. Also, all manner of institutions, corporations, government agencies, universities, hospitals and clinics, and correctional facilities may be clients or objects of testimony. Recently, even school psychologists have become involved in the forensic arena (Crespi, 1990).

History

In 1908, Hugo von Munsterberg published his book, *On the Witness Stand* (see Box 19-1). This was a notable event, but, unfortunately, psychology had relatively little direct influence on the law from then until 1954—the year the Supreme

Table 19-1

Examples of areas of testimony and expertise of forensic psychologists.

Commitment to mental hospitals
Child custody issues
Psychological damages suffered as the result of another's negligence
Release from involuntary confinement
Determination of the need for a conservator due to incapacity
Predicting dangerousness
Rights of mentally disabled person in an institution
Competency to stand trial
Criminal responsibility (insanity defense)
Determination of disability for social security claims
Workers' compensation claims
Conditions affecting accuracy of eyewitness testimony
Advice to attorneys regarding factors that will affect jurors' behavior
Extent to which advertising claims are misleading
Battered woman syndrome
Rape trauma syndrome
Accuracy of eyewitness identification
Sexual harassment
Police psychology
Jury selection
Offender treatment programs
Criminal profiling

Court finally paid attention to the social sciences in the *Brown v. Board of Education* desegregation case. This case certainly altered the course of human events in the United States. Then, in 1962, Judge Bazelon, writing for the majority on the United States Court of Appeals for the District of Columbia circuit, held for the first time that psychologists who were appropriately qualified could testify in court as experts on mental disorder. Finally, the forensic psychologist was about to appear on the scene, even though psychiatrists had enjoyed the privilege of providing expert testimony for many years. Now, some 30 years later, psychologists regularly testify as experts in virtually every area of criminal, civil, family, and administrative law. They also serve as consultants to agencies and individuals throughout the legal system.

Of course, the foregoing thumbnail sketch of forensic history from Munsterberg to Bazelon leaves out many details and controversies (Horowitz & Willging, 1984). Even before Munsterberg, William Stern reported in 1901 that he was studying the "correctness" of recollection, an early precursor of today's research on eyewitness testimony. And even Freud, in a 1906 speech to some Austrian judges, claimed that psychology has real applications to the law. Later, John Watson also asserted that the law and psychology have common interests.

Lest the reader think that forensic psychology marched inexorably toward professional respectability, it would be well to note that not everyone thought psychology had much to offer the legal system. Even Munsterberg was hardly without critics. Because he tended to promote the role of psychology before he had much empirical data to back his claims, many dismissed his book out of hand. In fact, Lewis Terman made a 1931 address in which he "suggested that Munsterberg's error was in exaggerating the importance of psychology's contributions based on research then at hand. He went on to suggest that in light of significant scientific advances the ultimate significance of psychology for the legal profession could not be overestimated" (Blau, 1984, p. 2). Box 19-1 provides one example of just how harsh some members of the legal community could be regarding Munsterberg's

■

Box 19-1
Munsterberg on trial

Munsterberg (1908) complained that no one—teacher, artist, businessman, physician, minister, politician, or soldier—could be as resistant to the idea that psychologists might be of help to them as could an attorney. He believed that lawyers, judges, and even members of juries seemed to think that all they needed in order to function correctly was their common sense.

To Professor John Wigmore (1909), an eminent professor of law at Northwestern University, this was the worst kind of arrogance. Reflecting the feelings of many attorneys, Wigmore wrote a clever yet scathing parody of Munsterberg. He sketched a fictional libel suit filed against Munsterberg. Munsterberg was accused of overstating what psychology had to offer, of ignoring the many disagreements that exist among psychologists themselves, and of failing to understand the differences between laboratory results and the realities of legal requirements.

The "suit" was filed in "Windyville" in "Wundt County." Munsterberg's attorneys were named R. E. Search, Si Kist, and X. Perry Ment. "Judge Wiseman" heard the case against Munsterberg and his claim that "lawyers are obdurate."

Of course, the proceedings went against Munsterberg. Indeed, the jury after only a few minutes of whispered consultation, agreed on the verdict and found for the plaintiffs. Munsterberg was fined one dollar in damages. All in all, Wigmore's attack was so clever and devastating that it took 25 years for psychologists to once again be considered fit as expert witnesses. However, shortly before his death some 30 years later, Wigmore softened his critique. He asserted that courts should be ready to use any methods that psychologists themselves agree are sound, accurate, and practical. Now, of course, Wigmore's change of heart is reflected in everyday court procedures; but it may well be true that, had Munsterberg been a little more restrained in his claims at that time, the entire Munsterberg-Wigmore episode would never have occurred.

■

thesis. Certainly into the 1950s before Judge Bazelon's ruling took hold, psychologists, as often as not, failed to be qualified by judges as experts in the courtroom.

The psychology-law standoff was characterized by Loh (1984) as a phase during which psychologists wanted to contribute to the legal system but attorneys were having none of it. In the 1930s, Loh believes that psychology was primarily applied to a critique of legal doctrine and decisions. In the 1950s, psychologists were mainly occupied in trying to serve as expert witnesses and in the 1970s and 1980s as consultants on matters pertaining to juror behavior (Loh, 1984).

Now, as noted at the outset, forensic psychology has arrived at a point where there are specialists in psycholegal research, where the development of interdisciplinary training programs are commonplace, and where numerous specialty books are being published. Many forensic psychology journals are now in print as well, including: *Law and Human Behavior, Criminal Justice Journal, Law and Psychology Review, Criminal Justice and Behavior, Behavioral Sciences and the Law, American Journal of Forensic Psychology,* and *Psychology, Public Policy, and Law.*

Professional issues

For some years, many were concerned that forensic psychologists lacked status and recognition in the eyes of their peers in other specialties (Kurke, 1980). Professional matters such as certification and licensing were also issues of importance to the forensic psychology field (Schwitzgebel & Schwitzgebel, 1980). To allay some of these concerns, the American Board of Forensic Psychology was established to help the public identify qualified practitioners and to promote the discipline as a whole.

Training. Some years ago, Poythress (1979) observed that forensic training should give the student a familiarity with legal tests and concepts, proper assessment, knowledge of relevant literature, and an orientation to the courtroom. To accomplish these goals, he recommended that students interested in forensic psychology be required to complete an introductory survey of the field, topical seminars in forensic psychology, and a field placement in a forensic setting. By 1988, forensic hospital settings were commonly involved in training at all levels, ranging from undergraduate practica to continuing professional education (Heilbrun & Annis, 1988).

Increasingly, academic departments are offering forensic courses. A 1994 brochure from Division 41 of the American Psychological Association (American Psychology-Law Society) identified six universities offering joint-degree (J.D. and Ph.D. or Psy.D.) programs in psychology and law, four universities offering Ph.D. programs with specialization in the areas of psychology and law, criminal justice, and corrections, and three programs offering doctorates in forensic psychology. In addition, several postdoctoral training opportunities now exist. Each year, the number and kinds of programs continue to grow.

Ethics and standards. All of the ethical principles and guidelines we explored in previous chapters are relevant here as well. In addition, it has been rec-

Table 19-2
Standards for financial arrangements applicable to the expert witness.

---

1. The psychologist should never accept a fee contingent upon the outcome of a case.

2. The fee structure and details of reimbursement should be established between the psychologist and the retaining attorney during the initial consultation. The understanding should be in writing between the two parties.

3. All outstanding fees should be paid before the psychologist testifies.

4. Misunderstandings or disagreements about fees should be resolved before proceeding in the case.

5. Psychologists who testify regularly as expert witnesses should devote some portion of their professional time to *pro bono publico*[*] cases.

[*]Cases without compensation for the purpose of advancing a social cause or representing someone who cannot otherwise afford it.

SOURCE: Blau 1984, p. 336.

---

ommended that the forensic scientist follow the code of the American Academy of Forensic Sciences (Curran, 1986). This code stresses (1) completeness and accuracy in stating professional qualifications, (2) technical and scientific accuracy and honesty in reports and testimony, and (3) impartiality. As another resource, Division 41 (American Psychology-Law Society) of the APA has developed a set of *Specialty Guidelines for Forensic Psychologists* (Committee on Ethical Guidelines for Forensic Psychologists, 1991) that elaborates on the APA's *Ethical Principles of Psychologists* as they apply to the practice of forensic psychology.

Finally, Blau (1984) has proposed several very explicit guidelines for the expert witness activities of psychologists. They involve matters of work quality, competence and decorum, and financial arrangements. In Table 19-2, Blau's standards for financial arrangements are presented as examples.

Still, the ethical issues encountered by forensic psychologists in the adversarial legal system can be formidable (Nietzel & Dillehay, 1986; Wrightsman, Nietzel, & Fortune, 1994). Issues of ethics and standards will weigh heavily in any professional arena that allows for so many role conflicts, biases, distortions, and subjectivity (Arcaya, 1987; Cornell, 1987; Homant & Kennedy, 1987). And forensic psychology is just such an arena.

■ Some Major Activities

The growth of forensic psychology has thrust the psychologist into many different roles. We shall focus on eight such roles and begin our discussion with the forensic psychologist as expert witness.

The expert witness

Consider the following scenario:

Ms. Ferris, an employee of the Diego Pan Co., was working at her desk on October 1, 1990. Her supervisor, Mr. Smith, stopped by her desk. He had a history of telling dirty jokes in her presence, commenting on her physical attributes, and asking about her dating activities. This day, however, he explicitly propositioned her and made it clear that if she wanted to advance in the company and, indeed, even remain employed, she had better agree to have sexual relations with him. She refused. Two weeks later she was fired. Subsequently, she filed sexual harassment charges against Mr. Smith and also sought damages for emotional suffering.

Dr. Miller, a clinical psychologist, was retained by Ms. Ferris's attorney. He conducted extensive interviews with Ms. Ferris and several of her coworkers. He also administered several tests. Mr. Wright, a coworker, had inadvertently overheard the October 1 conversation between Ms. Ferris and her supervisor and had also previously observed some of the alleged sexual harassment.

During the trial, Mr. Wright served as a witness testifying to the facts and with reference to his own observations. Dr. Miller testified as to his opinions and inferences about emotional damage that were within the scope of his training and experience. This illustrates the basic difference between a lay witness and an expert witness. The former may testify only to events witnessed; the latter may offer opinions and inferences. This goes beyond merely stating a conclusion—the expert witness must help the court understand and evaluate evidence or determine a fact at issue (Schwitzgebel & Schwitzgebel, 1980).

Qualifications.   An *expert witness* can be anyone who can provide information that, by its uniqueness in relation to some science, profession, training, or experience, is unlikely to be known to the average juror (Blau, 1984; Wrightsman et al., 1994). Initially, the court will decide whether the expert witness may, in fact, claim expert status. Often, in the case of physicians, psychologists, or psychiatrists, a license is taken as evidence of competence. But if opposing counsel objects to the witness's claim to be an expert, further evidence will typically be presented regarding competence. Ultimately, it is up to the judge to decide (Blau, 1984). In general, the bases of clinical psychological expertise include: (1) education, formal training, and subsequent learning; (2) relevant experience, including positions held; (3) research and publications; (4) knowledge and application of scientific principles; and (5) use of special tests and measurements (Maloney, 1985). What is accepted as evidence will vary from jurisdiction to jurisdiction.

A 1993 decision by the United States Supreme Court, *Daubert v. Merrell Dow,* established a more liberal standard for the admissibility of an expert's evidence. Briefly, the standard was changed from "general acceptance" in the relevant scientific community (the 1993 *Frye* v. *U.S.* standard) to one of "relevance and validity" as determined by the trial judge. In other words, the burden now falls on the judge to decide whether expert evidence is admissible or not (Bartol & Bartol, 1994).

Topics for expert testimony.   We have already seen from Table 19-1 how wide the range of topics suitable for expert testimony really is. This list is by no means exhaustive, and additional areas for expert psychological opinion exist (Nietzel & Dillehay, 1986; Wrightsman et al., 1994). However, experts are not allowed to state opinions that are the legal prerogatives of the jury. Thus, an expert could testify about the manner by which early child abuse might predispose the victim to later be aggressive toward others, but it is up to the jury to decide whether this is true in a particular case. Therefore, expert witnesses are prevented from providing "ultimate opinion" testimony (Wrightsman et al., 1994).

Testifying.   Regardless of the topic, testifying in court can be a harrowing experience for the expert witness. Anxiety and self-doubt may be the common accompaniments as the expert is tugged at by attorneys on both sides of the issue. Just as the neuropsychologist rarely gets the easy cases to diagnose, the behavioral expert in court rarely testifies about simple matters. Publicity, sensationalism, and the adversarial legal process are not conducive to making the life of the expert witness an easy one.

An important prelude to testifying is pretrial preparation. This can sometimes involve many hours of study, interviewing, testing, and conferences, depending on the case. The expert may be asked to testify by the court or by counsel for either a defendant or a plaintiff.

Cross-examination.   Consider the following two gems that illustrate what cross-examination can be like (Schwitzgebel & Schwitzgebel, 1980, p. 243):

> "Good morning, doctor. I see you are here on behalf of an accused killer (or 'your fellow psychologists') again. How are you today?"
> "Doctor, were you paid to perform your examination? [Yes] How much? [$200 an hour.] How many hours did you spend in all? [20 hours.] That's $4,000, isn't it doctor? [Yes]
> "And in your opinion the patient was insane on the night of January 26, 1975? [Yes] That's all doctor."

Additional, equally provocative questions that have been asked of psychologists serving as expert witnesses include:

> "Isn't it true that most of your experiments are done with rats?"
> "You are not a real doctor are you?"
> "You can't tell what's going on up here can you?" (opposing attorney points to his head)

Several authors (for example, Blau, 1984; Brodsky, 1991; Schwitzgebel & Schwitzgebel, 1980) provide numerous hints about how the expert witness should behave in the courtroom, even to the point of appropriate dress. For example, Schwitzgebel and Schwitzgebel (1980) summarize their recommended strategies for coping with cross-examination as follows:

- Be prepared
- Be honest
- Admit weaknesses
- Talk in personally meaningful terms
- Listen carefully to the wording of questions
- Take time to think

Criminal cases

For generations, society has grappled with questions of how to best deal with people who commit criminal acts and yet were so disturbed at the time that it is debatable whether they were personally responsible. Also difficult are decisions as to whether an accused person is competent to really understand the trial proceedings and thus cooperate in his or her own defense.

The insanity plea. If the accused is judged to have been sane at the time of the alleged crime, then conviction will bring with it imprisonment, fines, or probation. But the individual adjudged insane at the time of the alleged crime will, if convicted, be regarded as not responsible and thereby held for treatment rather than punishment. However, despite popular conceptions to the contrary, insanity pleas are seldom successful (Maloney, 1985; Wrightsman et al., 1994). Furthermore, the defendant is typically assumed to be responsible—thus, an *insanity plea* places the burden of its proof on the accused. In most states and the District of Columbia, the *burden of proof* is assigned to the defense; the defendant must prove insanity at the time of the criminal offense (Ogloff, 1991). It is also well to note that insanity is a legal term, not a medical, psychiatric, or psychological one. The legal system assumes that people make premeditated and rational choices. Therefore, to behave irrationally can be assumed to be evidence of insanity. But most psychologists would not agree that all normal behavior is rationally chosen. The deterministic view of science creates problems for such a simple notion.

So, then, how is it decided that the accused was insane? Although standards vary from state to state, one of three standards typically prevails. The oldest is the *M'Naghten Rule,* promulgated in England in 1843. It states that a successful insanity defense must prove that the person committed the unlawful act while "labouring under such a defect of reason, from disease of the mind, as not to know the nature and quality of the act he [sic] was doing; or, if he did know it, that he did not know he was doing what was wrong" (Brooks, 1974, p. 135). The second standard is the idea of an irresistible impulse. According to this test, although the person might have known the moral or legal ramifications of the act, it was impossible for the individual to resist the impulse—it was irresistible (Schwitzgebel & Schwitzgebel, 1980). The third standard is that the defendant is not responsible for a criminal act if it was the result of mental disease or defect such that substantial capacity to appreciate the criminality of the act or to conform to the law was lacking. The latter is the so-called *ALI standard* of the American Law Institute. The ALI standard is viewed as the most liberal or expansive in that criminal responsibility can be excused if mental illness causes a diminished capacity to understand what one is doing (that is, a cognitive deficit) or an inability to control one's behavior (that is, a volitional deficit) (Ogloff, 1991).

The famous *Hinckley* case (attempted assassination of President Reagan) changed the judicial scene in the U.S. Its first impact was to encourage a return to the M'Naghten Rule where cognitive factors rather than volitional ones are paramount. Its second impact is seen in the Supreme Court's ruling that it is constitutional to automatically and indefinitely confine those who are acquitted of a crime as the result of an insanity plea (Simon & Aaronson, 1988). Third, the verdict *guilty but mentally ill* was introduced into the defense statutes of several states as well as the federal government. Finally, more states began to place the burden of proving the defendant's insanity on the defense rather than requiring the pros-ecution to prove the defendant's sanity (Ogloff, 1991).

To conduct an evaluation for criminal insanity, the psychologist must address three questions: (1) does the person have a mental disorder or defect? (2) what is the person's present mental status? and (3) what was the person's mental status at the time of the alleged crime? (Maloney, 1985). In the process, the psychologist will assess many factors including the defendant's history (and that of the defendant's family), intellectual status, neuropsychological condition, competency to stand trial, reading skills, personality, and measures of faking or malingering (Blau, 1984).

Competency to stand trial.   The question of *competency to stand trial* addresses the defendant's state of mind at the time of the trial, not at the time the offense was allegedly committed. As a result, one could have been insane when the crime was committed but later be competent to stand trial. The reverse is also possible. In fact, issues of competency to stand trial are raised much more often than the insanity defense itself. To answer questions of competency, three basic issues commonly come to the fore (Maloney, 1985): (1) can the person appreciate the nature of the charges and can that person report factually on his or her behavior at the time of the alleged crime? (2) can the person cooperate in a reasonable way with counsel? and (3) can the person appreciate the proceedings of the court? In most instances, the evaluation factors noted in the preceding paragraph will apply here as well.

Civil cases

A very large number of civil issues engage the attention of forensic psychologists, running the gamut from trademark litigation to class action suits. But areas that are especially important for clinical psychologists involve commitment to and release from mental institutions as well as domestic issues such as child custody disputes. Let us focus on these areas as examples of activity in the civil arena.

Commitment to mental institutions.   Picture this scenario. Not too long ago, a disheveled man in his late thirties entered a restaurant and began haranguing customers who approached the cashier to pay their checks. He was incoherent but it was possible to pick out the obscenities and references to God that peppered his remarks. He did this for about five minutes, whereupon the manager appeared and unceremoniously escorted him to the door. Outside, he continued his tirade while pacing back and forth before the door. He repeatedly accosted customers and tried to make them listen to him. The manager finally called the police. After a brief interrogation they "helped" him into the patrol car and subsequently deposited him in the emergency ward of the local psychiatric hospital.

This and related scenarios are repeated thousands of times, day after day, across the nation. After an examination (sometimes a rather cursory one), the individual may be involuntarily detained for hours or days, depending upon particular state laws. (A few states do require judicial consent even for emergency detentions.)

Some 40% of hospitalizations occur against the will of the individual (Stone, 1976). This figure is dropping, however, as society increasingly pays attention to the civil rights of patients. Some, such as Szasz (1970), have argued strenuously that involuntary hospitalization is a dangerous and often misused power that has been repeatedly exercised by psychiatrists and others to maintain control over those who will not conform to certain social dictates. The permissible length of involuntary commitment typically varies from one day to three weeks or so, depending upon the jurisdiction. After that, a hearing must be held to decide whether detention should continue.

There is also *voluntary commitment*. Here, the individual agrees to admission and may leave at any time. Some hospitals require patients to sign a form stating that their leaving is "against medical advice." Others demand that such patients indicate several days in advance their intention to leave. This enables the hospital to initiate commitment proceedings if they believe the patient is dangerous to self or others or is so disturbed as not to be responsible. It might be noted, however, that voluntary admission is often not as voluntary as it might appear at first glance—most often, it is the result of strong pressure from relatives, friends, police or court authorities, or mental health personnel (Schwitzgebel & Schwitzgebel, 1980).

For the court to commit someone, a hearing must be held to determine whether the person meets the criteria laid out by law and whether treatment will be helpful. Usually, these criteria refer to a person who: (1) is dangerous to self or others; (2) is so disturbed or disabled as to be incapable of making responsible decisions about self-care and hospitalization; or (3) is in need of treatment or care in a hospital. But above all, the person must be determined to be mentally ill.

Literally anyone can petition the court for an examination of someone he or she believes requires commitment. Usually it is family or friends, or sometimes the police or welfare officials, who act as petitioners. If the court agrees, an order is issued and the person is required to submit to a professional examination. Such an examination should be based on personal observations of the individual by professionals and not just on what others have reported. Common matters to note are general appearance, clarity of thinking, presence of delusions or hallucinations, how well the patient understands the complaints, the person's use of drugs or alcohol, employment status, intelligence, prior history of mental and criminal problems, and kindred factors (Schwitzgebel & Schwitzgebel, 1980).

Domestic issues.   There are many domestic issues these days that require intervention by the courts. Child custody, parental fitness, visitation rights, child abuse, juvenile misbehavior, and adoption are but a few such issues. As an example of these issues, we shall discuss child custody in this section.

Because divorce has become so prevalent in our society in recent years, it is only natural that problems of child custody have proliferated as well. The fact that marital roles and norms have likewise changed also complicates matters. Increasingly, fathers are assuming child care responsibilities and mothers are commonly employed outside the home. These and other factors have made custodial questions much more complex than before.

Today, the doctrine of "the best interests of the child" always takes precedence in custody disputes. To better articulate exactly what standards are involved here, the Michigan Child Custody Act of 1970 established the following factors that are typically relied upon by the courts in making custodial decisions:

1. The love, affection, and other emotional ties existing between the competing parties and the child.
2. The capacity and disposition of competing parties to give the child love, affection, and guidance, and continuation of educating and raising the child in his [sic] religion or creed, if any.
3. The capacity and disposition of competing parties to provide the child with food, clothing, medical care, or other remedial care recognized and permitted under the laws of this state in lieu of medical care or other material needs.
4. The length of time the child has lived in a stable satisfactory environment and desirability of maintaining continuity.
5. The permanence, as a family unit, of the existing or proposed custodial home.
6. The moral fitness of the competing parties.
7. The home, school, and community record of the child.
8. The mental and physical health of the competing parties.
9. The reasonable preference of the child, if the court deems the child to be of sufficient age to express preference.
10. Any other factor considered by the court to be relevant to a particular child custody dispute.

Although 150 years ago children of divorce were automatically awarded to the father and 50 years ago almost always to the mother, such reflexive decisions no longer hold today (Blau, 1984). The present norm is *joint custody*, which rests on the belief that children should maintain ties with both parents. In fact, many divorces culminate in informal joint custody decisions by the divorced couple; a formal ruling by the court never occurs. When the court does issue an order for joint custody, this probably means that a dispute of some sort has arisen between competing parties. In the final analysis, however, the only way joint custody can really work is when competing parents set aside their animosity and anger toward each other and act in concert and with sensitivity to the best interests of the child.

It is worth reiterating that joint custody may not be in the best interest of the child in some cases. Specifically, joint custody may be contraindicated in situations where parents have an emotionally charged, conflictual relationship (Wrightsman et al., 1994). In these instances, legal custody might be granted to one parent while the other parent is granted visitation rights (Wrightsman et al., 1994).

In performing a child custody evaluation, the psychologist must remember that the critical element is a system of past, present, and future relationships among father, mother, children, and, sometimes, other relatives. Maloney (1985) has discussed both procedural and content issues relevant to the psychologist's preparation of reports on the evaluation of families facing custody problems. He has also listed the basic questions in child custody disputes that must be addressed in reports. These questions are based on a specific case but they do have relatively general implications.

1. Do any of the major parties in the child custody suit have a mental illness? How is such an illness manifested in terms of injuring or affecting the rights of others? Can the mental illness be defined in terms of interpersonal or relationship terms?
2. If a mental illness does exist, is it of such a type that would jeopardize the health, welfare, and safety of the children?

3. If such an illness does exist and it poses a danger to the children or spouse, is it treatable or remediable by drugs or other forms of psychological/psychiatric treatment?
4. Regardless of whether the illness is treatable or remediable, is it of such severity that it would make the other parent a better custodian?
5. If both parents are suffering from mental illness, which one would be better qualified to deal with the children? Would it be more appropriate to take the children away from both parents?
6. What effect might the mental illness have on the right of children to visit their mentally ill parents? What effect would the deprivation of visitation of the parents have on the children?
7. Are there ways that the examiner can suggest of controlling visitation or denying visitation if such recommendations are pertinent?
8. If the child were to be placed with a parent with homosexual or heterosexual promiscuity tendencies, how would the child be affected? (The judge goes on to spell out several other specific questions relating to the issue of placing children with parents with sexual problems.)
9. Who could best fill the emotional needs of the children? What is the basis for this judgment? What is the least detrimental alternative to this judgment, and what basis can be cited for this?
10. Do you recommend family counseling?* (Maloney, 1985, p. 156)

The ultimate goal of all the previous factors and questions is to identify a situation in which the best interests of the child are served. Other specific issues such as changes in previously established custody arrangements or visitation rights follow the same overriding principle.

Rights of patients

There is little doubt that the rights of hospitalized mental patients have come under increasing judicial scrutiny. We hear talk of the "hospitalized consumer" (Ladkin & Levine, 1976), arguments for the necessity of mental patient advisory boards (Morrison, 1976), and even a clients' "bill of rights" (Noll, 1974). Beginning in the early 1970s, courts have held that patients who are involuntarily hospitalized have a constitutional right to individualized treatment that offers them a realistic chance for cure or at least improvement (Schwitzgebel & Schwitzgebel, 1980). The courts have been less attentive to the rights of voluntary patients since it is assumed they can leave the hospital if they so choose.

Additional rights and standards involve the physical environment (for example, day rooms, lavatories, dining rooms, and so on), personal clothing, and personal activities (opportunities for physical exercise, regular outdoor opportunities, or social activities). In addition, involuntary labor is prohibited, and when labor is undertaken voluntarily, appropriate wages must be paid. Although many states recognize patients' rights to correspondence and visitation, institutional personnel often have wide discretion in controlling visits (except by lawyers, physicians, or

*SOURCE: Reprinted with permission of The Free Press, a division of Simon & Schuster from *A Clinician's Guide to Forensic Psychological Assessment,* by Michael P. Maloney. Copyright © 1985 by The Free Press.

clergy). Statutes have also generally asserted the patient's right to dignity and privacy, but in practice these rights tend to be subject to wide interpretation and discretion. Indeed, as observed earlier, statutes and court orders are one thing — their actual implementation in practice is another.

A controversial and complex issue is the patient's right to refuse treatment or medication (Schwitzgebel & Schwitzgebel, 1980; Wrightsman et al., 1994). The question is one of informed consent; not every involuntarily hospitalized patient is mentally incompetent and such individuals have the right to decide their own fate. But what about patients who are incompetent? Therein lies the rub. How can the rights of the competent be protected while also ensuring that the incompetent can experience the benefits of treatment? These are truly complex problems. In Box 19-2 are some examples of related issues dealing with the case of prison inmates that also tax good judgment.

Box 19-2
Recent legal controversies

A recent case, *Perry* v. *Louisiana* (1989) raised the issue of whether state officials may forcibly administer psychotropic medications to a death row inmate in order to render him mentally competent for his own execution. A macabre yet real-life question!

Who should decide whether prison inmates may be administered antipsychotic drugs against their will? This question was recently argued before the U. S. Supreme Court in the case of *Washington* v. *Harper* (1990). Harper is a convicted robber who initially accepted the medication voluntarily — later, he refused. A prison administrative committee concluded that Harper was both mentally ill and dangerous, and they authorized the antipsychotic medication. Harper then filed a suit that ultimately reached the Supreme Court. During oral arguments, several justices asked questions such as the following:

- Is it permissible to medicate an objecting inmate just to make the prison environment safer?
- As a ward of the state, how can a convicted criminal be presumed competent to make medication decisions?
- Why can't a dangerous inmate, even though competent, be medicated against his will?
- Because an inmate's competency may fluctuate over time, would not frequent judicial review be required for a given inmate? And would not such frequent review be an onerous burden to the court?

Ultimately, the Supreme Court ruled that mentally ill prisoners could not be medicated without their consent unless there was a consensus of professional opinion that safety would otherwise be compromised.

Predicting dangerousness

We saw in Chapter 2 that the *Tarasoff* case resulted in a California court decision that therapists have a duty to warn potential victims of their patients' violent behavior. Beyond that, many would agree that by law or moral imperative we all have the obligation to protect others from those who are deemed dangerous. But imperatives are one thing—the other is how well psychologists or anyone else can, in fact, accurately predict dangerous behavior! The reality is that to truly protect against those individuals who are dangerous would mean fishing with a very large net—a net that would snare large numbers of individuals who would never actually commit any violent acts. After all, the incidence of violence relative to the total population is quite low; so low, that in order to protect against the truly dangerous it would be necessary to confine many who are not (Rappaport, 1977). Therefore:

> If, in the criminal law, it is better that ten guilty men go free than one innocent man suffer, how can we say in the civil commitment area that it is better that 54 harmless people be incarcerated lest one dangerous man be free? (Livermore, Malmquist, & Meehl, 1968, p. 84)

According to Monahan (1976), violent acts are highly overpredicted, but many people seem willing to sacrifice many to protect society from one. There are undoubtedly many reasons why people tend to see dangerousness when none exists (Monahan, 1976). As much as anything, however, it is probably the television program or news story that describes how a mental patient was released only to kill someone, sexually abuse a child, or otherwise behave so as to lead the lay public to question the competency (and often the common sense) of the psychiatrist or psychologist involved in the release decision. All this leads to the conclusion that predicting dangerousness is very, very difficult. Although it is perhaps true that all of us have the potential to commit dangerous acts, given the right conditions, the fact remains that unless someone has previously behaved in a dangerous fashion, the ability to accurately predict such behavior is extremely limited (Shah, 1978).

Difficult though such predictions are, psychological evaluation for this purpose may constitute the largest single category of evaluation requested of the clinician by the criminal justice system (Blau, 1984). These evaluations are used for many decisions ranging from holding a prisoner without bail or granting work-release status to hospitalizing defendants or invoking special sentencing options for violent offenders (Shah, 1978). As noted by Wrightsman et al. (1994), research suggests that the most accurate predictions of violent behavior are:

1. predictions for the near, short-term future;
2. predictions for the same setting or circumstances for which the clinician already has historical data;
3. predictions based on the clinician's knowledge of the individual's past history of violent behavior; and
4. predictions for individuals from groups with relatively high base rates of violent behavior.

Because of the tremendous implications for public policy, to say nothing of human values, much more research is needed in this broad area of forensic psychology.

Psychological treatment

In the case of prisoners, legally established rights to psychological treatment or rehabilitation are still somewhat in a state of flux (Schwitzgebel & Schwitzgebel, 1980). Such persons have the right to medical treatment and, generally speaking, juvenile prisoners have the right to both psychological and medical treatment. When the right to psychological treatment for adult prisoners is recognized, it is most often for severely mentally disturbed individuals. Some experts are rather unwilling to promote treatment rights for prisoners because they believe that punishment and deprivation sometimes occur under labels like "treatment" and "behavior modification."

We have already observed that people have a right to refuse treatment, especially in the case of very intrusive forms such as psychosurgery or electroconvulsive therapy (ECT). But this right is most apparent in instances where the therapy may be considered punishing or manipulative. In such cases, the state must show a compelling interest that overrides the prisoner's right of refusal. Because of the ambiguities and the potential for violations of human rights, many correctional institutions now have committees to protect the rights of prisoners. Such bodies typically are composed of a majority of persons who are not affiliated with the institution.

There are wider forensic treatment implications, however (Cooke, 1984). In criminal cases, therapy may focus on restoring an incompetent person to a state of mental competency. Or therapy may be undertaken to provide emotional support for someone facing imprisonment. For criminal offenders, the focus is often on personality problems, sexual behavior, and aggressiveness. Sometimes therapy is conducted while the person is incarcerated, but other times it is on an outpatient basis as a condition of parole or probation. The forms of therapy employed include both individual and group methods that involve everything from insight-oriented and supportive methods to behavioral techniques, biofeedback, and cognitive approaches.

One of the major problems for the forensic clinician is the knowledge that testimony may be required later in court. What the court wants, what the client's attorney will permit, what is best for the client, and what the clinician sees as most desirable may conflict and lead to many problems. In child custody issues, the treatment problems and conflicts among parents and child may be especially difficult and poignant, and they can often lead to real professional dilemmas. For example, to best help the child, the clinician may recommend that the parents undergo therapy themselves, but sometimes one or both will refuse to do so.

Consultation

Another common activity of forensic psychologists is consultation (Nietzel & Dillehay, 1986). Of course, many of the activities discussed previously also involve some manner of consultation. In this section, we shall focus on several additional aspects of consultation.

Jury selection.   *Voir dire* is the legal term referring to that part of a trial in which a jury is impaneled. During this *jury selection* phase, attorneys have the opportunity to discover biases in potential jurors, obtain information for *peremptory* challenges (a set number of challenges allowed each side in a trial to remove jurors thought to be biased against a given side), ingratiate themselves with jurors or get jurors to identify with a given side, or to indoctrinate jurors so they will be receptive to an attorney's presentation of the case. All of this is designed to give the attorney an edge. The consulting psychologist works with attorneys to help them in a variety of ways to achieve better jury selection or deselection. Table 19-3 presents the goals and techniques of jury consultation.

Jury shadowing.   Another form of consultation is that of *jury shadowing*. Here the jury consultant hires analogous jurors (that is, individuals similar to those that actually serve on the jury) and monitors their reactions to the actual testimony as it is presented at the trial. In this way, the consultant and the attorneys can anticipate the reactions and impressions of the actual jurors and prepare a better-informed courtroom strategy.

Public opinion surveys.   Public opinion surveys have been used in many ways over the years. For example, in a trademark suit, a psychological consultant might be hired by an attorney to determine the public's recognition of some company name or symbol. One way to do this is through a survey. As another example, an opinion survey might be administered to a representative sample of people from the same geographical area in which a given trial is scheduled to be held. Respondents would give their opinions about the case in question and about the trial tactics planned by the attorney. In a sense, such a survey would allow the trial attorney to pretest the significant trial issues and to hone the proposed method of presentation of evidence. Another use for surveys is to determine whether a change in venue (location) for the trial might be in order. Attitudes in the community about the trial and particularly about the defendant can be elicited both to help convince the court to change the location and to help in the jury selection process (Nietzel & Dillehay, 1986).

Witness preparation.   It would be unethical for the consultant to work with a witness in any fashion that is designed to encourage an alteration in the facts of the testimony. Although the line is a very thin one, the idea is to help witnesses better present their testimony without, at the same time, changing the facts to which their testimony is directed. Because this is such a delicate matter, some consultants will not work with witnesses in criminal proceedings—only in civil cases. Again, Nietzel and Dillehay (1986) have discussed many aspects of *witness preparation,* including the manner of presentation of facts, associated emotions on the part of the witness, preparation for the sheer experience of being a witness in a courtroom, cross-examination matters, appearance, threats by the opposing attorney as to the credibility of the witness, and so on.

Convincing the jury.   Finally, the consultant can often help attorneys in the way they present their cases and evidence (within the allowable constraints of the judicial system) to jurors. They can likewise assist attorneys in predicting how jurors will respond to certain kinds of evidence or methods of presentation. This includes, especially, opening and closing arguments. The consultant will then help attorneys find the very best way to present their cases. In effect, the beliefs, feelings,

Table 19-3

Goals and techniques of jury consultation.

Stage of Consultation	Goals	Techniques
Stage I: Voir dire preparation	Learn about the case	Hold planning sessions with attorneys
	Educate attorneys about contributions that consultants can make	Review media, interview the client, observe courtroom procedures
	Develop instruments	If necessary, develop juror questionnaires, survey questionnaires, trial simulations, and interviews with key informants
	Formulate initial theory of jury selection	Analyze data from above and propose theory of jury selection that is integrated with attorneys' theory of the case
Stage II: Improving voir dire conditions	Structure voir dire in a manner that improves chances to uncover juror bias and to identify juror prejudice	Provide affidavits, expert testimony on: change of venue; individual, sequestered, attorney-conducted voir dire; struck versus "as-you-go" system; and composition challenge
	Improve voir dire skills of attorneys	Prepare voir dire topics and train attorneys in interviewing techniques
Stage III: Juror deselection	Develop final theory of jury selection	Coordinate pretrial data with in-court observation of venire persons
	Impanel a jury as favorably disposed toward the client and theory of the case as possible	Develop a rating system to identify jurors for peremptory challenge by juror experience, intelligence, sentiment, and social influence

SOURCE: From *Psychological Consultation in the Courtroom,* by M. T. Nietzel and R. C. Dillehay, p. 24. Copyright © 1986 by Pergamon Press. Reprinted by permission.

and behavior of jurors are the targets here. Within the legal and ethical constraints of the adversarial system, the consultant is there to be as helpful as possible.

Research and forensic psychology

In a real sense, virtually all research in psychology is relevant to some forensic issue. For example, research on the genetic components of schizophrenia may be very important in a mental competency hearing. Research on the nature of prejudice or the basic elements of the persuasive process is as germane to the attorney as it is to the social psychologist. Consumer research may have direct application to a product liability suit. And, recently, research on attributions and interpersonal relationships has been applied to the law on searches and seizures (Kagehiro, 1990). However, several research areas have become especially identified with forensic psychology, and we have chosen to sample two of them briefly in the next sections.

Eyewitness testimony.   Nothing can be so dramatic or damaging as an eyewitness who identifies the person accused of a crime. Such testimony has been a powerful factor in the conviction of countless individuals over the years (Cutler & Penrod, 1995). But such testimony has all too often convicted the innocent as well as the guilty (Loftus, 1979). The reason, put simply, is that *eyewitness testimony* is often unreliable and inaccurate. A case in point occurred in 1979 in Wilmington, Delaware. A Catholic priest was put on trial because a citizen told police that the priest looked very much like an artist's sketch of a robber being circulated by the police. Later, seven eyewitnesses to the robbery positively identified the priest as the robber. The trial was halted, however, when another man confessed to the crime. What had happened with these eyewitnesses? Apparently, before showing pictures of suspects to the witnesses, the police had quietly revealed that the robber might be a priest, and the priest's picture was the only one with the subject wearing a clerical collar!

Over the years, Loftus and her colleagues have conducted a number of experiments that, together, show that the eyewitness's memory can easily be distorted by subsequent information. For example, Loftus, Miller, and Burns (1978) had subjects view a series of color slides of an auto accident. Half the subjects were shown the series in which there was a stop sign present; the other half saw a yield sign. Afterward, subjects answered questions about the slides. The critical question mentioned whether a stop sign or a yield sign was present. For half the subjects the sign mentioned was consistent with what subjects had seen earlier; for the other half it was inconsistent. Still later, the subjects were shown 15 slides and were asked to pick out the one they had seen before. Interestingly, for subjects for whom the initial question was consistent with what they had seen, the correct slide was chosen 75% of the time. For the inconsistent group, the correct choice was made only 41% of the time.

It is clear that people often make inferences on the basis of their expectations. Also, as Loftus (1979) suggests, an eyewitness to an accident or crime is almost always questioned prior to the trial. In these conversations, something may easily be said to alter the witness's recollection. It is the role of the forensic psychologist to help identify the conditions in a specific case that might produce distortions in veridical testimony.

Experience has taught us that eyewitnesses to events all too often cannot agree among themselves. They differ in their descriptions of subjects' height, weight, hair color, clothing, and even race. A dramatic illustration of this axiom was provided by Buckhout (1975), who staged a demonstration as part of a television program. Viewers watched a staged purse-snatching episode that lasted but

12 seconds; following this, viewers saw a police lineup of six men that they were told, might contain the assailant. Viewers could call in and render their judgments. What happened? Over 2000 callers responded and 1800 were mistaken! Of course, none of the foregoing is meant to suggest that eyewitnesses are never correct. But it does suggest that caution should be exercised in accepting accounts automatically. At the very least, our legal system can use improvement in its procedures for identifying suspects (Loftus, 1983; Wells, 1995). Factors of perception, stress levels, information storage, identification procedures, and even unconscious integrative processes all need further study (Horowitz & Willging, 1984). Also important are prior experiences and conditioning as well as personal biases and stereotypes (Buckhout, 1980).

Jury behavior.   The better the conditions affecting how juries think and reach decisions are understood, the better the judicial system will be. A great deal of research has been done on just how jurors make sense out of evidence and process information, how they respond to instructions from the bench, and how they react to certain kinds of arguments (Kassin & Wrightsman, 1988; Wrightsman et al., 1994). Let us consider several examples.

Jurors are often confused by instructions from the judge. In one study, Severance and Loftus (1982) modified the pattern of instructions given to the jury — for example, instructions were written in active rather than passive sentences and the messages were short and concise. In addition, abstract notions such as "reasonable doubt" were given greater than usual elaboration. The result was a more accurate application of the law by jurors than is usual.

Even such a simple condition as the order in which the judge's instructions are presented can have an effect on jurors. For example, Kassin and Wrightsman (1979) used mock jurors who watched a videotaped trial. They found that informing jurors as to the requirements of proof prior to presentation of evidence, rather than after, had definite effects. Thus, jurors under the former condition were more likely to hold to the dictum of presumed innocence than jurors under the latter condition.

There are also many conditions that may bias jury decisions. An individual may be charged with several instances of a crime, which are sometimes joined into one indictment. In other cases, the defendant is tried separately for each instance. Greene and Loftus (1981) discovered that when charges are joined into one indictment, the jury is more likely to hand down harsher verdicts as compared to "severed" trials.

Much research on jury behavior has been simulated; that is, instead of studying real juries in real situations, subjects are placed in jurylike settings and their behavior is studied. Such studies have found that mock jurors who were exposed to a voir dire process were less prejudiced than jurors who did not have this experience (Padawer-Singer & Barton, 1975). Also, pretrial publicity colored those same mock jurors' understanding of the case. Likewise, Garcia and Griffitt (1978) found that the testimony of "likable" witnesses had a greater impact on mock jurors than did testimony from "dislikable" witnesses. Of course, the problem with simulated jury studies is that it is unclear how far one can generalize from them to real trials and real jurors (Kassin & Wrightsman, 1988); but simulations give researchers greater flexibility and allow them to exert more control over conditions and variables.

■ Focus Questions

1. What historical events influenced the development of the forensic psychology specialty?
2. What are the major roles engaged in by forensic psychologists?
3. What are the similarities and differences between the three major legal standards of insanity?
4. What role might a clinical psychologist play in a child custody decision?
5. How might a forensic psychologist contribute to the following processes: jury selection, preparing a witness, aiding an attorney who will cross-examine an eyewitness?

■ Key Terms

ALI standard
burden of proof
competency to stand trial
expert witness
eyewitness testimony
forensic psychology
insanity plea
joint custody

jury selection
jury shadowing
M'Naghten rule
peremptory challenges
voir dire
voluntary commitment
witness preparation

20

Pediatric and Clinical Child Psychology

Recently, it was estimated that at least eight million children in the United States need mental health services (Roberts, 1994). For years, the mental health needs of children and adolescents have not been adequately met. Unfortunately, this trend is likely to continue in the 1990s and beyond (Culbertson, 1993). Demographic projections for the United States suggest that, although the overall population growth rate is expected to decline for whites, the rates for groups of individuals that are currently underserved with regard to their mental health needs (for example, African American and Hispanic American children and adolescents) are expected to climb dramatically. Two subfields of clinical psychology — pediatric psychology and clinical child psychology — are uniquely qualified to address these needs.

■ Perspectives and History

Before touching on historical aspects of these child specialties, we should first discuss the distinction between clinical child psychology and pediatric psychology.

Definitions

At the outset it should be understood that distinctions between pediatric psychologists and clinical child psychologists are somewhat blurred at best. However, in *clinical child psychology,* a common activity over the years has been working with children and adolescents once psychopathological symptoms have developed. This work has often been conducted in either private practice settings or in child guidance clinics in the context of the traditional team of psychologist, psychiatrist, and social worker along with some collaboration with pediatricians (Kurz, 1987).

In contrast, *pediatric psychology* (or child health psychology, as it is often called) has been described as clinical child psychology conducted in medical settings including hospitals, developmental clinics, or medical group practice (Routh, 1988). Pediatric psychologists frequently intervene before psychopathology develops (or at least at an earlier stage of the disorder), and their referrals often come from pediatricians (Pruitt & Elliott, 1992). Specifically, Roberts, Maddox, and Wright (1984) have defined pediatric psychology as:

> . . . a field of research and practice [that] has been concerned with a wide variety of topics in the relationship between the psychological and physical well-being of children, including behavioral and emotional concomitants of disease and illness, the role of psychology in pediatric medicine, and the promotion of health and prevention of illness among healthy children. (pp. 56–57)

As suggested by the definitions above, surveys of pediatric and clinical child psychologists reveal several differences between the two areas, even though the overlap is considerable (for example, Kaufman, Holden, & Walker, 1989). First, a behavioral orientation with a related tendency to use short-term, immediate intervention strategies characterizes pediatric clinicians. In contrast, clinical child psychologists are more variable in their orientations (although psychodynamic and family systems approaches are more common in the case of clinical child specialists). Second, pediatric clinicians tend to place greater emphasis on medical and biological issues in their approaches to training, research, and service delivery. Their interests in behavioral medicine (see Chapter 17) and consultations with pediatricians are relevant here. Again, in contrast, clinical child specialists place greater emphasis on training in assessment, developmental processes, and family therapy.

Because of the increased relevance of pediatric psychology to clinical psychologists of the twenty-first century, we will focus much of our discussion in this chapter on this emerging specialty. Before reviewing the major activities of pediatric and clinical child psychologists, however, it is important to briefly survey the history of these specialties as well as some general training issues.

History

The history of clinical child psychology goes back to at least 1896, when Witmer stimulated the profession of clinical psychology by starting the first psychological clinic. Indeed, as noted in Chapter 2, this clinic was devoted to treating children who were, for example, having learning problems or were disruptive in the classroom.

The scientific study of childhood psychopathology probably can be dated to the early 1900s (Frame & Matson, 1989). For a long time, children were not recognized as being very different from adults in terms of their needs and abilities — they were pretty much regarded as miniature adults. However, by the later 1800s and early 1900s, several developments occurred to increase the focus on children (Ollendick & Hersen, 1989): (1) the identification and care of the mentally retarded, (2) the development of intelligence testing, (3) the formulation of psychoanalysis and behaviorism, (4) the child study movement, and (5) the emergence of child guidance clinics.

Even the classification of childhood disorders has changed greatly — especially in the last 30 years (Davison & Neale, 1996). For example, both the DSM-I and DSM-II regarded childhood problems as downward extensions of adult disorders. However, starting with the DSM-III and continuing today with DSM-IV, diagnostic

Table 20-1
Example of problems commonly addressed by pediatric psychologists.

Problems	Examples
Negative behaviors	Tantrums, crying
Toileting	Enuresis, toilet training
Developmental delays	Speech, overactivity
School	Reading, dislikes school
Sleeping	Nightmares, resists bedtime
Personality	Poor self-control, stealing
Siblings and peers	No friends, fighting
Divorce, separation, adoption	Visiting schedule, custody
Infant management	Feeding, colic
Family problems	Discipline, child abuse
Sex-related	Poor identification, no same-sexed friends
Food and eating	Picky eater, obesity
Specific fears	Dogs, trucks
Specific bad habits	Thumb sucking, tics

SOURCE: Roberts 1986, p.20

categories exist that are specifically relevant to children. Currently, there are 43 specific diagnoses contained in ten groups (APA, 1994). We will have more to say about diagnostic classification issues later in this chapter.

The foregoing trends have, over the years, culminated in what is now referred to as clinical child psychology. Indeed, the field is essentially oriented toward assessment, treatment, and prevention of a variety of problems.

Pediatric psychology evolved as a specialty when it became apparent that neither pediatrics nor clinical child psychology could handle all the problems presented in childhood (Roberts, 1986). Many well-child visits to pediatricians require mainly support and counseling rather than medical interventions. Often at issue are matters relevant to all child psychologists, including child rearing, behavioral management problems, or questions about academic performance. When these problems reflect the psychological-behavioral accompaniments of physical illness, handicap, or medical procedures, the pediatric psychologist typically has more relevant expertise than a traditional clinical child psychologist. In Table 20-1, some of the varieties of cases seen by pediatric psychologists are shown.

By 1966, there were some 300 psychologists in the U.S. working in pediatric settings (Routh, 1988). At about the same time, Wright (1967), in recognizing the marriage between pediatrics and psychology, called for a new specialty—pediatric psychology. Soon after, the Society of Pediatric Psychology was formed; this society now has over 1000 members, and the field has reached its adolescence (Peterson & Harbeck, 1988).

Table 20-2
Rankings of important training trends for the future.

Rank	Pediatric Experts	Clinical Child Experts
1	Brief treatment techniques	Specialty model
2	Residency model	Core curriculum
3	Biological and medical issues	Developmental processes
4	Specialty model	Assessment
5	Chronic illness	Prevention
6	Standard curriculum	Funding
7	Funding	Consultation/liaison
8	Consultation/liaison	Family therapy
9	Neuropsychology	Neuropsychology
10	Prevention	Research skills

SOURCE: From "Future Directions in Pediatric and Clinical Child Psychology," by K. L. Kaufman, E. W. Holden, and C. E. Walker, 1989, *Professional Psychology: Research and Practice, 20,* 148–152. Copyright © 1989 by the American Psychological Association. Reprinted by permission.

Professional issues

Issues of training and research in both clinical child and pediatric psychology have come to the fore in recent years. This is due in part to the growing interest in health and medical issues and to the developing collaboration between medicine and psychology. In the case of training, experts in both pediatric and clinical child psychology were asked about future directions (Kaufman, Holden, & Walker, 1989). The results of this survey are shown in Table 20-2 for both groups of experts. Again, several of the important items are common to both pediatric and clinical child psychology. All in all, the survey authors suggest that there will be a coevolution of the two areas and a continued blurring of their borders as well. As for research areas in the future, the Kaufman, Holden, and Walker survey results are summarized in Table 20-3. Clearly, this information on research trends is important since it can be expected to influence training models in the future.

Writing from the perspective of what they call *behavioral pediatrics,* Howard and Smith (1986) have addressed training issues in great detail, particularly in regard to course content and required skills. Others (for example, Winder, Michelson, & Diamond, 1985) have discussed practicum training for pediatric specialists. Writing largely from a child health perspective, Roberts, Fanurik, and Elkins (1988) recommend that several broad topical areas be covered in training programs (areas that usually seem equally relevant to the training of clinical child specialists as well). They are:

Child development
Psychopathology
Mental retardation and developmental disabilities
Psychotherapy and behavior change
Parent, family, and school intervention techniques

Table 20-3
Rankings of important research trends for the future.

Rank	Pediatric Experts	Clinical Child Experts
1	Chronic illness	Sexual abuse
2	Prevention	Childhood depression and suicide
3	Cost-benefit interventions	Developmental psychopathology
4	Treatment effectiveness	Prevention
5	Medical compliance	Treatment of conduct disorders
6	Neuropsychology	Custody and alternative living arrangements
7	Parenting issues	Parenting influences on development
8	Early intervention with children at risk	Diagnostic systems for children
9	Research strategies	Therapy effectiveness
10	Child abuse and neglect	Child neuropsychology

SOURCE: From "Future Directions in Pediatric and Clinical Child Psychology," by K. L. Kaufman, E. W. Holden, and C. E. Walker, 1989, *Professional Psychology: Research and Practice, 20,* 148–152. Copyright © 1989 by the American Psychological Association. Reprinted by permission.

Research methods
Ethical and legal issues
Health psychology
Assessment in child health
Interventions in child health
Clinical practica in health psychology

This list overlaps significantly with the recommendations of La Greca, Stone, Drotar, and Maddux (1988).

Major Activities

In newly developing areas such as pediatric or clinical child psychology, the activities are extremely diverse and steadily evolving. Therefore, to simplify matters a bit, we will group these activities under the headings of assessment, intervention, prevention, consultation, and research.

General issues
Before launching into the specifics of assessment, let us first consider several issues of general import.

The developmental perspective. Those who work with children quickly learn to adopt a developmental perspective (Campbell, 1989). Although conceptualizations of adult problems sometimes provide insight into children's difficulties, more often pediatric and clinical child psychologists must go beyond this. The age of children, their level of cognitive and social development, and their family and social situation must be considered as the psychologist tries to construe their problems. Indeed, failing to take into account the developmental stage of the child makes both assessment and treatment highly problematical. Bedwetting is a problem at age 12 but not at age 2. Aggressive behavior in 2-year-olds will likely be interpreted much differently than in the case of a 12-year-old. The prognostic implications of a behavior such as temper tantrums will be different for toddlers than for adolescents. Many such considerations help the psychologist decide who has a problem, how severe it is, how it is labeled, and what kind of intervention is to be recommended.

Epidemiology.   It is important to have some idea of how common various problems are across age groups and other segments of the population. Between the ages of one and two years, feeding and sleeping problems are very common. Hyperactivity and conduct disorders occur more frequently in boys than in girls. Even behaviors that might seem to indicate the presence of a mental disorder diagnosis occur commonly in nonclinical groups (Campbell, 1989). To properly understand and diagnose children's problems, the field must have information on how behaviors change over time, how they covary with one another, and how behaviors are distributed throughout the community (Yule, 1989).

The situation.   As noted by Yule (1989) and throughout this text, behavior is often situation-specific. A child may be quiet and withdrawn at home but not with peers. Another child may be compliant with authority figures but hostile with other children. This is not to say that general dispositional factors are unimportant; rather, to adequately conceptualize a child's problem (or presumed problem), those who work with the child must pay attention to the interaction between factors in the child's environment and generalized personality characteristics.

"Who is the client?"   In an earlier discussion of family therapy (see Chapter 15) it was noted that sometimes it is difficult to determine exactly who in the group is the real patient. That observation is equally true in the context of this chapter. In many instances, the most effective treatment is that which is directed at the parents, since it is they who are largely in control of the child. Furthermore, children do not refer themselves for assessment or therapy—they are referred by parents, physicians, teachers, or even court authorities. As Campbell (1989) puts it: "The first task of the clinician working with children and families is to determine whether a problem actually exists. Intolerance, ignorance, and misconceptions on the part of adults often lead to referral" (p. 7). For example, in a large epidemiological study of psychopathology in children, Shepherd, Oppenheim, and Mitchell (1971) compared children being seen in clinics with others matched in terms of severity of symptoms but whose parents had not sought help. What was the main factor differentiating the two groups? It was maternal perceptions of the problem as being serious. Certainly, then, parental concern, tolerance, and skill in managing children play a large part in defining childhood problem behavior.

Table 20-4
DSM-IV disorders usually first diagnosed in infancy, childhood, or adolescence.

Group	Diagnostic Examples
Mental retardation	Mild, moderate, or severe mental retardation
Learning disorders	Reading disorder, mathematics disorder
Motor skills disorder	Developmental coordination disorder
Communication disorders	Expressive language disorder, stuttering
Pervasive developmental disorders	Autistic disorder, Asperger's disorder
Attention deficit and disruptive behavior disorders	Attention deficit/hyperactivity disorder, conduct disorder
Feeding and eating disorders of infancy or early childhood	Pica, rumination disorder
Tic disorders	Tourette's disorder, transient tic disorder
Elimination disorders	Encopresis, enuresis
Other disorders of infancy, childhood, or adolescence	Separation anxiety disorder, selective mutism

SOURCE: From American Psychiatric Association, 1994, *Diagnostic and Statistical Manual of Mental Disorders,* 4th ed. Reprinted by permission.

DSM-IV.   Because we have already covered the DSM-IV (APA, 1994) in Chapter 5, only a few points with respect to children will be noted here. First, of course, the classification of childhood disorders has been of more interest to clinical child specialists than to pediatric psychologists since the former have historically more often had to deal with psychiatric cases. Second, the DSM-IV incorporates the growing interest in childhood disorders. There are ten major groups of disorders that are usually first diagnosed in infancy, childhood, or adolescence (APA, 1994). These groups, and diagnostic examples from each, are listed in Table 20-4. It is important to note two things. First, all of the disorders in Table 20-4 except those subtypes of mental retardation are coded on Axis I. Second, children and adolescents *can* receive diagnoses that are not listed in Table 20-4 (for example, major depressive disorder, dysthymic disorder, or bulimia nervosa). Often, however, diagnostic criteria or thresholds are modified so that they are more appropriate for children or adolescents. For example, to obtain a dysthymic disorder diagnosis, a child or adolescent can present with an irritable (versus depressed) mood, and the duration of all symptoms can be only one year (versus two years for adults).

Assessment

With children, it is almost always necessary to seek information from other people in addition to the child: parents, teachers, social workers, school psychologists, physicians, and others. Although parental consent is required, it is also important to obtain the child's permission to seek information from these other sources. This will help a great deal in building an atmosphere of trust and respect.

It should also be recognized, however, that these multiple sources of information may not agree with each other at times. For example, some have suggested that depressed mothers tend to exaggerate the nature and severity of child problems compared to other informants (Richters & Pelligrini, 1989). Although more recent evidence has challenged this claim (Tarullo, Richardson, Radke-Yarrow, & Martinez, 1995), the point is that there is currently no consensus as to how a clinician or researcher might integrate discrepant diagnostic information (Sher & Trull, 1996). This problem is compounded somewhat in the area of child clinical psychology because multiple sources of data are gathered routinely. Fortunately, researchers are now beginning to investigate how best to integrate assessment data from multiple informants (see Piacentini, Cohen, & Cohen, 1992).

When assessing children or adolescents, it is very important early on to estimate the nature and severity of the problem (Lindsay & Powell, 1989). The complaint may be as specific as vomiting or fear of walking to school or as general as a depression or lack of interest in schoolwork. In addition, the examiner will want to learn why help is being sought, how long the problem has existed, and what

other steps have been taken to resolve the problem. From all the sources available, a case history will then be generated in order to gain an understanding of exactly how the problems have developed. Again, all this is done to determine the nature of the problem and how best to deal with it.

Interviewing. Once again, the reader will recall that Chapter 6 dealt extensively with the interview process; that material is entirely relevant here. In the interest of brevity, this section will focus just on interviewing the parents and the child. According to Yule (1989), pediatric and clinical child psychologists interview parents to: (1) elicit information about behavior, events, and situations; (2) gauge parental feelings and emotions; and (3) establish the basis for subsequent therapeutic relationships.

When interviewing children, it is important to remember that they have not always been told why help is being sought, or else they understand what they have been told only imperfectly. Indeed, just being in a clinic without understanding why or without having been allowed to decide on treatment for themselves can be very anxiety-provoking for children (or anyone else). Therefore, it is important to find out how the child feels and what the child understands as the real purpose for the visit. As much as possible, the clinician must set a reassuring tone for the interview and then, within the limits of the child's understanding, explain what will take place and so on. In some cases, for example, it may be necessary to stress that the child will be going home after the visit to the clinic or that the specific diagnostic procedures will not hurt.

Interviewing children can be very difficult, as they cannot always communicate their feelings and thoughts in a precise fashion. Equally important to note is that children can be highly suggestible or fearful; consequently, they may tell the examiner what they think he or she wishes to hear or what others have told them. Or they may be so intimidated or nervous that they get their stories mixed up. The clinician must also bear in mind that the length of the interview with children may have to depend on such factors as age or intellectual level. Kanfer, Eyberg, &

Table 20-5

Tips for interviewing children.

General Communication Skills

1. Use descriptive statements (for example, "You look happy today")
2. Use reflective statements to help increase the amount of verbal interchange
3. Use praise
4. Avoid critical statements
5. Use open-ended questions (those that cannot be answered with a simple yes or no)
6. Use sentences and words that are age-appropriate

Conducting the Interview

1. Introduce yourself to parent(s) and child
2. Provide information about the plan for the session to both the child and parent(s)
3. Provide structure for the child to ease potential anxiety (for example, "Here, why don't we start by drawing some pictures")
4. Use an organizational format to gather information that focuses on the child's environment (peer relations, school, family); self (wishes, interests, fears); and presenting problem(s)
5. In wrapping up the interview, it is important to summarize for the child, to reinforce the child for his or her efforts, to ask for any additional information the child might want to offer, and to provide the child with information about what you plan to do from here on out

SOURCE: From "Interviewing Strategies in Child Assessment," by R. Kanfer, M. Eyberg, and G. L. Krahn in *Handbook of Clinical Child Psychology*, 2nd ed., edited by C. E. Walker and M. C. Roberts. Copyright © 1992 by John Wiley & Sons, Inc. Reprinted by permission.

Krahn (1992) have provided some good tips on interviewing children, a summary of which is presented in Table 20-5.

Finally, it should also be noted that a number of *structured diagnostic interviews* are available for assessing children and adolescents, including the Diagnostic Interview Schedule for Children (Costello, Edelbrock, Dulcan, Kalas, & Klaric, 1984), the Child Assessment Schedule (Hodges, Kline, Fitch, McKnew, & Cytryn, 1981), and the Diagnostic Interview for Children and Adolescents-Revised (Kaplan & Reich, 1991). These interviews are available in both child and parent (that is, informant) versions.

 Behavioral observations. As noted in Chapter 6, it is helpful to make *behavioral observations* during the interview. And, whenever possible, direct observations of the child at home and school should be undertaken (see Chapter 9). A variety of observational methods are available. For example, there are naturalistic, analog, participant, and self-observational techniques for use with children, and a variety of coding systems are available for rating behavior (LaGreca & Stone, 1992). As is true with all behavioral observations, child and pediatric psychologists need to keep in mind issues such as reliability of observations, reactivity to observation, and the validity of the observational data (LaGreca & Stone, 1992).

Intelligence tests.   When questions of intellectual achievement, academic deficits, or the development of an educational plan for the child are evident, *intelligence tests* are widely used for assessment. The most frequently employed tests are the Wechsler Intelligence Scale for Children-third edition (WISC-III), the Kaufman Assessment Battery for Children, the Wechsler Preschool and Primary Scale of Intelligence-revised, the Stanford-Binet Intelligence Scale-fourth edition, and the Peabody Picture Vocabulary Test-revised. These and other measures are well suited for test batteries assessing learning disabilities, mental retardation, neurological dysfunction, or pervasive developmental disorders in children (Sattler, 1992).

Achievement tests.   *Achievement tests* are used to assess past learning, particularly that which is associated with training or school programs. They can consist of a variety of different academic subjects from reading to arithmetic. Three widely used screening devices are the Peabody Individual Achievement Test, the Woodcock-Johnson Psychoeducational Battery, and the Wide Range Achievement Test-revised. A few commonly used test batteries are, for example, the Iowa Tests of Basic Skills, the SRA Achievement Series, the Stanford Achievement Test, and the Metropolitan Achievement Tests Survey Battery.

Special ability tests.   Sometimes psychologists want to go beyond an IQ or a specific achievement score in reading or spelling—they want a measure that will cover a specific ability, such as motor dexterity, vision, or creativity, and will do so with depth. Examples of *special ability tests* are the Differential Aptitude Test, the Primary Mental Abilities Test, and the General Aptitudes Test Battery.

Projective tests.   Although *projective tests* are somewhat controversial with children, some clinicians argue that they can be useful when a more dynamic picture of personality is required (for example, Levitt & French, 1992). One argument for the use of projective techniques in the assessment of children and adolescents is that the ambiguity of the stimuli in these tests or their use of animals as subject matter may be less threatening to those youngsters whose anxiety level is high. Both the Thematic Apperception Test and the Rorschach are often used, as well as the Children's Apperception Test, Incomplete Sentences Blank, or Draw-a-Person Test. As we mentioned in Chapter 8, however, clinicians who use projective techniques must consider the reliability and validity of their interpretations and guard against falling prey to interpretive errors based on illusory correlations.

Questionnaires and checklists.   Many scales, checklists, and questionnaires can be administered to adults who then respond in terms of their observations and inferences about the child's behavior and problems. With these tools, parents, teachers, and others who are in frequent contact with the child can

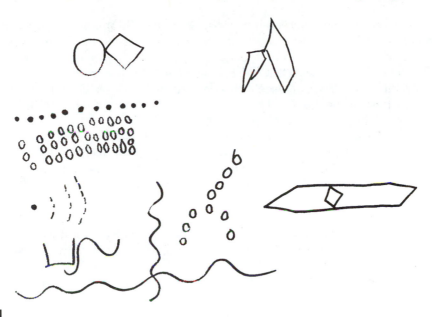

Figure 20-1

The Bender-Gestalt reproduction of Jim, a child aged 8 years and 6 months with low
average mental ability. He was a nonreading, learning-disabled child diagnosed
with minimal brain dysfunction and having a history of prenatal and birth trauma.
SOURCE: From Elizabeth M. Koppitz, *The Bender-Gestalt Test for Young
Children, Vol. II: Research and Application, 1963–1973,* Plate 19, p. 150.
Copyright © 1975 by Allyn & Bacon. Reprinted by permission.

provide information in terms of the child's personality characteristics, ranging
from the general to the very specific. Often-used measures include: the Personality Inventory for Children, the Child Behavior Checklist, the Teacher's Report
Form, the Revised Behavior Problem Checklist, and the Conners' Rating Scales.

Occasionally, self-report measures are administered directly to children when
it is felt they are capable of understanding directions and reporting properly on their
feelings, thoughts, or behavior. Two examples are the Children's Depression Inventory (said to be readable for first-grade children), the Perceived Competence Scales,
and, for adolescents, the MMPI-2 and the Youth Self-Report Test. McConaughy
(1992) provides an overview of these and other questionnaires and checklists.

Neuropsychological assessment. In recent years, the subspecialty
of child neuropsychology has grown considerably (Hynd, 1988; Tramontana &
Hooper, 1988). The recent growth of child neuropsychology as a specialty can be
attributed to an increased focus on neurodevelopmental disorders following the
passage of the Education for All Handicapped Children Act in 1976, as well as to
advances in medical care that have decreased mortality from devastating diseases
but *increased* the need for comprehensive assessment of the neurological effects

these conditions have on children (Hooper & Hynd, 1993). Some of the current research areas for child neuropsychologists include assessing the neurophysiological correlates of conduct disorder (Lahey, Hart, Pliska, Applegate, & McBurnett, 1993), of inattention/overactivity (McBurnett et al., 1993), of aggression/defiance (McBurnett et al., 1993), of anxiety disorders (Kushé, Cook, & Greenberg, 1993), and of a host of medical conditions (for example, Brown et al., 1993; Taylor, Barry, & Schatschneider, 1993; Wills, 1993).

Many of the issues, questions, and methods of neuropsychological assessment were touched upon in Chapter 18. Tests often used with children include: the Reitan-Indiana Battery, the Halstead Neuropsychological Battery for Children, the WISC-III, the Luria-Nebraska Neuropsychological Battery, and the Bender-Gestalt Test.

Cognitive assessment.   Increasingly, psychologists in this field have come to realize that many behavioral, emotional, and even medical problems in children are mediated by cognitive factors. For example, children with medical problems often do not understand the facts of their own condition nor do they appreciate the prescribed treatment. This can have an important impact on their recovery. Likewise, the child's self-efficacy can influence a host of reactions to medical problems and treatments. Finally, the child's cognitive appraisal can be vital in affecting behavior and feelings. For example, children's levels of stress or their responses to treatment may be partially controlled by the manner in which they process information. It is critical that clinical and pediatric child psychologists be able to understand and measure these cognitive variables (Eisenstein & Copeland, 1988).

Family systems assessment.   To a large extent, children's problems are embedded in the overall family context. The child is shaped by the family and, in turn, the family is shaped by the child. Therefore, if one is to understand the child's problems and intervene appropriately, one must also understand the family system. A variety of assessment devices exist for this purpose (McCubbin & McCubbin, 1988).

Interventions

In Part 3 we covered a variety of treatment approaches. In the case of children, the approaches are equally diverse and, in general, somewhat similar to those used with adults. However, child therapy is also different, for at least two reasons noted earlier: children do not typically refer themselves for treatment nor do they possess the same capacity for introspection and self-report as do most adults. Kazdin (1988) has conservatively estimated that there are over 230 therapeutic techniques used in treating children or adolescents. Below, we will briefly discuss some of the more commonly employed approaches.

Psychoanalytically oriented therapy.   Although psychoanalytically oriented treatments are frequently used in the treatment of children and adolescents, modification of the traditional techniques is often necessary. Children are unlikely to understand or be able to adhere to the strict requirements of an ortho-dox analysis in the same way that adults can; they usually cannot deal with the highly verbal, abstract, and introspective nature of the process. In addition, chil-dren who have particularly weak egos or else are living in extremely threatening home situations with unsupportive parents are not often good candidates for psy-choanalytic procedures. However, modified psychoanalytic approaches have been widely applied to children. Although Anna Freud (1946b) believed that children in therapy must achieve insight into their troubled feelings and defenses, other less traditional analysts have proceeded differently (Tuma, 1989). The frequency of meetings is usually reduced to once or twice per week, and the approach is more symptom oriented and designed to teach the child that certain behaviors are really defenses against anxiety. All of this may help the child negotiate a certain devel-opmental stage rather than "cure" a fixation, perhaps. In general, the differences in approaches are in degree rather than kind—for example, daydreams rather than nocturnal dreams might be solicited. In a greater departure, play rather than direct verbalization may be used as a communication vehicle, as we will see in the next section.

Play therapy.   Rather than employ dreams or free associations, some have chosen to study the psychic life of the child through play—either of a free or a structured variety. The child is brought to the playroom where a variety of ma-terials are present, such as a sandbox, clay, puppets, dolls, and toys of all kinds. How children play, what objects they choose, and the nature of their verbaliza-tions as they play can all be revealing, cathartic, and therapeutic. Sometimes the therapist enters into the play and makes comments and suggestions or otherwise guides the child toward certain conflict or problem areas. The nature of children's play may convey how they relate to significant other figures in their lives, how they handle their anxieties, and so on. In essence, play becomes a substitute for verbalization. An example of this might be Solomon's approach (1955). He brings the child into a room with a table on which have been placed a number of dolls. He selects one and then asks the child what to do with it. Sometimes the dolls are arrayed to represent the child's family. As the child arranges the dolls and plays, the therapist interprets what the child is doing, which then facilitates the expres-sion of feelings on the part of the child. Concrete family experiences, wishes, and even unconscious urges may be expressed in the process. In general, however, play therapy has evolved into a rather eclectic, amorphous set of techniques and procedures.

Behavior therapy.   The techniques of behavior therapy (which were reviewed in Chapter 14) have overtaken psychodynamic methods as the treatment of choice for childhood problems. For children, it has always seemed so evident that their problems are the direct outgrowth of environmental factors or the peo-ple who are in control of the various aspects of their lives. Either respondent prin-ciples (behavior is acquired through classical conditioning) or operant principles (behavior is maintained by its consequences) seem ideally suited to account for so many childhood behaviors. Moreover, these principles can easily be applied by

parents and teachers alike as part of the therapeutic plan. Most of these procedures, whether they be systematic desensitization, aversion therapy, or contingency management techniques, are highly efficient in comparison to older, more
traditional methods. Changes that once took months or even years to occur can
be achieved in 20 or fewer sessions. Parents and teachers can be trained in order
to enhance the effectiveness of the techniques and to help ensure that changes will
generalize outside the therapist's office.

For example, *parent management training* involves a set of therapeutic
procedures designed to "train" parents to modify a child's or adolescent's behavior at home. Parents master basic learning principles (for example, contingency
management, reinforcement) and then implement these at home. By enlisting parents in the treatment process, it becomes more likely that behavior change will
be effected in the child or adolescent. For example, Barkley (1987) has developed
a program for teaching child management skills to parents of children who are defiant and noncompliant. Table 20-6 presents a handout from this program that instructs parents on how to give effective commands.

Behavioral pediatrics.   Clinical child psychologists and pediatric psychologists can also contribute a great deal to the management of children during
their stay in the hospital (Yule, 1989). This includes help in preparing children for
particular medical procedures and in assisting the child and family in coping later
with their medical problems. Techniques employed here range from behavioral rehearsal and stress inoculation to various methods of cognitive reappraisal.
Whether the problem is a simple fear of needles or the stress and pain associated
with repeated changing of bandages for burn patients, behavioral methods can be
helpful. Managing pain and headaches as well as ensuring compliance with medical regimens are also important provinces of behavioral pediatrics (Krasnegor,
Arasteh, & Cataldo, 1986; Roberts, 1986).

Cognitive-behavioral therapy.   In recent years, cognitive-behavior
therapy has increasingly been applied to problems such as impulsivity, hyperactivity, anxiety, depression, and conduct disorders (Johnson, Rasbury, & Siegel, 1986;
Kendall, 1993). The basic idea is to improve problem solving and enhance planning and delay of gratification. Through internal assessments and self-statements,
children are taught to bring their previously distressing or problematic behavior
under rational control. The vehicle through which this is accomplished is the alteration of cognitions, and the ultimate goal is the creation of a new, more adaptive "coping template" (Kendall, 1993).

Family therapy.   Many of the approaches outlined as family therapy in
Chapter 15 are applicable to children's problems. Clearly, many of these problems are learned and even nourished in the family setting. To relieve them often
means the cooperation and understanding of the family unit is necessary. Because
children are the product of their families and are so much influenced by family
members, in some cases it only makes good sense to treat the entire family.

Table 20-6
Handout for parents of defiant/noncompliant children.

PARENT HANDOUT:
HOW TO GIVE EFFECTIVE COMMANDS

In our work with many behavior problem children, we have noticed that if parents simply change the way they give commands to their children, they can often achieve significant improvements in the child's compliance. When you are about to give a command or instruction to your child, be sure that you do the following:

1. *Make sure you mean it!* That is, never give a command that you do not intend to see followed up to its completion. When you make a request, plan on backing it up with appropriate consequences, either positive or negative, to show that you mean what you have said.

2. *Do not present the command as a question or favor.* State the command simply, directly, and in a businesslike tone of voice.

3. *Do not give too many commands at once.* Most children are able to follow only one or two instructions at a time. For now, try giving only one specific instruction at a time. If a task you want your child to do is complicated, then break it down into smaller steps and give only one step at a time.

4. *Make sure the child is paying attention to you.* Be sure that you have eye contact with the child. If necessary, gently turn the child's face toward yours to ensure that he or she is listening and watching when the command is given.

5. *Reduce all distractions before giving the command.* A very common mistake that parents make is to try to give instructions while a television, stereo, or video game is on. Parents cannot expect children to attend to them when something more entertaining is going on in the room. Either turn off these distractions yourself or tell the child to turn them off before giving the command.

6. *Ask the child to repeat the command.* This need not be done with each request, but it can be done if you are not sure your child heard or understood the command. Also, for children with a short attention span, having them repeat the command appears to increase the likelihood they will follow it through.

7. *Make up chore cards.* If your child is old enough to have jobs to do about the home, then you may find it useful to make up a chore card for each job. This can simply be a three-by-five file card. Listed on it are the steps involved in correctly doing that chore. Then, when you want your child to do the chore, simply hand the child the card and state that this is what you want done. Of course, this is only for children who are old enough to read. These cards can greatly reduce the amount of arguing that occurs over whether a child has done a job or chore properly. You might also indicate on the card how much time the chore should take and then set your kitchen timer for this time period so the child knows exactly when it is to be done.

If you follow these seven steps, you will find some improvement in your child's compliance with your requests. When used with the other methods your therapist will teach you, remarkable improvements can occur in how well your child listens and behaves.

SOURCE: From *Defiant Children: Parent-Teacher Assignments,* p. 43, by R. A. Barkley. Copyright © 1987 by Guilford Publications, Inc. Reprinted by permission.

Psychopharmacological treatment. Medications may be used as adjuncts to psychotherapy in the treatment of the child (Campbell, Cohen, Perry, & Small, 1989). The medications most frequently used are those that treat attention deficit/hyperactivity disorder, or ADHD (Pelham & Hinshaw, 1992). The most frequently prescribed medication for ADHD is the psychostimulant *methylphenidate* (Ritalin). Although studies have demonstrated the positive effects of Ritalin in treating ADHD symptoms, not all children and adolescents have a positive response (Pelham & Hinshaw, 1992). Further, the costs in the form of side effects may outweigh the benefits, and, to date, there are few demonstrations of long-term relief in the form of improved prognosis (Pelham & Hinshaw, 1992). These same points apply to other forms of medication that are used to treat the range of clinical problems presented by children and adolescents.

Are psychological interventions for children and adolescents effective?

To this point, we have presented descriptions of several of the more commonly employed psychological interventions for children and adolescents. However, how effective are these interventions? Recent reviews of the treatment outcome literature agree that, in general, psychological interventions for children and adolescents are effective (for example, Peterson & Bell-Dolan, 1995; Weisz, Donenberg, Han, & Weiss, 1995). This conclusion is based on the converging results of several major meta-analyses of the treatment outcome literature. Table 20-7 presents a summary of the results of four major meta-analytic studies.

The effect size estimates across these studies are quite consistent and are comparable to those reported for the psychological treatment of adults (Weisz, Donenberg, et al., 1995). Taken together, these meta-analytic results suggest that the average child or adolescent client who receives psychological treatment is functioning better than over 75% of those who did not receive treatment.

Although these findings are encouraging, more outcome research is necessary for several reasons. First, a disproportionately greater number of treatment outcome studies are conducted on adult versus child or adolescent patients. This relative paucity of child and adolescent outcome studies prohibits more fine-grained analyses aimed at comparing the effectiveness of competing forms of treatment for the same clinical problem (for example, cognitive-behavioral versus play therapy for childhood depression) as well as analyses identifying patient or therapist variables that may moderate treatment effects. In addition, there is some preliminary evidence suggesting that the effectiveness of more naturalistic "clinic therapy" is less effective than "research therapy" (Weisz, Donenberg, et al., 1995). Because the published literature typically reports on studies employing recruited (versus clinic-referred) patients, narrow problem focus (versus broad or multiproblem focus) in treatment, brief and time-limited (versus longer and time-unlimited) treatments, and treatments that are primarily behavioral (versus nonbehavioral), generalization from the meta-analytic results to situations involving psychotherapy as it is usually conducted may be problematic. Future research on psychological interventions for children and adolescents should attend to these and other methodological issues (Peterson & Bell-Dolan, 1995; Weisz, Donenberg et al., 1995).

Table 20-7

Average effect size (ES) and percentile equivalent for psychological interventions used to treat children and adolescents.

Meta-Analysis Study	$\overline{ES}$	Percentile Equivalent
Casey & Berman (1985)	0.71	76%
Weisz, Weiss, Alicke, & Klotz (1987)	0.79	79%
Kazdin, Bass, Ayers, & Rogers (1990)—no treatment control	0.88	81%
Kazdin et al. (1990)—active control	0.77	78%
Weisz, Weiss, Han, Granger, & Morton (1995)	0.71	76%

Note: Percentile equivalent indicates the percentage of those not receiving treatment whose outcome is exceeded by those receiving the treatment in question.

Prevention

Taking a page from the book of community psychology (see Chapter 16), pediatric psychologists have been especially concerned about the *prevention* of childhood problems (Roberts, 1986; Peterson & Harbeck, 1988). Of course, prevention and treatment are activities that blend and merge. For example, primary prevention was defined in Chapter 16 as counteracting problems before they have a chance to develop. Secondary prevention was said to be oriented toward the prompt treatment of problems while they are still manageable and the minimization of the impact of these problems. Certainly, then, the pediatric psychologist wants to either prevent the development of problems entirely, before they occur, or at least identify the problems before they get out of control. In any case, the stance of either the pediatric or clinical child psychologist is a proactive one (Peterson, Zink, & Farmer, 1992).

In the context of pediatric practice, Roberts (1986) likes to use the term *anticipatory guidance*—the use of counseling and education in advance of difficulties. For example, parents may be counseled about child-proofing their home at various stages of the child's development. This could cover almost anything from covering electrical outlets to blocking off stairways. At a more psychological level, this could involve providing information on preparing the child for the birth of a sibling or the death of a grandparent. In the case of a child with cystic fibrosis, for instance, it might take the form of counseling the youngster on how to respond to teasing from peers prompted by the physical limitations imposed by the disease.

One of the tenets of community psychology has always been the identification of people at risk for the development of subsequent problems. One such person is the child who is hospitalized. As we discussed earlier in the context of behavioral pediatrics, there is much that can be done for these children. For example, Elkins and Roberts (1983) have reviewed a number of programs designed to provide information to hospitalized children, to encourage emotional expression in such children, to offer coping strategies to them, or to just help build trusting relationships. Numerous films and videotapes also have been developed to help children cope with medical interventions (see Roberts, 1986).

To aid in the prevention of physical problems, safety programs have been created and directed toward children. Everything from crossing the street safely to avoiding abduction or molestation has been addressed (for example, Poche, Brouwer, & Swearingen, 1981; Yeaton & Bailey, 1978). Programs to train so-called latchkey children have also appeared (see Peterson, 1984). Similarly, programs designed to promote oral hygiene in children have been reviewed recently (Blount, Santilli, & Stokes, 1989). Research also suggests that specific recommendations and pediatric counseling with parents will increase the use of safety car seats (Christophersen & Gyulay, 1981). Finally, and more recently, attempts have been made to integrate child injury and child abuse-neglect research because similar interventions may be used to prevent harm in both domains (Peterson & Brown, 1994). Table 20-8 presents a model of an intervention sequence aimed at preventing child abuse-neglect in children from high-risk families (Peterson & Brown, 1994). These are but a brief sampling of the many approaches to prevention that characterize pediatric psychology today.

Consultation

Consultation-liaison relationships have long been typical in the professional lives of pediatric psychologists. Roberts (1986) has described this consultation process at some length, and we will follow his lead in this section. Although the focus here will be on the pediatric psychologist, many points apply equally to clinical child psychologists.

Because of the problems presented in the pediatric setting, *consultation* has become an integral part of the psychologist's role. Consultation occurs with parents, pediatricians, medical staff, school systems, welfare agencies, juvenile court systems, and other health or service agencies. The subjects of consultation may range from psychiatric, psychosomatic, or developmental problems to any kind of illness-related difficulties common to health care settings. In particular, pediatric psychologists consult with pediatricians. The latter call upon the psychologist much as they might consult with other medical specialists, such as cardiologists or oncologists. Because pediatricians encounter such a wide range of both well and ill children (probably more than any other specialist during the early stages of development), they often face problems for which they have little training, knowledge, or interest in treating. Hence, they may turn to the psychologist.

Consultation may occur in hospital practice or in outpatient settings. It may involve requests for immediate and very brief help in the form of hallway chats and quick telephone calls or for long-term interventions in the shape of case workups and written reports. Some interventions are directly with the child; others involve working with the family or with the pediatrician's staff. Indeed, several models of consultation have been offered by Roberts and Wright (1982). Let us consider them now.

Independent functions model.

The psychologist using the independent functions model acts as a specialist and independently carries out diagnostic

Table 20-8
Proposed treatment plan for prevention of child abuse-negelct in children from high-risk
    families.

Session	Content Areas
1	Introduction: Orientation to format, goals, reimbursement, meeting, and getting acquainted
2	I. Base problem solving (that is, recognize and define typical life problems, list a goal, evolve options, input plan, evaluate outcome) II. Positive parenting: enjoying the child

3–4	1. Reemphasize normative development and how to enjoy the child's unfolding abilities
	   2. Reciprocal activities: child-led play and mutual reinforcement
	   3. Seeing the world through the child's eyes
	III. Parenting skills

5–6	A. General skills
	     1. Defining behaviors and goals
	     2. Recognizing developmentally appropriate goals
	     3. Identifying antecedents and consequences
	     4. Identifying rewards
	     5. Identifying a reasonable level of control

7	B. Request skills
	     1. How to make requests to ensure compliance (alpha commands)
	     2. Reasonable requests

8–9	C. Response reduction
	     1. Ignoring
	     2. Reward the absence of negative behaviors
	     3. Time-out
	     4. Getting past the "testing the limits" phase

10	D. Response increasing
	     1. Use of Praise
	     2. Explicit rewards: appropriate rewards, token economy
	IV. Extending parenting

11	A. Child safety
	     1. Discipline and abuse: How discipline can slip into abuse, outcomes of abuse
	     2. Responsibility for selecting nonabusive care agents
	     3. Other kinds of injury "child proofing"
	     4. Supervision
	     5. Child as precious to mother: work to protect

12	B. Meeting the challenges of parenting: How to maintain parenting skills and other changes without group

13–14	V. Anger management
	  A. Seeing oneself through the child's eyes
	     1. Recalling one's own parents and parental anger
	     2. Characterization of how being the focus of anger feels
	  B. Neurolinguistic programming
	     1. Anger as feeling, color, or state
	     2. Power to alter that state

(continued)

■

Table 20-8 continued

Session	Content Areas
15	C. Behavioral treatment 1. Relaxation 2. Becoming aware of anger triggers 3. Safety valves 4. Self-esteem D. Successful parenting as anger reducing
16	VI. Open house and review

SOURCE: From "Integrating Child Injury and Abuse-neglect Research: Common Histories, Etiologies, and Solutions," by L. Peterson and D. Brown, 1994, *Psychological Bulletin, 116,* 293–315. Copyright © 1994 by the American Psychological Association. Reprinted by permission.

and treatment activities on patients referred by a pediatrician or other professional. This is really noncollaborative and is like any other referral process involving two independent professionals. Some psychologists occasionally get a bit suspicious of this model when they are confronted with what they see as purely diagnostic referrals because they feel this relegates them to the role of tester—a role secondary to the referring professional who then undertakes the more exciting activity of therapeutic intervention. However, the purely diagnostic role for psychologists has actually declined in recent years in favor of a more comprehensive one.

Indirect consultation model.   In the case of the indirect consultation model, the pediatrician retains chief responsibility for patient management. Indeed, the psychologist has, at best, limited contact with the actual patient and makes a contribution through analysis of information provided by the pediatrician (or other specialist). This kind of consultation is especially characteristic of medical center settings where teaching is a major function. Often, the role of the psychologist is then an educational or supervisory one, especially when pediatric residents are involved. The specific form of this kind of consultation can involve: (1) brief contacts (for example, phone calls); (2) presentations of information in seminars, conferences, workshops, or in service training for other professionals; or (3) situations where another professional carries out specific behavioral or psychosocial interventions recommended by the psychologist. For example, specific guidelines may be developed by the psychologist and given to the pediatrician, who either implements them or else supervises parents who do the actual intervention. These guidelines could involve how to handle temper tantrums in the child, bedwetting, mealtime problems, general behavioral management, and other problems. Roberts (1986) has provided a list of sample guidelines or protocols for the assessment and treatment of childhood problems.

Collaborative team model. In the collaborative team model, true collaboration is the watchword. Here, pediatrician, psychologist, nurse, or others work together, acting as functional equals, and share the responsibility and decision making. This might be referred to as *conjoint case management*. Of course, such a model is not often possible in nonteaching or nonresearch settings for several practical and financial reasons. However, such a model is especially appropriate for those cases that clearly involve both medical and psychological features; drug addiction, obesity, and physical handicaps are good examples. Thus, dealing with obesity requires not only insight into the psychological aspects of overeating but also the medical aspects of diet and health monitoring.

◼ The Future of Child Clinical and Pediatric Psychology

What lies ahead for child clinical and pediatric psychology? In closing, we note several trends and issues that will confront these specialties in the 1990s and beyond.

1. *Issues related to ethnicity, race, or culture.* As the population in the U.S. becomes increasingly diverse, clinicians and researchers alike must commit themselves to providing their services to those children and adolescents from underrepresented groups (Culbertson, 1993). Further, demographic trends suggest a great shortage of professionals to meet the needs of these children and adolescents. Finally, training programs need to provide the instruction and experience necessary to adequately prepare future child clinical and pediatric psychologists to meet these needs.

2. *Research.* As previously mentioned, more research on commonly employed interventions for children and adolescents is needed. Further, more research that evaluates the role of ethnicity, race, and culture in the treatment of children and adolescents is crucial as well. Foster and Martinez (1995) provide a thorough overview of conceptual and methodological issues that need to be considered in this line of research.

3. *Innovative treatment models.* Traditional interventions (for example, one-on-one therapy) may not be the most practical or effective in the treatment of children or adolescents. Recently, a task force report made a number of recommendations regarding mental health services for children, adolescents, and their families (Henggeler, 1994), including:

   (a) reduce the use of inpatient services and residential treatment and increase the use of home- and community-based services;
   (b) train providers in the delivery of cost-effective services and increase provider accountability;
   (c) increase the integration of services (for example, mental health, education, primary care); and
   (d) provide flexible, individualized services and elicit the support of families.

4. *Increased focus on injury prevention and prevention of child abuse-neglect.* Injury is the leading cause of death among children, and the safety and health of children is receiving more attention from psychologists and laypersons alike. The boundary between unintentional or inadvertent injury and injury due to neglect or abuse is often blurred (Peterson & Brown, 1994). Increasingly, interventions aimed at both caregivers and children are being developed and applied by psychologists (Peterson & Roberts, 1992), and this trend is likely to continue.

■ Focus Questions

1. What are the similarities and differences between pediatric and clinical child psychology?
2. What are the major differences between providing psychological services to children or adolescents versus adults?
3. What are the major assessment methods used in pediatric and clinical child psychology?
4. What major forms of intervention are employed in the treatment of children and adolescents? What evidence exists regarding the efficacy of these treatments?
5. What future trends have been identified for child clinical and pediatric psychology?

■ Key Terms

achievement tests
behavior therapy
behavioral observations
behavioral pediatrics
clinical child psychology
cognitive assessment
cognitive-behavioral therapy
consultation
family systems assessment
family therapy
intelligence tests

neuropsychological assessment
parent management training
pediatric psychology
play therapy
prevention
projective tests
psychoanalytically oriented therapy
questionnaires and checklists
special ability tests
structured diagnostic interviews

References

Abeles, N. (1990). Rediscovering psychological assessment. *The Clinical Psychologist, 10,* 3–4.

Ackerley, G. D., Burnell, J., Holder, D. C., & Kurdek, L. A. (1988). Burnout among licensed psychologists. *Professional Psychology: Research and Practice, 19,* 624–631.

Ackerman, N. W. (1958). *The psychodynamics of family life.* New York: Basic Books.

Ackerman, N. W. (1960). Family focused therapy of schizophrenia. In S. Scher & H. Davis (Eds.), *The outpatient treatment of schizophrenia.* New York: Grune and Stratton.

Ackerman, N. W. (1966). *Treating the troubled family.* New York: Basic Books.

Adams, K. M. (1996). President's message: "May you live in interesting times" Chinese proverb. *Division of Clinical Neuropsychology: Newsletter 40, 14,* 2–5, 10.

Ader, R., & Cohen, N. (1975). Behaviorally conditioned immuno-suppression. *Psychosomatic Medicine, 37,* 333–340.

Adler, A. (1930). *Guiding the child on the principles of individual psychology.* New York: Greenberg.

Akamatsu, T. J. (1988). Intimate relationships with former clients: National survey of attitudes and behavior among practitioners. *Professional Psychology: Research and Practice, 19,* 454–458.

Albee, G. W. (1959). *Mental health manpower trends.* New York: Basic Books.

Albee, G. W. (1968). Conceptual models and manpower requirements in psychology. *American Psychologist, 23,* 317–320.

Albee, G. W. (1986). Toward a just society: Lessons from observations on the primary prevention of psychopathology. *American Psychologist, 41,* 891–898.

Alberts, G., Edelstein, B. (1990). Therapist training: A critical review of skill training studies. *Clinical Psychology Review, 10,* 497–512.

Alden, L. E. (1988). Behavioral self-management controlled-drinking strategies in a context of secondary prevention. *Journal of Consulting and Clinical Psychology, 56,* 280–286.

Alexander, F. (1950). *Psychosomatic medicine.* New York: Norton.

Alexander, F., & French, T. M. (1946). *Psychoanalytic therapy.* New York: Ronald Press.

Alexander, J. F., Holtzworth-Munroe, A., & Jameson, P. (1994). The process and outcome of marital and family therapy: Research review and evaluation. In A. E. Bergin & S. L. Garfield (Eds.), *Handbook of psychotherapy and behavior change* (4th ed.) (pp. 595–630). New York: Wiley.

Allen, F. H. (1934). Therapeutic work with children. *American Journal of Orthopsychiatry, 4,* 193–202.

Allison, K. W., Crawford, I., Echemendia, R., Robinson, L., & Knepp, D. (1994). Human diversity and professional competence: Training in clinical and counseling psychology revisited. *American Psychologist, 49,* 792–796.

Allport, G. W. (1961). *Pattern and growth in personality.* New York: Holt, Rinehart and Winston.

Altrocchi, J. (1972). Mental health consultation. In S. E. Golann & C. Eisdorfer (Eds.), *Handbook of community mental health.* New York: Appleton-Century-Crofts.

American Group Psychotherapy Association, Committee on History. (1971). A brief history of the American Group Psychotherapy Association, 1943–1968. *International Journal of Group Psychotherapy, 21,* 406–435.

American Psychiatric Association. (1952). *Diagnostic and statistical manual of mental disorders.* Washington, DC: Author.

American Psychiatric Association. (1968). *Diagnostic and statistical manual of mental disorders* (2nd ed.). Washington, DC: Author.

American Psychiatric Association. (1980). *Diagnostic and statistical manual of mental disorders* (3rd ed.). Washington, DC: Author.

American Psychiatric Association. (1987). *Diagnostic and statistical manual of mental disorders* (3rd ed., rev.). Washington, DC: Author.

American Psychiatric Association. (1994). *Diagnostic and statistical manual of mental disorders* (4th ed.). Washington, DC: Author.

American Psychological Association. (1982). *Ethical principles in the conduct of research with human participants.* Washington, DC: Author.

American Psychological Association. (1985). *Standards for educational and psychological tests.* Washington, DC: Author.

American Psychological Association. (1992). Ethical principles of psychologists and code of conduct. *American Psychologist, 47,* 1597–1611.

American Psychological Association. (1996). *Standards for educational and psychological tests and manuals.* Washington, DC: Author.

Anastasi, A. (1988). *Psychological testing* (6th ed.). New York: Macmillan.

Anderson, H. H., & Anderson, G. L. (Eds.). (1951). *An introduction to projective techniques.* Englewood Cliffs, NJ: Prentice-Hall.

Anderson, N. B. (1995). Behavioral and sociocultural perspectives on ethnicity and health: Introduction to the special issue. *Health Psychology, 14,* 589–591.

Anderson, R. M., Jr. (1994). *Practitioner's guide to clinical neuropsychology.* New York: Plenum.

Anonymous. (1995). Hidden benefits of managed care. *Professional Psychology: Research and Practice, 26,* 235–237.

Ansbacher, H. L. (1951). The history of the leaderless group discussion technique. *Psychological Bulletin, 48,* 383–391.

Appelbaum, S. A. (1970). Science and persuasion in the psychological test report. *Journal of Consulting and Clinical Psychology, 35,* 349–355.

Arcaya, J. M. (1987). Role conflicts in coercive assessments: Evaluation and recommendations. *Professional Psychology: Research and Practice, 18,* 422–428.

Arkes, H. R. (1981). Impediments to accurate clinical judgment and possible ways to minimize their impact. *Journal of Consulting and Clinical Psychology, 49,* 323–330.

Arnhoff, F. N. (1968). Realities and mental health manpower. *Mental Hygiene, 52,* 181–189.

Arnkoff, D. B., & Glass, C. R. (1989). Cognitive assessment in social anxiety and social phobia. *Clinical Psychology Review, 9,* 61–74.

Arvey, R. D., et al. (1994, December 13). Mainstream science on intelligence. *Wall Street Journal,* p. A18.

Atkinson, L. (1986). The comparative validities of the Rorschach and MMPI: A meta-analysis. *Canadian Psychology, 27,* 238–247.

Babad, E. Y., Mann, M., & Mar-Hayim, M. (1975). Bias in scoring the WISC subtests. *Journal of Consulting and Clinical Psychology, 43,* 268.

Baer, L., Jacobs, D. G., Cukor, P., O'Laughlen, J., Coyle, J. T., & Magruder, K. M. (1995). Automated telephone screening survey for depression. *Journal of the American Medical Association, 273,* 1943–1944.

Baer, R., Wetter, M., & Berry, T. (1992). Detection of under reporting of psychopathology on the MMPI: A meta-analysis. *Clinical Psychology Review, 12,* 509–525.

Baird, K. A., & Rupert, P. A. (1987). Clinical management of confidentiality: A survey of psychologists in seven states. *Professional Psychology: Research and Practice, 18,* 347–352.

Bales, R. F. (1950). *Interaction process analysis.* Cambridge, MA: Addison-Wesley.

Ballou, M., & Gabalac, N. W. (1985). *A feminist position on mental health.* Springfield, IL: Charles C. Thomas.

Bandura, A. (1969). *Principles of behavior modification.* New York: Holt, Rinehart and Winston.

Bandura, A. (1971). Psychotherapy based upon modeling principles. In A. E. Bergin & S. L. Garfield (Eds.), *Handbook of psychotherapy and behavior change: An empirical analysis.* New York: Wiley.

Bandura, A. (1977). Self-efficacy: Toward a unifying theory of behavioral change. *Psychological Review, 84,* 191–215.

Bandura, A. (1989). Human agency in cognitive theory. *American Psychologist, 44,* 1175–1184.

Bandura, A., Adams, N. E., & Beyer, J. (1977). Cognitive processes mediating behavioral change. *Journal of Personality and Social Psychology, 35,* 125–139.

Bandura, A., Jeffrey, R. W., & Wright, C. L. (1974). Efficacy of participant modeling as a function of response induction aids. *Journal of Abnormal Psychology, 83,* 56–64.

Bangert-Drowns, R. L. (1986). Review of developments in meta-analytic method. *Psychological Bulletin, 99,* 388–399.

Banks, W. M. (1972). The differential effects of race and social class in helping. *Journal of Clinical Psychology, 28,* 90–92.

Barak, A., & Fisher, W. A. (1989). Counselor and therapist gender bias? More questions than answers. *Professional Psychology: Research and Practice, 20,* 377–383.

Barker, P. (1986). *Basic family therapy* (2nd ed.). New York: Oxford University Press.

Barker, R. G., & Wright, H. F. (1951). *One boy's day.* New York: Harper and Row.

Barker, S. L., Funk, S. C., & Houston, B. K. (1988). Psychological treatment versus nonspecific factors: A meta-analysis of conditions that engender comparable expectations for improvement. *Clinical Psychology Review, 8,* 579–594.

Barkley, R. A. (1987). *Defiant children: Parent-teacher assignments.* New York: Guilford.

Barlow, D. H. (1977). Assessment of sexual behavior. In A. R. Ciminero, K. S. Calhoun, & H. E. Adams (Eds.), *Handbook of behavioral assessment.* New York: Wiley.

Barlow, D. H. (1981). On the relation of clinical research to clinical practice: Current issues, new directions. *Journal of Consulting and Clinical Psychology, 49,* 147–155.

Barlow, D. H. (1994). Psychological interventions in the era of managed competition. *Clinical Psychology: Science and Practice, 1,* 109–122.

Barlow, D. H., & Abel, G. G. (1976). Sexual deviation. In W. E. Craighead, A. E. Kazdin, & M. J. Mahoney (Eds.), *Behavior modification: Principles, issues, and applications.* Boston: Houghton Mifflin.

Barlow, D. H., & Cerny, J. A. (1988). *Psychological treatment of panic.* New York: Guilford.

Baron, R. S., Cutrona, E. E., Hicklin, D., Russell, D. W., & Lubaroff, D. M. (1990). Social support and immune function among spouses of cancer patients. *Journal of Personality and Social Psychology, 59,* 344–352.

Barrom, C. P., Shadish, W. R., Jr., & Montgomery, L. M. (1988). PhDs, PsyDs, and real-world constraints on scholarly activity: Another look at the Boulder model. *Professional Psychology: Research and Practice, 19,* 93–101.

Barron, F. (1953). Some test correlates of response to psychotherapy. *Journal of Consulting Psychology, 17,* 235–241.

Bartell, P. A., & Rubin, L. J. (1990). Dangerous liaisons: Sexual intimacies in supervision. *Professional Psychology: Research and Practice, 21,* 442–450.

Bartelstone, J. H., & Trull, T. J. (1995). Personality, life events, and depression. *Journal of Personality Assessment, 64,* 279–294.

Bartol, C. R., & Bartol, A. M. (1994). *Psychology and law: Research and application* (2nd ed.). Pacific Grove, CA: Brooks/Cole.

Bates, C. M., & Brodsky, A. M. (1989). *Sex in the therapy hour: A case of professional incest.* New York: Guilford Press.

Bateson, G., Jackson, D. D., Haley, J., & Weakland, J. H. (1956). Toward a theory of schizophrenia. *Behavioral Science, 1,* 251–264.

Beck, A. T. (1972). *Depression: Causes and treatment.* Philadelphia: University of Pennsylvania Press.

Beck, A. T. (1983). Cognitive therapy of depression: New perspectives. In P. J. Clayton & J. E. Barrett (Eds.), *Treatment of depression: Old controversies and new approaches* (pp. 265–290). New York: Raven.

Beck, A. T. (1991). Cognitive therapy: A 30-year retrospective. *American Psychologist, 46,* 368–375.

Beck, A. T. (1993). Cognitive therapy: Past, present, and future. *Journal of Consulting and Clinical Psychology, 61,* 194–198.

Beck, A. T., & Emery, G. (1985). *Anxiety disorders and phobias.* New York: Basic Books.

Beck, A. T., Freeman, A., & Associates. (1990). *Cognitive therapy of personality disorders.* New York: Guilford.

Beck, A. T., Rush, A. J., Shaw, B. F., & Emery, G. (1979). *Cognitive therapy of depression.* New York: Guilford.

Beck, A. T., Ward, C. H., Mendelson, M., Mock, J. E., & Erbaugh, J. K. (1962). Reliability of psychiatric diagnoses: II. A study of consistency of clinical judgments and ratings. *American Journal of Psychiatry, 119,* 351–357.

Bednar, R. L., & Kaul, T. J. (1994). Experimental group research: Can the canon fire? In A. E. Bergin & S. L. Garfield (Eds.), *Handbook of psychotherapy and behavior change* (4th ed.) (pp. 631–663). New York: Wiley.

Beers, C. W. (1908). *A mind that found itself.* New York: Longmans, Green.

Belar, C. D., Deardorff, W. W., & Kelly, K. E. (1987). *The practice of clinical health psychology.* New York: Pergamon.

Bell, J. E. (1961). *Family group therapy* (No. 64). Washington, DC: U.S. Department of Health, Education, and Welfare.

Bender, L. (1938). *A visual motor Gestalt test and its clinical use.* New York: American Orthopsychiatric Association.

Benedict, R. H., Schretlen, D., & Bobholz, J. H. (1992). Concurrent validity of three WAIS-R short forms in psychiatric inpatients. *Psychological Assessment, 4,* 322–328.

Ben-Porath, Y. S., & Waller, N. G. (1992). "Normal" personality inventories in clinical assessment: General requirements and the potential for using the NEO Personality Inventory. *Psychological Assessment, 4,* 14–19.

Benton, A. L. (1963). *The revised visual retention test* (3rd ed.). New York: The Psychological Corporation.

Benton, A. L. (1974). *Revised visual retention test* (4th ed.). New York: The Psychological Corporation.

Bereiter, C., & Engleman, S. (1966). *Teaching disadvantaged children in the preschool.* Englewood Cliffs, NJ: Prentice-Hall.

Bergin, A. E. (1971). The evaluation of therapeutic outcomes. In A. E. Bergin & S. L. Garfield (Eds.), *Handbook of psychotherapy and behavior change.* New York: Wiley.

Bergin, A. E. (1980). Negative effects revisited: A reply. *Professional Psychology, 11,* 93–100.

Bergin, A. E., & Garfield, S. L. (1994). *Handbook of psychotherapy and behavior change* (4th ed.). New York: Wiley.

Bergin, A. E., & Suinn, R. M. (1975). Individual psychotherapy and behavior therapy. In M. R. Rosenzweig & L. W. Porter (Eds.), *Annual review of psychology.* Palo Alto, CA: Annual Reviews.

Berkman, L. F. (1986). Social networks, support, and health: Taking the next step forward. *American Journal of Epidemiology, 123,* 559–562.

Berman, J. S., & Norton, N. L. (1985). Does professional training make a therapist more effective? *Psychological Bulletin, 98,* 401–407.

Berne, E. (1961). *Transactional analysis in psychotherapy.* New York: Grove Press.

Berne, E. (1964). *Games people play.* New York: Grove Press.

Bernstein, B. L., & Lecomte, C. (1981). Licensure in psychology: Alternative directions. *Professional Psychology, 12,* 200–208.

Bernstein, D. A., & Nietzel, M. T. (1973). Procedural variation in behavioral avoidance tests. *Journal of Consulting and Clinical Psychology, 41,* 165–174.

Berry, D., Baer, R., & Harris, M. (1991). Detection of malingering on the MMPI: A meta-analysis. *Clinical Psychology Review, 11,* 585–598.

Berry, D., Wetter, M., Baer, R., Larsen, L., Clark, C., & Monroe, K. (1992). MMPI-2 random responding indices: Validation using a self-report methodology. *Psychological Assessment, 4,* 340–345.

Bersoff, D. N. (1995). *Ethical conflicts in psychology.* Washington, DC: American Psychological Association.

Beutler, L. E. (1990). Introduction to the special series on advances in psychotherapy process research. *Journal of Consulting and Clinical Psychology, 58,* 263–264.

Beutler, L. E. (1995). Integrating and communicating findings. In L. E. Beutler & M. R. Berren (Eds.), *Integrative assessment of adult personality* (pp. 25–64). New York: Guilford.

Beutler, L. E., & Fisher, D. (1994). Combined specialty training in counseling, clinical, and school psychology: An idea whose time has come. *Professional Psychology: Research and Practice, 25,* 62–69.

Beutler, L. E., Machado, P.P.P., & Neufeldt, S. A. (1994). Therapist variables. In A. E. Bergin & S. L. Garfield (Eds.), *Handbook of psychotherapy and behavior change* (4th ed.) (pp. 229–269). New York: Wiley.

Bieri, J., Atkins, A. L., Briar, S., Learman, R. L., Miller, H., & Tripodi, T. (1966). *Clinical and social judgment: The discrimination of behavioral information.* New York: Wiley.

Bijou, S. W., Peterson, R. F., & Ault, M. H. (1968). A method to integrate descriptive and experimental field studies at the level of data and empirical concepts. *Journal of Applied Behavior Analysis, 1,* 175–191.

Binet, A., & Henri, V. (1896). Psychologie individuelle. *Année Psychologie, 3,* 296–332.

Binswanger, L. (1963). *Being-in-the-world: Selected papers of Ludwig Binswanger.* New York: Basic Books.

Blanck, G., & Blanck, R. (1974). *Ego psychology: Theory and practice.* New York: Columbia University Press.

Blashfield, R. K., & Draguns, J. G. (1976). Evaluative criteria for psychiatric classification. *Journal of Abnormal Psychology, 85,* 140–150.

Blau, T. H. (1984). *The psychologist as expert witness.* New York: Wiley-Interscience.

Bliss, R. E., Barvey, A. J., Heinold, J. W., & Hitchcock, J. L. (1989). The influence of situation and coping on relapse crisis outcomes after smoking cessation. *Journal of Consulting and Clinical Psychology, 57,* 443–449.

Block, J. (1995). A contrarian view of the five-factor approach to personality description. *Psychological Bulletin, 117,* 187–215.

Bloom, B. L. (1973). *Community mental health: A historical and critical analysis.* Morristown, NJ: General Learning Press.

Bloom, B. L. (1981). Focused single-session therapy: Initial development and evaluation. In S. H. Budman (Ed.), *Forms of brief therapy.* New York: Guilford Press.

Bloom, B. L. (1992). Computer-assisted psychological intervention: A review and commentary. *Clinical Psychology Review, 12,* 169–197.

Blouin, A. G. (1991). *Computerized Diagnostic Interview Schedule-Revised DSM-III-R* (Version 2.0). Computer program. Ontario, Canada: C-DIS Management Group.

Blouin, A. G., Perez, E. L., & Blouin, J. H. (1988). Computerized administration of the Diagnostic Interview Schedule. *Psychiatry Research, 23,* 335–344.

Blount, R. L., Santilli, L., & Stokes, T. F. (1989). Promoting oral hygiene in pediatric dentistry: A critical review. *Clinical Psychology Review, 9,* 737–746.

Boll, T. J. (1983). Neuropsychological assessment. In I. B. Weiner (Ed.), *Clinical methods in psychology* (2nd ed.). New York: Wiley-Interscience.

Boll, T. J., & Bryant, B. K. (1988). *Clinical neuropsychology and brain function: Research, measurement, and practice.* Washington, DC: American Psychological Association.

Bootzin, R. R., Acocella, J. R., & Alloy, L. B. (1993). *Abnormal psychology: Current perspectives* (6th ed.). New York: McGraw-Hill.

Boss, M. (1963). *Psychoanalysis and daseinanalysis.* New York: Basic Books.

Bouchard, T. J., Jr., & McGue, M. (1981). Familial studies of intelligence: A review. *Science, 212,* 1055–1059.

Bouhoutsos, J. C., Goodchilds, J. D., & Huddy, L. (1986). Media psychology: An empirical study of radio call-in psychology programs. *Professional Psychology: Research and Practice, 17,* 408–414.

Bowen, M. (1960). A family concept of schizophrenia. In D. D. Jackson (Ed.), *Etiology of schizophrenia.* New York: Basic Books.

Brannon, L., & Feist, J. (1997). *Health psychology: An introduction to behavior and health* (3rd ed.). Pacific Grove, CA: Brooks/Cole.

Brentar, J., & McNamara, J. R. (1991). The right to prescribe medication: Considerations for professional psychology. *Professional Psychology: Research and Practice, 22,* 179–187.

Breuer, J., & Freud, S. (1955). *Studies on hysteria.* Standard edition (Vol. 2). London: Hogarth Press. (First German edition published 1895.)

Brewin, C. R. (1988). *Cognitive foundations of clinical psychology.* London: Erlbaum.

Brodsky, A. M. (1982). Sex, race, and class issues in psychotherapy research. In J. H. Harvey & M. M. Parks (Eds.), *The master lecture series. Vol. 1: Psychotherapy research and behavior change.* Washington, DC: American Psychological Association.

Brodsky, S. L. (1991). *Testifying in court: Guidelines and maxims for the expert witness.* Washington, DC: American Psychological Association.

Brody, C. (Ed.). (1987). *Women's therapy groups: Paradigms of feminist treatment.* New York: Springer.

Brody, E. B., & Brody, N. (1976). *Intelligence: Nature, determinants, and consequences.* New York: Academic Press.

Brody, E. M., & Farber, B. A. (1989). Effects of psychotherapy on significant others. *Professional Psychology: Research and Practice, 20,* 116–122.

Brom, D., Kleber, R. J., & Defares, P. B. (1989). Brief psychotherapy for posttraumatic stress disorders. *Journal of Consulting and Clinical Psychology, 57,* 607–612.

Brooks, A. D. (1974). *Law, psychiatry, and the mental health system.* Boston: Little, Brown.

Broskowski, A. T. (1991). Current mental health care environments: Why managed care is necessary. *Professional Psychology: Research and Practice, 22,* 6–14.

Broskowski, A. T. (1995). The evolution of health care: Implications for the training and careers of psychologists. *Professional Psychology: Research and Practice, 26,* 156–162.

Broverman, I., Broverman, D., Clarkson, F., Rosenkrantz, P., & Vogel, S. (1970). Sex-role stereotypes and clinical judgments of mental health. *Journal of Consulting and Clinical Psychology, 34,* 1–7.

Brown, D., & Schulte, A. C. (1987). A social learning model of consultation. *Professional Psychology: Research and Practice, 18,* 283–287.

Brown, L. S. (1990). Taking account of gender in the clinical assessment interview. *Professional Psychology: Research and Practice, 21,* 12–17.

Brown, R. T., Buchanan, I., Doepke, K., Eckman, J. R., Baldwin, K., Goonan, B., & Schoenherr, S. (1993). Cognitive and academic functioning in children with sickle-cell disease. *Journal of Clinical Child Psychology, 22,* 207–218.

Bruehl, S. (1994). A case of borderline personality disorder. In P. T. Costa, Jr., & T. A. Widiger (Eds.), *Personality disorders and the five-factor model of personality* (pp. 189–198). Washington, DC: American Psychological Association.

Brunink, S. A., & Schroeder, H. E. (1979). Verbal therapeutic behavior of expert psychoanalytically oriented, gestalt, and behavior therapists. *Journal of Consulting and Clinical Psychology, 47,* 567–574.

Brunswik, E. (1947). *Systematic and representative design of psychological experiments with results in physical and social perception.* Berkeley: University of California Press.

Buckhout, R. (1975). Nearly 2000 witnesses can be wrong. *Social Action and the Law, 2,* 7.

Buckhout, R. (1980). Eyewitness identification and psychology in the courtroom. In G. Cooke (Ed.), *The role of the forensic psychologist.* Springfield, IL: Charles C. Thomas.

Budman, S. H., & Gurman, A. S. (1983). The practice of brief therapy. *Professional Psychology: Research and Practice, 14,* 277–292.

Budman, S. H., & Gurman, A. S. (1988). *Theory and practice of brief therapy.* New York: Guilford.

Bugental, J.F.T. (1964). The person who is the psychotherapist. *Journal of Consulting Psychology, 28,* 272–277.

Bugental, J.F.T. (1965). *The search for authenticity.* New York: Holt, Rinehart and Winston.

Bugental, J.F.T. (1978). *Psychotherapy and process: The fundamentals of an existential-humanistic approach.* Reading, MA: Addison-Wesley.

Buhler, C. (1971). Basic theoretical concepts of humanistic psychology. *American Psychologist, 26,* 378–386.

Buhler, C., & Allen, M. (1971). *Introduction to humanistic psychology.* Pacific Grove, CA: Brooks/Cole.

Burke, M. J., & Normand, J. (1987). Computerized psychological testing: Overview and critique. *Professional Psychology: Research and Practice, 18,* 42–51.

Buros, O. K. (Ed.). (1972). *Seventh mental measurements yearbook.* Highland Park, NJ: Gryphon Press.

Burton, D. B., Ryan, J. J., Paolo, A. M., & Mittenberg, W. (1994). Structural equation analysis of the Wechsler Adult Intelligence Scale-Revised in a normal elderly sample. *Psychological Assessment, 6,* 380–385.

Butcher, J. N. (1971). *Objective personality assessment.* Morristown, NJ: General Learning Press.

Butcher, J. N. (1990). *MMPI-2 in psychological treatment.* New York: Oxford University Press.

Butcher, J. N. (1995a). *Clinical personality assessment: Practical approaches.* New York: Oxford.

Butcher, J. N. (1995b). Interpretation of the MMPI-2. In L. E. Beutler & M. R. Berren (Eds.), *Integrative assessment of adult personality* (pp. 206–239). New York: Guilford.

Butcher, J. N. (1995c). How to use computer-based reports. In J. N. Butcher (Ed.), *Clinical personality assessment: Practical approaches* (pp. 78–94). New York: Oxford.

Butcher, J. N., Dahlstrom, W. G., Graham, J. R., Tellegen, A., & Kaemmer, B. (1989). *Minnesota Multiphasic Personality Inventory MMPI-2: Manual for administration and scoring.* Minneapolis: University of Minnesota Press.

Butcher, J. N., Graham, J. R., & Ben-Porath, Y. S. (1995). Methodological problems and issues in MMPI, MMPI-2, and MMPI-A research. *Psychological Assessment, 7,* 320–329.

Butcher, J. N., Graham, J. R., Williams, C. L., & Ben-Porath, Y. S. (1990). *Development and use of the MMPI-2 content scales.* Minneapolis: University of Minnesota Press.

Butcher, J. N., Kendall, P. C., & Hoffman, N. (1980). MMPI short forms: Caution. *Journal of Consulting and Clinical Psychology, 48,* 275–278.

Butcher, J. N., & Koss, M. P. (1978). Research on brief and crisis-oriented therapies. In S. L. Garfield & A. E. Bergin (Eds.), *Handbook of psychotherapy and behavior change* (2nd ed.). New York: Wiley.

Butcher, J. N., Williams, C. L., Graham, J. R., Archer, R., Tellegen, A., Ben-Porath, Y. S., & Kaemmer, B. (1992). *Minnesota multiphasic personality inventory—Adolescent (MMPI-A): Manual for administration, scoring, and interpretation.* Minneapolis: University of Minnesota Press.

Campbell, D., & Draper, R. (Eds.). (1985). *Applications of systemic family therapy: The Milan approach.* London: Grune and Stratton.

Campbell, M., Cohen, I. L., Perry, R., & Small, A. M. (1989). Psychopharmacological treatment. In T. H. Ollendick & M. Hersen (Eds.), *Handbook of child psychopathology* (2nd ed.). New York: Plenum.

Campbell, S. B. (1989). Developmental perspectives. In T. H. Ollendick & M. Hersen (Eds.), *Handbook of child psychopathology* (2nd ed.). New York: Plenum.

Caplan, G. (1961). *Prevention of mental disorders in children.* New York: Basic Books.

Caplan, G. (1964). *Principles of preventive psychiatry.* New York: Basic Books.

Caplan, G. (1970). *The theory and practice of mental health consultation.* New York: Basic Books.

Carr, M. A., Sweet, J. J., & Rossini, E. (1986). Diagnostic validity of the Luria-Nebraska Neuropsychological Test Battery—Children's Revision. *Journal of Consulting and Clinical Psychology, 54,* 354–358.

Cartwright, D. S. (1956). Note on "changes in psychoneurotic patients with and without psychotherapy." *Journal of Consulting Psychology, 20,* 403–404.

Casey, R. J., & Berman, J. S. (1985). The outcome of psychotherapy with children. *Psychological Bulletin, 98,* 388–400.

Cattell, R. B. (1965). *The scientific analysis of personality.* Baltimore: Penguin.

Cattell, R. B. (1987). *Intelligence: Its structure, growth and action.* Amsterdam: North-Holland.

Cautela, J. R. (1967). Covert sensitization. *Psychological Reports, 20,* 459–468.

Cautela, J. R. (1971, September). *Covert modeling.* Paper presented at the fifth annual meeting of the Association for the Advancement of Behavior Therapy, Washington, DC.

Cautela, J., Flannery, R., & Hanley, E. (1974). Covert modeling: An experimental test. *Behavior Therapy, 5,* 494–502.

Centers for Disease Control and Prevention. (1994, November 18). Surveillance for selected tobacco use behaviors: United States, 1900–1994. *CDC surveillance summaries. Morbidity and Mortality Weekly Report, 43,* no. SS3.

Chambless, D. L., Caputo, G. C., Bright, P., & Gallagher, R. (1984). Assessment of fear in agoraphobics: The body sensations questionnaire and the agoraphobic cognitions questionnaire. *Journal of Consulting and Clinical Psychology, 52,* 1090–1097.

Chambless, D. L., Sanderson, W. C., Shoham, V., Bennett Johnson, S., Pope, K. S., Crits-Christoph, P., Baker, M., Johnson, B., Woody, S. R., Sue, S., Beutler, L., Williams, D.A., & McCurry, S. (1996). An update on empirically validated therapies. *The Clinical Psychologist, 49,* 5–18.

Chapman, L. J., & Chapman, J. P. (1967). Genesis of popular but erroneous psychodiagnostic observations. *Journal of Abnormal Psychology, 72,* 193–204.

Chapman, L. J., & Chapman, J. P. (1969). Illusory correlation as an obstacle to the use of valid psychodiagnostic signs. *Journal of Abnormal Psychology, 74,* 271–280.

Chapman, L. J., & Chapman, J. P. (1985). Psychosis proneness. In M. Alpert (Ed.), *Controversies in schizophrenia* (pp. 157–174). New York: Guilford.

Chase, M. (1975). The impact of correctional programs: Absconding. In R. Moos (Ed.), *Evaluating correctional and community environments.* New York: Wiley.

Chesney, M. A. (1993). Health psychology in the 21st century: Acquired immunodeficiency syndrome as a harbinger of things to come. *Health Psychology, 12,* 259–268.

Child, I. L. (1973). *Humanistic psychology and the research tradition: Their several virtues.* New York: Wiley.

Chipeur, H. M., Rovine, M., & Plomin, R. (1990). LISREL modelling: Genetic and environmental influences on IQ revisited. *Intelligence, 14,* 11–29.

Christensen, A., & Jacobson, N. S. (1994). Who (or what) can do psychotherapy: The status and challenge of nonprofessional therapies. *Psychological Science, 5,* 8–14.

Christophersen, E. R., & Gyulay, J. E. (1981). Parental compliance with car seat usage: A positive approach with long-term follow-up. *Journal of Pediatric Psychology, 6,* 301–312.

Cicchetti, D. V. (1994). Guidelines, criteria, and rules of thumb for evaluating normed and standardized instruments in psychology. *Psychological Assessment, 6,* 284–290.

Ciminero, A. R., Calhoun, K. S., & Adams, H. E. (Eds.). (1986). *Handbook of behavioral assessment.* New York: Wiley-Interscience.

Clark, L. A., & Watson, D. (1995). Constructing validity: Basic issues in objective scale development. *Psychological Assessment, 7,* 309–319.

Cleckley, H. (1964). *The mask of sanity* (4th ed.). St. Louis, MO: Mosby.

Coates, T. J., & Thoresen, C. E. (1981). Treating obesity in children and adolescents: Is there any hope? In J. M. Ferguson & C. B. Taylor (Eds.), *The comprehensive handbook of behavioral medicine* (Vol. 2). New York: Spectrum.

Cohen, J. (1960). A coefficient of agreement for nominal scales. *Educational and Psychological Measurement, 20,* 37–46.

Cohen, S., & Lichtenstein, E. (1990). Partner behaviors that support quitting smoking. *Journal of Consulting and Clinical Psychology, 58,* 304–309.

Cohen, S., & Syme, S. L. (Eds.). (1985). *Social support and health.* Orlando, FL: Academic Press.

Colby, K. M. (1951). *A primer for psychotherapists.* New York: Ronald Press.

Comas-Diaz, L. (1992). The future of psychotherapy with ethnic minorities. *Psychotherapy, 29,* 88–94.

Combs, A. W., & Snygg, D. (1959). *Individual behavior.* New York: Harper and Row.

Committee on Ethical Guidelines for Forensic Psychologists. (1991). Specialty guidelines for forensic psychologists. *Law and Human Behavior, 15,* 655–665.

Committee on Women in Psychology. (1989). If sex enters into the psychotherapy relationship. *Professional Psychology: Research and Practice, 20,* 112–115.

Condry, J. (1977). Enemies of exploration: Self-initiated versus other-initiated learning. *American Psychologist, 35,* 459–477.

Constantine, L. L. (1986). *Family paradigms: The practice of theory in family planning.* New York: Guilford Press.

Conte, H. R. (1986). Multivariate assessment of sexual dysfunction. *Journal of Consulting and Clinical Psychology, 54,* 149–157.

Conway, J. B. (1977). Behavioral self-control of smoking through aversive conditioning and self-management. *Journal of Consulting and Clinical Psychology, 45,* 348–357.

Cooke, G. (1984). Forensic psychology. In R. G. Corsini (Ed.), *Encyclopedia of psychology* (Vol. 2). New York: Wiley-Interscience.

Corbishley, M. A., & Yost, E. B. (1995). Integrative assessment: A workbook. In L. E. Beutler & M. R. Berren (Eds.), *Integrative assessment of adult personality* (pp. 320–420). New York: Guilford.

Cornell, D. G. (1987). Role conflict in forensic clinical psychology: Reply to Arcaya. *Professional Psychology: Research and Practice, 18,* 429–432.

Corsini, R. J. (1957). *Methods of group psychotherapy.* New York: McGraw-Hill.

Costa, P. T., Jr., & McCrae, R. R. (1988). Personality in adulthood: A six-year longitudinal study of self-reports and spouse ratings on the NEO Personality Inventory. *Journal of Personality and Social Psychology, 54,* 853–863.

Costa, P. T., Jr., & McCrae, R. R. (1990). Personality disorders and the five-factor model of personality. *Journal of Personality Disorders, 4,* 362–371.

Costa, P. T., Jr., & McCrae, R. R. (1992). *Revised NEO Personality Inventory (NEO-PI-R) and NEO Five Factor Inventory (NEO-FFI): Professional manual.* Odessa, FL: Psychological Assessment Resources.

Costa, P. T., Jr., & Widiger, T. A. (1994). *Personality disorders and the five-factor model of personality.* Washington, DC: American Psychological Association.

Costello, A. J., Edelbrock, C. S., Dulcan, M. K., Kalas, R., & Klaric, S. H. (1984). *Report on the NIMH Diagnostic Interview Schedule for Children (DIS-C).* Washington, DC: National Institute of Mental Health.

Cowen, E. L. (1967). An overview and directions for future work. In E. L. Cowen, E. A. Gardner, & M. Zax (Eds.), *Emergent approaches to mental health problems.* New York: Appleton-Century-Crofts.

Cowen, E. L. (1973). Social and community intervention. In P. H. Mussen & M. R. Rosenzweig (Eds.), *Annual review of psychology.* Palo Alto, CA: Annual Reviews.

Cowen, E. L. (1978). Some problems in community program evaluation research. *Journal of Consulting and Clinical Psychology, 46,* 792–805.

Cowen, E. L. (1982). Help is where you find it: Four informal helping groups. *American Psychologist, 3(7),* 385–395.

Cowen, E. L. (1983). Primary prevention in mental health: Past, present, and future. In R. D. Felner, L. A. Jason, J. N. Moritsugu, & S. S. Farber (Eds.), *Preventive psychology: Theory, research, and practice* (pp. 11–30). New York: Pergamon.

Cowen, E. L. (1991). In pursuit of wellness. *American Psychologist, 46,* 404–408.

Cowen, E. L., Hightower, A. D., Johnson, D. B., Sarno, M., & Weissberg, R. P. (1989). State-level dissemination of a program for early detection and prevention of school maladjustment. *Professional Psychology: Research and Practice, 20,* 309–314.

Craig, R. J., & Horowitz, M. (1990). Current utilization of psychological tests at diagnostic practicum sites. *The Clinical Psychologist, 43,* 29–36.

Crespi, T. D. (1990). School psychologists in forensic psychology: Converging and diverging issues. *Professional Psychology: Research and Practice, 21,* 83–87.

Crits-Christoph, P. (1992). The efficacy of brief dynamic psychotherapy: A meta-analysis. *American Journal of Psychiatry, 149,* 151–158.

Cronbach, L. J. (1946). Response sets and test validity. *Educational and Psychological Measurement, 6,* 475–494.

Cronbach, L. J. (1975). Five decades of public controversy over mental testing. *American Psychologist, 30,* 1–14.

Cronbach, L. J., & Meehl, P. E. (1955). Construct validity in psychological tests. *Psychological Bulletin, 52,* 281–302.

Cross, T. L., Bazron, B. J., Dennis, K. W., & Isaacs, M. R. (1989). *Toward a cultural competent system of care* (Vol. I). Washington, DC: Georgetown University Child Development Center.

Culbertson, J. L. (1993). Clinical child psychology in the 1990s: Broadening our scope. *Journal of Clinical Child Psychology, 22,* 116–122.

Cummings, N. A. (1986). The dismantling of our health system: Strategies for the survival of psychological practice. *American Psychologist, 41,* 426–431.

Cummings, N. A. (1995). Impact of managed care on employment and training: A primer for survival. *Professional Psychology: Research and Practice, 26,* 10–15.

Curran, W. J. (1986). Ethical perspectives: Formal codes and standards. In W. J. Curran, A. L. McGarry, & S. A. Shah (Eds.), *Forensic psychiatry and psychology.* Philadelphia: F. A. Davis.

Cutler, B. L., & Penrod, S. D. (1995). *Mistaken identification: The eyewitness, psychology, and the law.* New York: Cambridge University Press.

Dahlstrom, W. G., Welsh, G. S., & Dahlstrom, L. E. (1972). *An MMPI handbook. Vol. 1: Clinical interpretation* (rev. ed.). Minneapolis: University of Minnesota Press.

Dahlstrom, W. G., Welsh, G. S., & Dahlstrom, L. E. (1975). *An MMPI handbook. Vol. 2: Research developments and applications.* Minneapolis: University of Minnesota Press.

Dale, R. H. I. (1988). State psychological associations, licensing criteria, and the "master's issue." *Professional Psychology: Research and Practice, 19,* 589–593.

D'Amato, R. C., Dean, R. S., & Holloway, A. F. (1987). A decade of employment trends in neuropsychology. *Professional Psychology: Research and Practice, 18,* 653–655.

Dana, R. H., & May, W. T. (1986). Health care megatrends and health psychology. *Professional Psychology: Research and Practice, 17,* 251–255.

Danish, S. J., & Smyer, M. A. (1981). Unintended consequences of requiring a license to help. *American Psychologist, 36,* 13–21.

Davies, R. M. (1987). Demise of the 3rd-year internship: The changing role of the internship in graduate training. *Professional Psychology: Research and Practice, 18,* 481–484.

Davison, G. C., & Neale, J. M. (1996). *Abnormal psychology* (6th ed., rev.). New York: Wiley.

Davison, G. C., Robins, C., & Johnson, M. K. (1983). Articulated thoughts during simulated situations: A paradigm for studying cognition in emotion and behavior. *Cognitive Therapy and Research, 1,* 17–40.

Davison, G. C., & Wilson, G. T. (1973). Processes of fear reduction in systematic desensitization: Cognitive and social reinforcement factors in humans. *Behavior Therapy, 4,* 1–21.

Dawes, R. M. (1979). The robust beauty of improper linear models in decision making. *American Psychologist, 34,* 571–582.

Dawes, R. M. (1994). *House of cards: Psychology and psychotherapy built on myth.* New York: Free Press.

Dawes, R. M., Faust, D., & Meehl, P. E. (1989). Clinical versus actuarial judgment. *Science, 243,* 1668–1674.

deCharms, R., Levy, J., & Wertheimer, M. (1954). A note on attempted evaluations of psychotherapy. *Journal of Clinical Psychology, 10,* 233–235.

Decker, J. B., & Stubblebine, J. M. (1972). Crisis intervention and prevention and psychiatric disability: A follow-up study. *American Journal of Psychiatry, 129,* 725–729.

DeLeon, P. H. (1988). Public policy and public service: Our professional duty. *American Psychologist, 43,* 309–315.

DeLeon, P. H., Fox, R. E., & Graham, S. R. (1991). Prescription privileges: Psychology's next frontier? *American Psychologist, 46,* 384–393.

DeLeon, P. H., Frank, R. G., & Wedding, D. (1995). Health policy and public policy: The political process. *Health Psychology, 14,* 493–499.

DeNelsky, G. Y. (1991). Prescription privileges for psychologists: The case against. *Professional Psychology. Research and Practice, 22,* 188–193.

Dew, M. A., Bromet, E. J., Brent, D., & Greenhouse, J. B. (1987). A quantitative literature review of the effectiveness of suicide prevention centers. *Journal of Consulting and Clinical Psychology, 55,* 239–244.

Digman, J. M. (1990). Personality structure: Emergence of the five-factor model. *Annual Review of Psychology, 41,* 417–470.

DiMatteo, M. R., & DiNicola, D. D. (1982). *Achieving patient compliance: The psychology of the medical practitioner's role.* New York: Pergamon.

Dobson, K. S. (1989). A meta-analysis of the efficacy of cognitive therapy for depression. *Journal of Consulting and Clinical Psychology, 57,* 414–419.

Dollard, J., & Miller, N. E. (1950). *Personality and psychotherapy.* New York: McGraw-Hill.

Dorken, H. (1975). Private professional sector innovations in higher education: The California School of Professional Psychology. *Journal of Community Psychology, 3,* 15–21.

Dorken, H., & Cummings, N. A. (1977). A school of psychology as innovation in professional education: The California School of Professional Psychology. *Professional Psychology, 8,* 129–148.

Drabman, R. S. (1985). Graduate training of scientist practitioner-oriented clinical psychologists: Where we can improve. *Professional Psychology: Research and Practice, 16,* 623–633.

Dryden, W., & Golden, W. L. (Eds.). (1987). *Cognitive behavioral approaches to psychotherapy.* Cambridge, England: Hemisphere/Harper and Row.

Dumont, F., & Lecomte, C. (1987). Inferential processes in clinical work: Inquiry into logical errors that affect diagnostic judgments. *Professional Psychology: Research and Practice, 18,* 433–438.

Dunn, T. G., Lushene, R. E., & O'Neil, H. F., Jr. (1972). Complete automation of the MMPI and a study of its response latencies. *Journal of Consulting and Clinical Psychology, 39,* 381–387.

Durlak, J. A. (1979). Comparative effectiveness of paraprofessional and professional helpers. *Psychological Bulletin, 86,* 80–92.

Durlak, J. A. (1981). Evaluating comparative studies of paraprofessional and professional helpers: A reply to Nietzel and Fisher. *Psychological Bulletin, 89,* 566–569.

Dush, D. M., Hirt, M. L., & Schroeder, H. E. (1983). Self-statement modification with adults: A meta-analysis. *Journal of Consulting and Clinical Psychology, 94,* 408–442.

Edwards, N. B. (1972). Case conference: Assertive training in a case of homosexual pedophilia. *Journal of Behavior Therapy and Experimental Psychiatry, 3,* 55–63.

Eisenstein, J. L., & Copeland, A. P. (1988). Cognitive behavioral assessment of children in health settings. In P. Karoly (Ed.), *Handbook of child health assessment: Biopsychosocial perspectives.* New York: Wiley-Interscience.

Ekehammar, B. (1974). Interactionism in personality from a historical perspective. *Psychological Bulletin, 81,* 1026–1048.

Elkins, P. D., & Roberts, M. C. (1983). Psychological preparation for pediatric hospitalization. *Clinical Psychology Review, 3,* 275–295.

Elliott, C. H. (1983). Behavioral medicine: Background and implications. In C. E. Walker (Ed.), *The handbook of clinical psychology: Theory, research, and practice* (Vol. 2). Pacific Grove, CA: Brooks/Cole.

Ellis, A. (1962). *Reason and emotion in psychotherapy.* New York: Lyle Stuart.

Ellis, A. (1973). *Humanistic psychotherapy: The rational-emotive approach.* New York: McGraw-Hill.

Ellis, A. (1977). A basic clinical theory of rational-emotive therapy. In A. Ellis & R. Grieger (Eds.), *Handbook of rational-emotive therapy.* New York: Springer.

Ellis, A., & Dryden, W. (1987). *The practice of rational-emotive therapy (RET).* New York: Springer.

Ellis, A., & Grieger, R. M. (1986). *Handbook of rational emotive therapy* (Vol. 2). New York: Springer.

Ellis, H. C. (1992). Graduate education in psychology: Past, present, and future. *American Psychologist, 47,* 570–576.

Emmelkamp, P.M.G. (1982). *Phobic and obsessive-compulsive disorders: Theory, research, and practice.* New York: Plenum.

Emmelkamp, P.M.G. (1994). Behavior therapy with adults. In A. E. Bergin & S. L. Garfield (Eds.), *Handbook of psychotherapy and behavior change* (4th ed.) (pp. 379–427). New York: Wiley.

Endler, N. S., & Okada, M. (1975). A multidimensional measure of trait anxiety: The S-R Inventory of General Trait Anxiousness. *Journal of Consulting and Clinical Psychology, 43,* 319–329.

Engel, G. L. (1977). The need for a new medical model: A challenge for biomedicine. *Science, 196,* 129–136.

English, H. B., & English, A. C. (1958). *A comprehensive dictionary of psychological and psychoanalytic terms.* New York: Longmans, Green.

Epstein, L. H., Valoski, A., Wing, R. R., & McCurley, J. (1994). Ten-year outcomes of behavioral family-based treatment for childhood obesity. *Health Psychology, 13,* 373–383.

Epstein, N., Schlesinger, S. E., & Dryden, W. (Eds.). (1988). *Cognitive behavioral therapy with families.* New York: Brunner/Mazel.

Epstein, S., & O'Brien, E. J. (1985). The person-situation debate in historical perspective. *Psychological Bulletin, 98,* 513–537.

Erdman, H. P., Klein, M. H., & Greist, J. H. (1985). Direct patient computer interviewing. *Journal of Consulting and Clinical Psychology, 53,* 760–773.

Erikson, E. H. (1956). The problem of ego identity. *Journal of the American Psychoanalytic Association, 4,* 56–121.

Evans, R. I. (1976). Smoking in children: Developing a social psychological strategy of deterrence. *Preventive Medicine, 5,* 122–127.

Exner, J. E., Jr. (1974). *The Rorschach: A comprehensive system.* New York: Wiley.

Exner, J. E., Jr. (1983). Rorschach assessment. In I. B. Weiner (Ed.), *Clinical methods in psychology* (2nd ed.). New York: Wiley-Interscience.

Exner, J. E., Jr. (1991). *The Rorschach: A comprehensive system.* Vol. 2: *Interpretation* (2nd ed.). New York: Wiley.

Exner, J. E., Jr. (1993). *The Rorschach: A comprehensive system.* Vol. 1: *Basic foundations* (3rd ed.). New York: Wiley.

Exner, J. E., Jr. (1995). Why use personality tests? A brief historical view. In J. N. Butcher (Ed.), *Clinical personality assessment: Practical approaches* (pp. 10–18). New York: Oxford.

Exner, J. E., Jr., & Exner, D. E. (1972). How clinicians use the Rorschach. *Journal of Personality Assessment, 36,* 402–408.

Eyde, L. D., Robertson, G. J., Krug, S. E., Moreland, K. L., Robertson, A. G., Shewan, C. M., Harrison, P. L., Porch, B. E., & Hammer, A. L. (1993). *Responsible test use: Case studies for assessing human behavior.* Washington, DC: American Psychological Association.

Eysenck, H. J. (1952). The effects of psychotherapy: An evaluation. *Journal of Consulting Psychology, 16,* 319–324.

Eysenck, H. J. (1965). The effects of psychotherapy. *International Journal of Psychiatry, 1,* 99–142.

Eysenck, H. J. (1966). *The effects of psychotherapy.* New York: International Science Press.

Eysenck, H. J., & Rachman, S. (Eds.). (1980). *Advances in behavior research and therapy* (Vol. 2). Oxford, England: Pergamon Press.

Fairburn, C. G., Jones, R., Peveler, R. C., Carr, S. J., Solomon, R. A., O'Connor, M. E., Burton, J., & Hope, R. A. (1991). Three psychological treatments for bulimia nervosa: A comparative trial. *Archives of General Psychiatry, 48,* 463–469.

Fairweather, G. W. (1967). *Methods in experimental social innovation.* New York: Wiley.

Fairweather, G. W., Sanders, D. H., Maynard, H., & Cressler, D. L. (1969). *Community life for the mentally ill: An alternative to institutional care.* Chicago: Aldine Atherton.

Falloon, I.R.H. (Ed.). (1988). *Handbook of behavioral family therapy.* New York: Guilford Press.

Faris, R., & Dunham, H. (1939). *Mental disorders in urban areas.* Chicago: University of Chicago Press.

Farquhar, J. W., et al. (1977). Community education for cardiovascular health. *Lancet, 1,* 1192–1195.

Farrell, A. D. (1989). Impact of computers on professional practice: A survey of current practices and attitudes. *Professional Psychology: Research and Practice, 20,* 172–178.

Farrell, A. D., Complair, P. S., & McCullough, L. (1987). Identification of target complaints by computer interview: Evaluation of the computerized assessment system for psychotherapy evaluation and research. *Journal of Consulting and Clinical Psychology, 55,* 691–700.

Faust, D. (1986). Research on human judgment and its application to clinical practice. *Professional Psychology: Research and Practice, 17,* 420–430.

Felner, R. D., DuBois, D., & Adan, A. (1991). Community-based intervention and prevention: Conceptual underpinnings and progress towards a science of community intervention and evaluation. In C. E. Walker (Ed.), *Clinical psychology: Historical and research foundations* (pp. 459–510). New York: Plenum.

Felner, R. D., Jason, L. A., Moritsugu, J. N., & Farber, S. S. (Eds.). (1983). *Preventive psychology: Theory, research, and practice.* New York: Pergamon Press.

Fensterheim, H. (1972). Assertive methods and marital problems. In R. D. Rubin, H. Fensterheim, J. D. Henderson, & L. P. Ullman (Eds.), *Advances in behavior therapy.* New York: Academic Press.

Feuerstein, M., Labbé, E. E., & Kuczmierczyk, A. R. (1986). *Health psychology: A psychological perspective.* New York: Plenum.

Filskov, S. B., & Goldstein, S. G. (1974). Diagnostic validity of the Halstead-Reitan Neuropsychological Battery. *Journal of Consulting and Clinical Psychology, 42,* 382–388.

Finn, S. E., & Tonsager, M. E. (1992). Therapeutic effects of providing MMPI-2 test feedback to college students awaiting therapy. *Psychological Assessment, 4,* 278–287.

First, M. B., Spitzer, R. L., Gibbon, M., & Williams, J.B.W. (1995). *Structured Clinical Interview for DSM-IV Axis I Disorders-Patient Edition SCID-I/P* (version 2.0). New York: Biometrics Research Department, New York State Psychiatric Institute.

Fisher, S., & Greenberg, R. (1977). *The scientific credibility of Freud's theories and therapy.* New York: Basic Books.

Fishman, D. B., Rotgers, F., & Franks, C. M. (1988). *Paradigms in behavior therapy: Present and promise.* New York: Springer.

Fiske, D. W. (1983). The meta-analytic revolution in outcome research. *Journal of Consulting and Clinical Psychology, 51,* 71–75.

Fitzgerald, B. J. (1958). Some relationships among projective tests, interview, and sociometric measures of dependent behavior. *Journal of Abnormal and Social Psychology, 56,* 199–204.

Fitzgerald, L. F., & Osipow, S. H. (1988). We have seen the future, but is it us? The vocational aspirations of graduate students in counseling psychology. *Professional Psychology: Research and Practice, 19,* 575–583.

Fitzgerald, R. V. (1973). *Conjoint marital therapy.* New York: Jason Aronson.

Flack, J. M., Amaro, H., Jenkins, W., Kunitz, S., Levy, J., Mixon, M., & Yu, E. (1995). Panel I: Epidemiology of minority health. *Health Psychology, 14,* 592–600.

Flaugher, R. L. (1978). The many definitions of test bias. *American Psychologist, 33,* 671–679.

Floyd, F. J., & Widaman, K. F. (1995). Factor analysis in the development and refinement of clinical assessment instruments. *Psychological Assessment, 7,* 286–299.

Foa, E. B., & Emmelkamp, P.M.G. (Eds.). (1983). *Failures in behavior therapy.* New York: Wiley.

Foley, V. D. (1974). *An introduction to family therapy.* New York: Grune and Stratton.

Follette, W. C., & Hayes, S. C. (1992). Behavioral assessment in the DSM era. *Behavioral Assessment, 14,* 293–295.

Foster, S. L., Bell-Dolan, D. J., & Burge, D. A. (1988). Behavioral observation. In A. S. Bellack & M. Hersen (Eds.), *Behavioral assessment: A practical handbook* (pp. 119–160). New York: Pergamon.

Foster, S. L., & Martinez, C. R., Jr. (1995). Ethnicity: Conceptual and methodological issues in child clinical research. *Journal of Clinical Child Psychology, 24,* 214–226.

Fowler, R. D., & Butcher, J. N. (1986). Critique of Matarazzo's view on computerized testing: All sigma and no meaning. *American Psychologist, 41,* 94–96.

Fox, R. E. (1976). Family therapy. In I. B. Weiner (Ed.), *Clinical methods in psychology.* New York: Wiley-Interscience.

Fox, R. E. (1982). The need for a reorientation of clinical psychology. *American Psychologist, 3(7),* 1051–1057.

Fox, R. E. (1988). Prescription privileges: Their implications for the practice of psychology. *Psychotherapy, 25,* 501–507.

Fox, R. E., & Barclay, A. (1989). Let a thousand flowers bloom: Or, weed the garden? *American Psychologist, 44,* 55–59.

Frame, C. L., & Matson, J. L. (1989). Historical trends in the recognition and assessment of childhood psychopathology. In C. L. Frame & J. L. Matson (Eds.), *Handbook of assessment in childhood psychopathology: Applied issues in differential diagnosis and treatment evaluation.* New York: Plenum.

Frank, G. (1984). The Boulder model: History, rationale, and critique. *Professional Psychology: Research and Practice, 15,* 417–435.

Frank, J. D. (1971). Therapeutic factors in psychotherapy. *American Journal of Psychotherapy, 25,* 350–361.

Frank, J. D. (1973). *Persuasion and healing* (rev. ed.). Baltimore: The Johns Hopkins University Press.

Frank, J. D. (1979). The present status of outcome studies. *Journal of Consulting and Clinical Psychology, 47,* 310–316.

Frank, J. D. (1982). Therapeutic components shared by all psychotherapies. In J. H. Harvey & M. M. Parks (Eds.), *The master lecture series.* Vol. 1: *Psychotherapy research and behavior change.* Washington, DC: American Psychological Association.

Frank, L. K. (1939). Projective methods for the study of personality. *Journal of Psychology, 8,* 389–413.

Frank, R. G., & Ross, M. J. (1995). The changing workforce: The role of health psychology. *Health Psychology, 14,* 519–525.

Frank, R. G., & VandenBos, G. R. (1994). Health care reform: The 1993–1994 evolution. *American Psychologist, 49,* 851–854.

Frankenhaeuser, M. (1980). Psychological aspects of life stress. In S. Levine & H. Ursin (Eds.), *Coping and health.* New York: Plenum.

Frankl, V. E. (1953). Logos and existence in psychotherapy. *American Journal of Psychotherapy, 7,* 8–15.

Frankl, V. E. (1960). Paradoxical intention: A logotherapeutic technique. *American Journal of Psychotherapy, 14,* 520–535.

Frankl, V. E. (1963). *Man's search for meaning* (rev. ed.). New York: Washington Square Press.

Frankl, V. E. (1965). *The doctor and the soul* (2nd ed.). New York: Knopf.

Frankl, V. E. (1967). *Psychotherapy and existentialism: Selected papers on logotherapy.* New York: Washington Square Press.

Franzen, M. D. (1989). *Reliability and validity in neuropsychological assessment.* New York: Plenum.

Freud, A. (1946a). *The ego and the mechanisms of defense.* New York: International Universities Press. (Originally published 1936.)

Freud, A. (1946b). *The psychoanalytic treatment of children.* New York: International Universities Press.

Freud, S. (1938). *The basic writings of Sigmund Freud.* New York: Modern Library.

Freud, S. (1953a). The interpretation of dreams. In J. Strachey (Ed. and Trans.), *The standard edition of the complete psychological works of Sigmund Freud* (Vols. 4 and 5). London: Hogarth Press. (Original work published 1900.)

Freud, S. (1953b). Fragments of an analysis of a case of hysteria. In J. Strachey (Ed. and Trans.), *The standard edition of the complete psychological works of Sigmund Freud* (Vol. 7). London: Hogarth Press. (Original work published 1905.)

Freud, S. (1955). Analysis of a phobia in a five-year-old boy. In J. Strachey (Ed. and Trans.), *The standard edition of the complete psychological works of Sigmund Freud* (Vol. 10). London: Hogarth Press. (Original work published 1909.)

Freud, S. (1959). The question of lay analysis. In J. Strachey (Ed. and Trans.), *The standard edition of the complete psychological works of Sigmund Freud* (Vol. 20). London: Hogarth Press. (Original work published 1926.)

Freud, S. (1960). Psychopathology of everyday life. In J. Strachey (Ed. and Trans.), *The standard edition of the complete psychological works of Sigmund Freud* (Vol. 6). London: Hogarth Press. (Original work published 1901.)

Freud, S. (1966). The dynamics of transference. In J. Strachey (Ed. and Trans.), *The standard edition of the complete psychological works of Sigmund Freud* (Vol. 12). London: Hogarth Press. (Original work published 1912.)

Friedman, H. S., & Booth-Kewley, S. (1987). The "disease-prone personality": A meta-analytic view of the construct. *American Psychologist, 42,* 539–555.

Friedman, M., & Rosenman, R. H. (1974). *Type A behavior and your heart.* New York: Knopf.

Friedman, R., Sobel, D., Myers, P., Caudill, M., & Benson, H. (1995). Behavioral medicine, clinical health psychology, and cost offset. *Health Psychology, 14,* 509–518.

Fruzzetti, A. E., & Jacobson, N. S. (1991). Marital and family therapy. In M. Hersen, A. E. Kazdin, & A. Bellack (Eds.), *The clinical psychology handbook* (2nd ed.) (pp. 643–666). New York: Pergamon.

Fuller, G. D. (1978). Current status of biofeedback in clinical practice. *American Psychologist, 33,* 39–48.

Fuselier, G. D. (1989). Hostage negotiation consultant: Emerging role for the clinical psychologist. *Professional Psychology: Research and Practice, 19,* 175–179.

Gallagher-Thompson, D., & Thompson, L. W. (1995). Efficacy of psychotherapeutic interventions with older adults. *The Clinical Psychologist, 48,* 24–30.

Galton, F. (1879). Psychometric experiments. *Brain, 2,* 149–162.

Garb, H. N. (1989). Clinical judgment, clinical training, and professional experience. *Psychological Bulletin, 105,* 387–396.

Garcia, L. T., & Griffitt, W. (1978). Impact of testimonial evidence as a function of witness characteristics. *Bulletin of the Psychonomic Society, 11,* 37–40.

Gardner, H. (1983). *Frames of mind: The theory of multiple intelligences.* New York: Basic Books.

Garfield, S. L. (1989). *The practice of brief psychotherapy.* Elmsford, NY: Pergamon Press.

Garfield, S. L. (1990). Issues and methods in psychotherapy process research. *Journal of Consulting and Clinical Psychology, 58,* 273–280.

Garfield, S. L. (1994). Research on client variables in psychotherapy. In A. E. Bergin & S. L. Garfield (Eds.), *Handbook of psychotherapy and behavior change* (4th ed.) (pp. 190–228). New York: Wiley.

Garfield, S. L., & Kurtz, R. (1976). Clinical psychologists in the 1970s. *American Psychologist, 31,* 1–9.

Gatchel, R. J., Baum, A., & Krantz, D. S. (1989). *An introduction to health psychology* (2nd ed.). New York: Random House.

Gatchel, R. J., & Blanchard, E. B. (1993). *Psychophysiological disorders: Research and clinical applications.* Washington, DC: American Psychological Association.

Geen, R. G. (1976). *Personality: The skein of behavior.* St. Louis, MO: Mosby.

Geer, J. H. (1965). The development of a scale to measure fear. *Behavior Research and Therapy, 3,* 45–53.

Gendlin, E. T. (1969). Focusing. *Psychotherapy: Theory, Research, and Practice, 6(1).*

Gendlin, E. T. (1981). *Focusing* (2nd ed.). New York: Bantam Books.

Gendlin, E. T. (1988). Carl Rogers (1902–1987). *American Psychologist, 43,* 127–128.

Gesten, E. L., & Jason, L. A. (1987). Social and community interventions. In M. R. Rosenzweig & L. W. Porter (Eds.), *Annual review of psychology.* Palo Alto, CA: Annual Reviews.

Getz, W. L., Fujita, B. N., & Allen, D. (1975). The use of paraprofessionals in crisis intervention: Evaluation of an innovative program. *American Journal of Community Psychology, 3,* 135–144.

Gilandas, A., Touyz, S., Beaumont, P.J.V., & Greenberg, H. P. (1984). *Handbook of neuropsychological assessment.* New York: Grune and Stratton.

Gilbert, L. A. (1987). Educating about gender and sexuality issues in graduate training: Introduction. *Professional Psychology: Research and Practice, 18,* 554.

Glass, D. C. (1977). *Behavior patterns, stress, and coronary disease.* Hillsdale, NJ: Erlbaum.

Gleitman, H. (1981). *Psychology.* New York: Norton.

Glick, I. D., Clarkin, J. F., & Kessler, D. R. (1987). *Marital and family therapy* (3rd ed.). Orlando, FL: Grune and Stratton.

Golann, S. E., & Eisdorfer, C. (Eds.). (1972). *Handbook of community mental health.* New York: Appleton-Century-Crofts.

Goldberg, D. C. (Ed.) (1985). *Contemporary marriage: Special issues.* Pacific Grove, CA: Brooks/Cole.

Goldberg, L. R. (1965). Diagnosticians versus diagnostic signs: The diagnosis of psychosis versus neurosis from the MMPI. *Psychological Monographs, 79(9),* (whole no. 602).

Goldberg, L. R. (1971). A historical survey of personality scales and inventories. In P. McReynolds (Ed.), *Advances in psychological assessment* (Vol. 2). Palo Alto, CA: Science and Behavior Books.

Goldberg, L. R. (1991). Human mind versus regression equation: Five contrasts. In D. Cicchetti & W. M. Grove (Eds.), *Thinking clearly about psychology* (Vol. 1) (pp. 173–184). Minneapolis: University of Minnesota Press.

Golden, C. J. (1977). Validity of the Halstead-Reitan Neuropsychological Battery in a mixed psychiatric and brain-injured population. *Journal of Consulting and Clinical Psychology, 45,* 1043–1051.

Golden, C. J. (1981). *Diagnosis and rehabilitation in clinical neuropsychology.* Springfield, IL: Charles C. Thomas.

Golden, C. J. (1984). Neuropsychology. In R. J. Corsini (Ed.), *Encyclopedia of psychology.* New York: Wiley-Interscience.

Golden, C. J., Hammeke, T. A., & Purisch, A. O. (1978). Diagnostic validity of standardized neuropsychological battery derived from Luria's neuropsychological tests. *Journal of Consulting and Clinical Psychology, 46,* 1258–1265.

Golden, C. J., Purisch, A. D., & Hammeke, T. A. (1985). *Luria-Nebraska Neuropsychological Battery: Forms I and II manual.* Los Angeles: Western Psychological Services.

Golden, C. J., Zillmer, E., & Spiers, M. (1992). *Neuropsychological assessment and intervention.* Springfield, IL: Charles C. Thomas.

Golden, M. (1964). Some effects of combining psychological tests on clinical inferences. *Journal of Consulting Psychology, 28,* 440–446.

Goldfried, M. R. (1971). Systematic desensitization as training in self-control. *Journal of Consulting and Clinical Psychology, 37,* 228–234.

Goldfried, M. R. (1976). Behavioral assessment. In I. B. Weiner (Ed.), *Clinical methods in psychology.* New York: Wiley-Interscience.

Goldfried, M. R. (1984). Training the clinician as scientist professional. *Professional Psychology: Research and Practice, 15,* 477–481.

Goldfried, M. R., & Davison, G. C. (1976). *Clinical behavior therapy.* New York: Holt, Rinehart and Winston.

Goldfried, M. R., & Davison, G. C. (1994). *Clinical behavior therapy: Expanded edition.* New York: Wiley.

Goldfried, M. R., Greenberg, L. S., & Marmar, C. (1990). Individual psychotherapy: Process and outcome. In M. R. Rosenzweig & L. W. Porter (Eds.), *Annual review of psychology.* Palo Alto, CA: Annual Reviews.

Golding, S. L., & Rorer, L. G. (1972). Illusory correlation and subjective judgment. *Journal of Abnormal Psychology, 80,* 249–260.

Goldman, H. H., Skodol, A. E., & Lave, T. R. (1992). Revising Axis V for DSM-IV: A review of measures of social functioning. *American Journal of Psychiatry, 149,* 1148–1156.

Goldstein, A. P. (1973). *Structured learning therapy: Toward a psychotherapy for the poor.* New York: Academic Press.

Goldstein, A. P., Heller, K., & Sechrest, L. B. (1966). *Psychotherapy and the psychology of behavior change.* New York: Wiley.

Goldstein, G., & Shelly, C. (1984). Discriminative validity of various intelligence and neuropsychological tests. *Journal of Consulting and Clinical Psychology, 52,* 383–389.

Goldstein, K., & Scheerer, M. (1941). Abstract and concrete behavior. *Psychological Monographs, 53(2).*

Good, G. E., Borst, T. S., & Wallace, D. L. (1994). Masculinity research: A review and critique. *Applied and Preventive Psychology, 3,* 3–14.

Good, G. E., Gilbert, L. A., & Scher, M. (1990). Gender aware therapy: A synthesis of feminist therapy and knowledge about gender. *Journal of Counseling and Development, 68,* 376–380.

Goodrich, T. J., Rampage, C., Ellman, B., & Halstead, K. (1988). *Feminist family therapy: A casebook*. New York: Norton.

Goodstein, L. D. (1988). Report of the executive vice president: 1987. *American Psychologist, 43,* 491–498.

Goodwin, A. H., & Sher, K. J. (1993). Effects of induced mood on diagnostic interviewing: Evidence for a mood and memory effect. *Psychological Assessment, 5,* 197–202.

Gordon, L. V. (1967). Clinical, psychometric, and worksample approaches in the prediction of success in Peace Corps training. *Journal of Applied Psychology, 51,* 111–119.

Gordon, R. (1983). An operational classification of disease prevention. *Public Health Reports, 98,* 107–109.

Gordon, R. (1987). An operational classification of disease prevention. In J. A. Steinberg, & M. M. Silverman (Eds.), *Preventing mental disorders* (pp. 20–26). Rockville, MD: Department of Health and Human Services.

Gottesman, I. I., & Prescott, C. A. (1989). Abuses of the MacAndrew MMPI Alcoholism Scale: A critical review. *Clinical Psychology Review, 9,* 223–242.

Gottlieb, M. C. (1990). Accusation of sexual misconduct: Assisting in the complaint process. *Professional Psychology: Research and Practice, 21,* 455–461.

Gottlieb, M. C., Sell, J. M., & Schoenfeld, L. S. (1988). Social/romantic relationships with present and former clients: State licensing board actions. *Professional Psychology: Research and Practice, 19,* 459–462.

Gottman, J., Notarius, C., Gonso, J., & Markman, H. (1976). *A couple's guide to communication*. Champaign, IL: Research Press.

Gottschalk, L. A., Fox, R. A., & Bates, D. E. (1973). A study of prediction and outcome in a mental health crisis clinic. *American Journal of Psychiatry, 130,* 1107–1111.

Gough, H. C. (1962). Clinical versus statistical prediction in psychology. In L. Postman (Ed.), *Psychology in the making: Histories of selected research problems*. New York: Knopf.

Gould, S. J. (1981). *The mismeasure of man*. New York: Norton.

Graham, F. K., & Kendall, B. S. (1960). Memory-for-Designs Test: Revised general manual. *Perceptual and Motor Skills, 11,* 147–188.

Graham, J. R. (1990). *MMPI-2: Assessing personality and psychopathology*. New York: Oxford University Press.

Grayson, H. M., & Tolman, R. S. (1950). A semantic study of concepts of clinical psychologists and psychiatrists. *Journal of Abnormal and Social Psychology, 45,* 216–231.

Green, B. F., Jr. (1978). In defense of measurement. *American Psychologist, 33,* 664–670.

Greenberg, L., Elliott, R., & Lietaer, G. (1994). Research on experiential psychotherapies. In A. E. Bergin & S. L. Garfield (Eds.), *Handbook of psychotherapy and behavior change* (4th ed.) (pp. 509–539). New York: Wiley.

Greene, E., & Loftus, E. F. (1981). When crimes are joined at trial: Institutionalized prejudice. Paper presented at American Psychology-Law Society, Boston.

Grencavage, L. M., & Norcross, J. C. (1990). Where are the commonalities among the therapeutic common factors? *Professional Psychology: Research and Practice, 21,* 372–378.

Grieger, R., & Boyd, J. (1980). *Rational-emotive therapy: A skills-based approach*. New York: Van Nostrand Reinhold.

Griest, J. H., Klein, M. H., Erdman, H. P., Bires, J. K., Bass, S. M., Machtinger, P. E., & Kresge, D. G. (1987). Comparison of computer- and interview-administered versions of the Diagnostic Interview Schedule. *Hospital and Community Psychiatry, 38,* 1304–1311.

Grossberg, J. M. (1964). Behavior therapy: A review. *Psychological Bulletin, 62,* 73–88.

Guerin, P. J. (Ed.). (1976). *Family and therapy: Theory and practice*. New York: Gardner Press.

Guilford, J. P. (1959). *Personality*. New York: McGraw-Hill.

Guilford, J. P. (1967). *The nature of human intelligence*. New York: McGraw-Hill.

Gurin, G., & Gurin, P. (1970). Expectancy theory in the study of poverty. *Journal of Social Issues, 26,* 83–104.

Gurman, A. S. (1977). Therapist and patient factors influencing the patient's perception of facilitative therapeutic conditions. *Psychiatry, 40,* 16–24.

Guy, J. D., Poelstra, P. L., & Stark, M. J. (1989). Personal distress and therapeutic effectiveness: National survey of psychologists practicing psychotherapy. *Professional Psychology: Research and Practice, 20,* 48–50.

Guy, J. D., Stark, M. J., & Poelstra, P. L. (1988). Personal therapy for psychotherapists before and after entering professional practice. *Professional Psychology: Research and Practice, 19,* 474–476.

Gynther, M. D. (1972). White norms and black MMPIs: A prescription for discrimination. *Psychological Bulletin, 78,* 386–402.

Gynther, M. D., & Green, S. B. (1980). Accuracy may make a difference, but does a difference make for accuracy?: A response to Pritchard and Rosenblatt. *Journal of Consulting and Clinical Psychology, 48,* 268–272.

Haaga, D.A.F., & Davison, G. C. (1993). An appraisal of rational-emotive therapy. *Journal of Consulting and Clinical Psychology, 61,* 215–220.

Hadley, S. W., & Strupp, H. H. (1977). Evaluations of treatment in psychotherapy: Naivete or necessity? *Professional Psychology, 8,* 478–490.

Hagen, R. L. (1981). Behavioral treatment of obesity: Progress but not panacea. In J. M. Ferguson & C. B. Taylor (Eds.), *The comprehensive handbook of behavioral medicine* (Vol. 2). New York: Spectrum.

Hahlweg, K., & Markman, H. J. (1988). Effectiveness of behavioral techniques in preventing and alleviating marital distress. *Journal of Consulting and Clinical Psychology, 56,* 440–447.

Haley, J. (1971). *Changing families: A family therapy reader.* New York: Grune and Stratton.

Hall, G.C.N., & Malony, H. N. (1983). Cultural control in psychotherapy with minority clients. *Psychotherapy: Theory, Research, and Practice, 20,* 131–142.

Hall, R. V., Lund, D., & Jackson, D. (1968). Effects of teacher attention on study behavior. *Journal of Applied Behavior Analysis, 1,* 1–12.

Halstead, W. C. (1947). *Brain and intelligence.* Chicago: University of Chicago Press.

Handelsman, M. M. (1990). Do written consent forms influence clients' impressions of therapists? *Professional Psychology: Research and Practice, 21,* 451–454.

Handelsman, M. M., & Galvin, M. D. (1988). Facilitating informed consent for outpatient psychotherapy: A suggested written format. *Professional Psychology: Research and Practice, 19,* 223–225.

Handler, L. (1988). Monkey see, monkey do: The prescription-writing controversy. *The Clinical Psychologist, 41,* 44–49.

Hare-Mustin, R. T. (1983). An appraisal of the relationship between women and psychotherapy. *American Psychologist, 38,* 593–601.

Harrison, R. (1965). Thematic apperceptive methods. In B. B. Wolman (Ed.), *Handbook of clinical psychology.* New York: McGraw-Hill.

Hartlage, L. C. (1987). Neuropsychology: Definition and history. In L. C. Hartlage, M. J. Asken, & J. L. Homshy (Eds.), *Essentials of neuropsychological assessment.* New York: Springer.

Hartmann, D. P., Roper, B. L., & Bradford, D. C. (1979). Some relationships between behavioral and traditional assessment. *Journal of Behavioral Assessment, 1,* 3–21.

Hartmann, H. (1939). Psychoanalysis and the concept of health. *International Journal of Psychoanalysis, 20,* 308–321.

Hartshorne, H., & May, M. A. (1928). *Studies in deceit.* New York: Macmillan.

Hartshorne, H., May, M. A., & Maller, J. B. (1929). *Studies in service and self-control.* New York: Macmillan.

Hartshorne, H., May, M. A., & Shuttleworth, F. K. (1930). *Studies in the organization of character.* New York: Macmillan.

Hathaway, S. R. (1943). *The Minnesota Multiphasic Personality Inventory.* Minneapolis: University of Minnesota Press.

Hattie, J. A., Sharpley, C. F., & Rogers, H. J. (1984). Comparative effectiveness of professional and paraprofessional helpers. *Psychological Bulletin, 95,* 534–541.

Havens, R. A., Colliver, J. A., Dimond, R. E., & Wesley, R. M. (1982). Ph.D. and MA clinical psychologists and MSWs in public mental health settings: A nationwide comparison. *Professional Psychology, 13,* 654–660.

Hawkins, J. D., & Catalano, R. F. (1992). *Communities that care.* San Francisco: Jossey-Bass.

Hayes, S. C., Nelson, R. O., & Jarrett, R. B. (1987). The treatment utility of assessment: A functional approach to evaluating assessment quality. *American Psychologist, 42,* 963–974.

Haynes, S. N., Lemsky, C., & Sexton-Radek, K. (1987). Why clinicians infrequently do research. *Professional Psychology: Research and Practice, 18,* 515–519.

Haynes, S. N., & O'Brien, W. H. (1990). Functional analysis in behavior therapy. *Clinical Psychology Review, 10,* 649–668.

Haynes, S. N., Richard, D.C.S., & Kubany, E. S. (1995). Content validity in psychological assessment: A functional approach to concepts and methods. *Psychological Assessment, 7,* 238–247.

Hazelrigg, M. D., Cooper, H. M., & Borduin, C. M. (1987). Evaluating the effectiveness of family therapies: An integrative review and analysis. *Psychological Bulletin, 101,* 428–442.

Heaton, R. K. (1981). *A manual for the card sorting test.* Odessa, FL: Psychological Assessment Resources.

Hebb, D. O. (1978). Open letter: To a friend who thinks the IQ is a social evil [Comment]. *American Psychologist, 33,* 1143–1144.

Heilbrun, K. S., Annis, L. V. (1988). Research and training in forensic psychology: National survey of forensic facilities. *Professional Psychology: Research and Practice, 19,* 211–215.

Heitler, J. B. (1976). Preparatory techniques in initiating expressive psychotherapy with lower-class, unsophisticated patients. *Psychological Bulletin, 83,* 339–352.

Heller, K. (1990). Social and community intervention. In M. R. Rosenzweig & L. W. Porter (Eds.), *Annual review of psychology.* Palo Alto, CA: Annual Reviews.

Heller, K., & Monahan, J. (1977). *Psychology and community change.* Pacific Grove, CA: Brooks/Cole.

Heller, K., Price, R. H., Reinharz, S., Riger, S., & Wandersman, A. (1984). *Psychology and community change: Challenges of the future.* Pacific Grove, CA: Brooks/Cole.

Helmes, E., & Reddon, J. R. (1993). A perspective on developments in assessing psychopathology: A critical review of the MMPI and MMPI-2. *Psychological Bulletin, 113,* 453–471.

Henderson, D., & Gillespie, R. D. (1950). *A text-book of psychiatry for students and practitioners* (7th ed.). Oxford: Oxford University Press.

Henggeler, S. W. (1994). A consensus: Conclusions of the APA Task Force Report on innovative models of mental health services for children, adolescents, and their families. *Journal of Clinical and Child Psychology, 23(Suppl.),* 3–6.

Henricks, W. H., Stiles, W. B. (1989). Verbal processes on psychological call-in programs: Comparisons with other help-intended interactions. *Professional Psychology: Research and Practice, 20,* 315–321.

Henry, B., Moffitt, T. E., Caspi, A., Langley, J., & Silva, P. A. (1994). On the "Remembrance of Things Past": A longitudinal evaluation of the retrospective method. *Psychological Assessment, 6,* 92–101.

Henry, W. E., Sims, J. H., & Spray, S. L. (1973). *Public and private lives of psychotherapists.* San Francisco: Jossey-Bass.

Henry, W. P., Strupp, H. H., Schacht, T. E., & Gaston, L. (1994). Psychodynamic approaches. In A. E. Bergin & S. L. Garfield (Eds.), *Handbook of psychotherapy and behavior change* (4th ed.) (pp. 467–508). New York: Wiley.

Herrnstein, R. J., & Murray, C. A. (1994). *The bell curve: Intelligence and class structure in American life.* New York: Free Press.

Hershey, J. M., Kopplin, D. A., & Cornell, J. E. (1991). Doctors of psychology: Their career experiences and attitudes toward degree and training. *Professional Psychology: Research and Practice, 22,* 351–356.

Hill, C. E. (1990). Exploratory in-session process research in individual psychotherapy: A review. *Journal of Consulting and Clinical Psychology, 58,* 288–294.

Hobbs, N. (1964). Mental health's third revolution. *American Journal of Orthopsychiatry, 34,* 822–833.

Hodges, K., Kline, J., Fitch, P., McKnew, D., & Cytryn, L. (1981). The Child Assessment Schedule: A diagnostic interview for research and clinical use. *Catalogue of Selected Documents in Psychology, 11,* 56.

Hokanson, J. E. (1983). *Introduction to the therapeutic process.* Reading, MA: Addison-Wesley.

Hollingshead, A. B., & Redlich, F. C. (1958). *Social class and mental illness: A community study.* New York: Wiley.

Hollon, S. D., & Beck, A. T. (1994). Cognitive and cognitive-behavioral therapies. In A. E. Bergin & S. L. Garfield (Eds.), *Handbook of psychotherapy and behavior change* (4th ed.) (pp. 428–466). New York: Wiley.

Holmes, T. H., & Rahe, R. H. (1967). The Social Readjustment Scale. *Journal of Psychosomatic Research, 11,* 213–218.

Holub, E. A., & Lee, S. S. (1990). Therapists' use of nonerotic physical contact: Ethical concerns. *Professional Psychology: Research and Practice, 21,* 115–117.

Homant, R. J., & Kennedy, D. B. (1987). Subjective factors in clinicians' judgments of insanity: Comparison of a hypothetical case and an actual one. *Professional Psychology: Research and Practice, 18,* 439–446.

Honaker, L. M. (1988). The equivalency of computerized and conventional MMPI administration: A critical review. *Clinical Psychology Review, 8,* 561–577.

Hooper, S. R., & Hynd, G. W. (1993). The neuropsychological basis of disorders affecting children and adolescents: An introduction. *Journal of Clinical Child Psychology, 22,* 138–140.

Hops, H., Biglan, A., Sherman, L., Arthur, J., Friedman, L., & Osteen, V. (1987). Home observations of family interactions of depressed women. *Journal of Consulting and Clinical Psychology, 5,* 341–346.

Horney, K. (1967). *Feminine psychology.* New York: Norton.

Horowitz, I. A., & Willging, T. E. (1984). *The psychology of law: Integrations and applications.* Boston: Little, Brown.

Hothersall, D. (1984). *History of psychology* (2nd ed.). New York: McGraw-Hill.

Howard, B. J., & Smith, J. (1986). Concepts for training in behavioral pediatrics. In N. A. Krasnegor, J. D. Arasteh, & M. T. Cataldo (Eds.), *Child health behavior: A behavioral pediatrics perspective*. New York: Wiley-Interscience.

Huber, C. H., & Baruth, L. G. (1987). *Ethical, legal, and professional issues in the practice of marriage and family therapy*. Columbus, OH: Merrill.

Huessy, H. (1972). Tactics and targets in the rural setting. In S. E. Golann & C. Eisdorfer (Eds.), *Handbook of community mental health*. New York: Appleton-Century-Crofts.

Hunt, R. G. (1960). Social class and mental illness: Some implications for clinical theory and practice. *American Journal of Psychiatry, 116,* 1065.

Hunter, J. E., & Hunter, R. F. (1984). Validity and utility of alternative predictors of job performance. *Psychological Bulletin, 96,* 72–98.

Hynd, G. W. (1988). *Neuropsychological assessment in clinical child psychology*. Newbury Park, CA: Sage.

Insel, P. M., & Moos, R. H. (1974). Psychological environments: Expanding the scope of human ecology. *American Psychologist, 29,* 179–188.

Institute of Medicine. (1994). *Summary: Reducing risks for mental disorders: Frontiers for preventive intervention research*. Washington, DC: National Academy Press.

International Neuropsychological Society-Division 40 Task Force. (1987). Guidelines for doctoral training programs in clinical neuropsychology. *The Clinical Neuropsychologist, 1,* 29–34.

Isaacs, K. S., & Haggard, E. A. (1966). Some methods used in the study of affect in psychotherapy. In L. A. Gottschalk & A. H. Auerbach (Eds.), *Methods of research in psychotherapy*. New York: Appleton-Century-Crofts.

Isaacs, M. R., & Benjamin, M. P. (1991). *Toward a cultural competent system of care* (Vol. II). Washington, DC: Georgetown University Child Development Center.

Iscoe, I. (1982). Toward a viable community health psychology: Caveats from the experiences of the community mental health movement. *American Psychologist, 37,* 961–965.

Iscoe, I., & Harris, L. C. (1984). Social and community interventions. In M. R. Rosenzweig & L. W. Porter (Eds.), *Annual review of psychology*. Palo Alto, CA: Annual Reviews.

Jackson, D. D. (1957). The question of family homeostasis. *Psychiatric Quarterly Supplement, 31,* 79–90.

Jackson, D. D., & Weakland, J. H. (1961). Conjoint family therapy: Some considerations on theory, technique, and results. *Psychiatry, 24,* 30–45.

Jacobson, E. (1938). *Progressive relaxation*. Chicago: University of Chicago Press.

Jacobson, N. S., & Gurman, A. S. (Eds.). (1986). *Clinical handbook of marital therapy*. New York: Guilford Press.

Jacobson, N. S., & Margolin, G. (1979). *Marital therapy: Strategies based on social learning and behavior exchange principles*. New York: Brunner/Mazel.

Jampala, V., Sierles, F., & Taylor, M. (1988). The use of DSM-III in the United States: A case of not going by the book. *Comprehensive Psychiatry, 29,* 39–47.

Jay, S. M., Elliott, C. H., Katz, E., & Siegel, S. E. (1987). Cognitive-behavioral and phenomenological interventions for children's distress during painful medical procedures. *Journal of Consulting and Clinical Psychology, 55,* 860–865.

Jesness, C. F. (1975). Comparative effectiveness of behavior modification and transactional analysis programs for delinquents. *Journal of Consulting and Clinical Psychology, 43,* 758–779.

Jessor, R., Liverant, S., & Opochinsky, S. (1963). Imbalance in need structure and maladjustment. *Journal of Abnormal and Social Psychology, 66,* 271–275.

Johnson, J. (1984). Psychological interventions and coping with surgery. In A. Baum, S. E. Taylor, & J. E. Singer (Eds.), *Handbook of psychology and health* (Vol. 4). Hillsdale, NJ: Erlbaum.

Johnson, J. H., Rasbury, W. G., & Siegel, L. J. (1986). *Approaches to child treatment: Introduction to theory, research, and practice*. New York: Pergamon Press.

Johnstone, B., & Frank, R. G. (1995). Neuropsychological assessment in rehabilitation: Current limitations and applications. *NeuroRehabilitation, 5,* 75–86.

Jones, A. (1991). Psychological functioning in African Americans: A conceptual guide for use in psychotherapy. In R. L. Jones (Ed.), *Black psychology* (3rd ed.) (pp. 577–589). Berkeley, CA: Cobb & Henry.

Jones, B. P., & Butters, N. (1991). Neuropsychological assessment. In M. Hersen, A. E. Kazdin, & A. S. Bellack (Eds.), *The clinical psychology handbook* (2nd ed.) (pp. 406–429). New York: Pergamon.

Jones, M. C. (1924). The elimination of children's fears. *Journal of Experimental Psychology, 7,* 383–390.

Jones, R. R., Reid, J. B., & Patterson, G. R. (1975). Naturalistic observation in clinical assessment. In P. McReynolds (Ed.), *Advances in psychological assessment* (Vol. 3). San Francisco: Jossey-Bass.

Jourard, S. M. (1971). *Self-disclosure: An experimental analysis of the transparent self*. New York: Wiley.

Kagehiro, D. K. (1990). Psycholegal research on the Fourth Amendment. *Psychological Science, 1,* 187–193.

Kahneman, D., & Tversky, A. (1973). On the psychology of prediction. *Psychological Review, 80,* 237–251.

Kamphaus, R. W. (1993). *Clinical assessment of children's intelligence: A handbook for professional practice*. Boston, MA: Allyn & Bacon.

Kane, M. T. (1982). The validity of licensure examinations. *American Psychologist, 37,* 911–918.

Kane, R. L., Parsons, O. A., Goldstein, G., & Moses, J. A., Jr. (1987). Diagnostic accuracy of the Halstead-Reitan and Luria-Nebraska neuropsychological batteries: Performance of clinical raters. *Journal of Consulting and Clinical Psychology, 55,* 783–784.

Kanfer, F. H., & Phillips, J. S. (1970). *Learning foundations of behavior therapy*. New York: Wiley.

Kanfer, R., Eyberg, S., & Krahn, G. L. (1992). Interviewing strategies in child assessment. In C. E. Walker & M. C. Roberts (Eds.), *Handbook of clinical child psychology* (2nd ed.) (pp. 49–62). New York: Wiley.

Kaplan, E., Fine, D., Morris, R., & Delis, D. C. (1991). *WAIS-R NI: Manual*. San Antonio, TX: The Psychological Corporation.

Kaplan, M. (1983). A woman's view of DSM-III. *American Psychologist, 38,* 786–792.

Kaplan, L. M., & Reich, W. (1991). *Manual for Diagnostic Interview for Children and Adolescents-Revised (DICA-R)*. St. Louis, MO: Washington University.

Kaplan, R. M., Atkins, C. J., & Lenhard, L. (1982). Coping with a stressful sigmoidoscopy: Evaluations of cognitive and relaxation preparations. *Journal of Behavioral Medicine, 5,* 67–82.

Kass, F., Spitzer, R. L., & Williams, J. B. (1983). An empirical study of the issue of sex bias in the diagnostic criteria of DSM-III Axis II Personality Disorders. *American Psychologist, 38,* 799–801.

Kassin, S. M., & Wrightsman, L. S. (1979). On the requirements of proof: The timing of judicial instruction and mock juror verdicts. *Journal of Personality and Social Psychology, 37,* 1877–1887.

Kassin, S. M., & Wrightsman, L. S. (1988). *The American jury on trial: Psychological perspectives*. New York: Hemisphere.

Kaufman, A. S. (1990). *Assessing adolescent and adult intelligence*. Boston, MA: Allyn & Bacon.

Kaufman, K. L., Holden, E. W., & Walker, C. E. (1989). Future directions in pediatric and clinical child psychology. *Professional Psychology: Research and Practice, 20,* 148–152.

Kausler, D. H. (1991). *Experimental psychology, cognition, and human aging* (2nd ed.). New York: Springer-Verlag.

Kazdin, A. E. (1977). *The token economy: A review and evaluation*. New York: Plenum.

Kazdin, A. E. (1978). Evaluating the generality of findings in analogue therapy research. *Journal of Consulting and Clinical Psychology, 46,* 673–686.

Kazdin, A. E. (1979). Nonspecific treatment factors in psychotherapy outcome research. *Journal of Consulting and Clinical Psychology, 47,* 846–851.

Kazdin, A. E. (1985). Selection of target behaviors: The relationship of the treatment focus to clinical dysfunction. *Behavioral Assessment, 7,* 33–47.

Kazdin, A. E. (1987). Treatment of antisocial behavior in children: Current status and future directions. *Psychological Bulletin, 102,* 187–203.

Kazdin, A. E. (1988). *Child psychotherapy: Developing and identifying effective treatments*. Elmsford, NY: Pergamon Press.

Kazdin, A. E. (1989). *Behavior modification in applied settings* (4th ed.). Pacific Grove, CA: Brooks/Cole.

Kazdin, A. E. (1990). Psychotherapy for children and adolescents. *Annual Review of Psychology, 41,* 21–54.

Kazdin, A. E. (1992). *Methodological issues and strategies in clinical research*. Washington, DC: American Psychological Association.

Kazdin, A. E. (1994). Methodology, design, and evaluation in psychotherapy research. In A. E. Bergin & S. L. Garfield (Eds.), *Handbook of psychotherapy and behavior change* (4th ed.) (pp. 19–71). New York: Wiley.

Kazdin, A. E., & Bass, D. (1989). Power to detect differences between alternative treatments in comparative psychotherapy outcome research. *Journal of Consulting and Clinical Psychology, 57,* 138–147.

Kazdin, A. E., Bass, D., Ayers, W. A., & Rodgers, A. (1990). Empirical and clinical focus of child and adolescent psychotherapy research. *Journal of Consulting and Clinical Psychology, 58,* 729–740.

Kazdin, A. E., & Mascitelli, S. (1982). Covert and overt rehearsal and homework practice in developing assertiveness. *Journal of Consulting and Clinical Psychology, 50,* 250–258.

Keefe, R.S.E. (1995). The contribution of neuropsychology to psychiatry. *American Journal of Psychiatry, 152,* 6–15.

Keith-Spiegel, P., & Koocher, G. P. (1985). *Ethics in psychology: Professional standards and cases.* New York: Random House.

Keller, P. A., & Podrygula, S. (1990). Clinical psychology and the rural community. *The Clinical Psychologist, 10,* 5–9.

Kelly, G. A. (1955). *The psychology of personal constructs* (Vols. 1 and 2). New York: Norton.

Kelly, J. G., Snowden, L. R., & Muñoz, R. F. (1977). Social and community interventions. In M. R. Rosenzweig & L. W. Porter (Eds.), *Annual review of psychology.* Palo Alto, CA: Annual Reviews.

Kempel, L. T. (1973). Orientation errors during successive administration of the Memory-for-Designs Test. *Journal of Consulting and Clinical Psychology, 41,* 314.

Kempler, W. (1973). Gestalt therapy. In R. J. Corsini (Ed.), *Current psychotherapies.* Itasca, IL: Peacock.

Kendall, P. C. (1993). Cognitive-behavioral therapies with youth: Guiding theory, current status, and emerging developments. *Journal of Consulting and Clinical Psychology, 61,* 235–247.

Kendall, P. C., & Butcher, J. N. (Eds.). (1982). *Handbook of research methods in clinical psychology.* New York: Wiley.

Kendall, P. C., & Hollon, S. D. (Eds.). (1979). *Cognitive behavioral interventions: Theory, research, and procedures.* New York: Academic Press.

Kendall, P. C., & Hollon, S. D. (Eds.). (1981). *Assessment strategies for cognitive-behavioral interventions.* New York: Academic Press.

Kent, R. N., & Foster, S. L. (1977). Direct observational procedures: Methodological issues in naturalistic settings. In A. R. Ciminero, K. S. Calhoun, & H. E. Adams (Eds.), *Handbook of behavioral assessment.* New York: Wiley.

Kent, R. N., Miner, G., & Ray, B. (1974). *Clinic observer manual.* Stony Brook: State University of New York.

Kessler, R. C., McGonagle, K. A., Zhao, S., Nelson, C. B., Hughes, M., Eshleman, S., Wittchen, H., & Kendler, K. S. (1994). Lifetime and 12-month prevalence of DSM-III-R psychiatric disorders in the United States. *Archives of General Psychiatry, 51,* 8–19.

Kiesler, C. A. (1977). The training of psychiatrists and psychologists [Editorial]. *American Psychologist, 32,* 107–108.

Kiesler, C. A. (1982a). Mental hospitals and alternative care: Noninstitutionalization as potential public policy for mental patients. *American Psychologist, 37,* 349–360.

Kiesler, C. A. (1982b). Public and professional myths about mental hospitalization. *American Psychologist, 37,* 1323–1339.

Kiesler, C. A., & Morton, T. L. (1988). Psychology and public policy in the "health care revolution." *American Psychologist, 43,* 993–1003.

Kiesler, D. J. (1966). Some myths of psychotherapy research and the search for a paradigm. *Psychological Bulletin, 65,* 110–136.

Kinney, J. M., Madsen, B., Fleming, T., & Haapala, D. A. (1977). Homebuilders: Keeping families together. *Journal of Consulting and Clinical Psychology, 45,* 667–683.

Kleinmuntz, B. (1972). *Computers in personality assessment.* Morristown, NJ: General Learning Press.

Kleinmuntz, B. (1990). Why we still use our heads instead of formulas: Toward an integrative approach. *Psychological Bulletin, 107,* 296–310.

Klerman, G. L., Weissman, M. M., Rounsaville, B. J., & Chevron, E. S. (1984). *Interpersonal psychotherapy of depression.* New York: Basic Books.

Kline, P. (1981). *Fact and fantasy in Freudian theory* (2nd ed.). London: Methuen.

Klingman, A. (1987). A school-based emergency crisis intervention in a mass school disaster. *Professional Psychology: Research and Practice, 18,* 604–612.

Klosko, J. S., Barlow, D. H., Tassinari, R., & Cerny, J. A. (1990). A comparison of alprazolam and behavior therapy in treatment of panic disorder. *Journal of Consulting and Clinical Psychology, 58,* 77–84.

Kneisel, P. J., & Richards, G. P. (1988). Crisis intervention after the suicide of a teacher. *Professional Psychology: Research and Practice, 19,* 165–169.

Kobasa, S. C., & Maddi, S. R. (1977). Existential personality theory. In R. J. Corsini (Ed.), *Current personality theories.* Itasca, IL: Peacock.

Kohut, H. (1977). *The restoration of the self.* New York: International Universities Press.

Kolb, B., & Whishaw, I. Q. (1985). *Fundamentals of human neuropsychology* (2nd ed.). New York: W. H. Freeman.

Koocher, G. P. (1979). Credentialing in psychology: Close encounters with competence? *American Psychologist, 34,* 696–702.

Koppitz, E. M. (1964). *The Bender-Gestalt Test for young children.* New York: Grune and Stratton.

Koppitz, E. M. (1975). *The Bender-Gestalt Test for young children.* Vol. 11: *Research and application, 1963–1975.* New York: Grune and Stratton.

Korchin, S. J. (1976). *Modern clinical psychology.* New York: Basic Books.

Koss, M. P., Butcher, J. N., & Strupp, H. H. (1986). Brief psychotherapy methods in clinical research. *Journal of Consulting and Clinical Psychology, 54,* 60–67.

Koss, M. P., & Shiang, J. (1994). Research on brief psychotherapy. In A. E. Bergin & S. L. Garfield (Eds.), *Handbook of psychotherapy and behavior change* (4th ed.) (pp. 664–700). New York: Wiley.

Krantz, D. S., Grunberg, N. E., & Baum, A. (1985). Health psychology. In M. R. Rosenzweig & L. W. Porter (Eds.), *Annual review of psychology* (Vol. 36). Palo Alto, CA: Annual Reviews.

Krasnegor, N. A., Arasteh, J. D., & Cataldo, M. F. (Eds.). (1986). *Child health behavior: A behavioral pediatric perspective.* New York: Wiley-Interscience.

Krasner, L. (1963). *The therapist as a social reinforcer: Man or machine.* Paper presented at the meeting of the American Psychological Association, Philadelphia.

Krasner, L. (1971). The operant approach in behavior therapy. In A. E. Bergin & S. L. Garfield (Eds.), *Handbook of psychotherapy and behavior change.* New York: Wiley.

Krech, D. (1962). Cortical localization of function. In L. Postman (Ed.), *Psychology in the making.* New York: Knopf.

Kris, E. (1950). On preconscious mental processes. *Psychoanalytic Quarterly, 19,* 540–560.

Kurke, M. I. (1980). Forensic psychology: A threat and a response. *Professional Psychology, 11,* 72–77.

Kurz, R. B. (1987). Child health psychology. In G. C. Stone, S. M. Weiss, J. D. Matarazzo, N. E. Miller, J. Rodin, C. D. Belar, M. J. Follick, & J. E. Singer (Eds.), *Health psychology: A discipline and a profession.* Chicago: University of Chicago Press.

Kusché, C. A., Cook, E. T., & Greenberg, M. T. (1993). Neuropsychological and cognitive functioning in children with anxiety, externalizing, and comorbid psychopathology. *Journal of Clinical Child Psychology, 22,* 172–195.

L'Abate, L. (Ed.). (1985). *The handbook of family psychology and therapy* (Vols. 1 and 2). Pacific Grove, CA: Brooks/Cole.

L'Abate, L. (1986). *Systematic family therapy.* New York: Brunner/Mazel.

Lacks, P. (1984). *Bender-Gestalt screening for brain dysfunction.* New York: Wiley-Interscience.

Ladkin, J. F., & Levine, L. (1976). Interpreting psychological test results to the hospitalized consumer. *Professional Psychology, 7,* 161–166.

Lafferty, P., Beutler, L. E., & Crago, M. (1989). Differences between more and less effective psychotherapists: A study of select therapist variables. *Journal of Consulting and Clinical Psychology, 57,* 76–80.

La Greca, A. M., & Stone, W. L. (1992). Assessing children through interviews and behavioral observations. In C. E. Walker & M. C. Roberts (Eds.), *Handbook of clinical child psychology* (2nd ed.) (pp. 63–83). New York: Wiley.

La Greca, A. M., Stone, W. L., Drotar, D., & Maddux, J. (1988). Training in pediatric psychology: Survey results and recommendations. *Journal of Pediatric Psychology, 13,* 121–139.

Lahey, B. B., Hart, E. L., Pliska, S., Applegate, B., & McBurnett, K. (1993). Neurophychological correlates of conduct disorder: A rationale and review of research. *Journal of Clinical Child Psychology, 22,* 141–153.

Lahey, B. B., Hynd, G. W., Stone, P. A., Piacentini, J. C., & Frick, P. J. (1989). Neuropsychological test performance and the attention deficit disorders: Clinical utility of the Luria-Nebraska Neuropsychological Battery Children's Revision. *Journal of Consulting and Clinical Psychology, 57,* 112–116.

Lambert, M. J., & Bergin, A. E. (1994). The effectiveness of psychotherapy. In A. E. Bergin & S. L. Garfield (Eds.), *Handbook of psychotherapy and behavior change* (4th ed.) (pp. 143–189). New York: Wiley.

Lambert, M. J., DeJulio, S. S., & Stein, D. M. (1978). Therapist interpersonal skills: Process, outcome, methodological considerations and recommendations for future research. *Psychological Bulletin, 85,* 467–489.

Lambert, N. (1981). Psychological evidence in *Larry P. v. Wilson Riles:* An evaluation by a witness for the defense. *American Psychologist, 36,* 937–952.

Lamiell, J. T. (1987). *The psychology of personality: An epistemological inquiry.* New York: Columbia University Press.

Landman, J. T., & Dawes, R. M. (1982). Psychotherapy outcome: Smith and Glass' conclusions stand up under scrutiny. *American Psychologist, 37,* 504–516.

Lang, P. J., & Lazovik, A. D. (1963). Experimental desensitization of a phobia. *Journal of Abnormal and Social Psychology, 66,* 519–525.

Langer, E. J., & Rodin, J. (1976). The effects of choice and enhanced personal responsibility for the aged: A field experiment in an institutional setting. *Journal of Personality and Social Psychology, 34,* 191–198.

Lanyon, R. I., & Goodstein, L. D. (1982). *Personality assessment* (2nd ed.). New York: Wiley.

Lassen, C. L. (1973). Effect of proximity on anxiety and communication in the initial psychiatric interview. *Journal of Abnormal Psychology, 81,* 226–232.

Laurent, J., Swerdlik, M., & Ryburn, M. (1992). Review of the validity research on the Stanford-Binet Intelligence Scale: Fourth edition. *Psychological Assessment, 4,* 102–112.

Lazarus, A. A. (1961). Group therapy of phobic disorders by systematic desensitization. *Journal of Abnormal and Social Psychology, 63,* 504–510.

Lazarus, A. A. (1971). *Behavior therapy and beyond.* New York: McGraw-Hill.

Lazarus, A. A. (1975). Multimodal behavior therapy. In G. M. Gazda (Ed.), *Basic approaches to group psychotherapy and group counseling* (2nd ed.). Springfield, IL: Charles C. Thomas.

Lazarus, A. A. (1977). Has behavior therapy outlived its usefulness? *American Psychologist, 32,* 550–554.

Lazarus, A. A. (1980). Toward delineating some causes of change in psychotherapy. *Professional Psychology, 11,* 863–870.

Ledwidge, B. (1978). Cognitive behavior modification: A step in the wrong direction? *Psychological Bulletin, 85,* 353–375.

Lehman, A. K., & Salovey, P. (1990). Psychotherapist orientation and expectations for liked and disliked patients. *Professional Psychology: Research and Practice, 21,* 385–391.

Leitenberg, H., Agras, W. S., Barlow, D. H., & Oliveau, D. C. (1969). Contribution of selective positive reinforcement and therapeutic instructions to systematic desensitization therapy. *Journal of Abnormal Psychology, 74,* 113–118.

Leli, D. A., & Filskov, S. B. (1979). Relationship of intelligence to education and occupation as signs of intellectual deterioration. *Journal of Consulting and Clinical Psychology, 47,* 702–707.

Lemere, F., & Voegtlin, W. (1950). An evaluation of the aversion treatment of alcoholism. *Quarterly Journal of Studies on Alcohol, 11,* 199–204.

Levine, M. (1982). *The history and politics of community mental health.* New York: Oxford University Press.

Levine, M., & Perkins, D. V. (1987). *Principles of community psychology: Perspectives and applications.* New York: Oxford University Press.

Levitsky, A., & Perls, F. S. (1970). The rules and games of Gestalt therapy. In J. Fagan & I. L. Sheperd (Eds.), *Gestalt therapy now.* Palo Alto, CA: Science and Behavior Books.

Levitt, E. E., & French, J. (1992). Projective testing of children. In C. E. Walker & M. C. Roberts (Eds.), *Handbook of clinical child psychology* (2nd ed.) (pp. 149–162). New York: Wiley.

Levy, D. A. (1989). Social support and the media: Analysis of responses by radio psychology talk show hosts. *Professional Psychology: Research and Practice, 20,* 73–78.

Levy, J. (1938). Relationship therapy. *American Journal of Orthopsychiatry, 8,* 64–69.

Levy, L. H. (1963). *Psychological interpretation.* New York: Holt, Rinehart, and Winston.

Levy, L. H. (1984). The metamorphosis of clinical psychology: Toward a new charter as human services psychology. *American Psychologist, 39,* 486–494.

Lewinsohn, P. M., & Shaffer, M. (1971). Use of home observations as an integral part of the treatment of depression: Preliminary report and case studies. *Journal of Consulting and Clinical Psychology, 37,* 87–94.

Lezak, M. D. (1995). *Neuropsychological assessment* (3rd ed.). New York: Oxford University Press.

Liberman, R. P. (1970). Behavioral approaches to family and couple therapy. *American Journal of Orthopsychiatry, 40,* 106–118.

Liberman, R. P. (1972). Behavioral modification of schizophrenia: A review. *Psychological Bulletin, 1,* 37–48.

Lidz, T., Cornelison, A., Fleck, S., & Terry, D. (1957a). Intrafamilial environment of the schizophrenic patient: 1. The father. *Psychiatry, 20,* 329–342.

Lidz, T., Cornelison, A., Fleck, S., & Terry, D. (1957b). Intrafamilial environment of schizophrenic patients: 2. Marital schism and marital skew. *American Journal of Psychiatry, 114,* 241–248.

Lieberman, M. A., Yalom, I. D., & Miles, M. B. (1973). *Encounter groups: First facts.* New York: Basic Books.

Linden, W., & Wen, F. K. (1990). Therapy outcome research, health care policy, and the continuing lack of accumulated knowledge. *Professional Psychology: Research and Practice, 21,* 482–488.

Lindsay, S.J.E., & Powell, G. E. (1989). Practical issues of investigation in clinical child psychology. In S. Lindsay & G. Powell (Eds.), *An introduction to clinical child psychology.* Aldershot, England: Gower.

Lindsley, O. R., & Skinner, B. F. (1954). A method for the experimental analysis of the behavior of psychotic patients. *American Psychologist, 9,* 419–420.

Lindzey, G. (1961). *Projective techniques and cross-cultural research*. New York: Appleton-Century-Crofts.

Lindzey, G., Bradford, J., Tejessy, C., & Davids, A. (1959). Thematic Apperception Test: An interpretive lexicon for clinician and investigator. *Journal of Clinical Psychology Monograph Supplement* (No. 12).

Lipovsky, J. A. (1988). Internship year in clinical psychology training as a professional adolescence. *Professional Psychology: Research and Practice, 19,* 606–608.

Little, K. B., & Shneidman, E. S. (1959). Congruencies among interpretations of psychological test and anamnestic data. *Psychological Monographs, 73(6),* (whole no. 476).

Livermore, J. M., Malmquist, C. P., & Meehl, P. E. (1968). On the justifications for civil commitment. *University of Pennsylvania Law Review, 117,* 75–96.

Loftus, E. F. (1979). *Eyewitness testimony*. Cambridge, MA: Harvard University Press.

Loftus, E. F. (1983). Silence is not golden. *American Psychologist, 38,* 564–572.

Loftus, E. F., Miller, D. G., & Burns, H. J. (1978). Semantic integration of verbal information into a visual memory. *Journal of Experimental Psychology, 4,* 19–31.

Logue, M. B., Sher, K. J., & Frensch, P. A. (1992). Purported characteristics of adult children of alcoholics: A possible "Barnum effect." *Professional Psychology: Research and Practice, 23,* 226–232.

Loh, W. D. (1984). *Social research in the judicial process: Cases, readings, and text*. New York: Russell Sage Foundation.

Long, S. (Ed.). (1988). *Six group therapies*. New York: Plenum.

Lopez, S. R. (1989). Patient variable biases in clinical judgment: Conceptual overview and methodological considerations. *Psychological Bulletin, 106,* 184–203.

Lopez, S. R., Grover, K. P., Holland, D., Johnson, M. J., Kain, C. D., Kanel, K., Mellins, C. A., & Rhyne, M. C. (1989). Development of culturally sensitive psychotherapists. *Professional Psychology: Research and Practice, 20,* 369–376.

Lorion, R. P. (1974). Patient and therapist variables in the treatment of low-income patients. *Psychological Bulletin, 81,* 344–354.

Lorr, M. (1986). Classifying psychotics: Dimensional and categorical approaches. In T. Millon & G. L. Klerman (Eds.), *Contemporary directions in psychopathology: Toward the DSM-IV*. New York: Guilford Press.

Louttit, C. M. (1936). *Clinical psychology*. New York: Harper.

Lubin, B. (1976). Group therapy. In I. B. Weiner (Ed.), *Clinical methods in psychology*. New York: Wiley-Interscience.

Lubin, B., Larsen, R. M., & Matarazzo, J. D. (1984). Patterns of psychological test usage in the United States: 1935–1982. *American Psychologist, 39,* 451–454.

Luborsky, L., & Spence, D. P. (1978). Quantitative research on psychoanalytic therapy. In S. L. Garfield & A. E. Bergin (Eds.), *Handbook of psychotherapy and behavior change* (2nd ed.). New York: Wiley.

Luria, A. R. (1973). *The working brain*. New York: Basic Books.

MacGregor, R., Ritchie, A. M., Serrano, A. C., & Schuster, F. P. (1964). *Multiple impact therapy with families*. New York: McGraw-Hill.

MacLeod, R. B. (1964). Phenomenology: A challenge to experimental psychology. In T. W. Wann (Ed.), *Behaviorism and phenomenology: Contrasting bases for modern psychology*. Chicago: University of Chicago Press.

Maddi, S. R. (1989). *Personality theories: A comparative analysis* (5th ed.). Pacific Grove, CA: Brooks/Cole.

Madsen, C. H., Jr., & Becker, W. C. (1968). Rules, praise, and ignoring: Elements of elementary classroom control. *Journal of Applied Behavior Analysis, 1,* 139–150.

Magaro, P. (1969). A prescription treatment model based upon social class and pre-morbid adjustment. *Psychotherapy, 6,* 57–70.

Mahoney, M. J. (1977a). Some applied issues in self-monitoring. In J. D. Cone & R. P. Hawkins (Eds.), *Behavioral assessment: New directions in clinical psychology*. New York: Brunner/Mazel.

Mahoney, M. J. (1977b). Reflections on the cognitive-learning trend in psychotherapy. *American Psychologist, 32,* 5–13.

Mahoney, M. J., & Arnkoff, D. B. (1979). Self-management. In O. F. Pomerleau & J. P. Brady (Eds.), *Behavioral medicine: Theory and practice*. Baltimore: Williams and Wilkins.

Maloney, M. P. (1985). *A clinician's guide to forensic assessment*. New York: Free Press.

Maloney, M. P., & Ward, M. P. (1976). *Psychological assessment: A conceptual approach*. New York: Oxford University Press.

Mann, J. M. (1991). Global AIDS: Critical issues for prevention in the 1990s. *International Journal of Health Sciences, 21,* 553–559.

Mann, P. A. (1978). *Community psychology: Concepts and applications*. New York: Free Press.

Manne, S. L., Redd, W. H., Jacobsen, P. B., Gorfinkle, K., Schorr, O., & Rapkin, B. (1990). Behavioral intervention to reduce child and parent distress during venipuncture. *Journal of Consulting and Clinical Psychology, 58,* 565–572.

Margolin, G. (1982). Ethical and legal considerations in marital and family therapy. *American Psychologist, 37,* 788–801.

Margraf, J., Ehlers, A., Roth, W. T., Clark, D. B., Sheikh, J., Agras, W. S., & Taylor, C. B. (1991). How "blind" are double-blind studies? *Journal of Consulting and Clinical Psychology, 59,* 184–187.

Mariotto, M. J., & Paul, G. L. (1974). A multimethod validation of the Inpatient Multidimensional Psychiatric Scale with chronically institutionalized patients. *Journal of Consulting and Clinical Psychology, 42,* 497–508.

Maris, R. W., & Connor, H. E. (1973). Do crisis services work? A follow-up of a psychiatric outpatient sample. *Journal of Health and Social Behavior, 14,* 311–322.

Marlatt, G. A., & Gordon, J. R. (1985). *Relapse prevention maintenance strategies in the treatment of addictive behaviors.* New York: Guilford.

Marmar, C. R. (1990). Psychotherapy process research: Programs, dilemmas, and future directions. *Journal of Consulting and Clinical Psychology, 58,* 265–272.

Marston, A. R. (1989). Some data on the performance of the Boulder model in training successful clinical researchers. *The Clinical Psychologist, 42,* 89–92.

Martin, S. (1995). APA to pursue prescription privileges. *APA Monitor, 26,* 6.

Marx, A. J., Test, M. A., & Stein, L. I. (1973). Extrahospital management of severe mental illness. *Archives of General Psychiatry, 29,* 505–511.

Mash, E. J., Terdal, L., & Anderson, K. (1973). The response class matrix: A procedure for recording parent-child interactions. *Journal of Consulting and Clinical Psychology, 40,* 163–164.

Masling, J. (1960). The influence of situational and interpersonal variables in projective testing. *Psychological Bulletin, 57,* 65–85.

Maslow, A. H. (1962). *Toward a psychology of being.* Princeton, NJ: Van Nostrand.

Mason, J. (1971). A re-evaluation of the concept of "nonspecificity" in stress theory. *Journal of Psychiatric Research, 8,* 325–333.

Masserman, J. H. (1943). *Behavior and neurosis: An experimental psycho-analytic approach to psychobiologic principles.* Chicago: University of Chicago Press.

Massoth, N. A., McGrath, R. E., Bianchi, C., & Singer, J. (1990). Psychologists' attitudes toward prescription privileges. *Professional Psychology: Research and Practice, 21,* 147–149.

Masters, J. C., Burish, T. G., Hollon, S. D., & Rimm, D. C. (1987). *Behavioral therapy: Techniques and empirical findings* (3rd ed.). San Diego, CA: Harcourt Brace Jovanovich.

Matarazzo, J. D. (1972). *Wechsler's measurement and appraisal of adult intelligence* (5th ed.). Baltimore: Williams and Wilkins.

Matarazzo, J. D. (1980). Behavioral health and behavioral medicine: Frontiers for a new health psychology. *American Psychologist, 35,* 807–817.

Matarazzo, J. D. (1983). The reliability of psychiatric and psychological diagnosis. *Clinical Psychology Review, 3,* 103–145.

Matarazzo, J. D. (1986). Computerized clinical psychological test interpretations: Unvalidated plus all mean and no sigma. *American Psychologist, 41,* 14–24.

Matarazzo, J. D. (1987). There is only one psychology, no specialties, but many applications. *American Psychologist, 42,* 893–903.

Matarazzo, J. D. (1990). Psychological assessment versus psychological testing. *American Psychologist, 45,* 999–1017.

Matarazzo, J. D., & Carmody, T. P. (1983). Health psychology. In M. Hersen, A. E. Kazdin, & A. S. Bellack (Eds.), *The clinical psychology handbook.* New York: Pergamon Press.

Matarazzo, J. D., & Wiens, A. N. (1972). *The interview: Research on its anatomy and structure.* Chicago: Aldine-Atherton.

Mathews, A. M. (1971). Psychophysiological approaches to the integration of desensitization and related procedures. *Psychological Bulletin, 76,* 73–91.

Mathews, K. E., Jr., & Canon, L. K. (1975). Environmental noise level as a determinant of helping behavior. *Journal of Personality and Social Psychology, 32,* 571–577.

Maton, K. (1988). Social support, organizational characteristics, psychological well-being, and group appraisal in three self-help group populations. *American Journal of Community Psychology, 16,* 53–78.

Matthews, K. A. (1984). Assessment of Type A, anger, and hostility in epidemiological studies of cardiovascular disease. In A. Ostfeld & E. Eaker (Eds.), *Measuring psychosocial variables in epidemiologic studies of cardiovascular disease.* Bethesda, MD: National Institutes of Health.

Mayne, T. J., Norcross, J. C., & Sayette, M. A. (1994a). *Insider's guide to graduate programs in clinical psychology: 1994/1995 edition.* New York: Guilford.

Mayne, T. J., Norcross, J. C., & Sayette, M. A. (1994b). Admission requirements, acceptance rates, and financial assistance in clinical psychology programs: Diversity across the practice-research continuum. *American Psychologist, 49,* 806–811.

Mays, D. T., & Franks, C. M. (Eds.) (1985). *Negative outcomes in psychotherapy and what to do about it.* New York: Springer.

McAlister, A. L., Perry, C., Killen, J., Slinkard, L. A., & Maccoby, N. (1980). Pilot study of smoking, alcohol, and drug abuse and prevention. *American Journal of Public Health, 70,* 719–721.

McBurnett, K., Harris, S. M., Swanson, J. M., Pfiffner, L. J., Tamm, L., & Freeland, D. (1993). Neuropsychological and physiological differentiation of inattention/overactivity and aggression/defiance symptom groups. *Journal of Clinical Child Psychology,* 165–171.

McConaughy, S. H. (1992). Objective assessment of children's behavioral and emotional problems. In C. E. Walker & M. C. Roberts (Eds.), *Handbook of clinical child psychology* (2nd ed.) (pp. 163–180). New York: Wiley.

McConnell, S. C. (1984). Doctor of Psychology degree: From hibernation to reality. *Professional Psychology: Research and Practice, 15,* 362–370.

McCrae, R. R., & John, O. P. (1992). An introduction to the Five-Factor Model and its applications. *Journal of Personality, 60,* 175–215.

McCubbin, M. A., & McCubbin, H. I. (1988). Family systems assessment. In P. Karoly (Ed.), *Handbook of child health assessment: Biopsychosocial perspectives.* New York: Wiley-Interscience.

McFall, R. M. (1991). Manifesto for a science of clinical psychology. *The Clinical Psychologist, 44,* 75–88.

McFall, R. M., & Lillesand, D. V. (1971). Behavior rehearsal with modeling and coaching in assertive training. *Journal of Abnormal Psychology, 77,* 313–323.

McGee, R. K. (1974). *Crisis intervention in the community.* Baltimore: University Park Press.

McGue, M., Bouchard, T. J., Jr., Iacono, W. G., & Lykken, D. T. (1993). Behavioral genetics of cognitive ability: A life-span perspective. In R. Plomin & G. E. McClearn (Eds.), *Nature, nurture, and psychology* (pp. 59–76). Washington, DC: American Psychological Association.

McMullen, S., & Rosen, R. C. (1979). Self-administered masturbation training in the treatment of primary orgasmic dysfunction. *Journal of Consulting and Clinical Psychology, 47,* 912–918.

McReynolds, P. (1975). Historical antecedents of personality assessment. In P. McReynolds (Ed.), *Advances in psychological assessment* (Vol. 3). San Francisco: Jossey-Bass.

McReynolds, P. (1987). Lightner Witmer: Little-known founder of clinical psychology. *American Psychologist, 42,* 849–858.

McReynolds, P. (1989). Diagnosis and clinical assessment: Current status and major issues. In M. R. Rosenzweig & L. W. Porter (Eds.), *Annual review of psychology.* Palo Alto, CA: Annual Reviews.

Meador, B. D., & Rogers, C. R. (1984). Client-centered therapy. In R. J. Corsini (Ed.), *Current psychotherapies* (2nd ed.). Itasca, IL: Peacock.

Meehl, P. E. (1945). An investigation of a general normality or control factor in personality testing. *Psychological Monographs, 59(4),* (whole no. 274).

Meehl, P. E. (1954). *Clinical versus statistical prediction.* Minneapolis: University of Minnesota Press.

Meehl, P. E. (1956). Wanted—A good cookbook. *American Psychologist, 11,* 263–272.

Meehl, P. E. (1957). When shall we use our heads instead of the formula? *Journal of Counseling Psychology, 4,* 268–273.

Meehl, P. E. (1965). Seer over sign: The first good example. *Journal of Experimental Research in Personality, 1,* 27–32.

Meehl, P. E. (1977). Why I do not attend case conferences. In P. E. Meehl (Ed.), *Psychodiagnosis: Selected papers.* New York: Norton. (First published by the University of Minnesota, 1973.)

Meehl, P. E. (1986). Causes and effects of my disturbing little book. *Journal of Personality Assessment, 50,* 370–375.

Meehl, P. E., & Rosen, A. (1955). Antecedent probability and the efficiency of psychometric signs, patterns, or cutting scores. *Psychological Bulletin, 52,* 194–216.

Megargee, E. I. (1970). The prediction of violence with psychological tests. In C. Spielberger (Ed.), *Current topics in clinical and community psychology.* New York: Academic Press.

Meichenbaum, D. (1977). *Cognitive-behavior modification.* New York: Plenum.

Meichenbaum, D., & Jaremko, M. E. (Eds.). (1983). *Stress reduction and prevention.* New York: Plenum.

Meier, M. J., Benton, A. L., & Diller, L. (Eds.). (1987). *Neuropsychological rehabilitation.* New York: Guilford Press.

Melamed, B. G., & Siegel, L. J. (1975). Reduction of anxiety in children facing hospitalization and surgery by use of filmed modeling. *Journal of Consulting and Clinical Psychology, 43,* 511–521.

Meltzoff, J. (1984). Research training for clinical psychologists: Point-counterpoint. *Professional Psychology: Research and Practice, 15,* 203–209.

Meltzoff, J., & Kornreich, M. (1970). *Research on psychotherapy.* New York: Atherton.

Menninger, K. (1963). *The vital balance: The life process in mental health and illness.* New York: Viking Press.

Mermelstein, R., Cohen, S., Lichtenstein, E., Baer, J. S., & Kamarck, T. (1986). Social support for smoking cessation and maintenance. *Journal of Consulting and Clinical Psychology, 54,* 447–453.

Meyer, A. E. (1981). The Hamburg Short Psychotherapy Comparison Experiment. *Psychotherapy and Psychosomatics, 35,* 81–207.

Meyer, A. J., Nash, J. D., McAlister, A. L., Maccoby, N., & Farquhar, J. W. (1980). Skills training in a cardiovascular education campaign. *Journal of Consulting and Clinical Psychology, 48,* 129–142.

Meyer, J. M., & Stunkard, A. J. (1993). Genetics and human obesity. In A. J. Stunkard & T. A. Wadden (Eds.), *Obesity: Theory and therapy* (137–149). New York: Raven Press.

Meyer, R. G., & Smith, S. R. (1977). A crisis in group therapy. *American Psychologist, 32,* 638–643.

Meyers, H. F., Kagawa-Singer, M., Kumanyika, S. K., Lex, B. W., & Markides, K. S. (1995). Behavioral risk factors related to chronic diseases in ethnic minorities. *Health Psychology, 14,* 613–621.

Miller, J. O., & Gross, S. J. (1973). Curvilinear trends in outcome research. *Journal of Consulting Psychology, 41,* 242–244.

Miller, N. E. (1983). Behavioral medicine: Symbiosis between laboratory and clinic. In M. R. Rosenzweig & L. W. Porter (Eds.), *Annual review of psychology* (Vol. 34). Palo Alto, CA: Annual Reviews.

Minuchin, C. F. (1974). *Families and family therapy.* Cambridge, MA: Harvard University Press.

Mio, J. S., & Morris, D. R. (1990). Cross-cultural issues in psychology training programs: An invitation for discussion. *Professional Psychology: Research and Practice, 21,* 434–441.

Mischel, W. (1968). *Personality and assessment.* New York: Wiley.

Misiak, H., & Sexton, V. S. (1966). *History of psychology: An overview.* New York: Grune and Stratton.

Monahan, J. (1976). The prevention of violence. In J. Monahan (Ed.), *Community mental health and the criminal justice system.* New York: Pergamon Press.

Monroe, S. M., & Simons, A. D. (1991). Diathesis-stress theories in the context of life stress research: Implications for the depressive disorders. *Psychological Bulletin, 110,* 406–425.

Moos, R. H. (1975). *Evaluating and changing community settings.* Paper presented at American Psychological Association meetings, Chicago.

Moreland, K. L. (1985). Validation of computer-based test interpretations: Problems and prospects. *Journal of Consulting and Clinical Psychology, 53,* 816–825.

Moreno, J. L. (1946). *Psychodrama* (Vol. 1, 2nd ed.). New York: Beacon House.

Moreno, J. L. (1947). *The theatre of spontaneity.* New York: Beacon House.

Moreno, J. L. (1959). Psychodrama. In S. Arieti (Ed.), *American handbook of psychiatry* (Vol. 2). New York: Basic Books.

Morey, L., & Ochoa, E. (1989). An investigation of adherence to diagnostic criteria: Clinical diagnosis of the DSM-III personality disorders. *Journal of Personality Disorders, 3,* 180–192.

Morgan, C. D., & Murray, H. A. (1935). A method for investigating fantasies: The Thematic Apperception Test. *Archives of Neurology and Psychiatry, 34,* 289–306.

Morgan, G. D., Ashenberg, Z. S., & Fisher, E. B., Jr. (1988). Abstinence from smoking and the social environment. *Journal of Consulting and Clinical Psychology, 56,* 298–301.

Morris, R. J., & Suckerman, K. R. (1974). Therapist warmth as a factor in automated systematic desensitization. *Journal of Consulting and Clinical Psychology, 42,* 244–250.

Morrison, J. K. (1976). An argument for mental patient advisory boards. *Professional Psychology, 7,* 127–131.

Morrison, R. L. (1988). Structured interviews and rating scales. In A. S. Bellack & M. Hersen (Eds.), *Behavioral assessment: A practical handbook* (pp. 252–277). New York: Pergamon.

Munsterberg, H. (1908). *On the witness stand.* New York: Doubleday, Page.

Murray, B. (1995). Master's program growth spurs educational concerns. *APA Monitor, 26,* 47.

Murray, D. M., Richards, P. S., Luepker, R. V., & Johnson, C. A. (1987). The prevention of cigarette smoking in children: Two- and three-year follow-up comparisons of four prevention strategies. *Journal of Behavioral Medicine, 10,* 596–611.

Murray, H. A. (1943). *Thematic Apperception Test manual.* Cambridge, MA: Harvard University Press.

Murray, H. A. (1938). *Explorations in personality: A clinical and experimental study of fifty men of college age.* New York: Oxford University Press.

Murstein, B. I. (1963). *Theory and research in projective techniques (emphasizing the TAT).* New York: Wiley.

Naar, R. (1982). *A primer of group psychotherapy.* New York: Human Sciences Press.

Naranjo, C. (1970). Present-centeredness: Technique, prescription, and ideal. In J. Fagan & I. Sheperd (Eds.), *Gestalt therapy now.* Palo Alto, CA: Science and Behavior Books.

Nash, E. H., Hoehn-Saric, R., Battle, C. C., Stone, A. R., Imber, S. D., & Frank, J. D. (1965). Systematic preparation of patients for short-term psychotherapy: 2. Relation to characteristics of patient, therapist, and the psychotherapeutic process. *Journal of Nervous and Mental Disease, 140*, 388–399.

Neisser, U. (1979). The concept of intelligence. In R. J. Sternberg & D. K. Dettermen (Eds), *Human intelligence: Perspectives on its theory and measurement*. Norwood, NJ: Ablex.

Newmark, C. S., Woody, G. G., Finch, A. J., Jr., & Ziff, D. R. (1980). MMPI short forms: A different perspective. *Journal of Consulting and Clinical Psychology, 48*, 279–283.

Nichols, W. C. (1988). *Marital therapy: An integrative approach*. New York: Guilford Press.

Nichols, W. C., & Everett, C. A. (1986). *Systemic family therapy: An integrative approach*. New York: Guilford Press.

Nicholson, R. A., & Berman, J. S. (1983). Is follow-up necessary in evaluating psychotherapy? *Psychological Bulletin, 93*, 261–278.

Nickelson, D. W. (1995). The future of professional psychology in a changing health care marketplace: A conversation with Russ Newman. *Professional Psychology: Research and Practice, 26*, 366–370.

Nietzel, M. T., Bernstein, D. A., & Russell, R. L. (1988). Assessment of anxiety and fear. In A. S. Bellack & M. Hersen (Eds.), *Behavioral assessment: A practical handbook* (pp. 280–312). New York: Pergamon.

Nietzel, M. T., & Dillehay, R. C. (1986). *Psychological consultation in the courtroom*. New York: Pergamon Press.

Nietzel, M. T., & Fisher, S. G. (1981). Effectiveness of professional and paraprofessional helpers: A comment on Durlak. *Psychological Bulletin 89*, 555–565.

Nietzel, M. T., Winett, R. A., MacDonald, M. L., & Davidson, W. S. (1977). *Behavioral approaches to community psychology*. New York: Pergamon Press.

Nisbett, R. E., & Ross, L. (1980). *Human inference: Strategies and shortcomings of social judgment*. Englewood Cliffs, NJ: Prentice-Hall.

Noll, J. O. (1974). Needed—A bill of rights for clients. *Professional Psychology, 5*, 3–12.

Norcross, J. C., Karg-Bray, R. S., & Prochaska, J. O. (1995). *Clinical psychologists in the 1990's*. Unpublished manuscript.

Norcross, J. C., & Prochaska, J. O. (1982). A national survey of clinical psychologists: Characteristics and activities. *The Clinical Psychologist, 35(Winter)*, 1 and 5–8.

Norcross, J. C., Prochaska, J. O, & Gallagher, K. M. (1989a). Clinical psychologists in the 1980s: I. Demographics, affiliations, and satisfactions. *The Clinical Psychologist, 42*, 29–39.

Norcross, J. C., Prochaska, J. O., & Gallagher, K. M. (1989b). Clinical psychologists in the 1990s: II. Theory, research, and practice. *The Clinical Psychologist, 42*, 45–53.

Novaco, R. W. (1977). Stress inoculation: A cognitive therapy for anger and its application to a case of depression. *Journal of Consulting and Clinical Psychology, 45*, 600–608.

Nunes, E. V., Frank, K., & Kornfeld, D. S. (1987). Psychologic treatment for the Type A behavior pattern and for coronary heart disease: A meta-analysis of the literature. *Psychosomatic Medicine, 49*, 159–173.

Nunnally, J. C., & Bernstein, I. H. (1994). *Psychometric theory* (3rd ed.). New York: McGraw-Hill.

Oakland, T., & Glutting, J. J. (1990). Examiner observations of children's WISC-R test-related behaviors: Possible socioeconomic status, race, and gender effects. *Psychological Assessment: A Journal of Consulting and Clinical Psychology, 2*, 86–90.

Obrzut, J. E., & Hynd, G. W. (Eds.). (1986a). *Child neuropsychology*. Vol. 1: *Theory and research*. Orlando, FL: Academic Press.

Obrzut, J. E., & Hynd, G. W. (Eds.). (1986b). *Child neuropsychology*. Vol. 2: *Clinical practice*. Orlando, FL: Academic Press.

O'Donohue, W., Plaud, J. J., Mowatt, A. M., & Fearon, J. R. (1989). Current status of curricula of doctoral training programs in clinical psychology. *Professional Psychology: Research and Practice, 20*, 196–197.

Office of Demographic, Employment, and Educational Research (ODEER), American Psychological Association (1993). *Surveys of licensed psychologists, PhDs and PsyDs in clinical psychology, lists of professional schools, and characteristics of 1993 doctorate recipients in psychology*. Washington, DC: Author.

Ogloff, J.R.P. (1991). A comparison of insanity defense standards on juror decision making. *Law and Human Behavior, 15*, 509–531.

O'Leary, K. D., & Becker, W. C. (1967). Behavior modification of an adjustment class: A token reinforcement program. *Exceptional Children, 33*, 637–642.

O'Leary, K. D., & Wilson, G. T. (1987). *Behavior therapy: Application and outcome* (2nd ed.). Englewood Cliffs, NJ: Prentice-Hall.

Ollendick, T. H., & Hersen, M. (1989). Basic issues, I. In T. H. Ollendick & M. Hersen (Eds.), *Handbook of child psychopathology* (2nd ed.). New York: Plenum.

Olson, R. A., & Elliott, C. H. (1983). Behavioral medicine: Assessment, patient management, and treatment interventions. In C. E. Walker (Ed.), *The handbook of clinical psychology: Theory, research, and practice* (Vol. 2). Pacific Grove, CA: Brooks/Cole.

O'Malley, S. S., Foley, S. H., Rounsaville, B. J., Watkins, J. T., Sotsky, S. M., Imber, S. D., & Elkin, I. (1988). Therapist competence and patient outcome in interpersonal psychotherapy of depression. *Journal of Consulting and Clinical Psychology, 56,* 496–501.

O'Neill, P., & Trickett, E. J. (1982). *Community consultation.* San Francisco: Jossey-Bass.

Orford, J. (1992). *Community psychology: Theory and practice.* New York: Wiley.

Orne, M., & Wender, P. (1968). Anticipatory socialization for psychotherapy: Method and rationale. *American Journal of Psychiatry, 124,* 88–98.

OSS Assessment Staff. (1948). *Assessment of men: Selection of personnel for the Office of Strategic Services.* New York: Rinehart.

Overall, J. E., & Gorham, D. R. (1962). The brief psychiatric rating scale. *Psychological Reports, 10,* 799–812.

Overall, J. E., & Hollister, L. E. (1982). Decision rules for phenomenological classification of psychiatric patients. *Journal of Consulting and Clinical Psychology, 50,* 535–545.

Overholser, J. C., & Fine, M. A. (1990). Defining the boundaries of professional competence: Managing subtle cases of clinical competence. *Professional Psychology: Research and Practice, 21,* 462–469.

Pace, T. M., Chaney, J. M., Mullins, L. L., & Olson, R. A. (1995). Psychological consultation with primary care physicians: Obstacles and opportunities in the medical setting. *Professional Psychology: Research and Practice, 26,* 123–131.

Padawer-Singer, A. M., & Barton, A. H. (1975). The impact of pretrial publicity on jurors' verdicts. In R. J. Simon (Ed.), *The jury system in America.* Newbury Park, CA: Sage.

Parker, K.C.H. (1983). A meta-analysis of the reliability and validity of the Rorschach. *Journal of Personality Assessment, 47,* 227–231.

Parker, K.C.H., Hanson, R. K., & Hunsley, J. (1988). MMPI, Rorschach, and WAIS: A meta-analytic comparison of reliability, stability, and validity. *Psychological Bulletin, 103,* 367–373.

Parks, C. W., Jr., & Hollon, S. D. (1988). Cognitive assessment. In A. S. Bellack & M. Hersen (Eds.), *Behavioral assessment: A practical handbook* (pp. 161–212). New York: Pergamon.

Parloff, M. B., London, P., & Wolfe, B. (1986). Individual psychotherapy and behavior change. In M. R. Rosenzweig & L. W. Porter (Eds.), *Annual review of psychology* (Vol. 37). Palo Alto, CA: Annual Reviews.

Parsons, O. A. (1986). Overview of the Halstead-Reitan Battery. In T. Incagndi, G. Goldstein, & C. J. Golden (Eds.), *Clinical application of neuropsychological test batteries.* New York: Plenum.

Pascal, G., & Suttell, B. (1951). *The Bender-Gestalt Test.* New York: Grune and Stratton.

Patterson, G. R. (1971). *Families: Applications of social learning to family life.* Champaign, IL: Research Press.

Patterson, G. R. (1977). Naturalistic observation in clinical assessment. *Journal of Abnormal Child Psychology, 5,* 307–322.

Paul, G. L. (1966). *Insight versus desensitization in psychotherapy: An experiment in anxiety reduction.* Stanford, CA: Stanford University Press.

Paul, G. L. (1967). Strategy of outcome research in psychotherapy. *Journal of Consulting Psychology, 31,* 109–118.

Pavkov, T. W., Lewis, D. A., & Lyons, J. S. (1989). Psychiatric diagnoses and racial bias: An empirical investigation. *Professional Psychology: Research and Practice, 20,* 364–368.

Pechacek, T. F. (1979). Modification of smoking behavior. In *Smoking and health: A report of the Surgeon General* (DHEW Publication No. PHS 79-50065). Washington, DC: US Government Printing Office.

Pedersen, N. L., Plomin, R., Nesselroade, J. R., & McClearn, G. E. (1992). A quantitative genetic analysis of cognitive abilities during the second half of the life span. *Psychological Science, 3,* 346–353.

Pedersen, P. B., & Marsella, A. J. (1982). The ethical crisis for cross-cultural counseling and therapy. *Professional Psychology, 13,* 492–500.

Pelham, W. E. (1993). Pharmacotherapy for children with attention-deficit hyperactivity disorder. *School Psychology Review, 22,* 199–227.

Pelham, W. E., & Hinshaw, S. P. (1992). Behavioral intervention for attention deficit-hyperactivity disorder. In S. M. Turner, K. S. Calhoun, & H. E. Adams (Eds.), *Handbook of clinical behavior therapy* (2nd ed.) (pp. 259–283). New York: Wiley.

Penk, W. E., Charles, H. L., & Van Hoose, T. A. (1978). Comparative effectiveness of day hospital and inpatient psychiatric treatment. *Journal of Consulting and Clinical Psychology, 46,* 94–101.

Penn, L. S. (1990). When the therapist must leave: Forced termination of psychodynamic therapy. *Professional Psychology: Research and Practice, 21,* 379–384.

Penn, N. E., Snehendu, K., Kramer, J., Skinner, J., & Zambrana, R. (1995). Panel IV: Ethnic minorities, health care systems, and behavior. *Health Psychology, 14,* 641–646.

Perlman, B. (1985). A national survey of APA-affiliated master-level clinicians: Description and comparison. *Professional Psychology: Research and Practice, 16,* 553–564.

Perls, F. S. (1947). *Ego, hunger, and aggression.* London: Allen and Unwin.

Perls, F. S. (1969a). *Gestalt therapy verbatim.* Lafayette, CA: Real People Press.

Perls, F. S. (1969b). *In and out of the garbage pail.* Palo Alto, CA: Science and Behavior Books.

Perls, F. S. (1970). Four lectures. In J. Fagan & I. L. Sheperd (Eds.), *Gestalt therapy now.* Palo Alto, CA: Science and Behavior Books.

Perls, F. S. (1973). *The Gestalt approach and eyewitness to therapy.* Palo Alto, CA: Science and Behavior Books.

Perls, F. S., Hefferline, R. F., & Goodman, P. (1951). *Gestalt therapy.* New York: Julian Press.

Perry v. Louisiana, 111 S.Ct. 449 (1990).

Peterson, D. R. (1968). The doctor of psychology program at the University of Illinois. *American Psychologist, 23,* 511–516.

Peterson, D. R. (1971). Status of the doctor of psychology program. *Professional Psychology, 2,* 271–275.

Peterson, D. R., Eaton, M. M., Levine, A. R., & Snepp, F. P. (1982). Career experiences of doctors of psychology. *Professional Psychology, 13,* 268–276.

Peterson, D. R., & Fishman, D. B. (Eds.). (1987). *Assessment for decision.* New Brunswick, NJ: Rutgers University.

Peterson, D. R., & Knudson, R. M. (1979). Work preferences of clinical psychologists. *Professional Psychology, 10,* 175–182.

Peterson, J. (1995). How are psychologists perceived by the public? *APA Monitor, 26,* 31.

Peterson, L. (1984). Teaching home safety in latchkey children: A comparison of two manuals and methods. *Journal of Applied Behavior Analysis, 17,* 279–293.

Peterson, L. (1989). Special series: Coping with medical illness and medical procedures. *Journal of Consulting and Clinical Psychology, 57,* 331–332.

Peterson, L., & Bell-Dolan, D. (1995). Treatment outcome research in child psychology: Realistic coping with the "Ten Commandments of Methodology." *Journal of Clinical Child Psychology, 24,* 149–162.

Peterson, L., & Brown, D. (1994). Integrating child injury and abuse-neglect research: Common histories, etiologies, and solutions. *Psychological Bulletin, 116,* 293–315.

Peterson, L., & Harbeck, C. (1988). *The pediatric psychologist: Issues in professional development and practice.* Champaign, IL: Research Press.

Peterson, L., & Roberts, M. C. (1992). Complacency, misdirection, and effective prevention of children's injuries. *American Psychologist, 47,* 1040–1044.

Peterson, L., & Sobell, L. (1994). Introduction to the state-of-the-art review series: Research contributions to clinical assessment. *Behavior Therapy, 25,* 523–531.

Peterson, L., Zink, M., & Farmer, J. (1992). Prevention of disorders in children. In C. E. Walker & M. C. Roberts (Eds.), *Handbook of clinical child psychology* (2nd ed.) (pp. 951–965). New York: Wiley.

Pettit, I. B., Pettit, T. F., & Welkowitz, J. (1974). Relationship between values, social class, and duration of psychotherapy. *Journal of Consulting and Clinical Psychology, 42,* 482–490.

Pfohl, B., Blum, N., & Zimmerman, M. (1994). *Structured interview for DSM-IV personality: SIDP-IV.* Iowa City, IA: Author.

Phares, E. J. (1967). The deviant personality. In H. Helson & W. Bevan (Eds.), *Contemporary approaches to psychology.* Princeton, NJ: Van Nostrand.

Phares, E. J. (1976). *Focus of control in personality.* Morristown, NJ: General Learning Press.

Phares, E. J. (1991). *Introduction to personality* (3rd ed.). New York: HarperCollins.

Philipson, I. J. (1993). *On the shoulders of women: The feminization of psychotherapy.* New York: Guilford.

Phillips, E. L. (1988). *Patient compliance: New light on health delivery systems in medicine and psychotherapy.* Lewiston, NY: Hans Huber.

Piacentini, J. C., Cohen, P., & Cohen, J. (1992). Combining discrepant diagnostic information from multiple sources: Are complex algorithms better than simple ones? *Journal of Abnormal Child Psychology, 20,* 51–63.

Piaget, G. W., & Lazarus, A. A. (1969). The use of rehearsal-desensitization. *Psychotherapy: Theory, Research, and Practice, 6,* 264–266.

Piedmont, R. L., Sokolove, R. L., & Fleming, M. Z. (1989). An examination of some diagnostic strategies involving the Weschler scales. *Psychological Assessment: A Journal of Consulting and Clinical Psychology, 1,* 181–185.

Piercy, F. P., Sprenkle, D. H., & Associates. (1986). *Family therapy sourcebook.* New York: Guilford Press.

Pinkerton, S., Hughes, H., & Wenrich, W. W. (1982). *Behavioral Medicine: Clinical application.* New York: Wiley-Interscience.

Piotrowski, C., Sherry, D., & Keller, J. W. (1985). Psychodiagnostic test usage: A survey of the Society for Personality Assessment. *Journal of Personality Assessment, 49,* 115–119.

Pipes, R. B., & Davenport, D. S. (1990). *Introduction to psychotherapy: Common clinical wisdom.* Englewood Cliffs, NJ: Prentice-Hall.

Plant, W. T., & Southern, M. L. (1972). The intellectual and achievement effects of preschool cognitive stimulation on poverty Mexican-American children. *Genetic Psychology Monographs, 86,* 141–173.

Plomin, R., DeFries, J. C., & McClearn, G. E. (1990). *Behavioral genetics: A primer* (2nd ed.). New York: Freeman.

Plotkin, W. B., & Rice, K. M. (1981). Biofeedback as a placebo: Anxiety reduction facilitated by training in either suppression or enhancement of alpha brainwaves. *Journal of Consulting and Clinical Psychology, 49,* 590–596.

Poche, C., Brouwer, R., & Swearingen, M. (1981). Teaching self-protection to young children. *Journal of Applied Behavior Analysis, 14,* 169–176.

Pope, K. S. (1990). Therapist-patient sexual involvement: A review of the research. *Clinical Psychology Review, 10,* 477–490.

Pope, K. S., & Vetter, V. A. (1992). Ethical dilemmas encountered by members of the American Psychological Association: A national survey. *American Psychologist, 47,* 397–411.

Poythress, N. G., Jr. (1979). A proposal for training in forensic psychology. *American Psychologist, 34,* 612–621.

Premack, D. (1959). Toward empirical behavior laws: I. Positive reinforcement. *Psychological Review, 66,* 219–233.

Price, R. H., Cowen, E. L., Lorion, R. P., & Ramos-McKay, J. (Eds.). (1988). *14 ounces of prevention: A casebook for practitioners.* Washington, DC: American Psychological Association.

Pritchard, D. A., & Rosenblatt, A. (1980). Racial bias in the MMPI: A methodological review. *Journal of Consulting and Clinical Psychology, 48,* 263–267.

Pruitt, S. D., & Elliott, C. H. (1992). Pediatric psychology: Current issues and developments. In C. E. Walker & M. C. Roberts (Eds.), *Handbook of clinical child psychology* (2nd ed.) (pp. 859–872). New York: Wiley.

Quereshi, M. Y., & Kuchan, A. M. (1988). The master's degree in clinical psychology. *Professional Psychology: Research and Practice, 19,* 594–599.

Rachman, S. (1973). The effects of psychotherapy. In H. J. Eysenck (Ed.), *Handbook of abnormal psychology.* San Diego, CA: Knapp.

Raimy, V. C. (Ed.). (1950). *Training in clinical psychology.* Englewood Cliffs, NJ: Prentice-Hall.

Rapaport, D. (1946). *Diagnostic psychological testing* (Vol. II). Chicago: The Yearbook Publishers.

Rapaport, D. (1953). On the psychoanalytic theory of affects. *International Journal of Psycho-Analysis, 34,* 177–198.

Rappaport, J. (1977). *Community psychology: Values, research, and action.* New York: Holt, Rinehart and Winston.

Rappaport, J. (1981). In praise of paradox: A social policy of empowerment over prevention. *American Journal of Community Psychology, 9,* 1–25.

Rappaport, J. (1987). Terms of empowerment/exemplars of prevention: Toward a theory for community psychology. *American Journal of Community Psychology, 15,* 121–148.

Rappaport, J., & Seidman, E. (in press). *Handbook of community psychology.* New York: Plenum.

Rathus, S. A. (1973). A 30-item schedule for assessing assertive behavior. *Behavior Therapy, 4,* 398–406.

Raviv, A., Raviv, A., & Yunovitz, R. (1989). Radio psychology and psychotherapy: Comparison of client attitudes and expectations. *Professional Psychology: Research and Practice, 20,* 67–72.

Reid, J. B. (1970). Reliability assessment of observation data: A possible methodological problem. *Child Development, 41,* 1143–1150.

Reisman, J. M. (1976). *A history of clinical psychology* (enlarged ed.). New York: Irvington.

Reitan, R. M. (1969). *Manual for administration of neuropsychological test batteries for adults and children.* Indianapolis, IN: Author.

Reitan, R. M., & Davison, L. A. (1974). *Clinical neuropsychology: Current status and application.* New York: Winston/Wiley.

Resnick, J. H. (1991). Finally, a definition of clinical psychology: A message from the President, Division 12. *The Clinical Psychologist, 44,* 3–11.

Resnick, R. J. (1985). The case against the Blues: The Virginia challenge. *American Psychologist, 40,* 975–983.

Richardson, F. C., & Suinn, R. M. (1973). A comparison of traditional systematic desensitization, accelerated massed desensitization, and anxiety management training in the treatment of mathematics anxiety. *Behavior Therapy, 4,* 212–218.

Richters, J., & Pellegrini, D. (1989). Depressed mothers' judgments about their children: An examination of the depression-distortion hypothesis. *Child Development, 60,* 1068–1075.

Riley, W. T., Elliott, R. L., & Thomas, J. R. (1992). Impact of prescription privileging on psychology training: Training directors' survey. *The Clinical Psychologist, 45,* 63–71.

Rimm, D. C., & Masters, J. C. (1979). *Behavior therapy: Techniques and empirical findings* (2nd ed.). New York: Academic Press.

Roberts, A. H. (1985). Biofeedback: Research, training, and clinical roles. *American Psychologist, 40,* 938–941.

Roberts, M. C. (1986). *Pediatric psychology: Psychological intervention and strategies for pediatric problems.* New York: Pergamon Press.

Roberts, M. C. (1994). Models of service delivery in children's mental health: Common characteristics. *Journal of Clinical Child Psychology, 23,* 212–219.

Roberts, M. C., Fanurik, D., & Elkins, P. D. (1988). Training the child health psychologist. In P. Karoly (Ed.), *Handbook of child health assessment: Biopsychosocial perspectives.* New York: Wiley-Interscience.

Roberts, M. C., Maddux, J., & Wright, L. (1984). The development perspective in behavioral health. In J. D. Matarazzo, N. E. Miller, S. Weiss, J. A. Herd, & S. Weiss (Eds.), *Behavioral health: A handbook of health enhancement and disease prevention.* New York: Wiley.

Roberts, M. C., & Wright, L. (1982). Role of the pediatric psychologist as consultant to pediatricians. In J. Tuma (Ed.), *Handbook for the practice of pediatric psychology.* New York: Wiley-Interscience.

Robiner, W. N. (1991). How many psychologists are needed? A call for a national psychology human resource agenda. *Professional Psychology: Research and Practice, 22,* 427–440.

Robins, C. J. (1990). Congruence of personality and life events in depression. *Journal of Abnormal Psychology, 99,* 393–397.

Robins, L. N. (1985). Epidemiology: Reflections on testing the validity of psychiatric interviews. *Archives of General Psychiatry, 42,* 918–924.

Robins, L. N., & Guze, S. B. (1970). Establishment of diagnostic validity in psychiatric illness: Its application to schizophrenia. *American Journal of Psychiatry, 126,* 107–111.

Robins, L. N., & Helzer, J. E. (1986). Diagnosis and clinical assessment: The current state of psychiatric diagnosis. In M. R. Rosenzweig & L. W. Porter (Eds.), *Annual review of psychology* (Vol. 37). Palo Alto, CA: Annual Reviews.

Robinson, H. B., & Robinson, N. M. (1965). *The mentally retarded child.* New York: McGraw-Hill.

Robinson, L. A., Berman, J. S., & Neimeyer, R. A. (1990). Psychotherapy for the treatment of depression: A comprehensive review of controlled outcome research. *Psychological Bulletin, 108,* 30–49.

Rodin, J., & Salovey, P. (1989): Health psychology. In M. R. Rosenzweig & L. W. Porter (Eds.), *Annual review of psychology.* Palo Alto, CA: Annual Reviews.

Roe, A. (1953). A psychological study of eminent psychologists and anthropologists, and a comparison with biological and physical scientists. *Psychological Monographs General and Applied, 67,* (No. 352).

Rogers, C. R. (1939). *The clinical treatment of the problem child.* Boston: Houghton Mifflin.

Rogers, C. R. (1942). *Counseling and psychotherapy.* Boston: Houghton Mifflin.

Rogers, C. R. (1946). Significant aspects of client-centered therapy. *American Psychologist, 1,* 415–422.

Rogers, C. R. (1951). *Client-centered therapy.* Boston: Houghton Mifflin.

Rogers, C. R. (1957). The necessary and sufficient conditions of therapeutic personality change. *Journal of Consulting Psychology, 21,* 95–103.

Rogers, C. R. (1959). A theory of therapy, personality, and interpersonal relationships, as developed in the client-centered framework. In S. Koch (Ed.), *Psychology: A study of a science* (Vol. 3). New York: McGraw-Hill.

Rogers, C. R. (1961). *On becoming a person.* Boston: Houghton Mifflin.

Rogers, C. R. (1967). Autobiography. In E. Boring & G. Lindzey (Eds.), *A history of psychology in autobiography* (Vol. 5). New York: Appleton-Century-Crofts.

Rogers, C. R. (1970). *On encounter groups.* New York: Harper and Row.

Rogers, C. R. (1974). In retrospect: Forty-six years. *American Psychologist, 29,* 115–123.

Rogers, C. R. (1980). *A way of being.* Boston: Houghton Mifflin.

Rogers, C. R., & Dymond, R. F. (1954). *Psychotherapy and personality change.* Chicago: University of Chicago Press.

Rogers, C. R., Gendlin, E. T., Kiesler, D. J., & Truax, C. B. (1967). *The therapeutic relationship and its impact.* Madison: University of Wisconsin Press.

Rogers, R. (1995). *Diagnostic and structured interviewing: A handbook for psychologists.* Odessa, FL: Psychological Assessment Resources.

Rogers, R., Bagby, R., & Chakraborty, D. (1993). Feigning schizophrenic disorders on the MMPI-2: Detection of coached simulators. *Journal of Personality Assessment, 60,* 215–226.

Rogler, L. H., Malgady, R. G., Constantino, G., & Blumenthal, R. (1987). What do culturally sensitive mental health services mean? The case of Hispanics. *American Psychologist, 42,* 565–570.

Rorschach, H. (1921). *Psychodiagnostik.* Bern, Switzerland: Huber.

Rose, S. D. (1991). The development and practice of group treatment. In M. Hersen, A. E. Kazdin, & A. Bellack (Eds.), *The clinical psychology handbook* (2nd ed.) (pp. 627–642). New York: Pergamon.

Rosen, C. E. (1977). Why clients relinquish their rights to privacy under sign-away pressure. *Professional Psychology, 8,* 17–24.

Rosenbaum, M. (1965). Group psychotherapy and psychodrama. In B. B. Wolman (Ed.), *Handbook of clinical psychology.* New York: McGraw-Hill.

Rosenman, R. H. (1978). The interview method of assessment of the coronary-prone behavior pattern. In T. M. Dembroski, S. M. Weiss, J. L. Shields, S. G. Haynes, & M. Feinleib (Eds.), *Coronary-prone behavior.* New York: Springer-Verlag.

Rosenman, R. H., Brand, R. J., Jenkins, C. D., Friedman, M., Straus, R., & Wurm, M. (1975). Coronary heart disease in the Western Collaborative Group Study: Final follow-up of 8½ years. *Journal of the American Medical Association, 233,* 872–877.

Rosenthal, R. (1966). *Experimenter effects in behavioral research.* New York: Appleton-Century-Crofts.

Rosewater, L. B., & Walker, L.E.A. (Eds.). (1985). *Handbook of feminist therapy: Women's issues in psychotherapy.* New York: Springer.

Rosmann, M. R., Delworth, U. (1990). Clinical and community perspectives on the farm crisis. *The Clinical Psychologist, 10,* 10–16.

Rotter, J. B. (1946). Thematic Apperception Tests: Suggestions for administration and interpretation. *Journal of Personality, 15,* 70–92.

Rotter, J. B. (1954). *Social learning and clinical psychology.* Englewood Cliffs, NJ: Prentice-Hall.

Rotter, J. B. (1966). Generalized expectancies for internal versus external control of reinforcement. *Psychological Monographs, 80(1),* (Whole No. 609).

Rotter, J. B. (1970). Some implications of a social learning theory for the practice of psychotherapy. In D. J. Levis (Ed.), *Learning approaches to therapeutic behavior change.* Chicago: Aldine. (Also reprinted in Rotter, Chance, & Phares, 1972.)

Rotter, J. B. (1971). *Clinical psychology* (2nd ed.). Englewood Cliffs, NJ: Prentice-Hall.

Rotter, J. B. (1990). Internal versus external control of reinforcement: A case history of a variable. *American Psychologist, 45,* 489–493.

Rotter, J. B., Chance, J. E., & Phares, E. J. (Eds.). (1972). *Applications of a social learning theory of personality.* New York: Holt, Rinehart and Winston.

Rotter, J. B., & Rafferty, J. E. (1950). *Manual for the Rotter Incomplete Sentences Blank, college form.* New York: The Psychological Corporation.

Rotter, J. B., & Wickens, D. D. (1948). The consistency and generality of ratings of "social aggressiveness" made from observations of role playing situations. *Journal of Consulting Psychology, 12,* 234–239.

Routh, D. K. (1988). Prevention and life style in child health psychology. In B. G. Melamed, K. A. Matthews, D. K. Routh, B. Stabler, & N. Schneiderman (Eds.), *Child health psychology.* Hillsdale, NJ: Erlbaum.

Rubanowitz, D. E. (1987). Public attitudes toward psychotherapist-client confidentiality. *Professional Psychology: Research and Practice, 18,* 613–618.

Rudolfa, E. R., & Hungerford, L. (1982). Self-help groups: A referral resource for professional therapists. *Professional Psychology, 13,* 345–353.

Ryan, J. J., Paolo, A. M., & Brungardt, T. M. (1990). Standardization of the Wechsler Adult Intelligence Scale Revised for persons 75 years and older. *Psychological Assessment: A Journal of Consulting and Clinical Psychology, 2,* 404–411.

Ryan, W. (1971). *Blaming the victim.* New York: Random House.

Salter, A. (1949). *Conditioned reflex therapy.* New York: Farrar, Straus.

Sanchez, P. N., & Kahn, M. W. (1991). Differentiating medical from psychological disorders: How do medically and nonmedically trained clinicians differ? *Professional Psychology: Research and Practice, 22,* 124–126.

Sanford, N. (1965). The prevention of mental illness. In B. B. Wolman (Ed.), *Handbook of clinical psychology.* New York: McGraw-Hill.

Sarafino, E. P. (1990). *Health psychology: Biopsychosocial interactions.* New York: Wiley.

Sarbin, T. R. (1943). A contribution to the study of actuarial and individual methods of prediction. *American Journal of Sociology, 48,* 593–602.

Satir, V. (1967a). *Conjoint family therapy* (2nd rev. ed.). Palo Alto, CA: Science and Behavior Books.

Satir, V. (1967b). A family of angels. In J. Haley & L. Hoffman (Eds.), *Techniques of family therapy.* New York: Basic Books.

Satir, V. (1975). You as a change agent. In V. Satir, J. Satchowiak, & H. A. Tashman (Eds.), *Helping families to change.* New York: Jason Aronson.

Sattler, J. M. (1970). Racial "experimenter effects" in experimentation, testing, interviewing, and psychotherapy. *Psychological Bulletin, 73,* 137–160.

Sattler, J. M. (1992). Assessment of children's intelligence. In C. E. Walker & M. C. Roberts (Eds.), *Handbook of clinical child psychology* (2nd ed.) (pp. 85–100). New York: Wiley.

Sattler, J. M., & Gwynne, J. (1982). White examiners generally do not impede the intelligence test performance of black children: To debunk a myth. *Journal of Consulting and Clinical Psychology, 50,* 196–208.

Sawyer, J. (1966). Measurement and prediction, clinical and statistical. *Psychological Bulletin, 66,* 178–200.

Sayette, M. A., & Mayne, T. J. (1990). Survey of current clinical and research trends in clinical psychology. *American Psychologist, 45,* 1263–1266.

Schindler, F., Berren, M. R., Hanna, M. T., Beigel, A., & Santiago, J. M. (1987). How the public perceives psychiatrists, psychologists, nonpsychiatric physicians, and members of the clergy. *Professional Psychology: Research and Practice, 18,* 371–376.

Schmideberg, M. (1970). Psychotherapy with failures of psychoanalysis. *British Journal of Psychiatry, 116,* 195–200.

Schneider, S. F. (1990). Psychology at the crossroads. *American Psychologist, 45,* 521–529.

Schneider, S. F. (1991). No fluoride in our future. *Professional Psychology: Research and Practice, 22,* 456–460.

Schofield, W. (1964). *Psychotherapy: The purchase of friendship.* Englewood Cliffs, NJ: Prentice-Hall.

Schroeder, M. L., Wormworth, J. A., & Livesley, W. J. (1992). Dimensions of personality disorder and their relationships to the Big Five dimensions of personality. *Psychological Assessment, 4,* 47–53.

Schuerger, J. M., & Witt, A. C. (1989). The temporal stability of individually tested intelligence. *Journal of Clinical Psychology, 45,* 294–302.

Schulberg, H. C., & Killilea, M. (Eds.). (1982). *The modern practice of community mental health.* San Francisco: Jossey-Bass.

Schwartz, G. E., & Beatty, J. (Eds.) (1977). *Biofeedback: Theory and research.* New York: Academic Press.

Schwartz, G. E., & Weiss, S. (1977). What is behavioral medicine? *Psychosomatic Medicine, 36,* 377–381.

Schwartz, R. M., & Gottman, J. M. (1976). Toward a task analysis of assertive behavior. *Journal of Consulting and Clinical Psychology, 44,* 910–920.

Schweinhart, L. J., & Weikart, D. B. (1988). The High Scope/Perry Preschool Program. In R. H. Price, E. L. Cowen, R. P. Lorion, & J. Ramos-McKay (Eds.), *Fourteen ounces of prevention: A casebook for practitioners.* Washington, DC: American Psychological Association.

Schwitzgebel, R. L., & Schwitzgebel, R. K. (1980). *Law and psychological practice.* New York: Wiley.

Scogin, F., Bynum, J., Stephens, G., & Calhoon, S. (1990). Efficacy of self-administered treatment programs: Meta-analytic review. *Professional Psychology: Research and Practice, 21,* 42–47.

Scogin, F., & McElreath, L. (1994). Efficacy of psychosocial treatments for geriatric depression: A quantitative review. *Journal of Consulting and Clinical Psychology, 62,* 69–74.

Scott, N. E., & Borodovsky, L. G. (1990). Effective use of cultural role taking. *Professional Psychology: Research and Practice, 21,* 167–170.

Sears, J. D., Hirt, M. L., & Hall, R. W. (1984). A cross-validation of the Luria-Nebraska Neuropsychological Battery. *Journal of Consulting and Clinical Psychology, 52,* 309–310.

Sechrest, L. (1963). Incremental validity: A recommendation. *Educational and Psychological Measurement, 23,* 153–158.

Sechrest, L. B. (1985). President's message. *The Clinical Psychologist, 38,* 45, 47.

Seligman, M.E.P. (1994). *What you can change & what you can't.* New York: Knopf.

Seligman, M.E.P. (1995). The effectiveness of psychotherapy: The *Consumer Reports* study. *American Psychologist, 50,* 965–974.

Seligman, M.E.P., Castellon, C., Cacciola, J., Schulman, P., Luborsky, L., Ollove, M., & Downing, R. (1988). Explanatory style change during cognitive therapy for unipolar depression. *Journal of Abnormal Psychology, 97,* 13–18.

Semenoff, B. (1976). *Projective techniques.* New York: Wiley.

Severance, L. J., & Loftus, E. F. (1982). Improving the ability to comprehend and apply criminal jury instructions. *Law and Society Review, 17,* 153–198.

Shadish, W. R., Montgomery, L. M., Wilson, P., Wilson, M. R., Bright, I., & Okwumabua, T. (1993). Effects of family and marital psychotherapies: A meta-analysis. *Journal of Consulting and Clinical Psychology, 61,* 992–1002.

Shaffer, G. W., & Lazarus, R. S. (1952). *Fundamental concepts in clinical psychology.* New York: McGraw-Hill.

Shah, S. A. (1978). Dangerousness: A paradigm for exploring some issues in law and psychology. *American Psychologist, 33,* 224–238.

Shapiro, A. E., & Wiggins, J. G. (1994). A PsyD degree for every practitioner: Truth in labeling. *American Psychologist, 49,* 207–210.

Shapiro, D. A., & Shapiro, D. (1982). Meta-analysis of comparative therapy outcome studies: A replication and refinement. *Psychological Bulletin, 92,* 581–604.

Shapiro, D. A., & Shapiro, D. (1983). Comparative therapy outcome research: Methodological implications of meta-analysis. *Journal of Consulting and Clinical Psychology, 51,* 42–53.

Shemberg, K., Keeley, S. M., & Blum, M. (1989). Attitudes toward traditional and nontraditional dissertation research: Survey of directors of clinical training. *Professional Psychology: Research and Practice, 20,* 190–192.

Shepherd, M., Oppenheim, B., & Mitchell, S. (1971). *Childhood behavior and mental health.* New York: Grune and Stratton.

Sher, K. J., & Trull, T. J. (1996). Methodological issues in psychopathology research. *Annual Review of Psychology, 47,* 371–400.

Sher, K. J., Walitzer, K. S., Wood, P. K., & Brent, E. E. (1991). Characteristics of children of alcoholics: Putative risk factors, substance use and abuse, and psychopathology. *Journal of Abnormal Psychology, 100,* 427–448.

Sherman, R., & Fredman, N. (1986). *Handbook of structured techniques in marriage and family therapy.* New York: Brunner/Mazel.

Shneidman, E. S. (1951). *Thematic test analysis.* New York: Grune and Stratton.

Shneidman, E. S. (1965). Projective techniques. In B. Wolman (Ed.), *Handbook of clinical psychology.* New York: McGraw-Hill.

Shneidman, E. S., & Farberow, N. L. (1965). The Los Angeles suicide prevention center: A demonstration of public health feasibilities. *American Journal of Public Health, 55,* 21–26.

Shoham-Salomon, V., & Rosenthal, R. (1987). Paradoxical interventions: A meta-analysis. *Journal of Consulting and Clinical Psychology, 55,* 22–28.

Shrout, P. E., & Fleiss, J. L. (1979). Intraclass correlations: Uses in assessing rater reliability. *Psychological Bulletin, 86,* 420–428.

Sifneos, P. E. (1972). *Short-term psychotherapy and emotional crisis.* Cambridge, MA: Harvard University Press.

Silverstein, A. B. (1990). Short forms of individual intelligence tests. *Psychological Assessment: A Journal of Consulting and Clinical Psychology, 2,* 3–11.

Simon, R. J., & Aaronson, D. E. (1988). *The insanity defense: A critical assessment of law and policy in the post-Hinckley era.* New York: Praeger.

Singer, E. (1965). *Key concepts in psychotherapy.* New York: Random House.

Skinner, B. F. (1953). *Science and human behavior.* New York: Macmillan.

Skinner, B. F. (1971). *Beyond freedom and dignity.* New York: Knopf.

Slaikeu, K. A. (1984). *Crisis intervention: A handbook for practice and research.* Boston: Allyn and Bacon.

Slavson, S. R. (1964). *A textbook in analytic group psychotherapy.* New York: International Universities Press.

Sleek, S. (1995a). Managed care sharpens master's-degree debate. *APA Monitor, 26,* 8–9.

Sleek, S. (1995b). So talk shows exploit the profession? *APA Monitor, 26,* 6.

Sloane, R. B., Staples, F. R., Cristol, A. H., Yorkston, N. J., & Whipple, K. (1975a). *Psychotherapy versus behavior therapy.* Cambridge, MA: Harvard University Press.

Sloane, R. B., Staples, F. R., Cristol, A. H., Yorkston, N. J., & Whipple, K. (1975b). Short-term analytically oriented psychotherapy versus behavior therapy. *American Journal of Psychiatry, 132,* 373–377.

Smith, E.W.L. (Ed.). (1976). *The growing edge of Gestalt therapy.* New York: Brunner/Mazel.

Smith, G. T., & McCarthy, D. M. (1995). Methodological considerations in the refinement of clinical assessment instruments. *Psychological Assessment, 7,* 300–308.

Smith, M. B., & Hobbs, N. (1966). The community and the community mental health center. *American Psychologist, 21,* 499–509.

Smith, M. L., & Glass, G. V. (1977). Meta-analysis of psychotherapy outcome studies. *American Psychologist, 32,* 752–760.

Smith, M. L., Glass, G. V., & Miller, T. I. (1980). *The benefits of psychotherapy.* Baltimore: Johns Hopkins University Press.

Smith, T. W. (1992). Hostility and health: Currant status of a psychosomatic hypothesis. *Health Psychology, 11,* 139–150.

Smyer, M. A., Balster, R. L., Egli, D., Johnson, D. L., Kilbey, M. M., Leith, N. J., & Puente, A. E. (1993). Summary of the report of the Ad Hoc Task Force on Psychopharmacology of the American Psychological Association. *Professional Psychology: Research and Practice, 24,* 394–403.

Snepp, F. P., & Peterson, D. R. (1988). Evaluative comparison of PsyD and PhD students by clinical internship supervisors. *Professional Psychology: Research and Practice, 19,* 180–183.

Snyder, D. K., Widiger, T. A., & Hoover, D. (1990). Methodological considerations in validating computer-based test interpretations: Controlling for response bias. *Psychological Assessment: A Journal of Consulting and Clinical Psychology, 2,* 470–477.

Snyder, J. J. (1989). *Health psychology and behavioral medicine.* Englewood Cliffs, NJ: Prentice-Hall.

Snyder, W. U. (1961). *The psychotherapy relationship.* New York: Macmillan.

Snyderman, M., & Rothman, S. (1990). *The IQ controversy, the media, and public policy.* New Brunswick, NJ: Transaction.

Snygg, D., & Combs, C. W. (1949). *Individual behavior.* New York: Harper and Row.

Sobel, S. B., & Cummings, N. A. (1981). The role of professional psychologists in promoting equality. *Professional Psychology, 12,* 171–179.

Sobell, M. B., & Sobell, L. C. (1978). *Behavioral treatment of alcohol problems: Individualized therapy and controlled drinking.* New York: Plenum.

Soldz, S., Budman, S., Demby, A., & Merry, J. (1993). Representation of personality disorders in circumplex and five-factor space: Explorations with a clinical sample. *Psychological Assessment, 5,* 41–52.

Solomon, J. C. (1955). Play technique and the integrative process. *Journal of Orthopsychiatry, 25,* 591–600.

Spearman, C. (1927). *The abilities of man.* New York: Macmillan.

Speck, R. V., & Attneave, C. L. (1971). Social network intervention. In J. Haley (Ed.), *Changing families.* New York: Grune and Stratton.

Spence, D. P. (1987). *The Freudian metaphor: Toward paradigm change in psychoanalysis.* New York: Norton.

Spitzer, R. L. (1981). The diagnostic status of homosexuality in DSM-III: A reformulation of the issues. *American Journal of Psychiatry, 138,* 210–215.

Staples, F. R., Sloane, R. B., Whipple, K., Cristol, A. H., & Yorkston, N. (1976). Process and outcome in psychotherapy and behavior therapy. *Journal of Consulting and Clinical Psychology, 44,* 340–350.

Stein, D. J., Dodman, N. H., Borchelt, P., & Hollander, E. (1994). Behavioral disorders in veterinary practice: Relevance to psychiatry. *Comprehensive Psychiatry, 35,* 275–285.

Stein, M. I. (1948). *The Thematic Apperception Test: An introductory manual for its clinical use with adult males.* Cambridge, MA: Addison-Wesley.

Sterling, M. E. (1982). Must psychology lose its soul? *Professional Psychology, 13,* 789–796.

Stern, W. (1938). *General psychology from the personalistic point of view.* New York: Macmillan.

Sternberg, R. J. (1985). *Beyond IQ: A triarchic theory of human intelligence.* Cambridge, England: Cambridge University Press.

Sternberg, R. J. (1991). Theory-based testing of intellectual abilities: Rationale for the triarchic abilities test. In H. A. Rowe (Ed.), *Intelligence: Reconceptualization and measurement* (pp. 183–202). Hillsdale, NJ: LEA.

Sternberg, R. J., & Salter, W. (1982). Conceptions of intelligence. In R. J. Sternberg (Ed.), *Handbook of human intelligence.* New York: Cambridge University Press.

Sternberg, R. J., & Wagner, R. K. (Eds.). (1986). *Practical intelligence: Nature and origins of competence in the everyday world.* New York: Cambridge University Press.

Stevens, V. J., & Hollis, J. F. (1989). Preventing smoking relapse, using an individually tailored skills-training technique. *Journal of Consulting and Clinical Psychology, 57,* 420–424.

Stolorow, R. D., Bandchaft, B., & Atwood, G. E. (1987). *Psychoanalytic treatment: An intersubjective approach.* Hillsdale, NJ: Analytic Press.

Stone, A. A. (1976). *Mental health and law: A system in transition.* New York: Jason Aronson.

Stone, A. R., Frank, J. D., Nash, E. H., & Imber, S. D. (1961). An intensive five-year follow-up study of treated psychiatric outpatients. *Journal of Nervous and Mental Disease, 133,* 410–422.

Strasburg, E. L., & Jackson, D. N. (1977). Improving accuracy in a clinical judgmental task. *Journal of Consulting and Clinical Psychology, 45,* 303–309.

Strelnick, A. H. (1977). Multiple family group therapy: A review of the literature. *Family Process, 16,* 307–323.

Stricker, G. (1977). Implications of research for psychotherapeutic treatment of women. *American Psychologist, 32,* 14–22.

Strickland, B. R. (1979). Internal-external expectancies and cardiovascular functioning. In L. C. Perlmuter & R. A. Monty (Eds.), *Choice and perceived control.* Hillsdale, NJ: Erlbaum.

Strickland, B. R. (1988). Clinical psychology comes of age. *American Psychologist, 43,* 104–107.

Stroebe, W., & Stroebe, M. S. (1995). *Social psychology and health.* Pacific Grove, CA: Brooks/Cole.

Strupp, H. H. (1971). *Psychotherapy and the modification of abnormal behavior.* New York: McGraw-Hill.

Strupp, H. H. (1982). The outcome problem in psychotherapy: Contemporary perspectives. In J. H. Elarvey & M. M. Parks (Eds.), *The master lecture series. Vol. 1: Psychotherapy research and behavior change.* Washington, DC: American Psychological Association.

Strupp, H. H., & Bergin, A. E. (1969). Some empirical and conceptual bases for coordinated research in psychotherapy: A critical review of issues, trends, and evidence. *International Journal of Psychiatry, 7,* 18–90.

Strupp, H. H., & Binder, J. L. (1984). *Psychotherapy in a new key: A guide to time-limited dynamic therapy.* New York: Basic Books.

Stuart, R. B. (1969). Operant interpersonal treatment for marital discord. *Journal of Consulting and Clinical Psychology, 33,* 675–682.

Stuart, R. B. (1980). *Helping couples change: A social learning approach to marital therapy.* New York: Guilford.

Stunkard, A. J. (1979). Behavioral medicine and beyond: The example of obesity. In O. Pomerleau & J. Brady (Eds.), *Behavioral medicine: Theory and practice.* Baltimore: Williams and Wilkins.

Sturdivant, S. (1980). *Therapy with women: A feminist philosophy of treatment.* New York: Springer.

Sturgis, E. T., & Gramling, S. (1988). Psychophysiological assessment. In A. S. Bellack & M. Hersen (Eds.), *Behavioral assessment: A practical handbook* (pp. 213–251). New York: Pergamon.

Sue, D. W. (1990). Culture-specific strategies in counseling: A conceptual framework. *Professional Psychology: Research and Practice, 21,* 424–433.

Sue, S. (1988). Psychotherapeutic services for ethnic minorities: Two decades of research findings. *American Psychologist, 43,* 301–308.

Sue, S., Zane, N., & Young, K. (1994). Research on psychotherapy with culturally diverse populations. In A. E. Bergin & S. L. Garfield (Eds.), *Handbook of psychotherapy and behavior change* (4th ed.) (pp. 783–817). New York: Wiley.

Suinn, R. M. (1982). Intervention with Type A behaviors. *Journal of Consulting and Clinical Psychology, 50,* 797–803.

Sullivan, B. J., & Denney, D. R. (1977). Expectancy and phobic level: Effects on desensitization. *Journal of Consulting and Clinical Psychology, 45,* 763–771.

Suls, J., & Rittenhouse, J. D. (1987). Personality and physical health: An introduction. *Journal of Personality, 55,* 155–167.

Suls, J., & Wan, C. K. (1989). Effects of sensory and procedural information on coping with stressful medical procedures and pain: A meta-analysis. *Journal of Consulting and Clinical Psychology, 57,* 372–379.

Sundberg, N. D. (1977). *Assessment of persons.* Englewood Cliffs, NJ: Prentice-Hall.

Sundberg, N. D., Tyler, L. E., & Taplin, J. R. (1973). *Clinical psychology: Expanding horizons* (2nd ed.). Englewood Cliffs, NJ: Prentice-Hall.

Suomi, S. J. (1982). Relevance of animal models for clinical psychology. In P. C. Kendall & J. N. Butcher (Eds.), *Handbook of research methods in clinical psychology.* New York: Wiley.

Surgeon General. (1964). *Smoking and Health.* Washington, DC: U.S. Government Printing Office.

Sutton, R. G., & Kessler, M. (1986). National study of the effects of clients' socioeconomic status on clinical psychologists' professional judgments. *Journal of Consulting and Clinical Psychology, 54,* 275–276.

Svartberg, M., & Stiles, T. C. (1991). Comparative effects of short-term psychodynamic psychotherapy: A meta-analysis. *Journal of Consulting and Clinical Psychology, 59,* 704–714.

Swenson, C. H. (1971). Commitment and the personality of the successful therapist. *Psychotherapy: Theory, Research, and Practice, 8,* 31–36.

Symonds, P. M. (1949). *Adolescent fantasy: An investigation of the picture-story method of personality study.* New York: Columbia University Press.

Szasz, T. S. (1970). *The manufacture of madness.* New York: Harper and Row.

Talbert, F. S., & Pipes, R. B. (1988). Informed consent for psychotherapy: Content analysis of selected forms. *Professional Psychology: Research and Practice, 19,* 131–132.

Tallent, N. (1983). *Psychological report writing* (2nd ed.). Englewood Cliffs, NJ: Prentice-Hall.

Tarullo, L. B., Richardson, D. T., Radke-Yarrow, M., & Martinez, P. E. (1995). Multiple sources in child diagnosis: Parent-child concordance in affectively ill and well families. *Journal of Clinical Child Psychology, 24,* 173–183.

Task Force on Promotion and Dissemination of Psychological Procedures. (1995). Training in and dissemination of empirically-validated psychological treatments. *The Clinical Psychologist, 48,* 3–23.

Tauer, C. A. (1979). Freud and female inferiority. *International Journal of Women's Studies, 2,* 287–304.

Taylor, H. G., Barry, C. T., & Schatschneider, C. (1993). School-age consequences of *haemophilus influenzae* type B meningitis. *Journal of Clinical Child Psychology, 22,* 196–206.

Taylor, L., & Adelman, H. S. (1989). Reframing the confidentiality dilemma to work in children's best interests. *Professional Psychology: Research and Practice, 20,* 79–83.

Taylor, S. E. (1984). The developing field of health psychology. In A. Baum, S. E. Taylor, & J. E. Singer (Eds.), *Handbook of psychology and health* (Vol. 4). Hillsdale, NJ: Erlbaum.

Telch, M. J. (1981). The present status of outcome studies: A reply to Frank. *Journal of Consulting and Clinical Psychology, 49,* 472–475.

Tellegen, A. (1993). Folk concepts and psychological concepts of personality and personality disorder. *Psychological Inquiry, 4,* 122–130.

Tellegen, A., & Ben-Porath, Y. S. (1992). The new uniform T-scores for the MMPI-2: Rationale, derivation, and appraisal. *Psychological Assessment, 4,* 145–155.

Terestman, N., Miller, J., & Weber, J. (1974). Blue-collar patients at a psychoanalytic clinic. *American Journal of Psychiatry, 131,* 261–266.

Terman, L. M., & Merrill, M. A. (1937). *Measuring intelligence.* Boston: Houghton Mifflin.

Terman, L. M., & Merrill, M. A. (1960). *Stanford-Binet Intelligence Scale.* Boston: Houghton Mifflin.

Thigpen, C. H., & Cleckley, H. (1957). *The three faces of Eve.* New York: McGraw-Hill.

Thoits, P. A. (1986). Social support as coping assistance. *Journal of Consulting and Clinical Psychology, 54,* 416–423.

Thorndike, R. L., Hagen, E. P., & Sattler, J. M. (1986). *Stanford-Binet Intelligence Scale: Guide for administering and scoring the fourth edition.* Chicago: Riverside Publishing.

Thurstone, L. L. (1938). Primary mental abilities. *Psychometric Monographs* (No. 1).

Tibbits-Kleber, A. L., & Howell, R. J. (1987). Doctoral training in clinical psychology: A student's perspective. *Professional Psychology: Research and Practice, 18,* 634–639.

Timbrook, R. E., & Graham, J. R. (1994). Ethnic differences on the MMPI-2? *Psychological Assessment, 6,* 212–217.

Tipton, R. M. (1983). Clinical and counseling psychology: A study of roles and functions. *Professional Psychology: Research and Practice, 14,* 837–846.

Tramontana, M. G., & Hooper, S. R. (Eds.). (1988). *Assessment issues in neuropsychology.* New York: Plenum.

Travis, C. B. (1988). *Women and health psychology: Biomedical issues.* Hillsdale, NJ: Lawrence Erlbaum.

Truax, C. B., & Carkhuff, R. R. (1967). *Toward effective counseling and psychotherapy.* Chicago: Aldine Atherton.

Truax, C. B., & Mitchell, K. M. (1971). Research on certain therapist interpersonal skills in relation to process and outcome. In A. E. Bergin & S. L. Garfield (Eds.), *Handbook of psychotherapy and behavior change: An empirical analysis.* New York: Wiley.

Trull, T. J. (1992). DSM-III-R personality disorders and the Five-Factor Model of personality: An empirical comparison. *Journal of Abnormal Psychology, 101,* 553–560.

Trull, T. J., & Sher, K. J. (1994). Relationship between the Five-Factor Model of personality and Axis I disorders in a nonclinical sample. *Journal of Abnormal Psychology, 103,* 350–360.

Trull, T. J., Useda, J. D., Costa, P. T., Jr., & McCrae, R. R. (1995). Comparison of the MMPI-2 Personality Psychopathology Five (PSY-5), the NEO-PI, and NEO-PI-R. *Psychological Assessment, 7,* 508–516.

Trull, T. J., Widiger, T. A., & Guthrie, P. (1990). Categorical versus dimensional status of borderline personality disorder. *Journal of Abnormal Psychology, 99,* 40–48.

Tuma, J. M. (1989). Traditional therapies with children. In T. H. Ollendick & M. Hersen (Eds.), *Handbook of child psychopathology* (2nd ed.). New York: Plenum.

Turner, S. M., Calhoun, K. S., & Adams, H. E. (1992). *Handbook of clinical behavior therapy* (2nd ed.). New York: Wiley.

Twentyman, C. T., & McFall, R. M. (1975). Behavioral training of social skills in shy males. *Journal of Consulting and Clinical Psychology, 43,* 384–395.

Tyler, L. E. (1969). *The work of the counselor* (3rd ed.). New York: Appleton-Century-Crofts.

Tyler, L. E. (1972). Human abilities. In P. H. Mussen & M. R. Rosenzweig (Eds.), *Annual review of psychology.* Palo Alto, CA: Annual Reviews.

Tyler, L. E. (1976). The intelligence we test — an evolving concept. In L. B. Resnick (Ed.), *The nature of intelligence.* Hillsdale, NJ: Erlbaum.

Ullman, L. P., & Krasner, L. (Eds.). (1965). *Case studies in behavior modification.* New York: Holt, Rinehart and Winston.

Ullman, L. P., & Krasner, L. (1969). *A psychological approach to abnormal behavior.* Englewood Cliffs, NJ: Prentice-Hall.

United States Department of Health and Human Services. (1993). *Eighth special report to the U.S. Congress on alcohol and health.* Rockville, MD: U.S. Public Health Service.

Valins, S., & Ray, A. A. (1967). Effects of cognitive desensitization on avoidance behavior. *Journal of Personality and Social Psychology, 7,* 345–350.

Van Kaam, A. (1966). *Existential foundations of psychology.* Pittsburgh: Duquesne University Press.

Vernon, P. E. (1950). The validation of civil service selection board procedures. *Occupational Psychology, 24,* 75–95.

Vernon, P. E. (1960). *The structure of human abilities* (rev. ed.). London: Methuen.

Vinson, J. S. (1987). Use of complaint procedures in cases of therapist-patient sexual conduct. *Professional Psychology: Research and Practice, 18,* 159–164.

Voegtlin, W., & Lemere, F. (1942). The treatment of alcohol addiction. *Quarterly Journal of Studies on Alcohol, 2,* 717–803.

Wachtel, P. L. (1977). *Psychoanalysis and behavior therapy: Toward an integration.* New York: Basic Books.

Walfish, S., Stenmark, D. E., Shealy, J. S., & Shealy, S. E. (1989). Reasons why applicants select clinical psychology graduate programs. *Professional Psychology: Research and Practice, 20,* 350–354.

Wallace, J. (1966). An abilities conception of personality. Some implications for personality measurement. *American Psychologist, 21,* 132–138.

Ward, C. H., Beck, A. T., Mendelson, M., Mock, J. E., & Erbauch, J. K. (1962). The psychiatric nomenclature. *Archives of General Psychiatry, 7,* 198–205.

Washington v. Harper, **494** U.S. 210. (1990).

Watkins, C. E., Jr., Campbell, V. L., Nieberding, R., & Hallmark, R. (1995). Contemporary practice of psychological assessment by clinical psychologists. *Professional Psychology: Research and Practice, 26,* 54–60.

Watson, J. B., & Rayner, R. (1920). Conditioned emotional reactions. *Journal of Experimental Psychology, 3,* 114.

Watson, R. I. (1959). Historical review of objective personality testing: The search for objectivity. In B. M. Bass & I. A. Berg (Eds.), *Objective approaches to personality assessment.* Princeton, NJ: Van Nostrand.

Wechsler, D. (1939). *The measurement of adult intelligence.* Baltimore: Williams and Wilkins.

Wechsler, D. (1945). A standardized memory scale for clinical use. *Journal of Psychology, 19,* 87–95.

Wechsler, D. (1949). *Wechsler Intelligence Scale for Children.* New York: The Psychological Corporation.

Wechsler, D. (1974). *Manual: Wechsler Intelligence Scale for Children-Revised.* New York: The Psychological Corporation.

Wechsler, D. (1987). *Wechsler Memory Scale-Revised.* New York: The Psychological Corporation.

Wechsler, D. (1991). *WISC-III: Wechsler Intelligence Scale for Children-Third Edition Manual.* San Antonio, TX: The Psychological Corporation.

Weinberg, R. A. (1989). Intelligence and IQ: Landmark issues and great debates. *American Psychologist, 44,* 98–104.

Weiner, I. B. (1975). *Principles of psychotherapy.* New York: Wiley-Interscience.

Weiner, I. B. (1991). Editor's note: Interscorer agreement in Rorschach research. *Journal of Personality Assessment, 56,* 1.

Weiner, I. B. (1994). The Rorschach Inkblot Method (RIM) is not a test: Implications for theory and practice. *Journal of Personality Assessment, 62,* 498–504.

Weiner, I. B. (1995). Methodological considerations in Rorschach research. *Psychological Assessment, 7,* 330–337.

Weiner, J. P. (1994). Forecasting the effects of health care reform on U.S. physician workforce requirements: Evidence from HMO staffing patterns. *Journal of the American Medical Association, 272,* 222–229.

Weiss, R., & Margolin, G. (1977). Marital conflict and accord. In A. R. Ciminero, K. S. Calhoun, & H. E. Adams (Eds.), *Handbook of behavioral assessment.* New York: Wiley.

Weiss, R. L., Hops, H., & Patterson, G. R. (1973). A framework for conceptualizing marital conflict, technology for altering it, some data for evaluating it. In L. A. Hamerlynck, L. C. Handy, & E. J.

Mash (Eds.), *Behavioral change: Methodology, concepts, and practice* (pp. 309–342). Champaign, IL: Research Press.

Weissman, M. M., & Markowitz, J. C. (1994). Interpersonal psychotherapy: Current status. *Archives of General Psychiatry, 51,* 599–606.

Weisz, J. R., Donenberg, G. R., Han, S. S., & Weiss, B. (1995). Bridging the gap between laboratory and clinic in child and adolescent psychotherapy. *Journal of Consulting and Clinical Psychology, 63,* 688–701.

Weisz, J. R., Weiss, B., Alicke, M. D., & Klotz, M. L. (1987). Effectiveness of psychotherapy with children and adolescents: A meta-analysis for clinicians. *Journal of Consulting and Clinical Psychology, 55,* 542–549.

Weisz, J. R., Weiss, B., Han, S. S., Granger, D. A., & Morton, T. (1995). Effects of psychotherapy with children and adolescents revisited: A meta-analysis of treatment outcome studies. *Psychological Bulletin, 117,* 450–468.

Wells, G. L. (1995). Scientific study of witness memory: Implications for public and legal policy. *Psychology, Public Policy, and Law, 1,* 726–731.

Wessler, R. A., & Wessler, R. L. (1980). *The principles and practices of rational emotive therapy.* San Francisco: Jossey-Bass.

Westermeyer, J. (1987). Cultural factors in clinical assessment. *Journal of Consulting and Clinical Psychology, 55,* 471–478.

Wetter, M., Baer, R., Berry, D., Robinson, L., & Sumpter, J. (1993). MMPI-2 profiles of motivated fakers given specific symptom information. *Psychological Assessment, 5,* 317–323.

Wetter, M., Baer, R., Berry, D., Smith, G., & Larsen, L. (1992). Sensitivity of MMPI-2 validity scales to random responding and malingering. *Psychological Assessment, 4,* 369–374.

Whisman, M. A. (1990). The efficacy of booster maintenance sessions in behavior therapy: Review and methodological critique. *Clinical Psychology Review, 10,* 155–170.

White, R. W. (1976). *The enterprise of living: A view of personal growth* (2nd ed.). New York: Holt, Rinehart and Winston.

Widiger, T. A. (1991). Personality disorder dimensional models proposed for DSM-IV. *Journal of Personality Disorders, 5,* 386–398.

Widiger, T. A., & Settle, S. (1987). Broverman et al. revisited: An artifactual sex bias. *Journal of Personality and Social Psychology, 53,* 463–469.

Widiger, T. A., & Spitzer, R. L. (1991). Sex bias in the diagnosis of personality disorders: Conceptual and methodological issues. *Clinical Psychology Review, 11,* 1–22.

Widiger, T. A., & Trull, T. J. (1991). Diagnosis and clinical assessment. *Annual Review of Psychology, 42,* 109–133.

Wiens, A. N. (1983). The assessment interview. In I. B. Weiner (Ed.), *Clinical methods in psychology* (2nd ed.). New York: Wiley-Interscience.

Wierson, M., & Forehand, R. (1994). Introduction to the special section: The role of longitudinal data with child psychopathology and treatment: Preliminary comments and issues. *Journal of Consulting and Clinical Psychology, 62,* 883–886.

Wiggins, J. S. (1973). *Personality and prediction: Principles of personality assessment.* Reading, MA: Addison-Wesley.

Wiggins, J. S., & Pincus, A. L. (1989). Conceptions of personality disorders and dimensions of personality. *Psychological Assessment: A Journal of Consulting and Clinical Psychology, 1,* 305–316.

Wigmore, J. H. (1909). Professor Munsterberg and the psychology of testimony: Being a report of the case of Cokestone v. Munsterberg. *Illinois Law Review, 3,* 399–445.

Wilkins, W. (1971). Desensitization: Social and cognitive factors underlying the effectiveness of Wolpe's procedure. *Psychological Bulletin, 76,* 311–317.

Will, D., & Wrate, R. M. (1985). *Integrated family therapy: A problem-centered psychodynamic approach.* New York: Tavistock.

Willis, D. J. (1989). Expanding psychological practice to American Indians. *The Clinical Psychologist, 42,* 5–8.

Wills, K. E. (1993). Neuropsychological functioning in children with spina bifida and/or hydrocephalus. *Journal of Clinical Child Psychology, 22,* 247–265.

Wilson, G. T. (1981). Behavior therapy as a short-term therapeutic approach. In S. H. Budman (Ed.), *Forms of brief therapy.* New York: Guilford Press.

Wilson, G. T., & Davison, G. C. (1971). Processes of fear reduction in systematic desensitization: Animal studies. *Psychological Bulletin, 76,* 1–14.

Wilson, G. T., & Franks, C. M. (Eds.). (1982). *Contemporary behavior therapy: Conceptual and empirical foundations.* New York: Guilford Press.

Wilson, G. T., & Rachman, S. J. (1983). Meta-analysis and the evaluation of psychotherapy outcome: Limitations and liabilities. *Journal of Consulting and Clinical Psychology, 51,* 54–64.

Winder, A. E., Michelson, L. E., & Diamond, D. (1985). Practicum training for pediatric psychologists: A case study. *Professional Psychology: Research and Practice, 16,* 733–740.

Windholz, M. I., & Silberschatz, G. (1988). Vanderbilt Psychotherapy Process Scale: A replication with adult outpatients. *Journal of Consulting and Clinical Psychology, 56,* 56–60.

Witmer, L. (1907). Clinical psychology [Editorial]. *The Psychological Clinic, 1,* 1.

Wittenborn, J. R. (1955). *The Wittenborn Psychiatric Rating Scales.* New York: The Psychological Corporation.

Wolberg, L. R. (1967). *The technique of psychotherapy* (2nd ed.). New York: Grune and Stratton.

Wolf, A. (1975). Psychoanalysis in groups. In G. M. Gazda (Ed.), *Basic approaches to group psychotherapy and group consulting* (2nd ed.). Springfield, IL: Charles C. Thomas.

Wolff, W. T., & Merrens, M. R. (1974). Behavioral assessment. A review of clinical methods. *Journal of Personality Assessment, 38,* 3–16.

Wolpe, J. (1958). *Psychotherapy by reciprocal inhibition.* Stanford, CA: Stanford University Press.

Wolpe, J. (1973). *The practice of behavior therapy* (2nd ed.). New York: Pergamon Press.

Wolpe, J. (1981). Behavioral therapy versus psychoanalysis: Therapeutic and social implications. *American Psychologist, 36,* 159–164.

Wolpe, J., & Lazarus, A. A. (1966). *Behavior therapy techniques.* New York: Pergamon Press.

Wood, J. M., Nezworski, M. T., & Stejskal, W. J. (1996). The Comprehensive System for the Rorschach: A critical examination. *Psychological Science, 7,* 3–10.

Woodruff-Pak, D. (1988). *Psychology and aging.* Englewood Cliffs, NJ: Prentice-Hall.

Woolfolk, A. E., Woolfolk, R. L., & Wilson, G. T. (1977). A rose by any other name . . . : Labeling bias and attitudes toward behavior modification. *Journal of Consulting and Clinical Psychology, 45,* 184–191.

Wright, L. (1967). The pediatric psychologist: A role model. *American Psychologist, 22,* 323–325.

Wrightsman, L. S., Nietzel, M. T., & Fortune, W. H. (1994). *Psychology and the legal system* (3rd ed.). Pacific Grove, CA: Brooks/Cole.

Yalom, I. D. (1975). *The theory and practice of group psychotherapy.* New York: Basic Books.

Yeaton, W. H., & Bailey, J. S. (1978). Teaching pedestrian safety skills to young children: An analysis and one year follow-up. *Journal of Applied Behavior Analysis, 11,* 315–329.

Yoken, C., & Berman, J. S. (1987). Third-party payment and the outcome of psychotherapy. *Journal of Consulting and Clinical Psychology, 55,* 571–576.

Yule, W. (1989). An introduction to investigation in clinical child psychology. In S. Lindsay & G. Powell (Eds.), *An introduction to clinical child psychology.* Aldershot, England: Gower.

Zax, M., & Specter, G. A. (1974). *An introduction to community psychology.* New York: Wiley.

Zilboorg, G., & Henry, G. W. (1941). *A history of medical psychology.* New York: Norton.

Zimet, C. N. (1989). The mental health care revolution. *American Psychologist, 44,* 703–708.

Zook, A., II, & Walton, J. M. (1989). Theoretical orientations and work settings of clinical and counseling psychologists: A current perspective. *Professional Psychology: Research and Practice, 20,* 23–31.

Zubin, J., Eron, L. D., & Schumer, F. (1965). *An experimental approach to projective techniques.* New York: Wiley.

Name Index

Subject Index

TO THE OWNER OF THIS BOOK:

We hope that you have found *Clinical Psychology: Concepts, Methods, and Profession*, 5th Edition, useful. So that this book can be improved in a future edition, would you take the time to complete this sheet and return it? Thank you.

School and address: ─────────────────────────────────

Department: ──────────────────────────────────────

Instructor's name: ───────────────────────────────────

1. What I like most about this book is: ──────────────────────

───

───

2. What I like least about this book is: ──────────────────────

───

───

3. My general reaction to this book is: ──────────────────────

───

4. The name of the course in which I used this book is: ──────────

───

5. Were all of the chapters of the book assigned for you to read? ──────────

   If not, which ones weren't? ─────────────────────────

6. In the space below, or on a separate sheet of paper, please write specific suggestions for improving this book and anything else you'd care to share about your experience in using the book.

───

───

───

───

───

Optional:

Your name: _____ Date: _____

May Brooks/Cole quote you, either in promotion for *Clinical Psychology: Concepts, Methods, and Profession,* 5th Edition, or in future publishing ventures?

Yes: _____ No: _____

Sincerely,

E. Jerry Phares
TImothy J. Trull

FOLD HERE

BUSINESS REPLY MAIL

FIRST CLASS PERMIT NO. 358 PACIFIC GROVE, CA

POSTAGE WILL BE PAID BY ADDRESSEE

ATT: *E. Jerry Phares & Timothy J. Trull*

Brooks/Cole Publishing Company
511 Forest Lodge Road
Pacific Grove, California 93950-9968

FOLD HERE

IN-BOOK SURVEY

At Brooks/Cole, we are excited about creating new types of learning materials that are interactive, three-dimensional, and fun to use. To guide us in our publishing/development process, we hope that you'll take just a few moments to fill out the survey below. Your answers can help us make decisions that will allow us to produce a wide variety of videos, CD-ROMs, and Internet-based learning systems to complement standard textbooks. If you're interested in working with us as a student Beta-tester, be sure to fill in your name, telephone number, and address. We look forward to hearing from you!

In addition to books, which of the following learning tools do you currently use in your counseling/human services/social work courses?

_____ **Video** _____ in class _____ school library _____ own VCR

_____ **CD-ROM** _____ in class _____ in lab _____ own computer

_____ **Macintosh disks** _____ in class _____ in lab _____ own computer

_____ **Windows disks** _____ in class _____ in lab _____ own computer

_____ **Internet** _____ in class _____ in lab _____ own computer

How often do you access the Internet? _____

My own home computer is:

_____ Macintosh _____ DOS _____ Windows _____ Windows 95

The computer I use in class for counseling/human services/social work courses is:

_____ Macintosh _____ DOS _____ Windows _____ Windows 95

If you are NOT currently using multimedia materials in your counseling/human services/social work courses, but can see ways that video, CD-ROM, Internet, or other technologies could enhance your learning, please comment below:

_____

_____

_____

Other comments (optional): _____

_____

Name _____

Address _____

Telephone number (optional): _____

You can fax this form to us at (408) 375-6414; e:mail to: info@brookscole.com; or detach, fold, secure, and mail.